The Little, Brown Reader

Why Do You Need This New Edition?

If you're wondering why you should buy this new edition of *The Little, Brown Reader*, here are **6 good reasons**!

1. **New readings**—almost a third of the total—give you a wide range of contemporary writing models to engage your interest and help you understand what good writing looks like. Among the new writers in this edition: Thomas Hoving on Grant Wood's *American Gothic*, Peter Singer on Wal-Mart, Anar Ali on Muslims and terrorism, and Michael Ableman on food in public schools.

2. **A completely new chapter on immigration** (Chapter 8)—including Casebooks (collections of related readings) on recent immigrants and on poems about immigration—offers readings on one of the most controversial issues of our day.

3. **Additional new Casebooks**—on such subjects as whether poker-playing in college is harmful and whether torture is ever permissible—will challenge your assumptions. You'll also want to think about the issues in the popular Casebooks retained from earlier editions, on what should be taught in college, on testing and grading, and on race.

4. The chapter on **argument** (Chapter 4) has been substantially expanded to give you even more help in developing one of the most important skills you'll need, not only in your composition course, but also in your career beyond college. You'll find information here about appeals to reason and emotion, and new **debates**—paired readings—of particular interest to you as a new college student, on bringing laptops into the classroom and marketing credit cards to college students.

5. **Five new student essays** show you how your peers have tackled popular subjects in their college courses.

6. **Checklists** are one of this book's most popular features, offering condensed, step-by-step guidance for particular writing tasks. **New Checklists** in this edition provide help in Getting Started on writing a paper, Analyzing and Evaluating an Essay, Analyzing Your Own Analysis, and Critical Thinking.

The Little, Brown Reader

Eleventh Edition

Marcia Stubbs
Wellesley College

Sylvan Barnet
Tufts University

William E. Cain
Wellesley College

PEARSON
Longman

New York San Francisco Boston
London Toronto Sydney Tokyo Singapore Madrid
Mexico City Munich Paris Cape Town Hong Kong Montreal

Senior Sponsoring Editor: Virginia L. Blanford
Senior Marketing Manager: Sandra McGuire
Senior Supplements Editor: Donna Campion
Production Manager: Denise Phillip
Project Coordination, Text Design, and Electronic Page Makeup:
   GGS Book Services
Cover Design Manager: Wendy Ann Fredericks
Cover Designer: Kay Petronio
Cover Photos (from top to bottom): Amy Tan, Amy Tierney (Contributor)/
   WireImage/Getty Images; Martin Luther King Jr., Popperfoto/Alamy;
   Joan Didion, Victoria Will/Splash News/Newscorn; Brent Staples, James
   Keyser/Time Life Pictures/Getty Images; Jamaica Kincaid, Anne Katrine
   Senstad/Retna Ltd.; Dave Eggers, © Miriam Berkley; and Anar Ali, ©
   John W. MacDonald.
Photo Researcher: Ilene Bellovin
Manufacturing Buyer: Roy Pickering
Printer and Binder: R. R. Donnelley & Sons—Crawfordsville
Cover Printer: R. R. Donnelley & Sons—Crawfordsville

For permission to use copyrighted material, grateful acknowledgment is made to the copyright holders on the first pages of the respective selections, and photo acknowledgments on pages 659–660, which are hereby made part of this copyright page.

Library of Congress Cataloging-in-Publication Data

The Little Brown reader/[edited by] Marcia Stubbs, Sylvan Barnet,
William E. Cain.—11th ed.
    p. cm.
   Includes bibliographical references and index.
   ISBN 0-205-58966-9
   1. College readers. 2. English language—Rhetoric—Problems, exercises, etc.
3. Report writing—Problems, exercises, etc. I. Stubbs, Marcia. II. Barnet, Sylvan.
III. Cain, William E., 1952-

PE1417.L644 2009
808'.0427—dc22

                                                        2007029026

Copyright © 2009 by Pearson Education, Inc.

Visit us at www.ablongman.com

ISBN-13: 978-0-205-58966-1
ISBN-10:   0-205-58966-9

2 3 4 5 6 7 8 9 10—DOC—10 09 08

Brief Contents

Detailed Contents

3   Academic Writing   43

4 Writing an Argument 79

5   Reading and Writing about Pictures   121

6   All in the Family   143

7   Identities   195

A Casebook on Race   236

8 Immigrant Nation 257

A Casebook on What Colleges Should Teach   349

A Casebook on Testing and Grading   368

10   Work and Play   377

A Casebook on Virtual Worlds   486

12   Law and Order   501

A Casebook on Torture   548

14   Body and Soul   603

Rhetorical Contents

Argument

Cause and Effect

Comparison and Contrast

Definition

Description

Diction

Exposition

Evaluation

Exposition

Irony

Narration

Style

Preface

Overview

Books have been put to all sorts of unexpected uses. Tolstoy used Tatishef's dictionaries as a test of physical endurance, holding them in his outstretched hand for five minutes, enduring "terrible pain." Books (especially pocket-sized Bibles) have served as armor by deflecting bullets. And they have served as weapons: Two hundred years ago the poet and essayist Samuel Johnson knocked a man down with a large book.

In a course in writing, what is the proper use of the book in hand? This anthology contains some 140 essays, together with a few poems, stories, and fables, and numerous "Short Views," that is, paragraphs and aphorisms. But these readings are not the subject matter of the course; the subject matter of a writing course is writing, particularly the writing the students themselves produce. The responsibilities we felt as editors, then, were to include selections that encourage and enable students to write well, and to exclude selections that do not.

Our selections and writing exercises also reflect our own experience, over many years, as teachers of writing courses. We think it's important for the selections to lead not only to good written work by students, but also to lively discussion and debate. The more that students are engaged by the readings, and led to explore and examine their own responses in relation to those of their classmates, the more they feel there's something at stake in the writing they are doing. We have found, like all of our colleagues, that students improve the most when their work on papers is connected with lively classroom discussions about the readings, and we have tried to keep this point in mind in choosing selections and in preparing our topics for Joining the Conversation: Critical Thinking and Writing.

Purpose

To talk of "enabling" first: Students, like all other writers, write best when they write on fairly specific topics that can come within their experience and within their command in the time that they have available to write. A glance at our table of contents reveals the general areas within which, we believe, students can find topics they have already given some thought to and are likely to be encountering in other courses as well: family relationships; love and courtship; schools; work and play, immigration.

Although other sections ("Messages" and "Consuming Desires") are also on familiar subjects—language and popular culture—the selections themselves offer ways of thinking about these subjects that may be less familiar. Television commercials and films, for example, can be thought of as networks that articulate and transmit values implicit in a culture.

Other sections are about areas of experience that, while hardly remote from students' interest, are perhaps more difficult for all of us to grasp concretely: the tension between civil rights and liberties and the need for law and order; matters of gender and ethnic identity; relationships between mind and body or body and spirit. In these sections, therefore, we have taken particular care to exclude writing that is, for our purposes, too abstract, or too technical, or too elaborate.

As editors we have tried to think carefully about whether selections we were inclined to use—because they were beautifully written or on a stimulating topic—would encourage students to write. Such encouragement does not come, we feel, solely from the subject of an essay or from its excellence; it comes when the essay engenders in the reader a confidence in the writing process itself. No one quality in essays automatically teaches such confidence: not length or brevity, not difficulty or simplicity, not necessarily clarity, and almost certainly not brilliance. But essays that teach writing demonstrate, in some way, that the writers had some stake in what they were saying, took some pains to say what they meant, and took pleasure in having said it.

The selections we include vary in length, complexity, subtlety, tone, and purpose. Most were written by our contemporaries, but not all. The authors include historians, sociologists, scientists, saints, philosophers, and undergraduates, as well as journalists and other professional writers. And we have included some pictures in each section. The pictures, beautiful things in themselves, provide immediate or nearly immediate experiences for students to write about.

We offer substantial help to students who want to write about pictures: in Chapter 5, "Reading and Writing about Pictures," we set forth our own ideas about the topic; we reprint a helpful introductory essay, Lou Jacobs's "What Qualities Does a Good Photograph Have?"; and we print sample essays, including one by a first-year student.

We hope that everything in the book will allow students to establish connections between the activities that produced the words (and pictures) in these pages and their own work in putting critical responses to them on paper.

Flexible Arrangement

Although any arrangement of the selections—thematic, rhetorical, alphabetical, chronological, or random—would have suited our purposes, we prefer the thematic arrangement. For one thing, by narrowing our choices it helped us to make decisions. But more important, we know that in the real world what people write about is subjects, and we don't want to miss any opportunity to suggest that what goes on in writing courses is something like what goes on outside. The thematic categories are not intended to be rigid, however, and they do not pretend to be comprehensive; some of the questions following the selections suggest that leaping across boundaries is permitted, even encouraged. And, for instructors who prefer to organize their writing course rhetorically, we have added a selective table of contents organized rhetorically. Finally, we append a glossary of terms for students of writing.

What's New in the Eleventh Edition?

William Hazlitt said that he always read an old book when a new one was published. This new edition allows instructors to read both at once. We have of course retained those essays and the special features (for example Checklists for Writers, headnotes, and Joining the Conversation: Critical Thinking and Writing at the end of each essay) that in our experience and the experience of many colleagues have consistently been of value to instructors and to students. But, guided by suggestions from users of the tenth edition, we have made many changes and additions. Among the most evident changes in the five introductory chapters devoted to reading and writing are

- in Chapter 1, a new essay and a new checklist, "Analyzing and Evaluating an Essay";
- in Chapter 2, a new checklist, "Getting Started";
- in Chapter 3, a new note on writing a summary;
- in Chapter 4, an amplified discussion of arguments appealing to reason and arguments appealing to emotions, and an amplified discussion of introductory and concluding paragraphs, as well as two pairs of essays (one debating the use of laptops in the classroom, the other debating the marketing of credit cards to students); and
- in Chapter 5 ("Reading and Writing about Picutures"), a new essay on Grant Wood's *American Gothic*.

Almost one-third of the total readings are new to the book. These include

- a casebook on poker-playing in college,
- a casebook on virtual worlds,
- a casebook on torture,
- a new chapter, "Immigrant Nation," with two casebooks—one on recent immigrants and the other on poems about immigrants, and
- five additional essays by students.

We have retained the popular casebooks on testing and grading and on races.

An updated Instructor's Manual. *Teaching the Little, Brown Reader*, is available to instructors who adopt this eleventh edition.

Acknowledgments

As usual, we are indebted to readers-in-residence. Morton Berman, William Burto, and Judith Stubbs have often read our material and then told us what we wanted to hear. William Cain would like to thank his wife Barbara Harman and his daughters Julia and Isabel. All three of us wish to thank Pat Bellanca of Harvard University, Virginia L. Blanford of Longman, and the staff of GGS Book Services, all of whom have given us valuable assistance.

We are grateful also to colleagues at other institutions who offered suggestions for the eleventh edition: Robert Ford, Houston Community College; Amina Gautier, St. Joseph's University; Michael Hricik, Westmoreland County Community College; Irmagard Langmia, Bowie State University; Ronda K. Mehrer, Black Hills State University; Ida Nunley, Eastern Arizona College; Steven A. Remollino, College of the Mainland; and Marilyn Sahiba, Parkland College.

We are also indebted to colleagues at other institutions who offered suggestions for the tenth edition: Christine Berg, Nassau Community College; Cheryl Cardoza, Truckee Meadows Community College; Rose Day, Albuquerque TVI Community College; Paula-Eschliman, Richland College; Deborah Kirkman, University of Kentucky; Eleanor Q. Tignor, LaGuardia Community College; Lynn Wright, Pasadena City College.

Marcia Stubbs
Sylvan Barnet
William E. Cain

The Little, Brown Reader

CHAPTER 1

A Writer Reads

One reads well only when one reads with some personal goal in mind. It may be to acquire some power. It may be out of hatred for the author.

                                                                    Paul Valéry

Good writers are also good readers—of the works of other writers and of their own notes and drafts. The habits they develop as readers of others—for instance, evaluating assumptions, scrutinizing arguments, and perceiving irony—empower them when they write, read, and revise their own notes and drafts. Because they themselves are readers, when they write they have a built-in awareness of how their readers might respond. They can imagine an audience, and they write almost as if in dialogue with it.

Active reading (which is what we are describing) involves writing at the outset: annotating a text by highlighting or underlining key terms, putting question marks or brief responses in the margin, writing notes in a journal. Such reading, as you already may have experienced, helps you first of all to understand a text, to get clear what the writer seems to intend. Later, skimming your own notes will help you to recall what you have read.

But active reading also gives you confidence as a writer. It helps you to treat your own drafts with the same respect and disrespect with which you read the work of others. To annotate a text or a draft is to respect it enough to give it serious attention, but it is also to question it, to assume that the text or draft is not the last word on the topic.

But let's start at the beginning.

Previewing

By *previewing* we mean getting a tentative fix on a text before reading it closely.

If you know something about the **author, you probably already know something about a work even before you read the first paragraph.** An essay by Martin Luther King Jr. will almost surely be a deeply serious discussion centering on civil rights, and, since King was a Baptist clergyman, it is likely to draw on traditional religious values. An essay by Woody Allen will almost surely differ from King's in topic and tone. Allen usually writes about the arts, especially the art of film. Both writers are serious (though Allen also writes comic pieces), but they are serious about different things and serious in different ways. We can read both with interest, but when we begin with either of them, we know we will get something very different from the other.

King and Allen are exceptionally well known, but you can learn something about all of the authors represented in *The Little, Brown Reader* because they are introduced by means of biographical notes. Make it a practice to read these notes. They will give you some sense of what to expect. You may never have heard, for example, of J. H. Plumb—we include one of his essays later in this chapter—but when you learn from the note that he was a professor of history at the University of Cambridge and that he also taught in U.S. universities, you can tentatively assume that the essay will have a historical dimension. Of course, you may have to revise this assumption—the essay may be about the joys of trout fishing or the sorrows of being orphaned at an early age—but in all probability the biographical note will have given you some preparation for reading the essay.

The **original place of publication** may also give you some sense of what the piece will be about. The essays in *The Little, Brown Reader* originally were published in books, magazines, or newspapers, and these sources (specified, when relevant, in the biographical notes) may in themselves provide a reader with clues. For instance, since *The American Scholar* is published by Phi Beta Kappa and is read chiefly by college and university teachers or by persons with comparable education, articles in *The American Scholar* usually offer somewhat academic treatments of serious matters. They assume that the readers are serious and capable of sustained intellectual effort. Whereas a newspaper editorial runs about one thousand words, articles in *The American Scholar* may be eight or ten thousand words, running fifteen or so pages long.

Some journals have an obvious political slant, and the articles they publish are to some degree predictable in content and attitude. For instance, William Buckley's *National Review* is politically conservative. Its subscribers want to hear certain things, and *National Review* tells them what they want to hear. Its readers know, too, that the essays will be lively and can be read fairly rapidly. Similarly, subscribers to *Ms.* expect highly readable essays with a strong feminist slant.

The **form, or genre** (a literary term for type or kind of literature), may provide another clue as to what will follow. For instance, you can expect a letter to the editor to amplify or contradict an editorial or to comment approvingly or disapprovingly on some published news item. It will almost surely be concerned with a current issue. Martin Luther King Jr.'s "Letter from Birmingham Jail," a response to a letter from eight clergymen, is a famous example of a letter arguing on behalf of what was then a current action.

The **title, as we have already noted, may provide a clue.** Again, King provides an example; even before studying "I Have a Dream," a reader can assume that the essay will be about King's vision of the future. Another example of a title that announces its topic is "We Have No 'Right to Happiness.' " This title is straightforward and informative, but suppose you pick up an essay called "Do-It-Yourself Brain Surgery." What do you already know about the essay?

Skimming

"Some books are to be tasted, others to be swallowed, and some few to be chewed and digested." You may already have encountered this wise remark by Francis Bacon, a very good reader (and a good writer, too—though he did not write Shakespeare's plays). The art of reading includes the art of skimming, that is, the art of gliding rapidly over a piece of writing and getting its gist.

Skimming has three important uses: to get through junk mail and other lightweight stuff; to locate what is relevant to your purpose in a mass of material, as, for instance, when you are working on a research paper; and (our topic now) to get an overview of an essay, especially to get the gist of its argument. Having discovered what you can from the name of the author, the title of the work, and the place of publication, you may want to skim the essay before reading it closely.

The **opening paragraph** will often give you a good idea of the **topic** or general area of the essay (for instance, the family). And if the essay is essentially an argument, it may announce the writer's **thesis,** the point that the writer will argue (for instance, that despite the high divorce rate, the family is still in good shape). Here is an example from J. H. Plumb's "The Dying Family." (The entire essay is printed later in this chapter.)

> I was rather astonished when a minibus drove up to my house and out poured ten children. They had with them two parents, but not one child had them both in common as mother and father, and two of them belonged to neither parent, but to a former husband of the wife who had died. Both parents, well into middle age, had just embarked, one on his fourth, the other on her third marriage. The children, who came in all sizes, and ranged from blonde nordic to jet-haired Greek, bounded around the garden, young and old as happy as any children that I have seen. To them, as Californians, their situation was not particularly odd; most of their friends had multiple parents. Indeed to them perhaps the odd family was the one which Western culture has held up as a model for two thousand years or more—the life-long union of man and wife. But it took me a very long time to believe that they could be either happy or adjusted. And yet, were they a sign of the future, a way the world was going?

Taking into account the author's profession (a historian), the title ("The Dying Family"), and the first paragraph, a reader assumes that the essay probably will examine the new family in relation to the traditional Western model. A reader probably also assumes, on the basis of the first paragraph, that Plumb will not go on to scold this California family; we can't of course be certain of his position, but thus far he seems willing to grant that the family may really be happy.

If the title and first paragraph do not seem especially informative (the first paragraph may be a sort of warmup, akin to the speech maker's "A funny thing happened to me on my way here"), look closely at the second. Then, as you scan subsequent paragraphs, look especially for **topic sentences** (often the first sentence in a paragraph), which summarize the paragraph, and look for passages that follow **key phrases** such as "the important point to remember," "these two arguments can be briefly put thus," "in short," "it is essential to recall," and so on. Plumb's third paragraph begins thus:

> Basically the family has fulfilled three social functions—to provide a basic labor force, to transmit property and to educate and train children not only into

an accepted social pattern, but also in the work skills upon which their future subsistence would depend.

Not surprisingly, Plumb goes on to amplify—to support with details—these assertions, and you won't be wrong if you guess that later in the essay he will indicate that a change in historical conditions has changed the role of the family.

In skimming an essay, pay special attention to the **final paragraph,** which usually reformulates the writer's thesis. Plumb's final paragraph is long, and we need not quote it in full here, but it ends thus:

> Like any other human institution the family has always been molded by the changing needs of society, sometimes slowly, sometimes fast. And that bus load of children does no more than symbolize the failure, not of marriage, but of the role of the old-fashioned family unit in a modern, urbanized, scientific and affluent society.

Later, when you reread his essay carefully, you'll be on the lookout for the evidence that supports this view.

As you scan an essay, you'll find it useful to highlight phrases or sentences, or to draw vertical lines in the margin next to passages that seem to be especially concise bearers of meaning. In short, even while you are skimming you are using your pen.

If the essay is divided into sections, **headings** may give you an idea of the range of coverage. You probably won't need to highlight them—they already stand out—but there's no harm in doing so.

When you skim, you are seeking to get the gist of the author's **thesis, or point.** But you are also getting an idea of the author's **methods** and the author's **purpose.** For instance, skimming may reveal that the author is using statistics (or an appeal to common sense, or whatever) to set forth an unusual view. When Plumb begins by confessing he was "astonished" by the children in the minibus, he is using a bit of personal history to assure us that he is not a dry-as-dust historian whose understanding of life is based entirely on research in libraries. We immediately see that Plumb is writing for all of us, not just for professional historians, and we see that his purpose is to inform us in an engaging way. He will do a little preaching along the way, but even in skimming we can see that his chief purpose is to educate us, not to censure us for our high divorce rate. Another author might take the minibus as a symbol of what is wrong with the American family today, but such an author probably would, from the outset, let us sense what was coming, perhaps by depicting the children as quarreling or sulking.

During this preliminary trip through a piece of writing, you may get a pretty good idea of the writer's personality. More precisely, since you are not encountering the writer in the flesh but only the image that the writer presents in the essay, ~~you may form an impression of the~~ **voice,** ~~or persona, that speaks in the essay.~~ Something of Plumb's persona is evident in passages such as "I was rather astonished," "to them, as Californians, their situation was not particularly odd" (clearly the writer is *not* a Californian), and "it took me a very long time to believe that they could be either happy or adjusted." We will return to this important matter of persona later, on pages 16–17.

Let's now look at Plumb's essay. We suggest that in your first reading you skim it—perhaps highlighting, underlining, or drawing vertical lines next to passages that strike you as containing the chief ideas. To this extent, you are reading for information. But because you have ideas of your own and because you do not accept something as true simply because it appears in print, you may also want to put question marks or expressions of doubt ("Really?" "Check this") in the margin next to any passages that strike you as puzzling. Further, you may want to circle any words that you are not familiar with, but at this stage don't bother to look them up. In short, run through the essay, seeking to get the gist and briefly indicating your responses, but don't worry about getting every detail of the argument.

J. H. Plumb

The Dying Family

I was rather astonished when a minibus drove up to my house and out poured ten children. They had with them two parents, but not one child had them both in common as mother and father, and two of them belonged to neither parent, but to a former husband of the wife who had died. Both parents, well into middle age, had just embarked, one on his fourth, the other on her third marriage. The children, who came in all sizes, and ranged from blonde nordic to jet-haired Greek, bounded around the garden, young and old as happy as any children that I have seen. To them, as Californians, their situation was not particularly odd; most of their friends had multiple parents. Indeed to them perhaps the odd family was the one which Western culture has held up as a model for two thousand years or more—the lifelong union of man and wife. But it took me a very long time to believe that they could be either happy or

J. H. Plumb, "The Dying Family" from *In the Light of History* by J. H. Plumb. Published by Houghton Mifflin Company and Penguin Books Ltd. Reprinted by permission.

adjusted. And yet, were they a sign of the future, a way the world was going?

Unlike anthropologists or sociologists, historians have not studied family life very closely. Until recently we knew very little of the age at which people married in Western Europe in the centuries earlier than the nineteenth or how many children they had, or what the rates of illegitimacy might be or whether, newly wed, they lived with their parents or set up a house of their own. Few of these questions can be answered with exactitude even now, but we can make better guesses. We know even less, however, of the detailed sexual practices that marriage covered: indeed this is a subject to which historians are only just turning their attention. But we do know much more of the function of family life—its social role—particularly if we turn from the centuries to the millennia and pay attention to the broad similarities rather than the fascinating differences between one region and another: and, if we do, we realize that the family has changed far more profoundly than even the bus load of Californians might lead us to expect.

Basically the family has fulfilled three social functions—to provide a basic labor force, to transmit property and to educate and train children not only into an accepted social pattern, but also in the work skills upon which their future subsistence would depend. Until very recent times, the vast majority of children never went to any school: their school was the family, where they learned to dig and sow and reap and herd their animals, or they learned their father's craft of smith or carpenter or potter. The unitary family was particularly good at coping with the small peasant holdings which covered most of the world's fertile regions from China to Peru. In the primitive peasant world a child of four or five could begin to earn its keep in the fields, as they still can in India and Africa: and whether Moslem, Hindu, Inca or Christian, one wife at a time was all that the bulk of the world's population could support, even though their religion permitted them more. Indeed, it was the primitive nature of peasant economy which gave the family, as we know it, its wide diffusion and its remarkable continuity.

Whether or not it existed before the neolithic revolution we shall never know, but certainly it must have gained in strength as families became rooted to the soil. Many very primitive people who live in a pre-agrarian society of hunting and food-gathering often tend to have a looser structure of marriage and the women a far greater freedom of choice and easier divorce, as with the Esquimaux, than is permitted in peasant societies. There can be little doubt that the neolithic revolution created new opportunities for the family as we know it, partly because this revolution created new property relations. More importantly it created great masses of property, beyond anything earlier societies had known. True, there were a few hunting peoples, such as the Kwakiutl Indians, who had considerable possessions—complex lodges, great pieces of copper and piles of fibre blankets, which periodically they destroyed in great battles of raging pride—but the property, personal or communal, of most primitive hunting people is usually trivial.

After the revolution in agriculture, property and its transmission lay   5 at the very heart of social relations and possessed an actuality which we find hard to grasp. Although we are much richer, possessions are more anonymous, often little more than marks in a ledger, and what we own constantly changes. Whereas for the majority of mankind over this last seven thousand years property has been deeply personal and familial: a plot of land, if not absolute ownership over it, then valuable rights in it; sometimes a house, even though it be a hovel by our standards; perhaps no more than the tools and materials of a craft, yet these possessions were the route both to survival and to betterment. Hence they were endowed with manna, bound up with the deepest roots of personality. In all societies the question of property became embedded in every aspect of family life, particularly marriage and the succession and rights of children. Because of property's vital importance, subservience of women and children to the will of the father, limited only by social custom, became the pattern of most great peasant societies. Marriage was sanctified not only by the rites of religion, but by the transmission of property. Few societies could tolerate freedom of choice in marriage—too much vital to the success or failure of a family depended on it: an ugly girl with five cows was a far fairer prospect than a pretty girl with one. And because of the sexual drives of frail human nature, the customs of marriage and of family relationships needed to be rigorously enforced. Tradition sanctified them; religion blessed them. Some societies reversed the sexually restrictive nature of permanent marriage and permitted additional wives, but such permission was meaningless to the mass of the peasantry who fought a desperate battle to support a single family. And, as we shall see, the patterns of family life were always looser for the rich and the favored.

But a family was always more than property expressed clearly and visibly in real goods; it was for thousands of years both a school and a tribunal, the basic unit of social organization whose function in modern society has been very largely taken over by the state. In most peasant societies, life is regulated by the village community, by the patriarchs of the village, and the only officer of the central government these villagers see with any regularity is the tax-gatherer; but in societies that have grown more complex, and this is particularly true of the West during the last four hundred years, life has become regulated by the nation state or by the growth in power and importance of more generalized local communities—the town or county.

This has naturally weakened the authority of heads of families, a fact that can be symbolically illustrated by change in social custom. No child in Western Europe would sit unbidden in the presence of its parents until the eighteenth century: if it did it could be sure of rebuke and punishment. No head of a household would have thought twice about beating a recalcitrant young servant or apprentice before the end of the nineteenth century. For a younger brother to marry without the consent of his eldest brother would have been regarded as a social enormity; and sisters were disposable property. All of this power has vanished. Indeed the family ties of all of us have been so loosened that we find it hard to grasp the intensity of family relationships or their complexity, they have disintegrated so rapidly this last hundred years. Now nearly every child in the Western world, male or female, is educated outside the family from five years of age. The skills they learn are rarely, if ever, transmitted by parents: and what is more they learn about the nature of their own world, its social structure and its relationships in time outside the family. For millennia the family was the great transmitter and formulator of social custom; but it now only retains a shadow of this function, usually for very young children only.

Although the economic and education functions of the family have declined, most of us feel that it provides the most satisfactory emotional basis for human beings; that a secure family life breeds stability, a capacity not only for happiness, but also to adjust to society's demands. This, too, may be based on misjudgment, for family life in the past was not remarkable for its happiness. We get few glimpses into the private lives of men and women long dead, but when we do we often find strain, frustration, petty tyranny. For so many human beings family life was a prison from which they could not escape. And although it might create deep satisfactions here and there, the majority of the rich and affluent classes of the last four hundred years in Western Europe created for themselves a double standard, particularly as far as sex was concerned. In a few cities such as Calvin's Geneva, the purity of family life might be maintained, but the aristocracies of France, Italy and Britain tolerated, without undue concern, adultery, homosexuality and that sexual freedom which, for better or worse, we consider the hallmark of modern life. Indeed the family as the basic social group began firstly to fail, except in its property relations, amongst the aristocracy.

But what we think of as a social crisis of this generation—the rapid growth of divorce, the emancipation of women and adolescents, the sexual and educational revolutions, even the revolution in eating which is undermining the family as the basis of nourishment, for over a hundred years ago the majority of Europeans never ate in public in their lives—all of these things, which are steadily making the family weaker and weaker, are the inexorable result of the changes in society itself. The family as a unit of social organization was remarkably appropriate for a less complex world of agriculture and craftsmanship, a world which stretches back some seven thousand years, but ever since industry and highly urbanized societies began to take its place, the social functions of the family have steadily weakened—and this is a process that is unlikely to be halted. And there is no historical reason to believe that human beings could be less or more happy, less or more stable. Like any other human institution the family has always been molded by the changing needs of society, sometimes slowly, sometimes fast. And that bus load of children does no more than symbolize the failure, not of marriage, but of the role of the old-fashioned family unit in a modern, urbanized, scientific and affluent society.

Even a quick skimming reveals that Plumb offers, as you anticipated he would, a historical view. He begins with a glance at one contemporary family, but you probably noticed that by the second paragraph he speaks as a historian, tracing the origins and development of the institution of the family.

Highlighting, Underlining, Annotating

Now that you have the gist of Plumb's essay, go back and reread it; this time, highlight or underline key passages as though you were marking the text so that you might later easily review it for an examination. Your purpose now is simply to make sure that you know what Plumb is getting at. You may strongly disagree with him on details or even on large matters, and you would certainly make clear your differences with him if you were to write about his essay; but for the moment your purpose is to make sure that you know what his position is. See if in each paragraph you can find a sentence that contains the topic idea of the paragraph. If you find such sentences, mark them.

Caution: Do not allow yourself to highlight or underline whole paragraphs. Before you start to mark a paragraph, read it to the end, and then go back and mark what you now see as the key word, phrase, or passage. If you simply start marking a paragraph from the beginning, you may end up marking the whole and thus you will defeat your purpose, which is to make highly visible the basic points of the essay.

You may also want to jot down, in the margins, questions or objections, and you may want to circle any words that puzzle you.

Time's up. Let's talk about the underlinings and highlightings.

No two readers of the essay will make exactly the same annotations. To take a small example, a reader in Alaska would probably be more likely to mark the passage about "the Esquimaux" in paragraph 4 than would a reader in St Louis. But here is what one reader produced.

note
first
person
       ①was rather astonished when a minibus drove up to my house and out poured ten children. They had with them two parents, but not one child had them both in common as mother and father, and two of them belonged to neither parent, but to a former husband of the wife who had died. Both parents, well into middle age, had just embarked, one on his fourth, the other on her third marriage. The children, who came in all sizes, and ranged from blonde nordic to jet-haired Greek, bounded around the garden, young and old as happy

new (California) style

as any children that I have seen. To them, as
Californians, their situation was not particularly odd;
most of their friends had multiple parents. Indeed to
them perhaps the odd family was the one which
Western culture has held up as a model for two   *old style*
thousand years or more--the lifelong union of man and
wife. But it took me a very long time to believe that they
could be either happy or adjusted. And yet, were they   *who says*
a sign of the future, a way the world was going?   *they are*
first person Unlike anthropologists or sociologists, historians   *happy?*
again, but have not studied family life very closely. Until recently
less we knew very little of the age at which people married
"personal" in Western Europe in the centuries earlier than the
nineteenth or how many children they had, or what the
rates of illegitimacy might be or whether, newly wed,
they lived with their parents or set up a house of their
own. Few of these questions can be answered with
exactitude even now, but we can make better guesses.
We know even less, however, of the detailed sexual
practices that marriage covered: indeed this is a
subject to which historians are only just turning their
attention. But we do know much more of the function of
family life--its social role--particularly if we turn from
the centuries to the millennia and pay attention to the
broad similarities rather than the fascinating
differences between one region and another: and, if
we do, we realize that the family has changed far more   *change*
profoundly than even the bus load of Californians
might lead us to expect.
3 functions Basically the family has fulfilled three social   *1. provides*
functions--to provide a basic labor force, to transmit   *labor*
property and to educate and train children not only   *2. transmits*
into an accepted social pattern, but also in the work   *property*
skills upon which their future subsistence would   *3. educates*
depend. Until very recent times, the vast majority of   *children*
children never went to any school: their school was the
family, where they learned to dig and sow and reap
and herd their animals, or they learned their father's
craft of smith or carpenter or potter. The unitary family   *?*
was particularly good at coping with the small peasant
holdings, which covered most of the world's fertile
regions from China to Peru. In the primitive peasant
world a child of four or five could begin to earn its
keep in the fields, as they still can in India and Africa:
and whether Moslem, Hindu, Inca or Christian, one   *? couldn't*
wife at a time was all that the bulk of the world's   *wives earn*
population could support, even though their religion   *their keep?*
permitted them more. Indeed, it was the primitive
not also nature of peasant economy, which gave the family, as
religious we know it, its wide diffusion and its remarkable
teachings? continuity.

Whether or not it existed before the neolithic revolution we shall never know, but certainly it must have gained in strength as families became rooted to the soil. Many very primitive people who live in a pre-agrarian society of hunting and food-gathering often tend to have a looser structure of marriage and the women a far greater freedom of choice and easier divorce, as with the Esquimaux, than is permitted in peasant societies. There can be little doubt that the neolithic revolution created new opportunities for the family as we know it, partly because this revolution created new property relations. More importantly it created great masses of property, beyond anything earlier societies had known. True, there were a few hunting peoples, such as the Kwakiutl Indians, who had considerable possessions--complex lodges, great pieces of copper and piles of fibre blankets, which periodically they destroyed in great battles of raging pride--but the property, personal or communal, of most primitive hunting people is usually trivial.

Of course different readers will find different passages of special interest and importance. Our personal histories, our beliefs, our preconceptions, our current preoccupations, to some extent determine how we read. For instance, when they come to the fifth paragraph some readers may mark Plumb's sexist language ("mankind"), and some may highlight the assertion that "Marriage was sanctified not only by the rites of religion, but by the transmission of property." Readers who are especially interested in class relations might also highlight and underline this sentence:

> The patterns of family life were always looser for the rich and the favored.

Notice, by the way, that although Plumb makes this assertion he does not offer a value judgment. A reader might mark the sentence and add in the margin: *Still true, and outrageous!* Or, conversely, a reader may feel that the statement is false, and might write, *Really???*, or even *Not the rich, but the poor (free from bourgeois hangups) are sexually freer.*

As these last examples indicate, even when you simply set out to make a few notes that will help you to follow and to remember the essayist's argument, you may well find yourself making notes that record your **responses** (where you agree, what you question), notes that may start you thinking about the validity of the argument.

As we have already said, *what* you annotate will partly depend on what interests you, what your values are, and what your purpose is. True, you have read the essay because it was assigned, but Plumb's original readers read it for other reasons. It appeared first in a magazine and then in a collection of Plumb's essays. The original readers, then, were people who freely picked it up because they wanted to learn about the family or perhaps because they had read something else by Plumb, liked it, and wanted to hear more from this author.

Imagine yourself, for a moment, as a reader encountering this essay in a magazine that you have picked up. If you are reading because you want to know something about the family in an agrarian society, you'll annotate one sort of thing; if you are reading because as a child of divorced parents you were struck and possibly outraged by his first paragraph, you'll annotate another sort of thing; if you are reading because you admire Plumb as a historian, you'll annotate another sort of thing; and if you are reading because you dislike Plumb, you'll annotate something else. We remind you of a comment by Paul Valéry, quoted at the beginning of this chapter: "One reads well only when one reads with some personal goal in mind. It may be to acquire some power. It may be out of hatred for the author." An exaggeration, but there is something to it. (In the Book of Job, Job wishes that his "adversary had written a book.")

Summarizing

In your effort to formulate a brief version of what an essayist is saying, you may want to write a summary, especially if you found the essay difficult. A good way to begin is to summarize each paragraph in a sentence or two, or in some phrases. By summarizing each paragraph, you compile—without doing any additional work—an outline of the essay. Here is a student's outline of Plumb's essay.

1. Minibus in California: 10 children and 2 parents, but not one child was child of both adults. Different from traditional family. Sign of the way the world is going.
2. Many things not known about the past (age of marriage, sexual practices), but something known of the function of family life.
3. Three functions: providing a labor force, transmitting property, educating and training children. Peasant families today.
4, 5. After neolithic (agricultural?) revolution, family strengthened because people rooted to the soil (produced masses of property: land, house, or tools of a craft). Transmission of property sanctified marriage.
6, 7. Family was also school and basic social unit. Head of the household ruled (chose the mate for a child, etc.). In modern societies government has taken over many functions of patriarchs.
8. Despite loss of functions, most of us still feel that a family breeds stability, happiness. May be a misjudgment; family often was a prison. And for last 400 years the rich created a double standard, at least for sex.

9.   Decline of family (divorce, emancipation of women and adoles-
        cents, etc.) is result of historic <u>change in society itself</u>. Family ap-
        propriate for agricultural society but less in industrial and urban
        societies. Busload of kids symbolizes not the failure of marriage
        but the loss of role for old-fashioned family in a modern society.

Especially if an essay is complex, writing a summary of this sort can
help you to follow the argument. Glancing over your notes, you probably
can see, fairly easily, what the writer's *main* points are, as distinct from the
subordinate points and the examples that clarify the points. Furthermore,
since your summary is now a paragraph outline, you can look it over to see
not only what it adds up to, but also how the writer shaped the material.
Producing a summary, then, may be an activity that is useful to you when
you are *reading* an essay. It will almost surely help you to grasp the essay
and to remember its argument. And if you are *writing* about the essay—
perhaps to take issue with it or to amplify a point that it makes—you may
have to include in your essay a brief summary so that your readers will
know what you are writing about.

How long should the summary be? Just long enough to give readers
what they need in order to follow your essay. If in a fairly long essay you
are going to take issue with several of Plumb's points, you may want to
give a fairly detailed summary—perhaps a page long.

For a short essay, however, something like the following passage
might be appropriate:

In "The Dying Family," J. H. Plumb argues that when society was
primarily agricultural, the family provided education and training, a labor
force, and a way of transmitting property. In today's industrialized society,
however, these functions are largely provided by the government, and
the traditional family is no longer functional.

Critical Thinking: Analyzing the Text

Writing a summary requires that you pay attention to the text, but it does
not require you to question the text, to think about such issues as whether
the author's assumptions are plausible and whether evidence supports
the generalizations. In reading an essay, in addition to being able to summarize it accurately you must engage in **critical thinking.** "Critical" here
does not mean finding fault ("Don't be so critical") but, rather, it means
paying close attention to the ways in which the parts form the whole. In
this sense, to read critically is to read analytically.

We have already said that you will probably find yourself putting
question marks in the margins next to words that you don't know and that
don't become clear in the context, and next to statements that you find puzzling or dubious. These marks will remind you to take action—perhaps to

check a dictionary, to reread a paragraph, or to jot down your objection in the margin or at greater length in a journal.

But analytic readers also engage in another sort of questioning, though they may do so almost unconsciously. They are almost always asking themselves—or rather asking the text—several questions. You'll notice that these questions concern not only the writer's point but also the writer's craft. By asking such questions, you will learn about subject matter (for instance, about the history of the family in Plumb's essay) and also about some of the tricks of the writer's trade (for instance, effective ways of beginning). If you read actively, asking the following questions, you will find that reading is *not* a solitary activity; you are conversing with a writer.

- What is the writer's thesis?
- How does the writer support the thesis?
- What is the writer's purpose (to persuade, to rebut, to entertain, to share an experience, or whatever)?
- How do the writer's audience and purpose help shape the writing? (The place of publication is often a clue to the audience.) For instance, does the writer use humor or, on the other hand, speak earnestly? Are terms carefully defined, or does the writer assume that the audience is knowledgeable and does not need such information?
- What is the writer's tone?

These questions will help you to understand what you are reading and how writers go about their business. But you are also entitled to evaluate what you are reading, hence some other questions, of a rather different sort:

- How successful is the piece? What are its strengths and weaknesses? What do I especially like or dislike about it? Why?

We recommend that when you read an essay you ask each of these questions—not, of course, during an initial skimming, but during a second and third reading, after you have some sense of the essay.

These questions almost can be boiled down to one question:

What is the writer up to?

That is, a reader who is not content merely to take what the writer is handing out asks such questions as, Why *this* way of opening? Why *this* way of defining the term? The assumption that the writer has a purpose may be false. (We are reminded of a comment that Metternich, the keenly analytic Austrian statesman and diplomat, uttered when he learned that the Czar had died: "I wonder why he did that.") Yes, the writer may just be blundering along, but it's reasonable to begin with the assumption that the writer is competent. If under questioning the writer fails, you have at least learned that not everything in print is worthy.

Tone and Persona

Perhaps you know the line from Owen Wister's novel, *The Virginian:* "When you call me that, smile." Words spoken with a smile mean something different from the same words spoken through clenched teeth. But while speakers can communicate by facial gestures, body language, and changes in tone of voice, writers have only words in ink on paper. Somehow the writer has to help us to know whether, for instance, he or she is solemn, or joking, in earnest.

Consider the beginning of the first paragraph of J. H. Plumb's "The Dying Family."

> I was rather astonished when a minibus drove up to my house and out poured ten children. They had with them two parents, but not one child had them both in common as mother and father, and two of them belonged to neither parent, but to a former husband of the wife who had died. Both parents, well into middle age, had just embarked, one on his fourth, the other on her third marriage. The children, who came in all sizes, and ranged from blonde nordic to jet-haired Greek, bounded around the garden, young and old as happy as any children that I have seen.

Plumb's first sentence *could* have run thus:

> I noted with considerable surprise the fact that when a minibus drove up to my house, ten children got out of the vehicle.

This version contains nothing that is certifiably wrong—the grammar and spelling are satisfactory—but it lacks the energy of Plumb's version. In the original, Plumb is astonished rather than surprised, and the children don't just get out of the minibus, they "pour" out. Further, the original minibus is just a minibus; it doesn't become (as it unnecessarily does, in the revised version) a "vehicle." After all, who speaks of vehicles other than perhaps police officers when they say in an official report that they "apprehended the perpetrator in a speeding vehicle"?

Notice too, in the succeeding sentences, that the children "came in all sizes." If Plumb had said that the smallest child was about three feet tall, and the largest child must have been at least five feet tall, he might have been more exact, but he certainly would have been less engaging. As readers we probably enjoy the fairly colloquial tone that this distinguished professor is using.

What sort of person is Plumb? He seems to be a neighbor, chatting easily with us, not a remote professor delivering a lecture. And yet even in this paragraph, when he speaks of "two thousand years or more" of "Western culture" we realize that he is a historian who can speak with some authority. He may or may not be divorced, he may or may not be a loving parent, he may or may not be a good cook—there are countless things we don't know about him—so we can't really say what sort of person he is. We can, however, say what sort of *persona* (or personality) he conveys in his essay.

How do readers form an impression of a persona? By listening, so to speak, with a third ear, listening for the writer's attitude toward

- himself or herself,
- the subject, and
- the audience.

Still, different readers will, of course, respond differently. To take a simple example, readers who do not wish to hear arguments concerning new views of the family may dismiss Plumb as radical, or as lacking in basic moral values. But we think most readers will agree with us in saying that Plumb conveys the persona of someone who is (1) educated, (2) at least moderately engaging, (3) a good teacher, and (4) concerned with a significant issue. It's our guess, too, that Plumb hoped to be seen as this sort of person. If readers of his first paragraph conclude that he is conceited, stuffy, full of hot air, a threat to society, and so on, he has failed terribly, because he has turned his readers away.

There is a lesson for writers, too. When you reread your own drafts and essays, try to get out of yourself and into the mind of an imagined reader, say a classmate. Try to hear how your words will sound in this other person's ear; that is, try to imagine what impression this reader will form of your attitude toward yourself, your subject, and your reader.

Don't hesitate to demand that an essay give you pleasure. The author probably thought that he or she was writing well, and certainly hoped to hold your interest throughout the essay and to make you feel that you were learning something of interest. In short, the author hoped that you would like the essay. You have every right to evaluate the essay partly by considering the degree of pleasure that it affords.

Daniel Gilbert

Daniel Gilbert, a professor of psychology at Harvard, is the author of Stumbling on Happiness *(2006)—a best seller that won the Royal Society Prize ($20,000) for Science Books. Hearing of the award, Gilbert said, "There are very few countries, including my own, the U.S., where a somewhat cheeky book about happiness could win a science prize—but the British invented intellectual humor and have always understood that enlightenment and entertainment are natural friends."*

A high school dropout, Gilbert was nineteen when he visited a community college, intending to take a writing course but enrolling instead in the only course still open—a psychology course.

We reprint here an essay that appeared in Time *a few days before Father's Day.*

Does Fatherhood Make You Happy?

Sonora Smart Dodd was listening to a sermon on self-sacrifice when she decided that her father, a widower who had raised six children, deserved his very own national holiday. Almost a century later, people all over the world spend the third Sunday in June honoring their fathers with ritual offerings of aftershave and neckties, which leads millions of fathers to have precisely the same thought at precisely the same moment: "My children," they think in unison, "make me happy."

Could all those dads be wrong?

Studies reveal that most married couples start out happy and then become progressively less satisfied over the course of their lives, becoming especially disconsolate when their children are in diapers and in adolescence, and returning to their initial levels of happiness only after their children have had the decency to grow up and go away. When the popular press invented a malady called "empty-nest syndrome," it failed to mention that its primary symptom is a marked increase in smiling.

Psychologists have measured how people feel as they go about their daily activities, and have found that people are less happy when they are interacting with their children than when they are eating, exercising, shopping or watching television. Indeed, an act of parenting makes most people about as happy as an act of housework. Economists have modeled the impact of many variables on people's overall happiness and have consistently found that children have only a small impact. A small negative impact.

Those findings are hard to swallow because they fly in the face of our most compelling intuitions. We love our children! We talk about them to anyone who will listen, show their photographs to anyone who will look and hide our refrigerators behind vast collages of their drawings, notes, pictures and report cards. We feel confident that we are happy with our kids, about our kids, for our kids and because of our kids—so why is our personal experience at odds with the scientific data?

Three reasons.

First, when something makes us happy we are willing to pay a lot for it, which is why the worst Belgian chocolate is more expensive than the best Belgian tofu. But that process can work in reverse: when we pay a lot for something, we assume it makes us happy, which is why we swear to the wonders of bottled water and Armani socks. The compulsion to care for our children was long ago written into our DNA, so we toil and sweat, lose sleep and hair, play nurse, housekeeper, chauffeur and cook, and we do all that because nature just won't have it any other way. Given the high price we pay, it isn't surprising that we rationalize those costs and conclude that our children must be repaying us with happiness.

5

Second, if the Red Sox and the Yankees were scoreless until Manny Ramirez hit a grand slam in the bottom of the ninth, you can be sure that Boston fans would remember it as the best game of the season. Memories are dominated by their most powerful—and not their most typical—instances. Just as a glorious game-winning homer can erase our memory of 8½ dull innings, the sublime moment when our 3-year-old looks up from the mess she is making with her mashed potatoes and says, "I wub you, Daddy," can erase eight hours of no, not yet, not now and stop asking. Children may not make us happy very often, but when they do, that happiness is both transcendent and amnesic.

Third, although most of us think of heroin as a source of human misery, shooting heroin doesn't actually make people feel miserable. It makes them feel really, really good—so good, in fact, that it crowds out every other source of pleasure. Family, friends, work, play, food, sex—none can compete with the narcotic experience; hence all fall by the wayside. The analogy to children is all too clear. Even if their company were an unremitting pleasure, the fact that they require so much company means that other sources of pleasure will all but disappear. Movies, theater, parties, travel—those are just a few of the English nouns that parents of young children quickly forget how to pronounce. We believe our children are our greatest joy, and we're absolutely right. When you have one joy, it's bound to be the greatest.

Our children give us many things, but an increase in our average   10
daily happiness is probably not among them. Rather than deny that fact, we should celebrate it. Our ability to love beyond all measure those who try our patience and weary our bones is at once our most noble and most human quality. The fact that children don't always make us happy—and that we're happy to have them nonetheless—is the fact for which Sonora Smart Dodd was so grateful. She thought we would all do well to remember it, every third Sunday in June.

 ## Joining the Conversation: Critical Thinking and Writing

1. What is Gilbert's thesis? Does he state his thesis explicitly? If so, where?

2. How does Gilbert support his thesis?

3. What is Gilbert's purpose in this article (to persuade, to rebut, to entertain, or whatever)?

4. Where was the article first published, and on what date? How, in your opinion, do his audience and purpose affect his writing?

5. You may have been told that you should not write paragraphs consisting of only a sentence or two, but Gilbert's essay includes two such paragraphs, 2 and 6. Should Gilbert have revised these paragraphs? Or does their brevity serve a purpose? Explain.

6. Do you believe the "studies" that Gilbert mentions in his third paragraph? Why, or why not? Similarly, do you believe the "psychologists" of the fourth paragraph? Explain.

7. Describe Gilbert's tone to someone who has not read the article. Be sure to give examples of any traits you mention.

8. Gilbert's final paragraph begins, "Our children give us many things, but an increase in our average daily happiness is probably not among them." Having read his essay and thought about it—having, perhaps, thought about your own family—are you inclined to agree. Why, or why not?

✓ A Checklist: Analyzing and Evaluating an Essay

☐ What is the *topic* of the essay? Try to state the topic, preferably in writing, as specifically as possible. For example, broadly speaking, you might say that the topic of Plumb's essay is the family; more specifically his topic is the change in the nature of the family due to historical forces.

☐ What is the essay's *thesis*, its point, its argument?

☐ What does the title do?

☐ What is the function of the opening paragraph (or paragraphs)? What claim on your attention or beliefs does it make?

☐ What speaker or persona does the writer create, and how does the writer create it?

☐ What is the tone? Does the tone shift as the essay progresses? If so, why?

☐ What audience is the writer addressing? The general, literate public or a more specialized group?

☐ How is the argument set forth? By logic? By drawing on personal experience? What other kinds of evidence support the essay's claim? What are the author's underlying assumptions? Are they stated or implied, and are they acceptable to you, or can you challenge them?

☐ Is the essay persuasive (whether because of its logic or because of the power of the speaker's personality)?

☐ Does the essay give pleasure?

A Reader Writes

All there is to writing is having ideas. To learn to write is to learn to have ideas.

Robert Frost

So far, the only writing that we have suggested you do is in the form of annotating, summarizing, and responding to some basic and some specific questions about the essayist's thesis and methods. All of these activities help you to think about what you are reading. "It is thinking," the philosopher John Locke wrote, "that makes what we read ours." But ultimately your thoughts will manifest themselves in your own essays, which probably will take off from one or more of the essays that you have read. Before we discuss writing about more than one essay, let's look at another essay, this one by C. S. Lewis (1898–1963).

Lewis taught English literature at Oxford and at Cambridge, but he is most widely known not for his books on literature but for his books on Christianity (*The Screwtape Letters* is one of the most famous), his children's novels (collected in a seven-volume set called *The Chronicles of Narnia*), and his science fiction (for instance, *Perelandra*). Lewis also wrote autobiographical volumes and many essays on literature and on morality. The essay printed here—the last thing that he wrote—was published in *The Saturday Evening Post* in December 1963, shortly after his death.

C. S. Lewis

We Have No "Right to Happiness"

After all," said Clare, "they had a right to happiness."

We were discussing something that once happened in our own neighborhood. Mr. A. had deserted Mrs. A. and got his divorce in order to marry Mrs. B., who had likewise got her divorce in order to marry Mr. A. And there was certainly no doubt that Mr. A. and Mrs. B. were very much in love with one another. If they continued to be in love, and if nothing went wrong with their health or their income, they might reasonably expect to be very happy.

It was equally clear that they were not happy with their old partners. Mrs. B. had adored her husband at the outset. But then he got smashed up in the war. It was thought he had lost his virility, and it was known that he had lost his job. Life with him was no longer what Mrs. B. had bargained for. Poor Mrs. A., too. She had lost her looks—and all her liveliness. It might be true, as some said, that she consumed herself by bearing his children and nursing him through the long illness that overshadowed their earlier married life.

You mustn't, by the way, imagine that A. was the sort of man who nonchalantly threw a wife away like the peel of an orange he'd sucked dry. Her suicide was a terrible shock to him. We all knew this, for he told us so himself. "But what could I do?" he said. "A man has a right to happiness. I had to take my one chance when it came."

I went away thinking about the concept of a "right to happiness."   5

At first this sounds to me as odd as a right to good luck. For I believe—whatever one school of moralists may say—that we depend for a very great deal of our happiness or misery on circumstances outside all human control. A right to happiness doesn't, for me, make much more sense than a right to be six feet tall, or to have a millionaire for your father, or to get good weather whenever you want to have a picnic.

I can understand a right as a freedom guaranteed me by the laws of the society I live in. Thus, I have a right to travel along the public roads because society gives me that freedom; that's what we mean by calling the roads "public." I can also understand a right as a claim guaranteed me by the laws, and correlative to an obligation on someone else's part. If I have a right to receive £100 from you, this is another way of saying that you have a duty to pay me £100. If the laws allow Mr. A. to desert his wife and seduce his neighbor's wife, then, by definition, Mr. A. has a legal right to do so, and we need bring in no talk about "happiness."

But of course that was not what Clare meant. She meant that he had not only a legal but a moral right to act as he did. In other words, Clare is—or would be if she thought it out—a classical moralist after the style of Thomas Aquinas, Grotius, Hooker and Locke. She believes that behind the laws of the state there is a Natural Law.[1]

I agree with her. I hold this conception to be basic to all civilization. Without it, the actual laws of the state become an absolute, as in Hegel. They cannot be criticized because there is no norm against which they should be judged.

The ancestry of Clare's maxim, "They have a right to happiness," is   10 august. In words that are cherished by all civilized men, but especially by Americans, it has been laid down that one of the rights of man is a right to "the pursuit of happiness." And now we get to the real point.

What did the writers of that august declaration mean?

It is quite certain what they did not mean. They did not mean that man was entitled to pursue happiness by any and every means—including, say, murder, rape, robbery, treason and fraud. No society could be built on such a basis.

---

[1]**Thomas Aquinas . . . Natural Law** Lewis names some philosophers and theologians from the thirteenth century through the eighteenth who believed that certain basic moral principles are evident to rational people in all periods and in all cultures. (Editors' note)

They meant "to pursue happiness by all lawful means"; that is, by all means which the Law of Nature eternally sanctions and which the laws of the nation shall sanction.

Admittedly this seems at first to reduce their maxim to the tautology that men (in pursuit of happiness) have a right to do whatever they have a right to do. But tautologies, seen against their proper historical context, are not always barren tautologies. The declaration is primarily a denial of the political principles which long governed Europe: a challenge flung down to the Austrian and Russian empires, to England before the Reform Bills, to Bourbon France.[2] It demands that whatever means of pursuing happiness are lawful for any should be lawful for all; that "man," not men of some particular caste, class, status or religion, should be free to use them. In a century when this is being unsaid by nation after nation and party after party, let us not call it a barren tautology.

But the question as to what means are "lawful"—what methods of pursuing happiness are either morally permissible by the Law of Nature or should be declared legally permissible by the legislature of a particular nation—remains exactly where it did. And on that question I disagree with Clare. I don't think it is obvious that people have the unlimited "right to happiness" which she suggests.

For one thing, I believe that Clare, when she says "happiness," means simply and solely "sexual happiness." Partly because women like Clare never use the word "happiness" in any other sense. But also because I never heard Clare talk about the "right" to any other kind. She was rather leftist in her politics, and would have been scandalized if anyone had defended the actions of a ruthless man-eating tycoon on the ground that his happiness consisted in making money and he was pursuing his happiness. She was also a rabid teetotaler; I never heard her excuse an alcoholic because he was happy when he was drunk.

A good many of Clare's friends, and especially her female friends, often felt—I've heard them say so—that their own happiness would be perceptibly increased by boxing her ears. I very much doubt if this would have brought her theory of a right to happiness into play.

Clare, in fact, is doing what the whole western world seems to me to have been doing for the last forty-odd years. When I was a youngster, all the progressive people were saying, "Why all this prudery? Let us treat sex just as we treat all our other impulses." I was simple-minded enough to believe they meant what they said. I have since discovered that they meant exactly the opposite. They meant that sex was to be treated as no other impulse in our nature has ever been treated by civilized people. All the others, we admit, have to be bridled. Absolute obedience to your instinct for self-preservation is what we call cowardice; to your acquisitive impulse, avarice. Even sleep must be resisted if you're a sentry. But every

15

[2]**England ... France** England before the bills that liberalized representation in Parliament in the nineteenth century, and France before the French Revolution of 1789–99. (Editors' note)

unkindness and breach of faith seems to be condoned provided that the object aimed at is "four bare legs in a bed."

It is like having a morality in which stealing fruit is considered wrong—unless you steal nectarines.

And if you protest against this view you are usually met with chatter about the legitimacy and beauty and sanctity of "sex" and accused of harboring some Puritan prejudice against it as something disreputable or shameful. I deny the charge. Foam-born Venus . . . golden Aphrodite . . . Our Lady of Cyprus[3] . . . I never breathed a word against you. If I object to boys who steal my nectarines, must I be supposed to disapprove of nectarines in general? Or even of boys in general? It might, you know, be stealing that I disapproved of.

The real situation is skillfully concealed by saying that the question of Mr. A.'s "right" to desert his wife is one of "sexual morality." Robbing an orchard is not an offense against some special morality called "fruit morality." It is an offense against honesty. Mr. A.'s action is an offense against good faith (to solemn promises), against gratitude (toward one to whom he was deeply indebted) and against common humanity.

Our sexual impulses are thus being put in a position of preposterous privilege. The sexual motive is taken to condone all sorts of behavior which, if it had any other end in view, would be condemned as merciless, treacherous and unjust.

Now though I see no good reason for giving sex this privilege, I think I see a strong cause. It is this.

It is part of the nature of a strong erotic passion—as distinct from a transient fit of appetite—that it makes more towering promises than any other emotion. No doubt all our desires make promises, but not so impressively. To be in love involves the almost irresistible conviction that one will go on being in love until one dies, and that possession of the beloved will confer, not merely frequent ecstasies, but settled, fruitful, deep-rooted, lifelong happiness. Hence *all* seems to be at stake. If we miss this chance we shall have lived in vain. At the very thought of such a doom we sink into fathomless depths of self-pity.

Unfortunately these promises are found often to be quite untrue. Every experienced adult knows this to be so as regards all erotic passions (except the one he himself is feeling at the moment). We discount the world-without-end pretensions of our friends' amours easily enough. We know that such things sometimes last—and sometimes don't. And when they do last, this is not because they promised at the outset to do so. When two people achieve lasting happiness, this is not solely because they are great lovers but because they are also—I must put it crudely— good people; controlled, loyal, fairminded, mutually adaptable people.

[3]**Foam-born Venus . . . Aphrodite . . . Cyprus** The Roman goddess Venus was identified with the Greek goddess of love, Aphrodite. Aphrodite sprang from the foam (*aphros*), and was especially worshipped in Cyprus. (Editors' note)

If we establish a "right to (sexual) happiness" which supersedes all the ordinary rules of behavior, we do so not because of what our passion shows itself to be in experience but because of what it professes to be while we are in the grip of it. Hence, while the bad behavior is real and works miseries and degradations, the happiness which was the object of the behavior turns out again and again to be illusory. Everyone (except Mr. A. and Mrs. B.) knows that Mr. A. in a year or so may have the same reason for deserting his new wife as for deserting his old. He will feel again that all is at stake. He will see himself again as the great lover, and his pity for himself will exclude all pity for the woman.

Two further points remain.

One is this. A society in which conjugal infidelity is tolerated must always be in the long run a society adverse to women. Women, whatever a few male songs and satires may say to the contrary, are more naturally monogamous than men; it is a biological necessity. Where promiscuity prevails, they will therefore always be more often the victims than the culprits. Also, domestic happiness is more necessary to them than to us. And the quality by which they most easily hold a man, their beauty, decreases every year after they have come to maturity, but this does not happen to those qualities of personality—women don't really care twopence about our *looks*—by which we hold women. Thus in the ruthless war of promiscuity women are at a double disadvantage. They play for higher stakes and are also more likely to lose. I have no sympathy with moralists who frown at the increasing crudity of female provocativeness. These signs of desperate competition fill me with pity.

Secondly, though the "right to happiness" is chiefly claimed for the sexual impulse, it seems to me impossible that the matter should stay there. The fatal principle, once allowed in that department, must sooner or later seep through our whole lives. We thus advance toward a state of society in which not only each man but every impulse in each man claims *carte blanche*.[4] And then, though our technological skill may help us survive a little longer, our civilization will have died at heart, and will—one dare not even add "unfortunately"—be swept away.

Responding to an Essay

After you have read Lewis's essay at least twice, you may want to jot down your responses to the basic questions that we introduced on page 15 after J. H. Plumb's essay. Here they are yet again, slightly abbreviated:

- What is the writer's thesis?
- How does the writer support the thesis?
- What is the writer's purpose?

[4]*Carte blanche* Full permission to act (French for "blank card") (Editors' note)

- How does the writer shape the purpose to the audience?
- What is the writer's tone?
- How successful is the piece? What are its strengths and weaknesses?

And here, to help you to think further about Lewis's essay, are some specific questions to answer and points to consider:

- Having read the entire essay, look back at Lewis's first five paragraphs and point out the ways in which he is not merely recounting an episode but is already conveying his attitude and seeking to persuade.
- Lewis argues that we do not have a "right to (sexual) happiness." What *duty* or *duties* do we have, according to Lewis?
- In paragraph 25 Lewis writes:

  When two people achieve lasting happiness, this is not solely because they are great lovers but because they are also—I must put it crudely—good people; controlled, loyal, fairminded, mutually adaptable people.

  If you know of a couple who in your opinion have achieved "lasting happiness," do you agree with Lewis's view that their achievement is largely because they are "good people"?
- Evaluate Lewis's comment in paragraph 28 on the differences between men and women.

If you find yourself roughing out responses to any of these questions, you may be on the way toward writing a first draft of an essay.

The Writing Process

An essay is a response to experience. J. H. Plumb saw (or says that he saw) a busload of people and was prompted to think about them and ultimately to write an essay on the family (page 6); C. S. Lewis heard (or says that he heard) someone utter a comment about a right to happiness, and he was set to thinking and then to writing about it (page 22). Their essays came out of their experience. By *experience* we do not mean only what they actually saw (since we can suspect that Plumb and Lewis may have invented the episodes they use at the start of their essays); their experience included things they had read about and had reflected on. After all, Plumb's bus and Lewis's report of Clare's remark were at most only triggers, so to speak. A good deal of previous experience and a good deal of later experience—chiefly in the form of reading and of *thinking* about what they had read—went into the production of their essays.

In short, writers think about their responses to experience. You have been actively reading their responses—engaging in a dialogue with these authors—and so you have been undergoing your own experiences. You have things to say, though on any given topic you probably are not yet certain of *all* that you have to say or of how you can best say it. You need to get further ideas, to do further thinking. How do you get ideas? The short answer is that you will get ideas if you engage in an imagined dialogue with the authors whom you are reading. When you read an essay, you will find yourself asking such questions as, What evidence supports this assertion? Is the writer starting from assumptions with which I don't agree? Why do I especially like (or dislike) this essay?

Many writers—professionals as well as students—have found it useful to get their responses down on paper, either as annotations in the margins or as entries in a journal, or both. Here, as a sample, are the annotations that one student jotted next to Lewis's third and fourth paragraphs.

It was equally clear that they were not happy with their old partners. Mrs. B. had adored her husband at the outset. But then he got smashed up in the war. It was thought he had lost his virility, and it was known that he had lost his job. Life with him was no longer what Mrs. B. had bargained for. Poor Mrs. A., too. She had lost her looks--and all her liveliness. It might be true, as some said, that she consumed herself by bearing his children and nursing him through the long illness that overshadowed their earlier married life.

> *Loaded word. Makes her too calculating*

> *These examples are caricatures. They really defeat L's purpose*

You musn't, by the way, imagine that A. was the sort of man who nonchalantly threw a wife away like the peel of an orange he'd sucked dry. Her suicide was a terrible shock to him. We all knew this, for he told us so himself. "But what could I do?" he said. "A man has a right to happiness. I had to take my one chance when it came."

> *Is CSL making him too awful?*

Annotations of this sort often are the starting point for entries in a journal.

Keeping a Journal

A journal is not a diary, a record of what the writer did during the day ("Today I read Lewis's 'We Have No "Right to Happiness"'"). Rather, a journal is a place to store some of the thoughts that you may have scribbled on a bit of paper or in the margin of the text—for instance, your initial response to the title of an essay or to something you particularly liked or disliked. It is also a place to jot down further reflections. You can record your impressions as they come to you in any order—almost as though you are talking to yourself. Since no one else is going to read your notes, you can be entirely free and at ease. The student whose annotations we reproduced a moment ago wrote the following entry in his journal:

> I find Lewis's writing is very clear and in its way persuasive, but I also think that his people--A. and B. and Clare--are not real people. They are almost caricatures. Anyway, he certainly has chosen people (or invented them?) who help him make his case. What if Mrs. B.'s husband had been a wife-beater, or maybe someone who molested their daughter? Would Lewis still think Mrs. B. was wrong to leave Mr. B.?

A second student wrote a rather different entry in her journal:

> Lewis at first seems to be arguing against a "right to happiness," but really he is arguing against adultery and divorce, against what we can call the Playboy morality--the idea that if a middle-aged man divorces his middle-aged wife because he now finds his young secretary attractive, he is acting maturely.

Here is a third entry:

> Terrific. That story about A. and B. really got to me. But is it true? Does it matter if it isn't true? Probably not; there are people like the A.'s and the B.'s. Lewis really is awfully good at holding my interest. And I was really grabbed by that business about a right to happiness being as strange as a right to be six feet tall. But my question is this: I agree that we don't have a right to be six feet tall, but why, then, do we have <u>any</u> rights? Lewis talks about Natural Law, but what is that?
>
> Is the idea of one husband and one wife "Natural Law"? If so, how come so many societies don't obey it? When Bertrand Russell talks about natural instincts and emotions "which we inherit from our animal ancestors," is this like Natural Law?
>
> Still, I think Lewis is terrific. And I think he is probably right about the difference between men and women. It seems obvious to me that men care more about a woman's looks than women care about a man's looks. How can this be checked?

You might even make a journal entry in the form of a letter to the author or in the form of a dialogue. Or you might have Mr. A. and Mrs. B. give *their* versions of the story that Clare reports.

Questioning the Text Again

We have already suggested that one way to increase your understanding of an essay and to get ideas that you may use in an essay of your own is to ask questions of the selection that you have read. Let's begin by thinking about the questions we asked following C. S. Lewis's "We Have No 'Right to Happiness'" (pages 2–26). All of these could provide topics for your own essays. Some were questions that might be asked of any essay, you'll recall—about the author's thesis, the way in which the author supports the thesis, the author's purpose, the author's persona or tone, and your evaluation of the essay. And there were questions specifically about Lewis's essay, concerning Lewis's comments on rights and his comments about the differences between men and women.

Probably the most obvious topic for an essay such as Lewis's is

What is the author's thesis, and how sound is it?

One student formulated the thesis as follows:

> We not only do not have a "right" to sexual happiness, but we probably cannot achieve lasting happiness if we allow sex to govern behavior that otherwise "would be condemned as merciless, treacherous and unjust."

An essay concerning Lewis's thesis might be narrowed, for example, to

Does Lewis give a one-sided view of divorce?

or

Does Lewis underestimate (or overestimate) the importance of sexual satisfaction?

But other topics easily come to mind, for instance:

- Lewis's methods as a writer
- The logic of Lewis's argument

Take the matter of Lewis's methods, a topic of special interest if you are trying to become a better writer. One student who planned to write about this topic made the following notes.

Summaries, Jottings, Outlines, and Lists

(Parenthetic numbers refer to Lewis's paragraphs.)

1.   Purpose is obviously to persuade. How does he do it?
2.   Very informal manner:
     a. Begins by telling of a conversation he had (1).
     b. Often uses "I"; for instance, "I went away thinking" (5); "this sounds to me" (6); "I can understand" (7); "I was simple-minded

enough to believe" (18). So the tone is personal, as if he and the reader were having a conversation.

3.   Though informal, seems very educated:
        a. Cites authorities, apparently philosophers, in par. 8 (check these
           names); refers to Austrian, Russian, English, and French history (14).
        b. Educated vocabulary ("tautologies" in par. 14).

4.   But also uses easy examples: Mr. and Mrs. A. and Mr. and Mrs. B.
        in first paragraph; stealing fruit (19–21).

5.   Makes the abstract clear by being concrete. In par. 18, when he
        says that our impulses have to be controlled, he says, "Absolute
        obedience to your instinct for self-preservation is what we call
        cowardice. . . ."

6.   Sentences are all clear. Some are very short ("I agree with her" 9),
        but even the long sentences--several lines of type--are clear.
        Give one (or maybe two) examples?

7.   In next-to-last par., frankly speaks as a male: "domestic happiness
        is more necessary to them [that is, women] than to us." And "the
        quality by which they [that is, women] most easily hold a man," and
        "women don't really care twopence about our looks" (all in 28).
        Sense of a man talking heart-to-heart to men. But how might it strike
        a woman? Sexist? Ask Jane and Tina.

You may prefer to record your thoughts in the form of lists:

Methods:
        Examples
        Anecdote about A. and B. (par. 1)
        Stealing fruit (19–21)
Informal style:
        Uses "I" (many places)
        Also uses "we"
Clear sentences (give examples)
Vocabulary:
        Usually simple words
        A few hard words ("tautologies" in par. 14)
Beginning: an individual listening
End: rather authoritative: generalizes about men vs women

Further thinking and further readings of Lewis's essay produced more evidence, and of course the material then had to be reorganized into a clear and effective sequence, but these notes and lists were highly promising. The student who wrote them was well on the way to writing a strong first draft.

After converting his notes into a draft and then revising the draft, an interesting—yet rather common—thing happened. The student found himself dissatisfied with his point. He now felt that he wanted to say something different. The annotations and the drafts, it turned out, were a way of helping him to get to a deeper response to Lewis's essay, and so he rewrote his essay, changing his focus. But we are getting ahead of our story.

✓ A Checklist: Getting Started

- ☐ Have I adequately previewed the work?
- ☐ Can I state the thesis?
- ☐ If I have jotted down a summary,
    - ☐ Is the summary accurate?
    - ☐ Does the summary mention all the chief points?
    - ☐ If there are inconsistencies, are they in the summary or the original selection?
    - ☐ Will the summary be clear and helpful?

Getting Ready to Write a Draft

After jotting down notes (and further notes stimulated by rereading and further thinking), you probably will be able to formulate a tentative thesis, a point such as "Lewis argues with great skill," or "Lewis does not make clear the concept of Natural Law," or "Lewis generalizes too freely," or "Lewis has a narrow idea of why people divorce." At this point most writers find it useful to clear the air by glancing over their preliminary notes and by jotting down the thesis and a few especially promising notes—brief statements of what they think their key points may be. These notes may include some key quotations that the writer thinks will help support the thesis.

Draft of an Essay

On "We Have No 'Right to Happiness' "

When I first read the title of C. S. Lewis's essay, I was interested and also somewhat resistant. Without having given much thought to it, I believe that I do have a right to happiness. I don't want to give up this right or this belief. Still I was intrigued to know what Lewis had to say. After reading the essay, it seemed entirely reasonable to say that if there is a right to happiness there are also limits to it. So I decided to look at how Lewis managed to make me change my mind--at least part way.

C. S. Lewis is persuasive, especially because of three things. First, although Lewis (a professor) is obviously very learned, he uses an informal manner that sounds very natural and honest. Second, he gives clear examples. Three, his sentences are always clear. This is true even when they are not especially short. All of these things combine together to make his essay clear and interesting. Lewis is an Englishman, not an American.

Lewis's informal manner, especially seen in his use of the first-person pronoun, appears right away. In the second sentence, when he says "We were discussing something. . . ." He uses "I" in the fifth paragraph and in many later paragraphs.

Another sign of Lewis's informality is his use of such expressions as "It might be true, as some said," and "You mustn't, by the way, imagine," and "for one thing." It sounds like an ordinary person talking, even though Lewis also mentions the names of philosophers in paragraph 8, and in paragraph 14 mentions several historical matters.

Next I will deal with Lewis's examples. The examples help him to be clear to the reader. The essay begins with a story about four people. Two said they had a "right to happiness." In this story Lewis lets us see two people (Mr. A. and Mrs. B.) who behave very badly. They justify their behavior simply by saying they have a right to happiness. They behave so badly--Mr. A. deserts the wife who nursed him through a long illness, and Mrs. B. deserts her husband, who is a wounded veteran--that just to hear them talk about a "right to happiness" is almost enough to make you say they should not be happy and they certainly do not have a right to happiness. The example of Mr. and Mrs. A. and Mr. and Mrs. B. is the longest example that Lewis gives, but Lewis several times gives short examples. These short examples make his point clear. For instance, when he wants to show how silly it is to treat sex differently from all other impulses, he says that it is "like having a morality in which stealing fruit is considered wrong--unless you steal nectarines."

Another thing Lewis does to persuade the reader is to write very clear sentences. Some of his sentences are long--about three lines of print--but the reader has no trouble with them. Here is an example of this sort of sentence.

> A right to happiness doesn't, for me, make much more
> sense than a right to be six feet tall, or to have a
> millionaire for your father, or to get good weather
> whenever you want to have a picnic.

The only thing that causes any trouble is a few unfamiliar words such as "tautologies" (paragraph 14) and "tycoon" (paragraph 16), but you can understand the essay even without looking up such words.

Revising and Editing a Draft

To write a good essay you must be a good reader not only of the essay you are writing about, but also of the essay you yourself are writing. We're not talking about proofreading or correcting spelling errors, though you must engage in those activities as well.

Revising. In revising their work, writers ask themselves such questions as,

> Do I mean what I say?
>
> Do I say what I mean? (Answering this question will cause you to ask yourself such questions as, Do I need to define my terms, add examples to clarify, reorganize the material so that a reader can grasp it?)

During this part of the process of writing, you do your best to read the draft in a skeptical frame of mind. In taking account of your doubts, you will probably unify, organize, clarify, and polish the draft.

- **Unity** is achieved partly by eliminating irrelevancies. In the second paragraph of the draft, for example, the writer says that "Lewis is an Englishman, not an American," but the fact that Lewis is English is not clearly relevant to the student's argument that Lewis writes persuasively. The statement should be deleted—or its relevance should be demonstrated.
- **Organization** is largely a matter of arranging material into a sequence that will assist the reader to grasp the point. If you reread your draft and jot down a paragraph outline of the sort shown on pages 13–14. You can then see if the draft has a reasonable organization—a structure that will let the reader move easily from the beginning to the end.
- **Clarity** is achieved largely by providing concrete details, examples, and quotations to support generalizations and by providing helpful transitions ("for instance," "furthermore," "on the other hand," "however").
- **Polish** involves small-scale revision. For instance, you may delete unnecessary repetitions. In the first sentence of the second paragraph, "C. S. Lewis" can effectively be changed to "Lewis"—there really is no need to repeat his initials—and in the second sentence of the second paragraph "Lewis" can be changed to "he." Similarly, in polishing, a writer combines choppy sentences into longer sentences and breaks overly long sentences into shorter sentences.

Editing. After producing a draft that seems good enough to show to someone, writers engage in yet another activity. They edit; that is, they check the accuracy of quotations by comparing them with the original, check a dictionary for the spelling of doubtful words, check a handbook for doubtful punctuation—for instance, whether a comma or a semicolon is needed in a particular sentence.

A Revised Draft

Persuasive Strategies in C. S. Lewis's

~~On~~ "We Have No 'Right to Happiness' "

~~When I first read the title of C. S. Lewis's essay I was interested~~
~~and also somewhat resistant. Without having given much thought to it, I~~
~~believe that I do have a right to happiness. I don't want to give up this~~
~~right or this belief. Still I was intrigued to know what Lewis has to say. After~~
~~reading the essay it seemed entirely reasonable to say that if there is a~~
~~right to happiness there are also limits to it. So I decided to look at how~~
~~Lewis managed to make me change my mind, at least part way.~~

C. S. Lewis's "We Have No 'Right to Happiness'" is surprisingly persuasive-- "surprisingly" because I believe in the right to happiness which is mentioned in the Declaration of Independence. Lewis, an Englishman writing in an American magazine, probably knew he was facing an audience who did not hold his view, and he apparently decided to begin by stating his position as directly as possible in his title, "We Have No 'Right to Happiness'". How does he win his reader over?

C. S. Lewis is persuasive because in addition to thinking carefully, he writes effectively. Three features of his writing especially contribute to his effectiveness.

~~C. S. Lewis is persuasive especially because of three things.~~ First, although Lewis (a professor) is obviously very learned, he uses an informal
    helps to establish a bond between him and his reader
manner that ~~sounds very natural and honest~~. Second, he gives clear
       Third
examples. ~~Three~~, his sentences are always clear. This is true even when they are not especially short. All of these things combine together to make his essay clear and interesting. ~~Lewis is an Englishman, not an American~~.

Lewis's informal manner, especially seen in his use of the first-person pronoun, appears right away. ~~In~~ *in* the second sentence, when he says "We were discussing something. . . ." He uses "I" in the fifth paragraph and in many later paragraphs.

Another sign of Lewis's informality is his use of such expressions as "It might be true, as some said," and "You mustn't, by the way, imagine," and "for one thing." It sounds like an ordinary person talking, even though Lewis also mentions the names of philosophers in paragraph 8, and in paragraph 14 mentions several historical matters.

As for
~~Next I will deal with Lewis's~~ examples. *, which* ~~The examples~~ help him to be clear *, the story of Mr. & Mrs. A. and Mr. & Mrs. B. is a good illustration.* ~~to the reader. The essay begins with a story about four people.~~ *Mr. A. & Mrs. B. both of whom believed they* ~~Two said they~~ had a "right to happiness. ~~In this story Lewis lets us see two people (Mr. A. and Mrs. B.) who behave very badly. They justify their behavior simply by saying they have a right to happiness~~. They behave so badly--Mr. A. deserts the wife who nursed him through a long illness, and Mrs. B. deserts her husband, who is a wounded veteran--that just to hear them talk about a "right to happiness" is almost enough to make you *doubt that there can be such a right* ~~say they should not be happy and they certainly do not have a right to happiness~~. The example of Mr. and Mrs. A. and Mr. and Mrs. B. is the longest example that Lewis gives, but *he* ~~Lewis~~ several times gives short examples. *, that* ~~These short examples~~ make his point clear. For instance, when he wants to show how silly it is to treat sex differently from all other impulses, he says that it is "like having a morality in which stealing fruit is considered wrong--unless you steal nectarines."

Lewis's third persuasive technique
~~Another thing Lewis does to persuade the reader~~ is to write very clear sentences. Some of his sentences are long--about three lines of print--but the reader has no trouble with them. Here is an example of this sort of sentence.

> A right to happiness doesn't, for me, make much more sense than a right to be six feet tall, or to have a millionaire for your father, or to get good weather whenever you want to have a picnic.

The sentence is fairly long, partly because the second half gives three examples, but because these examples are given in a parallel construction ("to be," "or to have," "or to get") the reader easily follows the thought.

True,
~~The only thing that causes any trouble is~~ a few unfamiliar words such as

may cause a bit of trouble
tautologies (paragraph 14) and tycoon (paragraph 16), but ~~you~~ can

a reader
understand the essay even without looking up such words.

Of course Lewis has not absolutely proved that there is no "right to happiness," but he has made a good, clear case. The clarity, in fact, is part of the case. Everything that Lewis says here seems so obvious that a reader is almost persuaded by Lewis's voice alone.

Rethinking the Thesis: Preliminary Notes

You'll probably agree that the student improved his draft, for instance by deleting the original first paragraph and replacing it with a more focused paragraph. But, as we mentioned earlier, when the student thought further about his revision, he was still dissatisfied with it because he no longer fully believed his thesis.

He found that although he continued to admire Lewis's persuasive techniques, he remained unpersuaded by Lewis's argument. He therefore felt obliged to change the thesis of his essay from (approximately) "Lewis's chief persuasive techniques are . . . " to "Although Lewis is highly skilled as a persuasive writer, even his rhetorical skill cannot overcome certain weaknesses in his thesis."

Here are some of the annotations that the student produced after he recognized his dissatisfaction with his revised draft.

Mr. and Mrs. A. and B. may or may not be real people, but they certainly seem UNREAL: too neatly suited (all good or bad) to L's purpose.

> The villains: Mr. A. (he tosses out his wife after she loses her looks, despite the fact that she wore herself out with his children and nursed him through long illness; even after wife commits suicide he doesn't see that he continues to talk selfishly); Mrs. B. (she leaves her husband when he gets wounded and he loses his "virility" and loses his job). Aren't these people a bit too awful? Are they really typical of people who divorce?

> The heroes--or saints? Mrs. A. (nursed husband through long illness, wore self out with the children); Mr. B. (injured in war; loses job).

Clare: She also seems too suited to CSL's thesis; she's pretty terrible, and stupid too.

Lewis on Divorce: He seems to think it is always motivated by a desire for sex, and that it is always wrong. But what if a husband abuses his wife--maybe physically, or maybe verbally and emotionally? Maybe chronic alcoholic, refuses treatment, etc.? Or what if wife abuses husband--probably not physically, but verbally, and maybe she assaults kids? Or take another angle: what if woman married at too young an age, inexperienced, married to escape from an awful family, and now finds she made a mistake? Should she stay married to the man for life? In short, does Lewis see divorce from enough angles?

First five paragraphs are extremely interesting, but are unfair for three reasons:

1. Lewis loads the dice, showing us goodies and baddies, and then says (par. 5) that they set him to thinking about the "right to happiness";
2. He overemphasizes the importance of sex, neglects other possible reasons why people divorce;
3. His discussion of "Natural Law," is not convincing to me. I simply am not convinced that there is a "Law of Nature" that "eternally sanctions" certain things.

Sexist??? Although CSL seems to be defending women (esp. par. 28, in which he says that promiscuity puts women at a double disadvantage), there is something sort of sexist in the essay, and I imagine that this will turn off women, and maybe even men. I know that I'm a little bothered by it.

The Final Version

We won't take you through the drafts that the student wrote, but in reading the final version, below, you will notice that although some of the points from the draft are retained, the thesis, as we said, has shifted. Notice, for instance, that the first paragraph of the revised draft is used in the final version but with two significant changes: in the first sentence the student now adds that he finds Lewis's essay "finally unconvincing," and in the last sentence of the paragraph he implies that he will discuss why the essay is "not finally convincing."

Jim Weinstein

Professor Valdez

English Composition 12

Style and Argument:

An Examination of C. S. Lewis's

"We Have No 'Right to Happiness' "

C. S. Lewis's "We Have No 'Right to Happiness' " is, though

finally unconvincing, surprisingly persuasive--"surprisingly" because I believe in the right to happiness, which is mentioned in the Declaration of Independence. Lewis, an Englishman writing in an American magazine, probably knew he was facing an audience who did not hold his view, and he apparently decided to begin by stating his position as directly as possible in his title: "We Have No 'Right to Happiness.'" How does he nearly win his reader over? And why is he not finally convincing?

Lewis is highly (though not entirely) persuasive because he writes effectively. Three features of his writing especially contribute to his effectiveness. First, although Lewis (a professor) is obviously very learned, he uses an informal manner that helps to establish a bond between him and his reader. Second, he gives clear examples. Third, his sentences are always clear, even when they are not especially short. All of these things combine to make his essay clear and interesting--and almost convincing.

His informal manner, especially his use of the first-person pronouns, appears right away in the second sentence, when he says "We were discussing something. . . ." He uses "I" in the fifth paragraph and in many later paragraphs. Another sign of his informality is his use of such expressions as "It might be true, as some said," and "You mustn't, by the way, imagine." It sounds like an ordinary person talking.

Most of his examples, too, seem ordinary. They make his points seem almost obvious. For instance, when he wants to show how silly it is to treat sex differently from all other impulses, he says that it is "like having a morality in which stealing fruit is considered wrong--unless you steal nectarines" (p. 25). The touch of humor drives the point home.

Still, although Lewis seems thoughtful and he makes his argument very clear, the essay somehow does not finally persuade. The trouble may largely be Mr. and Mrs. A. and B., but there are other difficulties, too.

Mr. and Mrs. A. and B. are just too simple a case, too neat an illustration. Lewis of course wanted to make a clear-cut case, but a reader does not really believe in these people. They are caricatures: Mr. A. tosses out his wife after she loses her looks (and she lost them not only through the natural process of aging but through taking care of the family), and Mrs. B. leaves her husband, a wounded veteran. Of course it is conceivable that there really were a Mr. A. and a Mrs. B., but surely the pros and cons of divorce ought not to be based on cases like this, where it is so clear that Mr. A. and Mrs. B. are irresponsible. They are, one might say, as morally stupid as Clare is. But the fact that these people are selfish and stupid and that they each get a divorce does not prove that only selfish and stupid people seek divorce.

Nor do the experiences of the A.'s and the B.'s show that people who seek a divorce always are seeking sexual pleasure. We can imagine, for instance, a woman married to a wife-beater. Does she not have a right to be free of her abusive husband, a "right to happiness"? Nor need we limit our case to physical abuse. A husband (or a wife) can abuse a spouse verbally and emotionally and can be impossibly neglectful of the children. Or we can imagine a couple who married when very young-- perhaps partly for the sake of defying their parents, or maybe in order to escape from a bad family situation. In any case, we can imagine that one member of the couple now sees that a bad mistake was made. Need they stay tied to each other?

Lewis's essay is powerful, partly because it clearly advances a thesis that must seem strange to many Americans; and it is interesting, partly because Lewis makes his points clearly and he seems to be such a thoughtful and decent person. But in the end, the essay is not convincing. It is just a little too simple in its examples and in its suggestion that people who claim a right to happiness are really just saying that they want to get divorced so they can live legally with another sexual partner.

[New page]

Work Cited

Lewis, C. S. "We Have No 'Right to Happiness.'" The Little, Brown Reader.

Ed. Marcia Stubbs, Sylvan Barnet, and William E. Cain. 11th ed.

New York: Longman, 2008. 22–26.

A Brief Overview of the Final Version

- First, a mechanical matter: A bibliographic note, on a separate page headed "Work Cited," tells the reader where the essay can be found.
- The title, though not especially engaging, is informative—more so than, say, "On an Essay by C. S. Lewis." Readers know that the writer will discuss Lewis's style and argument in a particular essay.
- The student's final essay is *not* simply a balanced debate, a statement of the pros and cons that remains inconclusive. Rather, the student argues a thesis: Although Lewis's essay is in some ways admirable, it remains unconvincing.
- The student's thesis is stated early, in fact in the first paragraph. It's almost always a good idea to let your reader know early where you will be going.
- Quotations are used as evidence, not as padding. See, for example, paragraphs 3 and 4.
- The writer has kept his reader in mind. He has not summarized Lewis's essay in needless detail, but, on the other hand, he has not assumed that the reader knows the essay inside out. For instance, he does not simply assert that Mr. A. behaves very badly; rather, he reminds us that Mr. A. rejects his wife after she loses her looks. When he uses a quotation, he guides the reader to where in Lewis's essay the quotation can be found.
- He also keeps the reader in mind by using helpful transitions. In paragraph 2 notice "First," "Second," and "Third"; in paragraph 5, "Still" indicates a reversal of direction. Notice, too, that key words and phrases are repeated. Repetition of this sort, like transitions, makes it easy for the reader to follow the writer's train of thought. In the second paragraph, for example, he cites Lewis's "informal manner" as the first of three points of style. His next paragraph begins, "His informal manner. . . ." Similarly, the last sentence of paragraph 3 contains the words "ordinary person." The next paragraph begins, "Most of his examples, too, seem ordinary."
- So far we have talked about what is in the essay. But what is *not* in it is also worth comment. In the final essay, the student does *not* include all of the points he jotted down in his preliminary notes. He does not take up either Natural Law or the issue of sexism, probably because he felt unsure about both. Notes are points of departure; if when you get going you find you are going down a blind alley, don't hesitate to go back and drop the point.

⟨⟨ Joining the Conversation:
Thinking Further about an Essay

1. A scholar who generally admires Lewis's work has recently conceded, "One must admit that in some ways this essay, first published in 1963, has dated." Do you agree? Which features, if any, of the essay strike you as "dated," and which do not? Please point to evidence from the text to support your responses.

2. Another scholar, also an admirer of Lewis's work, has made a different claim about it: "The message of 'We Have No Right to Happiness' is as timely today as it was when Lewis wrote it." Do you agree, or disagree? Make sure that you cite evidence from the text of support your argument.

✓ A Checklist: Analyzing Your Analysis

☐ Have I fairly summarized the writer's thesis?

☐ Have I considered and evaluated the kinds of evidence—for instance, personal experience, statistics, authoritative testimony—the writer offers?

☐ Have I considered the writer's strategies from the beginning (the title) to the end, including the writer's tone?

☐ Is my essay organized so the reader can move through it easily, without wondering where I am going?

CHAPTER 3

Academic Writing

Kinds of Prose

Traditionally, prose is said to be of four kinds: **exposition** (its chief purpose is to explain), **description** (it sets forth a detailed account of appearances or sensations), **narration** (it recounts a sequence of events, telling a story), and **persuasion** or **argument** (it attempts to get readers to accept or act on the writer's views). Thus, an essay or a book on how to improve our game of tennis chiefly will be an

- *exposition*—a putting forth of information.
- In fact, however, the essay or book on how to improve our game probably will also include a good deal of *description* (it will describe as accurately as possible the motion of the arm),
- and it may include some *narration* ("Tennis seems to have originated in the courts of fourteenth-century France, originally was played with balls stuffed with horse hair, and from France the game traveled to Germany and England . . . ," or "You may already be familiar with the story of how Venus Williams became the great player that she now is, but the story is worth repeating here").
- The discussion of how to improve our tennis probably will not, however, contain much *persuasive* writing, because the author assumes that the readers are already sold on the game. On the other hand, we can reasonably say that simply by writing about how to improve your game, the author is in effect persuading you to stay with the game, implicitly telling you that, gee, even *you* can become a pretty good player.

When you think about it, almost *all* writing is persuasive, since it says, in effect, "I find this interesting and I want you to find it interesting too." Even a note on a refrigerator door, "Egg salad sandwich and apple on lower shelf," is partly an attempt to persuade the reader to leave the cold roast beef and the ice cream alone. Consider for a moment Thomas Jefferson's Declaration of Independence (page 506). On the surface, it is chiefly *expository*. Jefferson explains why the time has come for certain people to declare their independence from England; that's the expository part, the setting forth of information, though it also includes a good deal of narration, since Jefferson tells us that the King of England did this ("He has dissolved Representative Houses repeatedly") and the king did that ("He has kept among us, in times of peace, Standing Armies"). Jefferson offers this information because he wishes to *persuade* the international community—especially the French—to support the revolution.

Or consider a very different piece of writing, also by a political figure, Lincoln's Gettysburg Address (page 432). Surely Lincoln was not chiefly concerned with exposition or narration or description. True, he tells his hearers that "four score and seven years ago our fathers brought forth on this continent, a new nation" (narration), but they already knew *that* story; and he explains to them that they cannot dedicate the cemetery because the dead men have already hallowed it (exposition). But the speech essentially is meant to celebrate the heroism of the dead, and, by reminding the audience of the heroism of the fallen soldiers, the speech seeks to inspire—to persuade—the living to continue the battle. Of these two essays, The Declaration of Independence is closer to academic writing than is The Gettysburg Address.

A Note on Writing a Summary

In our discussion of J. H. Plumb's "The Dying Family" we talked a bit (pages 13–14) about writing a summary, but a few additional words may be useful.

In an academic essay you may want to summarize a position—for example, the gist of an essay that you will go onto analyze or to argue against. That is, you may want to offer a condensation or abridgment briefly giving the reader the gist of a longer work. Here are a few principles that govern summaries:

1. A summary is much briefer than the original. It is not a paraphrase—a word-by-word translation of someone's words into your own—for a paraphrase is usually at least as long as the original, whereas a summary is rarely longer than one-fourth the original and may even be much briefer, perhaps giving in a sentence or two an entire essay.
2. A summary usually achieves its brevity by omitting almost all the concrete details of the original, presenting only the sum that the details add up to.
3. A summary is accurate; it has no value if it misrepresents the point of the original.
4. The writer of a summary need not make the points in the same order as that of the original. In fact, a reader is occasionally driven to write a summary because the original author does not present the argument in an orderly sequence; the summary is an attempt to disengage the author's argument from the confusing presentation.
5. A summary normally is written in the present tense, because the writer assumes that although the author wrote the piece last year or a hundred years ago, the piece speaks to us today. (In other words, the summary is explicitly or implicitly prefaced by "The author says," and all that follows is in the present tense.)
6. Because a summary is openly based on someone else's views, not your own, you need not use quotation marks around any words that you take from the original.

Here is a summary of this discussion on *summary:*

A summary is a condensation or abridgment. These are some characteristics: (1) it is rarely more than one-fourth as long as the original; (2) its brevity is usually achieved by leaving out most of the concrete details of the original; (3) it is accurate; (4) it may rearrange the organization of the original, especially if a rearrangement will make things clearer; (5) it normally is in the present tense; (6) quoted words need not be enclosed in quotation marks.

More about Critical Thinking: Analysis and Evaluation

In Chapter 1 we talked briefly about critical thinking and about analysis. We now want to amplify our discussion, but first we should devote a few more words to the term "academic writing."

Exactly what is "academic writing"? *Academic* comes from the Greek *Academos,* a garden near Athens where the philosopher Plato taught. Because of its connection with a great teacher, the name of the garden came to refer to any place where the arts or sciences or both are taught or fostered. Academic writing is the sort of writing done in the academy—in colleges and universities. Since each academic discipline requires its own sort of writing, however, several kinds of writing are done in an academic setting. In literature courses, students chiefly analyze and evaluate works of literature—but they may also be required to write a story, poem, or play. In sociology courses, students may be asked to analyze and evaluate the views of a particular sociologist—but they may also be asked to interview authorities or perhaps ordinary folk, and to present their findings in writing.

Still, at the heart of most academic writing—most of the writing that you will do in college—is an activity that can be called *critical thinking,* which consists chiefly of *analyzing* and *evaluating.* Exactly what is analysis? Literally, it is "separating into parts," and a good way to get going on an analysis is to ask what the parts are. Let's talk briefly about "hate speech," a topic addressed in Derek Bok's "Protecting Freedom of Expression on the Campus" (page 538), an essay that was prompted by the display of a Confederate flag hung from the window of a dormitory. Is the display of a Confederate flag "hate speech"? It's not literally speech, of course, but probably most people would agree that the act of displaying the flag might be closely comparable to verbally expressing some ideas. But exactly what is hate speech? Suppose *X* uses an ethnic term that *Y* finds offensive, but *X* says he used it playfully? Or suppose *X* admits that the word was used aggressively, and suppose we all agree that such aggressive language is bad; we still have to think about *how bad* it is. Bad enough so that it ought to be regulated by the college? Punishable by a reprimand? Suspension? Expulsion?

If in an effort to think analytically we ask ourselves such questions (and perhaps even take notes to help us advance our thoughts), we might find we are thinking along these lines:

- What is hate speech? How is it distinguished from mere unthinking expression, or high spirits? Must the speech concern race, religion, ethnicity, or sexual preference? If *X* calls *Y* a fat pig, does this show an offensive hatred of obesity? (In asking the question, "What is . . . ?" we are getting into matters of *definition.*)

- The First Amendment to the Constitution guarantees freedom of speech, but it does *not* protect *all* speech (for instance, libel, false advertising, incitements to violence). Does hate speech belong to protected speech, or does it belong to *un*protected speech? (Here we are concerned with *classification,* with trying to see to what larger class of things something belongs.)
- How bad, after all, is hate speech? Bad, yes, but probably no one would suggest that it is as bad as murder or rape, or that it should be punished by long-term jail sentences. By one day in jail? By a reprimand? (Here we are concerned with quality, with evaluation.)

As you ask yourself questions such as these, and as you seek to answer them, you will probably find that your views are changing, perhaps slightly (maybe you are refining them), perhaps radically. The writer E. M. Forster tells of a little girl who, when instructed to think before she spoke, shrewdly replied, "How do I know what I think until I hear what I say?" Only by the process of hearing what we say, and then testing and pressing further in a mental conversation with ourselves, can we hope to have ideas that our fellow students and our instructors will value. When you write an academic paper, your instructor will expect you to have done this sort of work, and if you have done it, you will recognize that you have indeed been thinking, been educating yourself. If your paper is connected to Derek Bok's essay, you may begin with a brief summary of his essay in which your thinking doesn't go much beyond (1) understanding what Bok says, and (2) setting forth his thesis accurately and concisely; but soon you will get around to offering an *analysis* and probably an *evaluation,* to putting on paper the results of your serious, critical thinking.

The essays in *The Little, Brown Reader* contain a good deal of information, but chiefly you will read them not for the information they contain— the world is changing and today's facts will not be tomorrow's facts; rather, you read these essays chiefly for the ideas they advance, and for the habits of thought that they display. And you will respond to them largely by setting forth arguments of your own. Writing based on serious *thinking* is what is expected of you. One of the reasons you are attending college is to acquire practice in thinking. As William Cory said, one goes to school not only for knowledge—facts, we might say—but for

the art of assuming at a moment's notice a new intellectual posture, for the art of entering quickly into another person's thought, for the habit of submitting to censure and refutation, for the art of indicating assent or dissent in graduated terms. . . .

For a moment let's put aside the writings in this book, and look at a photograph of Sitting Bull and Buffalo Bill, taken in 1886 by William Notman. William Cody got his nickname from his work as a supplier of

Sitting Bull and Buffalo Bill, 1886

meat for workers on the Kansas Pacific Railway, but he got his fame from his exploits as an army scout and a fighter against the Sioux Indians. Sitting Bull, a chief of the Sioux Indians, had defeated Custer at the battle of Little Big Horn some ten years before this picture was taken, but he soon fled to Canada. In 1879 he was granted amnesty and he returned to the United States, where for a while he appeared in Buffalo Bill's Wild West Show. In 1890, whites, fearful of an Indian uprising, attempted to arrest Sitting Bull, and he was killed during the encounter.

What you have just read cannot pass for an example of critical thinking. We hope the writing is clear, but about the only thinking that we were forced to do was to decide how much information to give. Should we have added that Sitting Bull encouraged the Sioux not to sell their lands, and thus he enraged the whites? Should we have added that Buffalo Bill rode for the Pony Express? Or that he invented some of his greatest exploits? Probably none of these points needs to be made here, in a brief introduction to the photograph. In short, we made some choices—we decided to give minimal information—and that was that. But now let's think—think critically—about the picture. We can begin (and this may sound like a contradiction) with our emotional response, our gut feelings. We are interested in this picture—but why?

We begin to ask ourselves questions, a method that, we have seen, almost always helps to develop one's thoughts. What is going on here? There are two figures, but they are so different. Buffalo Bill, head brightly illuminated, is looking off into the distance, rather like a modern-day political candidate, whose upward and outward glance implies that he or she is looking into the future. His right hand is on his heart, in a patriotic or noble gesture; his left leg is thrust forward. He wears a mammoth buckle, a fancy jacket, and shiny hip boots. His hand is above Sitting Bull's on the gun, and he is both behind Sitting Bull and (by virtue of his left leg) in front of Sitting Bull. Buffalo Bill, in short, is all show biz. If we look closely at the setting, we see that the meeting is not taking place in the great outdoors; rather, the setting is a sort of stage set, presumably in a photographer's studio.

What of Sitting Bull? Whereas Buffalo Bill clearly was striking a pose for the camera, Sitting Bull seems indifferent to the camera. Later in this chapter we will discuss comparing at length, but here we want only to mention that comparing is an excellent way to perceive what is unique about each of the things being compared. By comparing these two figures, we can more clearly see Buffalo Bill's flamboyance—and Sitting Bull's reserve. Sitting Bull seems withdrawn; his face, tilted downward, is mostly in shadow; his body seems inert; his right arm hangs lifelessly; his headdress is splendid, but his trousers are baggy and his belt dangles beneath his shirt. His hand on the rifle is subordinated to Buffalo Bill's.

May we say that now we are really *thinking* about the picture? An *un*thinking description would say, "The picture shows the two figures, dividing the space approximately equally, each in costume." This statement is true, and it might indeed find a place in the early stage of an analytic essay on the photograph, but your teachers—you are writing in an academy— expect more than an accurate, neatly typed description.

Here is the final paragraph from one of the best student essays we have received on this photograph. (The earlier paragraphs specified the differences in pose, costume, and so on, along the lines that we have just set forth.)

> Buffalo Bill is obviously the dominant figure in this photograph, but he is not the outstanding one. His efforts to appear great only serve to make him appear small. His attempt to outshine Sitting Bull strikes us as faintly ridiculous. We do not need or want to know any more about Buffalo Bill's personality; it is spread before us in this picture. Sitting Bull's humility and dignity make him more interesting than Buffalo Bill, and make us wish to prove our intuition and to ascertain that this proud Sioux was a great chief.

Of course the photograph might lead a student to another, related topic. For instance, a student might want to know more about the photographer, William Notman. What did Notman think the photograph said to viewers? Was Notman setting forth a compassionate statement about the American Indian? Or was he just doing a job for Buffalo Bill? One might do some research on Notman, first, perhaps, by turning to a handsome book of his photographs, *Portrait of a Period,* edited by J. Russell Harper and Stanley Triggs. Research on Notman might lead you to conclude that his pictures often subtly undermine the pretensions of his heroic sitters, or you might find, on the contrary, that Notman celebrates heroism of all kinds, white and Indian. Or you might find that, for some strange reason, his pictures of Indians are far more interesting than his pictures of whites.

If a student writing about Notman's photographs does no more than tell us that the book has seventy-five pictures, that they are black and white, that all are portraits, that . . . , the student is not presenting the sort of writing expected in an academic community. Such information if presented briefly is acceptable as a start, acceptable as establishing a framework, but it is only a start; it is *not* critical thinking, it is *not* academic writing.

One last example of a related essay that would exemplify critical thinking. You might want to read the entries on Sitting Bull and Buffalo Bill in two versions of the *Encyclopaedia Britannica,* the 9th edition (1911) and the most recent edition. If you do, take note of the differences between the two versions, and then think about what these differences tell us about the early twentieth century and the last decade of the twentieth century.

✔ A Checklist: Critical Thinking

Attitudes

- ☐ Does my thinking show imaginative open-mindedness and intellectual curiosity?
  - ☐ Am I willing to examine my assumptions?
  - ☐ Am I willing to entertain new ideas—both those that I encounter while reading and those that come to mind while writing?
  - ☐ Am I willing to exert myself—for instance, to do research—to acquire information and to evaluate evidence?

Skills

- ☐ Can I summarize an argument accurately?
- ☐ Can I evaluate assumptions, evidence, and inferences?
- ☐ Can I present my ideas effectively—for instance, by organizing and by writing in a manner appropriate to my imagined audience?

Joining the Conversation: Writing about Differing Views

Your instructor will probably ask you to read more than one essay in some section of this book. The chief reason for such an assignment is to stimulate you to think about some complex issue. After all, no one essay on any topic of significance can claim to say all that needs to be said about the topic. Essays that advocate similar positions on, say, capital punishment may, because of slightly different emphases, usefully supplement one another; and even two radically opposed essays may both contain material that you find is essential to a thoughtful discussion of the topic.

Let's say that you read an essay supporting the death penalty. Perhaps, as an aid to grasping the author's argument, you prepared a summary of the essay, and you notice that the writer's chief points are these:

1. The death penalty serves as a deterrent.
2. Justice requires that murderers pay an appropriate price for their crimes.

These basic points probably are supported by some evidence, but you have been reading critically, and you have wondered whether this or that piece of evidence is compelling. You have also wondered if more can't be said on the other side—not only by specific refutation of certain arguments, but perhaps also by arguments that the first essayist has not raised. You turn to a second essayist, someone who opposes the death penalty, and who (you find when you summarize the essay) in effect offers these arguments:

1. The death penalty does not serve as a deterrent.
2. If the death penalty is inflicted mistakenly, the error cannot be corrected.
3. The death penalty is imposed unequally; statistics indicate that when blacks and whites are guilty of comparable offenses, blacks are more likely to be sentenced to death.

It is now evident that the two writers are and are not talking about the same thing. They are talking about the death penalty, but for the most part they are not confronting the same issues. On only one issue—deterrence—do they face each other. On this issue you will want to think hard about the evidence that each offers. Possibly you will decide that one author makes a compelling case at least on this issue, but it is also possible that you will decide that the issue cannot be resolved. Or you may find that you can make a better case than did either writer.

Think about the other arguments offered—on the one hand that justice requires the death penalty, and on the other hand that it can be mistakenly inflicted and is awarded unequally. You will not only want to think hard about each of these points, but you will also wonder why only one of the two essayists took them up. Is one or the other argument so clearly mistaken that it is not worth discussing? Or is a particular argument one that can't be proved either true or false? Or are the writers working from different **assumptions** (unexamined beliefs)? For instance, the writer who argues that the death penalty is capriciously enforced may assume that race prejudice cannot be overcome, whereas a writer who rejects the argument may assume that the courts can and will see to it that the death penalty is imposed impartially. As a critical reader, you will want to be alert to the assumptions that writers make. You'll have to ask yourself often, *What assumption lies beneath this assertion?* That is, what belief is so firmly held, and is assumed to be so self-evident, that the writer does not bother to assert it? Do I share this assumption? Why?

If you are asked to compare two essays that offer sharply differing views, you probably will want to point out where the two face each other and where they don't. You probably will want also to offer an evaluation of the two. Or, depending on the assignment, you may use the two merely as a point of departure for your own essay on the topic. That is, you may want to draw on one or both—giving credit of course—and then offer your own serious thoughts.

Writing about Essays Less Directly Related: A Student's Notes and Journal Entries

Let's assume that your instructor has asked you to read Plumb's "The Dying Family" (page 6) and Lewis's "We Have No 'Right to Happiness' " (page 22), and has asked you to compare them. Both of these essays concern family relationships, but they do not take distinctly different positions on a single controversial topic. They are, we might say, thoughtful voices in a conversation that is consistently interesting but is wide-ranging rather than sharply focused.

Let's say that you settle on Plumb's and Lewis's attitudes toward their material. Perhaps your first thought is that Lewis very obviously offers value judgments, whereas Plumb, as a historian, simply reports what has happened in history.

On rereading the two essays, you may find yourself making notes somewhat like these notes that a student made:

1. Some of Plumb's assumptions:
    Family evolves: history a process (not static, not cyclical).
    Idea of parents wedded until death no longer needed in our urban, industrial society.
    Happiness not increasing or decreasing.
2. I'm surprised to find so many assumptions in the writings of a historian.
    I thought history was supposed to be an account, the "story" of what happened: in Social Studies we learned history is "value-free."

3.   Some of Lewis's assumptions:

>   Lewis very clearly makes assumptions, for instance, belief in
>   the existence of "Natural Law" (par. 8) and belief that
>   "domestic happiness is more necessary to them than to us"
>   (to women, than to men), par. 28. Also assumes that women
>   don't care much about men's looks (28)--but is this true?
>   How might someone be able to prove it?

4.   Big difference between Plumb and Lewis on assumptions. I think

>   that Plumb makes assumptions but is hardly aware of them,
>   whereas Lewis makes them and puts them right up front.
>   With Lewis we know exactly where he stands. For instance,
>   he obviously believes that we can use our free will to
>   behave in ways that he considers proper. He even talks
>   about "good people; controlled, loyal, fairminded" (25). (It's
>   hard to imagine Plumb talking about "good people"; he only
>   talks about whether people are "happy" or "stable.") Lewis
>   pretty clearly believes not only that it's our job to act
>   decently but that we can act decently. Seems not to accept
>   the idea that we can be overwhelmed by passion or by the
>   unconscious. Probably very anti-Freud. Anyway, his position
>   is clear (and I agree with it). With Plumb we can hardly
>   argue--at least I can't--since I'm not a historian. I don't know
>   if what he says about the past really is true, but his opening
>   paragraph strikes me as completely made up.

5.   Attitudes toward change in family:

>   For Lewis, a moralist, breakdown of family is a disaster; for Plumb,
>   a fact of social evolution.

One student, whose thoughts were something like those that we have
just presented, wrote two entries in his journal.

>   Plumb: As I see it, he makes assumptions that pretty much go
>   against what Lewis is arguing. Plumb looks at this family in
>   California, and he says they are happy and he thinks everything is
>   just fine. Well, maybe not fine, but at least he says that these chil-
>   dren seem "as happy as any children that I have seen." I'm not so
>   sure they are as happy as most. I know (from my own experience
>   and from what I hear from friends) what divorced kids go through.
>   Divorce may be normal (common, ordinary), but is it right? It
>   seems to lead to so much unhappiness (for parents and children).
>   Putting aside my own feelings, I can certainly see that my parents
>   aren't especially happy with their new families. But there is Plumb,
>   with his happy busload. Is he kidding? Or trying to fool us?
>
>   Lewis: Lewis says we have no right to happiness--no right to
>   divorce, remarry several times, and have families like that bus-
>   load of people Plumb talks about. Lewis seems to be saying that
>   divorce is morally wrong. Why? What are his reasons? I think he
>   gives two: 1) it makes people unhappy (for instance, Mr. B., the
>   wounded veteran, must have been miserable when Mrs. B. left

him), and 2) it is against "Natural Law." But come to think of it, what is Natural Law? What makes divorce contrary to Natural Law? Is it really "unnatural"? Why? Lots of religions--maybe most of them--accept divorce. And certainly governments accept it. So what makes it unnatural? What is it that Bertrand Russell said about our animal instinct? Check this.

The next day, after rereading Lewis's essay and the two entries, he wrote two additional entries in his journal:

I think that I agree with Lewis that we don't have a right to happiness, just as we don't have a right to be rich and handsome. But I wish Lewis had given some clear reasons instead of just saying that we have to remain for life with one spouse--even if we see that we have made a bad choice--because "Natural Law" tells us that we can't change. Come to think of it, Lewis does give some reasons against giving sex a special privilege: we hurt others, and we kid ourselves if we think each passion will last.

Both Lewis and Plumb use short stories to make their points: Plumb's busload of Californians, Lewis's Mr. and Mrs. A. and Mr. and Mrs. B. Suppose these stories aren't true and Lewis and Plumb made these stories up. Does that matter?

The Student's Final Version

Drawing on this material, the student drafted and revised an essay and then submitted it to peer review. Then, in light of the comments and further thinking, he wrote the final version, which we give here. Our marginal comments summarize some of the strengths that we find in the finished essay. (*Note:* The original essay was, of course, double-spaced.)

Title gives a clue to topic.

Opening paragraph names authors and essays, and indicates thesis— that the essays strongly differ.

Two Ways of Thinking about Today's Families

J. H. Plumb in "The Dying Family" and C. S. Lewis in "We Have No 'Right to Happiness' " both note that today's families often consist of adults who have been divorced. But that is about as much as they would agree on. Judging from an example Plumb gives of a minibus with ten happy children, none of whom had both parents in common, Plumb thinks there is no reason to regret, much less to condemn, the behavior that presumably has produced this sort of family. And judging from the examples Lewis gives of Mrs. B. who left her wounded husband and of Mr. A. who left his worn-out wife, Lewis thinks that the pursuit of happiness--sexual happiness at the expense of marriage--is immoral.

Clear transition
("Despite these
great
differences").

Details support
generalization.

Despite these great differences, there are interesting similarities in the essays. The essays are both by Englishmen, are about the same length, were both written around the middle of the twentieth century, and both begin with an example. Plumb begins with his minibus of ten children and two adults, Lewis with his Mr. and Mrs. A. and Mr. and Mrs. B. Certainly both examples are striking. I'm not sure that, on rereading the essays, I believe either example is real, but they caught my attention. I must say, however, that I have more trouble believing in Plumb's happy busload than in Lewis's two couples. Putting aside my own experience as the child of divorced parents (each of whom has remarried), ten children--no two of whom have the same two parents--just seems like too many.

Again a clear
transition ("In
addition to").

In addition to these relatively superficial resemblances, there is also a deeper resemblance. Plumb and Lewis are both talking about the great change in sexual behavior that came about in the twentieth century, especially in the middle of the century when divorce became respectable and common. But there is a big difference in their response. Plumb, writing as a historian, tries to understand why the change came about. Having concluded that the family no longer serves the purposes that it served in earlier periods, Plumb is not disturbed by the change. He ends his essay by saying,

Quotation is used
as evidence to
support student's
assertion that
Plumb "is not
disturbed."

"And that busload of children does no more than symbolize the failure, not of marriage, but of the role of the old-fashioned family unit in a modern, urbanized, scientific and affluent society" (9). Lewis, on the other hand, writes as a moralist. He tries to understand why the A.'s and B.'s of this world do what they do, and he sees that they behave as they do because of "the sexual impulse" (23). But Lewis does more than see what they do; he judges what they do, in particular he judges behavior against what he calls "Natural Law" (21) and "the Law of Nature" (22). And he makes it clear that he is not speaking only of sexual behavior. After saying that women are at a disadvantage in a society that tolerates conjugal infidelity, he makes a final point that goes far beyond matters of sex:

Cites evidence.

Quotation of more
than four lines is
indented five
spaces at left.

> Secondly, though the "right to happiness" is chiefly claimed for the sexual impulse, it seems to me impossible that the matter should stay there. The fatal principle, once allowed in that department, must sooner or later seep through the whole of our lives. (24)

Transition ("For Plumb, then") by means of brief summary.

Parallel construction ("For Plumb. . . For Lewis") highlights similarities and differences.

Student briefly offers objections to each essay.

Discloses reasons.

Student imaginatively extends the discussion.

For Plumb, then, the family is something produced by history, and it changes as history goes on. For Lewis, the family--two adults wedded for life--is something in accordance with Natural Law, and since this law does not change, the nature of the family does not change, or, rather, <u>should not</u> change. This difference between the essays, of course, is far more important than all of the similarities. Each essay is interesting to read, and maybe each is even convincing during the moments that someone is reading it. But finally the essays are strongly opposed to each other, and it is impossible to agree with both of them.

How is a reader to decide between the two essays? Doubtless the earlier experience of a reader predisposes that reader to believe certain things and not to believe other things. Reading Plumb's essay, I find, drawing on my experience, that I cannot believe in his busload of happy children. Plumb does not seem to be aware that children are greatly pained by the divorce and remarriage of their parents. In short, Plumb seems to me to be too satisfied that everything is just fine and that we need not regret the loss of the old-style family. On the other hand, Lewis does not think that everything is just fine with the family. He sees the selfishness behind the "right to [sexual] happiness" that for the most part has destroyed the old-fashioned family. But Lewis rests his case entirely on Natural Law, something that perhaps not many people today believe in.

I can imagine Lewis and Plumb meeting and having a debate. Lewis points out to Plumb that divorce causes more unhappiness than Plumb has admitted, and Plumb points out to Lewis that if modern divorce causes much suffering, there must also have been much suffering when parents did <u>not</u> get divorced. Plumb and Lewis each grant the truth of these objections, and then, in my imagined debate, Plumb says to Lewis, "Furthermore, you build your case on 'Natural Law,' but I don't think there really is any such thing. I will grant that Mr. A. and Mrs. B. seem irresponsible, but I won't grant that married adults must for their entire lives remain with each other." Lewis replies: "If you don't think that some things are right--<u>always</u> right--and that some things are wrong-- <u>always</u> wrong--what guides actions? You seem to care whether or not people are happy. But isn't it clear to you that some people seek their own happiness at the expense of others? What gives them such a right? If you don't believe in Natural Law, what do you believe in? Where do 'rights' come from?"

Transition and conclusion about the two essays.

And so the debate ends, not so much because they differ about whether people today are happier than people in the past, but because they differ in their assumptions. Plumb's assumption that history determines the rightness or wrongness of the family is unacceptable to Lewis, and Lewis's assumption that the family is based on Natural Law is unacceptable to Plumb.

Student introduces a personal note, but relates it closely to the two readings.

What is my own position? For the moment, I find both assumptions unacceptable. Intellectually I feel the force of Plumb's argument, but my experience tells me that he accepts the change in the family too easily. Intellectually I feel the force of Lewis's argument, but somehow I cannot convince myself that there is such a thing as Natural Law. Still, of the two writers, I feel that Lewis has a clearer picture of what people are like. I do know lots of people like Mr. and Mrs. A and Mr. and Mrs. B, but I don't know that busload of California kids.

Concludes with succinct references to both essays.

Documentation.

Works Cited

Lewis, C. S. "We Have No 'Right to Happiness.'" The Little, Brown Reader. Ed. Marcia Stubbs, Sylvan Barnet, William E. Cain. 11th ed. New York: Longman, 2008. 22–26.

Plumb, J. H. "The Dying Family." The Little, Brown Reader. Ed. Marcia Stubbs, Sylvan Barnet, and William E. Cain. 11th ed. New York: Longman, 2008. 6–10.

Interviewing

In preparing to write about some of the essays in *The Little, Brown Reader*, you may want to interview faculty members or students, or persons not on the campus. For instance, if you are writing about the essays by Plumb and Lewis, you may want to talk to instructors who teach sociology or ethics—or you may simply want to collect the views of people who have no special knowledge but who may offer thoughtful responses. Obviously topics such as divorce and the value of computers in the classroom and almost all of the other topics addressed in this book are matters that you might profitably discuss with someone whose experience is notably different from your own.

A college campus is an ideal place to practice interviewing. Faculties are composed of experts in a variety of fields, and distinguished visitors are a regular part of extracurricular life. In the next few pages, we'll offer some advice on conducting interviews and writing essays based on them. If you take our advice, you'll acquire a skill you may well put to further, more specialized use in social science courses; at the same time you'll be developing skill in asking questions and shaping materials relevant to all research and writing.

Guidelines for Conducting the Interview and Writing the Essay

You can conduct interviews over the telephone or online using electronic mail, but in the following pages we assume that you are conducting the interview face to face.

  1. *Finding a subject for an interview.* If you are looking for an expert, in the college catalog scan the relevant department and begin to ask questions of students who have some familiarity with the department. Then, with a name or two in mind, you may want to see if these faculty members have written anything on the topic. Department secretaries are good sources of information not only about the special interests of the faculty, but also about guest speakers scheduled by the department in the near future. Investigate the athletic department if you're interested in sports; or the departments of music, art, and drama, for the names of resident or visiting performing artists. Other sources of newsworthy personalities or events: the publicity office, the president's office, the college newspaper, bulletin boards. All are potential sources for information about recent awards, or achievements, or upcoming events that may lead you to a subject for an interview, and a good story.

  2. *Doing preliminary homework.* Find out as much as you can about your potential interviewee's work, from the sources we mentioned above. If the subject of your interview is a faculty member, ask the department secretary if you may see a copy of that person's vita (Latin for "life," and pronounced vee-ta). Many departments have these brief biographical sketches on file for publicity purposes. The vita will list, among other things, publications and current research interests.

  3. *Requesting the interview.* In making your request, don't hesitate to mention that you are fulfilling an assignment, but also make evident your own interest in the person's work or area of expertise. (Showing that you already know something about the work, that you've done some preliminary homework, is persuasive evidence of your interest.) Request the interview, preferably in writing, at least a week in advance, and ask for ample time (probably an hour to an hour and a half) for a thorough interview.

  4. *Preparing thoroughly.* If your subject is a writer, read and take notes on the publications that most interest you. Read book reviews, if available; read reviews of performances if your subject is a performing artist. As you read, write out the questions that occur to you. As you work on them, try to phrase your questions so that they require more than a yes or no answer. A "why" or "how" question is likely to be productive, but don't be afraid of a general question such as "Tell me something about . . ."

Revise your questions and put them in a reasonable order. Work on an opening question that you think your subject will find both easy and interesting to answer. "How did you get interested in . . . " is often a good start. Type your questions or write them boldly so that you will find them easy to refer to.

Think about how you will record the interview. Although a tape recorder may seem like a good idea, there are good reasons not to rely on one. First of all, your subject may be made uneasy by its presence and freeze up. Second, the recorder (or the operator) may malfunction, leaving you with a partial record, or nothing at all. Third, even if all goes well, when you prepare to write you will face a mass of material, some of it inaudible, and all of it daunting to transcribe.

If, despite these warnings, you decide (with your subject's permission) to tape, expect to take notes anyway. It's the only way you can be sure you will have a record of what was important to you out of all that was said. Think beforehand, then, of how you will take notes, and if you can manage to, practice by interviewing a friend. You'll probably find that you'll want to devise some system of shorthand, perhaps no more than using initials for names that frequently recur, dropping the vowels in words that you transcribe—whatever assists you to write quickly but legibly. But don't think you must transcribe every word. Be prepared to do a lot more listening than writing.

5. *Presenting yourself for the interview.* Dress appropriately, bring your prepared questions and a notebook or pad for your notes, and appear on time.

6. *Conducting the interview.* At the start of the interview, try to engage briefly in conversation, without taking notes, to put your subject at ease. Even important people can be shy. Remembering that will help keep you at ease, too. If you want to use a tape recorder, ask your subject's permission, and if it is granted, ask where the microphone may be conveniently placed.

As the interview proceeds, *keep your purpose in mind.* Are you trying to gain information about an issue or a topic, or are you trying to get a portrait of a personality? Listen attentively to your subject's answers and be prepared to follow up with your own responses and spontaneous questions. Here is where your thorough preparation will pay off.

A good interview develops like a conversation. Keep in mind that your prepared questions, however essential, are not sacred. At the same time don't hesitate to steer your subject, courteously, from apparent irrelevancies (what one reporter calls "sawdust") to something that interests you more. "I'd like to hear a little more about . . . " you can say. Or "Would you mind telling me about how you . . . ." It's also perfectly acceptable to ask your subject to repeat a remark so that you can record it accurately, and if you don't understand something, don't be afraid to admit it. Experts are accustomed to knowing more than others do and are particularly happy to explain even the most elementary parts of their lore to an interested listener.

7. Concluding the interview. Near the end of the time you have agreed upon, ask your subject if he or she wishes to add any material, or to clarify something said earlier. Express your thanks and, at the appointed time, leave promptly.

8. Preparing to write. As soon as possible after the interview, review your notes, amplify them with details you wish to remember but might have failed to record, and type them up. You might have discovered during the interview, or you might see now, that there is something more that you want to read by or about your subject. Track it down and take further notes.

9. Writing the essay. In writing your first draft, think about your audience. Unless a better idea occurs to you, consider your college newspaper or magazine, or a local newspaper, as the place you hope to publish your story. Write with the readers of that publication in mind. Thinking of your readers will help you to be clear—for instance to identify names that have come up in the interview but which may be unfamiliar to your readers.

As with other writing, begin your draft with any idea that strikes you, and write at a fast clip until you have exhausted your material (or yourself).

When you revise, remember to keep your audience in mind; your material should, as it unfolds, tell a coherent and interesting story. Interviews, like conversations, tend to be delightfully circular or disorderly. But an essay, like a story, should reveal its contents in a sequence that captures and holds attention.

If you've done a thorough job of interviewing you may find that you have more notes than you can reasonably incorporate without disrupting the flow of your story. Don't be tempted to plug them in anyway. If they're really interesting, save them, perhaps by copying them into your journal; if not, chuck them out.

In introducing direct quotations from your source, choose those that are particularly characteristic, or vivid, or memorable. Paraphrase or summarize the rest of what is usable. Although the focus of your essay is almost surely the person you interviewed, it is your story, and most of it should be in your own words. Even though you must keep yourself in the background, your writing will gain in interest if your reader hears your voice as well as your subject's.

You might want to use a particularly good quotation for your conclusion. (Notice that both essays we've chosen as examples conclude this way.) Now make sure that you have an attractive opening paragraph. Identifying the subject of your interview and describing the setting is one way to begin. Give your essay an attractive title. Before you prepare your final draft, read your essay aloud. You're almost certain to catch phrases you can improve, and places where a transition will help your reader to follow you without effort. Check your quotations for accuracy; check with your subject any quotations or other details you're in doubt about. Type your final draft, then edit and proofread carefully.

10. *Going public.* Make two copies of your finished essay, one for the person you interviewed, one for yourself. The original is for your instructor; hand it in on time.

Topics for Writing

Write an essay based on an interview. You needn't be limited in your choice of subject by the examples we've given. A very old person, a recent immigrant, the owner or manager of an interesting store or business, a veteran of the war in Afghanistan or Iraq, a gardener are only a few of the possibilities. If you can manage to do so, include a few photographs of your subject, with appropriate captions.

Using Quotations

Our marginal comments briefly call your attention to the student's use of quotations, but here we remind you of procedures for using quotations. These procedures are not noteworthy when handled properly, but they become noticeable and even ruinous to your essay when bungled. Read over the following reminders, check them against the student's essay that you have just read, and consult them again the first few times you write about an essay.

- *Quote.* Quotations from the work under discussion provide evidence and indispensable support for your analysis. Quotations that strike you as especially engaging will also provide your readers with a welcome change of voice.
- *Don't overquote.* Most of your essay should consist of your own words.
- *Quote briefly.* Use quotations as evidence, not as padding.
- *Comment on what you quote*—immediately before or immediately after the quotation. Make sure your reader understands why you find the quotation relevant. Don't count on the quotation to make your point for you.
- *Take care with embedded quotations* (quotations within a sentence of your own). A quotation must make good sense and must fit grammatically into the sentence of which it is a part.

Incorrect:

> Plumb says he was "astonished when a minibus drove up to my house."

(In this example, the shift from Plumb to "my" is bothersome, especially since the student uses the first person in his essay.)

Improved:

> Plumb says that he was "astonished" when he saw a minibus arrive at his house.

Or:

> Plumb says, "I was astonished when a minibus drove up to my house."

Incorrect:

> Plumb implies he is well read because "Unlike anthropologists or sociologists, historians have not studied family life very closely."

Improved:

> Plumb implies he is well read in his assertion that "unlike anthropologists or sociologists, historians have not studied family life very closely."

- Don't try to fit a long quotation into the middle of one of your own sentences. It is almost impossible for the reader to come out of the quotation and pick up the thread of your sentence. It is better to lead into a long quotation with "Plumb says," followed by a colon, and then, after quoting, to begin a new sentence of your own.
- *Quote exactly.* Any material that you add (to make the quotation coherent with your sentence) must be in square brackets. Thus:

> Plumb says that he "was rather astonished when a minibus drove up to [his] house and out poured ten children."

An ellipsis (any material that you omit from a quotation) must be indicated by three spaced periods:

> Plumb says he "was rather astonished when a minibus drove up . . . and out poured ten children."

If you end the quotation before the end of the author's sentence, add a period and then three spaced periods to indicate the omission:

> Plumb says he "was rather astonished when a minibus drove up. . . ."

- *Quote fairly.* It would not be fair, for instance, to say that Lewis says, "After all, . . . they had a right to happiness." The words do in fact appear in Lewis's essay, but he is quoting them in order, ultimately, to refute them.

- *Identify the quotation* clearly for your reader. Use such expressions as "Lewis says," "Plumb argues."
- *Identify the source of quotations* in a list called "Works Cited."
- *Check your punctuation.* Remember: Periods and commas go *inside* the closing quotation marks, semicolons and colons go outside. Question marks and exclamation points go inside if they are part of the quotation, outside if they are your own.

Avoiding Plagiarism

Acknowledging Sources

Your purpose as an academic writer is to develop your own ideas about the topic you are writing about. Secondary sources will help you shape and develop your thoughts about your topic, but your purpose is to develop an argument and an analysis that is your own. It is crucial, then, to be clear about the distinction between your words and ideas and those of your sources. Not to do so is to risk charges of **plagiarism.** To plagiarize is to use someone else's words or ideas without attributing them to a source; it is to pass off someone else's work as your own. It is, in short, theft. The institutional consequences of plagiarism vary from school to school, and from case to case. In the university where one of us teaches, students who are found guilty of plagiarism are, among other things, banned from the campus for a year. At other schools, students can be expelled permanently; at still others, they simply receive a failing grade for the course and are put on academic probation.

Respect for your readers and for your sources requires that you acknowledge your indebtedness for material when

- you quote directly from a work, or
- you paraphrase or summarize someone's words (the words of your paraphrase or summary are your own, but the ideas are not), or
- you use an idea that is not common knowledge.

Most commonly, the words, ideas, and information you'll cite in a research essay will come from printed and electronic sources. But you must also acknowledge the advice of peer editors and ideas that come from lectures and class discussions, unless your instructor tells you not to do so. (Consult a handbook for instructions on formatting citations of sources.)

Let's suppose you want to make use of William Bascom's comment on the earliest European responses to African art:

> The first examples of African art to gain public attention were the bronzes and ivories which were brought back to Europe after the sack of Benin by a British military expedition in 1987. The superb technology of the Benin bronzes won the praise of experts like Felix von Luschan who wrote in 1899, "Cellini himself

could not have made better casts, nor anyone else before or since the present day." Moreover, their relatively realistic treatment of human features conformed to the prevailing European aesthetic standards. Because of their naturalism and technical excellence, it was at first maintained that they have been produced by Europeans—a view that was still current when the even more realistic bronze heads were discovered at Ife in 1912. The subsequent discovery of new evidence has caused the complete abandonment of this theory of European origins of the bronzes of Benin and Ife, both of which are in Nigeria.

—William Bascom, *African Art in Cultural Perspective*
(New York: Norton, 1973), p. 4

Acknowledge a direct quotation. A student wanting to use some or all of Bascom's words might write something like this:

According to William Bascom, when Europeans first encountered Benin and Ife works of art in the late nineteenth century, they thought that Europeans had produced them, but the discovery of new evidence "caused the complete abandonment of this theory of European origins of the bronzes of Benin and Ife, both of which are cities in Nigeria." (4)

In this example, the writer introduces Bascom with a signal phrase ("According to William Bascom"); then she summarizes several sentences from Bascom; then she uses quotation marks to indicate the passage that comes directly from Bascom's book. Note that the summary does not borrow Bascom's language; the words are all the writer's own. Note also that what appears inside the quotation marks is an exact transcription of Bascom's words: The writer has not changed any word endings or omitted any words, or any punctuation of her own. (The "4" inside parentheses at the end of the passage is the page reference.)

Acknowledging a paraphrase or summary. Summaries (abridgments) are usually superior to paraphrases (rewordings, usually phrase by phrase, of approximately the same length as the original) because summaries are briefer. When you are using sources, you will for the most part be writing summaries, *not* paraphrases—unless the language of the source is especially complex. If Bascom's sentences had been obscure—for instance, if they used highly technical language—there would have been a reason to paraphrase them, to translate them (so to speak) into clearer English. In that case, the writer of the essay would explicitly have said she was paraphrasing Bascom, and she would have explained why.

Occasionally you may find that you cannot summarize a passage in your source and yet you don't want to quote it word for word—perhaps because it is too technical or because it is poorly written. In that case, you need to paraphrase the passage—that is, you need to put it into your own words. Even though you have put the idea into your own words, you must give credit to the source because the idea is not yours. *Both summaries and paraphrases must be acknowledged.* In both case, the author must be identified by name, and the location of the source—a page reference if you are using a print source—must be given.

Here is an example of an **acceptable summary:**

> William Bascom, in *African Art in Cultural Perspective*, points out that the first examples of African art brought to Europe—Benin bronzes and ivories— were thought by Europeans to be of European origin, because they were realistic and well made, but evidence was later discovered that caused this theory to be abandoned (4).

The summary is adequate, and the page reference indicates where the source is to be found. But if the writer had omitted the signal phrase "William Bascom, in African Art, points out that," the result would have been plagiarism. Not to give Bascom credit would be to plagiarize, even if the words are the writer's own. The offense is just as serious as not acknowledging a direct quotation.

The following paragraph is an example of an **unacceptable summary.** Why is it unacceptable, since the writer cites Bascom as her source? It is unacceptable because she uses too much of Bascom's language, and she follows his organization of the material: She has not turned the material into her own writing.

> William Bascom points out that the earliest examples of African art to become widely known in Europe were bronzes and ivories that were brought to Europe in 1897. These works were thought to be of European origin, and one expert said that Cellini could not have done better work. Their technical excellence, as well as their realism, fulfilled the European standards of the day. The later discovery of new evidence at Benin and Ife, both in Nigeria, refuted this belief.

Again, all the ideas are Bascom's, and so is the way in which the ideas are presented. The writer simply substitutes one phrase for another, maintaining much of the structure and organization of Bascom's sentences. The writing is Bascom's, in a thin disguise. She substitutes

> "The earliest examples of African art"

for Bascom's

> "The first examples of African art";

she substitutes

> "to become widely known"

for

> "to gain public attention";

she substitutes

> "Their technical excellence, as well as their realism"

for

> "their naturalism and technical excellence."

The writer here is plagiarizing—perhaps without even knowing it. But it should be clear that neither the words nor the ideas in this passage are the writer's own. This form of plagiarism, where a writer simply substitutes his or her own phrases here and there but retains the form and content of the original passage, is one of the most common forms of plagiarism that writing instructors see. Much of it occurs, we believe, because students don't know it's wrong—and because they don't see their job as developing their own ideas in relation to their sources.

As we have noted, it is unlikely that a writer would paraphrase a passage that is as straightforward and as free of technical language as Bascom's: The main reason for paraphrasing is to clarify a text that might be confusing to a reader—a literary text, for example, or a particularly complex or technical piece of writing.

Acknowledging an idea. Let's say you have read an essay in which Irving Kristol argues that journalists who pride themselves on being tireless critics of national policy are in fact irresponsible critics because they have no policy they prefer. If this strikes you as a new idea and you adopt it in an essay—even though you set it forth entirely in your own words and with examples not offered by Kristol—you must acknowledge your debt to Kristol. Not to acknowledge such borrowing is plagiarism. Your readers will not think the less of you for naming your source; rather, they will be grateful to you for telling them about an interesting writer.

Fair Use of Common Knowledge

If in doubt as to whether or not to give credit (either with formal documentation or merely in a phrase such as "Carol Gilligan says . . ."), give credit. But as you begin to read widely in your field or subject, you will develop a sense of what is considered common knowledge.

Unsurprising definitions in a dictionary can be considered common knowledge, and so there is no need to say "According to Webster, a novel is a long narrative in prose." (That's weak in three ways: It's unnecessary, it's uninteresting, and it's inexact since "Webster" appears in the titles of several dictionaries, some good and some bad.)

Similarly, the date of Freud's death can be considered common knowledge. Few can give it when asked, but it can be found out from innumerable sources, and no one need get the credit for providing you with the date. Again, if you simply know from your reading of Freud that Freud was interested in literature, you need not cite a specific source for an assertion to that effect, but if you know only because some commentator on Freud said so, and you have no idea whether or not the fact is well known, you should give credit to the source that gave you the information. Not to give credit—for ideas as well as for quoted words—is to plagiarize.

"But How Else Can I Put It?"

If you have just learned—say, from one of the readings in this book, or from an encyclopedia—something that you sense is common knowledge, you may wonder how to change into your own words the simple, clear words that this source uses in setting forth this simple fact. For example, if before writing an analysis of a photograph of Buffalo Bill and Sitting Bull (p. 48), you look up these names in the *Encyclopaedia Britannica*, you will find this statement about Buffalo Bill (William E Cody): "In 1883 Cody organized his first Wild West exhibition." You could not use this statement as your own, word for word, without feeling uneasy. But to put in quotation marks such a routine statement of what can be considered common knowledge, and to cite a source for it, seems pretentious. After all, the *Encyclopedia Americana* says much the same thing in the same routine way: "In 1883 . . . Cody organized Buffalo Bill's Wild West." It may be that the word "organized" is simply the most obvious and the best word, and perhaps you will end up using it. Certainly, to change "Cody organized" into "Cody presided over the organization of" or "Cody assembled" or some such thing in an effort to avoid plagiarizing would be to make a change for the worse and still to be guilty of plagiarism. What, then, can you do? You won't get yourself into this mess of wondering whether to change clear, simple wording into awkward wording if in the first place, when you take notes, you summarize your sources, thus: "1883: organized Wild West," or "first Wild West: 1883." Later (even if only thirty minutes later), when drafting your paper, if you turn this nugget—probably combined with others—into the best sentence you can, you will not be in danger of plagiarizing, even if the word "organized" turns up in your sentence. The sentence will be your own sentence, not your source's sentence.

Of course, even when dealing with material that can be considered common knowledge—and even when you have put it into your own words—you probably will cite your source if you are drawing more than just an occasional fact from a source. For instance, if your paragraph on Buffalo Bill uses half a dozen facts from a source, cite the source. You do this both to avoid charges of plagiarism and to protect yourself in case your source contains errors of fact.

Joining the Conversation: Critical Thinking and Writing

1. Write a paragraph that acknowledges the author of an essay in this book but nevertheless illustrates plagiarism. (Your instructor will probably choose the paragraph.)

2. Write a paragraph in which you make honest use of a source, quoting some words and summarizing a passage or an idea. (Your instructor will probably choose the paragraph.)

✓ A Checklist: Avoiding Plagiarism

☐ In my sources, did I *summarize* (rather than paraphrase) material, and did I give credit to the source for the facts and ideas? (A paraphrase in the student's essay, even if a source is cited, is considered plagiarism because the sequence of ideas is the source's, not the student's. The writing is essentially the source's, translated into the student's language.)

☐ Is *all* quoted material—in notes and in the submitted essay— enclosed within quotation marks, and is the source cited?

☐ Are all borrowed *ideas* credited to the appropriate sources?

☐ Common knowledge—the term includes indisputable material that can be found in countless sources, such as the date of the Battle of the Bulge and the fact that Lincoln was assassinated— is *not* cited, but if you are in doubt about whether something is "common knowledge," choose the safer course and cite your source.

✓ A Checklist: Thirteen Questions to Ask Yourself When Editing

☐ Is the title of my essay at least moderately informative?

☐ Do I identify the subject of my essay (author and title) early?

☐ What is my thesis? Do I state it soon enough (perhaps even in the title) and keep it in view?

☐ Is the organization reasonable? Does each point lead into the next, without irrelevancies and without anticlimaxes?

☐ Is each paragraph unified by a topic sentence or a topic idea? Are there adequate transitions from one paragraph to the next?

- ☐ Are generalizations supported by appropriate concrete details, especially by brief quotations from the text?
- ☐ Is the opening paragraph interesting and, by its end, focused on the topic? Is the final paragraph conclusive without being repetitive?
- ☐ Is the tone appropriate? No sarcasm, no apologies, no condescension?
- ☐ If there is a summary, is it as brief as possible, given its purpose?
- ☐ Are the quotations accurate? Do they serve a purpose other than to add words to the essay?
- ☐ Is documentation provided where necessary?
- ☐ Are the spelling and punctuation correct? Are other mechanical matters (such as margins, spacing, and citations) in correct form? Have I proofread carefully?
- ☐ Is the paper properly identified—author's name, instructor's name, course number, and date?

A Student's Documented Essay

Jason Green

Jason Green wrote this essay not for an art history course but for an introductory course in composition. Notice that Green draws not only on his experience as an amateur photographer but also on material that he found in the college library.

Did Dorothea Lange Pose Her Subject for <u>Migrant Mother</u>?

In doing research for this essay, I was surprised to find that Dorothea Lange's <u>Migrant Mother</u> (figure 1) is one of six pictures of this woman and her children. <u>Migrant Mother</u> is so much an image of the period, an icon of the Depression, that it is hard to believe it exists in any other form than the one we all know.[1]

---

1 Curiously, Lange in her short essay on the picture, "The Assignment I'll Never Forget: Migrant Mother," in <u>Popular Photography</u> 46 (February 1960): 43, says that she made five exposures. A slightly abridged version of the essay is reprinted in Milton Meltzer, <u>Dorothea Lange: A Photographer's Life</u> (New York: Farrar Straus Giroux 1978): 132–33. Because Meltzer's book is more available than the magazine, when I quote from the article I quote from his book.

Figure 1   *Migrant Mother, Nipomo, California*
                           Dorothea Lange, 1936

In addition to the famous picture, four other pictures of this
subject (figures 2–5) are illustrated in a recent book, Vincent Virga's Eyes
of the Nation, and still another picture (figure 6) is illustrated in Karen
Tsujimoto's Dorothea Lange. When you think about it, it is not surprising
that Lange would take several pictures of this woman and her children.
Anyone who takes snapshots knows that if photographers have the
opportunity they will take several pictures of a subject. What is surprising
is that the picture we all know, the one that has become an icon for the
period, is so much more moving than the others.

Two of the pictures include an older child, apparently a teenager,
sitting in a chair, so in a sense they are "truer" to the fact, because
they give us more information about the family. The trunk, for instance,

Figure 2

Figure 3

tells us that these people are on the move, and the setting--a messy field, with a shabby tent or lean-to--tells us that they are homeless. But sometimes less is more; the pictures showing the tent, trunk, and all of the children seem to sprawl. Perhaps we find ourselves wondering why people who seem to have only a trunk and some canvas would carry with them so bulky an object as a rocker. In saying that the two more inclusive pictures are less effective--less impressive, less moving--than the others, then, I don't think that I am simply expressing a personal preference. I think that most or maybe even all viewers would agree.

Putting aside the two pictures that show the setting, and also putting aside for the moment the most famous picture, we probably can agree that the three remaining pictures of the woman are approximately equally effective, one viewer might prefer one picture, another viewer another, but compared with the two that show the larger setting, all three of these pictures have the advantage of emphasizing the mother-and-child motif. But the remaining picture, the famous one, surely is far more memorable than even the other three close-up pictures. Why? Partly, perhaps, because it is a closer view, eliminating the tent pole and most of the hanging cloth. Partly it is more effective because the children have turned their faces from the camera, thereby conveying their isolation from everything in the world except their mother. And partly it is more effective because the woman, touching the side of her face, has a faraway look of anxiety.

Thinking about this picture in the context of the other five, if one has a cynical mind one might wonder if Lange staged it. And this is exactly what Charles J. Shindo says she did, in his recent book:

> In the course of this encounter Lange took six exposures, starting with a long shot of the lean-to with the mother and four children inside. . . . For the final shot Lange called back another of the children and had the children lean

Figure 4

upon their mother with their backs to the camera. The
woman raised her hand to her chin and struck the now
famous pose of the <u>Migrant Mother</u>. . . . (50)

What evidence does Shindo give for his claim that "Lange called
back another of the children" and that she "had the children lean upon their
mother"? Absolutely none. He does not cite Lange, or an eyewitness, or
anyone who suggests that Lange customarily posed her subjects. He ignores
the basic evidence, Lange's own words about how she took the picture:

I saw and approached the hungry and desperate mother,
as if drawn by a magnet. I do not remember how I
explained my presence or my camera to her, but I do

Figure 5

Figure 6

remember she asked me no questions. I made five exposures, working closer and closer from the same direction. I did not ask her name or her history. She told me her age, that she was thirty-two. She said that they had been living on frozen vegetables from the surrounding fields, and birds that the children killed. She had just sold the tires from her car to buy food. There she sat in that lean-to tent with her children huddled around her, and seemed to know that my pictures might help her, and so she helped me. There was a sort of equality about it.

The pea crop at Nipomo had frozen and there was no work for anybody. But I did not approach the tents and shelters of other stranded pea-pickers. It was not necessary; I knew I had recorded the essence of my assignment. . . . (qtd. in Meltzer 133)

This is the <u>only</u> eye-witness account of how Lange photographed the woman and her children. Of course she may not have been telling the truth, but none of her contemporaries ever challenged the truth of her statement. Furthermore, everything that we know about Lange suggests that she did not pose her subjects. For instance, Rondal Partridge, a longtime friend and sometimes a co-worker, gave this description of Lange's method: "She did not ask people to hold a pose or repeat an action, instead she might ask a question: 'How much does that bag of cotton weigh?' And the man, wanting to give her a precise answer, would lift it onto the scales and Lange would make her photograph" (qtd. in Ohrn 61).

Rondal Partridge's comment harmonizes with comments that Lange herself made about her method. Asked about her approach to photography, she said, "First--hands off! Whatever I photograph, I do not molest or tamper with or arrange" (qtd. in Dixon 68). Elsewhere she explained that since she worked with a large camera, "You have to wait until certain decisions are made by the subject--what he's going to give to the camera, which is a very important decision; and the photographer--what he's going to choose to take" (qtd. in Ohrn 233). If I may add a personal comment, I want to say that as an amateur portrait photographer I know from my experience and from talking to other photographers, that posed photographs just don't come out successfully. You can't say to children, "Turn your faces toward your mother," and then say to the mother, "Please put your hand on your cheek," and get a good picture. Every photographer quickly learns that when the photographer specifies the poses, the pictures will be lifeless. The way to get a picture that is convincing is, as Lange's friend said, for the photographer to engage in some talk with the subject, which allows the subject to respond in some significant way. I imagine that while Lange talked, the children may have become uneasy at the sight of the woman with the big camera, and they may have turned and sought the security of their mother. (This is only a guess, but it is very different from Shindo's assertion, made without evidence, that "Lange called back another of the children and had the children lean upon their mother with their backs to the camera"). And perhaps Lange asked the woman something like, "What do you think you will do now?" or "Do you think you can get a friend to give your family a hitch to another work-site?" or some such thing, and the woman responded naturally. Again my view is different from Shindo's, who says that the woman "struck the pose of the Migrant Mother," where "struck the pose," in the context of his preceding sentences about Lange coldly setting up the image, suggests that the whole thing is a performance, with Lange as stage-manager and the woman as the chief actor.

Anyone who has read a book about Dorothea Lange, and has studied Lange's numerous comments about her ways of working in Dorothea Lange, ed. Howard M. Levin and Katherine Northrup, knows that posing figures was utterly foreign to her. In 1923 she posted on her darkroom door these words from Francis Bacon, and they guided her for the remaining thirty-odd years of her career:

> The contemplation of things as they are
> without substitution or imposture
> without error or confusion
> is in itself a nobler thing
> than a whole harvest of invention. (qtd. in Stein 59)

In her photography Lange sought to show the viewer "things as they are." She believed it was nobler to show life as it is than it is to invent compositions.

There are, of course, questions about this picture, such as "Exactly what is the mother thinking about?" Is she thinking that the situation is hopeless? Or that somehow she and the children will get through? Does her face show despair, or does it show determination? These are questions that we cannot answer definitively. But if we ask the question, "Did Lange tell the children and the woman how to position themselves?" we must answer that all of the evidence suggests that she did not set the scene. She spoke to the woman, and she moved about, looking for the best shot, but a picture as great as this one can only have come from (to repeat Lange's own belief) what the subject is "going to give to the camera" and what the photographer is "going to choose to take."

Works Cited

Dixon, Daniel. "Dorothea Lange." Modern Photography 16 (Dec 1952).
    68–77, 138–41.

Levin, Howard M., and Katherine Northrup. Dorothea Lange. 2 vols.
    Glencoe: Text-Fiche Press, 1980.

Meltzer, Milton. Dorothea Lange: A Photographer's Life. New York: Farrar,
    1978.

Ohrn, Karin Becker. <u>Dorothea Lange and the Documentary Tradition</u>.
    Baton Rouge: Louisiana State UP, 1980.

Shindo, Charles J. <u>Dust Bowl Migrants in the American Imagination</u>.
    Lawrence: UP of Kansas, 1997.

Stein, Sally. "Peculiar Grace: Dorothea Lange and the Testimony of the
    Body." <u>Dorothea Lange: A Visual Life</u>. Ed. Elizabeth Partridge.
    Washington, D.C.: Smithsonian Institution, 1994. 57–89.

CHAPTER 4

Writing an Argument

Although in common usage an **argument** can be a noisy wrangle—baseball players argue about the umpire's decision, spouses argue about who should put out the garbage—in this chapter we mean a discourse that uses *reasons*—rather than, say, appeals to pity, or, for that matter, threats—in order to persuade readers to hold the writer's opinion, or at least to persuade readers that the writer's opinion is thoughtful and reasonable. In this sense, argument is a thoroughly respectable activity.

What distinguishes argument from **exposition** (for instance, the explanation of a process) is this: Argument and exposition both consist of statements, but in argument some statements are offered as *reasons* for other statements. Essentially one builds an argument on the word *because*. Another characteristic of argument is that argument assumes there may be a substantial disagreement among informed readers. Exposition assumes that the reader is unfamiliar with the subject matter—let's say, the origins of jazz or the law concerning affirmative action—but it does *not* assume that the reader holds a different opinion. The writer of an argument, however, seeks to overcome disagreement (for instance about the value or the fairness of something) by offering reasons that are convincing or at least worth considering carefully. Here is Supreme Court Justice Louis Brandeis concluding a justly famous argument that government may not use evidence illegally obtained by wiretapping:

> Decency, security, and liberty alike demand that government officials shall be subjected to the same rules of conduct that are commands to the citizen. In a government of laws, existence of the government will be imperilled if it fails to observe the law scrupulously. Our Government is the potent, the omnipresent teacher. For good or for ill, it teaches the whole people by its example. Crime is contagious. If the Government becomes a lawbreaker, it breeds contempt for law; it invites every man to become a law unto himself; it invites anarchy. To declare that in the administration of the criminal law the end justifies the means—to declare that the Government may commit crimes in order to secure the conviction of a private criminal—would bring terrible retribution. Against that pernicious doctrine the Court should resolutely set its face.

Brandeis's reasoning is highlighted by his forceful style. Note the resonant use of parallel constructions ("Decency, security, and liberty," "For good or for ill," "it breeds . . . it invites," "To declare . . . to declare"), which convey a sense of dignity and authority. Notice, too, the effective variation between short and long sentences. The sentences range from three words ("Crime is contagious"—forceful because of its brevity and its alliteration) to thirty-seven words (the next-to-last sentence—impressive because of its length and especially because the meaning is suspended until the end, when we get the crucial verb and its object, "would bring terrible retribution"). Later in our discussion of argument we will talk about the importance of the writer's style.

The Aims of an Argumentative Essay

The aim might seem obvious—to persuade the reader to accept the writer's opinion. In fact, often there are other aims. First, writers draft argumentative essays partly in order to find out what they believe. In drafting a paper they come to see that certain of their unformed beliefs can't really be supported or that their beliefs need to be considerably modified. This point should not come as a surprise; in earlier chapters we have said that writers get ideas and refine their beliefs by the act of writing. Second, if you read argumentative essays in, say, *National Review* (a conservative magazine), in *The Nation* (a liberal magazine), or in just about any magazine, you will see that much of the writing is really a matter of preaching to the converted. Good arguments may be offered, but they are offered not to persuade readers but to reassure them that the views they already hold are sound. After all, few liberals read *National Review*, few conservatives read *The Nation*, and so on.

When you write an argumentative essay, although you may hope to convince all readers to adopt your view, you probably also realize that the subject is complex, and that other opinions are possible. What you want to do is to set forth your viewpoint as effectively as possible, not because you believe all readers will say, "Yes, of course, you have converted me," but because *you want your view to be given a hearing. You want to show that it is one that can be held by a reasonable person.* Because you are a person of goodwill, with an open mind, you realize that most issues are very complicated. You have formed some ideas, and now you are taking a stand and arguing on its behalf. However, you probably are not saying that no other view can possibly have the tiniest scrap of merit. As Virginia Woolf put it (with perhaps a bit of self-irony),

> When a subject is highly controversial . . . one cannot hope to tell the truth. One can only show how one came to hold whatever opinion one does hold. One can only give one's audience the chance of drawing their own conclusions as they observe the limitations, the prejudices, the idiosyncrasies of the speaker.

Again, we want to say that in drafting the paper your chief aim is to educate yourself; in offering it to readers your chief aim is to let others know that your views are worth considering because they are supported by reason. If you persuade your readers to accept your views, great; but you should at least persuade them that a reasonable person can hold these views.

Negotiating Agreements: The Approach of Carl R. Rogers

Carl R. Rogers (1902–87), best known for his book entitled *On Becoming a Person,* was a psychotherapist, not a writer, but he has exerted a great influence on teachers of writing. Rogers originally intended to become a

Protestant minister, but, as he tells in *On Becoming a Person*, during the course of a six-month visit to East Asia he came to recognize "that sincere and honest people could believe in very divergent religious doctrines." He turned to the study of psychology, and in the course of time developed the idea that a therapist must engage in "reflection," by which he meant that the therapist must reflect—must give back an image—of what the client said. (Rogers's use of the word "client" rather than "patient" is itself a clue to his approach; the therapist is not dealing with someone who is supposed passively to accept treatment from the all-powerful doctor.)

What has this to do with seeking to persuade a reader? Consider two lawyers arguing a case in court. Lawyer A may seem to be arguing with lawyer B, but neither lawyer really is trying to convince the other, and neither lawyer has the faintest interest in learning from the other. The lawyers are trying to persuade not each other, but the judge or jury. Similarly, the writer of a letter to a newspaper, taking issue with an editorial, probably has no thought of changing the newspaper's policy. Rather, the letter is really directed to another audience, readers of the newspaper. And we hear this sort of thing on radio and television shows with titles like *Crossfire, Firing Line,* and *Point Counterpoint.* For the most part the participants are not trying to learn from each other and are not trying to solve a complex problem, but rather are trying to convince the audience that one side is wholly right and the other side is wholly wrong. If they are talking about an issue that we don't know much about, the arguments on both sides may seem to be equally strong, and we are likely to side with the speaker whose *style* of talk (and maybe of dress) we prefer. This point is important, and we will return to it when we talk about the *persona* or character of the writer of an argument.

Suppose that unlike a participant on a radio or television show, and unlike a lawyer arguing a case, speaker X really does want to persuade speaker Y; that is, X really wants to bring Y around to X's point of view, or if X is mistaken in his or her views, X really is willing to learn from Y in the course of the give and take. Rogers points out that when we engage in an argument, if we feel that our integrity or our identity is threatened, we stiffen our resistance. Normally we may *want* to grow, to develop our thoughts, to act in accordance with sound reasons, but when we are threatened we erect defenses that in fact shut us off from communication. That is, we find ourselves within a circle that not only shuts others out but that also has the unintended effect of shutting us in. We—or our opponent—may have given very good reasons, but because each party has behaved in a threatening manner, and has felt threatened by the other side, we have scarcely listened to each other, and therefore little or nothing has been communicated. (If you think about your own experience, you probably can confirm Rogers's view.)

To avoid this deplorable lack of opportunity for growth, Rogers suggests that participants in arguments need to become partners, not adversaries. Here, with Rogers's insight in mind, we can digress for a moment, and call attention to the combative terms normally associated with argument. *Debate,* for instance, is from Latin *de-* (down) and *battere* (to beat), the same word that gives us *battery,* as in "assault and battery." We *marshal* our arguments (arrange them into a military formation), and we *attack our opponents,* seeking to *rebut* (from a Latin word meaning "to butt back") or *refute* (again from a Latin word, this time meaning "to drive back") their assertions. When we are engaged in these activities, (1) we are scarcely in a position to learn from those we are talking with—really, talking *at*—and (2) we are not likely to teach them anything, because, like us, they are busy *defending* (still another military word) their own position.

Rogers suggests, therefore, that a writer who wishes to communicate (as opposed to a lawyer or a debater who merely wishes to win) needs to reduce the threat. To repeat: The participants in an argument need to become partners rather than adversaries. "Mutual communication," he says, "tends to be pointed toward solving a problem rather than attacking a person or a group."

Take abortion, for instance. We hear about "pro-life" (or "anti-abortion") people, and about "pro-choice" (or "pro-abortion") people. It may seem that there is no common ground, nothing they can agree on. But polls reveal considerable ambiguity within some people. Consider, for instance, a finding of a New York Times/CBS News poll of representative Americans, in January 1998. Participants were asked which question came nearer to their opinion: Is abortion the same thing as murdering a child? Or, is abortion not murder because the fetus really isn't a child? Half the sample chose "the same thing as murdering a child," and 38 percent chose "the fetus really isn't a child." At the same time, however, 58 percent, including a third of those who chose "murdering a child," agreed that abortion was "sometimes the best course in a bad situation."

These apparently inconsistent responses have been fairly consistent for the last twenty years; some people who consider abortion equivalent to murdering a child will grant that there are situations in which abortion is "the best course," and, we should add, many pro-choice people, people who insist that a woman has a right to choose and that her choice is not the government's business, also agree that abortion should not be lightly entered into. Take a particular case: A pregnant woman who regards abortion as "the same thing as murdering a child" learns that her baby will probably have Down syndrome (such persons have an average IQ of about 50, are prone to hearing problems and vision problems, and have an increased risk of heart disease and leukemia). Despite her opposition to abortion, she may become one of the people who feel abortion is "sometimes the best course in a bad situation." Given the choice of bearing or aborting, she may very reluctantly decide to abort. Yet on the day we were drafting these pages we happened to come across a letter in a newspaper making a point that, however obvious, we had not thought of. The writer, Maureen K. Hogan, Executive Director of Adopt a Special Kid, reported in her letter that "there are thousands of families around the United States that would be happy to adopt such a child. . . . In 25 years, there hasn't been a single child for whom we have not been able to find a home." We can imagine that a woman who dreaded the idea of aborting a fetus but felt that she had no choice but abortion, might, on hearing this information, modify her intention and engage in a course of behavior that she and all others concerned will find more satisfactory.

We should mention, too, that open-minded discussion between persons who hold differing views may reveal that some of their differences are verbal rather than substantial. One can wonder, for instance, if the poll would have produced the same results if the question had asked about "killing" rather than "murdering" a child. Patient, well-intentioned discussion may reveal that the parties are not as far apart as they at first seemed to be; they share some ground, and once this common ground is acknowledged, differences can be discussed.

Consider, as another example, a proposal in 1997 by President Clinton to introduce voluntary national tests in reading and mathematics. Some people think such testing is a Bad Idea. Why?

- What is tested is what will get taught; teachers will soon start preparing students for the test, rather than teaching the things they think are important. Why would teachers do this? Because they want to look good, they want their school to stand high in the national ratings.
- A second objection is that testing introduces an unhealthy spirit of competition.
- A third objection concerns the issue of who will make the tests. Administrators? Professors of education? The teachers who are on the firing line?
- A fourth objection is that, no matter who makes the test, the testing board would have too much power, since it would in effect determine not only what things get taught but which students get to go on to college.
- A fifth objection is that a national test would have little meaning; some states have a relatively homogenous population, whereas others have a relatively heterogenous population. A sixth objection is that test scores don't have much value. After all, we know (or do we?) that the SAT is not really a good predictor of success in school, and that tests are especially likely to fail to recognize the offbeat creative students—just look at X, who had poor grades and dropped out of school and is now recognized as a genius.

Probably all of these objections have some weight, but replies (also of varying weight) can be made to them. To take only the first two: It may be a good thing if teachers are jolted out of their parochialism and are made to become aware of the values of others, and, second, what is wrong with some competition? Competition sometimes is healthy. But after all of the pros and the cons are laid out, a Rogerian thinker will want to see what the two sides can *agree* on. They can agree, probably, that American school children ought to do better in reading and in mathematics. They can also agree, probably, that testing has some validity. And they can also agree, probably, that national testing by itself will not solve the problem. For instance, other possibilities include a longer school year, better pay for teachers (to attract better teachers), national tests for teachers, and so on. If the disputants can first establish the positions they *share,* and realize that both sides are people of goodwill endowed with some good ideas, they may better be able to work out their differences.

Rogers was drawing on his experience as a psychotherapist, which means he was mostly writing about the relationship between two people who were literally talking to each other, whereas a writer can at best imagine a reader. But good writers do in fact bring their readers into their writings, by such devices as "It may be said that . . ."—here one summarizes or quotes a view other than one's own. Writers genuinely interested in contributing to the solution of a problem will not merely busy themselves in asserting their position but will also inform themselves of a variety of views, by listening and by reading. And when they listen and read, they must do so with an open mind, giving the speaker or author (at least at first) the benefit of the doubt. (Rogers's term for this sort of activity is "empathic listening," i.e., comprehension so complete that it grasps not only the thoughts but also the feelings and motives of another.) That is, they will listen and read sympathetically, and they will not be too quick to evaluate. They may even, in an effort to do justice to the material, listen and read with the mind of a believer. Or, if this is asking too much, they will act in the spirit advocated by the seventeenth-century essayist Francis Bacon: "Read not to contradict and confute; nor to believe and take for granted; nor to find talk and discourse; but to weigh and consider."

Writers genuinely interested in persuading others will educate themselves, by listening and reading. In their own writing, where they wish to contribute their views on a disputed matter, they simultaneously can reduce the psychological threat to those who hold views different from their own by doing several things: They can show sympathetic understanding of the opposing argument; they can recognize what is valid in it; and they can recognize and demonstrate that those who take a different view are nonetheless persons of goodwill.

A writer who takes Rogers seriously will, usually, in the first part of an argumentative essay

- state the problem, suggesting that it is an issue of concern, and that the reader has a stake in it;
- show respect for persons who hold differing views;
- set forth opposing positions, *stated in such a way that their proponents will agree that the statements of their positions are fair;* and
- find some shared values—that is, grant whatever validity the writer finds in those positions, for instance, by recognizing the circumstances in which they would indeed be acceptable.

Having accurately summarized other views and having granted some concessions, the writer presumably has won the reader's attention and goodwill; the writer can now

- show how those who hold other positions will benefit if they accept the writer's position.

This last point is essentially an appeal to self-interest. In the example we gave a moment ago, concerning a pregnant woman who has contemplated aborting a fetus that, if born, probably will be a baby with Down syndrome, the appeal to self-interest might run along the lines that if she bears the child she will be free from the remorse she might feel if she had aborted it.

Sometimes, of course, the differing positions will be so far apart that no reconciliation can be proposed, in which case the writer will probably seek to show how the issue can best be solved by adopting the writer's own position. But even in such an essay it is desirable to state the opposing view in such a way that proponents of that view will agree that that is indeed their position and not a caricature of it.

Rogers, again, was a psychologist, not a teacher of writing and not a logician. In fact, his writing shares with some recent feminist theory a distrust of logic, which can be seen as masculine and aggressive, concerned with winning, even with "annihilating the opposition." Rogers offers advice not so much on winning (in the sense of conquering) but in the sense of winning over, that is, gaining converts, or at least allies.

✓ A Checklist: Rogerian Argument

- ☐ Have I treated other views with **respect?**
- ☐ Have I stated at least one other view **in a way that would satisfy its proponents, and thus demonstrated my familiarity with the issue?**
- ☐ Have I granted **validity to any aspects of other positions, and thus demonstrated my openmindedness?**
- ☐ Have I pointed out the **common ground,** the ground that we share, and thus prepared the reader to listen attentively to my proposals?
- ☐ Have I shown how the other position will be strengthened, at least in some contexts, by accepting some aspects of my position? (In short, have I **appealed to the reader's self-interest,** by showing that proponents of the other view(s) will benefit from accepting at least part of my view?

Some Ways of Arguing: Appeals to Reason and Appeals to Emotions

Appeals to Reason: Deduction and Induction

Deduction is the process of reasoning from premises to a logical conclusion. Here is the classic example:

> All men are mortal (*major premise*).
>
> Socrates is a man (*minor premise*).
>
> Therefore Socrates is mortal (*conclusion*).

Such an argument, which takes two truths and joins them to produce a third truth, is called a **syllogism.** Deduction (from the Latin *deducere*, for "lead down from") moves from a general statement to a specific application.
Here is a second example:

> All teachers of Spanish know that *hoy* means "today" (*major premise*)
>
> John is a teacher of Spanish (*minor premise*)
>
> John knows that *hoy* means today (*conclusion*)

If indeed all teachers of Spanish know the meaning of *hoy*, and if indeed John is a teacher of Spanish, the conclusion *must* be true.
Notice, however, that *if a premise of a syllogism is not true*, one can reason logically and still come to a *false* conclusion. Example:

> All teachers are members of a union (*major premise*)
>
> John is a teacher (*minor premise*)
>
> John is a member of a union (*conclusion*)

The *process* of reasoning is correct here, *the major premise is false*—but all teachers are not members of a union—and so the conclusion is worthless. John may or may not be a member of the union.
Another point: Some arguments superficially appear logical but are not. Let's take this attempt at a syllogism:

> All teachers of Spanish know that in Spanish *hoy* means today (*major premise*)
>
> John knows that in Spanish *hoy* means today (*minor premise*)
>
> Therefore John is a teacher of Spanish (*conclusion*).

Both of the premises are correct, but the conclusion does not follow. What's wrong? Valid deduction requires that the subject or condition of the major premise (in this case, teachers of Spanish) appear also in the minor premise, but here it does not. The minor premise should be "John is a teacher of Spanish," and the valid conclusion, of course, would be "therefore John knows that *hoy* means today."

Let's now turn to another process of reasoning, **induction.** Whereas deduction moves from a general statement ("All men are mortal") to a particular conclusion ("Socrates is mortal"), induction moves from particular instances to a general conclusion.

> I saw an elephant and it was grayish. Six months later I saw another elephant and it was grayish. In fact, every elephant I have seen is grayish, so by induction (from Latin *inducere,* "lead into," "lead up to") I conclude that all elephants are grayish.

Now consider a second example: I have met ten graduates of Vassar College and all are females, so I conclude that all Vassar graduates are females. This conclusion, however, happens to be incorrect: Vassar was founded as a women's college, but it now admits men; so although male graduates are notably fewer than female graduates, they do exist. Induction is valid only if the sample is representative.

Because we can rarely be certain that a sample is representative, induced conclusions are usually open to doubt. Still, we live our lives largely by induction: We have dinner with a friend, we walk the dog, we write home for money—all because these actions have produced certain results in the past and we assume that actions of the same sort will produce results consistent with our earlier findings. Nelson Algren's excellent advice must have been arrived at inductively: "Never eat at a place called Mom's, and never play cards with a man called Doc."

Appeals to Emotions

"Tears are not arguments," the Brazilian writer Machado de Assis said. We understand the point, and we remember the old joke about the youngster who killed his parents and then pleaded for mercy on the grounds that he was an orphan. Still, under certain conditions, something can be said on behalf of appeals to the emotions.

An emotional appeal is legitimate if it heightens the facts rather than obscures them. In an argument about legislation that would govern police actions, surely it is legitimate to show a photograph of the battered, bloodied face of an alleged victim of police brutality. True, such a photograph cannot tell the whole truth; it cannot tell us if the subject threatened the officer with a gun or repeatedly resisted an order to surrender. But it can tell us that the victim was severely beaten, and (like a comparable description in words) it can evoke in us emotions that may properly enter into our decision about the permissible use of force.

The emotional appeals that one is most likely to encounter are

- appeals to pity
- appeals to fear
- appeals to tradition

Consider an appeal to *pity*. An animal rights activist who is arguing that calves are cruelly confined might reasonably tell us about the size of the pen in which the calf is kept (too small for the calf to turn around or even to lie down). Now, someone might argue that calves don't like to lie down or to turn around, or that calves have no right to lie down or turn around, but the verbal description and the picture of the calf in the pen, which unquestionably make an emotional appeal, can hardly be called irrelevant or illegitimate.

Appeals to *fear* are commonly found in advertisements and other publications issued by insurance companies, where the argument, such as it is, plays on our concern with our property, our health, and our responsibility to provide for our spouse and our children. Appeals to *tradition* draw on our nostalgia, our fondness for and respect for the past, such as the America of the Founding Fathers—but a world, we must remember that accepted slavery and that allowed only males to vote. The emotional appeal to tradition is not, by itself, a convincing argument.

In appealing to the emotions, then, the important things are

- not to falsify the issue (for instance, by oversimplifying it),
- not to distract attention from the facts of the case, and
- not to let the emotional appeal take the place of appeals to reason.

Focus on the facts, and concentrate on offering *reasons* (essentially, statements linked explicitly or implicitly with *because*). But you may also legitimately bring the facts home to your readers by seeking to induce in them the appropriate emotions. Your words will be fallacious (illegitimate, deceptive) only if you stimulate emotions that are not rightly connected to the facts of the case.

As a reader, by attentive to emotional appeals, but recognize arguments that offer *only* emotional appeals. Be especially aware of arguments that offer emotional appeals designed to keep the reader from accurately perceiving the facts, the real evidence.

Three Kinds of Evidence: Examples, Testimony, Statistics

Writers of arguments seek to persuade by showing that they themselves are persons of goodwill, and—our topic here—by offering evidence to support their thesis. The chief forms of evidence used in argument are

- examples
- testimony (the citation of authorities)
- statistics

We'll briefly consider each of these.

Examples

Example is from the Latin *exemplum*, which means "something taken out." An **example** is the sort of thing, taken from among many similar things, that one selects and holds up for view, perhaps after saying "for example" or "for instance."

Three sorts of examples are especially common in written arguments:

- Real examples
- Invented instances
- Analogies

Real examples are just what they sound like—instances that have occurred. If we are arguing that gun control won't work, we point to those states that have adopted gun control laws and that nevertheless have had no reduction in crimes using guns. Or, if one wants to support the assertion that a woman can be a capable head of state, one may find oneself pointing to women who have actually served as heads of state, such as Cleopatra, Queen Elizabeth I of England, Golda Meir (prime minister of Israel), Indira Ghandi (prime minister of India), Margaret Thatcher (prime minister of England), and Angela Merkel (German chancellor).

The advantage of using real examples is, clearly, that they are real. Of course, an opponent might stubbornly respond that the persons whom you name could not, for some reason or other, function as the head of state in *our* country. One might argue, for instance, that the case of Golda Meir proves nothing, since the role of women in Israeli society is different from the role of women in the United States (a country in which a majority of the citizens are Christians). And one might argue that much of Indira Gandhi's power came from her being the daughter of Nehru, an immensely popular Indian statesman. Even the most compelling real example inevitably will be in some ways special or particular, and in the eyes of some readers may not seem to be a fair example.

Consider, for instance, a student who is arguing that peer review should be part of the writing course, pointing out that he or she found it of great help in high school. An opponent argues that things in college are different: College students should be able to help themselves, even highly gifted college students are not competent to offer college-level instruction, and so on. Still, as the feebleness of these objections (and the objections against Meir and Gandhi) indicates, real examples can be very compelling.

Invented instances are exempt from the charge that, because of some detail or another, they are not relevant as evidence. Suppose you are arguing against capital punishment, on the grounds that if an innocent person is executed, there is no way of even attempting to rectify the injustice. If you point to the case of X, you may be met with the reply that X was not in fact innocent. Rather than get tangled up in the guilt or innocence of a particular person, it may be better to argue that we can suppose—we can imagine—an innocent person being convicted and executed, and we can imagine that evidence later proves the person's innocence.

Invented instances have the advantage of presenting an issue clearly, free from all of the distracting particularities (and irrelevancies) that are bound up with any real instance. But invented instances have the disadvantage of being invented, and they may seem remote from the real issues being argued.

Analogies are comparisons pointing out several resemblances between two rather different things. For instance, one might assert that a government is like a ship, and in times of stress—if the ship is to weather the storm—the authority of the captain must not be questioned.

But don't confuse an analogy with proof. An analogy is an extended comparison between two things: It can be useful in exposition, for it explains the unfamiliar by means of the familiar: "A government is like a ship, and just as a ship has a captain and a crew, so a government has . . ."; "Writing an essay is like building a house; just as an architect must begin with a plan, so the writer must. . . ." Such comparisons can be useful, helping to clarify what otherwise might be obscure, but their usefulness goes only so far. Everything is what it is, and not something else. A government is not a ship, and what is true of a captain's power need not be true of a president's power; and a writer is not an architect. Some of what is true about ships may be roughly true of governments, and some of what is true about architects may be (again, roughly) true of writers, but there are differences too. Consider the following analogy between a lighthouse and the death penalty:

> The death penalty is a warning, just like a lighthouse throwing its beams out to sea. We hear about shipwrecks, but we do not hear about the ships the lighthouse guides safely on their way. We do not have proof of the number of ships it saves, but we do not tear the lighthouse down.
>
> J. Edgar Hoover

How convincing is Hoover's analogy as an argument—that is, as a reason for retaining the death penalty?

Testimony

Testimony, or the citation of authorities, is rooted in our awareness that some people are recognized as experts. In our daily life we constantly turn to experts for guidance: We look up the spelling of a word in the dictionary, we listen to the weather forecast on the radio, we take an ailing cat to the vet for a checkup. Similarly, when we wish to become informed about controversial matters, we often turn to experts, first to help educate ourselves and then to help convince our readers.

Don't forget that *you* are an authority on many things. For example, today's newspaper includes an article about the cutback in funding for teaching the arts in elementary and secondary schools. Educators are responding that arts education is not a frill, and that in fact the arts provide the analytical thinking, teamwork, motivation, and self-discipline that most people agree are needed to reinvigorate American schools. If you have studied the arts in school—for instance, if you painted pictures or learned to play a musical instrument—you are in a position to evaluate these claims. Similarly, if you have studied in a bilingual educational program, your own testimony will be invaluable.

There are at least two reasons for offering testimony in an argument. The obvious reason is that expert opinion does (and should) carry some weight with the audience; the less obvious one is that a change of voice (if the testimony is not your own) in an essay may afford the reader a bit of pleasure. No matter how engaging our own voice may be, a fresh voice—whether that of Thomas Jefferson, Albert Einstein, or Toni Morrison—may provide a refreshing change of tone.

But there are dangers. The chief dangers are that the words of authorities may be taken out of context or otherwise distorted, or that the authorities may not be authorities on the topic at hand. We are concerned quite rightly with what the framers of the U.S. Constitution said, but it is not entirely clear that their words can be fairly applied, on one side or the other, to such an issue as abortion. We are concerned quite rightly with what Einstein said, but it is not entirely clear that his eminence as a physicist qualifies him as an authority on, say, world peace. In a moment, when we discuss errors in reasoning, we'll have more to say about the proper and improper use of authorities.

Statistics

Statistics, another important form of evidence, are especially useful in arguments concerning social issues. If we want to argue for (or against) raising the driving age, we will probably do some research in the library, and will offer statistics about the number of accidents caused by people in certain age groups.

But a word of caution: The significance of statistics may be difficult to assess. For instance, opponents of gun control legislation have pointed out, in support of the argument that such laws are ineffectual, that homicides in Florida *increased* after Florida adopted gun control laws. Supporters of gun control laws cried "foul," arguing that in the years after adopting these laws Miami became (for reasons having nothing to do with the laws) the cocaine capital of the United States, and the rise in homicide was chiefly a reflection of murders involved in the drug trade. That is, a significant change in the population has made a comparison of the figures meaningless. This objection seems plausible, and probably the statistics therefore should carry little weight.

How Much Evidence Is Enough?

If you allow yourself ample time to write your essay, you probably will turn up plenty of evidence to illustrate your arguments, such as examples drawn from your own experience and imagination, from your reading, and from your talks with others. Examples not only will help to clarify and to support your assertions, but also will provide a concreteness that will be welcome in a paper that might be, on the whole, fairly abstract. Your sense of your audience will have to guide you in making your selection of examples. Generally speaking, a single example may not fully illuminate a difficult point, and so a second example—a clincher—may be desirable. If you offer a third or fourth example, you probably are succumbing to a temptation to include something that tickles your fancy. If it is as good as you think it is, the reader probably will accept the unnecessary example and may even be grateful. But before you pile on examples, try to imagine yourself in your reader's place, and ask if an example is needed. If not, ask yourself if the reader will be glad to receive the overload.

One other point: On most questions—say on the value of bilingual education or on the need for rehabilitation programs in prisons—it's not possible to make a strictly logical case, in the sense of an absolutely airtight proof. Don't assume that it is your job to make an absolute proof. What you are expected to do is to offer a reasonable argument. Remember Virginia Woolf's words: "When a subject is highly controversial . . . one cannot hope to tell the truth. One can only show how one came to hold whatever opinion one does hold."

Avoiding Fallacies

Let's further examine writing reasonable arguments by considering some obvious errors in reasoning. In logic these errors are called **fallacies** (from a Latin verb *fallere*, meaning "to deceive"). As Tweedledee says in *Through the Looking-Glass,* "If it were so, it would be; but as it isn't, it ain't. That's logic."

To persuade readers to accept your opinions you must persuade them that you are reliable; if your argument includes fallacies, thoughtful readers will not take you seriously. More important, if your argument includes fallacies, you are misleading yourself. When you search your draft for fallacies, you are searching for ways to improve the quality of your thinking.

Here are the most common fallacies:

1. *False Authority.* Don't try to borrow the prestige of authorities who are not authorities on the topic in question—for example, a heart surgeon speaking on politics. Similarly, some former authorities are no longer authorities because the problems have changed or because later knowledge has superseded their views. Adam Smith, Thomas Jefferson, Eleanor Roosevelt, and Albert Einstein remain persons of genius, but an attempt to use their opinions when you are examining modern issues— even in their fields—may be questioned. Remember the last words of John B. Sedgwick, a Union Army general at the Battle of Spotsylvania in 1864: "They couldn't hit an elephant at this dist—."

In short, before you rely on an authority, ask yourself if the person in question *is* an authority on the topic. And don't let stereotypes influence your idea of who is an authority. There is an apt Yiddish proverb: "A goat has a beard, but that doesn't make him a rabbi."

2. *False Quotation.* If you do quote from an authority, don't misquote. For example, you may find someone who grants that "there are strong arguments in favor of abolishing the death penalty"; but if she goes on to argue that, on balance, the arguments in favor of retaining it seem stronger to her, it is dishonest to quote her words so as to imply that she favors abolishing it.

3. *Suppression of Evidence.* Don't neglect evidence that is contrary to your own argument. You owe it to yourself and your reader to present all the relevant evidence. Be especially careful not to assume that every question is simply a matter of *either/or.* There may be some truth on both sides. Take the following thesis: "Grades encourage unwholesome competition and should therefore be abolished." Even if the statement about the evil effect of grading is true, it may not be the whole truth, and therefore it may not follow that grades should be abolished. One might point out that grades do other things, too: They may stimulate learning, and they may assist students by telling them how far they have progressed. One might nevertheless conclude, on balance, that the fault outweighs the benefits. But the argument will be more persuasive now that the benefits of grades have been considered.

Concede to the opposition what it deserves and then outscore the opposition. Failure to confront the opposing evidence will be noticed; your readers will keep wondering why you do not consider some particular point, and may consequently dismiss your argument. However, if you confront the opposition, you will almost surely strengthen your own argument. As Edmund Burke said two hundred years ago, "He that wrestles with us strengthens our nerves, and sharpens our skill. Our antagonist is our helper."

4. *Generalization from Insufficient Evidence.* In rereading a draft of an argument that you have written, try to spot your own generalizations. Ask yourself if a reasonable reader is likely to agree that the generalization is based on an adequate sample.

A visitor to a college may sit in on three classes, each taught by a different instructor, and may find all three stimulating. That's a good sign, but can we generalize and say that the teaching at this college is excellent? Are three classes a sufficient sample? If all three are offered by the Biology Department, which includes only five instructors, perhaps we can tentatively say that the teaching of biology at this institution is good. If the Biology Department contains twenty instructors, perhaps we can still say—though more tentatively—that this sample indicates that the teaching of biology is good. But what does the sample say about the teaching of other subjects at the college? It probably does say something—the institution may be much concerned with teaching across the board—but then again it may not say a great deal, since the Biology Department may be exceptionally concerned with good teaching.

5. *The Genetic Fallacy.* Don't assume that something can necessarily be explained in terms of its birth or origin. "He wrote the novel to make money, so it can't be any good" is not a valid inference. The value of a novel does not depend on the author's motivations in writing it. Indeed, the value or worth of a novel needs to be established by reference to other criteria. Neither the highest nor the lowest motivations guarantee the quality of the product. Another example: "Capital punishment arose in days when men sought revenge, so now it ought to be abolished." Again, an unconvincing argument: Capital punishment may have some current value; for example, it may serve as a deterrent to crime. But that's another argument, and it needs evidence if it is to be believed. Be on guard, too, against the thoughtless tendency to judge people by their origins: Mr. *X* has a foreign accent, so he is probably untrustworthy or stupid or industrious.

6. *Begging the Question and Circular Reasoning.* Don't assume the truth of the point that you should prove. The term "begging the question" is a trifle odd. It means, in effect, "You, like a beggar, are asking me to grant you something at the outset."

Examples: "The barbaric death penalty should be abolished"; "This senseless language requirement should be dropped." Both of these statements assume what they should prove—that the death penalty is barbaric, and that the language requirement is senseless. You can, of course, make such assertions, but you must go on to prove them.

Circular reasoning is usually an extended form of begging the question. What ought to be proved is covertly assumed. Example: "*X* is the best-qualified candidate for the office, because the most informed people say so." Who are the most informed people? Those who recognize *X*'s superiority. Circular reasoning, then, normally includes intermediate steps absent from begging the question, but the two fallacies are so closely related that they can be considered one. Another example: "I feel sympathy for her because I identify with her." Despite the "because," no reason is really offered. What follows "because" is merely a restatement, in slightly different words, of what precedes; the shift of words, from *feel sympathy* to *identify with* has misled the writer into thinking she is giving a reason.

Other examples: "Students are interested in courses when the subject matter and the method of presentation are interesting"; "There cannot be peace in the Middle East because the Jews and the Arabs will always fight." In each case, an assertion that ought to be proved is reasserted as a reason in support of the assertion.

7. *Post hoc ergo propter hoc.* Latin: "after this, therefore because of this." Don't assume that because X precedes Y, X must cause Y. For example: "He went to college and came back a boozer; college corrupted him." He might have taken up liquor even if he had not gone to college. Another example: "When a fifty-five-mile-per-hour speed limit was imposed in 1974, after the Arab embargo on oil, the number of auto fatalities decreased sharply, from 55,000 deaths in 1973 to 46,000 in 1974. Therefore, it is evident that a fifty-five-mile-per-hour speed limit—still adhered to in some states—saves lives." Not quite. Because gasoline was expensive after the embargo, the number of miles traveled decreased. The number of fatalities *per mile* remained constant. The price of gas, not the speed limit, seems responsible for the decreased number of fatalities. Moreover, the national death rate has continued to fall. Why? Several factors are at work: seat-belt and child-restraint laws, campaigns against drunk driving, improved auto design, and improved roads. Medicine, too, may have improved, so that today doctors can save accident victims who in 1974 would have died. In short, it probably is impossible to isolate the correlation between speed and safety.

8. *Argumentum ad hominem.* Here the argument is directed toward the person (*hominem* is Latin for *man*) rather than toward the issue. Don't shift from your topic to your opponent. A speaker argues against legalizing abortions, and her opponent, instead of facing the merits of the argument, attacks the character or the associations of the opponent: "You're a Catholic, aren't you?"

9. *False Assumption.* Consider the Scot who argued that Shakespeare must have been a Scot. Asked for his evidence, he replied, "The ability of the man warrants the assumption." Or take such a statement as "She goes to Yale, so she must be rich." Possibly the statement is based on faulty induction (the writer knows four Yale students, and all four are rich), but more likely he is just passing on a cliché. The Yale student in question may be on a scholarship, may be struggling to earn the money, or may be backed by parents of modest means who for eighteen years have saved money for her college education. Other examples: "I haven't heard him complain about French 10, so he must be satisfied"; "She's a writer, so she must be well read." A little thought will show how weak such assertions are; they *may* be true, but they may not.

The errors we have discussed are common. In revising your writing, try to spot them and eliminate or correct them. You have a point to make, and you should make it fairly. If you can only make it unfairly, you are doing an injustice to your reader and yourself; you should try to change your view of the topic. You don't want to be like the politician whose speech had a marginal note: "Argument weak; shout here."

Drafting an Argument

Imagining an Audience

A writer's job is made easier if the audience is known. Thus, if you are writing for the college newspaper, you can assume that your readers know certain things, and you can adopt a moderately familiar tone. Similarly, if you are writing a letter to the college trustees, you can assume that they know certain things—you will not have to tell them that the institution is a small, coeducational, undergraduate college located in northern Georgia—but you will probably adopt a somewhat more formal tone than you would use in writing for your fellow students.

Your instructor may tell you to imagine a particular audience—readers of the local newspaper, alumni, high school students, your representative in Congress, or any other group. But if your instructor does not specify an audience, you will probably do best if you imagine one of two possibilities: either write for the general reader (the person who reads *Time* or *Newsweek*) or for your classmates. Although these two audiences are similar in many respects, there is a significant difference. All of your classmates may be of the same gender or the same religion, they may be of approximately the same age, and they may come from the same area. In an essay written for your classmates, then, you may not have to explain certain things that you will indeed have to explain if you are writing for the general reader. To cite an obvious example: If the school is specialized (for instance, if it is a religious school or a military school), you can assume that your readers know certain things and share certain attitudes that you cannot assume in the general public.

Getting Started

If your essay is related to one or more of the readings in this book, of course you will read the essay(s) carefully—perhaps highlighting, underlining, annotating, summarizing, and outlining, as we suggest in our first chapter. You will question the text, and you probably will make entries in a journal, as we suggest in the second and third chapters. These entries may be ideas that come to you out of the blue, or they may emerge from conscious, critical thinking, perhaps in conversations with some of your classmates. (Critical thinking means, among other things, that you will question your own assumptions and evaluate your evidence as objectively as possible.)

Discussions—with yourself and with others—will help you to improve your ideas. At this stage, you will probably have some ideas that you did not have when you began thinking about the topic, and you will probably want to abandon some of your earlier ideas which now seem less strong than you had originally thought.

Writing a Draft

By now you probably have a fair idea of the strengths and (as you see it) the weaknesses of other positions. You also have a fair idea of what your thesis—your claim—is and what reasons you will offer to support it. And you also probably have at hand some of the supporting evidence—examples, statements by authorities, or personal experiences—that you intend to offer as support.

Some people, at this point—especially if they are writing on a word processor—like to sit down and write freely, pouring out their ideas. They then print out the material and, on rereading, highlight what seems useful, perhaps indicating in the margins how the material should be reorganized. They then (again, we are speaking of writing on a word processor) move blocks of material into some reasonable organization.

Our own preference (even though we also use a word processor when we write a first draft) is to prepare a rough outline on paper—really a list of topics. Then, after further thought, we add to it, circling items on the list and indicating (by means of arrows) better positions for these items.

Next, when we have a rough outline (perhaps a list of five or six chief items, under each of which we have written a word or phrase indicating how the point might be developed), we start writing on the word processor. It happens that our rough outline (later, much changed) for this section ran thus:

audience

   assigned? or general? or classmates

starting

   annotating, journal? Refer to earlier chapters?

writing

   brainstorming? outline first, then word processor

Revising a Draft

After you have written a first draft, you will read it and, almost surely, make extensive revisions. Some points will now strike you as not really worth making; others that do survive the cut you will now see as needing to be developed. You may see that you have not adequately set forth a commonly held view that you will in effect be largely rejecting. You now realize that you must summarize this view fairly, because many people hold it, and you now see the need to indicate that you are familiar with the view, that you see its merits, and that you think your own view is better and may at least in part be attractive even to those who hold this other view.

You may also see that the organization needs improvement. For instance, if you notice that a point you have made in the second paragraph is pretty much the same as one in the sixth paragraph, the two should be combined, rewritten, and perhaps put into an entirely new position.

Reorganizing, and providing the transitional words and phrases that make the organization clear to the reader ("moreover," "a second example," "on the other hand"), is usually not difficult, especially if you outline your draft. When you look at the outline of what you have written, you will probably see that portions of the draft have to be moved around or (in some cases) amplified or deleted, and new transitions written. Organizing an argument is so important that we will treat it separately, at some length, in a moment.

In revising, think carefully about how you use **quotations.** Keep in mind the following principles:

- Most quotations should be brief; present a long quotation only if it is extremely interesting and cannot be summarized effectively.
- Let the reader know who wrote the quotation. Identify an author who is not widely known, for example: "Judith Craft, a lawyer who specializes in constitutional matters, argues . . ."; "The warden of a maximum security prison, John Alphonso, testified that . . ."; "Anne Smith, a lesbian who has given birth to one child and adopted a second, suggests that families headed by lesbians. . . ." This sort of lead-in gives authority to the quotation.
- Let the reader know how the quotation was originally used. Examples: "The editor of the journal *Nature* argues . . ."; "The Pope rejects this view, saying . . ."; "Dr. Joycelyn Elders interprets the statistics as indicating that. . . ."
- Use the present tense: "*X* says," *not* "*X* said," though of course if you are treating the passage as something from the past, use the past tense: "*X* wrote, twenty years ago, that . . . , but today he argues that. . . ."

After revising your draft, you may want to show it to some classmates or friends; they will doubtless give you helpful advice if you make it clear that you really do want their assistance.

Organizing an Argument

The writer of a persuasive essay almost always has to handle, in some sequence or other, the following matters:

- The background (for instance, the need to consider the issue)
- The readers' preconceptions
- The thesis (claim)
- The evidence that supports the claim
- The counterevidence

- Responses to counterclaims and counterevidence (perhaps a refutation, but probably a concession that there *is* merit in the counterclaims although not as much as in the writer's thesis)
- Some sort of reaffirmation—for instance, that the topic needs attention, that the thesis advanced is the most plausible or the most workable or the most moral, and that even holders of other views may find their own values strengthened by adopting the writer's view

And here we repeat the organization that we suggested (page 85) for Rogerian argument:

- state the problem, suggesting that it is an issue of concern, and that the reader has a stake in it;
- show respect for persons who hold differing views;
- set forth opposing positions, *stated in such a way that their proponents will agree that the statements of their positions are fair;* and
- find some shared values—that is, grant whatever validity the writer finds in those positions, for instance, by recognizing the circumstances in which they would indeed be acceptable.

Having accurately summarized other views and having granted some concessions, the writer presumably has won the reader's attention and goodwill; the writer can now

- show how those who hold other positions will benefit if they accept the writer's position.

Introductory and Concluding Paragraphs

Introductory Paragraphs

In the **introduction** (the first paragraph or first few paragraphs) you will usually indicate what the issue is, why it is of significance, and what your thesis is. You will also seek to gain your reader's attention and introduce yourself—which is to say that you will convey some sort of engaging personality to the reader. Obviously, it is in your interest to come across as courteous, reasonable, and well informed. We will talk about this matter in a moment, when we discuss the writer's persona.

When writing a first draft, you merely need something to break the ice, something to get you going, but in your finished paper the opening cannot be mere throat-clearing. The opening should be interesting. Here are some common *un*interesting openings to *avoid*:

- A dictionary definition ("Webster says . . . " or "According to Webster").
- A restatement of your title. The title is (let's assume) "Poker Playing May Be Harmful to Your Health," and the first sentence says, "This

essay will study the harmful effects of poker playing." True, the sentence announces the topic of the essay, but it gives no information about the topic beyond what the title already offers, and it provides no information about you either—that is, no sense of your response to the topic, such as might be present in, say, "The people least aware of the harmful effects of poker seem to be those who play the most."

- A broad generalization, such as "Ever since the beginning of time, human beings have been violent." Again, such a sentence may be fine if it helps you to start drafting, but it should not remain in your final version: It's dull—and it tells your readers almost nothing about the essay they're about to read. (Our example, after all, could begin anything from an analysis of a video game to a term paper on Darfur.) To put it another way, the ever-since-the-beginning-of-time opening lacks substance—and if your opening lacks substance, it will not matter what you say next. You've already lost your reader's attention.

What is left? What is an *effective* way for an introductory paragraph to begin?

- It will be at least moderately interesting if it provides **information.**
- It will be pleasing if the information provides **focus**—that is, if it lets the reader know what your topic is and it indicates what you will say about it.
- It will capture a reader's attention if it articulates a problem and suggests why the essay is worth reading.

When you write, *you* are the teacher; it won't do to begin with a vague statement:

George Orwell says he shot the elephant because. . . .

We need some information, identifying the text you are writing about:

George Orwell, in "Shooting an Elephant," says he shot the elephant because . . .

Even better is

In "Shooting an Elephant," George Orwell set forth his reflections on his service as a policeman in Burma. He suggests that he once shot an elephant because . . . but his final paragraph suggests that we must look for additional reasons.

Why is this opening better? Because it suggests that the writer has something interesting to say. It points to a contradiction in the Orwell piece, a problem worth examining: Orwell says one thing, but that thing may not be entirely true.

Of course you can provide interest and focus by other means, among them the following:

- A quotation
- An anecdote or other short narrative
- An interesting fact (a statistic, for instance, showing the reader that you know something about your topic)
- A definition of an important term—but not merely one derived from a dictionary
- A question—but an interesting one, such as "Why do we call some words obscene?"
- A glance at the opposition
- An assertion that a problem exists

Concluding Paragraphs

Concluding paragraphs, like opening paragraphs, are especially difficult if only because they are so conspicuous. Fortunately, you are not always obliged to write one. Descriptive essays, for example, may end merely with a final paragraph, not with a paragraph that draws a conclusion. In an expository essay explaining a process or mechanism, you may simply stop when you have finished.

But if you need to write a concluding paragraph (and an argumentative essay usually calls for one), say something interesting. It is of little interest to say "Thus we see . . . " and then echo your title and first paragraph. A good concluding paragraph rounds out the previous discussion. Such a paragraph may offer a few sentences that summarize but it should not begin with the dull phrase, "in summary"); it might also draw an inference that has not previously been expressed. To draw such an inference is not to introduce an entirely new idea—the end of an essay is hardly the place for that. Rather it is to see the previous material in a fresh perspective, to take the discussion perhaps one step further.

Because all writers must find out what they think about any given topic, and must find the appropriate strategies for presenting their thoughts to a particular audience, we hesitate to offer a do-it-yourself kit for final paragraphs, but the following devices often work:

- End with a quotation, especially a quotation that amplifies or varies a quotation used in the opening paragraph, but be careful not to use a quotation that is too long or too complex, and that your reader would expect you to analyze.
- End with some idea or detail from the beginning of the essay and thus bring it full circle.
- End with a new (but related) point, one that takes your discussion a step further.

- End with an allusion, say to a historical or mythological figure or event, putting your topic in a larger framework.
- End with a glance at the readers—not with a demand that they mount the barricades, but with a suggestion that the next move is theirs.

If you adopt any of these devices, do so quietly; the aim is not to write a grand finale, but to complete or round out a discussion.

All essayists must find their own ways of ending each essay; the five strategies we have suggested are common—you will often encounter them in the essays that you read in *The Little, Brown Reader*—but these strategies are not for you if you don't find them congenial or useful. And so, rather than ending this section with rules about how to end essays, we suggest how not to end them: *Don't* merely summarize, *don't* say "in conclusion," *don't* introduce a totally new point, and *don't* apologize.

✓ A Checklist: Revising Paragraphs

- ☐ Does the paragraph say anything? Does it have substance?
- ☐ Does the paragraph have a topic sentence? If so, is it in the best place? If the paragraph doesn't have a topic sentence, would the paragraph be improved by adding one? Or does the paragraph have a clear topic idea?
- ☐ If the paragraph is an opening paragraph, is it interesting enough to attract and to hold a reader's attention? If it is a later paragraph, does it easily evolve out of the previous paragraph and lead into the next paragraph?
- ☐ Does the paragraph contain some principle of development— for instance, from cause to effect or from general to particular? What is the purpose of the paragraph? Does the paragraph fulfill the purpose?
- ☐ Does each sentence clearly follow from the preceding sentence? Have you provided transitional words or cues to guide your reader? Would it be useful to repeat certain key words, for clarity?
- ☐ Is the closing paragraph effective, or is it an unnecessary restatement of the obvious?

Persona and Style

In Chapter 1 we talked about the writer's **persona**—the personality that the writer conveys through his or her words. More exactly, the persona is the image of the writer that *the readers* imagine. The writer tries to convey a certain image (courteous, fair-minded, authoritative, or all of the above, and more), but if readers find the writer discourteous, well, the writer *is* discourteous (or mean-spirited, or uninformed). It won't do for the writer, hearing of the readers' response, to insist that he or she did not mean to be discourteous (is not mean-spirited or is well informed).

The persona is created by the impression that the words make—both the individual words and the kinds of sentences (long or short, complex or simple) in which they appear. A writer who says something like "It behooves us to exert all of our mental capacities on what I deem the primary issue of our era" may have a heart of gold and be well informed, but he or she will still strike readers as a pompous ass—and the writer's argument will not get a very attentive hearing. A writer who uses many short sentences, much direct address to the reader, and lots of colloquial diction ("Let's get down to nuts and bolts. You've got to stop kidding yourselves. We all know what the problem is.") probably will strike readers as aggressive—someone they are not keen on associating with. In short, the wrong persona can alienate readers. Even though the arguments are thoughtful, readers will be put off. We would live in a better world if we could listen objectively and separate the argument (very good) from the speaker (very unpleasant), but we can't usually do so. A hundred years ago Samuel Butler put it this way (he is overstating the case, but there is much to what he says): "We are not won by arguments that we can analyze but by tone and temper, by the manner."

Now, in fact one often *does* find aggressive writing in magazines, but this writing is, as we said earlier, a sermon addressed to the converted. The liberal readers of *The Nation* derive pleasure from seeing conservatives roughed up a bit, just as the conservative readers of *National Review* derive pleasure from seeing liberals similarly handled. But again, these writers—utterly ignoring the principles of Carl Rogers, which we set forth on pages 81–86—are not trying to gain a hearing for their ideas; rather, they are reassuring their readers that the readers' ideas are just fine.

What kind of persona should you, as the writer of an argument, try to project? You will want to be (you will *have to be*) yourself. But, just as you have different kinds of clothes, suitable for different purposes, you have several or even many selves—for instance, the self you are with a close friend, the self you are with your teachers, the self you are with customers (if you have a job), and so forth. The self that you will present in your essays—the self that you hope the readers will see from the words you put down on the page—will probably include certain specific qualities. You probably want your readers to see that you are informed and fair and are presenting a thoughtful case. You want them to be interested in hearing what you have to say. If you browse through the essays in this book, you will of course hear different voices. Although some may have an academic tone and some may sound folksy, almost all of them have one thing in common: they are the voices of people whom we would like to get to know.

An Overview: An Examination of an Argument

Now that we have covered the ground from a more or less theoretical point of view, let's look at a specific argument. The writer is Richard Rhodes, a journalist who has written for many newspapers and magazines, including the *New York Times, Newsweek, Harper's, Playboy,* and *Rolling Stone.* Rhodes is also known as a novelist and as a writer of books about science and technology. We reprint an essay that first appeared in the *New York Times* on September 17, 2000.

Richard Rhodes

Hollow Claims about Fantasy Violence

The moral entrepreneurs are at it again, pounding the entertainment   1
industry for advertising its Grand Guignolesque confections[1] to children.
If exposure to this mock violence contributes to the development of violent behavior, then our political leadership is justified in its indignation at
what the Federal Trade Commission has reported about the marketing of
violent fare to children. Senators John McCain and Joseph Lieberman
have been especially quick to fasten on the FTC report as they make an issue of violent offerings to children.

But is there really a link between entertainment and violent behavior?   2

The American Medical Association, the American Psychological Association, the American Academy of Pediatrics, and the National Institute of   3
Mental Health all say yes. They base their claims on social science research
that has been sharply criticized and disputed within the social science
profession, especially outside the United States. In fact, no direct, causal link
between exposure to mock violence in the media and subsequent violent behavior has ever been demonstrated, and the few claims of modest correlation
have been contradicted by other findings, sometimes in the same studies.

History alone should call such a link into question. Private violence   4
has been declining in the West since the media-barren late Middle Ages,
when homicide rates are estimated to have been 10 times what they are
in Western nations today. Historians attribute the decline to improving

[1]*Grand Guignolesque confections* The Grand Guignol was a Parisian theater specializing in
plays dealing with brutality.

social controls over violence—police forces and common access to courts of law—and to a shift away from brutal physical punishment in child-rearing (a practice that still appears as a common factor in the background of violent criminals today).

The American Medical Association has based its endorsement of the   5
media violence theory in major part on the studies of Brandon Centerwall, a psychiatrist in Seattle. Dr. Centerwall compared the murder rates for whites in three countries from 1945 to 1974 with numbers for television set ownership. Until 1975, television broadcasting was banned in South Africa, and "white homicide rates remained stable" there, Dr. Centerwall found, while corresponding rates in Canada and the United States doubled after television was introduced.

A spectacular finding, but it is meaningless. As Franklin E. Zimring   6
and Gordon Hawkins of the University of California at Berkeley subsequently pointed out, homicide rates in France, Germany, Italy, and Japan either failed to change with increasing television ownership in the same period or actually declined, and American homicide rates have more recently been sharply declining despite a proliferation of popular media outlets—not only movies and television but also video games and the Internet.

Other social science that supposedly undergirds the theory, too, is   7
marginal and problematic. Laboratory studies that expose children to selected incidents of televised mock violence and then assess changes in the children's behavior have sometimes found more "aggressive" behavior after the exposure—usually verbal, occasionally physical.

But sometimes the control group, shown incidents judged not to be vi-   8
olent, behaves more aggressively afterward than the test group; sometimes comedy produces the more aggressive behavior; and sometimes there's no change. The only obvious conclusion is that sitting and watching television stimulates subsequent physical activity. Any kid could tell you that.

As for those who claim that entertainment promotes violent behavior   9
by desensitizing people to violence, the British scholar Martin Barker offers this critique: "Their claim is that the materials they judge to be harmful can only influence us by trying to make us be the same as them. So horrible things will make us horrible—not horrified. Terrifying things will make us terrifying—not terrified. To see something aggressive makes us feel aggressive—not aggressed against. This idea is so odd, it is hard to know where to begin in challenging it."

Even more influential on national policy has been a 22-year study by   10
two University of Michigan psychologists, Leonard I. Eron and L. Rowell Huesmann, of boys exposed to so-called violent media. The Telecommunications Act of 1996, which mandated the television V-chip, allowing parents to screen out unwanted programming, invoked these findings, asserting, "Studies have shown that children exposed to violent video programming at a young age have a higher tendency for violent and aggressive behavior later in life than children not so exposed."

Well, not exactly. Following 875 children in upstate New York from   11
third grade through high school, the psychologists found a correlation
between a preference for violent television at age 8 and aggressiveness at
age 18. The correlation—0.31—would mean television accounted for about
10 percent of the influences that led to this behavior. But the correlation only
turned up in one of three measures of aggression: the assessment of students
by their peers. It didn't show up in students' reports about themselves or in
psychological testing. And for girls, there was no correlation at all.

Despite the lack of evidence, politicians can't resist blaming the me-   12
dia for violence. They can stake out the moral high ground confident that
the First Amendment will protect them from having to actually write legislation that would be likely to alienate the entertainment industry. Some
use the issue as a smokescreen to avoid having to confront gun control.

But violence isn't learned from mock violence. There is good evidence—   13
causal evidence, not correlational—that it's learned in personal violent
encounters, beginning with the brutalization of children by their parents or
their peers.

The money spent on all the social science research I've described was di-   14
verted from the National Institute of Mental Health budget by reducing
support for the construction of community mental health centers. To this
day there is no standardized reporting system for emergency-room findings
of physical child abuse. Violence is on the decline in America, but if we want
to reduce it even further, protecting children from real violence in their real
lives—not the pale shadow of mock violence—is the place to begin.

The Analysis Analyzed

Let's go through Rhodes's argument step by step, looking not only at the
points he makes, but also at the ways he makes them.

The title does not clearly announce the topic and the thesis, but it
does give the reader a hint: Rhodes will be concerned with "hollow
claims" (i.e., with assertions he thinks are insubstantial) about something
he calls "fantasy violence." At this stage the reader doesn't know what
"fantasy violence" is—could it be fantasies of violence that some or all of
us have, or could it be fantastic violence in films, or what? But "fantasy"
and "violence" are words that interest most people, and the writer has
therefore probably hooked the reader. (Give him a B+ for the title.)

The first paragraph begins with a world-weary voice: "The moral entrepreneurs are at it again. . . ." The readers do not know exactly who "the
moral entrepreneurs" are, and what they are doing again, but Rhodes's
first words are catchy, and by the end of the sentence the readers know
the main point: People who seem to be in the business of making moral
judgments—"moral entrepreneurs"—are yet again criticizing the entertainment industry because it advertises its "Grand Guignolesque confections" to children. Notice how Rhodes *diminishes* or trivializes the violent
productions, by calling them "Grand Guignolesque confections." For him,

they are theatrical (showy but insubstantial) candies or pastries. He is already preparing us for his thesis.

The second sentence in this paragraph introduces the term "mock violence," and it makes clear Rhodes's topic: He will be concerned not with the real violence of life—assaults, robberies, rapes, murders—but with the fictional, unreal or "mock" violence of the media. If indeed "mock violence contributes to the development of violent behavior," then the moral entrepreneurs (he will name some names in a moment) are "justified" in their indignation. But readers by now can guess that Rhodes will argue that "mock violence" (the "fantasy violence" of his title) does *not* contribute to violent behavior. By the end of the paragraph we know what his topic is, and we have a pretty good idea of what his thesis will be. (Give him an A for his opening paragraph.)

The second paragraph consists of only one sentence: "But is there really a link between entertainment and violent behavior?" Your instructor has probably already told you, rightly, to beware of writing one-sentence paragraphs. A paragraph of one sentence is usually underdeveloped. But Rhodes knows what he is doing here. Since in an essay each paragraph is of roughly equal weight, a one-sentence paragraph must indeed contain a weighty sentence, a big point, and this one does. By letting a single sentence stand as a paragraph, Rhodes is telling us that it is very important. And clearly the answer to his question, "But is there really a link between entertainment and violent behavior?" will be "No." (Give him an A for knowing how to make effective use of a short paragraph.)

The third paragraph shows us the opposing view. Rhodes cites the heavyweights, the medical associations that "all say yes," that all say there is a link between entertainment and violent behavior in real life. What is Rhodes doing, citing these groups that hold a view different from his own? He is letting us know that of course he is familiar with the opposing view; his position is not (he thus assures us) based on ignorance of the other view. And then he firmly rejects this view: "In fact, no direct causal link between exposure to mock violence in the media and subsequent violent behavior has ever been demonstrated." Gosh, readers think, we didn't know that; we thought that there are all sort of studies that prove. . . . But Rhodes's statement is so strong that it causes us to doubt what we thought we knew, and we realize that in fact we have not read the studies, we do *not* know of any study that really proves the connection. Gee, maybe he is right, after all. (Give him an A for writing a vigorous paragraph that begins to win us to his side.)

The fourth paragraph tells us to think about history, and it offers a statistic, admittedly an uncertain one ("homicide rates are estimated to have been 10 times what they are"). By now we can stop grading his paragraphs; he has probably won a writer's most important battle—not the battle to convince a reader, but the battle to keep a reader's attention. Almost surely the reader who has come this far will continue to read the essay to the end, and that's really as much as a writer can hope for. If the reader is also convinced, that's great, but it's an extra. When writers offer an argument, they want to tell people what their ideas are, and they want to explain why they hold these ideas. They offer reasons based on evidence, but they can offer them only to those readers who stay with them, so writers must write in ways that hold the attention of readers. The job of a writer is to make readers mentally say, "Very interesting, tell me more."

The fifth paragraph sets forth opposing evidence, statistics accepted by no less an authority than the American Medical Association. Why does he do this? Because, again, if writers are to be at all convincing they must show awareness of opposing viewpoints. We can be pretty sure, however, that Rhodes will go on to dispute this opposing view.

The sixth paragraph does exactly what the reader expects it to do: It rejects the AMA position. The statistical findings are "spectacular"—but they are "meaningless." Of course Rhodes cannot merely assert this, he must provide evidence. And he does. Whether this evidence is totally convincing is not our concern here; we are merely pointing out the techniques Rhodes uses in setting forth his argument.

The seventh paragraph returns to the strategy of setting forth the view Rhodes rejects, and we know what he will do in the eighth paragraph.

The eighth paragraph predictably offers evidence rejecting the view set forth in the preceding paragraph. It tells the reader that the experiments don't really prove what they are supposed to prove, and that they prove only that "sitting and watching television stimulates subsequent physical activity." And then, since Rhodes's aim is to discredit the experiments, he firmly dismisses the results with "Any kid could tell you that."

The ninth paragraph glances at a variation of the opposing view, and dismisses it by quoting an authority. Rhodes doubtless could have dismissed the view himself, but he wisely thought it was appropriate to let the reader know that someone else shares his view.

The tenth paragraph gives yet another glance at the opposing view—and we know what is coming next.

The eleventh paragraph dismisses the gist of the tenth, with "Well, not exactly." And Rhodes now offers statistics to support his position.

The twelfth paragraph begins by mentioning "politicians." Probably we are meant to recall Senators McCain and Lieberman, who were specifically named in the opening paragraph.

The thirteenth paragraph assumes that the reader has been following the argument, taking in the evidence, and perhaps is now convinced. It offers no evidence—doubtless Rhodes feels that he has made his case; the paragraph is content to state the thesis bluntly: "But violence isn't learned from mock violence."

The fourteenth (final) paragraph mentions the National Institute of Mental Health—an organization we met in paragraph 3—but the point now is that the money used for wrong-headed social science research could have been used more wisely by the NIMH "for the construction of community mental health centers." The paragraph ends by returning to the "mock violence" of the first paragraph, a variation on the "fantasy violence" of the title.

In short,

- Rhodes's opening paragraph gets attention, though perhaps he took a risk by referring to the Grand Guignol, an allusion that not everyone will get;
- he shows he is familiar with arguments other than his own;
- his language, except for the reference to "Grand Guignolesque confections," is easily intelligible to the ordinary reader;
- his paragraphs are coherent and unified; readers are never confused about the point of a paragraph;
- his organization is clear; readers are never uncertain of how a paragraph is related to the previous paragraph;
- his concluding paragraph, with its reference to "mock violence," neatly ties things up by glancing back to the beginning of the essay.

You may strongly disagree with Rhodes's position, but if so, you ought to be able to offer some evidence. The evidence need not be the statements of authorities, or statistics that you have encountered; it may be your own experience. But whether or not you disagree with Rhodes's position, we hope you will agree with our view that he sets forth his position effectively.

 ## Joining the Conversation: Critical Thinking and Writing

1. Rhodes sets forth views other than his own, but he makes no effort to suggest that they have any merit, or that they can be held by reasonable people. His essay shows no awareness of the principles that Carl Rogers set forth (see pages 81–86). Do you think Rhodes comes across as overly aggressive, arrogant, stubborn, rude? Or on this issue can there be no middle ground? In an essay of 250 words discuss Rhodes's tone as you perceive it, and its effectiveness here.

2. One reader of Rhodes's essay wrote a letter to the *New York Times,* asserting that even if violent movies and violent music cannot be directly tied to real violence, "they do set a tone and a mood. And they do send the message that in America, violence is an answer to almost any problem." If Rhodes were to write to this person, what do you think he would say? (Put your response in a letter of about 500 words.)

3. Another letter-writer said that, unfortunately, athletes are role models for young boys: "We continue to train boys to be violent men by offering them [as role models] highly paid athletes who fight, trash-talk, and assault officials." Write a 500-word essay supporting or taking issue with this position.

4. A third letter-writer said that "society at large; endorses violence and killing," and went on to cite the death penalty as "society's ultimate violence." This "socially approved real violence," the letter-writer asserted, encourages violent behavior. In a 500-word essay, set forth your response to this position.

Two Debates (Four Arguments) for Analysis

After reading the following essays, consider these points:

- What assumptions does the writer make? Do you accept these assumptions?
- What evidence does the writer offer? Is the evidence convincing?
- What (if any) counterevidence can you offer?
- Does the wirter seem fair to you? What has the writer done to make you hold the view that you hold? (For instance, has the writer faced objections to his or her view and answered them satisfactorily.)
- Putting aside your own views on the legality of downloading from the Internet, which of the two authors seems to you to argue the case more strongly? Explain why you view one of the essays as stronger argument than the other.

A Debate: Should Laptops Be Banned from the Classroom?

Andrew Goldstein

Andrew Goldstein, a student at Tufts University, submitted this essay in a first-year composition course.

Keep Online Poker Out of the Classroom: Why Professors Should Ban Laptops

Can it really be that all those students who are earnestly taking notes in my Econ class, never looking up for a moment but always tapping away, are trying to get down every word the lecturer is saying? Certainly that's the way it must seem to Prof. X, who, seeing plenty of the uplifted tops of laptops, keeps talking, and maybe even occasionally slows down so that the typists can get every detail.

From my view, behind the students and facing the professor, I see something else. I see screens that show that students are playing poker, or are shopping online, or are reading or writing e-mails. And I confess that I myself have done all these things in this course, and also in Poly Sci, another large lecture. It's not that these courses are especially boring; they aren't, they are pretty good courses. But I can get notes from my roommate, and, when you really think about it, there is no reason why both of us have to spend the hour taking notes that will be pretty much the same, so I sometimes do a little extra-curricular activity.

Actually, there *is* a reason why I should not be playing poker or surfing the web or instant messaging, and it is very simple: I should be paying attention to the lecturer, and *thinking* about what she is saying. True, there is very little discussion in the class—once in a while, maybe twice during the hour—the prof will ask if we have any questions, and maybe twice she will even toss out a question and ask for a response—but for the most part the course is a straight lecture course. Still, I know from my own experience that when I pay attention I do find myself thinking about what she is saying, sometimes wondering why I had never thought of this or that, sometimes wondering if the point also could be applied to X or Y, and so forth.

I have therefore come to the conclusion—based on my experience in the only two large lecture courses that I am taking—that professors should ban laptops from the lecture hall. There are several good reasons to support this position.

First, I'd say that when other students use laptops, they distract *me*. I cannot help but see games on the screen to my left and on the screen of the girl in front of me, and it's very distracting. The tapping noise is also distracting, and I think, that as a member of the class, I have a right to be protected from such distractions.

But what about the students who are *not* using laptops for such purposes, but who are genuinely taking notes? Well, the tapping is still an annoyance, but I suppose someone might complain that when I turn the page of the spiral notepad in which I am scribbling notes, the sound of the paper is distracting. I can only say that I don't think the two are really comparable. My noise is for a fraction of a second, not a constant sound throughout the lecture.

Second, as for the students who are using laptops in class only to take notes, not to play games or to shop or write letters, you might ask, "Why shouldn't students take advantage of technology to help them learn?" With laptops they can get down in their notes much more than they could by writing by hand. Furthermore, the notes will be easily legible when they review for the exam, and with some software the notes can easily be reorganized efficiently for certain specific purposes. All of this is true, but I think one can argue that the very fact that one can take extensive notes, almost word for word, is not good but is bad. I know from my own experience that when I take detailed notes I am *not* thinking. Instead, I am doing stenography, and it seems to me that most professors want us to *think* about what they are saying. And then, when I am reviewing for an examination and I look at my very full notes, I find lots of material that is in the textbook, and I wonder why I bothered to write all of those things down. I should have been thinking, and taking only a few notes about especially challenging ideas.

Third, in my smaller course in American Lit, where there is discussion, the five or six students (out of maybe twelve or fifteen) who are busy typing away on their laptops never contribute to the discussion. In fact, when one was called on in a recent class, he said he didn't hear the question because he was busy typing what the instructor had been saying a few minutes earlier.

In short, I don't think there are any good reasons for students to use laptops in class, and I think there are *several* good reasons why they should not use laptops. If professors want to ban laptops, that's fine with me. The only thing I would add is this: If a course is required, a professor should not ban laptops. Although I personally find laptops distracting, and I think that students probably learn less when they take extensive notes—and certainly when they IM or they surf the web, in the final analysis, that's their business. True, I object to the distracting noise and the distracting screens, and I suppose the prof must object to the lack of eye-contact with these students, but I think that if a course is required, a professor should allow students to take notes however they wish. But in an elective course, I think the professor can and should set the rules for the best learning conditions—and that includes banning laptops. If students want to use laptops, let them choose another course.

 ## Joining the Conversation: Critical Thinking and Writing

1. List each argument that Golden offers in defense of his position, and then, in two or three sentences, evaluate each of these arguments.

2. Can you think of arguments that he does not raise that would strengthen his thesis? If so what are they?

3. What grade would you give this essay? Please explain your evaluation.

Elena Choy

Elena Choy has taught economics at several community colleges. She wrote this essay at the request of the editors of The Little, Brown Reader.

Laptops in the Classroom? No Problem

Someone—I forget who—said, "A teacher is someone who never says anything once." I myself have quoted this comment many times—in the classroom, during conferences, at faculty meetings, and now in print. We teachers are a varied bunch, some of us are much more interesting than others, but probably all of us repeat ourselves more than we should or are sometimes boring in other ways, at least to certain students. If, then, during one of our lectures a student wants to surf the web or to play poker online, well, who am I to say that she or he hasn't the right to do so? We all claim that we value individual thinking, that we want students to think for themselves. Why, then, do we object when they decide they want to tune us out?

Let me try to give a reasoned statement of my position, a statement that will take account of the contrary position. In fact, I'll begin with what I take to be the arguments in *favor* of banning laptops. I believe the chief arguments are these: (1) the upraised lids of laptops distract the instructor, and they often prevent the instructor from making eye-contact with the students; (2) laptops distract other students, who cannot help but see what is on the screens—for instance video games; (3) students who use laptops to take notes take overly extensive notes, so they are doing stenography rather than thinking—rather, one might almost say, than paying real attention to the significant content of the course; (4) because they are so busy taking notes, laptop users tend not to participate in whatever discussion there may be in the course because they are too busy taking notes.

Let's look at each of these arguments, beginning with the first. I grant that I am not keen about seeing lots of upraised tops, but (a) the large majority of my students, even in a big lecture course, are not using laptops, and I therefore can make plenty of eye-contact; (b) I am delighted to see that students are taking notes, or at least I think they are taking notes; (c) if they are playing poker or shopping online, well, that's their business. They have paid their tuition, and it's up to them to decide how to spend their money and their time. I am not Big Brother; I don't think it is appropriate for me to assume that those with laptops are not taking notes. In any case, if they are not, it surely is not for me to tell them how to use their time in class, provided they are not disturbing others.

Which gets to the second argument offered in favor of banning laptops, that they distract other students. Do the users of laptops in class significantly damage other students? If so, of course laptops should be banned, just as we ban smoking in the classroom. I have heard students say that the poker games they see on the screens of other students prevent them from paying attention to the lecturer, but I find it hard to take this objection seriously. Such students should stop peeking, should discipline themselves, should look at the lecturer, and should occupy themselves by taking their own notes.

The third objection, that students who use laptops are engaged in stenography rather than in thoughtful thinking, seems to me to be equally without force. Different students have different methods of learning: Some students find it useful to take abundant notes, others take very few notes, perhaps preferring to think about what is being said while it is being said. Indeed, some students have different methods for different courses: I can easily imagine hearing a lecture that I would like a preserve fairly extensively, a lecture perhaps filled with facts and figures, but I can also easily imagine hearing an equally stimulating lecture that is not of the sort that I would find myself taking extensive notes—an occasional memorable phrase might be all that I might jot down. A wise student might well adopt different methods for different lecturers. It doesn't follow, then that every student who uses a laptop will take too many notes.

The fourth reason offered on behalf of banning laptops is that the note-takers tend not to participate in whatever discussion there may be in class. My response is twofold: First, in lecture classes the discussion inevitably is an extremely minor part of the class, perhaps a few minutes of discussion at the end, or possibly one or two questions that are handled during the course of the lecture. At most only three or four students can participate, so we cannot in good faith argue that the laptop user, by remaining relatively silent, is hurting himself of herself, or is depriving other students of the benefit of his or her contribution. And, for that matter, even in smaller classes, let's say of ten or fifteen, we should respect the wishes of a student who prefers not to speak much in class. In many twenty years of teaching I have had three students who approached me after the first meeting of a smallish class, and explained that for one reason or another they preferred not to be called on. Ordinarily in such classes I say that part of the grade will depend upon class participation, but in their cases, because they raised the matter at the outset, I respected their wishes—I do not think it is my job to demand that shy people overcome their shyness—and I based the grade entirely on their three papers, their midterm and their final examinations—just as I base the grades in my large lecture courses. Obviously some courses—let's say Spoken Spanish—require oral participation, but in most classes I think we can comply with a student who requests that he or she not be called on to speak.

Finally, and with some hesitation, at this late stage in my essay I want to introduce a new point. It has been my experience that the call to ban laptops chiefly comes not from students but from their professors, my colleagues. Sometimes my colleagues say that they are disturbed by the lack of eye-contact, and I sympathize with them; I know what it is to see a raised lid rather than a student's face. Sometimes they say that the students are engaged in stenography, not in thinking, and I can understand this objection too, though, as I have indicated, I think different methods of note-taking work well for different students. When I was a student, in pre-laptop days, I confess, I took abundant notes in certain courses. My colleagues may say that they are concerned with helping students to *learn*, or *think*, not to be stenographers, but this sort of stenography served me well I think in some of the courses I took. It is not up to professors to prohibit students from taking the kinds of notes that the students think will be useful. We can give advice about taking notes, about preparing for the examination, and so forth, but we go too far when we prohibit students from taking notes in the way they find most useful.

In any case, and here I come to a dangerous point, I think that the chief reason instructors suggest that laptops be banned is one that they do not state, and maybe they are not even aware of. I think they fear that most students who use laptops are not taking notes, but are engaged in activities unrelated to the course—instant messaging, e-mailing, shopping, playing poker, and so on. But if students are in fact doing these things, what is the cure? Banning laptops? I don't think so. If the instructor is so boring that the students use laptops to shop and to write letters, well, when the laptops are banned the students will probably bring in crossword puzzles or exercises from other courses (for instance, Spanish vocabulary lists to be memorized) or whatever, and continue to ignore the lecturer.

I am saying, with much embarrassment, that a professor should ask himself a hard question: If students in my courses are using laptops for purposes unrelated to the course, what am I doing wrong? Perhaps we should videotape a lecture or two so that we can see hear what we look like and sound like, or perhaps ask a colleague to visit our class and evaluate it. It may be that if we saw ourselves, we would understand why the student has chosen to act independently. It might be that we too would prefer online poker.

Joining the Conversation: Critical Thinking and Writing

1. Can you think of any significant arguments *against* her case that Choy omits? If so, what are they—and how might she (or you) respond to them?

2. If you were the editor of your college newspaper, would you print this essay? Why, or why not?

3. Basing your view on this essay, do you think you would want to take a course with Professor Choy? Explain your reasoning.

A Second Debate: Do Credit Companies Market Too Aggressively to Youths?

Travis B. Plunkett

Travis B. Plunkett, the Legislative Director of Consumer Federation of America, wrote this essay for CQ Researcher *in 2006.*

Yes, Credit Companies Market Too Aggressively to Youths

Many credit card issuers have targeted the least sophisticated and riskiest consumers in recent years, including young people, and encouraged them to run up high, often unsustainable levels of debt. This practice has proven to be very profitable for many credit card issuers, but it can have devastating consequences for consumers.

Starting in the early 1990s, card issuers targeted massive marketing efforts at college campuses across the country, resulting in a sharp growth in credit card debt among college-age and younger Americans. As a result, Americans under age 35 continue to show more signs of trouble managing credit card debt than other age group.

Between the mid-1990s and 2004, the amount of credit card debt held by students graduating from college more than doubled, to $3,262. Americans under 35 are less likely to pay off their card balances every month than average Americans. They are paying more for debt obligations than in the past and are increasingly likely to pay more than 40 percent of their incomes on credit card debt.

Not surprisingly, more young Americans are declaring bankruptcy than in the past. Moreover, there is increasing evidence that credit card companies are now targeting high-school students, students with card offers. They are also marketing branded debit cards to adolescents, in part to encourage these young consumers to use similarly branded credit cards when they are older.

Young people are also financially vulnerable to the questionable pricing and business practices adopted by issuers to increase the profitability of lending to riskier customers. These abusive practices include "universal default," in which a consumer must suddenly pay a sharply higher interest rate on their outstanding balance with one credit card company because of a minor problem with another creditor.

Many creditors have also significantly increased their penalty fees, even for small transgressions like a payment that is made only a few hours late. Until recently, issuers also decreased the size of minimum payments that consumers had to pay, encouraging them to carry more debt for longer periods.

Several pieces of legislation have been introduced in Congress in recent years that would prevent credit card companies from targeting young people with unsustainable offers of credit and prohibit abusive fee and interest-rate practices. Unless credit card issuers adopt considerably more restraint in marketing and extending credit to less-sophisticated borrowers, the Consumer Federation of America will continue to urge Congress to adopt such restrictions.

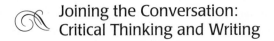

Joining the Conversation: Critical Thinking and Writing

1. In his first paragraph Plunkett says that issuers of credit cards encourage "young people" to run up high levels of debt. Does your experience support this assertion? Explain your answer.

2. Do you believe (with Plunkett) that legislation should be introduced to "prevent credit card companies from targeting young people with unsuitable offers of credit"? Explain your answer.

3. Whether you agree or disagree with Plunkett, give some suggestions about how he might strengthen his argument, even within the space limits that governed his comments? Be specific.

Louis J. Freeh

Louis L. Freeh is Vice Chairman and General Consel, MBNA Corporation, testified before the U. S. Senate Banking Committee in 2005. CQ Researcher *printed the following excerpt in 2006.*

No, Credit Companies Do Not Market Too Aggressively to Youths

In discussing student marketing, it is important to note that we make every effort to ensure that credit card offers are not sent to people under the age of 18.

MBNA does promote its products to college-aged customers by partnering with more than 700 colleges and universities, primarily through the college alumni associations. By working closely with school administrators, we have earned the confidence and trust of most of America's premier educational institutions. . . .

Before granting credit to a college student, analysts familiar with the needs and abilities of college students review each application and decline more than half. . . . Most college student applicants report a separate income, and many already have an established credit history.

"Do Credit Companies Market Too Aggressively to Youths?" (Con) by Louis J. Freeh, published in *CQ Researcher*, May 26, 2006. Reprinted by permission of CQ Press.

When evaluating an application, we consider the college student's projected performance as an alumnus, and when we grant credit, we typically assign a line of between $500 and $1,000. If a college student attempts to use his or her card beyond the credit line, we typically refuse the charge. And we do not re-price these accounts based on behavior.

Once a college student becomes a cardholder, MBNA delivers its "Good Credit, Great Future" brochure in a Welcome Package. The brochure highlights sound money-management habits, including guidance on how to handle a credit card responsibly. We also maintain a Web site aimed at college-aged consumers, highlighting many of the same tips. MBNA also conducts on-campus credit-education seminars, and we provide articles concerning responsible credit use for student and parent publications.

The performance of our college-student portfolio mirrors closely that of the national experience, as reported in [Government Accountability Office] reports and several independent studies. However, our accounts have much smaller credit limits and much smaller balances than the norm, our college student customers utilize their cards less often than the norm and these accounts are less likely to incur fees. Our experience has also been that college students are no more likely to mishandle their accounts than any other group of customers.

When we grant a card to college student, we think of it as the beginning of what we hope will be a long relationship. . . . Given this, we have absolutely no interest in encouraging poor credit habits. In fact, everyone's interest is best served when college students make responsible use of credit. That is our goal in every situation, and certainly when dealing with college-aged customers.

Joining the Conversation: Critical Thinking and Writing

1. Freeh says that his organization denies credit to more than half of the applicants. (He doesn't give details, but in paragraph 4 he explains that the company considers the student's projected performance as an alumnus.) Have you been denied credit? If so, do you think this action was fair and reasonable? Explain your answer. If you have been granted credit, do you think, on balance, that perhaps you should have been denied? Explain.

2. What differences do you find between Plunkett's and Freeh's accounts of college students' use of credit cards? Can you explain the differences? If not, which account are you more likely to believe, and why?

3. Whether you agree or disagree with Freeh, give some suggestions about how he might strengthen his argument, even within the space limits that governed his comments. Be specific.

4. Putting aside your own stand, which essay seems to you to be more convincing? Why?

✓ A Checklist: Revising Drafts of Arguments

☐ Does the introduction let the audience know what the topic is, why the topic is of some importance, and what your thesis is?

☐ Are the terms clearly defined?

☐ Are the assumptions likely to be shared by your readers? If not, are they reasonably argued rather than merely asserted?

☐ Does the essay summarize other views fairly, and grant that they have some merit, at least in some contexts?

☐ Are the facts verifiable? Is the evidence reliable?

☐ Is the reasoning sound?

☐ Are the authorities really authorities on this matter?

☐ Are quotations no longer than they need to be, are they introduced with useful lead-ins, and do they make good reading?

☐ Are all of the substantial counterarguments recognized and effectively responded to?

☐ Is the organization effective? Does the essay begin interestingly, keep the thesis in view, and end interestingly?

☐ Is the tone appropriate? (Avoid sarcasm, present yourself as fair-minded, and assume that people who hold views opposed to yours are also fair-minded.)

CHAPTER 5

Reading and Writing about Pictures

I am after the one unique picture whose composition possesses such vigor and richness, and whose content so radiates outwards from it, that this single picture is a whole story in itself.

Henri Cartier-Bresson

The Language of Pictures

It may sound odd to talk about "reading" pictures and about the "language" of pictures, but pictures, like words, convey messages. Advertisers know this, and that's why their advertisements for soft drinks include images of attractive young couples frolicking at the beach. The not-so-hidden message is that consumers of these products are healthy, prosperous, relaxed, and sexually attractive.

Like compositions made of words—stories, poems, even vigorous sentences—many pictures are carefully constructed things, built up in a certain way in order to make a statement. To cite an obvious example, in medieval religious pictures Jesus or Mary may be shown larger than the surrounding figures to indicate their greater spiritual status. But even in realistic paintings the more important figures are likely to be given a greater share of the light or a more central position than the lesser figures. Such devices of composition are fairly evident in paintings, but we occasionally forget that photographs too are almost always constructed things. The photographer—even the amateur just taking a candid snapshot—adjusts a pillow under the baby's head, or suggests that the subject may want to step out of the shadow, and then the photographer backs up a little and bends his or her knees before clicking the shutter. Even when photographing something inanimate, the photographer searches for the best view, waits for a cloud to pass, and perhaps pushes out of the range of the camera some trash that would spoil the effect of a lovely fern growing beside a rock. Minor White was speaking for almost all photographers when he said, "I don't take pictures, I make them."

And we often make our photographs for a particular purpose—perhaps to have a souvenir of a trip, or to show what we look like in uniform, or to show grandparents what the new baby looks like. Even professional photographers have a variety of purposes—for instance, to provide wedding portraits, to report the news, to sell automobiles, or to record some visual phenomena that they think must be recorded. Sometimes these purposes can be mingled. During the depression of the early 1930s, for instance, the Resettlement Administration employed photographers such as Dorothea Lange to help convince the nation that migrant workers and dispossessed farmers needed help. These photographers were, so to speak, selling something, but they were also reporting the news and serving a noble social purpose. (In Chapter 3 we reproduced Lange's most famous picture, *Migrant Mother*, along with some comments on it that students wrote in journals.)

Here are some questions that may help you to think about pictures.

Writing about Art

What are some of the basic things to look for in understanding the language of pictures? One can begin almost anywhere, but let's begin with the relationship among the parts:

- Do the figures share the space evenly, or does one figure overpower another, taking most of the space or the light?
- Are the figures harmoniously related, perhaps by a similar stance or shared action? Or are they opposed, perhaps by diagonals thrusting at each other? Generally speaking, diagonals may suggest instability, except when they form a triangle resting on its base. Horizontal lines suggest stability, as do vertical lines when connected by a horizontal line. Circular lines are often associated with motion, and sometimes—especially by men—with the female body and fertility. These simple formulas, however, must be applied cautiously, for they are not always appropriate.
- In a landscape, what is the relation between humans and nature? Are the figures at ease in nature, or are they dwarfed by it? Are they earthbound, beneath the horizon, or (because the viewpoint is low) do they stand out against the horizon and perhaps seem in touch with the heavens, or at least with open air? Do the natural objects in the landscape somehow reflect the emotions of the figures in it?
- If the picture is a portrait, how do the furnishings and the background and the angle of the head or the posture of the head and body (as well, of course, as the facial expression) contribute to our sense of the character of the person portrayed?
- What is the effect of light in the picture? Does it produce sharp contrasts, brightly illuminating some parts and throwing others into darkness? Or does it, by means of gentle gradations, unify most or all of the parts? Does the light seem theatrical or natural, disturbing or comforting? If the picture is in color, is the color realistic or is it expressive, or both?

You can stimulate responses to pictures by asking yourself two kinds of questions:

- *What is this doing?* Why is this figure here and not there, why is this tree so brightly illuminated, why are shadows omitted, why is this seated figure leaning forward like that?
- *Why do I have this response?* Why do I find this figure pathetic, this landscape oppressive, this child revoltingly sentimental but that child fascinating?

The first of these questions, "What is this doing?" requires you to identify yourself with the artist, wondering perhaps whether the fence or the side of the house is the better background for this figure, or whether both figures should sit or stand. The second question, "Why do I have this response?" requires you to trust your feelings. If you are amused, repelled, unnerved, or soothed, assume that these responses are appropriate and follow them up—at least until further study of the work provides other responses.

Writing about an Advertisement

Most advertisements in magazines and newspapers rely heavily on pictures: We see a happy family standing by an automobile and a few lines of text tell us that we should buy such-and-such a car, or we see a sexy body and a few lines tell us to use such-and-such perfume or to put on such-and-such underwear, or we see a starving child and a few lines tell us to contribute to such-and-such charitable foundation.

Putting aside for the moment advertisements for charities, most of the ads that we see are images not so much of the product (a car, perfume) as they are images of a desirable condition, a state, for instance affluence or happiness or sexual attractiveness or health. The ads are first of all selling an *idea*, such as "You deserve to be happy" (or healthy, or sexy), and this idea is chiefly what is depicted. Once the ad has conveyed this point, it then hooks the product to it: If you buy this particular car, you and your family will have lots of fun; if you use this particular perfume or this particular underwear, you will attract a sexual partner. Again, the implication is that something is missing from your life, but you can remedy this defect if you buy X. Is cleaning the stove too much of a chore? Use X oven cleaner. Are you worried that you won't have enough money to pay for your child's college tuition? Just open a savings plan with Bank X, and you will have peace of mind. Frequently, the appeal is to our vanity: "Be the first to own," "Use the cosmetic used by stars."

Sometimes, there is no clear relation at all between the image in an advertisement and the product being promoted. This may seem odd, but it is intentional. Perhaps the basic point, or goal, of all advertisements is to prompt the viewer to remember the product. The image has served its purpose if it catches your attention, and hence leads you to see and remember the name of the product. There have even been some very successful advertisements that make no mention of the product. There's just an image, usually one that is highly unusual, or explicitly sexual or violent, and shocking. The image creates buzz, and the discussion (and controversy) gets people talking. Who placed the ad? Why did they choose such an image? Haven't they gone too far? Isn't this an outrage? Most of the time, advertisers are pleased when such questions are raised and debated: These mean that the product is receiving lots of notice.

Of course other kinds of ads make *logical claims* ("proven," "doctors recommend," "more economical," "better value," "longer lasting"), but claims of this sort are usually impossible to validate. In any case, the picture rather than the text is usually the hook, the thing that catches the viewer's attention.

Ads for charities often work differently: The pictures are still the hooks (a starving child, a battered woman, a maltreated animal), but the pictures and the texts usually appeal to our sense of decency rather than to our vanity or to logic. They often appeal to our emotions—for instance, to our sense of pity, or of fairness—and although we commonly hear that emotional appeals are an illegitimate form of argument, one can question this view. Human beings are not merely logical creatures, but compassionate as well; and most people would agree that compassion is a virtue.

If your instructor asks you to analyze an advertisement, be sure to include the image with your essay. In your opening paragraph you will probably offer some sort of lead-in ("Among the most annoying ads in the current issue of . . . ," or "A good deal of today's advertising is highly sexual," rather than the bland "In this advertisement . . ."). In the body of the essay describe the ad accurately enough so that someone who hasn't seen it can visualize it, and then analyze how the ad works. You will consider such issues as

- To whom is the ad addressed?
- Is the appeal of the text logical ("tests prove," "doctors recommend"), or emotional (for instance, addressing our sympathy, our patriotism, our love of family)?
- What is the relationship between the image and the text? How does the design of the ad make that relationship?

In your conclusion you will probably evaluate the ad, perhaps on two grounds: How honest is the ad? Honest or not, how effective do you find it?

✓ A Checklist: Analyzing Advertisements

☐ What is the viewer's first impression of the ad? Excitement, perhaps conveyed by a variety of colors and large type? Dignity, perhaps conveyed chiefly by grays, lots of empty space, and smaller type?

☐ What is the audience for the ad? Affluent young women? College students? Housewives? Retired persons?

- ☐ Does the image appeal to an emotion—for instance to our sense of fairness, pity, patriotism, envy ("You too can get admiring looks"), fear ("Worried about aging skin? Use . . .")?

- ☐ Is the image intentionally shocking (for instance, a fetus being aborted, a brain being fried, lungs coated with tar)?

- ☐ Does the text make a logical, rational appeal ("Three out of four doctors recommend . . . ," "tests at a leading university show . . .")?

- ☐ What does the text do? Is it chiefly devoted to giving information? To being entertaining?

- ☐ What is the relationship of image to text? Does the image do most of the work, or is its job simply to get us to read the text?

- ☐ How successful is the ad? And how honest is it?

Writing about a Political Cartoon

Most editorial pages print political cartoons as well as editorials. These cartoons may use words in speech balloons or in captions, but generally the drawing does most of the work. Cartoonists almost always caricature their subjects because their aim is to satirize; that is, they exaggerate the subject's distinctive features to the point where the subject becomes grotesque and ridiculous—absurd, laughable, contemptible. True, it is scarcely fair to suggest that because, say, the politician who proposes such-and-such a measure is short, fat, and bald, his proposal is ridiculous, but that is the way cartoonists work.

In addition to (in effect) saying that the figures in the cartoon are ridiculous and therefore their ideas are contemptible, cartoonists often use symbolism, for instance symbolic figures (Uncle Sam), animals (the Democratic donkey and the Republican elephant), buildings (the White House stands symbolically for the president of the United States), things (a bag with a dollar sign on it symbolizes a bribe). For anyone brought up in our culture, these symbols (like the human figures who are represented) are obvious, and cartoonists assume that viewers will instantly recognize the symbols and figures, will get the joke, will see the absurdity of whatever it is that they are seeking to demolish.

In writing about a cartoon, normally you will lead into your analysis with a sentence or two that sets the context: the date, the publication, the cartoonist's name. Then, even though you will include a photocopy of the cartoon with your paper, you will offer a brief but clear *description* of the picture. From that description your reader ought to have a pretty good idea of what the picture looks like. You will then offer some *exposition*—that is, you will explain (interpret) the drawing by identifying the persons depicted and the event or the issue the cartoonist comments on. You will then devote most of the essay to an *analysis* of the cartoon. That is, you will discuss the ways in which the cartoon makes it point. Caricature, we have said, usually says in effect, "This is ridiculous, as you can plainly see by the absurdity of the figures depicted." "What *X*'s proposal adds up to, despite its apparent complexity, is nothing more than . . ."). This sort of persuasion—chiefly by ridicule—probably is unfair (a thoughtful political proposal can be offered by a funny-looking person), but this is largely the way cartoons work, and we should not reject the possibility that the cartoonist has indeed put his or her finger on the absurdity of the issue. Probably your essay will include an *evaluation* of the cartoon; indeed the *thesis* underlying the essay may be (for instance) that the cartoon is effective for such-and-such reasons, but it is also unfair for such-and-such reasons.

In analyzing the cartoon—in grasping the attitude of the cartoonist—consider such things as

- the relative size of the figures in the image
- the quality of the lines—thin and spidery, or thick and seemingly aggressive
- the amount of empty space in comparison with the amount of heavily inked space (obviously a drawing with lots of inky areas will convey a more oppressive sense than a drawing that is largely open)
- the degree to which text is important—and what the text says (Is it witty? Heavy-handed?)

Caution: If your instructor lets you choose a cartoon, be sure to choose one with sufficient complexity to make the exercise worthwhile.

✓ A Checklist: Analyzing Political Cartoons

☐ Have I provided a lead-in?

☐ Have I provided a brief but accurate description of the drawing?

☐ Have I included a brief report of the event or issue that the cartoon is dealing with and an explanation of all of the symbols?

☐ Have I included an analysis of the ways in which the content and style of the drawing help to convey the message?

☐ Have I provided an adequate evaluation of the effectiveness of the drawing?

☐ Have I provided an adequate evaluation of the effectiveness of the text (caption or speech balloons), and of the fairness of the cartoon?

Lou Jacobs Jr.

Lou Jacobs Jr., photographer and the author of several books on photography, is a frequent contributor of essays on the topic to the New York Times, *where this piece originally appeared.*

What Qualities Does a Good Photograph Have?

When amateur and professional photographers get together they often discuss equipment and techniques at some length, but it is not often that photographers take time to consider what makes a good picture.

Many photographic organizations list criteria similar to those described below when judging pictures submitted in a competition. Judges may offer opinions like "The composition is off balance," or "The expressions on peoples' faces tell the story well." But photographic criticism is not an exact art. In the media, critics tend to use esoteric terms that even an "in" group doesn't always grasp.

Therefore it's important to the average photographer that he or she develop a basis for understanding and verbalizing how pictures succeed or fail in their visual way, or how they happen to be a near-miss. The latter term describes an image that has some, but not enough, of the visual virtues discussed below.

Of course "a good picture" is a relative description because it's subjective, as is the judgment of all the qualities mentioned in the list that follows. However, there is enough agreement in the tastes of a variety of people to make certain standards general and valid, though the characteristics of a good picture are subject to flexible interpretation. A little honest controversy about the visual success of a print or slide can be a healthy thing.

Impact: This descriptive word comprises a collection of the qualities that help make a photograph appealing, interesting, impressive, or memorable. For instance, Ansel Adams's "Moonrise, Hernandez, NM" is a famous image that has been selling for astronomical prices at auctions because it has enormous pictorial or visual impact—among other reasons. The picture's impact evolves from many qualities such as the drama of the light, the mood invoked, and the magic sense of realism.   5

It is possible to translate such qualities into your own photographs when you consider how the subjects were treated, whether landscapes or people. Too seldom do we meet dramatic opportunities in nature as grand as those in "Moonrise," but with a well developed artistic sensitivity, ideal conditions can be captured on film.

Human Interest: Here is another rather general term to encompass emotional qualities, action, and things that people do which appeal to a lot of viewers. A shot of your children laughing or a picture of vendors in a marketplace might both show outstanding human interest. The success of such a photograph depends on how you compose it, on lighting, on timing to catch vivid expressions, and perhaps on camera angle or choice of lens. All of these ingredients of a good picture are coming up on the list.

Moonrise, Hernandez, New Mexico, 1941
Ansel Adams

There is another aspect of human interest in your own or others' photographs. Sometimes the unusualness of a subject and the way it's presented overshadows adequate technique. For instance, a good sports picture showing peak action in a scrimmage or a definitive play in baseball has intrinsic appeal.

A photograph of a pretty girl, a baby, and a sunset are in the same category, because in each case the subject matter grabs the viewer's attention. As a result, a mediocre composition, inferior lighting, a messy background, or other technical or esthetic weaknesses are ignored or excused because the subject is striking.

It's a good feeling when you can distinguish between the subject in a photograph and the way it was treated.   10

Galleries and museums often hang photographs that are "different," but they're not necessarily worthy of distinction. Many offbeat photographs we see are likely not to have lasting visual value, while fine photographs like those of Ansel Adams or Cartier-Bresson will still be admired in future decades.

Effective Composition: Like other qualities that underlie a good picture, composition can be controversial. There are somewhat conventional principles of design that we follow because they seem "natural," like placing the horizon line or a figure off-center to avoid a static effect.

But really effective composition is usually derived from the subject, and generally the urge to keep composition as simple as possible pays off. That's why plain backgrounds are often best for portraits, and if you relate someone to his/her environment, simplicity is also a virtue. Composition may be dynamic, placid, or somewhere between.

Study the compositional tendencies of fine photographers and painters for guidance. Be daring and experimental at times too, because a "safe" composition may also be dull.

Spontaneity: This characteristic of a good picture is related to human   15
interest, realism and involvement. When you are involved with the subject, as you might be in photographing an aged father or mother, you prize most the images that include spontaneous expressions and emotional reactions. Get people involved with each other, too, so they forget the camera and your pictures are likely to be more believable—and credibility is often a pictorial asset.

If your camera lens is not fast enough to shoot at let's say 1/60th of a second of f/2.8, then you need flash. But you get more spontaneity when people aren't posed, waiting for the flash to go off. Natural light also adds to the realistic impression you capture of people and places, since flash-on-camera has an unavoidably artificial look in most cases.

Lighting: Certainly we have to shoot sometimes when the light is not pictorial, so we do the best we can. A tripod is often the answer to long exposures and exciting photographs. In some situations the light improves if we have the time and patience to wait. Outdoors plan to shoot when the sun is low in the early morning, and at sunset time. Mountains, buildings and people are more dramatic in low-angle light. Details lost in shadows don't seem to matter when the light quality itself is beautiful.

Lighting also helps to create mood, another element of a good picture. Mood is understandably an ethereal quality which includes mystery, gaiety, somberness, and other emotional aspects. Effective photographs may capitalize on the mood of a place especially when it's dramatic.

Color: In a painting a pronounced feeling of light and shadow is called chiaroscuro, and in photographs such effects are augmented by color which may be in strong contrasts, or part of important forms. Outstanding pictures may also be softly colored in pastels that can be as appealing as bright hues.

We tend to take color in photographs for granted, but we don't have to   20
settle for literal color when a colored filter or a switch in film may improve a situation. Next time it rains, shoot some pictures through a car window or windshield, or keep your camera dry and shoot on foot—using indoor

color film. The cold blue effects, particularly in slides, are terrific. You may later use an 85B filter to correct the color for normal outdoor or flash use.

Keep in mind that "pretty" or striking color may influence us to take pictures where there really is no worthwhile image. And when you view prints and slides, realize that theatrical color can influence your judgment about the total quality of a picture. A beautiful girl in brightly colored clothes, or an exotic South Seas beach scene may be photographed with creative skill, or insensitively, no matter how appealing the color is.

Contrast: Outstanding pictures may be based on the fact that they contain various contrasting elements, such as large and small, near and far, old and new, bright and subtle color, etc. In taking pictures and evaluating them, keep the contrast range in mind, although these values are often integral with other aspects of the picture.

Camera Angle and Choice of Lens: If someone standing next to you shoots a mid-town Manhattan street with a 50mm lens on a 35mm camera, and you do the same scene with a 35mm or 105mm lens from a crouch rather than standing, you might get a better picture. You can dramatize a subject through your choice of camera angle and lens focal length to alter perspective as well as the relationship of things in the scene. Distortion created this way can be pictorially exciting—or awkward and distracting. You may get good pictures by taking risks in visual ways, and later deciding if what you tried seems to work.

Imagination and Creativity: These two attributes of people who take pictures might have been first on the list if they were not abused words. Look each one up in the dictionary. Ponder how you would apply the definitions to your own pictures and to photographs you see in books or exhibitions.

It takes imagination to see the commonplace in an artistic way, but a certain amount of imagination and creativity should be involved every time we press the shutter button. These human capabilities are basic to understanding the other qualities that make good pictures. 25

Joining the Conversation: Critical Thinking and Writing

1. Evaluate the title and the first paragraph.

2. In paragraph 4 Jacobs says, "Of course 'a good picture' is a relative description because it's subjective. . . ." Do you agree? Look, for instance, at Dorothea Lange's photographs of a migrant laborer and her children, on pages 70–71 and 73–76. Would you be willing to argue that the famous picture (the one showing the children turned away from the camera) is clearly—objectively—a better picture than one of the other pictures? Explain.

3. In paragraph 5 Jacobs praises Ansel Adams's *Moonrise, Hernandez, NM*, but this picture, showing a cemetery with crosses illumined by a silvery moon, has been disparaged by some critics on the grounds that it is sentimental. How would you define sentimentality? And is it a bad thing in a photograph? Explain.

4. In paragraph 7 Jacobs speaks of "human interest," and he cites a picture of "children laughing or a picture of vendors in a marketplace." Given these examples, what does "human interest" seem to mean? What might be some examples of photographs of people that do *not* have "human interest"?

5. In paragraph 23 Jacobs says that "you can dramatize a subject through your choice of camera angle. . . ." Find an example of such a photo in a newspaper or newsmagazine, or perhaps in this book, and explain how the camera angle "dramatizes" the subject.

6. Take a photo, perhaps one in this book, and in 500 words analyze and evaluate it in Jacobs's terms. Then consider whether Jacobs's essay has helped you to see and enjoy the photograph.

7. Write your own short essay (250–500 words) on Jacobs's topic, "What Qualities Does a Good Photograph Have?" Illustrate it with photocopies of two or three photographs, from this book or from any other source that you wish to draw on. (You may want to choose two examples of good photographs, or one of a good photograph and one of a poor photograph.)

Sample Analyses of Pictures

A Sample Essay by a Student

If you take a course in art history, you will probably be asked to write a formal analysis. In such a context, the word *formal* is not the opposite of *informal*, as in a formal dance or a formal dinner, but simply means "related to the form or structure." Here we print a short formal analysis of a photograph. Formal analysis, however, is by no means limited to courses in art history; we follow the student's essay with a professional writer's examination—largely a formal analysis—of an advertisement.

Zoe Morales

Zoe Morales wrote the following essay in a first-year composition course at Tufts University. She is planning to go to law school, probably in her native Texas.

The instructor distributed copies of three pictures and asked students to write an analysis of any one of the three. Morales has kindly let us reproduce her final set of notes—that is, the organized notes that she jotted down after she reread material that she generated, almost at random, by asking herself questions such as "What interests me about this picture?" "What puzzles me here?" "What is the relation of one figure to another?" and "What does this all add up to?"

Dancing at Durango

(Preliminary Jottings)

Title: tourists, Navajo, in Colorado

The tourists (white) on the train are gawking at the Navajo, and the boy seems to be interested (at least he is smiling), BUT the man with the boy looks pretty grim, looks straight ahead, *not* at dancers. Superior? Uptight?

The Navajo are doing their stuff, at least the dancers are, BUT the girl (she's a Navajo too) is not part of the act (not dressed "Indian-style"). At side; not center-stage. Not being looked at— but she looks coolly at the photographer.

The whole thing seems pretty grim—these Navajo (one at right even in a war bonnet) perform for a couple of minutes when the train pulls in, then probably wait an hour or maybe many hours, until the next train. They probably depend on coins or if they are lucky dollar bills that whites toss to them out of the train.

Navajo Dancers Entertaining a Tourist Train, June 1963, Durango, Colorado
George Hight

The Navajo in the war bonnet seems to be drummer. Anyway, he is sort of offstage, with the girl.

Pretty strong separation of whites from Navajo. A white man and a boy are on the ground with Navajo, but whites' clothes clearly separate them from Navajo. These whites belong to the group on the train, that is, to the world on wheels that will soon pull out of this town.

Lettering on train is like lettering on a "Wanted Poster"—to make the tourists think they are in the Wild West of the nineteenth century, even though reality is 1963!

These jottings served, with considerable amplification and reorganization, as the basis of an essay on the picture. Here is the finished essay.

Dancing at Durango: White Tourists and Navajo Performers

Today when people who are not Native Americans think about Native Americans, they probably think first of their terrible mistreatment by whites. The lands of the Native Americans were stolen, and many of the tribes were nearly annihilated by diseases introduced by whites. But this view seems to be fairly recent. A common older view, forcefully presented in the Indian Wars of the nineteenth century, can be summarized in the blunt words, "The only good Indian is a dead Indian." These words are reported to have been spoken by General Philip Henry Sheridan, who achieved fame and acclaim as one of Lincoln's generals, and even more fame and even more acclaim as an Indian fighter after the Civil War.

By the beginning of the twentieth century the Native Americans, their populations and their territories greatly reduced by war and disease, were no longer a military threat to the whites. In the popular white mind in the first half of the twentieth century, Native Americans chiefly were of two sorts, bad guys in cowboy films and quaint feather-wearing people in tourist attractions. In films they were sometimes brave but more often were cunning, and they were always defeated by whites; in tourist sites they wore their feathers and beads and moccasins, and they danced their dances, representing a colorful past that the civilized world had outgrown.

George Hight's photograph, Navajo Dancers Entertaining a Tourist Train, June 1963, Durango, Colorado, shows two contrasting worlds, the white world with its railroad train, and the Native American world with its costumes worn for the sake of the tourists. But this railroad train is itself a bit of a fake, a twentieth-century machine that, for the pleasure of white people, uses a style of lettering that looks like a Wanted Poster to call to mind the Wild West of a bygone day.

The train has stopped, some people have stepped off it, but the strong diagonal line conveys a sense that this self-contained world, this world which is decidedly separate from the Navajo, will soon speed away, leaving the Navajo behind. Although a white man and a boy are off the train and on the ground with the Navajo—they are in Navajo territory for a minute, so to speak—clearly there is no real intermingling. Their clothing separates them, and so do their expressions: The man is grim-faced, the boy is smiling and to that degree he is sympathetically entering into the Navajo world, but there is no real contact between the two dancers and the people safe in their train or the two whites who have stepped off the train. This grim white man at the left faces the same way that the Navajo in the bonnet at the right faces, but this similarity only emphasizes the difference between them. The chief connection between the two worlds, interestingly, is made by the Navajo girl at the right, who is dressed like a white and looks at the photographer and at us, that is, at the tourist world in front of the picture. She lives in what we can call the real Navajo world, the modern world, which whites dominate. And this is the world to which the Navajo performers probably will return. After the last performance the costumed men will put on jeans and cotton shirts, and they will replace their beaded and feathered moccasins with sneakers. But the girl, standing at the side, dressed like a white, not performing, is a Native American who scarcely exists so far as the tourists are concerned.

I find the photograph disturbing, and not simply because of the separation suggested between the worlds of the whites and the Navajo. The white man and the boy stride toward a dancer who leans, knees flexed, in their direction: Will the whites and this dancer collide? Certainly the white man does not look as though he is going to change his direction. Furthermore, the other dancer, in profile, bends forward and, as the scene is caught by the camera, blocks the movement of the white man. All of this troubling placement of the figures on the left-hand side is set in contrast to the firm vertical stances of the Indian wearing the headdress and the little girl on the right. A little to the right of the center of the picture, a man walks away (he seems to be wearing a cap, so he probably is a trainman of some sort), and further to the right two white women, also with their backs toward us, flank the bonneted Navajo and the girl. The man in the center and the two white women at the right take us in one direction, the white man and the boy at the left take us in the opposite direction. And as if all this contradictory motion were not enough, the train cars, which are stationary so that the tourists can take pictures, seem propelled forward to the left and also veering backward into the sharply receding right.

Most Native American dances had a social function: The Bear Dance was danced to appease the soul of the animal which they would kill; the Scalp Dance was a dance of victory; the Sun Dance was danced in an effort to achieve divine guidance. Judging from the hoops that hang on a post in the foreground, these Navajo perform some sort of Hoop Dance. (According to Gladys A. Reichard, Navaho Religions: A Study of Symbolism [1950], hoops are used in many kinds of Navaho sacred dances.) But this dance is performed not for any ritual that is an important part of the life of the dancers; rather, it is performed for the entertainment of outsiders. It has utterly lost its religious or healing function. But not quite. It is still life-giving, since it gains some money, helping the Native Americans to survive in the narrow world that the whites have pushed them into—the space between the train and the presumably white tourist who took the picture.

To my eye and mind, it is tragic that these Navajo are performing their dances not as religious rites but just to entertain outsiders and to make a few dollars. Imagine if some Christians, Jews, Muslims, or Buddhists were so poor that today they had to make money by performing their sacred ceremonies to entertain people who do not have the faintest knowledge of or interest in their religion, but who look at the ceremonies as the strange doings of people who are not part of the modern world. On the other hand, we don't know how these Indians felt when they were dancing for tourists. Maybe they believed—and maybe they were right—that they were communicating at least some of their culture to strangers, were showing that although much of their traditional way of life had been forcibly taken from them, they nevertheless retained important parts of it, and were willing to share these with the whites. The whites in a moment will be speeding down the railroad tracks to the next tourist attraction, but maybe some of them will be mysteriously touched by what they saw. We can't know, but we can guess that the photographer was touched enough to record the image.

Joining the Conversation: Critical Thinking and Writing

1. What do the first two paragraphs contribute to the essay? What would be the effect if these were omitted?

2. Does this essay present a thesis? Does an analysis of a picture require one?

3. Do you find the ending too indefinite, or just right?

A Sample Essay by an Art Historian

Thomas Hoving

Thomas Hoving was born in New York City in 1931, into a socially prominent family. In 1959, after receiving a Ph.D. in art history at Princeton University, he began work in the medieval department of the Metropolitan Museum of Art. In 1966 he left the Metropolitan to become the parks commissioner of New York City, but he returned to the Metropolitan the following year, as director of the museum. In 1977 he left the museum to become an independent consultant and writer. Among his publications are an autobiography called Making the Mummies Dance *(1993),* Art for Dummies *(1999), and* American Gothic: Biography of Grant Wood's American Masterpiece *(2005). We reprint his essay on Grant Wood's painting.*

American Gothic
Grant Wood, 1930

So, Does It Speak to You?

It's been 75 years since Grant Wood's *American Gothic* was exhibited to appreciative crowds at the Art Institute in Chicago, where it won a prize of $300 and was acquired by the museum. The painting has been lavishly praised, brutally condemned (called a "corpse" by one feckless critic), waved aloft as a symbol of the gloriously down-to-earth Midwest, vilified as Satan's work and satirized in myriad parodies and advertisements. No matter what has been said about it or done to it, *American Gothic* has become a preeminent American art icon.

Why? What's it got going for it? Is it a serious work of art or just a hyped-up cliche? I mean, *is it any good?* To find out, you have to dissect it by means of the "secret" art connoisseurs' checklist. There are about 20 items on this checklist, including a battery of scientific tests, iconographic analyses and provenance searches, but I won't bore you with all that stuff. Three items in the checklist suffice: The "blink test," or your 100th-of-a-second first impression; a ponderously detailed description of the painting intended to force you to look at every pore of the work; and the artist's own words. To get to the heart and soul of *American Gothic* you don't have to read art critics' jargon or delve into the often convoluted theories of art historians. As we used to joke in grad school, *"kunstgeschichte* [the German word for art history] *ist horsegeschichte"* Well, almost.

If a work of art is any good, it will talk to you. Art will talk quicker if you happen to be able to recognize all sorts of influences—but essentially a great work will reach your own heart and do it on its own. For instance, you don't need to know a lot about the Old Testament to know that Michelangelo's David is the image of a splendid, possibly royal youth facing an adversary with resolve and about to launch a large stone from his sling. The breathtaking sculpture stands on its own. And to get at the quality of *American Gothic*, you don't need to know that Wood thought the Gothic house (still existing, in Eldon, Iowa) was pretentious and silly, or that the man is his dentist, Byron Mckeeby, whose long, oval face and huge hands obsessed the artist, or that the woman is Wood's sister, Nan Wood Graham, or that Wood added hair to Mckeeby's head.

When I first saw *American Gothic* in the flesh in 1961 I wrote down my "blink" impression: "Nicely tight. Powerful reality and witty visuals combined. Late Gothic European style." When I wrote my long, long and studiously boring description of it (I'll not inflict it on you), I spotted certain details that helped me asses its quality. One was the sky, utterly without blemish, without a smidgen of haze. Perhaps Wood didn't intend this to be a real sky at all but something better than real, something spiritual. I was reminded of the religious works of artists such as Jan van Eyck and Hans Memling (artists, it turns out, that Wood idolized). In all these late 15th-century Northern European works, the skies are clear azure whenever Christ, the Virgin Mary or God the Father appears and cloudy when mankind shows up. Wood's sky is about the spiritual and the good.

The faces are marvelously painted, and the dentist's visage—with   5
those perfect lines in that long, Gothic face, with thin, firm but not inimical lips, with the wattles of age—is as well conceived as anything by Thomas Eakins or John Singleton Copley. The woman is in her early 30s with a face too oval—Gothicized—to be natural. I am fascinated by her naturally blond hair pulled back so severely yet softened by that provocative curl. Beneath the impassive expression, she could be a lot of fun.

Other details that grabbed me:

The way the peaked roof of the house binds the pair together.

His gold collar tack, which reflects the gold bulb on the lightning rod atop the house.

The amusing "reflection" of the pitchfork in the overalls, which is reminiscent of a reflection of the Virgin in the silver breastplate of the Archangel Michael in a Memling that Wood adored.

Then there are Wood's own descriptions of the work. After he found the Carpenter Gothic house in Eldon, he said, "I simply invented some *American Gothic* people to stand in front of [it]." And, "I admit the fanaticism and false taste of the characters in *American Gothic*, but to me, they are basically good and solid people."

After sweating through my detailed description and picking up what the painter himself said, I went back to my "blink" impression and made my judgment. *American Gothic* is an exquisitely painted portrait of the highest quality that ranks with any of America's great portraits. It is gentle, mischievous and satirical. It is packed with sophisticated visual puns and renders homage to a golden age of art—the Northern European late Gothic period—without slavishly aping it.

In short, it's a crackling, iron-hard yet sinuously soft, killer-diller study of a slice of humanity, perhaps of a bygone era but one that resonates today, proclaiming something ancient and enduring—and something sacred too.

 ## Joining the Conversation: Critical Thinking and Writing

1. Hoving says (paragraph 3) that art "will talk to you." One of the things Grant Wood's depiction of the woman apparently says to him is "she could be a lot of fun" (paragraph 5). Does the picture say this to you? If it doesn't say this to you, does that mean that any viewer can say anything he or she wishes about a work of art, and no one can suggest that the comment is nonsense? Please explain.

2. As mentioned in the headnote to this essay, Hoving was the director of America's greatest art museum, the Metropolitan Museum of Art. Given his background, are there passages in his essay that surprise you? Look closely, for instance at the second paragraph. Does his manner of writing—for instance his tone—surprise you? Why or why not? Do you think the essay is a successful piece of writing?

3. Look again at Hoving's comment in paragraph 3, about art talking to viewers: "If a work of art is any good, it will talk to you. Art will talk quicker if you happen to be able to recognize all sorts of influences—but essentially a great work will reach your own heart and do it on its own." Do you think he is right? Can you point to some work of art that reached your heart "on its own"? Presumably Hoving is talking about paintings and sculptures, but we can extend his term "work of art" to include poems, stories, plays, films, and all sorts of musical compositions. If some work reached you immediately, briefly describe the work and its effect on you. And tell the reader if, as the days, months, years have passed, the work has deepened—or has faded—in significance and value for you.

4. Hoving describes the "blink test" (paragraph 2) as the "100th-of-a-second first impression," and in paragraph 4 he puts into words his "blink" impression of

American Gothic. Take a picture that you like and would be familiar to most readers—for instance the painting commonly called *Whistler's Mother* (the artist's own title for it was *Arrangement in Grey and Black No. 1: The Artist's Mother*)—and put into a few words your blink impression. Next write a somewhat fuller account, about 250 words (one page of double-spaced typing), indicating to readers *why* you like the picture. Or if you have a favorite that is not widely known, take that picture and give your blink impression and your more extended account but accompany your words with a copy of the picture. (You can find almost any work of art on the Internet, or you can photocopy the picture from a book.)

CHAPTER 6

All in the Family

The Acrobat's Family with a Monkey
Pablo Picasso, 1905

Sonia
Joanne Leonard, 1966

Short Views

Higamus hogamus,
Woman's monogamous;
Hogamus higamus,
Man is polygamous.
      Anonymous (often attributed to William James)

After a certain age, the more one becomes oneself, the more obvious one's family traits become.
      Marcel Proust

All happy families resemble one another; every unhappy family is unhappy in its own fashion.
      Leo Tolstoy

Marriage is the best of human statuses and the worst, and it will continue to be. And that is why, though its future in some form or other is as assured as anything can be, this future is as equivocal as its past. The demands that men and women make on marriage will never be fully met; they cannot be.
      Jessie Bernard

Nobody who has not been in the interior of a family can say what the difficulties of any individual of that family may be.
      Jane Austen

Lewis Coser

Lewis Coser, born in Berlin in 1913, was educated at the Sorbonne in Paris and at Columbia University, where he received a Ph.D. in sociology in 1954. For many years he taught at the State University of New York, Stony Brook, where he held the title Distinguished Professor. The passage below is from a textbook for college students.

The Family

Following the French anthropologist Claude Lévi-Strauss, we can define the family as a group manifesting these characteristics: it finds its origin in marriage; it consists of husband, wife and children born in their wedlock—though other relatives may find their place close to that nuclear group; and the members of the group are united by moral, legal, economic, religious, and social rights and obligations. These include a network of sexual rights and prohibitions and a variety of socially patterned feelings such as love, attraction, piety, awe, and so on.

The family is among the few universal institutions of mankind. No known society lacks small kinship groups of parents and children related through the process of reproduction. But recognition of the universality of this institution must immediately be followed by the acknowledgment that its forms are exceedingly varied. The fact that many family organizations are not monogamic, as in the West, led many nineteenth-century observers to the erroneous conclusion that in "early" stages of evolution there existed no families, and that "group marriage," institutionalized promiscuity, prevailed. This is emphatically not the case; even though patterned wife-lending shocked the sensibilities of Victorian anthropologists, such an institution is evidently predicated on the fact that men have wives in the first place. No matter what their specific forms, families in all known societies have performed major social functions—reproduction, maintenance, socialization, and social placement of the young.

Families may be monogamous or polygamous—there are systems where one man is entitled to several wives and others where several husbands share one wife. A society may recognize primarily the small nuclear, conjugal unit of husband and wife with their immediate descendants or it may institutionalize the large extended family linking several generations and emphasizing consanguinity more than the conjugal bond. Residence after marriage may be matrilocal, patrilocal or neolocal; exchanges of goods and services between families at the time of marriage

---

Lewis Coser, "The Family" from Lewis Coser, *Sociology Through Literature*. Prentice-Hall, 1963, pp. 250–251. Reprinted by permission.

may be based on bride price, groom price or an equal exchange; endogamous or exogamous regulations may indicate who is and who is not eligible for marriage; the choice of a mate may be controlled by parents or it may be left in large measure to the young persons concerned. These are but a few of the many differences which characterize family structures in variant societies.

 ## Joining the Conversation:
Critical Thinking and Writing

1. At the end of paragraph 2, Coser writes: "No matter what their specific forms, families in all known societies have performed major social functions—reproduction, maintenance, socialization, and social placement of the young." What does "socialization" mean? How does it differ from "social placement of the young"? What specific forms does each take in our society?

2. What examples can you give of "moral, legal, economic, religious, and social rights and obligations" (paragraph 1) that unite members of a family?

3. Compare Coser and J. H. Plumb (page 6) on the social functions of the family. According to Plumb, what responsibility does the family in our society have in performing the social functions Coser lists? How do other institutions compete with the family in performing some of these functions?

4. As you read other selections in this chapter, what variations in form of the family do you encounter? Are there any variations in form that Coser did not mention or anticipate?

Joan Didion

Joan Didion, born in Sacramento in 1934 and educated at the University of California, Berkeley, worked for a while as a features editor at Vogue *but then turned to freelance writing. Among her novels are* Play It as It Lays *(1970),* A Book of Common Prayer *(1977), and* The Last Thing He Wanted *(1996). Collections of her magazine essays include* Slouching Towards Bethlehem *(1968), which is the source of the piece we reprint,* The White Album *(1979), and* The Year of Magical Thinking, *which won the U.S. National Book Award in 2005.*

On Going Home

I am home for my daughter's first birthday. By "home" I do not mean the house in Los Angeles where my husband and I and the baby live, but the place where my family is, in the Central Valley of California. It is a vital although troublesome distinction. My husband likes my family but is uneasy in their house, because once there I fall into their ways, which are difficult, oblique, deliberately inarticulate, not my husband's ways. We live in dusty houses ("D-U-S-T," he once wrote with his finger on surfaces all over the house, but no one noticed it) filled with mementos quite without value to him (what could the Canton dessert plates mean to him? how could he have known about the assay scales, why should he care if he did know?), and we appear to talk exclusively about people we know who have been committed to mental hospitals, about people we know who have been booked on drunk-driving charges, and about property, particularly about property, land, price per acre and C-2 zoning and assessments and freeway access. My brother does not understand my husband's inability to perceive the advantage in the rather common real-estate transaction known as "sale-leaseback," and my husband in turn does not understand why so many of the people he hears about in my father's house have recently been committed to mental hospitals or booked on drunk-driving charges. Nor does he understand that when we talk about sale-leasebacks and right-of-way condemnations we are talking in code about the things we like best, the yellow fields and the cottonwoods and the rivers rising and falling and the mountain roads closing when the heavy snow comes in. We miss each other's points, have another drink and regard the fire. My brother refers to my husband, in his presence, as "Joan's husband." Marriage is the classic betrayal.

Or perhaps it is not any more. Sometimes I think that those of us who are now in our thirties were born into the last generation to carry the burden of "home," to find in family life the source of all tension and drama. I had by all objective accounts a "normal" and a "happy" family situation, and yet I was almost thirty years old before I could talk to my family on the telephone without crying after I had hung up. We did not fight. Nothing was wrong. And yet some nameless anxiety colored the emotional charges between me and the place that I came from. The question of whether or not you could go home again was a very real part of the sentimental and largely literary baggage with which we left home in the fifties; I suspect that it is irrelevant to the children born of the fragmentation after World War II. A few weeks ago in a San Francisco bar I saw a pretty young girl on crystal take off her clothes and dance for the cash prize in an "amateur-topless" contest. There was no particular sense of moment about this, none of the effect of romantic degradation, of "dark journey," for which my generation strived so assiduously. What sense could that girl possibly make of, say, *Long Day's Journey into Night*? Who is beside the point?

That I am trapped in this particular irrelevancy is never more apparent to me than when I am home. Paralyzed by the neurotic lassitude engendered by meeting one's past at every turn, around every corner, inside every cupboard, I go aimlessly from room to room. I decide to meet it head-on and clean out a drawer, and I spread the contents on the bed.

A bathing suit I wore the summer I was seventeen. A letter of rejection from *The Nation*, an aerial photograph of the site for a shopping center my father did not build in 1954. Three teacups hand-painted with cabbage roses and signed "E.M.," my grandmother's initials. There is no final solution for letters of rejection from *The Nation* and teacups hand-painted in 1900. Nor is there any answer to snapshots of one's grandfather as a young man on skis, surveying around Donner Pass in the year 1910. I smooth out the snapshot and look into his face, and do and do not see my own. I close the drawer, and have another cup of coffee with my mother. We get along very well, veterans of a guerrilla war we never understood.

Days pass. I see no one. I come to dread my husband's evening call, not only because he is full of news of what by now seems to me our remote life in Los Angeles, people he has seen, letters which require attention, but because he asks what I have been doing, suggests uneasily that I get out, drive to San Francisco or Berkeley. Instead I drive across the river to a family graveyard. It has been vandalized since my last visit and the monuments are broken, overturned in the dry grass. Because I once saw a rattlesnake in the grass I stay in the car and listen to a country-and-Western station. Later I drive with my father to a ranch he has in the foothills. The man who runs his cattle on it asks us to the roundup, a week from Sunday, and although I know that I will be in Los Angeles I say, in the oblique way my family talks, that I will come. Once home I mention the broken monuments in the graveyard. My mother shrugs.

I go to visit my great-aunts. A few of them think now that I am my cousin, or their daughter who died young. We recall an anecdote about a relative last seen in 1948, and they ask if I still like living in New York City. I have lived in Los Angeles for three years, but I say that I do. The baby is offered a horehound drop, and I am slipped a dollar bill "to buy a treat." Questions trail off, answers are abandoned, the baby plays with the dust motes in a shaft of afternoon sun.

It is time for the baby's birthday party: a white cake, strawberry-marshmallow ice cream, a bottle of champagne saved from another party. In the evening, after she has gone to sleep, I kneel beside the crib and touch her face, where it is pressed against the slats, with mine. She is an open and trusting child, unprepared for and unaccustomed to the ambushes of family life, and perhaps it is just as well that I can offer her little of that life. I would like to give her more. I would like to promise her that she will grow up with a sense of her cousins and of rivers and of her great-grandmother's teacups, would like to pledge her a picnic on a river with fried chicken and her hair uncombed, would like to give her *home* for her birthday, but we live differently now and I can promise her nothing like that. I give her a xylophone and a sundress from Madeira, and promise to tell her a funny story.

5

Joining the Conversation: Critical Thinking and Writing

1. Didion reveals that members of her family are difficult, inarticulate, poor housekeepers, and so forth. Do you find these revelations about her family distasteful? Would you mind seeing in print similarly unflattering things you had written about your own family? How might such revelations be justified? Are they justified in this essay?

2. Summarize the point of the second paragraph. Do you find Didion's speculations about the difference between her generation and succeeding generations meaningful? Are they accurate for your generation?

3. Do you think that growing up necessarily involves estrangement from one's family? Explain.

Sam Schulman

Sam Schulman writes on politics and culture for Commentary, *the* Wall Street Journal, *and other publications. We reprint an essay that appeared in the* WSJ *in 2006.*

Letting Go

In the midst of my 1950s childhood, the playwright Robert Paul Smith published a quirky little book that became a best seller called *Where Did You Go? Out. What Did You Do? Nothing*. It was a laconic evocation of the independent lives that Depression children contrived for themselves in the era before postwar affluence. And its subtitle—"How it was when you were a kid, and how things have deteriorated since"—condemned, by contrast, the coddled, structured, supervised and superabundant childhoods of my own generation.

Though *Where Did You Go?* was written for our parents, every child I knew made sure to get hold of a copy. A year after its publication, we children were the target of a sequel: *How to Do Nothing with Nobody All Alone by Yourself*. It featured seductively grim drawings of spare little toys and games you could make out of wooden matchsticks, empty spools of thread, tin cans and rubber bands. I, for one, went right to work. Trying to carve a boat out of a wine cork, I cut my thumb to the bone with my Cub Scout pocketknife. My quest for the simple life of an earlier time ended, sitting with my disgusted father, in a Chicago hospital emergency room.

But any envy that we children of the '50s felt toward the sparse childhood of our grandparents faded quickly. Now we have children of our own, and we're determined that they should never be alone, should never go out and must never do nothing. Despite all the opportunities for independence that our way of life should give them—with both parents working and huge increases in disposable income—the fact is that our children are part of the most closely watched generation in history.

The watching begins in primary school. The days are no more when knots of children wandered erratically to their schoolhouse or back home. They step out of sliding minivan doors in the morning and are quickly whisked away the moment the bell rings, driven in quick succession to gymnastics, soccer, karate or violin lessons.

And the lazy days of summer are over, too. Not only will few kids be playing out on the street when the weather warms up, but the ones who go away to summer camp will be in constant contact with their parents, sending daily emails with pictures and reporting on each of their activities. 5

As kids grow older and begin to take an interest in something more than kickball, it turns out that even romance isn't off-limits. Today's parents don't want to be the strict, distant types of yesteryear, handing down judgments that may cause moments of unpleasantness. They want to be "friends" who hear about—and show sympathy for—the travails of dating and "relationships." As social commentator Leonard Steinhorn boasts in a recent book on the baby boomers: "Candor and openness—not rigidity and distance—have become the norms in American families today."

The parental connection does not wither away after high-school graduation. Cell phones keep college students tethered to their parents—parents who might have been sent off to college, like my freshman roommate in 1967, with 12 stamped, preaddressed envelopes in which to insert a weekly letter home. Email and text-messages now allow for minute-by-minute updates. One recent study by a college revealed that its freshmen were in touch with their parents by cell phone as many as 15 times a day.

Parental hovering has not simply produced a large number of inane conversations—"I'm on my way to class, I'm walking into the building"—it has destroyed the private lives of children. Kids no longer have the privilege of making their own worlds and participating in a separate culture. This kind of childhood was celebrated not only by Robert Paul Smith but by Peter and Iona Opie in *Lore and Language of Schoolchildren* (1959). The Opies discovered that teasing games, hide-and seek and tag, have been around at least since the time of Chaucer.

Another version of childhood as a separate realm is visible in Booth Tarkington's Penrod books, which were published in 1914 and 1916 and remained best sellers until midcentury. The American childhood that Tarkington's children experienced was beset by grown-ups, but they wanted to impose adult responsibilities on the young ones, not supervise their childhood adventures. Penrod's traumas came from haircuts, dancing lessons, school arithmetic and mixed-sex parties where he was expected to act like "a little gentleman." His parents—a stern father and a sentimental mother—knew that there were certain things he needed to be taught but generally let Penrod look after his own childhood.

So why can't parents today leave their children alone for five minutes? 10
There are probably a number of reasons. Some no doubt worry that the
coarse surrounding culture is a constant threat—and indeed it is. But it is
much more likely to intrude on the computer or on television—two aspects
of life often unmonitored by parents—than at a playground or summer
camp. Another reason may be an exaggerated sense of our own importance
in producing the persons our children are destined to become.

A recent *Wall Street Journal* story about the growing reluctance of affluent families to send their children to boarding schools illustrates the
point. One couple, who chose not to send their daughter to a famous New
England prep school, rationalized their decision like this: "We just want
to spend a couple of more years imparting our values to our daughter."

Yes, parents impart values. But values come from other useful
sources, too. Hovering parents undermine the influence not only of other
institutions like schools and churches but of peers. Being picked for a
sports team, facing the first day at school or at a job, learning to handle
the ups and downs of courtship, enduring the apprenticeship of almost
any career—these are not only signs that our children are becoming independent adults, but acts of initiation that take them out of the family
embrace and into the wider world.

The seemingly obvious notion that kids need to be left alone sometimes if they are to grow up has been so lost that more than one
American university has been forced to station security guards outside
freshmen orientation sessions to keep anxious parents out. There are no
reports, encouragingly, of freshmen on the other side trying to pull their
parents in.

Joining the Conversation: Critical Thinking and Writing

1. Comment on the first three paragraphs of Schulman's essay. Do you think
   that it opens effectively? Why or why not?

2. Schulman claims that "parental hovering" has "destroyed the private lives of
   children." Does he provide convincing evidence to support this claim?

3. Do you think Schulman is describing such a small section of the population—
   folks who read the *Wall Street Journal* and whose kids take violin and karate
   lessons—that his essay has nothing to say to most of America? Explain your
   answer.

4. If you agree with Schulman, write an essay of 1 to 2 pages in which you develop and provide further support for his argument. If you disagree, write an
   essay in which you state and give evidence for your argument against him.

5. One student who read Schulman's essay criticized it, saying that "he doesn't
   tell us what should be done to make things better." Another student replied,
   "But that's the point of the essay." What is your view?

Stephanie Coontz

Stephanie Coontz, the director of public education for the Council on Contemporary Families, is the author of numerous books, including The Way We Really Are: Coming to Terms with America's Changing Families *(1997) and* Marriage, a History: From Obedience to Intimacy, or How Love Conquered Marriage *(2006). We reprint an Op-Ed piece here from the* New York Times.

The Heterosexual Revolution

The last week has been tough for opponents of same-sex marriage. First Canadian and then Spanish legislators voted to legalize the practice, prompting American social conservatives to renew their call for a constitutional amendment banning such marriages here. James Dobson of the evangelical group Focus on the Family has warned that without that ban, marriage as we have known it for 5,000 years will be overturned.

My research on marriage and family life seldom leads me to agree with Dr. Dobson, much less to accuse him of understatement. But in this case, Dr. Dobson's warnings come 30 years too late. Traditional marriage, with its 5,000-year history, has already been upended. Gays and lesbians, however, didn't spearhead that revolution: heterosexuals did.

Heterosexuals were the upstarts who turned marriage into a voluntary love relationship rather than a mandatory economic and political institution. Heterosexuals were the ones who made procreation voluntary, so that some couples could choose childlessness, and who adopted assisted reproduction so that even couples who could not conceive could become parents. And heterosexuals subverted the long-standing rule that every marriage had to have a husband who played one role in the family and a wife who played a completely different one. Gays and lesbians simply looked at the revolution heterosexuals had wrought and noticed that with its new norms, marriage could work for them, too.

The first step down the road to gay and lesbian marriage took place 200 years ago, when Enlightenment thinkers raised the radical idea that parents and the state should not dictate who married whom, and when the American Revolution encouraged people to engage in "the pursuit of happiness," including marrying for love. Almost immediately, some thinkers, including Jeremy Bentham and the Marquis de Condorcet, began to argue that same-sex love should not be a crime.

Same-sex marriage, however, remained unimaginable because marriage had two traditional functions that were inapplicable to gays and lesbians. First, marriage allowed families to increase their household labor force by having children. Throughout much of history, upper-class men divorced their wives if their marriage did not produce children, while peasants often wouldn't marry until a premarital pregnancy confirmed

5

the woman's fertility. But the advent of birth control in the 19th century permitted married couples to decide not to have children, while assisted reproduction in the 20th century allowed infertile couples to have them. This eroded the traditional argument that marriage must be between a man and a woman who were able to procreate.

In addition, traditional marriage imposed a strict division of labor by gender and mandated unequal power relations between men and women. "Husband and wife are one," said the law in both England and America, from early medieval days until the late 19th century, "and that one is the husband."

This law of "coverture" was supposed to reflect the command of God and the essential nature of humans. It stipulated that a wife could not enter into legal contracts or own property on her own. In 1863, a New York court warned that giving wives independent property rights would "sow the seeds of perpetual discord," potentially dooming marriage.

Even after coverture had lost its legal force, courts, legislators and the public still cleaved to the belief that marriage required husbands and wives to play totally different domestic roles. In 1958, the New York Court of Appeals rejected a challenge to the traditional legal view that wives (unlike husbands) couldn't sue for loss of the personal services, including housekeeping and the sexual attentions, of their spouses. The judges reasoned that only wives were expected to provide such personal services anyway.

As late as the 1970s, many American states retained "head and master" laws, giving the husband final say over where the family lived and other household decisions. According to the legal definition of marriage, the man was required to support the family, while the woman was obligated to keep house, nurture children, and provide sex. Not until the 1980s did most states criminalize marital rape. Prevailing opinion held that when a bride said, "I do," she was legally committed to say, "I will" for the rest of her married life.

I am old enough to remember the howls of protest with which some defenders of traditional marriage greeted the gradual dismantling of these traditions. At the time, I thought that the far-right opponents of marital equality were wrong to predict that this would lead to the unraveling of marriage. As it turned out, they had a point.

Giving married women an independent legal existence did not destroy heterosexual marriage. And allowing husbands and wives to construct their marriages around reciprocal duties and negotiated roles—where a wife can choose to be the main breadwinner and a husband can stay home with the children—was an immense boon to many couples. But these changes in the definition and practice of marriage opened the door for gay and lesbian couples to argue that they were now equally qualified to participate in it.

Marriage has been in a constant state of evolution since the dawn of the Stone Age. In the process it has become more flexible, but also more optional. Many people may not like the direction these changes have taken in recent years. But it is simply magical thinking to believe that by banning gay and lesbian marriage, we will turn back the clock.

⌘ Joining the Conversation: Critical Thinking and Writing

1. According to Coontz, what events—ideas, inventions, and laws—have contributed in the last 200 years to "changes in the definition and practice of marriage"? Does she indicate whether or not she approves of these changes? If so, where? Do you approve of these changes? Explain.

2. How have these changes, according to Coontz, "opened the door to gay and lesbian couples"?

3. What is Coontz's thesis? How does she support it? In your opinion, how well does she succeed?

Gabrielle Glaser

Gabrielle Glaser is the author of the book, Strangers to the Tribe: Portraits of Interfaith Marriage *(1997). We reprint an essay that was originally published in the* New York Times Magazine *in 1997.*

Scenes from an Intermarriage

As Alfred and Eileen Ono sit down late one evening to discuss their family's religious life, even the seating arrangement seems to reveal their spiritual divide. On one side of their sumptuous living room in Portland, Ore., Eileen settles into a comfortable wing chair. Al is across from her, on the couch, next to their 22-year-old daughter, Sarah. From time to time during the conversation, father and daughter link hands.

Sarah and her 18-year-old brother, Alistair, a college freshman, have been raised in the Buddhist faith of their Japanese-American father. Eileen, a Middle Westerner with Dutch, Lithuanian and German roots, has remained a Catholic. The Onos decided how to raise the children long ago, even before they were married, and Eileen insists that her solitary spirituality is of little import. But the religious differences in this family, in which both children shave their heads in the style of Buddhist monks and nuns, exert a gravitational pull on each relationship—between the parents and the children, between the siblings and between husband and wife.

Gabrielle Glaser, "Faith Is a Gamble: Scenes from an Intermarriage," *New York Times Magazine,* December 7, 1997. Reprinted by permission of the author.

Perhaps surprisingly, it is Eileen who is most relaxed about the family's complicated spiritual life. Over the years, her husband has become more doctrinaire. When Sarah was in her early teens and interested in Catholicism, for example, Al insisted that she continue to attend temple every Sunday. Then, in college, when she dated a devout Irish Catholic and began going to Mass with him, Al expressed his disappointment outright.

The Onos say that they try to live up to the ideal of tolerance in all matters. But it isn't any easier for them than it is for the other 33 million Americans who live in interfaith households. The United States, founded by religious dissidents and shaped by a Christian revival in the 19th century, has evolved into a rich religious pluralism. As racial and ethnic barriers have become hazier, intermarriage has become more common: according to recent surveys, 52 percent of Jews, 32 percent of Catholics and 57 percent of Buddhists marry outside the faith.

Many couples split their religious differences in the interest of family harmony, but the Onos' choice not to is evident the moment you enter their splendid turn-of-the-century home. A gold Japanese panel rests on the living room mantel, and in the library sits a black lacquer *obutsudan,* or Buddhist shrine, where Alistair, Sarah and Al recite chants over prayer beads. The three practice Jodoshinshu, a form of Japanese Buddhism, although in recent years Sarah has also included elements of Tibetan Buddhism. (Alistair refers teasingly to Sarah's interest in Tibetan Buddhism as an "upper-middle-class white thing.")

Al, a gentle man with thick gray hair and a kind but intense face, speaks in the drawn-out vowels of his native Minnesota. His parents, George and Masaye, were born in California; their marriage was arranged by a match-maker. They later settled in St. Louis Park, and helped to found the state's first Buddhist temple. Growing up, Al flourished there and relished the simple truths of his faith: There is suffering. There is a cause for suffering. Suffering can be overcome by thinking and living in the right way. His Buddhism, which he describes as "logical and linear," built on wisdom, knowledge, truth and compassion, filters into all aspects of his life: as a doctor—he has a thriving OB-GYN practice in Portland—a father and a husband. "When patients come to me and say, 'Oh, my God, it's cancer, I should have come to you sooner,'" Al says, "I say: 'This is not because you've done anything wrong or because you missed your last appointment. Don't blame yourself. Bodies are always changing. Now it's time to put it back on track.'"

Eileen, on the other hand, has always had questions about her faith. A plain-spoken woman with pale, luminous skin and large, hazel eyes, she was raised in a Minnesota farming town where about half the population was Catholic. As a child, she liked the music and pageantry the church offered, but some things didn't make sense to her. "I'd go to confession and have to make up sins," she says. "I just hadn't done anything horrible." By the time she married, Eileen had also begun to find much of church

5

doctrine—on birth control and the role of women, for example—outdated. Still, she considers herself Catholic. "It's how I was brought up, and it's in my soul," she says.

From time to time, she has second thoughts about the choice she made 27 years ago to raise children in a religion not her own. "I sometimes wish we could be all the same thing," she says softly. "Sure, I do." Sometimes an "Our Father" or "Hail, Mary" will cross her lips before she falls asleep, or when she learns that someone has died. But she rarely goes to church, and like the crossword puzzles she does on Sunday mornings when the rest of her family is at temple, or the meticulous squares of fabric she sews together in her award-winning quilts, Eileen's faith lies apart, boxed and separate, from the rest of her family. "I'm happy with how my spiritual life is," she says. She pauses, then adds, "It's others who have a problem with it."

Those others included her relatives, at least at first. When Al and Eileen began dating in the late 1960's as students at the University of Minnesota, their parents couldn't believe the relationship was serious. When Al told his parents of the couple's plans to marry, his parents accepted the announcement with grim resignation. Eileen's parents reacted with similar reticence.

The wedding was to take place in Minneapolis, and the closest   10
English-speaking Buddhist clergyman lived hundreds of miles away, in Chicago, so the couple settled on a Catholic priest. They were married in a campus chapel, amid burlap banners reading "Peace" and "Love." Led by the priest, they recited Buddhist wedding vows, emphasizing not love or miracles but truth, honor and respect.

Yet the occasion did not flow as smoothly as they had hoped. Eileen's father, an Army veteran, had been stationed in the Philippines during World War II, and after the surrender had hunted the country for Japanese deserters. After several glasses of champagne at the reception, he approached George Ono's best friend with a powerful slap on the back. "Whoever would have guessed that my daughter would be marrying a Jap 25 years after I was over there shooting at them?" he declared. Eileen and Al stared at each other in disbelief. "We'd been so worried about the religious aspects of the wedding that we had overlooked the racial ones," Eileen says. "Our families had always been very cordial to each other." There were other not-so-subtle messages. As a gift, an aunt gave them a plaster statue of Christ, engraved with their names and wedding date.

The couple moved to Portland, and a few years after Sarah's birth the family started going to the Oregon Buddhist Temple there. But at first it was Eileen who took the children to and from services—while Al, caught up in building his medical practice, rarely went. Over time, she began to feel a resistance to being so involved and told Al that he would have to take the lead. "I don't care if you're in the middle of a delivery, you're going to have to be the point man on this," she finally said to him. When Al started going, she stopped.

Sometimes during the ride to temple an image would flash through his head. Of all things, he envisioned a Norman Rockwell painting he once saw, of a family driving off to church, all together. He would dismiss the picture by reminding himself: "But she's not Japanese! She doesn't even relate to this stuff. This was the agreement."

These days, Eileen attends temple occasionally and has incorporated Buddhist thought into her life as a *hakujin*, or white person, as she jokingly calls herself. Indeed, the flies she once swatted are now gently shooed outdoors, in keeping with the Buddhist belief that all forms of life deserve dignity and respect. "They get several chances," she says with a smile. But she has retained a few of her rituals, and Christmas is one of them. The family chooses a tree together, and on Dec. 24 Al and Sarah attend midnight Mass—because they like the music. Eileen doesn't go. "I'm not practicing Catholicism, so I don't feel good just going to church for the highlights," she says, "but I do encourage them to go." The next morning, the whole family opens presents together.

Al says that Christ embodied the wisdom and compassion to which   15
Buddhists aspire, so honoring his birthday has never been an issue. Even so, the holiday Eileen loved as a child, and dreamed of sharing someday with her children, is a bit of a compromise. But religious differences can't take all of the blame: Dec. 25 is also Alistair's birthday, and at noon the day turns from celebrating Christ's arrival to celebrating Alistair's.

Other holidays follow Japanese tradition. For New Year's, Al spends days preparing a feast of special rice cakes and sashimi, and the family toasts one another with sake. "It's never been, 'Well, if you get sushi, tomorrow we have to have schnitzel,'" Eileen says. "I never denied my heritage. It just wasn't a big deal."

Her children's upbringing was a world away from memorizing catechism lessons. Sarah and Alistair spent Sundays at dharma school, learning to chant and meditate. At home, they drank green tea and, as toddlers, learned to use chopsticks. (So accustomed was the family to eating rice at every meal that Alistair thought mashed potatoes were a delicacy. "I thought there was a religious meaning to having them at Thanksgiving," he says with a grin. "That's the only time we ever had them.")

Yet growing up Buddhist in Portland wasn't easy. Children taunted Sarah and Alistair on the playground. In his advanced-placement English class, Alistair once suggested that perhaps not everyone was able to recognize Biblical allusions in literature. The teacher replied, "If you don't know the story of Moses, you don't belong here."

Sarah, a recent graduate of Connecticut College, is back at home doing part-time work while she looks for a job. As a child, she could see only what her religion didn't offer her. "Buddhism didn't have any perks," she says. "Until high school, it was weird. There's no Buddhist rite of passage. My Jewish friends got bas mitzvahs, my Catholic friends got big parties at their first Communion. When you're 9 or 10, you don't want to be anything but what your friends are." So she "tried out"

Catholicism and at night would drop to her knees, hands clasped together, and pray at her bedside. She thought it might be easier to "talk to God" than to sit in silent meditation and clear her head of all thoughts. She even attended Catholic summer camp. Her friends taught her prayers, walked her through the steps of Mass, including Communion. She wanted, she says, "to pass," and told people that her mother was Catholic. When a counselor found out that Sarah had taken Communion without being Catholic, she scolded her. Sarah was mortified.

In time, Sarah, a small woman with delicate Asian features, made peace with Buddhism. She studied in Asia for several months and welcomed living in a Buddhist society. Her faith, she says, has taught her one true thing: "to focus on the present."

20

In some ways, Eileen and Al's decision to raise their children as Buddhists was reinforced by society at large. Because of their Japanese surname and their tea-with-cream-colored skin, both Alistair and Sarah say that they found themselves identifying more readily with their Asian roots than their European ones. Alistair in particular has immersed himself in Japanese culture and credits the dynamic young minister at the Portland temple with inspiring his deeper involvement in Buddhism. At a special ceremony last spring, he received his Buddhist name, a great honor. Days later, he had the name, Gu-Sen—"widespread proclamation"—tattooed in Japanese on his lower back.

Yet guilt also lurks behind Alistair's enthusiasm for his father's faith and heritage. He half-facetiously calls himself a "mama's boy," and frequently E-mails Eileen from college; he worries that he has neglected her in some way. When a high-school history teacher gave out an assignment to research family trees, Alistair filled out the Ono branches practically by heart. When he asked his mother for help with her side, she pulled out photo albums and scrapbooks and recounted details of little-known relatives. "I had never asked about them before," he says. "I felt kind of bad."

Al, too, wonders quietly if he has inadvertently dampened his wife's religious life or her ties to her culture. They don't talk about it much; Al shies from confrontation. But he does remember that on a trip to Ireland some years ago they stumbled one afternoon into a stone church in the middle of Mass. Al turned to Eileen and asked, "Do you want to take Communion?" She brushed him off, he says, by saying she couldn't, since she hadn't been to confession in years. "Was it that she didn't want to be bothered?" he wonders. "Or was it just too complicated with me there, and she didn't want to mess with it?"

What may become of the religious divide between Al and Eileen now, with both children grown, is hard to say. Their marriage is a solid one. They take trips together, go to movies, make elaborate meals, enjoy their children. As middle age gives way to senior discounts, however, the Onos are likely to have disquieting moments. For them, death poses yet another separation. "I don't necessarily believe that God will forgive all at the last minute," Eileen says. "But I do think our spirits go somewhere." Al shakes his head gently. "I'm not so sure there's any connection between this life and another one. The Buddhist perspective doesn't believe we'll all be together again somewhere. I kid Eileen sometimes, telling her: 'Gee, Eileen, if you get last rites, you'll go to heaven. We'll all go to hell, so we'll still be in different places.'"

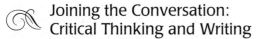

Joining the Conversation: Critical Thinking and Writing

1. Glaser writes of the Ono family's "complicated spiritual life" (paragraph 3). What are the complications, and what produces them?

2. Glaser casts her first paragraph in the present tense. What advantage does this focus give her?

3. Think of an intermarriage with which you are acquainted, in your family or among your friends. Then jot down a list of "scenes" that represent it; for example, religious services, holidays, weddings, funerals. Would you label the intermarriage "complicated"?

4. In an essay of 750 to 1,000 words, write your own "Scenes from an Intermarriage" through which you reveal its ease, or strains, or both.

Anonymous

The anonymous author of this essay has revealed only that he was forty years old when he wrote it, is married, and is the father of three children. The essay originally appeared in the New Republic, *a magazine that was, at the time (1974), regarded as liberal.*

Confessions of an Erstwhile Child

Some years ago I attempted to introduce a class of Upward Bound students to political theory via More's *Utopia*. It was a mistake: I taught precious little theory and earned More a class full of undying enemies on account of two of his ideas. The first, that all members of a Utopian family were subject to the lifelong authority of its eldest male. The second, the Utopian provision that should a child wish to follow a profession different from that of his family, he could be transferred by adoption to a family that practiced the desired trade. My students were not impressed with my claim that the one provision softened the other and made for a fair compromise—for what causes most of our quarrels with our parents

---

but our choice of life-patterns, of occupation? In objecting to the first provision my students were picturing themselves as children, subject to an unyielding authority. But on the second provision they surprised me by taking the parents' role and arguing that this form of ad lib adoption denied them a fundamental right of ownership over their children. It occurred to me that these reactions were two parts of the same pathology: having suffered the discipline of unreasonable parents, one has earned the right to be unreasonable in turn to one's children. The phenomenon has well-known parallels, such as frantic martinets who have risen from the ranks. Having served time as property, my Upward Bound students wanted theirs back as proprietors. I shuddered. It hardly takes an advanced course in Freudian psychology to realize that the perpetuation, generation after generation, of psychic lesions must go right to this source, the philosophically dubious notion that children are the property of their biological parents, compounded with the unphilosophic certitude so many parents harbor, that their children must serve an apprenticeship as like their own as they can manage.

The idea of the child as property has always bothered me, for personal reasons I shall outline. I lack the feeling that I own my children and I have always scoffed at the idea that what they are and do is a continuation or a rejection of my being. I like them, I sympathize with them, I acknowledge the obligation to support them for a term of years—but I am not so fond or foolish as to regard a biological tie as a lien on their loyalty or respect, nor to imagine that I am equipped with preternatural powers of guidance as to their success and happiness. Beyond inculcating some of the obvious social protocols required in civilized life, who am I to pronounce on what makes for a happy or successful life? How many of us can say that we have successfully managed our own lives? Can we do better with our children? I am unimpressed, to say no more, with parents who have no great track record, presuming to oracular powers in regard to their children's lives.

The current debate over the Equal Rights Amendment frequently turns to custody questions. Opponents of ERA have made the horrifying discovery that ERA will spell the end of the mother's presumed rights of custody in divorce or separation cases, and that fathers may begin custody rights. Indeed a few odd cases have been so settled recently in anticipation of the ratification of ERA. If ratified, ERA would be an extremely blunt instrument for calling the whole idea of custody into question, but I for one will applaud anything that serves to begin debate. As important as equal rights between adults may be, I think that the rights of children are a far more serious and unattended need. To me, custody by natural parents, far from being a presumed right only re-examined in case of collapsing marriages, should be viewed as a privilege.

At this point I have to explain why I can so calmly contemplate the denial of so-called parental rights.

I am the only child of two harsh and combative personalities who married, seemingly, in order to have a sparring partner always at hand. My   5 parents have had no other consistent or lasting aim in life but to win out over each other in a contest of wills. They still live, vigorous and angry sep-tuagenarians, their ferocity little blunted by age or human respect. My earli-est memories—almost my sole memories—are of unending combat, in which I was sometimes an appalled spectator, more often a hopeless nego-tiator in a war of no quarter, and most often a bystander accused of covert belligerency on behalf of one side or the other, and frequently of both! I grew up with two supposed adults who were absorbed in their hatreds and recriminations to the exclusion of almost all other reality. Not only did I pass by almost unnoticed in their struggle, the Depression and World War II passed them by equally unnoticed. I figured mainly as a practice target for sarcasm and invective, and occasionally as the ultimate culprit responsible for their unhappiness. ("If it weren't for you," my mother would sometimes say, "I could leave that SOB," a remark belied by her refusal to leave the SOB during these 20 long years since I left their "shelter.")

The reader may ask, "How did you survive if your parents' house was all that bad?" I have three answers. First, I survived by the moral equivalent of running away to sea or the circus, i.e., by burying myself in books and study, especially in the history of faraway and (I thought) more idealistic times than our own, and by consciously shaping my life and tastes to be as different as possible from those of my parents (this was a re-proach to them, they knew, and it formed the basis of a whole secondary area of conflict and misunderstanding). Second, I survived because statis-tically most people "survive" horrible families, but survival can be a qual-ified term, as it is in my case by a permanently impaired digestive system and an unnatural sensitivity to raised voices. And third, though I found solace in schooling and the rationality, cooperation and basic fairness in teachers that I missed in my parents, I must now question whether it is healthy for a child to count so heavily on schooling for the love and ap-proval that he deserves from his home and family. Even if schooling can do this well, in later life it means that one is loyal and affectionate toward schooling, not toward parents, who may in some sense need affection even if they don't "deserve" it. I am not unaware that however fair and rational I may be in reaction to my parents' counter-examples, I am a very cold-hearted man. I might have done better transferred to a new family, not just by receiving love, but through learning to give it—a lack I mourn as much or more than my failure to receive.

It is little wonder then that I have an acquired immunity to the notion that parental custody is by and large a preferable thing. In my case, almost anything else would have been preferable, including even a rather callously run orphanage—anything for a little peace and quiet. Some people are simply unfit, under any conditions, to be parents, even if, in-deed especially if, they maintain the charade of a viable marriage. My parents had no moral right to custody of children, and I cannot believe that my experience is unique or particularly isolated. There are all too many such marriages, in which some form of horror, congenial enough to adults too sick or crazed to recognize it, works its daily ruination on children. Surely thousands of children conclude at age 10 or 11, as I did, that marriage is simply an institution in which people are free to be as beastly as they have a mind to, which may lead either to a rejection of marriage or to a decision to reduplicate a sick marriage a second time, with another generation of victims. It is time to consider the rights of the victims.

How to implement a nascent theory of justice for children is difficult to say. One cannot imagine taking the word of a five-year-old against his parents, but what about a ten- or twelve-year-old? At *some* point, children should have the right to escape the dominance of impossible parents. The matter used to be easier than it has been since World War I. The time-honored solution—for boys—of running away from home has been made infeasible by economic conditions, fingerprints, social security and minimum wage laws. No apprenticeship system exists any more, much less its upper-class medieval version—with required exchange of boys at puberty among noble families to serve as pages and so forth. The adoption system contemplated in More's *Utopia* is a half-remembered echo of a medieval life, in which society, wiser than its theory, decreed a general exchange of children at or just before puberty, whether through apprenticeship or page-service, or more informal arrangements, like going to a university at 14 or running away with troubadors or gypsies.

Exchanging children is a wisely conceived safety valve against a too traumatic involvement between the biological parent and the child. Children need an alternative to living all their formative life in the same biological unit. They should have the right to petition for release from some sorts of families, to join other families, or to engage in other sorts of relationships that may provide equivalent service but may not be organized as a family. The nuclear family, after all, is not such an old or proven vehicle. Phillippe Aries' book, *Centuries of Childhood*, made the important point that the idea of helpless childhood is itself a notion of recent origin, that grew up simultaneously in the 16th and 17th centuries with the small and tight-knit nuclear family, sealed off from the world by another recent invention, "privacy." The older *extended* family (which is the kind More knew about) was probably more authoritarian on paper but much less productive of dependency in actual operation. There ought to be more than one way a youngster can enter adult society with more than half of his sanity left. At least no one should be forced to remain in a no-win game against a couple of crazy parents for 15–18 years. At 10 or 12, children in really messy situations should have the legal right to petition for removal from impossible families, and those rights should be reasonably easy to exercise. (This goes on de facto among the poor, of course, but it is not legal, and usually carries both stigma and danger.) The minimum wage laws should be modified to exempt such persons, especially if they wish to continue their education, working perhaps for public agencies, if they have no other means of support. If their parents can support them, then the equivalent of child support should be charged them to maintain their children, not in luxury, but adequately. Adoption of older children should be facilitated by easing of legal procedures (designed mainly to govern the adoption of *infants*) plus tax advantages for those willing to adopt older children on grounds of goodwill. Indeed children wishing to escape impossible family situations should be allowed a fair degree of initiative in finding and negotiating with possible future families.

Obviously the risk of rackets would be very high unless the exact terms of such provisions were framed very carefully, but the possibility of rackets is less frightening to anyone who thinks about it for long than the dangers of the present situation, which are evident and unrelieved by any signs of improvement. In barely a century this country has changed from a relatively loose society in which Huckleberry Finns were not uncommon, to a society of tense, airless nuclear families in which unhealthy and neurotic tendencies, once spawned in a family, tend to repeat themselves at a magnifying and accelerating rate. We may soon gain the distinction of being the only nation on earth to need not just medicare but "psychi-care." We have invested far too heavily in the unproved "equity" called the nuclear family; that stock is about to crash and we ought to begin finding escape options. In colonial days many New England colonies passed laws imposing fines or extra taxes on parents who kept their children under their own roofs after age 15 or 16, on the sensible notion that a person of that age ought to be out and doing on his own, whether going to Yale or apprenticing in a foundry. Even without the benefit of Freud, the colonial fathers had a good sense of what was wrong with a closely bound and centripetal family structure—it concentrates craziness like compound interest, and so they hit it with monetary penalties, a proper Protestant response, intolerant at once of both mystery and excuses. But this was the last gasp of a medieval and fundamentally Catholic idea that children, God help them, while they may be the children of *these* particular parents biologically, spiritually are the children of God, and more appositely are the children of the entire community, for which the entire community takes responsibility. The unguessed secret of the middle ages was not that monasteries relieved parents of unwanted children; more frequently, they relieved children of unwanted parents!

10

Joining the Conversation: Critical Thinking and Writing

1. What is the author's thesis? (Quote the thesis sentence.) Apart from his own experience, what evidence or other means does he offer to persuade you to accept his thesis?

2. What part does the *tone* of his article play in persuading you to agree with him or in alienating you? Does his tone strike you, perhaps, as vigorous or belligerent, as ironic or bitter, as reasonable or hysterical?

3. The author admits (paragraph 6) that he is "a very cold-hearted man." Do you remember your initial reaction to that sentence? What was it? Overall, does the author strengthen or jeopardize his argument by this admission? Explain.

4. If you did not find the article persuasive, did you find it interesting? Can you explain why?

Arlie Hochschild

Its a she you idiot publishers ... even wikipedia got that one right

Arlie Hochschild, born in Boston in 1940, holds a bachelor's degree from Swarthmore College and a Ph.D. from the University of California, Berkeley, where he is now a professor in the Department of Sociology. He is the author of several important books, including The Second Shift: Working Parents and the Revolution at Home *(1989, written with Anne Machung). The material below comes from this book.*

The Second Shift: Employed Women Are Putting in Another Day of Work at Home

Every American household bears the footprints of economic and cultural trends that originate far outside its walls. A rise in inflation eroding the earning power of the male wage, an expanding service sector opening up jobs for women, and the inroads made by women into many professions—all these changes do not simply go on around the American family. They occur *within* a marriage or living-together arrangement and transform it. Problems between couples, problems that seem "unique" or "marital," are often the individual ripples of powerful economic and cultural shock waves. Quarrels between husbands and wives in households across the nation result mainly from a friction between faster-changing women and slower-changing men.

The exodus of women from the home to the workplace has not been accompanied by a new view of marriage and work that would make this transition smooth. Most workplaces have remained inflexible in the face of the changing needs of workers with families, and most men have yet to really adapt to the changes in women. I call the strain caused by the disparity between the change in women and the absence of change elsewhere the "stalled revolution."

If women begin to do less at home because they have less time, if men do little more, and if the work of raising children and tending a home requires roughly the same effort, then the questions of who does what at home and of what "needs doing" become a source of deep tension in a marriage.

Over the past 30 years in the United States, more and more women have begun to work outside the home, and more have divorced. While some commentators conclude that women's work *causes* divorce, my research into changes in the American family suggests something else. Since all the wives in the families I studied (over an eight-year period) worked outside the home, the fact that they worked did not account for why some marriages were happy and others were not. What *did* contribute to happiness was the husband's willingness to do the work at home. Whether they were traditional or more egalitarian in their relationship, couples were happier when the men did a sizable share of housework and child care.

In one study of 600 couples filing for divorce, researcher George 5 Levinger found that the second most common reason women cited for wanting to divorce—after "mental cruelty"—was their husbands' "neglect of home or children." Women mentioned this reason more often than financial problems, physical abuse, drinking, or infidelity.

A happy marriage is supported by a couple's being economically secure, by their enjoying a supportive community, and by their having compatible needs and values. But these days it may also depend on a shared appreciation of the work it takes to nurture others. As the role of the homemaker is being abandoned by many women, the homemaker's work has been continually devalued and passed on to low-paid housekeepers, baby-sitters, or day-care workers. Long devalued by men, the contribution of cooking, cleaning, and care-giving is now being devalued as mere drudgery by many women, too.

In the era of the stalled revolution, one way to make housework and child care more valued is for men to share in that work. Many working mothers are already doing all they can at home. Now it's time for men to make the move.

If more mothers of young children are working at full-time jobs outside the home, and if most couples can't afford household help, who's doing the work at home? Adding together the time it takes to do a paid job and to do housework and child care and using estimates from major studies on time use done in the 1960s and 1970s, I found that women worked roughly 15 more hours each week than men. Over a year, they worked an extra month of 24-hour days. Over a dozen years, it was an extra year of 24-hour days. Most women without children spend much more time than men on housework. Women with children devote more time to both housework and child care. Just as there is a wage gap between men and women in the workplace, there is a "leisure gap" between them at home. Most women work one shift at the office or factory and a "second shift" at home.

In my research, I interviewed and observed 52 couples over an eight-year period as they cooked dinner, shopped, bathed their children, and in general struggled to find enough time to make their complex lives work. The women I interviewed seemed to be far more deeply torn between the demands of work and family than were their husbands. They talked more about the abiding conflict between work and family. They felt the second shift was *their* issue, and most of their husbands agreed. When I telephoned one husband to arrange an interview with him, explaining that I wanted to ask him how he managed work and family life, he replied genially, "Oh, this will *really* interest my *wife.*"

Men who shared the load at home seemed just as pressed for time as their wives, and as torn between the demands of career and small children. But of the men I surveyed, the majority did not share the load at home. Some refused outright. Others refused more passively, often offering a loving shoulder to lean on, or an understanding ear, as their working wife faced the conflict they both saw as hers. At first it seemed to me that the problem of the second shift *was* hers. But I came to realize that those husbands who helped very little at home were often just as deeply affected as their wives—through the resentment their wives felt toward them and through their own need to steel themselves against that resentment.

A clear example of this phenomenon is Evan Holt, a warehouse furniture salesman who did very little housework and played with his four-year-old son, Joey, only at his convenience. His wife, Nancy, did the second shift, but she resented it keenly and half-consciously expressed her frustration and rage by losing interest in sex and becoming overly absorbed in Joey.

Even when husbands happily shared the work, their wives *felt* more responsible for home and children. More women than men kept track of doctor's appointments and arranged for kids' playmates to come over. More mothers than fathers worried about a child's Halloween costume or a birthday present for a school friend. They were more likely to think about their children while at work and to check in by phone with the baby-sitter.

Partly because of this, more women felt torn between two kinds of urgency, between the need to soothe a child's fear of being left at day-care and the need to show the boss she's "serious" at work. Twenty percent of the men in my study shared housework equally. Seventy percent did a substantial amount (less than half of it, but more than a third), and 10 percent did less than a third. But even when couples more equitably share the work at home, women do two thirds of the daily jobs at home, such as cooking and cleaning up—jobs that fix them into a rigid routine. Most women cook dinner, for instance, while men change the oil in the family car. But, as one mother pointed out, dinner needs to be prepared every evening around six o'clock, whereas the car oil needs to be changed every six months, with no particular deadline. Women do more child care than men, and men repair more household appliances. A child needs to be tended to daily, whereas the repair of household appliances can often wait, said the men, "until I have time." Men thus have more control over

10

when they make their contributions than women do. They may be very busy with family chores, but, like the executive who tells his secretary to "hold my calls," the man has more control over his time.

Another reason why women may feel under more strain than men is that women more often do two things at once—for example, write checks and return phone calls, vacuum and keep an eye on a three-year-old, fold laundry and think out the shopping list. Men more often will either cook dinner *or* watch the kids. Women more often do both at the same time.

Beyond doing more at home, women also devote proportionately more of their time at home to housework than men and proportionately less of it to child care. Of all the time men spend working at home, a growing amount of it goes to child care. Since most parents prefer to tend to their children than to clean house, men do more of what they'd rather do. More men than women take their children on "fun" outings to the park, the zoo, the movies. Women spend more time on maintenance, such as feeding and bathing children—enjoyable activities, to be sure, but often less leisurely or "special" than going to the zoo. Men also do fewer of the most undesirable household chores, such as scrubbing the toilet.

As a result, women tend to talk more intensely about being over-tired, sick, and emotionally drained. Many women interviewed were fixated on the topic of sleep. They talked about how much they could "get by on": six and a half, seven, seven and a half, less, more. They talked about who they knew who needed more or less. Some apolo-gized for how much sleep they needed—"I'm afraid I need eight hours of sleep"—as if eight was "too much." They talked about how to avoid fully waking up when a child called them at night, and how to get back to sleep. These women talked about sleep the way a hungry person talks about food.

If, all in all, the two-job family is suffering from a speedup of work and family life, working mothers are its primary victims. It is ironic, then, that often it falls to women to be the time-and-motion experts of family life. As I observed families inside their homes, I noticed it was often the mother who rushed children, saying, "Hurry up! It's time to go." "Finish your cereal now," "You can do that later," or "Let's go!" When a bath needed to be crammed into a slot between 7:45 and 8:00, it was often the mother who called out. "Let's see who can take their bath the quickest!" Often a younger child would rush out, scurrying to be first in bed, while the older and wiser one stalled, resistant, sometimes resentful: "Mother is always rushing us." Sadly, women are more often the lightning rods for family tensions aroused by this speedup of work and family life. They are the villains in a process in which they are also the primary victims. More than the longer hours and the lack of sleep, this is the saddest cost to women of their extra month of work each year.

Raising children in a nuclear family is still the overwhelming prefer-ence of most people. Yet in the face of new problems for this family model we have not created an adequate support system so that the nuclear family can do its job well in the era of the two-career couple. Corporations have done little to accommodate the needs of working parents, and the government has done little to prod them.

We really need, as sociologist Frank Furstenberg has suggested, a Marshall Plan for the family. After World War II we saw that it was in our best interests to aid the war-torn nations of Europe. Now—it seems obvious in an era of growing concern over drugs, crime, and family instability—it is in our best interests to aid the overworked two-job families right here at home. We should look to other nations for a model of what could be done. In Sweden, for example, upon the birth of a child every working couple is entitled to 12 months of paid parental leave—nine months at 90 percent of the worker's salary, plus an additional three months at about three hundred dollars a month. The mother and father are free to divide this year off between them as they wish. Working parents of a child under eight have the opportunity to work no more than six hours a day, at six hours' pay. Parental insurance offers parents money for work time lost while visiting a child's school or caring for a sick child. That's a true pro-family policy.

A pro-family policy in the United States could give tax breaks to companies that encourage job sharing, part-time work, flex time, and family leave for new parents. By implementing comparable worth policies we could increase pay scales for "women's" jobs. Another key element of a pro-family policy would be instituting fewer-hour, more flexible options—called "family phases"—for all regular jobs filled by parents of young children.

Day-care centers could be made more warm and creative through generous public and private funding. If the best form of day-care comes from the attention of elderly neighbors, students, or grandparents, these people could be paid to care for children through social programs.

In these ways, the American government would create a safer environment for the two-job family. If the government encouraged corporations to consider the long-range interests of workers and their families, they would save on long-range costs caused by absenteeism, turnover, juvenile delinquency, mental illness, and welfare support for single mothers.

These are real pro-family reforms. If they seem utopian today, we should remember that in the past the eight-hour day, the abolition of child labor, and the vote for women seemed utopian, too. Among top-rated employers listed in *The 100 Best Companies to Work for in America* are many offering country-club memberships, first-class air travel, and million-dollar fitness centers. But only a handful offer job sharing, flex time, or part-time work. Not one provides on-site day-care, and only three offer child-care deductions: Control Data, Polaroid, and Honeywell. In his book *Megatrends*, John Naisbitt reports that 83 percent of corporate executives believed that more men feel the need to share the responsibilities of parenting; yet only 9 percent of corporations offer paternity leave.

Public strategies are linked to private ones. Economic and cultural trends bear on family relations in ways it would be useful for all of us to understand. The happiest two-job marriages I saw during my research were ones in which men and women shared the housework and parenting. What couples called good communication often meant that they were good at saying thanks to one another for small aspects of taking care of the family. Making it to the school play, helping a child read, cooking dinner in good spirit, remembering the grocery list, taking responsibility for cleaning up the bedrooms—these were the silver and gold of the marital exchange. Until now, couples committed to an equal sharing of housework and child care have been rare. But, if we as a culture come to see the urgent need of meeting the new problems posed by the second shift, and if society and government begin to shape new policies that allow working parents more flexibility, then we will be making some progress toward happier times at home and work. And as the young learn by example, many more women and men will be able to enjoy the pleasure that arises when family life is family life, and not a second shift.

Joining the Conversation: Critical Thinking and Writing

1. Here is Hochschild's opening sentence: "Every American household bears the footprints of economic and cultural trends that originate far outside its walls." Explain what Hochschild means and then, using the household you know best, test the truth of Hochschild's sentence.

2. What does Hochschild mean by the phrase "stalled revolution"?

3. Hochschild writes that "most workplaces have remained inflexible in the face of the changing needs of workers with families" (second paragraph). Assuming that he is correct, why do you think this is so?

4. The rest of the sentence we just quoted is "and most men have yet to really adapt to the changes in women." To what changes does he refer? And do you think he is right? If so, how do you account for the failure of men to adapt?

5. According to Hochschild, women "are the villains in a process in which they are also the primary victims." What does he mean? In your own experience, have you been aware that women have been cast as the villains?

6. Hochschild lists conditions in Sweden for working families and refers to them as a "pro-family policy." What are some of the conditions? Why, in your opinion, does a similar pro-family policy not exist in the United States?

7. In your own family, what was the division of labor for raising children and doing household chores? Who did what (and how often)? Write a brief essay (500–750 words) in which you reveal both the division of labor and your attitude toward it.

A Debate (Two Arguments) for Analysis

Andrew Sullivan versus William J. Bennett

Andrew Sullivan

Andrew Sullivan grew up in England, but he earned a doctorate in government at Harvard University. Sullivan for several years served as the editor of the New Republic, *where the following essay was originally published in 1989.*

Here Comes the Groom

A (Conservative) Case for Gay Marriage

Last month in New York, a court ruled that a gay lover had the right to stay in his deceased partner's rent-control apartment because the lover qualified as a member of the deceased's family. The ruling deftly annoyed almost everybody. Conservatives saw judicial activism in favor of gay rent control: three reasons to be appalled. Chastened liberals (such as the *New York Times* editorial page), while endorsing the recognition of gay relationships, also worried about the abuse of already stretched entitlements that the ruling threatened. What neither side quite contemplated is that they both might be right, and that the way to tackle the issue of unconventional relationships in conventional society is to try something both more radical and more conservative than putting courts in the business of deciding what is and is not a family. That alternative is the legalization of civil gay marriage.

The New York rent-control case did not go anywhere near that far, which is the problem. The rent-control regulations merely stipulated that a "family" member had the right to remain in the apartment. The judge ruled that to all intents and purposes a gay lover is part of his lover's family, inasmuch as a "family" merely means an interwoven social life, emotional commitment, and some level of financial interdependence.

It's a principle now well established around the country. Several cities have "domestic partnership" laws, which allow relationships that do not fit into the category of heterosexual marriage to be registered with the city and qualify for benefits that up till now have been reserved for straight married couples. San Francisco, Berkeley, Madison, and Los Angeles all have legislation, as does the politically correct Washington, D.C. suburb, Takoma Park. In these cities, a variety of interpersonal arrangements qualify for health insurance, bereavement leave, insurance, annuity and pension rights, housing rights (such as rent-control apartments), adoption and inheritance rights. Eventually, according to gay lobby groups, the aim is to include federal income tax and veterans' benefits as well. A recent

---

Andrew Sullivan, "Here Comes the Groom: A (Conservative) Case for Gay Marriage," the *New Republic*, August 28, 1989. Reprinted by permission.

case even involved the right to use a family member's accumulated frequent-flier points. Gays are not the only beneficiaries; heterosexual "live-togethers" also qualify.

There's an argument, of course, that the current legal advantages extended to married people unfairly discriminate against people who've shaped their lives in less conventional arrangements. But it doesn't take a genius to see that enshrining in the law a vague principle like "domestic partnership" is an invitation to qualify at little personal cost for a vast array of entitlements otherwise kept crudely under control.

To be sure, potential DPs have to prove financial interdependence, shared living arrangements, and a commitment to mutual caring. But they don't need to have a sexual relationship or even closely mirror old-style marriage. In principle, an elderly woman and her live-in nurse could qualify. A couple of uneuphemistically confirmed bachelors could be DPs. So could two close college students, a pair of seminarians, or a couple of frat buddies. Left as it is, the concept of domestic partnership could open a Pandora's box of litigation and subjective judicial decision-making about who qualifies. You either are or are not married; it's not a complex question. Whether you are in a "domestic partnership" is not so clear.

More important, the concept of domestic partnership chips away at the prestige of traditional relationships and undermines the priority we give them. This priority is not necessarily a product of heterosexism. Consider heterosexual couples. Society has good reason to extend legal advantages to heterosexuals who choose the formal sanction of marriage over simply living together. They make a deeper commitment to one another and to society; in exchange, society extends certain benefits to them. Marriage provides an anchor, if an arbitrary and weak one, in the chaos of sex and relationships to which we are all prone. It provides a mechanism for emotional stability, economic security, and the healthy rearing of the next generation. We rig the law in its favor not because we disparage all forms of relationships other than the nuclear family, but because we recognize that not to promote marriage would be to ask too much of human virtue. In the context of the weakened family's effect upon the poor, it might also invite social disintegration. One of the worst products of the New Right's "family values" campaign is that its extremism and hatred of diversity has disguised this more measured and more convincing case for the importance of the marital bond.

The concept of domestic partnership ignores these concerns, indeed directly attacks them. This is a pity, since one of its most important objectives—providing some civil recognition for gay relationships—is a noble cause and one completely compatible with the defense of the family. But the way to go about it is not to undermine straight marriage; it is to legalize old-style marriage for gays.

The gay movement has ducked this issue primarily out of fear of division. Much of the gay leadership clings to notions of gay life as essentially outsider, antibourgeois, radical. Marriage, for them, is co-optation into straight society. For the Stonewall[1] generation, it is hard to see how this vision of conflict will ever fundamentally change. But for many other gays—my guess, a majority—while they don't deny the importance of rebellion twenty years ago and are grateful for what was done, there's now the sense of a new opportunity. A need to rebel has quietly ceded to a desire to belong. To be gay and to be bourgeois no longer seems such an absurd proposition. Certainly since AIDS, to be gay and to be responsible has become a necessity.

Gay marriage squares several circles at the heart of the domestic partnership debate. Unlike domestic partnership, it allows for recognition of gay relationships, while casting no aspersions on traditional marriage. It merely asks that gays be allowed to join in. Unlike domestic partnership, it doesn't open up avenues for heterosexuals to get benefits without the responsibilities of marriage, or a nightmare of definitional litigation. And unlike domestic partnership, it harnesses to an already established social convention the yearnings for stability and acceptance among a fast-maturing gay community.

Gay marriage also places more responsibilities upon gays: It says for the first time that gay relationships are not better or worse than straight relationships, and that the same is expected of them. And it's clear and dignified. There's a legal benefit to a clear, common symbol of commitment. There's also a personal benefit. One of the ironies of domestic partnership is that it's not only more complicated than marriage, it's more demanding, requiring an elaborate statement of intent to qualify. It amounts to a substantial invasion of privacy. Why, after all, should gays be required to prove commitment before they get married in a way we would never dream of asking of straights?

Legalizing gay marriage would offer homosexuals the same deal society now offers heterosexuals: general social approval and specific legal advantages in exchange for a deeper and harder-to-extract-yourself-from commitment to another human being. Like straight marriage, it would foster social cohesion, emotional security, and economic prudence. Since there's no reason gays should not be allowed to adopt or be foster parents, it could also help nurture children. And its introduction would not be some sort of radical break with social custom. As it has become more acceptable for gay people to acknowledge their loves publicly, more and more have committed themselves to one another for life in full view of their families and their friends. A law institutionalizing gay marriage would merely reinforce a healthy social trend. It would also, in the wake of AIDS, qualify as a genuine public health measure. Those conservatives who deplore promiscuity

10

[1]The Stonewall Inn was a gay bar in New York City. When the police closed it in June 1966, the gays did not submit (as they had done in the past) but attacked the police. The event is regarded as a turning point in gay history. (All notes are by the editors.)

among some homosexuals should be among the first to support it. Burke[2] could have written a powerful case for it.

The argument that gay marriage would subtly undermine the unique legitimacy of straight marriage is based upon a fallacy. For heterosexuals, straight marriage would remain the most significant—and only legal—social bond. Gay marriage could only delegitimize straight marriage if it were a real alternative to it, and this is clearly not true. To put it bluntly, there's precious little evidence that straights could be persuaded by any law to have sex with—let alone marry—someone of their own sex. The only possible effect of this sort would be to persuade gay men and women who force themselves into heterosexual marriage (often at appalling cost to themselves and their families) to find a focus for their family instincts in a more personally positive environment. But this is clearly a plus, not a minus: Gay marriage could both avoid a lot of tortured families and create the possibility for many happier ones. It is not, in short, a denial of family values. It's an extension of them.

Of course, some would claim that any legal recognition of homosexuality is a de facto attack upon heterosexuality. But even the most hardened conservatives recognize that gays are a permanent minority and aren't likely to go away. Since persecution is not an option in a civilized society, why not coax gays into traditional values rather than rail incoherently against them?

There's a less elaborate argument for gay marriage: It's good for gays. It provides role models for young gay people who, after the exhilaration of coming out, can easily lapse into short-term relationships and insecurity with no tangible goal in sight. My own guess is that most gays would embrace such a goal with as much (if not more) commitment as straights. Even in our society as it is, many lesbian relationships are virtual textbook cases of monogamous commitment. Legal gay marriage could also help bridge the gulf often found between gays and their parents. It could bring the essence of gay life—a gay couple—into the heart of the traditional straight family in a way the family can most understand and the gay off-spring can most easily acknowledge. It could do as much to heal the gay-straight rift as any amount of gay rights legislation.

If these arguments sound socially conservative, that's no accident. It's   15
one of the richest ironies of our society's blind spot toward gays that essentially conservative social goals should have the appearance of being so radical. But gay marriage is not a radical step. It avoids the mess of domestic partnership: it is humane; it is conservative in the best sense of the word. It's also practical. Given the fact that we already allow legal gay relationships, what possible social goal is advanced by framing the law to encourage those relationships to be unfaithful, undeveloped, and insecure?

[2]Edmund Burke (1729–97), conservative British politician.

Joining the Conversation:
Critical Thinking and Writing

1. In his second paragraph Sullivan summarizes a judge's definition of a family. How satisfactory do you find the definition? Explain.

2. What is "conservative"—Sullivan's word, in his title—about this case for gay and lesbian marriages?

3. A common argument in support of the financial privileges that the state awards to the traditional family is that it is in the state's interest for children to be brought up by adults committed to each other. However, divorce is now common, and, of course, many married couples do not have children, for one reason or another. Can any justification, then, be offered for allowing a spouse—but not an unmarried heterosexual or homosexual lover—to inherit without payment of taxes the partner's share of property jointly held?

4. In Sullivan's view why is marriage better than mere cohabitation? What is your view of this matter?

5. In paragraph 11 Sullivan says that "there's no reason gays should not be allowed to adopt or be foster parents." This issue is highly controversial. Construct the strongest argument you can, on one side or the other. (Remember, a strong argument faces the opposing arguments.)

6. In his next-to-last paragraph Sullivan says that "legal gay marriage could also help bridge the gulf often found between gays and their parents." If you are aware of gays who are separated from their parents by a "gulf," do you think that legal marriage might reduce that gulf? Explain.

William J. Bennett

William J. Bennett, born in 1943, served as U.S. Secretary of Education under President Ronald Reagan and as "Drug Czar" under the first President Bush. He is a popular author and speaker and the host of a weekday radio program, Morning in America.

Gay Marriage: Not a Very Good Idea

We are engaged in a debate which, in a less confused time, would be considered pointless and even oxymoronic: the question of same-sex marriage.

Now, anyone who has known someone who has struggled with his homosexuality can appreciate the poignancy, human pain and sense of

---

William J. Bennett, "Gay Marriage: Not a Very Good Idea" published in the *Washington Post*, May 21, 1996. Reprinted by permission of the author.

exclusion that are often involved. One can therefore understand the effort to achieve for homosexual unions both legal recognition and social acceptance. Advocates of homosexual marriages even make what appears to be a sound conservative argument: Allow marriage in order to promote faithfulness and monogamy. This is an intelligent and politically shrewd argument. One can even concede that it might benefit some people. But I believe that overall, allowing same-sex marriages would do significant, long-term social damage.

Recognizing the legal union of gay and lesbian couples would represent a profound change in the meaning and definition of marriage. Indeed, it would be the most radical step ever taken in the deconstruction of society's most important institution. It is not a step we ought to take.

The function of marriage is not elastic; the institution is already fragile enough. Broadening its definition to include same-sex marriages would stretch it almost beyond recognition—and new attempts to broaden the definition still further would surely follow. On what principled grounds could the advocates of same-sex marriage oppose the marriage of two consenting brothers? How could they explain why we ought to deny a marriage license to a bisexual who wants to marry two people? After all, doing so would be a denial of that person's sexuality. In our time, there are more (not fewer) reasons than ever to preserve the essence of marriage.

Marriage is not an arbitrary construct; it is an "honorable estate" based on the different, complementary nature of men and women—and how they refine, support, encourage and complete one another. To insist that we maintain this traditional understanding of marriage is not an attempt to put others down. It is simply an acknowledgment and celebration of our most precious and important social act.   5

Nor is this view arbitrary or idiosyncratic. It mirrors the accumulated wisdom of millennia and the teaching of every major religion. Among worldwide cultures, where there are so few common threads, it is not a coincidence that marriage is almost universally recognized as an act meant to unite a man and a woman.

To say that same-sex unions are not comparable to heterosexual marriages is not an argument for intolerance, bigotry or lack of compassion (although I am fully aware that it will be considered so by some). But it is an argument for making distinctions in law about relationships that are themselves distinct.

Even Andrew Sullivan,[1] among the most intelligent advocates of same-sex marriage, has admitted that a homosexual marriage contract will entail a greater understanding of the need for "extramarital outlets." He argues that gay male relationships are served by the "openness of the contract," and he has written that homosexuals should resist allowing their "varied and complicated lives" to be flattened into a "single, moralistic model."

---

[1]Editors note: We include an essay by Sullivan, but Bennett is referring to other comments by Sullivan.

But this "single, moralistic model" is precisely the point. The marriage commitment between a man and a woman does not—it cannot—countenance extramarital outlets. By definition it is not an open contract; its essential idea is fidelity. Obviously that is not always honored in practice. But it is normative, the ideal to which we aspire precisely because we believe some things are right (faithfulness in marriage) and others are wrong (adultery). In insisting that marriage accommodate the less restrained sexual practices of homosexuals, Sullivan and his allies destroy the very thing that supposedly has drawn them to marriage in the first place.

There are other arguments to consider against same-sex marriage— 10 for example, the signals it would send, and the impact of such signals on the shaping of human sexuality, particularly among the young. Former Harvard professor E. L. Pattullo has written that "a very substantial number of people are born with the potential to live either straight or gay lives." Societal indifference about heterosexuality and homosexuality would cause a lot of confusion. A remarkable 1993 article in *The Post* supports this point. Fifty teenagers and dozens of school counselors and parents from the local area were interviewed. According to the article, teenagers said it has become "cool" for students to proclaim they are gay or bisexual—even for same who are not. Not surprisingly, the caseload of teenagers in "sexual identity crisis" doubled in one year. "Everything is front page, gay and homosexual," according to one psychologist who works with the schools. "Kids are jumping on it . . . [counselors] are saying, 'What are we going to do with all these kids proclaiming they are bisexual or homosexual when we know they are not?' "

If the law recognizes homosexual marriages as the legal equivalent of heterosexual marriages, it will have enormous repercussions in many areas. Consider just two: sex education in the schools and adoption. The sex education curriculum of public schools would have to teach that heterosexual and homosexual marrige are equivalent. *Heather Has Two Mommies* would no longer be regarded as an anomaly; it would more likely become a staple of a sex education curriculum. Parents who want their children to be taught (for both moral and utilitarian reasons) the privileged status of heterosexual marriage will be portrayed as intolerant bigots; they will necessarily be at odds with the new law of matrimony and its derivative curriculum.

Homosexual couples will also have equal claim with heterosexual couples in adopting children, forcing us (in law at least) to deny what we know to be true: that it is far better for a child to be raised by a mother and a father than by, say, two male homosexuals.

The institution of marriage is already reeling because of the effects of the sexual revolution, no-fault divorce and out-of-wedlock births. We have reaped the consequences of its devaluation. It is exceedingly imprudent to conduct a radical, untested and inherently flawed social experiment on an institution that is the keystone in the arch of civilization. That we have to debate this issue at all tells us that the arch has slipped. Getting it firmly back in place is, as the lawyers say, a "compelling state interest."

⟡ Joining the Conversation:
Critical Thinking and Writing

1. Evaluate Bennett's first paragraph as an opening paragraph. What does it do, and how effectively does it do it?

2. At the end of the second paragraph Bennett says he believes that "allowing same-sex marriage would do significant, long-term social damage." Putting aside whatever views you held before reading Bennett's essay, do you think his essay offers convincing evidence to support his view? Explain your answer.

3. In paragraph 4 Bennett speaks of "the function of marriage." What, in your view, is the function (or are the functions) of marriage?

4. In paragraph 10 Bennett sets forth his view of an undesirable consequence of same-sex marriage. How convincing do you find his point? Why?

5. In paragraph 11 Bennett sets forth what he takes to be another undesirable consequence. Suppose someone replied that research does *not* demonstrate that children raised by homosexual couples are at a disadvantage. What might Bennett reply? What is your own reply?

6. In his final paragraph Bennett says, "The institution of marriage is already reeling because of the effects of the sexual revolution, no-fault divorce and out-of-wedlock births." Could one argue that Bennett's very statement can be used *against* his argument? That is, can one use this statement to point out that despite the talk about "the accumulated wisdom of millennia" and "the teaching of every major religion" (paragraph 5), marriage as we have known it is in bad shape and needs to be rethought?

Judy Brady

Born in San Francisco in 1937, Judy Brady married in 1960 and two years later earned a bachelor's degree in painting at the University of Iowa. Active in the women's movement and in other political causes, she has worked as an author, an editor, and a secretary. The essay reprinted here, written before she and her husband separated, appeared originally in the first issue of Ms. *in 1972, when the author used her married name, Judy Syfers.*

I Want a Wife

I belong to that classification of people known as wives. I am A Wife. And, not altogether incidentally, I am a mother.

Not too long ago a male friend of mine appeared on the scene fresh from a recent divorce. He had one child, who is, of course, with his ex-wife. He is looking for another wife. As I thought about him while I was ironing one evening, it suddenly occurred to me that I, too, would like to have a wife. Why do I want a wife?

I would like to go back to school so that I can become economically independent, support myself, and, if need be, support those dependent upon me. I want a wife who will work and send me to school. And while I am going to school I want a wife to take care of my children. I want a wife to keep track of the children's doctor and dentist appointments. And to keep track of mine, too. I want a wife to make sure my children eat properly and are kept clean. I want a wife who will wash the children's clothes and keep them mended. I want a wife who is a good nurturant attendant to my children, who arranges for their schooling, makes sure that they have an adequate social life with their peers, takes them to the park, the zoo, etc. I want a wife who takes care of the children when they are sick, a wife who arranges to be around when the children need special care, because, of course, I cannot miss classes at school. My wife must arrange to lose time at work and not lose the job. It may mean a small cut in my wife's income from time to time, but I guess I can tolerate that. Needless to say, my wife will arrange and pay for the care of the children while my wife is working.

I want a wife who will take care of *my* physical needs. I want a wife who will keep my house clean. A wife who will pick up after my children, a wife who will pick up after me. I want a wife who will keep my clothes clean, ironed, mended, replaced when need be, and who will see to it that my personal things are kept in their proper place so that I can find what I need the minute I need it. I want a wife who cooks the meals, a wife who is a *good* cook. I want a wife who will plan the menus, do the necessary grocery shopping, prepare the meals, serve them pleasantly, and then do the cleaning up while I do my studying. I want a wife who will care for me when I am sick and sympathize with my pain and loss of time from school. I want a wife to go along when our family takes a vacation so that someone can continue to care for me and my children when I need a rest and change of scene.

I want a wife who will not bother me with rambling complaints about a wife's duties. But I want a wife who will listen to me when I feel the need to explain a rather difficult point I have come across in my course of studies. And I want a wife who will type my papers for me when I have written them.

I want a wife who will take care of the details of my social life. When my wife and I are invited out by my friends, I want a wife who will take care of the babysitting arrangements. When I meet people at school that I like and want to entertain, I want a wife who will have the house clean, will prepare a special meal, serve it to me and my friends, and not interrupt when I talk about things that interest me and my friends. I want a wife who will have arranged that the children are fed and ready for bed before my guests arrive so that the children do not bother us. I want a wife who takes care of the needs of my guests so that they feel comfortable, who makes sure that they have an ashtray, that they are passed the hors d'oeuvres, that they are

5

offered a second helping of the food, that their wine glasses are replenished when necessary, that their coffee is served to them as they like it. And I want a wife who knows that sometimes I need a night out by myself.

I want a wife who is sensitive to my sexual needs, a wife who makes love passionately and eagerly when I feel like it, a wife who makes sure that I am satisfied. And, of course, I want a wife who will not demand sexual attention when I am not in the mood for it. I want a wife who assumes the complete responsibility for birth control, because I do not want more children. I want a wife who will remain sexually faithful to me so that I do not have to clutter up my intellectual life with jealousies. And I want a wife who understands that *my* sexual needs may entail more than strict adherence to monogamy. I must, after all, be able to relate to people as fully as possible.

If, by chance, I find another person more suitable as a wife than the wife I already have, I want the liberty to replace my present wife with another one. Naturally, I will expect a fresh, new life; my wife will take the children and be solely responsible for them so that I am left free.

When I am through with school and have a job, I want my wife to quit working and remain at home so that my wife can more fully and completely take care of a wife's duties.

My God, who *wouldn't* want a wife?   10

ℛ Joining the Conversation: Critical Thinking and Writing

1. Brady uses the word "wife" in sentences where one ordinarily would use "she" or "her." Why? And why does she begin paragraphs 4, 5, 6, and 7 with the same words, "I want a wife"?

2. Drawing on your experience as observer of the world around you (and perhaps as husband, wife, or ex-spouse), do you think Brady's picture of a wife's role is grossly exaggerated? Or is it (allowing for some serious playfulness) fairly accurate, even though it was written in 1971? If grossly exaggerated, is the essay therefore meaningless? If fairly accurate, what attitudes and practices does it encourage you to support? Explain.

3. Whether or not you agree with Brady's vision of marriage in our society, write an essay (500 words) titled "I Want a Husband," imitating her style and approach. Write the best possible essay, and then decide which of the two essays makes a fairer comment on current society. Or, if you believe Brady is utterly misleading, write an essay titled "I Want a Wife," seeing the matter in a different light.

4. If you feel that you have been pressed into an unappreciated, unreasonable role—built-in babysitter, listening post, or girl (or boy or man or woman) Friday—write an essay of 500 words that will help the reader to see both your plight and the injustice of the system. (*Hint:* A little humor will help to keep your essay from seeming to be a prolonged whine.)

Black Elk

Black Elk, a wichasha wakon *(holy man) of the Oglala Sioux, as a small boy witnessed the bat-tle of the Little Bighorn (1876). He lived to see his people all but annihilated and his hopes for them extinguished. In 1931, toward the end of his life, he told his life story to the poet and scholar John G. Neihardt to preserve a sacred vision given him.*

"High Horse's Courting" is a comic interlude in Black Elk Speaks, *a predominantly tragic memoir.*

High Horse's Courting

You know, in the old days, it was not very easy to get a girl when you wanted to be married. Sometimes it was hard work for a young man and he had to stand a great deal. Say I am a young man and I have seen a young girl who looks so beautiful to me that I feel all sick when I think about her. I cannot just go and tell her about it and then get married if she is willing. I have to be a very sneaky fellow to talk to her at all, and after I have managed to talk to her, that is only the beginning.

Probably for a long time I have been feeling sick about a certain girl because I love her so much, but she will not even look at me, and her parents keep a good watch over her. But I keep feeling worse and worse all the time; so maybe I sneak up to her tepee in the dark and wait until she comes out. Maybe I just wait there all night and don't get any sleep at all and she does not come out. Then I feel sicker than ever about her.

Maybe I hide in the brush by a spring where she sometimes goes to get water, and when she comes by, if nobody is looking, then I jump out and hold her and just make her listen to me. If she likes me too, I can tell that from the way she acts, for she is very bashful and maybe will not say a word or even look at me the first time. So I let her go, and then maybe I sneak around until I can see her father alone, and I tell him how many horses I can give him for his beautiful girl, and by now I am feeling so sick that maybe I would give him all the horses in the world if I had them.

Well, this young man I am telling about was called High Horse, and there was a girl in the village who looked so beautiful to him that he was just sick all over from thinking about her so much and he was getting sicker all the time. The girl was very shy, and her parents thought a great deal of her because they were not young any more and this was the only child they had. So they watched her all day long, and they fixed it so that she would be safe at night too when they were asleep. They thought so much of her that they had made a rawhide bed for her to sleep in, and

---

after they knew that High Horse was sneaking around after her, they took rawhide thongs and tied the girl in bed at night so that nobody could steal her when they were asleep, for they were not sure but that their girl might really want to be stolen.

Well, after High Horse had been sneaking around a good while and hiding and waiting for the girl and getting sicker all the time, he finally caught her alone and made her talk to him. Then he found out that she liked him maybe a little. Of course this did not make him feel well. It made him sicker than ever, but now he felt as brave as a bison bull, and so he went right to her father and said he loved the girl so much that he would give two good horses for her—one of them young and the other one not so very old.

But the old man just waved his hand, meaning for High Horse to go away and quit talking foolishness like that.

High Horse was feeling sicker than ever about it; but there was another young fellow who said he would loan High Horse two ponies and when he got some more horses, why, he could just give them back for the ones he had borrowed.

Then High Horse went back to the old man and said he would give four horses for the girl—two of them young and the other two not hardly old at all. But the old man just waved his hand and would not say anything.

So High Horse sneaked around until he could talk to the girl again, and he asked her to run away with him. He told her he thought he would just fall over and die if she did not. But she said she would not do that; she wanted to be bought like a fine woman. You see she thought a great deal of herself too.

That made High Horse feel so very sick that he could not eat a bite, and he went around with his head hanging down as though he might just fall down and die any time.

Red Deer was another young fellow, and he and High Horse were great comrades, always doing things together. Red Deer saw how High Horse was acting, and he said: "Cousin, what is the matter? Are you sick in the belly? You look as though you were going to die."

Then High Horse told Red Deer how it was, and said he thought he could not stay alive much longer if he could not marry the girl pretty quick.

Red Deer thought awhile about it, and then he said: "Cousin, I have a plan, and if you are man enough to do as I tell you, then everything will be all right. She will not run away with you; her old man will not take four horses; and four horses are all you can get. You must steal her and run away with her. Then afterwhile you can come back and the old man cannot do anything because she will be your woman. Probably she wants you to steal her anyway."

So they planned what High Horse had to do, and he said he loved the girl so much that he was man enough to do anything Red Deer or anybody else could think up. So this is what they did.

5

10

That night late they sneaked up to the girl's tepee and waited until it   15
sounded inside as though the old man and the old woman and the girl
were sound asleep. Then High Horse crawled under the tepee with a
knife. He had to cut the rawhide thongs first, and then Red Deer, who
was pulling up the stakes around that side of the tepee, was going to help
drag the girl outside and gag her. After that, High Horse could put her
across his pony in front of him and hurry out of there and be happy all
the rest of his life.

When High Horse had crawled inside, he felt so nervous that he
could hear his heart drumming, and it seemed so loud he felt sure it
would 'waken the old folks. But it did not, and afterwhile he began cutting the thongs. Every time he cut one it made a pop and nearly scared
him to death. But he was getting along all right and all the thongs were
cut down as far as the girl's thighs, when he became so nervous that his
knife slipped and stuck the girl. She gave a big, loud yell. Then the old
folks jumped up and yelled too. By this time High Horse was outside,
and he and Red Deer were running away like antelope. The old man and
some other people chased the young men but they got away in the dark
and nobody knew who it was.

Well, if you ever wanted a beautiful girl you will know how sick High
Horse was now. It was very bad the way he felt, and it looked as though
he would starve even if he did not drop over dead sometime.

Red Deer kept thinking about this, and after a few days he went to
High Horse and said: "Cousin, take courage! I have another plan, and I am
sure, if you are man enough, we can steal her this time." And High Horse
said: "I am man enough to do anything anybody can think up, if I can only
get that girl."

So this is what they did.

They went away from the village alone, and Red Deer made High   20
Horse strip naked. Then he painted High Horse solid white all over, and
after that he painted black stripes all over the white and put black rings
around High Horse's eyes. High Horse looked terrible. He looked so terrible that when Red Deer was through painting and took a good look at
what he had done, he said it scared even him a little.

"Now," Red Deer said, "if you get caught again, everybody will
be so scared they will think you are a bad spirit and will be afraid to
chase you."

So when the night was getting old and everybody was sound asleep,
they sneaked back to the girl's tepee. High Horse crawled in with his
knife, as before, and Red Deer waited outside, ready to drag the girl out
and gag her when High Horse had all the thongs cut.

High Horse crept up by the girl's bed and began cutting at the thongs.
But he kept thinking, "If they see me they will shoot me because I look so
terrible." The girl was restless and kept squirming around in bed, and
when a thong was cut, it popped. So High Horse worked very slowly and
carefully.

But he must have made some noise, for suddenly the old woman awoke and said to her old man: "Old Man, wake up! There is somebody in this tepee!" But the old man was sleepy and didn't want to be bothered. He said: "Of course there is somebody in this tepee. Go to sleep and don't bother me." Then he snored some more.

But High Horse was so scared by now that he lay very still and as flat to the ground as he could. Now, you see, he had not been sleeping very well for a long time because he was so sick about the girl. And while he was lying there waiting for the old woman to snore, he just forgot everything, even how beautiful the girl was. Red Deer who was lying outside ready to do his part, wondered and wondered what had happened in there, but he did not dare call out to High Horse.

Afterwhile the day began to break and Red Deer had to leave with the two ponies he had staked there for his comrade and girl, or somebody would see him.

So he left.

Now when it was getting light in the tepee, the girl awoke and the first thing she saw was a terrible animal, all white with black stripes on it, lying asleep beside her bed. So she screamed, and then the old woman screamed and the old man yelled. High Horse jumped up, scared almost to death, and he nearly knocked the tepee down getting out of there.

People were coming running from all over the village with guns and bows and axes, and everybody was yelling.

By now High Horse was running so fast that he hardly touched the ground at all, and he looked so terrible that the people fled from him and let him run. Some braves wanted to shoot at him, but the others said he might be some sacred being and it would bring bad trouble to kill him.

High Horse made for the river that was near, and in among the brush he found a hollow tree and dived into it. Afterwhile some braves came there and he could hear them saying that it was some bad spirit that had come out of the water and gone back in again.

That morning the people were ordered to break camp and move away from there. So they did, while High Horse was hiding in his hollow tree.

Now Red Deer had been watching all this from his own tepee and trying to look as though he were as much surprised and scared as all the others. So when the camp moved, he sneaked back to where he had seen his comrade disappear. When he was down there in the brush, he called, and High Horse answered, because he knew his friend's voice. They washed off the paint from High Horse and sat down on the river bank to talk about their troubles.

High Horse said he never would go back to the village as long as he lived and he did not care what happened to him now. He said he was going to go on the war-path all by himself. Red Deer said: "No, cousin, you are not going on the war-path alone, because I am going with you."

So Red Deer got everything ready, and at night they started out on the war-path all alone. After several days they came to a Crow camp just about sundown, and when it was dark they sneaked up to where the Crow horses were grazing, killed the horse guard, who was not thinking about enemies because he thought all the Lakotas were far away, and drove off about a hundred horses.

They got a big start because all the Crow horses stampeded and it was probably morning before the Crow warriors could catch any horses to ride. Red Deer and High Horse fled with their herd three days and nights before they reached the village of their people. Then they drove the whole herd right into the village and up in front of the girl's tepee. The old man was there, and High Horse called out to him and asked if he thought maybe that would be enough horses for his girl. The old man did not wave him away that time. It was not the horses that he wanted. What he wanted was a son who was a real man and good for something.

So High Horse got his girl after all, and I think he deserved her.

 ## Joining the Conversation: Critical Thinking and Writing

Although High Horse's behavior is amusing and at times ridiculous, how does Black Elk make it clear that he is not ridiculing the young man, but is instead in sympathy with him? Consider the following questions:

1. What is the effect of the first three paragraphs? Think about the first two sentences, and then the passage beginning "Say I am a young man . . ." and ending ". . . I would give him all the horses in the world if I had them."

2. Describe the behavior of the young girl and of her father and mother. How do they contribute to the comedy? How does their behavior affect your understanding of Black Elk's attitude toward High Horse?

3. What is the function of Red Deer?

4. The narrative consists of several episodes. List them in the order in which they occur and then describe the narrative's structure. How does this structure affect the tone?

Celia E. Rothenberg

Celia E. Rothenberg graduated from Wellesley College in 1991. A history major with a special interest in the lives of Middle Eastern women, she was awarded a Marshall fellowship and studied modern Middle Eastern history at the University of Oxford. She has served as an intern in an Israeli-Palestinian women's peace group in Jerusalem, and she plans to continue working for understanding between these two groups.

Rothenberg wrote the following essay while she was an undergraduate.

Child of Divorce

Over this past winter vacation my parents, brother, and I spent a few days together—a rare event now that the four of us live in four different states. As I watched my parents and brother engage in our usual laughter and reminiscing, accompanied by an occasional tear at a past both bitter and sweet, I listened more closely than ever before to what is a frequent topic of discussion, our relationship as a family.

Perhaps because my parents divorced when I was a small child, it seems to surprise my friends that my family's recollections of those years are filled with many pleasant memories. After all, those who don't know my family have reason to assume that the memories of growing up with divorced parents in some tough economic times might be rather dreary. In fact, however, my memories center on the results of the thoughtfulness and conscious effort exerted by both my parents to create a sense of love and protection for my brother and me. I have always felt that my family was a team, a team that sometimes fumbled, and sometimes seemed to have two, three, or even four captains, and a team that underwent a change in plan mid-game, but a team nevertheless. It is only recently, how-ever, that I have realized how much patience and understanding went into achieving that sense of belonging and love, and how achieving it was part of the long and often painful process for us of divorce and healing.

My parents divorced, after fifteen years of marriage, when I was six. I have nearly no memories of living in a two-parent household. From the time of my earliest memories, my mother has always studied or worked full time. Immediately after the divorce, she, like many women who find themselves single after many years as a "housewife," went back to school. My brother at the time was twelve. Although I remember my Cinderella-shaped cake for my seventh birthday, a few of my favorite pets, and a well-loved school teacher, I remember very little of my mom's return to school, or my own or brother's adjustment to our new sur-roundings. Perhaps the gaps in my memory serve as some kind of mental defense mechanism to protect me from the reality of the harder times; no matter the reason for my memory voids, however, my brother's recollec-tions are so vivid, and my mom and dad so open about those years, that my scattered memories have been augmented by their story-telling—to the point that I often confuse my memories with theirs.

It is only recently, in fact, that I have realized how difficult the initial years following the divorce were for my mother, brother and father. Over this past winter vacation, my mom told me for the first time how taxing even the simplest tasks seemed to be. For example, locking the doors to our new, small house conjured up all the difficulties and sad-nesses of this new beginning. Because my dad had customarily locked

Celia E. Rothenberg, "Child of Divorce." By permission of the author.

up, she had rarely been the one to lock each lock and turn off each light. Doing these tasks in a new house in a new city was a constant reminder of her changed circumstances. Late in the evening she would carefully plot the order in which to turn off the lights, so as not to be alone in the dark. She would lock a door, and then a window, pausing in between the locks to distract her mind from the task at hand—and the frightening and lonely feelings these new responsibilities brought with them.

My family now openly recalls that those years were a difficult time of   5
adjustment to new schools, a new city, and a new life. We had moved from a small suburb of St. Louis to Champaign-Urbana, a community largely centered on the life of the University of Illinois. Our first house in Champaign and my mom's tuition for the Master's degree in Library and Information Science were largely financed by the sale of the lovely Steinway baby grand piano that had graced my parents' living room since before I was born. Before the divorce, my father was an attorney until he found himself in legal difficulties, which ultimately led him to give up the practice of law. His reduced income and my mom's tuition bills placed us under a great financial strain.

My brother, who was twelve at the time of the divorce, particularly recalls how difficult communication was between the three of us and my father, and at times even among the three of us. To help ease the tension of my dad's monthly visits and maintain a relationship which included some fun, my brother and dad played checkers through the mail. They carefully conceived of a plan of multiple paper copies of the checker board and colored pencils for their game. One of my few early memories of those years focusses on the checker board we set up on the dining room table to represent the game my brother and dad played on paper. One evening, the cat we brought with us from (as my mother often said) our "other life," jumped on the board, knocking the pieces all over the table. Steve was inconsolable, and only a prolonged long-distance phone call to figure out where each piece belonged resolved the situation.

That first year my brother escaped into a world of books, often reading fiction and plays when he should have been doing homework, a coping behavior he practiced until he was nearly through high school.

But even the deepest hurts can heal over time. With encouragement and support from both my parents, Steve channeled his considerable energy and anger into planning for an early graduation from high school and a year in Israel between high school and college. The only conditions set were that he had to earn enough money to buy his own plane ticket and he had to have a college acceptance letter in hand before he left. These goals gave him something to work for at a time when he felt that he had lost friends and status in coming to a new, very different, and less comfortable environment than had been part of his early days.

As for me, perhaps because I was six years younger, I appeared to go blithely along, oblivious to most of the tensions and strains that Steve seemed to feel. With my mother studying for her classes and Steve spending almost all his time reading, I became an avid reader myself, almost in self defense. I found new friends and reveled in my new elementary school, a magnet school where we studied French every day. I wrote long, detailed stories of a young girl who lived on a farm with both parents and a dozen brothers and sisters and a beautiful horse. Perhaps I, too, was seeking some consolation in an imaginary life far removed from our little house.

It can take years for wounds to heal, and I am happy to say that my family healed more quickly than most. Perhaps we got past that initial phase early on because my parents did not make too many mistakes. They avoided some common pitfalls of divorcing families. The divorce was quick—the process was completed a few months after my parents sold their house and moved to their new homes—there were no court battles, no screaming fights, no wrenching decisions that we children were required to make. Steve and I were never asked—or allowed—to choose sides or express a preference for one parent over the other. Although my own memories are blurry, the few recollections I have of those first five years focus on my dad's regular monthly visits (he lived a few hours away by car). By the time I was ten, he was spending nearly every weekend with us at the house, a pattern which continued for the next decade, until I was out of high school and off to Wellesley.

Nothing worthwhile, my mother has always told me, is ever easy. It could not have always been easy for either of my parents to spend so much of their free time together when they had chosen to create separate lives, but at the time Steve and I rarely saw anything but civility and fondness. As parents they were determined not to let their children suffer for mistakes they may have made in their marriage. It is one of their greatest gifts to Steve and me, for it was the ultimate lesson in learning about the commitment and cost of love and the lifelong responsibilities of family.

The stories we have accumulated over the years have become more hilarious as I have grown older. My dad, determined not to be a "Disneyland daddy," showing up on the weekends for shopping and dinners out, was not uncomfortable in our new home. In fact, he helped us figure out how to do various home improvement projects. Under his direction, we rewired our house (and nearly electrocuted Steve in the process), insulated our attic (the family story lingers that we nearly blew off the roof), and painted the house (and, of course, ourselves). Our projects probably didn't save us very much money, since we seemed to spend as much money on fixing the mistakes we made as on the project itself, yet we were not merely building the house, or growing gardens, or mowing the lawn. We were rebuilding our lives, making memories, and creating a sense of togetherness.

My own clear and more complete memories begin at the age of eleven, when my mother, brother, and I began a new life-style, which reflected a newly achieved flexibility and confidence in our ability to manage our lives. When my brother entered the University of Illinois, we moved into a big old

10

house and I began high school. The house was what a real estate broker fondly calls a "fixer-upper," and was perfect for my mom's income (she worked for the University after she finished her Master's degree) and our need for space for friends of mine and Steve's. Steve, in particular, brought home countless Jewish college students whom he knew from his involvement in the campus Jewish student organization. They often needed a good meal, a shoulder to lean on, an opinion on a paper, or a good night's sleep.

I remember our dining room on Shabbos, furnished with a dining room set probably beautiful in my grandmother's day but battered after three generations of use, packed with college students eating dinner. I remember vividly the talk and the laughter, the jesting and the endless debates. My mom was not only an intellectual support for those students but also an inspiration, someone who had experienced a marriage gone bad, the trials and tribulations of parenting alone (at least during the week), and the tough economics of a single-parent household. Conversations stretched from the abstract to the concrete, from the politics of the Eastern bloc to the intricacies of love and sex.

Over the years it has become clear that the divorce, although traumatic, opened our minds, enriched our relationships with each other, and loosened restraints we did not know we were subject to. I vividly remember my high school years as a busy time full of my friends and my brothers' who simply enjoyed being around the house. The slightly chaotic, easygoing atmosphere of the house was fostered in large part by our mom; she had disliked the isolated feeling of life in suburbia when she was married. She wanted to create a different atmosphere for Steve and me, a place where young people were comfortable to come and go.

My friends in high school were fascinated by my home, and I enjoyed it as much as they did. My dad was able to watch us grow and change from weekend to weekend, his place secure and comfortable at the head of the Shabbos table surrounded by students. He helped us with science projects, participated in countless car-pools, and, most of all, was there when we needed him. Although from the point of view of the Census Bureau we were a "single parent household," in actuality we were a *family* that happened to have divorced parents. Perhaps our experience was not typical of some families in which there has been a divorce, but the labels obscure our understanding of the needs and hopes of all families, which I think are probably the same, divorced or not. My parent's expectations for Steve and me were not altered by their marital status, nor do I think that Steve and I let them get away with very much on the excuse that they were divorced!

I have always loved my family, but I find that I admire each of them increasingly as time goes on. Now, when we gather from different corners of the country and world during vacations a few times a year, we admit that the best and the worst, but always the most precious times, were when we were together on the weekends in that big old house, sometimes with the students and sometimes with only each other. On special occasions, we have a (very patient) long-distance operator connect the four of us on the same phone line, and we talk as if there is no tomorrow. We are fiercely

15

proud of one another; I often have to restrain myself from blurting out the merits of my exceptional family to my unsuspecting friends.

At times I wonder how different we would be if we had not gone through the divorce, but for that question I can conjure up no really meaningful speculation. I know that we immensely value our time together, freely share our money (or, I should say, our student loans, as my brother is now in law school, my mom is a full-time doctoral student and my father shoulders the Wellesley burden), and exorbitantly rejoice in each other's company. What more could any of us want from family? So often, it seems to me, I see families that do not realize they possess a great wealth—time. They are together all the time. They don't miss the moments of their mother/father/brother/sister's lives that are irreplaceable.

There is no question that it is often difficult to be a family. My own family's life took a path with an unexpected curve. We weathered times of tough adjustments, economic difficulties, and typical adolescent rebellion. Through it all, though, there was a guiding (if unspoken until many years later) principle of life: family is family forever, and there is no escaping either the trials or the rewards. My parents expect my brother and me to extend ourselves and do work that in some way will bring more light into the world. I have parents who, on modest incomes and budgets, have endowed me with dreams and a sense that the impossible is possible. I have parents for whom I am extremely grateful.

When I told my family that Wellesley asked me to write an article on growing up in a single parent household, they responded in their typical chaotic fashion. My brother forced each of us to sit and write a page about the "Single-Parent Thing" before he let us eat dinner. My mother began plotting a book made up of chapters written from the different perspectives of mother, father, son, and daughter in the single-parent household. My dad insisted we discuss it over dinner (and promised to write his page immediately after dessert). In the end, I took their contributions with me back to Wellesley and wrote down my own feelings, late at night in Munger Hall.

20

Joining the Conversation: Critical Thinking and Writing

1. What are your earliest memories of your family? How would you account for the fact that Rothenberg has "nearly no memories of living in a two-parent household"?

2. Rothenberg calls her family "exceptional." What do you find to be her strongest evidence for this claim?

3. In paragraph 2 Rothenberg refers to assumptions that her friends make about a child who grew up with divorced parents. What are or were your assumptions? On what are (or were) they based?

4. A highly personal essay runs the risk of being of little interest to persons other than the author. If you found this essay interesting, try to account for its appeal.

Jamaica Kincaid

Jamaica Kincaid was born in 1949 in St. Johns, Antigua, in the West Indies. She was educated at the Princess Margaret School in Antigua and, briefly, at Westchester Community College and Franconia College. Since 1974 she has been a contributor to the New Yorker, *where "Girl" first was published. "Girl" was later included in the first of Kincaid's six books,* At the Bottom of the River.*

Kincaid informs us that "benna," mentioned early in "Girl," refers to "songs of the sort your parents didn't want you to sing, at first calypso and later rock and roll."

Girl

Wash the white clothes on Monday and put them on the stone heap; wash the color clothes on Tuesday and put them on the clothesline to dry; don't walk barehead in the hot sun; cook pumpkin fritters in very hot sweet oil; soak your little clothes right after you take them off; when buying cotton to make yourself a nice blouse, be sure that it doesn't have gum on it, because that way it won't hold up well after a wash; soak salt fish overnight before you cook it; is it true that you sing benna in Sunday school?; always eat your food in such a way that it won't turn someone else's stomach; on Sundays try to walk like a lady and not like the slut you are so bent on becoming; don't sing benna in Sunday school; you mustn't speak to wharf-rat boys, not even to give directions; don't eat fruits on the street—flies will follow you; *but I don't sing benna on Sundays at all and never in Sunday school*; this is how to sew on a button; this is how to make a buttonhole for the button you have just sewed on; this is how to hem a dress when you see the hem coming down and so to prevent yourself from looking like the slut I know you are so bent on becoming; this is how you iron your father's khaki shirt so that it doesn't have a crease; this is how you iron your father's khaki pants so that they don't have a crease; this is how you grow okra—far from the house, because okra tree harbors red ants; when you are growing dasheen, make sure it gets plenty of water or else it makes your throat itch when you are eating it; this is how you sweep a corner; this is how you sweep a whole house; this is how you sweep a yard; this is how you smile to someone you don't like too much; this is how you smile to someone you don't like at all; this is how you smile to someone you like completely; this is how you set a table for tea; this is how you set a table for dinner; this is how you set a table for dinner with an important guest; this is how you set a table for lunch; this is how you set a table for breakfast; this is how to behave in the presence of men who don't know you very well, and this way they won't recognize immediately the slut I have warned you against becoming; be sure to wash every day, even if it is with your own spit; don't squat down to play marbles—you are not a boy, you know; don't pick people's flowers— you might catch something; don't throw stones at blackbirds, because it might not be a blackbird at all; this is how to make a bread pudding; this is how to make doukona; this is how to make pepper pot; this is how to make a good medicine for a cold; this is how to make a good medicine to throw away a child before it even becomes a child; this is how to catch a fish; this is how to throw back a fish you don't like, and that way something bad won't fall on you; this is how to bully a man; this is how a man bullies you; this is how to love a man, and if this doesn't work there are other ways, and if they don't work don't feel too bad about giving up; this is how to spit up in the air if you feel like it, and this is how to move quick so that it doesn't fall on you; this is how to make ends meet; always squeeze bread to make sure it's fresh; *but what if the baker won't let me feel the bread?*; you mean to say that after all you are really going to be the kind of woman who the baker won't let near the bread?

Joining the Conversation: Critical Thinking and Writing

1. In a paragraph, identify the two characters whose voices we hear in this story. Explain what we know about them (their circumstances and their relationship). Cite specific evidence from the text. For example, what is the effect of the frequent repetition of "this is how"? Are there other words or phrases frequently repeated?

2. Try reading a section of "Girl" out loud in a rhythmical pattern, giving the principal and the second voices. Then reread the story, trying to incorporate this rhythm mentally into your reading. How does this rhythm contribute to the overall effect of the story? How does it compare to or contrast with speech rhythms that are familiar to you?

Robert Hayden

Robert Hayden (1913–1980) was born in Detroit, Michigan. His parents divorced when he was a child, and he was brought up by a neighboring family, whose name he adopted. In 1942, at the age of 29, he graduated from Detroit City College (now Wayne State University), and he received a master's degree from the University of Michigan. He taught at Fisk University from 1946 to 1969 and after that, for the remainder of his life, at the University of Michigan. In 1979 he was appointed Consultant in Poetry to the Library of Congress, the first African-American to hold the post.

Those Winter Sundays

Sundays too my father got up early
and put his clothes on in the blueblack cold,
then with cracked hands that ached
from labor in the weekday weather made
banked fires blaze. No one ever thanked him.   5

I'd wake and hear the cold splintering, breaking.
When the rooms were warm, he'd call,
and slowly I would rise and dress,
fearing the chronic angers of that house.

Speaking indifferently to him,   10
who had driven out the cold
and polished my good shoes as well.
What did I know, what did I know
of love's austere and lonely offices?

Joining the Conversation:
Critical Thinking and Writing

1. In line 1, what does the word "too" tell us about the father? What does it suggest about the speaker and the implied hearer of the poem?

2. How old do you believe the speaker was at the time he recalls in the second and third stanzas? What details suggest this age?

3. What is the meaning of "offices" in the last line? What does this word suggest that other words Hayden might have chosen do not?

4. What do you take to be the speaker's present attitude toward his father? What circumstances, do you imagine, prompted his memory of "Those Winter Sundays"?

5. In a page or two, try to get down the exact circumstances when you spoke "indifferently," or not at all, to someone who had deserved your gratitude.

CHAPTER 7

Identities

Grandfather and Grandchildren Awaiting Evacuation Bus,
Hayward, California, May 9, 1942
Dorothea Lange

Behind the Bar, Birney, Montana
Marion Post Wolcott, 1941

Short Views

In every known society, the male's need for achievement can be recognized. Men may cook, or weave, or dress dolls or hunt hummingbirds, but if such activities are appropriate occupations of men, then the whole society, men and women alike, votes them as important. When the same occupations are performed by women, they are regarded as less important.
>   *Margaret Mead*

There is no female mind. The brain is not an organ of sex. As well speak of a female liver.
>   **Charlotte Perkins Gilman**

This has always been a man's world, and none of the reasons hitherto brought forward in explanation of this fact has seemed adequate.
>   **Simone de Beauvoir**

America is God's crucible, the great melting pot where all the races of Europe are melting and re-forming.
>   **Israel Zangwill**

Capitalism is a machine for the suppression of one class by another.
>   **Vladimir I. Lenin**

Through our own efforts and concerted good faith in learning to know, thus to respect, the wonderfully rich and diverse subcommunities of America, we can establish a new vision of America: a place where "community" may mean many things, yet retains its deeper spiritual significance. We may even learn to coincide with the 500th anniversary of the "discovery" of America by Columbus, that America, in its magnificent variety, has yet to be discovered.
>   *Joyce Carol Oates*

I have a dream that my four little children will one day live in a nation where they will not be judged by the color of their skin but by the content of their character.

   Martin Luther King Jr.

Racism is so universal in this country, so wide-spread and deep-seated, that it is invisible because it is so normal.

   Shirley Chisholm

Rogelio R. Gomez

Rogelio R. Gomez at the age of six was brought by his family from Mexico to the United States. His lack of competence in English caused him to fail first grade and to be labeled learning-disabled. He nevertheless earned a bachelor's degree from the University of Texas at Austin, where he majored in history, and in 1990 he earned a master's degree in English.

Foul Shots

Now and then I can still see their faces, snickering and laughing, their eyes mocking me. And it bothers me that I should remember. Time and maturity should have diminished the pain, because the incident happened more than 20 years ago. Occasionally, however, a smug smile triggers the memory, and I think, "I should have done something," Some act of defiance could have killed and buried the memory of the incident. Now it's too late.

In 1969, I was a senior on the Luther Burbank High School basketball team. The school is on the south side of San Antonio, in one of the city's many barrios. After practice one day our coach announced that we were going to spend the following Saturday scrimmaging with the ball club from Winston Churchill High, located in the city's rich, white north side. After the basketball game, we were to select someone from the opposing team and "buddy up"—talk with him, have lunch with him and generally spend the day attempting friendship. By telling us that this experience would do both teams some good, I suspect our well-intentioned coach was thinking about the possible benefits of integration and of learning to appreciate the differences of other people. By integrating us with this more prosperous group, I think he was also trying to inspire us.

But my teammates and I smiled sardonically at one another, and our sneakers squeaked as we nervously rubbed them against the waxed hardwood floor of our gym. The prospect of a full day of unfavorable comparisons drew from us a collective groan. As "barrio boys," we were already acutely aware of the differences between us and them. Churchill meant "white" to us: It meant shiny new cars, two-story homes with fireplaces, pedigreed dogs and manicured hedges. In other words, everything that we did not have. Worse, travelling north meant putting up a front, to ourselves as well as to the Churchill team. We felt we had to pretend that we were cavalier about it all, tough guys who didn't care about "nothin."

Rogelio R. Gomez, "Foul Shots," *New York Times*, 1991.

It's clear now that we entered the contest with negative images of ourselves. From childhood, we must have suspected something was inherently wrong with us. The evidence wrapped itself around our collective psyche like a noose. In elementary school, we were not allowed to speak Spanish. The bladed edge of a wooden ruler once came crashing down on my knuckles for violating this dictum. By high school, however, policies had changed, and we could speak Spanish without fear of physical reprisal. Still, speaking our language before whites brought on spasms of shame—for the supposed inferiority of our language and culture—and guilt at feeling shame. That mixture of emotions fueled our burning sense of inferiority

After all, our mothers in no way resembled the glamorized models of   5 American TV mothers—Donna Reed baking cookies in high heels. My mother's hands were rough and chafed, her wardrobe drab and worn. And my father was preoccupied with making ends meet. His silence starkly contrasted with the glib counsel Jim Anderson offered in "Father Knows Best." And where the Beaver worried about trying to understand some difficult homework assignment, for me it was an altogether different horror, when I was told by my elementary school principal that I did not have the ability to learn.

After I failed to pass the first grade, my report card read that I had a "learning disability." What shame and disillusion it brought my parents! To have carried their dream of a better life from Mexico to America, only to have their hopes quashed by having their only son branded inadequate. And so somewhere during my schooling I assumed that saying I had a "learning disability" was just another way of saying that I was "retarded." School administrators didn't care that I could not speak English.

As teen-agers, of course, my Mexican-American friends and I did not consciously understand why we felt inferior. But we might have understood if we had fathomed our desperate need to trounce Churchill. We viewed the prospect of beating a white, north-side squad as a particularly fine coup. The match was clearly racial, our need to succeed born of a defiance against prejudice. I see now that we used the basketball court to prove our "blood." And who better to confirm us, if not those whom we considered better? In retrospect, I realize the only thing confirmed that day was that we saw ourselves as negatively as they did.

After we won the morning scrimmage, both teams were led from the gym into an empty room where everyone sat on a shiny linoleum floor. We were supposed to mingle—rub the colors together. But the teams sat separately, our backs against concrete walls. We faced one another like enemies, the empty floor between us a no man's land. As the coaches walked away, one reminded us to share lunch. God! The mere thought of offering them a taco from our brown bags when they had refrigerated deli lunches horrified us.

Then one of their players tossed a bag of Fritos at us. It slid across the slippery floor and stopped in the center of the room. With hearts beating anxiously, we Chicanos stared at the bag as the boy said with a sneer, "Y'all probably like 'em"—the "Frito Bandito" commercial being popular then. And we could see them, smiling at each other, giggling, jabbing their elbows into one another's ribs at the joke. The bag seemed to grow before our eyes like a monstrous symbol of inferiority.

We won the afternoon basketball game as well. But winning had   10
accomplished nothing. Though we had wanted to, we couldn't change their perception of us. It seems, in fact, that defeating them made them meaner. Looking back, I feel these young men needed to put us "in our place," to reaffirm the power they felt we had threatened. I think, moreover, that they felt justified, not only because of their inherent sense of superiority, but because our failure to respond to their insult underscored our worthlessness in their eyes.

Two decades later, the memory of their gloating lives on in me. When a white person is discourteous, I find myself wondering what I should do, and afterward, if I've done the right thing. Sometimes I argue when a deft comment would suffice. Then I reprimand myself, for I am no longer a boy. But my impulse to argue bears witness to my ghosts. For, invariably, whenever I feel insulted I'm reminded of that day at Churchill High. And whenever the past encroaches upon the present, I see myself rising boldly, stepping proudly across the years and crushing, underfoot, a silly bag of Fritos.

Joining the Conversation: Critical Thinking and Writing

1. Gomez is describing an experience that occurred twenty years earlier. What did he feel then, and what does he feel now?

2. How does the author make his past experiences come alive for the reader? What, more generally, does it mean to say that in a piece of writing an author has succeeded in making an experience "come alive?"

3. Have you ever suffered from a sense of inferiority similar to the one that Gomez describes? What was the situation? How did you feel at the time, and how do you feel about it now?

4. When something bad or upsetting happens to us, we are often told, "You'll have to get over it—put it behind you." Do you think that someone should offer this advice to Gomez? How do you respond when someone gives such advice to you? In your view, how would Gomez respond to someone who gave this advice to him?

Marianne J. Legato

Marianne J. Legato, born in New York in 1935, is a medical doctor. She is a professor of clinical medicine at Columbia University, the director of the Partnership for Women's Health, the founder and editor of the Journal of Gender-Specific Medicine, *and the author of several books.*

The Weaker Sex

When I say I study gender-specific medicine, most people assume I mean women's health. Patients ask me, "Do you take care of men too?"

I may be partly to blame for the confusion: in the years since the revolutionary 1985 report on women's health from the United States Public Health Service, I—along with many of my colleagues—have tried to atone for the fact that for so long the majority of diseases that afflicted both genders were studied exclusively in men.

Over the past two decades, we've radically revised how we conduct medical research and take care of our female patients. And we've made valuable discoveries about how gender helps determine vulnerability to illness and, ultimately, the timing and causes of death. But I now believe that we doctors and researchers may have focused too much on women.

What emerges when one studies male biology in a truly evenhanded way is the realization that from the moment of conception on, men are less likely to survive than women. It's not just that men take on greater risks and pursue more hazardous vocations than women. There are poorly understood—and underappreciated—vulnerabilities inherent in men's genetic and hormonal makeup. This Father's Day, we need to rededicate ourselves to deepening our knowledge of male physiology.

Men's troubles begin during the earliest days in the womb. Even though there are more male than female embryos, there are more miscarriages of male fetuses. Industrial countries are also witnessing a decline in male to female birth ratios, and we don't know why.   5

Some scientists have argued that the probability of a male child declines as parents (especially fathers) age. Still others have cited the prevalence of pesticides, which produce more birth defects in male children.

Even when a boy manages to be born, he's still behind the survival eight ball: he is three to four times more likely than girls to have developmental disorders like autism and dyslexia; girls learn language earlier, develop richer vocabularies and even hear better than boys. Girls demonstrate insight and judgment earlier in adolescence than boys, who are more impulsive and take more risks than their sisters. Teenage boys are more likely to commit suicide than girls and are more likely to die violent deaths before adulthood.

As adults, too, men die earlier than women. Twice as many men as women die of coronary artery disease, which manifests itself a decade earlier in men than women; when it comes to cancer, the news for men is almost as bad. Women also have more vigorous immune systems than men: of the 10 most common infections, men are more likely to have serious encounters with seven of them.

While depression is said to be twice as frequent in women as in men, I'm convinced that the diagnosis is just made more frequently in women, who show a greater willingness to discuss their symptoms and to ask for help when in distress. Once, at a dinner party, I asked a group of men whether they believed men were depressed as often as women, but were simply conditioned to be silent in the face of discomfort, sadness or fear. "Of course!" replied one man. "Why do you think we die sooner?"

Considering the relative fragility of men, it's clearly counterintuitive   10
for us to urge them, from boyhood on, to cope bravely with adversity, to ignore discomfort, to persevere in spite of pain and to accept without question the most dangerous jobs and tasks we have to offer. Perhaps the reason many societies offer boys nutritional, educational and vocational advantages over girls is not because of chauvinism—it's because we're trying to ensure their survival.

It's possible, too, that we've simply been sexist. We've complained bitterly that until recently women's health was restricted to keeping breasts and reproductive organs optimally functional, reflecting the view that what made women valuable was their ability to conceive and bear children. But aren't we doing the same thing with men? Read the questions posed on the cover of men's magazines: how robust is your sexuality? How well-developed are your abs? The only malignancy I hear discussed with men is prostate cancer.

It's time to focus on the unique problems of men just the way we have learned to do with women. In 2004, the National Institutes of Health spent twice as much on studies done only on women as only on men. We are not devoting nearly enough money to men's health; worse yet, we may be spending those insufficient funds to answer exactly the wrong questions.

The National Institutes of Health should therefore convene a consensus conference to identify the most important threats to men's well-being and longevity and issue a request for research proposals to address them. Would an estrogen-like molecule postpone the onset of coronary artery disease in susceptible males? Are there ways to strengthen the male immune system?

Thinking about how we might correct the comparative vulnerability of men instead of concentrating on how we have historically neglected women's biology will doubtless uncover new ways to improve men's health—and ultimately, every human's ability to survive.

◌ Joining the Conversation:
Critical Thinking and Writing

1. "The weaker sex"—what do we usually understand this description to mean? And why, according to Legato, does it more accurately apply to men than to women?

2. What evidence does Legato offer to support her claim that men are in fact the weaker sex?

3. In paragraph 10 Legato says that "Perhaps the reason many societies offer boys nutritional, educational and vocational advantages over girls is not because of chauvinism—it's because we're trying to ensure their survival." First, define *chauvinism*, and then explain your reaction to the reason Legato here offers.

4. What does Legato propose that we should do to improve men's health? Does her argument support her conclusion that improving men's health would also improve "every human's ability to survive"? Explain.

Zora Neale Hurston

Zora Neale Hurston (1891–1960) was brought up in Eatonville, Florida, a town said to be the first all-black self-governing town in the United States. Her early years were spent working at odd jobs (domestic servant, manicurist, waitress), but she managed to attend Howard University and then, with the aid of a scholarship, entered Barnard College, where she was the first black student. At Barnard, influenced by anthropologists Franz Boas and Ruth Benedict, she set out to study the folklore of Eatonville. Later she published several volumes of folklore, as well as stories, novels, and an autobiography entitled Dust Tracks on a Road *(1942).*

In the 1950s Hurston's writing seemed reactionary, almost embarrassing in an age of black protest, and she herself—working as a domestic, a librarian, and a substitute teacher—was almost forgotten. She died in a county welfare home in Florida and was buried in an unmarked grave. In the 1980s Hurston was, so to speak, rediscovered, partly because of the attention given to her by Alice Walker.

How It Feels to Be Colored Me

I am colored but I offer nothing in the way of extenuating circumstances except the fact that I am the only Negro in the United States whose grandfather on the mother's side was *not* an Indian chief.

I remember the very day that I became colored. Up to my thirteenth year I lived in the little Negro town of Eatonville, Florida. It is exclusively a colored town. The only white people I knew passed through the town

Zora Neale Hurston, "How It Feels to Be Colored Me." Used with the permission of Zora Neale Hurston Trust.

going to or coming from Orlando. The native whites rode dusty horses, the Northern tourists chugged down the sandy village road in automobiles. The town knew the Southerners and never stopped cane chewing when they passed. But the Northerners were something else again. They were peered at cautiously from behind curtains by the timid. The more venturesome would come out on the porch to watch them go past and got just as much pleasure out of the tourists as the tourists got out of the village.

The front porch might seem a daring place for the rest of the town, but it was a gallery seat to me. My favorite place was atop the gate-post. Proscenium box for a born first-nighter. Not only did I enjoy the show, but I didn't mind the actors knowing that I liked it. I usually spoke to them in passing. I'd wave at them and when they returned my salute, I would say something like this: "Howdy-do-well-I-thank-you-where-you-goin'?" Usually the automobile or the horse paused at this, and after a queer exchange of compliments, I would probably "go a piece of the way" with them, as we say in farthest Florida. If one of my family happened to come to the front in time to see me, of course negotiations would be rudely broken off. But even so, it is clear that I was the first "welcome-to-our-state" Floridian, and I hope the Miami Chamber of Commerce will please take notice.

During this period, white people differed from colored to me only in that they rode through town and never lived there. They liked to hear me "speak pieces" and sing and wanted to see me dance the parse-me-la, and gave me generously of their small silver for doing these things, which seemed strange to me for I wanted to do them so much that I needed bribing to stop. Only they didn't know it. The colored people gave no dimes. They deplored any joyful tendencies in me, but I was their Zora nevertheless. I belonged to them, to the nearby hotels, to the county—everybody's Zora.

But changes came in the family when I was thirteen, and I was sent to 5 school in Jacksonville. I left Eatonville, the town of the oleanders, as Zora. When I disembarked from the river-boat at Jacksonville, she was no more. It seemed that I had suffered a sea change. I was not Zora of Orange County any more, I was now a little colored girl. I found it out in certain ways. In my heart as well as in the mirror, I became a fast brown—warranted not to rub nor run.

But I am not tragically colored. There is no great sorrow dammed up in my soul, nor lurking behind my eyes. I do not mind at all. I do not belong to the sobbing school of Negrohood who hold that nature somehow has given them a lowdown dirty deal and whose feelings are all hurt about it. Even in the helter-skelter skirmish that is my life, I have seen that the world is to the strong regardless of a little pigmentation more or less. No, I do not weep at the world—I am too busy sharpening my oyster knife.

Someone is always at my elbow reminding me that I am the granddaughter of slaves. It fails to register depression with me. Slavery is sixty years in the past. The operation was successful and the patient is doing well, thank you. The terrible struggle that made me an American out of a potential slave said "On the line!" The Reconstruction said "Get set!"; and the generation before said "Go!" I am off to a flying start and I must not halt in the stretch to look behind and weep. Slavery is the price I paid for civilization, and the choice was not with me. It is a bully adventure and worth all that I have paid through my ancestors for it. No one on earth ever had a greater chance for glory. The world to be won and nothing to be lost. It is thrilling to think—to know that for any act of mine, I shall get twice as much praise or twice as much blame. It is quite exciting to hold the center of the national stage, with the spectators not knowing whether to laugh or to weep.

The position of my white neighbor is much more difficult. No brown specter pulls up a chair beside me when I sit down to eat. No dark ghost thrusts its leg against mine in bed. The game of keeping what one has is never so exciting as the game of getting.

I do not always feel colored. Even now I often achieve the unconscious Zora of Eatonville before the Hegira. I feel most colored when I am thrown against a sharp white background.

For instance at Barnard. "Beside the waters of the Hudson" I feel my race. Among the thousand white persons, I am a dark rock surged upon, overswept by a creamy sea. I am surged upon and overswept, but through it all, I remain myself. When covered by the waters, I am; and the ebb but reveals me again.

10

Sometimes it is the other way around. A white person is set down in our midst, but the contrast is just as sharp for me. For instance, when I sit in the drafty basement that is The New World Cabaret with a white person, my color comes. We enter chatting about any little nothing that we have in common and are seated by the jazz waiters. In the abrupt way that jazz orchestras have, this one plunges into a number. It loses no time in circumlocutions, but gets right down to business. It constricts the thorax and splits the heart with its tempo and narcotic harmonies. This orchestra grows rambunctious, rears on its hind legs and attacks the tonal veil with primitive fury, rending it, clawing it until it breaks through to the jungle beyond. I follow those heathen—follow them exultingly. I dance wildly inside myself; I yell within, I whoop; I shake my assegai[1] above my head, I hurl it true to the mark *yeeeeooww!* I am in the jungle and living in the jungle way. My face is painted red and yellow and my body is painted blue. My pulse is throbbing like a war drum. I want to slaughter something— give pain, give death to what, I do not know. But the piece ends. The men of the orchestra wipe their lips and rest their fingers. I creep back slowly to the veneer we call civilization with the last tone and find the white friend sitting motionless in his seat, smoking calmly.

"Good music they have here," he remarks, drumming the table with his fingertips.

[1] **assegai** An African spear

Music! The great blobs of purple and red emotion have not touched him. He has only heard what I felt. He is far away and I see him but dimly across the ocean and the continent that have fallen between us. He is so pale with his whiteness then and I am *so* colored.

At certain times I have no race, I am *me*. When I set my hat at a certain angle and saunter down Seventh Avenue, Harlem City, feeling as snooty as the lions in front of the Forty-Second Street Library, for instance. So far as my feelings are concerned, Peggy Hopkins Joyce on the Boule Mich[2] with her gorgeous raiment, stately carriage, knees knocking together in a most aristocratic manner, has nothing on me. The cosmic Zora emerges. I belong to no race nor time. I am the eternal feminine with its string of beads.

I have no separate feeling about being an American citizen and colored.   15
I am merely a fragment of the Great Soul that surges within the boundaries. My country, right or wrong.

Sometimes, I feel discriminated against, but it does not make me angry. It merely astonishes me. How *can* any deny themselves the pleasure of my company! It's beyond me.

But in the main, I feel like a brown bag of miscellany propped against a wall. Against a wall in company with other bags, white, red and yellow. Pour out the contents, and there is discovered a jumble of small things priceless and worthless. A first-water diamond, an empty spool, bits of broken glass, lengths of string, a key to a door long since crumbled away, a rusty knife-blade, old shoes saved for a road that never was and never will be, a nail bent under the weight of things too heavy for any nail, a dried flower or two, still a little fragrant. In your hand is the brown bag. On the ground before you is the jumble it held—so much like the jumble in the bags, could they be emptied, that all might be dumped in a single heap and the bags refilled without altering the content of any greatly. A bit of colored glass more or less would not matter. Perhaps that is how the Great Stuffer of Bags filled them in the first place—who knows?

Joining the Conversation: Critical Thinking and Writing

1. Do you think that Hurston has chosen an effective title? In a sentence or two, can you summarize what she says about "how it feels to be colored me"? (Note that when Hurston wrote this essay in 1928, "colored" was the term commonly used for persons whom today we call African-American or black.)

---

[2] **Peggy Hopkins Joyce on the Boule Mich** Joyce (1893–1957), an actress in racy musicals, was famous for her marriages to (and her divorces from) rich men; "Boule Mich" (pronounced "Bull Mish") refers to Michigan Avenue, in Chicago, grandly compared to Boulevard St. Michel, a fashionable street in Paris.

2. Explain the following sentence: "But I am not tragically colored."

3. At one point, Hurston writes: "At certain times I have no race, I am me." What does she mean? Does her distinction here make sense to you, or do you find it confusing?

4. How would you describe Hurston's style? Do you think it works well in this essay, or would a different style be more effective? Explain.

5. One reader of this essay has said. "By telling us who she isn't, Hurston tells us who she is." Do you agree? If so, in a sentence or two explain who she is.

6. Hurston was the first student of color to attend Barnard College, and this is the background for this essay, which she wrote in 1928. Do you think that the essay as it stands is still relevant?

7. Do you feel that your race, religion, ethnicity, or something else identifies you as "different"? Is this something you talk about? With whom? Or do you keep this feeling to yourself?

Stephen Jay Gould

Stephen Jay Gould (1941–2002) taught paleontology, biology, and the history of science at Harvard University. The essays he wrote for the magazine Natural History *have been collected in several highly readable books.*

Women's Brains

In the Prelude to *Middlemarch*, George Eliot lamented the unfulfilled lives of talented women:

> Some have felt that these blundering lives are due to the inconvenient indefiniteness with which the Supreme Power has fashioned the natures of women: if there were one level of feminine incompetence as strict as the ability to count three and no more, the social lot of women might be treated with scientific certitude.

Eliot goes on to discount the idea of innate limitation, but while she wrote in 1872, the leaders of European anthropometry were trying to measure "with scientific certitude" the inferiority of women. Anthropometry, or measurement of the human body, is not so fashionable a field these days, but it dominated the human sciences for much of the nineteenth century and remained popular until intelligence testing replaced skull measurement as a favored device for making invidious comparisons among races, classes, and sexes. Craniometry, or measurement of the skull, commanded the most attention and respect. Its unquestioned leader, Paul Broca (1824–80), professor of clinical surgery at the Faculty of Medicine in Paris, gathered a school of disciples and imitators around himself. Their work, so meticulous and apparently irrefutable, exerted great influence and won high esteem as a jewel of nineteenth-century science.

Broca's work seemed particularly invulnerable to refutation. Had he not measured with the most scrupulous care and accuracy? (Indeed, he had. I have the greatest respect for Broca's meticulous procedure. His numbers are sound. But science is an inferential exercise, not a catalog of facts. Numbers, by themselves, specify nothing. All depends upon what you do with them.) Broca depicted himself as an apostle of objectivity, a man who bowed before facts and cast aside superstition and sentimentality. He declared that "there is no faith, however respectable, no interest, however legitimate, which must not accommodate itself to the progress of human knowledge and bend before truth." Women, like it or not, had smaller brains than men and, therefore, could not equal them in intelligence. This fact, Broca argued, may reinforce a common prejudice in male society, but it is also a scientific truth. L. Manouvrier, a black sheep in Broca's fold, rejected the inferiority of women and wrote with feeling about the burden imposed upon them by Broca's numbers:

> Women displayed their talents and their diplomas. They also invoked philosophical authorities. But they were opposed by *numbers* unknown to Condorcet or to John Stuart Mill. These numbers fell upon poor women like a sledge hammer, and they were accompanied by commentaries and sarcasms more ferocious than the most misogynist imprecations of certain church fathers. The theologians had asked if women had a soul. Several centuries later, some scientists were ready to refuse them a human intelligence.

Broca's argument rested upon two sets of data: the larger brains of men in modern societies, and a supposed increase in male superiority through time. His most extensive data came from autopsies performed personally in four Parisian hospitals. For 292 male brains, he calculated an average weight of 1,325 grams; 140 female brains averaged 1,144 grams for a difference of 181 grams, or 14 percent of the male weight. Broca understood, of course, that part of this difference could be attributed to the greater height of males. Yet he made no attempt to measure the effect of size alone and actually stated that it cannot account for the entire difference because we know, a priori, that women are not as intelligent as men (a premise that the data were supposed to test, not rest upon):

> We might ask if the small size of the female brain depends exclusively upon the small size of her body. Tiedemann has proposed this explanation. But we

must not forget that women are, on the average, a little less intelligent than men, a difference which we should not exaggerate but which is, nonetheless, real. We are therefore permitted to suppose that the relatively small size of the female brain depends in part upon her physical inferiority and in part upon her intellectual inferiority.

In 1873, the year after Eliot published *Middlemarch*, Broca measured the cranial capacities of prehistoric skulls from L'Homme Mort cave. Here he found a difference of only 99.5 cubic centimeters between males and females, while modern populations range from 129.5 to 220.7. Topinard, Broca's chief disciple, explained the increasing discrepancy through time as a result of differing evolutionary pressures upon dominant men and passive women:

> The man who fights for two or more in the struggle for existence, who has all the responsibility and the cares of tomorrow, who is constantly active in combating the environment and human rivals, needs more brain than the woman whom he must protect and nourish, the sedentary woman, lacking any interior occupations, whose role is to raise children, love, and be passive.

In 1879, Gustave Le Bon, chief misogynist of Broca's school, used these data to publish what must be the most vicious attack upon women in modern scientific literature (no one can top Aristotle). I do not claim his views were representative of Broca's school, but they were published in France's most respected anthropological journal. Le Bon concluded:

> In the most intelligent races, as among the Parisians, there are a large number of women whose brains are closer in size to those of gorillas than to the most developed male brains. This inferiority is so obvious that no one can contest it for a moment; only its degree is worth discussion. All psychologists who have studied the intelligence of women, as well as poets and novelists, recognize today that they represent the most inferior forms of human evolution and that they are closer to children and savages than to an adult, civilized man. They excel in fickleness, inconstancy, absence of thought and logic, and incapacity to reason. Without doubt there exist some distinguished women, very superior to the average man, but they are as exceptional as the birth of any monstrosity, as, for example, of a gorilla with two heads; consequently, we may neglect them entirely.

Nor did Le Bon shrink from the social implications of his views. He was horrified by the proposal of some American reformers to grant women higher education on the same basis as men:

> A desire to give them the same education, and, as a consequence, to propose the same goals for them, is a dangerous chimera . . . . The day when, misunderstanding the inferior occupations which nature has given her, women leave the home and take part in our battles; on this day a social revolution will begin, and everything that maintains the sacred ties of the family will disappear.

5

Sound familiar?[1]

I have reexamined Broca's data, the basis for all this derivative pronouncement, and I find his numbers sound but his interpretation ill-founded, to say the least. The data supporting his claim for increased difference through time can be easily dismissed. Broca based his contention on the samples from L'Homme Mort alone—only seven male and six female skulls in all. Never have so little data yielded such far ranging conclusions.

In 1888, Topinard published Broca's more extensive data on the Parisian hospitals. Since Broca recorded height and age as well as brain size, we may use modern statistics to remove their effect. Brain weight decreases with age, and Broca's women were, on average, considerably older than his men. Brain weight increases with height, and his average man was almost half a foot taller than his average woman. I used multiple regression, a technique that allowed me to assess simultaneously the influence of height and age upon brain size. In an analysis of the data for women, I found that, at average male height and age, a woman's brain would weigh 1,212 grams. Correction for height and age reduces Broca's measured difference of 181 grams by more than a third, to 113 grams.

I don't know what to make of this remaining difference because I cannot assess other factors known to influence brain size in a major way. Cause of death has an important effect: degenerative disease often entails a substantial diminution of brain size. (This effect is separate from the decrease attributed to age alone.) Eugene Schreider, also working with Broca's data, found that men killed in accidents had brains weighing, on average, 60 grams more than men dying of infectious diseases. The best modern data I can find (from American hospitals) records a full 100-gram difference between death by degenerative arteriosclerosis and by violence or accident. Since so many of Broca's subjects were very elderly women, we may assume that lengthy degenerative disease was more common among them than among the men.

More importantly, modern students of brain size still have not agreed on a proper measure for eliminating the powerful effect of body size. Height is partly adequate, but men and women of the same height do not share the same body build. Weight is even worse than height, because most of its variation reflects nutrition rather than intrinsic size—fat versus skinny exerts little influence upon the brain. Manouvrier took up this subject in the 1880s and argued that muscular mass and force should be used. He tried to measure this elusive property in various ways and found a marked difference in favor of men, even in men and women of the same height. When he corrected for what he called "sexual mass," women actually came out slightly ahead in brain size.

---

[1]When I wrote this essay, I assumed that Le Bon was a marginal, if colorful, figure. I have since learned that he was a leading scientist, one of the founders of social psychology, and best known for a seminal study on crowd behavior, still cited today (*La psychologie des foules*, 1895), and for his work on unconscious motivation.

Thus, the corrected 113-gram difference is surely too large; the true figure is probably close to zero and may as well favor women as men. And 113 grams, by the way, is exactly the average difference between a 5 foot 4 inch and a 6 foot 4 inch male in Broca's data. We would not (especially us short folks) want to ascribe greater intelligence to tall men. In short, who knows what to do with Broca's data? They certainly don't permit any confident claim that men have bigger brains than women.

To appreciate the social role of Broca and his school, we must recognize that his statements about the brains of women do not reflect an isolated prejudice toward a single disadvantaged group. They must be weighed in the context of a general theory that supported contemporary social distinctions as biologically ordained. Women, blacks, and poor people suffered the same disparagement, but women bore the brunt of Broca's argument because he had easier access to data on women's brains. Women were singularly denigrated but they also stood as surrogates for other disenfranchised groups. As one of Broca's disciples wrote in 1881: "Men of the black races have a brain scarcely heavier than that of white women." This juxtaposition extended into many other realms of anthropological argument, particularly to claims that, anatomically and emotionally, both women and blacks were like white children—and that white children, by the theory of recapitulation, represented an ancestral (primitive) adult stage of human evolution. I do not regard as empty rhetoric the claim that women's battles are for all of us.

Maria Montessori did not confine her activities to educational reform for young children. She lectured on anthropology for several years at the University of Rome, and wrote an influential book entitled *Pedagogical Anthropology* (English edition, 1913). Montessori was no egalitarian. She supported most of Broca's work and the theory of innate criminality proposed by her compatriot Cesare Lombroso. She measured the circumference of children's heads in her schools and inferred that the best prospects had bigger brains. But she had no use for Broca's conclusions about women. She discussed Manouvrier's work at length and made much of his tentative claim that women, after proper correction of the data, had slightly larger brains than men. Women, she concluded, were intellectually superior, but men had prevailed heretofore by dint of physical force. Since technology has abolished force as an instrument of power, the era of women may soon be upon us: "In such an epoch there will really be superior human beings, there will really be men strong in morality and in sentiment. Perhaps in this way the reign of women is approaching, when the enigma of her anthropological superiority will be deciphered. Woman was always the custodian of human sentiment, morality and honor."

This represents one possible antidote to "scientific" claims for the constitutional inferiority of certain groups. One may affirm the validity of biological distinctions but argue that the data have been misinterpreted by prejudiced men with a stake in the outcome, and that disadvantaged groups are truly superior. In recent years, Elaine Morgan has followed this strategy in her *Descent of Woman*, a speculative reconstruction of

15

human prehistory from the woman's point of view—and as farcical as more famous tall tales by and for men.

I prefer another strategy. Montessori and Morgan followed Broca's philosophy to reach a more congenial conclusion. I would rather label the whole enterprise of setting a biological value upon groups for what it is: irrelevant and highly injurious. George Eliot well appreciated the special tragedy that biological labeling imposed upon members of disadvantaged groups. She expressed it for people like herself—women of extraordinary talent. I would apply it more widely—not only to those whose dreams are flouted but also to those who never realize that they may dream—but I cannot match her prose. In conclusion, then, the rest of Eliot's prelude to *Middlemarch:*

> The limits of variation are really much wider than anyone would imagine from the sameness of women's coiffure and the favorite love stories in prose and verse. Here and there a cygnet is reared uneasily among the ducklings in the brown pond, and never finds the living stream in fellowship with its own oary-footed kind. Here and there is born a Saint Theresa, foundress of nothing, whose loving heartbeats and sobs after an unattained goodness tremble off and are dispersed among hindrances instead of centering in some long-recognizable deed.

Joining the Conversation: Critical Thinking and Writing

1. What is your understanding of anthropometry from paragraph 2? According to Gould, what does intelligence testing have in common with anthropometry? Characterize his attitude toward both. How does he reveal his attitude in this paragraph?

2. In paragraph 3, what does Gould mean when he says, "But science is an inferential exercise, not a catalog of facts"?

3. In paragraph 14 Gould says, "I do not regard as empty rhetoric the claim that women's battles are for all of us." What does he mean? What foundation for this opinion have this paragraph and paragraph 2 provided?

4. Who was Maria Montessori, and what does her work have to do with Gould's argument? If her relevance is not entirely clear to you, or was not on first reading, what might Gould have done to make it clearer?

5. What, according to Gould, are the social consequences of what he calls in paragraph 17 *biological labeling*? If on the whole you agree with him, what is the basis of your agreement?

6. In paragraph 14 Gould refers to the "social role of Broca and his school." What does he mean by that? On the basis of this essay (and others of Gould's that you may have read) formulate in a sentence or two the social role of Gould.

Katha Pollitt

Katha Pollitt (b. 1949) writes chiefly on literary, political, and social topics. In addition to writing essays, she writes poetry; her first collection of poems, Antarctic Traveller *(1982), won the National Book Critics Circle Award. She publishes widely, especially in the* Nation, *the* New Yorker, *and the* New York Times. *We reprint an article that originally appeared in the* New York Times Magazine.

Why Boys Don't Play with Dolls

It's twenty-eight years since the founding of NOW,[1] and boys still like trucks and girls still like dolls. Increasingly, we are told that the source of these robust preferences must lie outside society—in prenatal hormonal influences, brain chemistry, genes—and that feminism has reached its natural limits. What else could possibly explain the love of preschool girls for party dresses or the desire of toddler boys to own more guns than Mark from Michigan?

True, recent studies claim to show small cognitive differences between the sexes: He gets around by orienting himself in space; she does it by remembering landmarks. Time will tell if any deserve the hoopla with which each is invariably greeted, over the protests of the researchers themselves. But even if the results hold up (and the history of such research is not encouraging), we don't need studies of sex-differentiated brain activity in reading, say, to understand why boys and girls still seem so unalike.

The feminist movement has done much for some women, and something for every woman, but it has hardly turned America into a playground free of sex roles. It hasn't even got women to stop dieting or men to stop interrupting them.

Instead of looking at kids to "prove" that differences in behavior by sex are innate, we can look at the ways we raise kids as an index to how unfinished the feminist revolution really is, and how tentatively it is embraced even by adults who fully expect their daughters to enter previously male-dominated professions and their sons to change diapers.

I'm at a children's birthday party. "I'm sorry," one mom silently mouths to the mother of the birthday girl, who has just torn open her present—Tropical Splash Barbie. Now, you can love Barbie or you can hate Barbie, and there are feminists in both camps. But *apologize* for Barbie? Inflict Barbie, against your own convictions, on the child of a friend you know will be none too pleased?

Every mother in that room had spent years becoming a person who had to be taken seriously, not least by herself. Even the most attractive, I'm willing to bet, had suffered over her body's failure to fit the impossible American ideal. Given all that, it seems crazy to transmit Barbie to the

5

[1]**NOW** National organization for Women (Editors' note)

next generation. Yet to reject her is to say that what Barbie represents—being sexy, thin, stylish—is unimportant, which is obviously not true, and children know it's not true.

Women's looks matter terribly in this society, and so Barbie, however ambivalently, must be passed along. After all, there are worse toys. The Cut and Style Barbie styling head, for example, a grotesque object intended to encourage "hair play." The grown-ups who give that probably apologize, too.

How happy would most parents be to have a child who flouted sex conventions? I know a lot of women, feminists, who complain in a comical, eye-ball-rolling way about their sons' passion for sports: the ruined weekends, obnoxious coaches, macho values. But they would not think of discouraging their sons from participating in this activity they find so foolish. Or do they? Their husbands are sports fans, too, and they like their husbands a lot.

Could it be that even sports-resistant moms see athletics as part of manliness? That if their sons wanted to spend the weekend writing up their diaries, or reading, or baking, they'd find it disturbing? Too antisocial? Too lonely? Too gay?

Theories of innate differences in behavior are appealing. They let parents off the hook—no small recommendation in a culture that holds moms, and sometimes even dads, responsible for their children's every misstep on the road to bliss and success.

They allow grown-ups to take the path of least resistance to the dominant culture, which always requires less psychic effort, even if it means more actual work: Just ask the working mother who comes home exhausted and nonetheless finds it easier to pick up her son's socks than make him do it himself. They let families buy for their children, without *too* much guilt, the unbelievably sexist junk that the kids, who have been watching commercials since birth, understandably crave.

But the thing the theories do most of all is tell adults that the *adult* world—in which moms and dads still play by many of the old rules even as they question and fidget and chafe against them—is the way it's supposed to be. A girl with a doll and a boy with a truck "explain" why men are from Mars and women are from Venus, why wives do housework and husbands just don't understand.

The paradox is that the world of rigid and hierarchical sex roles evoked by determinist theories is already passing away. Three-year-olds may indeed insist that doctors are male and nurses female, even if their own mother is a physician. Six-year-olds know better. These days, something like half of all medical students are female, and male applications to nursing school are inching upward. When tomorrow's three-year-olds play doctor, who's to say how they'll assign the roles?

With sex roles, as in every area of life, people aspire to what is possible, and conform to what is necessary. But these are not fixed, especially today. Biological determinism may reassure some adults about their present, but it is feminism, the ideology of flexible and converging sex roles, that fits our children's future. And the kids, somehow, know this.

That's why, if you look carefully, you'll find that for every kid who fits   15
a stereotype, there's another who's breaking one down. Sometimes it's the
same kid—the boy who skateboards *and* takes cooking in his after school
program; the girl who collects stuffed animals *and* A-pluses in science.

Feminists are often accused of imposing their "agenda" on children.
Isn't that what adults always do, consciously and unconsciously? Kids
aren't born religious, or polite, or kind, or able to remember where they
put their sneakers. Inculcating these behaviors, and the values behind
them, is a tremendous amount of work, involving many adults. We don't
have a choice, really, about *whether* we should give our children messages
about what it means to be male and female—they're bombarded with
them from morning till night.

Joining the Conversation: Critical Thinking and Writing

1. In a paragraph set forth Pollitt's answer to the question she poses in her title.

2. In paragraph 7 Pollitt says, "Women's looks matter terribly in this society." Do you agree with this generalization? If they do matter "terribly," do they matter more than men's? What evidence can you give, one way or the other? Set forth your answer in an essay of 250 words.

3. Look at the last sentence in paragraph 12: "A girl with a doll and a boy with a truck 'explain' why men are from Mars and women are from Venus, why wives do housework and husbands just don't understand." Why does Pollitt put "explain" within quotation marks? What is she getting at by speaking of Mars and Venus? "Do housework" and "don't understand" are not the parallel construction that a reader probably expects. Do you think Pollitt's writing is deficient here, or is the variation purposeful? Explain.

4. In paragraph 14 Pollitt says that "the ideology of flexible and converging sex roles" is the one that "fits our children's future." What would be examples of "flexible and converging sex roles"? And do you agree that this ideology is the one that suits the immediate future? Why?

5. Do you believe that you have been influenced by Barbie or by any other toy? Explain.

6. In her final paragraph Pollitt says that adults always impose an "agenda" on their children, consciously or unconsciously. What agenda did your parents (or other adults charged with your upbringing) impose or try to impose? What was your response? As you think back on it, were the agenda and the responses appropriate? Set forth your answers in an essay of 500 to 750 words.

7. If you have heard that "brain chemistry" or "genes" (paragraph 1) account for "innate differences in behavior" (paragraph 10) in boys and girls, in a paragraph set forth the view, and in another paragraph evaluate it, drawing perhaps on your reading of Pollitt's essay.

Paul Theroux

Paul Theroux was born in 1941 in Medford, Massachusetts, and was educated at the University of Maine, the University of Massachusetts, and Syracuse University. He served as a Peace Corps volunteer in Africa and has spent much of his adult life abroad, in Africa, Asia, Europe, and Central America. Though best known as a novelist and writer of travel books, he is also a poet and essayist. This essay originally appeared in the New York Times Magazine.

The Male Myth

There is a pathetic sentence in the chapter "Fetishism" in Dr. Norman Cameron's book *Personality Development and Psychopathology*. It goes: "Fetishists are nearly always men; and their commonest fetish is a woman's shoe." I cannot read that sentence without thinking that it is just one more awful thing about being a man—and perhaps it is the most important thing to know about us.

I have always disliked being a man. The whole idea of manhood in America is pitiful, a little like having to wear an ill-fitting coat for one's entire life. (By contrast, I imagine femininity to be an oppressive sense of nakedness.) Even the expression "Be a man!" strikes me as insulting and abusive. It means: Be stupid, be unfeeling, obedient and soldierly, and stop thinking. Man means "manly"—how can one think "about men" without considering the terrible ambition of manliness? And yet it is part of every man's life. It is a hideous and crippling lie; it not only insists on difference and connives at superiority, it is also by its very nature destructive—emotionally damaging and socially harmful.

The youth who is subverted, as most are, into believing in the masculine ideal is effectively separated from women—it is the most savage tribal logic—and he spends the rest of his life finding women a riddle and a nuisance. Of course, there is a female version of this male affliction. It begins with mothers encouraging little girls to say (to other adults), "Do you like my new dress?" In a sense, girls are traditionally urged to please adults with a kind of coquettishness, while boys are enjoined to behave like monkeys toward each other. The 9-year-old coquette proceeds to become womanish in a subtle power game in which she learns to be sexually indispensable, socially decorative and always alert to a man's sense of inadequacy.

Femininity—being ladylike—implies needing a man as witness and seducer; but masculinity celebrates the exclusive company of men. That is why it is so grotesque; and that is also why there is no manliness without inadequacy—because it denies men the natural friendship of women.

It is very hard to imagine any concept of manliness that does not be-
little women, and it begins very early. At an age when I wanted to meet
girls—let's say the treacherous years of 13 to 16—I was told to take up a
sport, get more fresh air, join the Boy Scouts, and I was urged not to read
so much. It was the 1950's and, if you asked too many questions about
sex, you were sent to camp—boy's camp, of course; the nightmare.
Nothing is more unnatural or prisonlike than a boys' camp, but if it were
not for them, we would have no Elks' Lodges, no pool-rooms, no boxing
matches, no marines.

And perhaps no sports as we know them. Everyone is aware of how
few in number are the athletes who behave like gentlemen. Just as high-
school basketball teaches you how to be a poor loser, the manly attitude
toward sports seems to be little more than a recipe for creating bad
marriages, social misfits, moral degenerates, sadists, latent rapists and
just plain louts. I regard high-school sports as a drug far worse than
marijuana, and it is the reason that the average tennis champion, say, is a
pathetic oaf.

Any objective study would find the quest for manliness essentially
right wing, puritanical, cowardly, neurotic and fueled largely by a fear of
women. It is also certainly philistine. There is no book hater like a Little
League coach. But, indeed, all the creative arts are obnoxious to the manly
ideal, because at their best the arts are pursued by uncompetitive and essentially solitary people. It makes it very hard for a creative youngster, for
any boy who expresses the desire to be alone seems to be saying that
there is something wrong with him.

It ought to be clear by now that I have an objection to the way we
turn boys into men. It does not surprise me that when the President of the
United States has his customary weekend off, he dresses like a cowboy—
it is both a measure of his insecurity and his willingness to please. In
many ways, American culture does little more for a man than prepare
him for modeling clothes in the L. L. Bean catalogue. I take this as a personal insult because for many years I found it impossible to admit to myself that I wanted to be a writer. It was my guilty secret, because being a
writer was incompatible with being a man.

There are people who might deny this, but that is because the
American writer, typically, has been so at pains to prove his manliness.
But first there was a fear that writing was not a manly profession—
indeed, not a profession at all. (The paradox in American letters is that it
has always been easier for a woman to write and for a man to be published.) Growing up, I had thought of sports as wasteful and humiliating,
and the idea of manliness as a bore. My wanting to become a writer was
not a flight from that oppressive role playing, but I quickly saw that it
was at odds with it. Everything in stereotyped manliness goes against the
life of the mind. The Hemingway personality is too tedious to go into here,
but certainly it was not until this aberrant behavior was examined by
feminists in the 1960's that any male writer dared question the pugnacity

in Hemingway's fiction. All that bullfighting and arm-wrestling and elephant shooting diminished Hemingway as a writer: One cannot be a male writer without first proving that one is a man.

It is normal in America for a man to be dismissive or even somewhat apologetic about being a writer. Various factors make it easier. There is a heartiness about journalism that makes it acceptable—journalism is the manliest form of American writing and, therefore, the profession the most independent-minded women seek (yes, it is an illusion, but that is my point). Fiction writing is equated with a kind of dispirited failure and is only manly when it produces wealth. Money is masculinity. So is drinking. Being a drunkard is another assertion, if misplaced, of manliness. The American male writer is traditionally proud of his heavy drinking. But we are also very literal-minded people. A man proves his manhood in America in old-fashioned ways. He kills lions, like Hemingway; or he hunts ducks, like Nathanael West; or he makes pronouncements, like "A man should carry enough knife to defend himself with," as James Jones is said to have once told an interviewer. And we are familiar with the lengths to which Norman Mailer is prepared, in his endearing way, to prove that he is just as much a monster as the next man.

10

When the novelist John Irving was revealed as a wrestler, people took him to be a very serious writer. But what interests me is that it is inconceivable that any woman writer would be shown in such a posture. How surprised we would be if Joyce Carol Oates were revealed as a sumo wrestler or Joan Didion enjoyed pumping iron. "Lives in New York City with her three children" is the typical woman-writer's biographical note, for just as the male writer must prove he has achieved a sort of muscular manhood, the woman writer—or rather her publicists—must prove her motherhood.

There would be no point in saying any of this if it were not generally accepted that to be a man is somehow—even now in feminist-influenced America—a privilege. It is on the contrary an unmerciful and punishing burden. Being a man is bad enough; being manly is appalling. It is the sinister silliness of men's fashions that inspires the so-called dress code of the Ritz-Carlton Hotel in Boston. It is the institutionalized cheating in college sports. It is a pathetic and primitive insecurity.

And this is also why men often object to feminism, but are afraid to explain why: Of course women have a justified grievance, but most men believe—and with reason—that their lives are much worse.

Joining the Conversation: Critical Thinking and Writing

1. In paragraph 6 Theroux says that "high-school basketball teaches you how to be a poor loser." Think about this, and then write a paragraph that in effect offers a definition of a "poor loser" but that also shows how a high school sport teaches one to be a poor loser.

2. Theroux speaks of "the Hemingway personality" and of "the pugnacity in Hemingway's fiction." If you have read a work by Hemingway, write a paragraph in which you explain (to someone unfamiliar with Hemingway) what Theroux is talking about.

3. Let's assume that a reader says he or she doesn't quite understand Theroux's final paragraph. Write a paragraph explaining it.

4. Theroux makes some deliberately provocative statements, for example:

> Nothing is more unnatural or prisonlike than a boys' camp (paragraph 5).

> Everyone is aware of how few in number are the athletes who behave like gentlemen (paragraph 6).

> The quest for manliness . . . [is] fueled largely by a fear of women (paragraph 7).

Choose one such statement from the essay and consider what you would need to do to argue effectively against it. You needn't produce the argument, but simply consider how such an argument might be constructed.

Emily Tsao

Emily Tsao wrote this essay when she was a sophomore at Yale University. It was originally published in Newsday.

Thoughts of an Oriental Girl

I am an Oriental girl. Excuse me, I forgot to use my politically correct dictionary. Let me rephrase that, I am an Asian-American woman. Yes, that sounds about right. Excuse me again; I mean politically correct.

When I first stepped onto the campus scene last year, I, like many other anxious freshmen, wanted to fit in. I wanted to wear the right clothes, carry the right bookbag and, most important, say the right things. Speaking to upperclassmen, however, I realized that I had no command of the proper "PC" language.

Girls, it became clear, were to be called women. Freshmen who were girls were to be called freshwomen. Mixed groups of both sexes were to be labeled freshpeople, and upperclassmen were to be referred to as upper-classpeople. Orientals were to be called Asian Americans, blacks were to be called African Americans and Hispanics Latinos.

To me, most of this seemed pointless. Being called a girl doesn't bother   5
me. I'm 18 years old. My mom is a woman. I'm her kid. I don't expect her to refer to me as a woman.

I have always referred to my female friends as girls, and still do. I want my boyfriend to call me his girlfriend, not his woman friend.

My friends and I refer to the male students at college as boys or guys. Never men. Kevin Costner and Robert Redford are men. Men don't drink themselves sick at keg parties every weekend, ask Dad for money, or take laundry home to Mom.

For 12 years of high school and grade school, the female students were always girls and the males were boys. Why does going to college with these same peers suddenly make me a woman and the boys men? I certainly don't feel much older or wiser than I did last year. When people refer to me as a woman, I turn around to see who might be standing behind me.

Another fad now is for people to spell women with a "y" in place of the "e"—"womyn." These people want to take the "men" out of "women." Next perhaps they'll invent "fcmylc."

I've always been gender conscious with my language when it seemed   10
logical. In third grade I referred to the mailman as a mailperson because our mail was sometimes delivered by a woman. I don't think I ever said mailwoman, though, because it just didn't sound right.

From elementary through high school, I told people I was Chinese, and if I wanted to refer to all Asians, I used the word "Orientals." I guess I was young and foolish and didn't know any better.

At college I was told that the proper label for me was Asian American, that "Oriental" was a word to describe furniture, not people. But what is the difference? All Asians are still being clumped together, even though each group—Chinese, Korean, Japanese, Indians, Vietnamese and Filipinos, to name just a few—comes from a different country with a different language and culture.

The new "PC" term to describe Asian Americans and all other minorities is "people of color." The reason, I am told, is that the "minority" population has grown to be the majority. But even if that's true, the phrase seems contradictory. Since many African Americans no longer want to be referred to as blacks, why should the term for minorities once again refer to skin color? The same is true for Asians, most of whom find the label "yellow" more offensive than Oriental. And isn't white also a color?

As long as we're throwing out all the old labels, why not replace "white" with "European American." Wasps could be EAASPS (European-American Anglo Saxon Protestants). Well, maybe not. Minority groups want new labels to give themselves a more positive image, but unless the stereotypes disappear as well, is it really going to help very much?

Look at the word "sophomore," which comes from Greek roots meaning "wise fool." PC-conscious sophomores ought to revolt against this offensive phrase. I, however, will not be among them. Changing the word won't make me any smarter, humbler or wiser.

Joining the Conversation: Critical Thinking and Writing

1. Tsao doesn't comment on stereotypical views of persons of Asian background, but one commonly hears that the chief stereotypes are these: The men are asexual, effeminate, and sly; the women are malevolent (Dragon Lady) or passive (Madam Butterfly). If you are familiar with any of the images that perhaps have helped to perpetuate these or other stereotypes, set forth your response, for instance to a Charlie Chan film (the clever Asian).

2. In paragraph 11 Tsao rightly insists that "each group—Chinese, Korean, Japanese, Indians, Vietnamese and Filipinos, to name just a few—comes from a different country with a different language and culture." If we can speak of "culture"—whether Chinese or Anglo or Italian or Italian American—how does culture differ from stereotypical behavior?

3. In her first three paragraphs Tsao says that the word "Oriental" is now in disfavor, but she doesn't say why. The reasons apparently are two: (1) The word (from Latin *oriri*, "to arise") means, in effect, the east, where the sun arises. The word is now regarded as Eurocentric; China, Korea, and Japan are eastern relative to Europe, but they are not eastern in an absolute sense. (2) "Oriental," used of Chinese, Koreans, Japanese, Indonesians, and others, suggests racial identity, and overlooks important cultural differences. The preferred terms today are East Asia and East Asian. Given this background, do you think it is foolish to abandon the terms "Orient" and "Oriental"? In an essay of 250 words set forth your response.

4. In paragraph 3 Tsao talks about the word "freshman." If you were a college dean or president, in other words someone in a position to set the tone for the institution, would you abandon "freshman" and "freshwoman" for "freshperson," or perhaps for "first-year student"? In a paragraph explain why you would or would not drop "freshman" for all first-year students.

5. In paragraph 12 Tsao comments on the use of the term "people of color." Does the term seem to you to have some value, or is it something we should avoid using? Set forth your views in one or two paragraphs.

Gloria Naylor

Gloria Naylor—university teacher, essayist, and novelist—holds an M.A. in African-American Studies from Yale University. Her first novel, The Women of Brewster Place *(1983), won an American Book Award. "A Question of Language" originally appeared in the* New York Times Magazine.

A Question of Language

Language is the subject. It is the written form with which I've managed to keep the wolf away from the door and, in diaries, to keep my sanity. In spite of this, I consider the written word inferior to the spoken, and much of the frustration experienced by novelists is the awareness that whatever we manage to capture in even the most transcendent passages falls far short of the richness of life. Dialogue achieves its power in the dynamics of a fleeting moment of sight, sound, smell, and touch.

I'm not going to enter the debate here about whether it is language that shapes reality or vice versa. That battle is doomed to be waged whenever we seek intermittent reprieve from the chicken and egg dispute. I will simply take the position that the spoken word, like the written word, amounts to a nonsensical arrangement of sounds or letters without a consensus that assigns "meaning." And building from the meanings of what we hear, we order reality. Words themselves are innocuous; it is the consensus that gives them true power.

I remember the first time I heard the word *nigger*. In my third-grade class, our math tests were being passed down the rows, and as I handed the papers to a little boy in back of me, I remarked that once again he had received a much lower mark than I did. He snatched his test from me and spit out that word. Had he called me a nymphomaniac or a necrophiliac, I couldn't have been more puzzled. I didn't know what a nigger was, but I knew that whatever it meant, it was something he shouldn't have called me. This was verified when I raised my hand, and in a loud voice repeated what he had said and watched the teacher scold him for using a "bad" word. I was later to go home and ask the inevitable question that every black parent must face—"Mommy, what does 'nigger' mean?"

And what exactly did it mean? Thinking back, I realize that this could not have been the first time the word was used in my presence. I was part of a large extended family that had migrated from the rural South after World War II and formed a close-knit network that gravitated around my maternal grandparents. Their ground-floor apartment in one of the buildings they owned in Harlem was a weekend mecca for my immediate family, along with countless aunts, uncles, and cousins who brought along assorted friends. It was a bustling and open house with assorted neighbors and tenants popping in and out to exchange bits of gossip, pick up an old quarrel or referee the ongoing checkers game in which my grandmother cheated shamelessly. They were all there to let down their hair and put up their feet after a week of labor in the factories, laundries, and shipyards of New York.

Amid the clamor, which could reach deafening proportions—two or
three conversations going on simultaneously, punctuated by the sound of
a baby's crying somewhere in the back rooms or out on the street—there
was still a rigid set of rules about what was said and how. Older children
were sent out of the living room when it was time to get into the juicy details about "you-know-who" up on the third floor who had gone and gotten herself "p.r.e.g.n.a.n.t!" But my parents, knowing that I could spell
well beyond my years, always demanded that I follow the others out to
play. Beyond sexual misconduct and death, everything else was considered harmless for our young ears. And so among the anecdotes of the triumphs and disappointments in the various workings of their lives, the
word *nigger* was used in my presence, but it was set within contexts and
inflections that caused it to register in my mind as something else.

In the singular, the word was always applied to a man who had distinguished himself in some situation that brought their approval for his
strength, intelligence, or drive:

"Did Johnny really do that?"

"I'm telling you, that nigger pulled in $6,000 of overtime last year.
Said he got enough for a down payment on a house."

When used with a possessive adjective by a woman—"my nigger"—
it became a term of endearment for husband or boyfriend. But it could be
more than just a term applied to a man. In their mouths it became the
pure essence of manhood—a disembodied force that channeled their past
history of struggle and present survival against the odds into a victorious
statement of being: "Yeah, that old foreman found out quick enough—
you don't mess with a nigger."

In the plural, it became a description of some group within the community that had overstepped the bounds of decency as my family defined
it: Parents who neglected their children, a drunken couple who fought in
public, people who simply refused to look for work, those with exces-
sively dirty mouths or unkempt households were all "trifling niggers."
This particular circle could forgive hard times, unemployment, the occasional bout of depression—they had gone through all of that themselves—
but the unforgivable sin was lack of self-respect.

A woman could never be a *nigger* in the singular, with its connotation
of confirming worth. The noun *girl* was its closest equivalent in that
sense, but only when used in direct address and regardless of the gender
doing the addressing. *Girl* was a token of respect for a woman. The one-
syllable word was drawn out to sound like three in recognition of the extra ounce of wit, nerve or daring that the woman had shown in the situation under discussion.

"G.i.r.l, stop. You mean you said that to his face?"

But if the word was used in a third-person reference or shortened so
that it almost snapped out of the mouth, it always involved some element
of communal disapproval. And age became an important factor in these
exchanges. It was only between individuals of the same generation, or

5

10

from an older person to a younger (but never the other way around), that "girl" would be considered a compliment.

I don't agree with the argument that use of the word *nigger* at this social stratum of the black community was an internalization of racism. The dynamics were the exact opposite: the people in my grandmother's living room took a word that whites used to signify worthlessness or degradation and rendered it impotent. Gathering there together, they transformed *nigger* to signify the varied and complex human beings they knew themselves to be. If the word was to disappear totally from the mouths of even the most liberal of white society, no one in that room was naive enough to believe it would disappear from white minds. Meeting the word head-on, they proved it had absolutely nothing to do with the way they were determined to live their lives.

So there must have been dozens of times that the word *nigger* was   15
spoken in front of me before I reached the third grade. But I didn't "hear" it until it was said by a small pair of lips that had already learned it could be a way to humiliate me. That was the word I went home and asked my mother about. And since she knew that I had to grow up in America, she took me in her lap and explained.

 ## Joining the Conversation: Critical Thinking and Writing

1. Why, according to Naylor (in paragraph 1) is written language inferior to spoken language? Can you think of any way or any circumstance in which written language is superior? How does Naylor's essay support her position here? Or does it?

2. In paragraph 2 Naylor says, "Words themselves are innocuous; it is the consensus that gives them true power." What does this mean? In the rest of the essay Naylor discusses meanings of the word *nigger*. To what extent does her discussion demonstrate that consensus "assigns meaning" and gives words power?

3. If as a child you were the victim of an ethnic slur, explain how you reacted to it and how others (perhaps a parent or teacher) reacted to it. Or, if you ever delivered an ethnic slur, explain how you felt then and how you feel now about the incident or incidents.

Richard Rodriguez, with Scott London

Richard Rodriguez, born in San Francisco in 1944, is often seen and heard as a commentator on the NewsHour with Jim Lehrer. *His memoir,* Hunger of Memory: The Education of Richard Rodriguez *(1982), is an account of the experience of a Chicano growing up in a neighborhood that was chiefly white. We reprint part of an interview with Rodriguez (interviewed by Scott London), conducted in Santa Barbara in 1997.*

A View from the Melting Pot

Scott London: In *Hunger of Memory*, you suggest that supporters of bilingual education are misguided. You write, "What they don't seem to recognize is that, as a socially disadvantaged child, I considered Spanish to be a private language." In what way was Spanish a private language for you?

Richard Rodriguez: In some countries, of course, Spanish is the language spoken in public. But for many American children whose families speak Spanish at home, it becomes a private language. They use it to keep the English-speaking world at bay.

Billingual-education advocates say it's important to teach a child in his or her family's language. I say you can't use family language in the classroom—the very nature of the classroom requires that you use language publicly. When the Irish nun said to me, "Speak your name loud and clear so that all the boys and girls can hear you," she was asking me to use language publicly, with strangers. That's the appropriate instruction for a teacher to give. If she were to say to me, "We are going to speak now in Spanish, just like you do at home. You can whisper anything you want to me, and I am going to call you by a nickname, just like your mother does," that would be inappropriate. That is not what classrooms are about.

Scott London: Some would argue that students are stripped of their cultural identity by being instructed in the dominant language. Isn't there some truth to that?

Richard Rodriguez: My grandmother would always tell me that I was hers, that I was Mexican. That was her role. It was not my teacher's role to tell me I was Mexican. It was my teacher's role to tell me I was an American. The notion that you go to a public institution in order to learn private information about yourself is absurd. We used to understand that when students went to universities, they would become cosmopolitan. They were leaving their neighborhoods. Now we have this idea that, not only do you go to first grade to learn your family's language, but you go to a university to learn about the person you were before you left home. So rather than becoming multicultural, rather than becoming confident in your knowledge of the world, you become just the opposite. You end up in college having to apologize for the fact that you no longer speak your native language.

I worry these days that Latinos in California speak neither Spanish nor English very well. They are in a kind of linguistic limbo between the two. They don't really have a language, and are, in some deep sense homeless.

Scott London: Many people feel that the call for diversity and multiculturalism is one reason the American educational system is collapsing.

Scott London, "A View from the Melting Pot: An Interview with Richard Rodriguez" from the public radio series, *Insight & Outlook,* 1997. Reproduced by permission.

Richard Rodriguez: It's no surprise that at the same time that American universities have engaged in a serious commitment to diversity, they have been thought-prisons. We are not talking about diversity in any real way. We are talking about brown, black, white versions of the same political ideology. It is very curious that the United States and Canada both assume that diversity means only race and ethnicity. They never assume it might mean more Nazis, or more Southern Baptists. That's diversity too, you know.

Scott London: What do you mean by diversity?

Richard Rodriguez: For me, diversity is not a value. Diversity is what you find in Northern Ireland. Diversity is Beirut. Diversity is brother killing brother. Where diversity is shared—where I share with you my difference—that can be valuable. But the simple fact that we are unlike each other is a terrifying notion. I have often found myself in foreign settings where I became suddenly aware that I was not like the people around me. That, to me, is not a pleasant discovery.

Scott London: You've said that it's tough in America to lead an intellectual life outside the universities. Yet you made a very conscious decision to leave academia.

Richard Rodriguez: My decision was sparked by affirmative action. There was a point in my life when affirmative action would have meant something to me—when my father was working-class, and we were struggling. But very early in life I became part of the majority culture and now don't think of myself as a minority. Yet the university said I was one. Anybody who has met a real minority—in the economic sense, not the numerical sense—would understand how ridiculous it is to describe a young man who was already at the university, already well into his studies in Italian and English Renaissance literature, as a minority. Affirmative action ignores society's real minorities—members of the disadvantaged classes, no matter what their race. We have this ludicrous bureaucratic sense that certain racial groups, regardless of class, are minorities. So what happens is those "minorities" at the very top of the ladder get chosen for everything.

Scott London: Is that what happened to you?

Richard Rodriguez: Well, when it came time for me to look for jobs, the jobs came looking for me. I had teaching offers from the best universities in the country. I was about to accept one from Yale when the whole thing collapsed on me.

Scott London: What do you mean?

Richard Rodriguez: I had all this anxiety about what it meant to be a minority. My professors—the same men who taught the intricacies of language—just shied away from the issue. They didn't want to talk about it, other than to suggest I could be a "role model" to other Hispanics— when I went back to my barrio, I suppose. I came from a white middle-class neighborhood. Was I expected to go back there and teach the woman next door about Renaissance sonnets? The embarrassing truth of the matter was that I was being chosen because Yale University had some peculiar idea about [what] my skin color or ethnicity signified. Who knows what Yale thought it was getting when it hired Richard Rodriguez?

The people who offered me the job thought there was nothing wrong with that. I thought there was something very wrong with that. I still do. I think race-based affirmative action is crude and absolutely mistaken.

Scott London: I noticed that some university students had put up a poster outside the lecture hall where you spoke the other night. It said "Richard Rodriguez is a disgrace to the Chicano community."

Richard Rodriguez: I sort of like that. I don't think writers should be convenient examples. I don't think we should make people feel settled. I don't try to be a gadfly, but I do think that real ideas are troublesome. There should be something about my work that leaves the reader unsettled. I intend that. The notion of the writer as a kind of sociological sample of a community is ludicrous. Even worse is the notion that writers should provide an example of how to live. Virginia Woolf ended her life by putting a rock in her sweater one day and walking into a lake. She is not a model of how I want to live my life. On the other hand, the bravery of her syntax, of her sentences, written during her deepest depression, is a kind of example for me. But I do not want to become Virginia Woolf. That is not why I read her.

Scott London: What's wrong with being a role model?   20

Richard Rodriguez: The popular idea of a role model implies that an adult's influence on a child is primarily occupational, and that all a black child needs is to see a black doctor, and then this child will think, "Oh, I can become a doctor too." I have a good black friend who is a doctor, but he didn't become a doctor because he saw other black men who were doctors. He became a doctor because his mother cleaned office buildings at night, and because she loved her children. She grew bowlegged from cleaning office buildings at night, and in the process she taught him something about courage and bravery and dedication to others. I became a writer not because my father was one—my father made false teeth for a living. I became a writer because the Irish nuns who educated me taught me something about bravery with their willingness to give so much to me.

Scott London: Why do we always talk about race in this country strictly in terms of black and white?

Richard Rodriguez: America has never had a very wide vocabulary for miscegenation. We say we like diversity, but we don't like the idea that our Hispanic neighbor is going to marry our daughter. America has nothing like the Spanish vocabulary for miscegenation. Mulatto, *mestizo,* Creole—these Spanish and French terms suggest, by their use, that miscegenation is a fact of life. America has only black and white. In eighteenth-century America, if you had any drop of African blood in you, you were black.

After the O.J. Simpson trial there was talk about how the country was splitting in two—one part black, one part white. It was ludicrous: typical gringo arrogance. It's as though whites and blacks can imagine America only in terms of each other. It's mostly white arrogance, in that it places whites always at the center of the racial equation. But lots of emerging racial tensions in California have nothing to do with whites: Filipinos and Samoans are fighting it out in San Francisco high schools. Merced is becoming majority Mexican and Cambodian. They may be fighting in gangs right now, but I bet they are also learning each other's language. Cultures, when they meet, influence one another, whether people like it or not. But Americans don't have any way of describing this secret that has been going on for over two hundred years. The intermarriage of the Indian and the African in America, for example, has been constant and thorough. Colin Powell tells us in his autobiography that he is Scotch, Irish, African, Indian, and British, but all we hear is that he is African.

Scott London: The latest census figures show that two-thirds of children who are the products of a union between a black and a white call themselves black.   25

Richard Rodriguez: The census bureau is thinking about creating a new category because so many kids don't know how to describe themselves using the existing categories. I call these kids the "Keanu Reeves Generation," after the actor who has a Hawaiian father and a Welsh mother. Most American Hispanics don't belong to one race, either. I keep telling kids that, when filling out forms, they should put "yes" to everything—yes, I am Chinese; yes, I am African; yes, I am white; yes, I am a Pacific Islander; yes, yes, yes—just to befuddle the bureaucrats who think we live separately from one another.

Scott London: There is a lot of talk today about the "hyphenating" of America. We no longer speak of ourselves as just Americans—now we're Italian-Americans, African-Americans, Mexican-Americans, even Anglo-Americans.

Richard Rodriguez: The fact that we're all hyphenating our names suggests that we are afraid of being assimilated. I was talking on the BBC recently, and this woman introduced me as being "in favor of assimilation." I said. "I'm not in favor of assimilation." I am no more in favor of assimilation than I am in favor of the Pacific Ocean. Assimilation is not something to oppose or favor—it just happens.

Scott London: Time magazine did a special issue on the global village a couple of years ago. The cover photo was a computer composite of different faces from around the world. It was a stunning picture—neither man nor woman, black nor white. This is the kind of assimilation that many worry about—the loss of things that make us separate and unique.

Richard Rodriguez: Jose Vasconcelos, Mexico's great federalist and   30
apologist, has coined a wonderful term, *la raza cosmica,* "the cosmic race," a new people having not one race but many in their blood.

But Mexicans who come to America today end up opposing assimilation. They say they are "holding on to their culture," To them, I say, "If you really wanted to hold on to your culture, you would be in favor of assimilation. You would be fearless about swallowing English and about becoming Americanized. You would be much more positive about the future, and much less afraid. That's what it means to be Mexican.

I'm constantly depressed by the Mexican gang members I meet in East LA who essentially live their lives inside five or six blocks. They are caught in some tiny ghetto of the mind that limits them to these five blocks because, they say, "I'm Mexican. I live here." And I say, "What do you mean you live here—five blocks? Your granny, your *abualita*, walked two thousand miles to get here. She violated borders, moved from one language to another, moved from a sixteenth-century village to a twenty-first-century city, and you live within five blocks? You don't know Mexico, man. You have trivialized Mexico. You are a fool about Mexico if you think that Mexico is five blocks. That is not Mexico; that is some crude Americanism you have absorbed."

Scott London: You have described Los Angeles as the symbolic capital of the United States.

Richard Rodriguez: I find LA very interesting, partly because I think something new is forming there, but not in a moment of good fellowship as you might think from all this "diversity" claptrap. It's not as if we'll all go down to the Civic Center in our ethnic costumes and dance around.

After the LA riots in 1992, my sense was not that the city was dying, as the expert opinion had it, but that the city was being formed. What was dying was the idea that LA was a city of separate suburbs and freeway exits. What burned in that riot was the idea that the east side was far away from the west side. People went to bed that first night watching television, watching neighborhoods they had never seen before, streets they had never been on, and they were chagrined and horrified by what they saw. Sometime in the middle of the night they could hear the sirens and smell the smoke, and realized that the fire was coming toward them—that the street they lived on, the boulevard they used everyday, was in fact connected to a part of town where they had never been before, and that part of town was now a part of their lives.

That moment of fear, of terror, of sleeplessness, was not a death, but the birth of the idea that LA is a single city, a single metropolitan area.

What we have seen in the last three or four years is, if not optimistic, at least something very young and full of possibility. Women have been telling men forever that childbirth is painful, that life begins with a scream, not with little butterflies and little tweeting birds; life begins with a scream. In 1992, LA came to life with a scream.

Scott London: If LA represents the future, does that mean we're looking at more riots?

35

Richard Rodriguez: We're looking at complexity. We're looking at blond kids in Beverley Hills who can speak Spanish because they have been raised by Guatemalan nannies. We're looking at Evangelicals coming up from Latin America to convert the U.S. at the same time that LA movie stars are taking up Indian pantheism. We're looking at such enormous complexity and variety that it makes a mockery of "celebrating diversity." In the LA of the future, no one will need to say, "Let's celebrate diversity." Diversity is going to be a fundamental part of our lives.

If you want to live in Tennessee, God bless you, I wish for you a long life   40
and starry evenings. But that is not where I want to live my life. I want to live my life in Carthage, in Athens. I want to live my life in Rome. I want to live my life in the center of the world. I want to live my life in Los Angeles.

Joining the Conversation: Critical Thinking and Writing

1. What does Rodriguez mean when he says that for many families Spanish is a "private language"?

2. Why does Rodriguez say, "We are not talking about diversity in any real way?" Does he give evidence to support this claim? Does he explain what would be the "real way" to talk about diversity?

3. Do you think that Rodriguez presents a new perspective on affirmative action? What is the strongest argument you can make *for* affirmative action? What is the strongest argument you can make *against* it? Which is closer to your own view?

4. Do you agree with Rodriguez that Americans "are afraid of being assimilated?" Do you feel that you have "assimilated" into American society and culture? What is your evidence that you have or have not?

5. Imagine that you have been assigned to do "part two" of an interview with Richard Rodriguez. List five questions that you would like him to respond to.

Amy Tan

Amy Tan was born in Oakland, California, in 1952, of Chinese immigrant parents. When she was eight years old, she won first prize among elementary students with an essay entitled, "What the Library Means to Me." In due time she attended Linfield College in Oregon, then transferred to San Jose State University where, while working two part-time jobs, she became an honors student and a President's Scholar. In 1973 she earned an M.A. in linguistics, also at San Jose, and she later enrolled as a doctoral student at the University of California, Berkeley, though she left this program after the murder of a close friend. In 1989 her novel, The Joy Luck Club, *was published. Other books include* The Kitchen God's Wife *(1991),* The Hundred Secret Senses *(1995),* The Bonesetter's Daughter *(2001), and* Saving Fish from Drowning *(2005). She has also written two books for children,* The Moon Lady *(1992) and* SAGWA the Chinese Siamese Cat *(1994).*
The essay that we reprint appeared in Life *magazine in April 1991.*

Snapshot: Lost Lives of Women

When I first saw this photo as a child, I thought it was exotic and remote, of a faraway time and place, with people who had no connection to my American life. Look at their bound feet! Look at that funny lady with the plucked forehead!

The solemn little girl is, in fact, my mother. And leaning against the rock is my grandmother, Jingmei. "She called me Baobei," my mother told me. "It means Treasure."

The picture was taken in Hangzhou, and my mother believes the year was 1922, possibly spring or fall, judging by the clothes. At first glance, it appears the women are on a pleasure outing.

But see the white bands on their skirts? The white shoes? They are in mourning. My mother's grandmother, known to the others as Divong, "The Replacement Wife," has recently died. The women have come to this place, a Buddhist retreat, to perform yet another ceremony for Divong. Monks hired for the occasion have chanted the proper words. And the women and little girl have walked in circles clutching smoky sticks of incense. They knelt and prayed, then burned a huge pile of spirit money so that Divong might ascend to a higher position in her new world.

Courtesy Amy Tan

This is also a picture of secrets and tragedies, the reasons that warnings have been passed along in our family like heirlooms. Each of these women suffered a terrible fate, my mother said. And they were not peasant women but big city people, very modern. They went to dance halls and wore stylish clothes. They were supposed to be the lucky ones.

Look at the pretty woman with her finger on her cheek. She is my mother's second cousin, Nunu Aiji, "Precious Auntie." You cannot see this, but Nunu Aiyi's entire face was scarred from smallpox. Lucky for her, a year or so after this picture was taken, she received marriage proposals from two families. She turned down a lawyer and married another man. Later she divorced her husband, a daring thing for a woman to do. But then, finding no means to support herself or her young daughter, Nunu eventually accepted the lawyer's second proposal—to become his number two concubine. "Where else could she go?" my mother asked. "Some people said she was lucky the lawyer still wanted her."

Now look at the small woman with a sour face (*third from left*). There's a reason that Jyou Ma, "Uncle's Wife," looks this way. Her husband, my great-uncle often complained that his family had chosen an ugly woman for his wife. To show his displeasure, he often insulted Jyou Ma's cooking. One time Great-Uncle tipped over a pot of boiling soup, which fell all over his niece's four-year-old neck and nearly killed her. My mother was the little niece, and she still has that soup scar on her neck. Great-Uncle's family eventually chose a pretty woman for his second wife. But the complaints about Jyou Ma's cooking did not stop.

Doomma, "Big Mother," is the regal-looking woman seated on a rock. (The woman with the plucked forehead, far left, is a servant, remembered only as someone who cleaned but did not cook.) Doomma was the daughter of my great-grandfather and Nu-pei, "The Original Wife." She was shunned by Divong, "The Replacement Wife," for being "too strong," and loved by Divong's daughter, my grandmother. Doomma's first daughter was born with a hunchback—a sign, some said, of Doomma's own crooked nature. Why else did she remarry, disobeying her family's orders to remain a widow forever? And why did Doomma later kill herself, using some mysterious means that caused her to die slowly over three days? "Doomma died the same way she lived," my mother said, "strong, suffering lots."

Jingmei, my own grandmother, lived only a few more years after this picture was taken. She was the widow of a poor scholar, a man who had the misfortune of dying from influenza when he was about to be appointed a vice-magistrate. In 1924 or so, a rich man, who liked to collect pretty women, raped my grandmother and thereby forced her into becoming one of his concubines. My grandmother, now an outcast, took her young daughter to live with her on an island outside of Shanghai. She left her son behind, to save his face. After she gave birth to another son she killed herself by swallowing raw opium buried in the New Year's rice cakes. The young daughter who wept at her deathbed was my mother.

At my grandmother's funeral, monks tied chains to my mother's an-   10
kles so she would not fly away with her mother's ghost. "I tried to take
them off," my mother said. "I was her treasure. I was her life."

My mother could never talk about any of this, even with her closest
friends. "Don't tell anyone," she once said to me. "People don't understand. A concubine was like some kind of prostitute. My mother was a
good woman, high-class. She had no choice."

I told her I understood.

"How can you understand?" she said, suddenly angry. "You did not
live in China then. You do not know what it's like to have no position in
life. I was her daughter. We had no face! We belonged to nobody! This is a
shame I can never push off my back." By the end of the outburst, she was
crying.

On a recent trip with my mother to Beijing, I learned that my uncle
found a way to push the shame off his back. He was the son my grandmother left behind. In 1936 he joined the Communist party—in large part,
he told me, to overthrow the society that forced his mother into concubi-
nage. He published a story about his mother. I told him I had written about
my grandmother in a book of fiction. We agreed that my grandmother is
the source of strength running through our family. My mother cried to
hear this.

My mother believes my grandmother is also my muse, that she helps me   15
write. "Does she still visit you often?" she asked while I was writing my
second book. And then she added shyly, "Does she say anything about me?"

"Yes," I told her. "She has lots to say. I am writing it down."

This is the picture I see when I write. These are the secrets I was
supposed to keep. These are the women who never let me forget why
stories need to be told.

Joining the Conversation: Critical Thinking and Writing

1. Consider the title of this essay. Why are the women's lives described as
   "lost lives"? Can you imagine a companion piece, "Lost Lives of Men"? If
   not, why not?

2. In paragraph 5, what does Tan communicate by "and they were not peasant women but big city people, very modern"? What does she imply about
   the lives of those who *were* peasants?

3. In the fifth paragraph and in the last, Tan refers to "secrets" that she "was
   supposed to keep." What were the secrets? Why does she reveal them?

4. In the first paragraph Tan reports, "When I first saw this photo as a child, I
   thought it was exotic and remote, of a faraway time and place, with people
   who had no connection to my American life." What does she imply in this
   paragraph about their "connection to [her] American life" now? Where in
   the essay is that connection revealed or explained?

5. If you are lucky enough to have photographs of your ancestors, explore the images of the people in them and what you have been told about their lives. Do you feel "connected" or not? Explain.

A Casebook on Race

Columbia Encyclopedia

Because The Columbia Encyclopedia *is amazingly comprehensive and, for its size, relatively inexpensive, many people rightly believe that (like a good dictionary) it should be part of one's home reference library. We reprint the unsigned essay on "Race."*

Race

Race, one of the group of populations constituting humanity. The differences among races are essentially biological and are marked by the hereditary transmission of physical characteristics. Genetically a race may be defined as a group with gene frequencies differing from those of the other groups in the human species (see heredity; genetics; gene). However, the genes responsible for the hereditary differences between humans are extremely few when compared with the vast number of genes common to all human beings regardless of the race to which they belong. Many physical anthropologists believe that, because there is as much genetic variation among the members of any given race as there is between different racial groups, the concept of race is ultimately unscientific and racial categories are arbitrary designations. The term *race* is inappropriate when applied to national, religious, geographic, linguistic, or ethnic groups, nor can the biological criteria of race be equated with any mental characteristics such as intelligence, personality, or character.

All human groups belong to the same species (*Homo sapiens*) and are mutually fertile. Races arose as a result of mutation, selection, and adaptational changes in human populations. The nature of genetic variation in human beings indicates that there has been a common evolution for all races and that differentiation occurred relatively late in the history of *Homo sapiens*. Theories postulating the very early emergence of racial differentiation have been advanced (e.g., C. S. Coon, *The Origin of Races*, 1962), but they are now scientifically discredited.

To classify humans on the basis of physiological traits is difficult, for the coexistence of races through conquests, invasions, migrations, and mass deportations has produced a heterogeneous world population. Nevertheless, by limiting the criteria to such traits as skin pigmentation, color and form of hair, shape of head, stature, and form of nose, most anthropologists agree on the existence of three relatively distinct groups: the Caucasoid, the Mongoloid, and the Negroid.

The Caucasoid, found in Europe, North Africa, and the Middle East to North India, is characterized as pale reddish white to olive brown in skin color, of medium to tall stature, with a long or broad head form. The hair is light blond to dark brown in color, of a fine texture, and straight or wavy. The color of the eyes is light blue to dark brown, and the nose bridge is usually high.

The Mongoloid race, including most peoples of East Asia and the indigenous peoples of the Americas, has been described as saffron to yellow or reddish brown in skin color, of medium stature, with a broad head form. The hair is dark, straight, and coarse; body hair is sparse. The eyes are black to dark brown. The epicanthic fold, imparting an almond shape to the eye, is common, and the nose bridge is usually low or medium.

The Negroid race is characterized by brown to brown-black skin, usually a long head form, varying stature, and thick, everted lips. The hair is dark and coarse, usually kinky. The eyes are dark, the nose bridge low, and the nostrils broad. To the Negroid race belong the peoples of Africa south of the Sahara, the Pygmy groups of Indonesia, and the inhabitants of New Guinea and Melanesia.

Each of these broad groups can be divided into subgroups. General agreement is lacking as to the classification of such people as the aborigines of Australia, the Dravidian people of South India, the Polynesians, and the Ainu of North Japan.

Attempts have been made to classify humans since the 17th century, when scholars first began to separate types of flora and fauna. Johann Friedrich Blumenbach was the first to divide humanity according to skin color. In the 19th and early 20th centuries, men such as Joseph Arthur Gobineau and Houston Stewart Chamberlain, mainly interested in pressing forward the supposed superiority of their own kind of culture or nationality, began to attribute cultural and psychological values to race. This approach, called racism, culminated in the vicious racial doctrines of Nazi Germany, and especially in anti-Semitism. This same approach complicated the integration movement in the United States and underlay the former segregation policies of the Republic of South Africa (see apartheid).

See R. Benedict, *Race: Science and Politics* (rev. ed. 1943, repr. 1968); C. Lévi-Strauss, *Race and History* (1962); M. Mead et al., ed., *Science and the Concept of Race* (1968); S. M. Garn, ed., *Readings on Race* (2d ed. 1968) and *Human Races* (3d ed. 1971); J. C. King, *The Biology of Race* (1971); L. L. Cavalli-Sforza, *The Origin and Differentiation of Human Races* (1972); S. J. Gould, *The Mismeasure of Man* (1981); I. F. Haney Lopez, *White by Law: The Legal Construction of Race* (1996); A. Montagu, *Man's Most Dangerous*

Myth: The Fallacy of Race (6th ed. 1998); G. M. Frederickson, *Racism: A Short History* (2002).

Joining the Conversation: Critical Thinking and Writing

1. The author refers to inappropriate applications of the word "race." What applications are listed as inappropriate?

2. The author reports that physical anthropologists believe that "the concept of race is ultimately unscientific and racial categories are arbitrary designations." On what evidence does the author base this belief?

3. The author also states that "biological criteria of race" cannot "be equated with any mental characteristics such as intelligence, personality, or character." If, in a conversation, you were to hear an inappropriate use of the word "race" or an equation of race with mental characteristics, what would you do?

Armand Marie Leroi

Armand Marie Leroi, a Dutch citizen, was born in New Zealand in 1964, and educated in New Zealand, South Africa, Canada, and the United Sates. An evolutionary developmental biologist, he now teaches at Imperial College in London. He is the author of Mutants: On Genetic Variety and the Human Body *(2007).*

A Family Tree in Every Gene

Shortly after last year's tsunami devastated the lands on the Indian Ocean, *The Times* of India ran an article with this headline: "Tsunami May Have Rendered Threatened Tribes Extinct." The tribes in question were the Onge, Jarawa, Great Andamanese and Sentinelese—all living on the Andaman Islands—and they numbered some 400 people in all. The article, noting that several of the archipelago's islands were low-lying, in the direct path of the wave, and that casualties were expected to be high, said, "Some beads may have just gone missing from the Emerald Necklace of India."

The metaphor is as colorful as it is well intentioned. But what exactly does it mean? After all, in a catastrophe that cost more than 150,000 lives, why should the survival of a few hundred tribal people have any special claim on our attention? There are several possible answers to this question. The people of the Andamans have a unique way of life. True, their material culture does not extend beyond a few simple tools, and their visual art is confined to a few geometrical motifs, but they are hunter-gatherers and so a rarity in the modern world. Linguists, too, find them interesting since they collectively speak three languages seemingly unrelated to any others. But *The Times* of India took a slightly different tack. These tribes are special, it said, because they are of "Negrito racial stocks" that are "remnants of the oldest human populations as Asia and Australia."

It's an old-fashioned, even Victorian, sentiment. Who speaks of "racial stocks" anymore? After all, to do so would be to speak of something that many scientists and scholars say does not exist. If modern anthropologists mention the concept of race, it is invariably only to warn against and dismiss it. Likewise many geneticists. "Race is social concept, not a scientific one," according to Dr. Craig Venter—and he should know, since he was first to sequence the human genome. The idea that human races are only social constructs has been the consensus for at least 30 years.

But now, perhaps, that is about to change. Last fall, the prestigious journal *Nature Genetics* devoted a large supplement to the question of whether human races exist and, if so, what they mean. The journal did this in part because various American health agencies are making race an important part of their policies to best protect the public—often over the protests of scientists. In the supplement, some two dozen geneticists offered their views. Beneath the jargon, cautious phrases and academic courtesies, one thing was clear: the consensus about social constructs was unraveling. Some even argued that, looked at the right way, genetic data show that races clearly do exist.

The dominance of the social construct theory can be traced to a 1972 article by Dr. Richard Lewontin, a Harvard geneticist, who wrote that most human genetic variation can be found within any given "race." If one looked at genes rather than faces, he claimed, the difference between an African and a European would be scarcely greater than the difference between any two Europeans. A few years later he wrote that the continued popularity of race as an idea was an "indication of the power of socioeconomically based ideology over the supposed objectivity of knowledge." Most scientists are thoughtful, liberal-minded and socially aware people. It was just what they wanted to hear.

5

Three decades later, it seems that Dr. Lewontin's facts were correct, and have been abundantly confirmed by ever better techniques of detecting genetic variety. His reasoning, however, was wrong. His error was an elementary one, but such was the appeal of his argument that it was only a couple of years ago that a Cambridge University statistician, A. W. F. Edwards, put his finger on it.

The error is easily illustrated. If one were asked to judge the ancestry of 100 New Yorkers, one could look at the color of their skin. That would do much to single out the Europeans, but little to distinguish the Senegalese from the Solomon Islanders. The same is true for any other feature of our bodies. The shapes of our eyes, noses and skulls; the color of our eyes and our hair; the heaviness, height and hairiness of our bodies are all, individually, poor guides to ancestry.

But this is not true when the features are taken together. Certain skin colors tend to go with certain kinds of eyes, noses, skulls and bodies. When we glance at a stranger's face we use those associations to infer what continent, or even what country, he or his ancestors came from—and we usually get it right. To put it more abstractly, human physical variation is correlated; and correlations contain information.

Genetic variants that aren't written on our faces, but that can be detected only in the genome, show similar correlations. It is these correlations that Dr. Lewontin seems to have ignored. In essence, he looked at one gene at a time and failed to see races. But if many—a few hundred—variable genes are considered simultaneously, then it is very easy to do so. Indeed, a 2002 study by scientists at the University of Southern California and Stanford showed that if a sample of people from around the world are sorted by computer into five groups on the basis of genetic similarity, the groups that emerge are native to Europe, East Asia, Africa, America and Australasia—more or less the major races of traditional anthropology.

One of the minor pleasures of this discovery is a new kind of genealogy. Today it is easy to find out where your ancestors came from—or even when they came, as with so many of us, from several different places. If you want to know what fraction of your genes are African, European or East Asian, all it takes is a mouth swab, a postage stamp and $400—though prices will certainly fall.

Yet there is nothing very fundamental about the concept of the major continental races; they're just the easiest way to divide things up. Study enough genes in enough people and one could sort the world's population into 10, 100, perhaps 1,000 groups, each located somewhere on the map. This has not yet been done with any precision, but it will be. Soon it may be possible to identify your ancestors not merely as African or European, but Ibo or Yoruba, perhaps even Celt or Castilian, or all of the above.

The identification of racial origins is not a search for purity. The human species is irredeemably promiscuous. We have always seduced or coerced our neighbors even when they have a foreign look about them and we don't understand a word. If Hispanics, for example, are composed of a recent and evolving blend of European, American Indian and African genes, then the Uighurs of Central Asia can be seen as a 3,000-year-old mix of West European and East Asian genes. Even homogenous groups like native Swedes bear the genetic imprint of successive nameless migrations.

Some critics believe that these ambiguities render the very notion of race worthless. I disagree. The physical topography of our world cannot be accurately described in words. To navigate it, you need a map with elevations, contour lines and reference grids. But it is hard to talk in numbers, and so we give the world's more prominent features—the mountain ranges and plateaus and plains—names. We do so despite the inherent ambiguity of words. The Pennines of northern England are about one-tenth

10

as high and long as the Himalayas, yet both are intelligibly described as mountain ranges.

So, too, it is with the genetic topography of our species. The billion or so of the world's people of largely European descent have a set of genetic variants in common that are collectively rare in everyone else; they are a race. At a smaller scale, three million Basques do as well; so they are a race as well. Race is merely a shorthand that enables us to speak sensibly, though with no great precision, about genetic rather than cultural or political differences.

But it is a shorthand that seems to be needed. One of the more painful spectacles of modern science is that of human geneticists piously disavowing the existence of races even as they investigate the genetic relationships between "ethnic groups." Given the problematic, even vicious, history of the word "race," the use of euphemisms is understandable. But it hardly aids understanding, for the term "ethnic group" conflates all the possible ways in which people differ from each other. 15

Indeed, the recognition that races are real should have several benefits. To begin with, it would remove the disjunction in which the government and public alike defiantly embrace categories that many, perhaps most, scholars and scientists say do not exist.

Second, the recognition of race may improve medical care. Different races are prone to different diseases. The risk that an African-American man will be afflicted with hypertensive heart disease or prostate cancer is nearly three times greater than that for a European-American man. On the other hand, the former's risk of multiple sclerosis is only half as great. Such differences could be due to socioeconomic factors. Even so, geneticists have started searching for racial differences in the frequencies of genetic variants that cause diseases. They seem to be finding them.

Race can also affect treatment. African-Americans respond poorly to some of the main drugs used to treat heart conditions—notably beta blockers and angiotensin-converting enzyme inhibitors. Pharmaceutical corporations are paying attention. Many new drugs now come labeled with warnings that they may not work in some ethnic or racial groups. Here, as so often, the mere prospect of litigation has concentrated minds.

Such differences are, of course, just differences in average. Everyone agrees that race is a crude way of predicting who gets some disease or responds to some treatment. Ideally, we would all have our genomes sequenced before swallowing so much as an aspirin. Yet until that is technically feasible, we can expect racial classifications to play an increasing part in health care.

The argument for the importance of race, however, does not rest purely on utilitarian grounds. There is also an aesthetic factor. We are a physically variable species. Yet for all the triumphs of modern genetics, we know next to nothing about what makes us so. We do not know why some people have prominent rather than flat noses, round rather than pointed skulls, wide rather than narrow faces, straight rather than curly hair. We do not know what makes blue eyes blue. 20

One way to find out would be to study people of mixed race ancestry. In part, this is because racial differences in looks are the most striking that we see. But there is also a more subtle technical reason. When geneticists map genes, they rely on the fact that they can follow our ancestors' chromosomes as they get passed from one generation to the next, dividing and mixing in unpredictable combinations. That, it turns out, is much easier to do in people whose ancestors came from very different places.

The technique is called admixture mapping. Developed to find the genes responsible for racial differences in inherited disease, it is only just moving from theory to application. But through it, we may be able to write the genetic recipe for the fair hair of a Norwegian, the black-verging-on-purple skin of a Solomon Islander, the flat face of an Inuit, and the curved eyelid of a Han Chinese. We shall no longer gawp ignorantly at the gallery; we shall be able to name the painters.

There is a final reason race matters. It gives us reason—if there were not reason enough already—to value and protect some of the world's most obscure and marginalized people. When *The Times* of India article is referred to the Andaman Islanders as being of ancient Negrito racial stock, the terminology was correct. Negrito is the name given by anthropologists to a people who once lived throughout Southeast Asia. They are very small, very dark, and have peppercorn hair. They look like African pygmies who have wandered away from Congo's jungles to take up life on a tropical isle. But they are not.

The latest genetic data suggest that the Negritos are descended from the first modern humans to have invaded Asia, some 100,000 years ago. In time they were overrun or absorbed by waves of Neolithic agriculturalists, and later nearly wiped out by British, Spanish and Indian colonialists. Now they are confined to the Malay Peninsula, a few islands in the Philippines and the Andamans.

Happily, most of the Andamans' Negritos seem to have survived December's tsunami. The fate of one tribe, the Sentinelese, remains uncertain, but an Indian coast guard helicopter sent to check up on them came under bow and arrow attack, which is heartening. Even so, Negrito populations, wherever they are, are so small, isolated and impoverished that it seems certain that they will eventually disappear.

Yet even after they have gone, the genetic variants that defined the Negritos will remain, albeit scattered, in the people who inhabit the littoral of the Bay of Bengal and the South China Sea. They will remain visible in the unusually dark skin of some Indonesians, the unusually curly hair of some Sri Lankans, the unusually slight frames of some Filipinos. But the unique combination of genes that makes the Negritos so distinctive, and that took tens of thousands of years to evolve, will have disappeared. A human race will have gone extinct, and the human species will be the poorer for it.

25

David Fitch, Herbert J. Gans, Mary T. Bassett, Lynn M. Morgan, Martin E. Fuller, John Waldman

Letters Responding to Armand Marie Leroi

To the Editor:

Re "A Family Tree in Every Gene," by Armand Marie Leroi (Op-Ed, March 14):

Biological diversity is real and should be celebrated, not pushed under the carpet and ignored.

This is not just about race, either. A Harvard president is being criticized for proposing that biological differences might explain why certain propensities are more common among men or women. If true, it would be important to understand what these differences are.

Understanding differences does not mean we must then use such differences to practice discrimination. The great thing about us humans is our ability to transcend biological differences, particularly if we understand them.

David Fitch
New York, March 16, 2005
*The writer is an associate professor of biology
at New York University.*

To the Editor:

Race remains a social construct. And no matter how Armand Marie Leroi defines it ("A Family Tree in Every Gene," Op-Ed, March 14), it is still widely used, not only to describe, but also to judge and stigmatize people.

Why not choose a nonjudgmental construct like DNA type?

Herbert J. Gans
New York, March 14, 2005
*The writer is a professor of sociology at
Columbia University.*

Letters to the editor by David Fitch, Herbert J. Gans, Mary T. Bassett, M.D., Lynn M. Morgan, Martin E. Fuller, and John Waldman, published in the *New York Times*, March 20, 2005. Reprinted by permission of the authors.

To the Editor:

Now we hear that the Victorian notion of "racial stocks" could lead to improved health. Such thinking will not advance public health, which is well acquainted with the enduring impact of race. Indeed, ever since the first crude tabulation of vital statistics in Colonial America, blacks have been sicker and died younger than whites.

There has been progress: in 1981, black infants in New York City had an infant mortality rate of 22.3 per 1,000 live births. By 2003, a black in fant's risk of death had fallen by almost half.

What happened? Our society changed, not our genes.

Today health disparities persist. But we can end the unfair odds by changing how people live, not by insisting on genetic explanations for these differences.

Mary T. Bassett, M.D.
Deputy Commissioner
Dept. of Health and Mental Hygiene
New York, March 15, 2005

To the Editor:

Race is not a fact rooted in nature, but an ideology that justifies treating people differently based on the meanings we attribute to physical differences.

When people are subjected to poor treatment, diagnostic delay and unhealthy environments because of the color of their skin, "race" impairs their health. The ideology of race can have real biological consequences.

Lynn M. Morgan
South Hadley, Mass.
March 15, 2005
The writer is an anthropology professor at
Mount Holyoke College.

To the Editor:

Armand Marie Leroi (Op-Ed, March 14) brings us a celebration of human genetic variability. That variability has enabled the human race to survive, and even thrive, in so many different and not always friendly habitats.

It would be a sad world were the races homogenized into one amorphous mass. Let us rejoice in and be grateful for our differences. They are beautiful.

Martin E. Fuller
Albuquerque, March 16, 2005

To the Editor:

Is there such a thing as "race"?

Mix 10 native Central Africans and 10 native Scandinavians together, and I'll sort them out every time. Race is real. The problem is that this easily answered question is often confounded with the far trickier and far touchier question of "how much does race matter?"

John Waldman
Flushing, Queens, March 15, 2005
The writer is a professor of biology
at Queens College, CUNY.

Joining the Conversation: Critical Thinking and Writing

1. In paragraph 3, Leroi writes of the "idea that human races are only social constructs." What does this mean? With what idea about races does this idea contrast?

2. In paragraph 4, Leroi claims that the idea that races are only social constructs is about to change. What evidence does he offer to support this claim?

3. What benefits does Leroi claim for "the recognition that races are real" (paragraph 15)?

4. Leroi both begins and ends his article referring to the Negritos. Who are they? What recent event threatened their existence? Why, according to Leroi, should they claim our attention?

5. How does Leroi's focus on the Negritos both at the beginning and end of his essay help to define and strengthen his argument?

6. We reprint six responses to Leroi's article received by the *New York Times*. Which letter do you find most (or least) interesting and persuasive? Explain why.

Sharon Begley

Sharon Begley, a senior writer for Newsweek, *published this essay in an issue (February 13, 1995) whose cover story was "What Color Is Black?"*

Three Is Not Enough

To most Americans race is as plain as the color of the nose on your face. Sure, some light-skinned blacks, in some neighborhoods, are taken for Italians, and some Turks are confused with Argentines. But even in the children of biracial couples, racial ancestry is writ large—in the hue of the skin and the shape of the lips, the size of the brow and the bridge of the nose. It is no harder to trace than it is to judge which basic colors in a box of Crayolas were combined to make tangerine or burnt umber. Even with racial mixing, the existence of primary races is as obvious as the existence of primary colors.

Or is it? C. Loring Brace has his own ideas about where race resides, and it isn't in skin color. If our eyes could perceive more than the superficial, we might find race in chromosome 11: there lies the gene for hemoglobin. If you divide humankind by which of two forms of the gene each person has, then equatorial Africans, Italians and Greeks fall into the "sickle-cell race"; Swedes and South Africa's Xhosas (Nelson Mandela's ethnic group) are in the healthy-hemoglobin race. Or do you prefer to group people by whether they have epicanthic eye folds, which produce the "Asian" eye? Then the !Kung San (Bushmen) belong with the Japanese and Chinese. Depending on which trait you choose to demarcate races, "you won't get anything that remotely tracks conventional [race] categories," says anthropologist Alan Goodman, dean of natural science at Hampshire College.

The notion of race is under withering attack for political and cultural reasons—not to mention practical ones like what to label the child of a Ghanaian and a Norwegian. But scientists got there first. Their doubts about the conventional racial categories—black, white, Asian—have nothing to do with a sappy "we are all the same" ideology. Just the reverse. "Human variation is very, very real," says Goodman. "But race, as a way of organizing [what we know about that variation], is incredibly simplified and bastardized." Worse, it does not come close to explaining the astounding diversity of humankind—not its origins, not its extent, not its meaning. "There is no organizing principle by which you could put 5 billion people into so few categories in a way that would tell you anything important about humankind's diversity," says Michigan's Brace, who will lay out the case against race at the annual meeting of the American Association for the Advancement of Science.

About 70 percent of cultural anthropologists, and half of physical anthropologists, reject race as a biological category, according to a 1989 survey by Central Michigan University anthropologist Leonard Liebermnan and colleagues. The truths of science are not decided by majority vote, of course. Empirical evidence, woven into a theoretical whole, is what - matters. The threads of the argument against the standard racial categories:

• **Genes:** In 1972, population biologist Richard Lewontin of Harvard   5
University laid out the genetic case against race. Analyzing 17 genetic markers in 168 populations such as Austrians, Thais and Apaches, he found that there is more genetic difference within one race than there is between that race and another. Only 6.3 percent of the genetic differences could be explained by the individuals' belonging to different races. That is, if you pick at random any two "blacks" walking along the street, and analyze their 23 pairs of chromosomes, you will probably find that their genes have less in common than do the genes of one of them with that of a random "white" person. Last year the Human Genome Diversity Project used 1990s genetics to extend Lewontin's analysis. Its conclusion: genetic variation from one individual to another of the same "race" swamps the average differences between racial groupings. The more we learn about humankind's genetic differences, says geneticist Luca Cavalli-Sforza of Stanford University, who chairs the committee that directs the biodiversity project, the more we see that they have almost nothing to do with what we call race.

• **Traits:** As sickle-cell "races" and epicanthic-fold "races" show, there are as many ways to group people as there are traits. That is because "racial" traits are what statisticians call non-concordant. Lack of concordance means that sorting people according to *these* traits produces different groupings than you get in sorting them by *those* (equally valid) traits. When biologist Jared Diamond of UCLA surveyed half a dozen traits for a recent issue of *Discover* magazine, he found that, depending on which traits you pick, you can form very surprising "races." Take the scooped-out shape of the back of the front teeth, a standard "Asian" trait. Native Americans and Swedes have these shovel-shaped incisors, too, and so would fall in the same race. Is biochemistry better? Norwegians, Arabians, north Indians and the Fulani of northern Nigeria, notes Diamond, fall into the "lactase race" (the lactase enzyme digests milk sugar). Everyone else—other Africans, Japanese, Native Americans— forms the "lactase-deprived race" (their ancestors did not drink milk from cows or goats and hence never evolved the lactase gene). How about blood types, the familiar A, B and O groups? Then Germans and New Guineans, populations that have the same percentages of each type, are in one race; Estonians and Japanese comprise a separate one for the same reason, notes anthropologist Jonathan Marks of Yale University. Depending on which traits are chosen, "we could place Swedes in the same race as either Xhosas, Fulani, the Ainu of Japan or Italians," writes Diamond.

• **Subjectivity:** If race is a valid biological concept, anyone in any culture should be able to look at any individual and say, Aha, you are a . . . It should not be the case, as French tennis star Yannick Noah said a few years ago, that "in Africa I am white, and in France I am black" (his mother is French and his father is from Cameroon). "While biological traits give the impression that race is a biological unit of nature," says anthropologist George Armelagos of Emory University, "it remains a cultural construct. The boundaries between races depend on the classifier's own cultural norms."

• **Evolution:** Scholars who believe in the biological validity of race argue that the groupings reflect human pre-history. That is, populations that evolved together, and separately from others, constitute a race. This school of thought holds that blacks should all be in one race because they are descended from people who stayed on the continent where humanity began. Asians, epitomized by the Chinese, should be another race because they are the children of groups who walked north and east until they reached the Pacific. Whites of the pale, blond variety should be another because their ancestors filled Europe. Because of their appearance, these populations represent the extremes, the archetypes, of human diversity—the reds, blues and yellows from which you can make every other hue. "But if you use these archetypes as your groups you have classified only a very tiny proportion of the world's people, which is not very useful," says Marks, whose incisive new book "Human Biodiversity" deconstructs race. "Also, as people walked out of Africa, they were differentiating along the way. Equating 'extreme' with 'primordial' is not supported by history."

Often, shared traits are a sign of shared heritage—racial heritage. "Shared traits are not random," says Alice Brues, an anthropologist at the University of Colorado. "Within a continent, you of course have a number of variants [on basic traits], but some are characteristic of the larger area, too. So it's natural to look for these major divisions. It simplifies your thinking." A wide distribution of traits, however, makes them suspect as evidence of a shared heritage. The dark skin of Somalis and Ghanaians, for instance, indicates that they evolved under the same elective force (a sunny climate). But that's all it shows. It does *not* show that they are any more closely related, in the sense of sharing more genes, than either is to Greeks. Calling Somalis and Ghanaians "black" therefore sheds no further light on their evolutionary history and implies—wrongly—that they are more closely related to each other than either is to someone of a different "race." Similarly, the long noses of North Africans and northern Europeans reveal that they evolved in dry or cold climates (the nose moistens air before the air reaches the lungs, and longer noses moisten more air). The tall, thin bodies of Kenya's Masai evolved to dissipate heat; Eskimos evolved short, squat bodies to retain it. Calling these peoples "different races" adds nothing to that understanding.

Where did the three standard racial divisions come from? They entered the social, and scientific, consciousness during the Age of Exploration. Loring Brace doesn't think it's a coincidence that the standard races represent peoples who, as he puts it, "lived at the end of the

Europeans' trade routes"—in Africa and China—in the days after Prince Henry the Navigator set sail. Before Europeans took to the seas, there was little perception of races. If villagers began to look different to an Englishman riding a horse from France to Italy and on to Greece, the change was too subtle to inspire notions of races. But if the English sailor left Lisbon Harbor and dropped anchor off the Kingdom of Niger, people looked so different he felt compelled to invent a scheme to explain the world—and, perhaps, distance himself from the Africans.

This habit of sorting the world's peoples into a small number of groups got its first scientific gloss from Swedish taxonomist Carolus Linnaeus. (Linnaeus is best known for his system of classifying living things by genus and species—*Escherichia coli, Homo sapiens* and the rest.) In 1758 he declared that humanity falls into four races: white (Europeans), red (Native Americans), dark (Asians), and black (Africans). Linnaeus said that Native Americans (who in the 1940s got grouped with Asians) were ruled by custom. Africans were indolent and negligent, and Europeans were inventive and gentle, said Linnaeus. Leave aside the racist undertones (not to mention the oddity of ascribing gentleness to the group that perpetrated the Crusades and Inquisition): that alone should not undermine its validity. More worrisome is that the notion and the specifics of race predate genetics, evolutionary biology and the science of human origins. With the revolutions in those fields, how is it that the 18th-century scheme of race retains its powerful hold? Consider these arguments:

• **If I parachute into Nairobi, I know I'm not in Oslo:** Colorado's Alice Brues uses this image to argue that denying the reality of race flies in the face of common sense. But the parachutists, if they were familiar with the great range of human diversity, could also tell that they were in Nairobi rather than Abidjan—east Africans don't look much like west Africans. They could also tell they were in Istanbul rather than Oslo, even though Turks and Norwegians are both called Caucasian.

• **DOA, male, 58119 ... black:** When U.S. police call in a forensic anthropologist to identify the race of a skeleton, the scientist comes through 80 to 85 percent of the time. If race has no biological validity, how can the sleuths get it right so often? The forensic anthropologist could, with enough information about bone structure and genetic markers, identify the region from which the corpse came—south and west Africa, Southeast Asia and China, Northern and Western Europe. It just so happens that the police would call corpses from the first two countries black, from the middle two Asian, and the last pair white. But lumping these six distinct populations into three groups of two serves no biological purpose, only a social convention. The larger grouping may reflect how society views humankind's diversity, but does not explain it.

• **African-Americans have more hypertension:** If race is not real, how can researchers say that blacks have higher rates of infant mortality, lower rates of osteoporosis and a higher incidence of hypertension? Because a social construct can have biological effects, says epidemiologist Robert Hahn of the U.S. Centers for Disease Control and Prevention. Consider hypertension among African-Americans. Roughly 34 percent have high blood pressure, compared with about 16 percent of whites. But William Dressler finds the greatest incidence of hypertension among blacks who are upwardly mobile achievers. "That's probably because in mundane interactions, from the bank to the grocery store, they are treated in ways that do not coincide with their self-image as respectable achievers," says Dressler, an anthropologist at the University of Alabama. "And the upwardly mobile are more likely to encounter discriminatory white culture." Lab studies show that stressful situations—like being followed in grocery stores as if you were a shoplifter—elevate blood pressure and lead to vascular changes that cause hypertension. "In this case, race captures social factors such as the experience of discrimination," says sociologist David Williams of the University of Michigan. Further evidence that hypertension has more to do with society than with biology: black Africans have among the lowest rates of hypertension in the world.

If race is not a biological explanation of hypertension, can it offer a biological explanation of something as complex as intelligence? Psychologists are among the strongest proponents of retaining the three conventional racial categories. It organizes and explains their data in the most parsimonious way, as Charles Murray and Richard Herrnstein argue in "The Bell Curve." But anthropologists say that such conclusions are built on a foundation of sand. If nothing else, argues Brace, every ethnic group evolved under conditions where intelligence was a requirement for survival. If there are intelligence "genes," they must be in all ethnic groups equally: differences in intelligence must be a cultural and social artifact.   15

Scientists who doubt the biological meaningfulness of race are not nihilists. They just prefer another way of capturing, and explaining, the great diversity of humankind. Even today most of the world's peoples marry within their own group. Intramarriage preserves features—fleshy lips, small ears, wide-set eyes—that arose by a chance genetic mutation long ago. Grouping people by geographic origins—better known as ethnicity—"is more correct both in a statistical sense and in understanding the history of human variation," says Hampshire's Goodman. Ethnicity also serves as a proxy for differences—from diet to a history of discrimination—that can have real biological and behavioral effects.

In a 1942 book, anthropologist Ashley Montagu called race "Man's Most Dangerous Myth." If it is, then our most ingenuous myth must be that we sort humankind into groups in order to understand the meaning and origin of humankind's diversity. That isn't the reason at all; a greater number of smaller groupings, like ethnicities, does a better job. The obsession with broad categories is so powerful as to seem a neurological imperative. Changing our thinking about race will require a revolution in thought as profound, and profoundly unsettling, as anything science has ever demanded. What these researchers are talking about is changing the way in which we see the world—and each other. But before that can happen, we must do more than understand the biologist's suspicions about race. We must ask science, also, why it is that we are so intent on sorting humanity into so few groups—us and Other—in the first place.

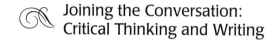 ## Joining the Conversation: Critical Thinking and Writing

1. Begley quotes George Armelagos as saying that race is "a cultural construct" (paragraph 7). What does Armelagos mean? Begley also quotes Robert Hahn (paragraph 14) as saying that "a social construct can have biological effects." What does Hahn mean? What examples of this phenomenon does Begley offer?

2. How does Begley define ethnicity? What advantages does Begley claim for this way of grouping people?

Shelby Steele

Shelby Steele, a research fellow at the Hoover Institution, was educated at Coe College, Southern Illinois University, and the University of Utah. In 1990 one of his books, The Content of Our Character: A New Vision of Race in America, *was awarded the National Book Critics Circle Award for nonfiction. His most recent book is* A Dream Deferred: The Second Betrayal of Black Freedom in America. *Steele publishes widely in major journals, including the* New York Times *and (the source of the following article)* Time *magazine.*

Hailing While Black

In Manhattan recently I attempted something that is thought to be all but impossible for a black man: I tried to hail a cab going uptown toward Harlem after dark. And I'll admit to feeling a new nervousness. This simple action—black man hailing cab—is now a tableau in America's ongoing culture war. If no cab swerves in to pick me up, America is still a racist country, and the entire superstructure of contemporary liberalism is bolstered. If I catch a ride, conservatives can breath easier. So, as I raise my hand and step from the curb, much is at stake.

It's all the talk these days of racial profiling that has set off my nerves in this way. Having grown up in the era of segregation, I know I can survive the racial profiling of a cabby. What makes me most nervous is the anxiety that I have wrongly estimated the degree of racism in American life. I am a conservative. But conservatism is a misunderstood identity in blacks that would be much easier to carry in a world where New York City cab drivers stopped for black fares, even after dark.

It is easy to believe that racial profiling is a serious problem in America. It fits the American profile, and now politicians have stepped forward to give it credence as a problem. But is it a real problem? Is dark skin a shorthand for criminality in the mind of America's law-enforcement officers? Studies show that we blacks are stopped in numbers higher than our percentage in the population but lower than our documented involvement in crime. If you're trying to measure racism, isn't it better to compare police stops to actual black involvement in crime than to the mere representation of blacks in the population? The elephant in the living room—and the tragedy in black America—is that we commit crimes vastly out of proportion to our numbers in society.

But I can already hear "so what?" from those who believe profiling is a serious problem. And I know that the more energetic among them will move numbers and points of reference around like shells in a shill game to show racism. In other words, racial profiling is now an "identity" issue like affirmative action, black reparations or even O.J.'s innocence. It is less a real issue than a coded argument over how much racism exists in society today. We argue these issues fiercely—make a culture war around them—because the moral authority of both the left and right political identities hangs in the balance.

Racial profiling is a boon to the left because this political identity justifies its demand for power by estimating racism to be high. The more racism, the more power the left demands for social interventions that go beyond simple fairness under the law. Profiling hurts the right because it makes its fairness-under-the-law position on race seem inadequate, less than moral considering the prevalence of racism. The real debate over racial profiling is not about stops and searches on the New Jersey Turnpike. It is about the degree of racism in America and the distribution of power it justifies.

Even as individuals, we Americans cannot define our political and moral identities without making them accountable to an estimate of racism's potency in American life. Our liberalism or conservatism, our faith in government intervention or restraint and our concept of social responsibility on issues from diversity to school reform—all these will be,

5

in part, a response to how bad we think racism is. The politically liberal identity I was born into began to fade as my estimate of American racism declined. I could identify with a wider range of American ideas and possibilities when I thought they were no longer tainted by racism. Many whites I know today, who are trying to separate themselves from the shame of America's racist past, will overestimate racism to justify a liberal identity that they hope proves that separateness. First the estimation, then the identity.

Recently, after a talk on a college campus, a black girl stood up and told me that she was "frequently" stopped by police while driving in this bucolic and liberal college town. A professor on the same campus told me that blacks there faced an "unwelcome atmosphere"—unwelcomeness being a newly fashionable estimation of racism's potency on college campuses today. Neither of these people offered supporting facts. But I don't think they were lying so much as "spinning" an estimation of racism that shored up their political identities.

We are terrible at discussing our racial problems in America today because we just end up defending our identities and the political power we hope those identities will align us with. On that day in Manhattan, I caught the first cab that came along. And I should have been happy just for the convenience of good service. That I also saw this minor event as evidence of something, that I was practicing a kind of political sociology as well as catching a cab—that is the problem.

Joining the Conversation: Critical Thinking and Writing

1. In his essay, Steele refers to "racial profiling." What is "racial profiling," and how, according to Steele, does it affect what he calls "the left" and "the right"?

2. Explain Steele's last sentence to someone who has read the article but didn't get it.

3. Have you ever been the victim, the perpetrator, or a witness to racial or ethnic profiling or prejudice? If so, in an essay of 750–1,000 words, recount the circumstances of the event, and your reaction to it, then and now. Use Steele's essay as a model, if that is helpful.

Brent Staples

Brent Staples, born in 1951, holds a Ph.D. in psychology from the University of Chicago. He taught briefly, then turned to journalism, and now is on the editorial board of the New York Times. *We reprint an essay that appeared in this paper in 2007.*

On Race and the Census: Struggling with Categories That No Longer Apply

Imagine the Census Bureau announcing that it would end the practice of asking people to identify themselves by race beginning in 2010. Black elected officials and their allies in the civil rights community would fight the proposal tooth and nail by arguing that racial statistics were necessary for enforcing civil rights laws—especially the Voting Rights Act—and that dropping race from the census would dilute black political strength. Enemies of affirmative action would jump for joy, believing that they had finally won.

But these antagonists aren't the only factions in the fight. A growing number of demographers and historians who are fully sympathetic to the civil rights struggle would probably be happy to see the word "race" disappear from the census as well. There seems to be an emerging consensus that the system of racial classification that has dominated national politics and the census for nearly two centuries is so fraught with imprecision—and so tainted by racist ideas that have been disproved by science—that it should eventually be dropped altogether.

This view has been percolating among census historians for years. But it has gained traction since the 1990s, when there was a pitched battle over a proposal that would have added a "multiracial" category to the 2000 census. A compromise allowed people to check more than one box for race. But that change only fueled the debate by revealing a conflict between the fixed racial categories that have long dominated American life and a different sense of identity that's clearly on the rise among younger Americans.

Most Americans think of racial categories as objective, even benign, descriptions that are part of the social fabric. But the historian Margo Anderson writes that official statistics on "race" or "color" were inaugurated into the federal statistical system in the early 19th century. By then the government had embraced the view that people of African descent were from genetically inferior ancestral groups and could never escape subordinate status.

Armed with this view, the Census Bureau became the fountainhead 5 of 19th-century racist dogma. The bureau reported, for example, that free black people were disproportionately insane, thus supporting the view that slavery was the only suitable status for them. It actively promoted the eugenicist view that Americans of African descent were so inferior and ill equipped to survive that they would eventually become extinct.

The bureau during this period was obsessed with the notion that sexual contact between people of African and European descent was polluting the theoretically "pure" white society. The belief that the so-called "races" had been set apart by God and nature led to the popular theory that children of mixed ancestry were akin to mules, which are sterile, and would die out after a single generation.

With an eye out for what the government saw as racial abomination, census wardens went house to house, eyeballing ostensibly white people for traces of creeping "blackness." This period marked the rise of the so-called "one-drop rule"—which defined as black anyone with any African heritage at all. That often meant banishment from jobs, housing and public schools set aside for whites. The "one-drop rule" has been stripped of its worst penalties. But it is still evident in the census, as Kim Williams of Harvard points out in her recent book, "Mark One or More: Civil Rights in Multiracial America." For example, people who checked both "white" and one minority race in 2000 were counted in a single-race minority group.

The system of racial classification used in this country will never be scrubbed clean of its racist origins. Indeed, the seemingly innocuous act of assigning people to "races" still sets them sociologically and biologically apart in a way that scientists and anthropologists have long since rejected. The Americans who checked more than one box in 2000 seem to reject this fixed, "one drop" formulation of race.

Many people now see race as a facet of personal identity that changes from time to time or even from place to place. In a follow-up survey just a year after the initial 2000 census, for example, about 4 of 10 people who had listed more than one race decided to change their responses. Kenneth Prewitt, a Columbia University professor and former census director, wrote in the journal *Daedalus* in 2005 that these people seem to see race not as a fixed demographic fact, but as "something closer to an attitude toward oneself."

The 2000 census suggests that we are gradually moving away from   10
the rigid, racialist system of classification that has long dominated this country and toward a system that sees racial identity as more fluid. Even historians and demographers who sympathize with the civil rights struggle and who recognize the need to document discrimination now see that the "one-drop rule" will not be sustainable in the new, multiracial America. We may be stuck with the old formulation for the moment. But it's no longer a matter of if it will fall away. It's a matter of when.

Joining the Conversation: Critical Thinking and Writing

1. What is the main point that Staples is making here?

2. To support his argument, Staples provides historical background. In what ways does it support his argument?

3. What is Staples's conclusion? Do you agree?

4. If you were assigned to debate Staples, which features of his argument might you seek to call into question or raise objections to?

5. Sometimes it is said that Americans should "move beyond race." What does this claim mean? Do you think it can be achieved?

Countee Cullen

Countee Cullen (1903–1946) was born Countee Porter in New York City, raised by his grand-mother, and then adopted by the Reverend Frederick A. Cullen, a Methodist minister in Harlem. Cullen received a bachelor's degree from New York University (Phi Beta Kappa) and a master's degree from Harvard University. He earned his living as a high school teacher of French, but his literary gifts were recognized in his own day.

Incident
(For Eric Walrond)

Once riding in old Baltimore,
    Heart-filled, head-filled with glee.
I saw a Baltimorean
    Keep looking straight at me.

Now I was eight and very small.   5
    And he was no whit bigger.
And so I smiled, but he poked out
    His tongue, and called me, "Nigger."

I saw the whole of Baltimore
    From May until December;   10
Of all the things that happened there
    That's all that I remember.

Joining the Conversation: Critical Thinking and Writing

1. How would you define an "incident"? A serious occurrence? A minor occurrence, or what? Think about the word, and then think about Cullen's use of it as a title for the event recorded in this poem. Test out one or two other possible titles as a way of helping yourself to see the strengths or weaknesses of Cullen's title.

2. The dedicatee, Eric Walrond (1898–1966), was an African-American essayist and writer of fiction, who in an essay, "On Being Black," had described his experiences of racial prejudice. How does the presence of the dedication bear on our response to Cullen's account of the "incident"?

3. What is the tone of the poem? Indifferent? Angry? Or what? What do you think is the speaker's attitude toward the "incident"? What is your attitude?

4. Ezra Pound, poet and critic, once defined literature as "news that *stays* news." What do you think he meant by this? Do you think that the definition fits Cullen's poem?

CHAPTER 8

Immigrant Nation

New U.S. Citizens at a Citizenship Ceremony, Pomona, California
Christopher J. Morris

Short Views

Every ship that comes to America got its chart from Columbus.
Ralph Waldo Emerson

America is God's crucible, the great melting pot where all the races of Europe are melting and re-forming.
Israel Zangwill

Melting pot? Don't kid yourself: Every politician knows that the secret of success is an awareness of ethnicity.
Jack Strong

Every immigrant who comes here should be required within five years to learn English or leave the country.
Theodore Roosevelt

I cannot say too often—any man who carries a hyphen about him carries a dagger which he is ready to plunge into the vitals of the Republic.
Woodrow Wilson

There is nothing less to our credit than our neglect of the foreigner and his children, unless it be the arrogance most of us betray when we set out to "americanize" him.
Charles Horton Cooley

My literary agenda begins by acknowledging that America has transformed me. It does not end until I show how I (and hundreds of thousands like me) have transformed America.
Bharati Mukherjee

All the problems we face in the United States today can be traced to an unenlightened immigration policy on the part of the American Indian.
Pat Paulsen

This country was a lot better off when the Indians were running it.
Vine Deloria

We didn't cross the border into the U.S., the border crossed into us.
  Anonymous Mexican American

We become not a melting pot but a beautiful mosaic. Different
people, different beliefs, different earnings, different hopes,
different dreams.
  Jimmy Carter

O brave new world,
That hath such people in't
  William Shakespeare, **The Tempest**

Whither thou goest, I will go; and where thou lodgest, I will
lodge: thy people shall be my people, and thy God my God.
  Hebrew Bible, The Book of Ruth

Bharati Mukherjee

Bharati Mukherjee, born in Calcutta, India, in 1940, spent much of her childhood in London with her parents and sisters, but returned to India in 1951. She earned a bachelor's and a master's degree in India, then moved to London, and to the United States, where she studied for a doctorate at the University of Iowa Writers Workshop. At the University of Iowa she met and married a novelist, and the couple later moved to Canada. While living in Canada she published two novels, and in 1980 she came to the United States to teach at the University of Iowa. She has also taught at Skidmore College, Queens College, and Columbia University. We reprint an essay that originally appeared in the New York Times.

Two Ways to Belong in America

This is a tale of two sisters from Calcutta, Mira and Bharati, who have lived in the United States for some 35 years, but who find themselves on different sides in the current debate over the status of immigrants. I am an American citizen and she is not. I am moved that thousands of long-term residents are finally taking the oath of citizenship. She is not.

Mira arrived in Detroit in 1960 to study child psychology and pre-school education. I followed her a year later to study creative writing at the University of Iowa. When we left India, we were almost identical in appearance and attitude. We dressed alike, in saris; we expressed identical views on politics, social issues, love and marriage in the same Calcutta convent-school accent. We would endure our two years in America, secure our degrees, then return to India to marry the grooms of our father's choosing.

Instead, Mira married an Indian student in 1962 who was getting his business administration degree at Wayne State University. They soon acquired the labor certifications necessary for the green card of hassle-free residence and employment.

Mira still lives in Detroit, works in the Southfield, Mich., school system, and has become nationally recognized for her contributions in the fields of pre-school education and parent-teacher relationships. After 36 years as a legal immigrant in this country, she clings passionately to her Indian citizenship and hopes to go home to India when she retires.

In Iowa City in 1963, I married a fellow student, an American of Canadian parentage. Because of the accident of his North Dakota birth, I bypassed labor-certification requirements and the race-related "quota" system that favored the applicant's country of origin over his or her merit. I was prepared for (and even welcomed) the emotional strain that came with marrying outside my ethnic community. In 33 years of marriage, we have lived in every part of North America. By choosing a husband who was not my father's selection, I was opting for fluidity, self-invention, blue jeans and T-shirts, and renouncing 3,000 years (at least) of caste-observant, "pure culture" marriage in the Mukherjee family. My books have often

5

been read as unapologetic (and in some quarters over-enthusiastic) texts for cultural and psychological "mongrelization." It's a word I celebrate.

Mira and I have stayed sisterly close by phone. In our regular Sunday morning conversations, we are unguardedly affectionate. I am her only blood relative on this continent. We expect to see each other through the looming crises of aging and ill health without being asked. Long before Vice President Gore's "Citizenship U.S.A." drive, we'd had our polite arguments over the ethics of retaining an overseas citizenship while expecting the permanent protection and economic benefits that come with living and working in America.

Like well-raised sisters, we never said what was really on our minds, but we probably pitied one another. She, for the lack of structure in my life, the erasure of Indianness, the absence of an unvarying daily core. I, for the narrowness of her perspective, her uninvolvement with the mythic depths or the superficial pop culture of this society. But, now, with the scapegoating of "aliens" (documented or illegal) on the increase, and the targeting of long-term legal immigrants like Mira for new scrutiny and new self-consciousness, she and I find ourselves unable to maintain the same polite discretion. We were always unacknowledged adversaries, and we are now, more than ever, sisters.

"I feel used," Mira raged on the phone the other night. "I feel manipulated and discarded. This is such an unfair way to treat a person who was invited to stay and work here because of her talent. My employer went to the I.N.S. and petitioned for the labor certification. For over 30 years, I've invested my creativity and professional skills into the improvement of *this* country's pre-school system. I've obeyed all the rules, I've paid my taxes, I love my work, I love my students, I love the friends I've made. How dare America now change its rules in midstream? If America wants to make new rules curtailing benefits of legal immigrants, they should apply only to immigrants who arrive after those rules are already in place."

To my ears, it sounded like the description of a long-enduring, comfortable yet loveless marriage, without risk or recklessness. Have we the right to demand, and to expect, that we be loved? (That, to me, is the subtext of the arguments by immigration advocates.) My sister is an expatriate, professionally generous and creative, socially courteous and gracious, and that's as far as her Americanization can go. She is here to maintain an identity, not to transform it.

I asked her if she would follow the example of others who have decided to become citizens because of the anti-immigration bills in Congress. And here, she surprised me. "If America wants to play the manipulative game, I'll play it too," she snapped. "I'll become a U.S. citizen for now, then change back to Indian when I'm ready to go home. I feel some kind of irrational attachment to India that I don't to America. Until all this hysteria against legal immigrants, I was totally happy. Having my green card meant I could visit any place in the world I wanted to and then come back to a job that's satisfying and that I do very well."

10

In one family, from two sisters alike as peas in a pod, there could not be a wider divergence of immigrant experience. America spoke to me—I married it—I embraced the demotion from expatriate aristocrat to immigrant nobody, surrendering those thousands of years of "pure culture," the saris, the delightfully accented English. She retained them all. Which of us is the freak?

Mira's voice, I realize, is the voice not just of the immigrant South Asian community but of an immigrant community of the millions who have stayed rooted in one job, one city, one house, one ancestral culture, one cuisine, for the entirety of their productive years. She speaks for greater numbers than I possibly can. Only the fluency of her English and the anger, rather than fear, born of confidence from her education, differentiate her from the seamstresses, the domestics, the technicians, the shop owners, the millions of hard-working but effectively silenced documented immigrants as well as their less fortunate "illegal" brothers and sisters.

Nearly 20 years ago, when I was living in my husband's ancestral homeland of Canada, I was always well-employed but never allowed to feel part of the local Quebec or larger Canadian society. Then, through a Green Paper that invited a national referendum on the unwanted side effects of "nontraditional" immigration, the Government officially turned against its immigrant communities, particularly those from South Asia.

I felt then the same sense of betrayal that Mira feels now. I will never forget the pain of that sudden turning, and the casual racist outbursts the Green Paper elicited. That sense of betrayal had its desired effect and drove me, and thousands like me, from the country.

Mira and I differ, however, in the ways in which we hope to interact   15
with the country that we have chosen to live in. She is happier to live in America as expatriate Indian than as an immigrant American. I need to feel like a part of the community I have adopted (as I tried to feel in Canada as well). I need to put roots down, to vote and make the difference that I can. The price that the immigrant willingly pays, and that the exile avoids, is the trauma of self-transformation.

 ## Joining the Conversation:
Critical Thinking and Writing

1. Analyze the first paragraph as an opening paragraph. Why do you think it is or is not effective? (Some suggestions: Does the phrase "a tale of two sisters" ring a bell? Do the variations in the lengths of the sentences contribute to the meaning?)

2. Given what you now know about Mira, do you think she has a case? List her arguments and evaluate each. If you believe they don't add up to much, do you think she should be required to leave? Set forth your evaluation of her arguments, and your view about granting permanent status to aliens who do not wish to become citizens, in an essay of 500 words.

3. If you are an American citizen, can you imagine living most of your adult life in another country—perhaps because you believe you are contributing a needed skill, or perhaps because your spouse is a citizen of that country—and *not* becoming a citizen, even though you enjoy your life there? Or put the reverse question: Can you imagine *becoming* a citizen of that country? Perhaps much would depend on the country. Choose a country that you are likely to find highly attractive, and in an essay of 500 words set forth your position.

4. Mukherjee in her final paragraph speaks of the "price" that the immigrant willingly pays when he or she becomes a citizen. Interview two immigrants who have become citizens, and report their views on what (if anything) it cost them spiritually to become a citizen. (On interviewing, see pages 57–61.)

Anar Ali

Anar Ali's family, residents of Tanzania, fled to Canada to escape anti-Indian persecution. Anar, who grew up in Alberta and now lives in Toronto, is the author of Baby Khaki's Wings, *a collection of short stories about an Ismaili (Muslim) community in exile. We reprint an essay that originally appeared in the* New York Times *in 2006.*

The Person Behind the Muslim

I went to a school in rural Alberta from sixth grade onward, and each year I had to endure the annual school rodeo. Most of the students at my school were avid 4-H members, so the rodeo was the highlight of their year. It was an opportunity for them to exhibit their award-winning cattle or show off their skills in events like barrel racing and bronco riding. In an effort to convert the few city slickers among us, the school also provided less challenging events like the greased pig race.

I wasn't interested in participating. My parents owned a motel, not a farm; my skills were honed as a chambermaid, not a cowgirl. I told my teacher that I was Muslim and it was against my religion to touch a pig.

"I thought you just couldn't eat them," she said.

"No, I can't have anything to do with them," I retorted, knowing full well that I was stretching the truth.

When Mrs. Ritchie refused to excuse me from the rodeo, I took the   5
matter up with my father, certain he would side with me, not because of religion, but for hygiene and safety reasons. (Only recently, he called me at 11 p.m. to let me know he wanted to install anti-slip strips in my bathtub.)

But I was wrong. My father insisted I join the rodeo, even bought me cowboy gear from Kmart. Each year I tried protesting, emphasizing my inability to a catch a pig (let alone drag it across the finish line) as proof that I was wasting my time. But none of that mattered to my father. He was keen for me (and my sisters) to participate in all things Canadian. He refused to let me eat the hot dogs at the rodeo barbecue, but I had to enter the greased pig race.

This battle portended the many I would have in the future—not only with my father, but also with myself on where to set the dial between assimilation and retaining my own culture. I grew up living between worlds, in the hyphenated spaces of Indo-Canadian, Tanzanian-Canadian, and Ismaili Muslim-Canadian. It was a fractured existence, and one that was often unsatisfying. I never belonged anywhere completely.

Meena Alexander, an Indian-born poet who has lived in Sudan and the United States, puts it eloquently: "I am, a woman cracked by multiple migrations. Uprooted so many times she can connect nothing with nothing." But I did not want to live in the cracks; it was exhausting. I wanted to live in a place that held all my multiplicities.

After years of hard work (and 30 years in Canada), I finally arrived in a new geography. It wasn't a physical space, although being in Toronto, a city made of many cultures, helps. But it was a cultural and psychological place, one that coalesced my identities into one and gave me a sense of home. I called this place Canadian.

Sept. 11 changed all that. So have subsequent acts of terrorism—or attempted acts of terrorism, like the ones authorities said were planned by the members of Islamic terrorist cells arrested here last week. These events have all, in one way or another, expelled me from my new home. It was dismantled; my Muslim identity was teased out like code from a DNA strand. One piece of code does not tell you the whole story, but it is only one placed under the microscope for investigation.   10

This is all you are. Muslim Magnified.

After 9/11, I soon became used to the new rules: double-checking at borders, detentions at airports, suspicious glances on subways, especially if you are carrying a backpack. One memorable incident: I was detained for three hours en route from Calgary to Los Angeles when the South Asian Arts festival I was attending in 2004 was suspected of being a radical Muslim group. The festival's name, Art-wallah, is a play on words, a mix of the words "art" and "wallah." Wallah is a Hindi-derived word that denotes a profession; examples include taxi-wallah and chai-wallah. The presence of (w)Allah in the festival name raised flags.

I had to do a lot of explaining. Something, as an immigrant or person of color, you get used to from a very young age. (Where are you from? What does your name mean?) After a thorough investigation and phone calls to England to confirm the whereabouts of an "evil person" with a name similar to mine—"Ali," I reassured the officer, was akin to "Smith"—I was finally released.

Whether you want it or not, as a Muslim (secular and otherwise) you are automatically pulled into the debate on terrorism. Not that I don't want to discuss it, I do. But I want to discuss it as a citizen, not just a Muslim.

As a Muslim, people expect you to be an expert, to have special inside knowledge on the topic. They want your opinion on the issue, your help in explaining and analyzing complex political issues, the history of Islam, the psychology of suicide bombers. 15

I have no sense of what motivates a terrorist (except maybe as a fiction writer, since it's my job to enter the hearts and minds of characters). Terrorists and radical Islamists live in a different place from me, psychologically and culturally, even if they were raised in Canada just as I was. To better understand these young men and why they turn to violence as a means to an end, it might make more sense to ask someone who was a skinhead, a member of the Irish Republican Army, a Tamil Tiger, or a Weatherman.

If you asked me, I would have to speculate, as most people do, from the sidelines.

Joining the Conversation: Critical Thinking and Writing

1. Ali's essay explains a series of challenges she has faced since childhood. What have been the sources of those challenges?

2. Ali's essay is, for the most part, expository. What argument do you find implicit in it?

3. Ali writes that because she is a Muslim, people expect her to "have special inside knowledge" on such things as terrorism, the history of Islam, and the psychology of suicide bombers. If you have experienced similar challenges because of your identity, write an essay of 500 words explaining the circumstances and your responses.

A Casebook on Recent Immigrants

Barry R. Chiswick

Barry R. Chiswick holds a Ph.D. in economics from Columbia University. A specialist in the labor market, Chiswick is head of the economics department at the University of Illinois at Chicago. We reprint an essay that originally appeared in the New York Times *in 2006.*

The Worker Next Door

It is often said that the American economy needs low-skilled foreign workers to do the jobs that American workers will not do. These foreign workers might be new immigrants, illegal aliens or, in the current debate, temporary or guest workers. But if low-skilled foreign workers were not here, would lettuce not be picked, groceries not bagged, hotel sheets not changed, and lawns not mowed? Would restaurants use disposable plates and utensils?

On the face of it, this assertion seems implausible. Immigrants and low-skilled foreign workers in general are highly concentrated in a few states. The "big six" are California, Florida, Illinois, New Jersey, New York and Texas. Even within those states, immigrants and low-skilled foreign workers are concentrated in a few metropolitan areas—while there are many in New York City and Chicago, relatively few are in upstate New York or downstate Illinois.

Yet even in areas with few immigrants, grass is cut, groceries are bagged and hotel sheets are changed. Indeed, a large majority of low-skilled workers are native to the United States. A look at the 2000 census is instructive: among males age 25 to 64 years employed that year, of those with less than a high school diploma, 64 percent were born in the United States and 36 percent were foreign born.

Other Americans nominally graduated from high school but did not learn a trade or acquire the literacy, numeracy or decision-making skills needed for higher earnings. Still others suffer from a physical or emotional ailment that limits their labor productivity. And some low-skilled jobs are performed by high school or college students, housewives or the retired who wish to work part time. Put simply, there are no low-skilled jobs that American workers would not and do not do.

Over the past two decades the number of low-skilled workers in the United States has increased because of immigration, both legal and illegal. This increase in low-skilled workers has contributed to the stagnation of wages for all such workers. The proposed "earned legalization" (amnesty) and guest worker programs would allow still more low-skilled workers into the country, further lowering their collective wages.

True, the prices of the goods and services that these new immigrants produce are reduced for the rich and poor alike. But the net effect of this dynamic is a decline in the purchasing power of low-skilled families and a rise in the purchasing power of high-income families—a significant factor behind the increase in income inequality that has been of considerable public concern over the past two decades.

In short, the continued increase in the flow of unskilled workers into the United States is the economic and moral equivalent of a regressive tax.

5

If the number of low-skilled foreign workers were to fall, wages would increase. Low-skilled American workers and their families would benefit, and society as a whole would gain from a reduction in income inequality.

Employers facing higher labor costs for low-skilled workers would raise their prices, and to some extent they would change the way they operate their businesses. A farmer who grows winter iceberg lettuce in Yuma County, Ariz., was asked on the ABC program "Nightline" in April what he would do if it were more difficult to find the low-skilled hand harvesters who work on his farm, many of whom are undocumented workers. He replied that he would mechanize the harvest. Such technology exists, but it is not used because of the abundance of low-wage laborers. In their absence, mechanical harvesters—and the higher skilled (and higher wage) workers to operate them—would replace low-skilled, low-wage workers.

But, you might ask, who would mow the lawns in suburbia? The higher wages would attract more lower-skilled American workers (including teenagers) to these jobs. Facing higher costs, some homeowners would switch to grass species that grow more slowly, to alternative ground cover or to flagstones. Others would simply mow every other week, or every 10 days, instead of weekly. And some would combine one or more of these strategies to offset rising labor costs.

Few of us change our sheets and towels at home every day. Hotels and motels could reduce the frequency of changing sheets and towels from every day to, say, every third day for continuing guests, perhaps offering a price discount to guests who accept this arrangement.

Less frequent lawn mowing and washing of hotel sheets and towels would reduce air, noise and water pollution in the bargain.

With the higher cost of low-skilled labor, we would import more of some goods, in particular table-quality fruits and vegetables for home consumption (as distinct from industrial use) and lower-priced off-the-rack clothing. But it makes no sense to import people to produce goods in the United States for which we lack a comparative advantage—that is, goods that other countries can produce more efficiently.

The point is that with a decline in low-skilled foreign workers, life would go on. The genius of the American people is their ingenuity, and the genius of the American economy is its flexibility. And throughout our nation's history, this flexibility, the finding of alternative ways of doing things, has been a prime engine of economic growth and change.

Joining the Conversation: Critical Thinking and Writing

1. What is Chiswick's topic? What is his thesis?

2. What kinds of evidence does Chiswick present in order to support his argument? Do you find his evidence to be convincing? Explain your answer.

3. A student who read this essay in an economics course said she found it "confusing." Another student in the same course said he found it "persuasive." Which of these observations do you think is more accurate? Why?

4. Define a "low-skilled" worker. Have you ever worked in a "low-skilled" job? Describe this experience in detail.

5. How would you define a "high-skilled" worker? Identify some kinds of work that require "high skills."

6. Do you think a person who holds a high-skilled job is likely to be happier than a person who holds a low-skilled job? Explain your answer.

Jeff Jacoby

Jeff Jacoby is a columnist for the Boston Globe, *where this essay originally was published on the Op-Ed page on March 19, 2007.*

What If We Deport Them All?

"**N**ot often do I disagree with your views, but on illegal aliens we are a world apart," writes V., one of many readers I heard from after suggesting last week that the best solution to our illegal immigration problem is to make more immigration legal. "My view, unlike yours, is to secure the borders by whatever means possible. Arrest, imprison, and heavily fine employers who hire illegals. Apprehend and deport illegals no matter how long it takes—years, if necessary.

"The American people," V. concludes, "overwhelmingly want these illegals out of the country."

Actually, only about one American in four feels that way. According to a new Gallup poll, when asked to choose among three options—deporting all illegal immigrants, allowing them to remain temporarily in the United States to work, or allowing them to stay permanently and become US citizens after meeting certain conditions—a majority, 59 percent, chose permanent legalization. Fifteen percent favored the temporary-worker option. Just 24 percent supported deportation.

What the throw-'em-out school lacks in numbers it more than makes up for in vehemence. But the raucous demand for ever-tougher border security tends to drown out a disconcerting fact: It doesn't work. The harder we make it for illegal immigrants to enter the country, the more unwilling they are to leave once they get here.

"Between 1986 and 2002 the number of Border Patrol officers tripled," notes Princeton sociologist Douglas Massey, an expert on Mexican migration, "and the number of hours they spent patrolling the borders . . . grew by a factor of about eight."

Yet driving up the risks and costs of crossing the border hasn't shrunk the number of illegal immigrants crossing the border—only the number prepared to run that gauntlet more than once. Historically, Mexican migrants came to the United States sporadically, working for a while, then heading home. Now, millions figure it is better to stay put and risk deportation than to go back to Mexico and risk being unable to return. In 1986, the probability that an illegal entering from Mexico would leave within 12 months was around 45 percent. Today it is half that.

Nevertheless, suppose that V. and others got their wish, and 12 million illegal immigrants were forced out. What then?

As millions of farm hands, busboys, chambermaids, and garment workers vanished, who would take their places? Unemployed US citizens? With unemployment down to 4.5 percent, there aren't 12 million of them to spare. Even if there were, not many native-born Americans are prepared to accept the low wages and hard conditions that characterize so much illegal-immigrant labor.

Hard-liners insist that there are no "jobs Americans won't do" if the pay is right. Well, how much would an employer have to pay *you* to pick lettuce or clean hotel rooms for a living? A lot of jobs that pay, say, $8 an hour and are acceptable to a Mexican or Guatemalan alien with little education, few skills, and a fear of being deported would evaporate at the $16 an hour Americans would demand. With more expensive labor would come more reliance on machines instead of people, more outsourcing to cheaper labor markets, more closing of no-longer-profitable ventures. If illegal immigrants disappeared, countless jobs would disappear with them.

Pull 12 million low-skilled workers out of the economy, and the cost of everything from yardwork to restaurant meals would soar. Higher costs would mean lower profits and disposable income, less investment, weaker growth.   10

"Some 1.2 million illegals are believed to work in construction," Holman Jenkins wrote in the *Wall Street Journal* last June. "If the cost of home building goes up, demand goes down: Less wood is sold, fewer nails, fewer power tools, fewer pickup trucks. Contractors would make less profit; ergo, Harley-Davidson would sell fewer Road Kings with all the chrome and finery."

The United States creates more than 400,000 new low-skill jobs each year, a tremendous employment magnet for hundreds of thousands of foreign workers. But because US law authorizes only 5,000 visas annually for low-skilled immigrants, there is no lawful way for most of the workers we need to enter the country. So they enter unlawfully—a wrongful act, perhaps, but hardly an evil one.

Immigration is good for America. So is respect for the law. Nothing forces us to choose between them. As long as there is work for them to do here, immigrants will keep crossing the border. We'd all be better off if we let them cross it legally.

Joining the Conversation: Critical Thinking and Writing

1. In paragraph 3 Jacoby says that only about a quarter of the American public favors deporting illegal aliens. Is this information effective in his essay? Is this fact relevant to your own view of the issue of illegal immigration? Explain your position.

2. Rogerian argument (see pages 81–86) emphasizes the need to find common ground, to become a partner rather than an adversary. Do you think Jacoby's essay would be more convincing if he showed greater sympathy for views other than his own? Explain.

3. Jacoby raises issues that Barry Chiswick also raises (pages 268–269). Putting aside your own view of the issue, which essay do you think is more convincing? Why? Again, put aside our own views, and, in the role of neutral umpire, evaluate the essays as though the two authors were participating in a debate. Which essay is more convincing? Why?

4. Read or reread Chiswick's essay, and then write a dialogue (about 500 words) in which Chiswick and Jacoby discuss the issue.

5. Prepare an argument in which you refute the position that Jacoby presents. Then, prepare an argument in which you refute Chiswick's position. Which of the two is more difficult for you to refute? Explain why, as carefully as you can.

Victor Davis Hanson

Victor Davis Hanson, born in 1953 in Fowler, California, is a classicist and historian at the Hoover Institution, Stanford University. His most recent book is A War Like No Other: How the Athenians and Spartans Fought the Peloponnesian War *(2005). You can read many of his publications by entering his name in a search engine.*

Socrates on Illegal Immigration

After Socrates was convicted by a court of questionable charges, his friends planned to break him out of his jail in Athens. But the philosopher refused to flee. Instead, he insisted that a citizen who lived in a consensual society should not pick and choose which laws he finds convenient to obey.

Selective compliance, Socrates warned, would undermine the moral integrity of the entire legal system, ensuring anarchy. And so, as Plato tells us, the philosopher accepted the court's death sentence and drank the deadly hemlock.

Socrates' final lesson about the sanctity of the law is instructive now in our current debate over illegal immigration.

There are, of course, many objections to illegal immigration besides that it is against the law: Unlawful workers undermine the wages of our own citizen entry-level workers. Employers who depend on imported labor find common ground with ethnic chauvinists; they both exploit a large, vulnerable and unassimilated constituency. And security analysts warn us that it is insane to allow a 2,000-mile open border at a time when terrorist infiltrators are planning to kill us.

Yet few have criticized illegal immigration solely because millions have, with impunity, flouted the law—aliens, their employers and the officials who look the other way.   5

But Socrates would do just that, and also point to our hypocrisy.

The alien from Mexico chooses which American laws he finds convenient. He wants our border police to leave him alone—until he becomes lost in the desert or is attacked by robbers.

The employer expects trespassing laws to be enforced to keep vagrants off his premises, but then assumes that the same vigilant police will ignore the illegal status of his cheap labor force.

And does the city council that orders its policemen not to turn over arrested illegal aliens to the border patrol similarly allow townspeople to ignore their municipal tax bills?

When thousands operate cars without state-mandated licenses and car insurance, why should other drivers bother to purchase them? If police pull over motorists and do not verify the legal status of aliens, why do they check for outstanding arrest warrants of citizens?   10

Ignoring the law is not only hypocritical and anarchical; it also creates cynicism. Recently, I listened to friends relate that the government had indicted some Indian immigrants on charges of arranging bogus marriages to gain citizenship. My friends half-jokingly wondered why the culprits hadn't simply flown to Mexico and tried to sneak across the border!

So, besides the money to be made on both sides of the border, why do we disregard the immigration laws?

Are the laws wrong and cruel, and even if they are, would it be moral to ignore them? The answers are no and no.

Employing illegal workers drives down the wages of the legal poor. Cutting ahead in the immigration line is unfair to immigrants who wait years to enter America legally. Mexico wants money from aliens to prop up its failures at home but cares little how such remittances burden poorer Mexican wage earners abroad. In other words, breaking the immigration law is not really civil disobedience but, typically, an expression of jaded self-interest by workers, employers and government officials.

Nevertheless, what distinguishes the U.S. from nations in the Middle   15 East, Africa and, yes, Mexico is the sanctity of our legal system. The terrain of Mexico may be indistinguishable from the landscape across the border in the U.S. But when it comes to the law, there is a grand canyon between us.

Only on one side of the border is title to private property sacrosanct, are police held accountable and is banking conducted transparently. Public hiring in America is based on civil service law, and judges are autonomous. And the American public has a legal right to investigate and even sue its government. That maze of legality helps to explain everything from why the water is safer to drink in San Diego than in Tijuana to why a worker makes $12 an hour in Fresno but less than $1 in Oaxaca.

Yet once we as a nation choose to ignore our keystone laws of sovereignty and citizenship, the entire edifice of a once unimpeachable legal system will collapse. Ironically, we would then become no different from those nations whose citizens are now fleeing to our shores to escape the wages of lawlessness.

That worry is why Socrates, 2,400 years ago, taught us that the deliberate violation of the rule of law would have been worse for ancient Athens even than losing its greatest philosopher.

Joining the Conversation: Critical Thinking and Writing

1. Speaking of Socrates' acceptance of the death sentence imposed upon him by the Athenian court, Hanson says (paragraph 3) that "Socrates' final lesson about the sanctity of the law is instructive now in our current debate over illegal immigration." We reprint Plato's account of Socrates on page 630, but even if you have not read it, does Hanson's essay convince you that the law—whether we like it or not—must be obeyed?

2. In paragraph 4 Hanson asserts, among other things, that "unlawful workers undermine the wages of our own citizen entry-level workers." Think of some people who have recently entered the job market. Do you think that their wages have been lowered by the presence of "unlawful workers"? Explain.

3. In paragraphs 7 through 9 Hanson gives examples of what he calls hypocrisy. Do you agree that the actions illustrate hypocrisy? Can you imagine that you might behave in this manner? If so, what is to be done?

4. In paragraph 17 Hanson suggests that "once we as a nation choose to ignore our keystone laws of sovereignty and citizenship, the entire edifice of a once unimpeachable legal system will collapse." Do you think Hanson overstates the issue? Explain.

5. Evaluate Hanson's strategy of beginning and ending with Socrates. Do you think his use of Socrates is effective? Explain.

Cardinal Roger Mahony

Roger Mahony, born in Hollywood, California, in 1936, was ordained a priest in 1962. In 1975 Governor Jerry Brown appointed Mahony as the first chair of the California Agricultural Labor Relations Board, where he worked to resolve disputes between the United Farm Workers and the growers. Mahony was appointed bishop in 1980, archbishop in 1985, and cardinal in 1991. He has made controversial statements, sometimes disturbing liberals and sometimes disturbing conservatives. This essay originally appeared as an Op-Ed piece in the New York Times.

Called by God to Help

I've received a lot of criticism for stating last month that I would instruct the priests of my archdiocese to disobey a proposed law that would subject them, as well as other church and humanitarian workers, to criminal penalties. The proposed Border Protection, Antiterrorism and Illegal Immigration Control bill, which was approved by the House of Representatives in December and is expected to be taken up by the Senate next week, would among other things subject to five years in prison anyone who "assists" an undocumented immigrant "to remain in the United States."

Some supporters of the bill have even accused the church of encouraging illegal immigration and meddling in politics. But I stand by my statement. Part of the mission of the Roman Catholic Church is to help people in need. It is our Gospel mandate, in which Christ instructs us to clothe the naked, feed the poor and welcome the stranger. Indeed, the Catholic Church, through Catholic Charities agencies around the country, is one of the largest nonprofit providers of social services in the nation, serving both citizens and immigrants.

Providing humanitarian assistance to those in need should not be made a crime, as the House bill decrees. As written, the proposed law is so broad that it would criminalize even minor acts of mercy like offering a meal or administering first aid.

Current law does not require social service agencies to obtain evidence of legal status before rendering aid, nor should it. Denying aid to a fellow human being violates a law with a higher authority than Congress—the law of God.

That does not mean that the Catholic Church encourages or supports illegal immigration. Every day in our parishes, social service programs, hospitals and schools, we witness the baleful consequences of illegal immigration. Families are separated, workers are exploited and migrants are left by smugglers to die in the desert. Illegal immigration serves neither the migrant nor the common good.

What the church supports is an overhaul of the immigration system so that legal status and legal channels for migration replace illegal status

5

and illegal immigration. Creating legal structures for migration protects not only those who migrate but also our nation, by giving the government the ability to better identify who is in the country as well as to control who enters it.

Only comprehensive reform of the immigration system, embodied in the principles of another proposal in Congress, the Secure America and Orderly Immigration bill, will help solve our current immigration crisis.

Enforcement-only proposals like the Border Protection act take the country in the opposite direction. Increasing penalties, building more detention centers and erecting walls along our border with Mexico, as the act provides, will not solve the problem.

The legislation will not deter migrants who are desperate to survive and support their families from seeking jobs in the United States. It will only drive them further into the shadows, encourage the creation of more elaborate smuggling networks and cause hardship and suffering. I hope that the Senate will not take the same enforcement-only road as the House.

The unspoken truth of the immigration debate is that at the same time our nation benefits economically from the presence of undocumented workers, we turn a blind eye when they are exploited by employers. They work in industries that are vital to our economy yet they have little legal protection and no opportunity to contribute fully to our nation.

While we gladly accept their taxes and sweat, we do not acknowledge or uphold their basic labor rights. At the same time, we scapegoat them for our social ills and label them as security threats and criminals to justify the passage of anti-immigrant bills.

This situation affects the dignity of millions of our fellow human beings and makes immigration, ultimately, a moral and ethical issue. That is why the church is compelled to take a stand against harmful legislation and to work toward positive change.

It is my hope that our elected officials will understand this and enact immigration reform that respects our common humanity and reflects the values—fairness, compassion and opportunity—upon which our nation, a nation of immigrants, was built.

Joining the Conversation: Critical Thinking and Writing

1. Why does the cardinal object to the law that the House of Representatives approved? Do you agree with him?

2. Putting aside your own personal views, set forth the best possible argument against the view that Mahony gives here.

3 Do you agree with Mahony that there is a "higher authority"—the law of God—that should take precedence over the laws of a state or a nation? Explain your position.

4. Suppose someone said, "If everyone believed what Cardinal Mahony believes, there would be a breakdown of civil society. No one would feel obligated to obey the laws of the land. We would have utter chaos." What reply might be made to this objection?

5. Suppose someone said, "People who hold strong religious views should keep these out of politics. Religion is one thing, and politics is something else." Do you agree or disagree? Explain your position.

A Casebook of Poems about Immigrants

Emma Lazarus

Emma Lazarus (1849–1887) was of German-Jewish descent on her mother's side, and of Sephardic descent on her father's side. (Sephardic Jews trace their ancestry back to Spain under Muslim rule, before the Jews were expelled by the Christians in 1492.)

In 1883 a committee was formed to raise funds for a pedestal for the largest statue in the world, Liberty Enlightening the People, *to be installed on a small island in New York Harbor. Authors were asked to donate manuscripts that were then auctioned to raise money. Emma Lazarus, keenly aware of ancient persecutions and of contemporary Jewish refugees fleeing Russian persecution, contributed the following poem. It was read when the statue was unveiled in 1886, and the words of Liberty, spoken in the last five lines, were embossed on a plaque inside the pedestal.*

For the ancients, a colossus was a statue larger than life. "The brazen giant of Greek fame," mentioned in Lazarus's first line, was a statue of the sun god, erected in the harbor of the Greek island of Rhodes, celebrating the island's success in resisting the Macedonians in 305–304 B.C. More than 100 feet tall, it stood in the harbor until it toppled during an earthquake in 225 B.C. In later years its size became mythical; it was said to have straddled the harbor (Lazarus speaks of "limbs astride from land to land"), so that ships supposedly entered the harbor by sailing between its legs.

In Lazarus's poem, the "imprisoned lightning" (line 5) in the torch is electricity. The harbor is said to be "air-bridged" because in 1883, the year of the poem, the Brooklyn Bridge was completed, connecting Brooklyn with New York. (These are the "twin cities" of the poem.)

The New Colossus

Not like the brazen giant of Greek fame,
With conquering limbs astride from land to land;
Here at our sea-washed, sunset gates shall stand
A mighty woman with a torch, whose flame
Is the imprisoned lightning, and her name   5
Mother of Exiles. From her beacon-hand
Glows world-wide welcome; her mild eyes command

The air-bridged harbor that twin cities frame.
"Keep, ancient lands, your storied pomp!" cries she
With silent lips. "Give me your tired, your poor,   10
Your huddled masses yearning to breathe free,
The wretched refuse of your teeming shore.
Send these, the homeless, tempest-tost to me,
I lift my lamp beside the golden door!"

Joining the Conversation: Critical Thinking and Writing

1. Do you find this poem to be clear, or confusing, or both? Point to details that either are clear in their meaning or that are confusing to you.

2 Lazarus uses the word "new" in her title. What is the relationship between the old Colossus and this new one?

3. Have you ever visited the Statue of Liberty? If you have, describe this experience. If you have not, describe a visit you have made to some other important historical or cultural site.

4. Does this poem have a message? In a paragraph, state what this message is.

5. A prominent historian has said that the Statue of Liberty is the nation's "greatest monument to the true meaning of America." Do you agree with this statement? Argue for or against this statement.

Pat Mora

Pat Mora did her undergraduate work at Texas Western College and then earned a master's degree at the University of Texas at El Paso, where she later served as Assistant to the Vice President for Academic Affairs, Director of the University Museum, and then (1981–1989) as Assistant to the President. She has published essay on Hispanic culture as well as a children's book, Tomás and the Library Lady, *but she is best known for her books of poems. Mora has received several awards, including one from the Southwest Council of Latin American Studies.*

Immigrants

wrap their babies in the American flag,
feed them mashed hot dogs and apple pie,

name them Bill and Daisy,
buy them blonde dolls that blink blue
eyes or a football and tiny cleats   5
before the baby can even walk,
speak to them in thick English,
   hallo, babee, hallo.
whisper in Spanish or Polish
when the babies sleep, whisper   10
in a dark parent bed, that dark
parent fear, "Will they like
our boy, our girl, our fine american
boy, our fine american girl?"

 Joining the Conversation:
Critical Thinking and Writing

1. To say that someone—for example, a politician—"wraps himself in the American flag" is to suggest disapproval or even anger or contempt. What behavior does the phrase usually describe? What does Mora mean when she says that immigrants "wrap their babies in the American flag"?

2. We often use the phrase "tone of voice" when we respond to and discuss a poem, essay or story. How would you describe the speaker's tone of voice in this poem? Does the tone stay the same throughout, or does it change?

3. Sometimes the word "american" in the final two lines is mistakenly printed as "American." Would this make a difference in your response? Explain your answer.

4. What do you suppose is Mora's attitude toward the immigrants? Do you think she fully approves of their hopes? On what do you base your answer?

5. Do you think that someone could say, "I find this poem offensive"? Present an argument in which you take this position. Then, present an argument in which you take the opposite view. Remember in both cases to point to evidence in the text to support your argument.

6. What does "dark/parent fear" mean? Do all parents—immigrants and non-immigrants alike—have fears? What kinds of fears? Is there one fear in particular that all parents share? Explain, perhaps drawing upon family experiences and memories of your own.

7. Does Mora's description of the behavior of immigrants ring true of the immigrant group you are part of or know best? What is your attitude toward their efforts to assimilate? Explain in an essay of 750 to 1,000 words.

Dudley Randall

Born in Washington, D.C., in 1914, Randall graduated from Wayne State University and the University of Michigan, and worked as a reference librarian and as poet in residence at the University of Detroit. In 1965 he founded the Broadside Press, widely recognized as influential far beyond its size, publishing excellent small books and single sheets with poems by African-Americans.

The Melting Pot

There is a magic melting pot
where any girl or man
can step in Czech or Greek or Scot,
step out American.

Johann and *Jan* and *Jean* and *Juan,*   5
Giovanni and *Ivan*
step in and then step out again
all freshly christened *John.*

Sam, watching, said, "Why, I was here
even before they came,"   10
and stepped in too, but was tossed out
before he passed the brim.

And every time Sam tried that pot
they threw him out again.
"Keep out. This is our private pot   15
We don't want your black stain."

At last, thrown out a thousand times,
Sam said, "I don't give a damn.
Shove your old pot. You can like it or not,
but I'll be just what I am."   20

Joining the Conversation:
Critical Thinking and Writing

1. When you read the first two stanzas for the first time, what was your response to them? When you reread them after finishing the poem and giving it some thought, what was your response? The same? Different?

2. In the final stanza, what is Sam saying? What is his tone of voice?

Dudley Randall, "The Melting Pot" from *Cities Burning*. Broadside Press, 1968. Reprinted by permission of the Estate of Dudley Randall.

3. Does the image of "the melting pot" accurately reflect what happens to immigrants in the United States? Is this a good thing, or a bad thing, or both? Can you think of a better image?

4. What is "the American Dream"? Is anyone excluded from it? Do you believe in it yourself?

5. Does everyone in the United States have the same chance to succeed? If not, do you think that the government should make certain that every person does have the same chance? Explain how this might be done.

CHAPTER 9

Teaching and Learning

Blackboard
Winslow Homer, 1877

The Lesson—Planning a Career
Rom James, 1963

Short Views

Knowledge is power.
Francis Bacon

In my opinion, the only justification for high schools is as therapeutic halfway houses for the deranged. Normal adolescents can find themselves and grow further only by coping with the jobs, sex, and chances of the real world—it is useless to feed them curricular imitations. I would simply abolish the high schools, substituting apprenticeships and other alternatives and protecting the young from gross exploitation by putting the school money directly in their pockets. The very few who have authentic scholarly interests will gravitate to their own libraries, teachers, and academies, as they always did in the past, when they could afford it. In organic communities, adolescents cluster together in their own youth houses, for their fun and games and loud music, without bothering sober folk. I see no reason whatsoever for adults to set up or direct such nests or to be there at all unless invited.
Paul Goodman

How people keep correcting us when we are young! There's always some bad habit or other they tell us we ought to get over. Yet most bad habits are tools to help us through life.
Johann Wolfgang von Goethe

Supposing anyone were to suggest that the best results for the individual and society could be derived through compulsory feeding, would not the most ignorant rebel against such a stupid procedure? And yet the stomach has far greater adaptability to almost any situation than the brain. With all that, we find it quite natural to have compulsory mental feeding.

Indeed, we actually consider ourselves superior to other nations, because we have evolved a compulsory brain tube through which, for a certain number of hours every day, and for so many years, we can force into the child's mind a large quantity of mental nutrition.

. . . The great harm done by our system of education is not so much that it teaches nothing worth knowing, that it helps to perpetuate privileged classes, that it assists them in the criminal procedure of robbing and exploiting the masses; the harm of the system lies in its boastful proclamation that it stands for true

education, thereby enslaving the masses a great deal more than could an absolute ruler.
  Emma Goldman

If Johnny can't learn because he is hungry, that's the fault of poverty. But if Johnny can't pay attention because he is sleepy, that's the fault of parents.

   What does it matter if we have a new book or an old book, if we open neither?
  Jesse Jackson

Universities are, of course, hostile to geniuses.
  Ralph Waldo Emerson

Education! Which of the various me's do you propose to educate, and which do you propose to suppress?
  D. H. Lawrence

Think about the kind of world you want to live and work in. What do you need to know to build the world? Demand that your teachers teach you that.
  Prince Kropotkin

The entire object of true education is to make people not merely do the right things, but enjoy the right things.
  John Ruskin

Learning without thought is labor lost; thought without learning is dangerous.
  Confucius

I think [Raymond Weaver] first attracted my attention as someone worth watching when, while we were both new instructors, I heard from a bewildered freshman about the quiz he had just given. The first question written on the blackboard was, "Which of the required readings in this course did you find least interesting?" Then, after members of the class had had ten minutes in which to expatiate on what was certainly to many a congenial topic, he wrote the second question: "To what defect in yourself do you attribute this lack of interest?"
  Joseph Wood Krutch

It is not sufficiently understood that a child's education should include at least a rudimentary grasp of religion, sex, and money. Without a basic knowledge of these three primary facts in a normal human being's life—subjects which stir the emotions, create events and opportunities, and if they do not wholly decide must greatly influence an individual's personality—no human being's education can have a safe foundation.

Phyllis Bottome

David Brooks

David Brooks, senior editor at the Weekly Standard *(a conservative journal), publishes frequently in* Atlantic Monthly, Newsweek, *and the* New York Times, *where he writes an op-ed column. He is the author of* Bobos in Paradise: The New Upper Class and How They Got There *(2000)—a "bobo" is a bourgeois bohemian—and* On Paradise Drive: How We Live Now (and Always Have) in the Future Tense *(2004). Brooks appears regularly on the* NewsHour with Jim Lehrer.

The Gender Gap at School

There are three gender-segregated sections in any airport: the restrooms, the security pat-down area and the bookstore. In the men's sections of the bookstore, there are books describing masterly men conquering evil. In the women's sections there are novels about . . . well, I guess feelings and stuff.

The same separation occurs in the home. Researchers in Britain asked 400 accomplished women and 500 accomplished men to name their favorite novels. The men preferred novels written by men, often revolving around loneliness and alienation. Camus's "The Stranger," Salinger's "Catcher in the Rye" and Vonnegut's "Slaughterhouse-Five" topped the male list. The women leaned toward books written by women. The women's books described relationships and are a lot better than the books the men chose. The top six women's books were "Jane Eyre," "Wuthering Heights," "The Handmaid's Tale," "Middlemarch," "Pride and Prejudice" and "Beloved."

There are a couple of reasons why the two lists might diverge so starkly. It could be men are insensitive dolts who don't appreciate subtle human connections and good literature. Or, it could be that the part of the brain where men experience negative emotion, the amygdala, is not well connected to the part of the brain where verbal processing happens, whereas the part of the brain where women experience negative emotion, the cerebral cortex, is well connected. It could be that women are better at processing emotion through words.

Over the past two decades, there has been a steady accumulation of evidence that male and female brains work differently. Women use both sides of their brain more symmetrically than men. Men and women hear and smell differently (women are much more sensitive). Boys and girls process colors differently (young girls enjoy an array of red, green and orange crayons whereas young boys generally stick to black, gray and blue). Men and women experience risk differently (men enjoy it more).

It could be, in short, that biological factors influence reading tastes, even after accounting for culture. Women who have congenital adrenal hyperplasia, which leads to high male hormone secretions, are more

5

likely to choose violent stories than other women. This wouldn't be a problem if we all understood these biological factors and if teachers devised different curriculums to instill an equal love of reading in both boys and girls.

(The problem is that even after the recent flurry of attention about why boys are falling behind, there is still intense social pressure not to talk about biological differences between boys and girls) (ask Larry Summers). There is still resistance, especially in the educational world, to the findings of brain researchers. Despite some innovations here and there, in most classrooms boys and girls are taught the same books in the same ways.

Young boys are compelled to sit still in schools that have sacrificed recess for test prep. Many are told in a thousand subtle ways they are not really good students. They are sent home with these new-wave young adult problem novels, which all seem to be about introspectively morose young women whose parents are either suicidal drug addicts or fatally ill manic depressives.

(It shouldn't be any surprise that according to a National Endowment for the Arts study, the percentage of young men who read has plummeted over the past 14 years.) Reading rates are falling three times as fast among young men as among young women. Nor should it be a surprise that men are drifting away from occupations that involve reading and school (Men now make up a smaller share of teachers than at any time in the past 40 years.)

Dr. Leonard Sax, whose book "Why Gender Matters" is a lucid guide to male and female brain differences, emphasizes that men and women can excel at any subject. (They just have to be taught in different ways.) Sax is a big believer in single-sex schools, which he says allow kids to open up and break free from gender stereotypes. But for most kids it would be a start if they were assigned books they might actually care about. For boys, that probably means more Hemingway, Tolstoy, Homer and Twain.

During the 1970's, it was believed that gender is a social construct and   10
that gender differences could be eliminated via consciousness-raising. But it turns out gender is not a social construct. Consciousness-raising doesn't turn boys into sensitively poetic pacifists. It just turns many of them into high school and college dropouts who hate reading.

Joining the Conversation: Critical Thinking and Writing

1. Brooks begins his essay with a description of three "sections in any airport," but his essay is not about airports. What is it about? How does his first paragraph introduce his argument?

2. What evidence does Brooks offer to support his argument? Where do you find this evidence?

3. Brooks says (in paragraph 6) "that even after the recent flurry of attention about why boys are falling behind, there is still intense social pressure not to talk about biological differences between boys and girls." What, in your opinion, accounts for that "intense social pressure"? In the same sentence, Brooks refers to Larry Summers. Who is Larry Summers and why does Brooks refer to him here?

4. In the next-to-last paragraph Brooks suggests that boys and girls might be assigned different books because they have different interests. Does he have a good point—or should he be reminded that one of the aims of education is to broaden one's interests, to get out of one's own mind, to see things from another point of view.

5. In the last paragraph Brooks argues against the idea that gender is a "social construct." How does something become a social construct? What does it mean to say that gender is a social construct? (*Hint*: In today's usage, "gender" is commonly distinguished from biological sex. "Male" and "female" are said to be matters of sex, but "masculinity" and "femininity" are said to be matters of gender.) Does Brook offer reasonable evidence that gender is not a social construct?

A Debate (Two Arguments) for Analysis

A Debate: Do Video Games Significantly Enhance Literacy?

James Paul Gee

James Paul Gee, a professor of reading in the School of Education at the University of Wisconsin at Madison, is the author of numerous books, including What Video Games Have to Teach Us about Learning and Literacy *(2003).*

Pro

Popular culture today often involves quite complex language, and that matters because the biggest predictor of children's school success is the size of their early vocabularies and their abilities to deal with complex language.

Consider, for example, a typical description of a "Pokémon" ("pocket monsters" found in video games, cards, books, movies and television shows): "Bulbasaur are a combination of Grass-type and Poison-type Pokémon. Because they are Grass-type Pokémon, Bulbasaur have plant-like characteristics." Or consider this from a Web site for "Yu-Gi-Oh" (another card, game, book, movie phenomenon): "The effect of '8-Claws Scorpion' is a Trigger Effect that is applied if the condition is correct on activation." Lots of low-frequency words here; complex syntax, as well. Children as young as 6 and 7 play "Pokémon" and "Yu-Gi-Oh." To play they have to read—and read complex language.

The biggest barrier to school success is the child's ability to deal with complex "academic" language, the sort of language in textbooks. Such language starts to kick in about fourth grade and ever increases thereafter in school. Children who learn to decode, but can't read to learn in the content areas later on, are victims of the well-known "fourth-grade slump." Worse yet, research shows that even children who can pass tests in the content areas often can't apply their knowledge to real problem-solving.

Without lots of practice, humans are poor at learning from words out of their contexts of application. Good video games put young people in worlds composed of problems to be solved. They almost always give verbal information "just in time"—when players need and can use it—and "on demand," when the player asks for it. They show how language applies to the world it is about.

Research suggests that people really know what words mean only   5
when they can hook them to the sorts of actions, images or dialogues to which they apply. That is why a game manual or strategy guide makes much more sense after someone has played a game for a while than before. So, too, science textbooks, cut off from the images and actions science is about, are like a technical game manual without any game.

But, a warning: Good video games—good commercial ones like "Civilization 4" and good "serious games" made around academic content—will not work by themselves. Mentors are needed to encourage strategic thinking about the game and the complex language connected to them.

Joining the Conversation: Critical Thinking and Writing

1. Does your own experience confirm Gee's assertion (paragraph 2) that in order to play video games youngsters "have to read"? A few games? Many games? Most games? Explain.

2. In the final paragraph Gee speaks about the importance of mentors. If you were mentored or have served as a mentor in an enterprise involving games, briefly narrate the background and then argue that the experience did or did not serve a larger educational purpose.

Howard Gardner

Howard Gardner, a professor of cognition in the Harvard Graduate School of Education, has written numerous books. Among his recent publications are The Development and Education of the Mind: The Selected Works of Howard Gardner *(2006) and* Multiple Intelligences: New Horizons *(2006).*

Con

It's difficult to argue with many of Gee's points, and the jury is still out on others. Yet I'd point to several biases in the cited examples. (1) They are oriented toward competition (despite the fact that some also entail cooperation); (2) The literacy highlighted is that used in technical manuals; (3) These games, and the epistemology underlying them, are more likely to appeal to boys rather than to girls, and to "techies" rather than dreamers, humanists and conversationalists; (4) The foreground simulation, a very powerful technique, but it's not the same as real life.

I am happy to have medical students or future airplane pilots train on simulations—but they also require real, high-stake experience. Patients have feelings; simulacra and robots don't. And note that these are two areas where simulation makes sense. In many other professions, from poets to priests, they don't.

Which leads to the most important point. Literacy is far more than expertise in technical manuals or even in understanding science and technology, important as they are. It entails the capacity to immerse oneself and, ultimately, to love long, imaginative pieces of fiction, such as *Madame Bovary* or *One Hundred Years of Solitude;* poring over difficult philosophical texts and returning time and again to key passages (Kant, Wittgenstein); and spending time and exercising emotional imagination with challenging poets (Gerard Manley Hopkins, Jorie Graham).

Literacy involves linear thinking over many pages—an entirely different mental faculty than is exploited when one surfs the Web from one link to another, often randomly encountered one. I want all young persons to learn how to think like a historian, a philosopher, an economist, a literary critic (four very different "frames of mind"). I want to stimulate their imaginations to create their own worlds, not just that conjured up by the makers of "World of Warcraft."

In sum, the treasures and skills entailed in the video games of today are impressive, but they still represent only a very partial sampling of the kinds of minds that young people have and the kinds that can and should be cultivated. Some can be cultivated in front of a screen. But too much time there is not healthy on any criterion and any slice of life—no matter how engrossing—is only partial at best. So two cheers for Jim Gee—but two cheers as well for Mark Hopkins[1] on one end of a log, and an eager questioner and listener on the other.

[1]Mark Hopkins (1802–87) was president of Williams College.

"Do Video Games Significantly Enhance Literacy?" (Con) by Howard Gardner, published in *CQ Researcher*, November 10, 2006. Reprinted by permission of CQ Press.

ℰ Joining the Conversation: Critical Thinking and Writing

1. Gardner's opening sentence is courteous, but he goes on to say that Gee's examples are biased. Do you agree that the examples Gee cites are severely limited and that his argument therefore is not as strong as it seems to be? Explain.

2. Gardner's "most important point" (paragraph 3) is that "Literacy is far more than expertise in technical manuals or even in understanding science." He amplifies this point in his next paragraph. Does your experience support his position? Explain.

3. Evaluate paragraph 5 as a final paragraph in an argumentative essay. Do you think it is effective? Why, or why not?

Plato

Plato (427–347 B.C.), born in Athens, into an aristocratic family, wrote thirty dialogues in which Socrates is the chief speaker. Socrates, about twenty-five years older than Plato, was a philosopher who called himself a gadfly to Athenians. For his efforts at stinging them into thought the Athenians executed him in 399 B.C. "The Myth of the Cave" is the beginning of Book 7 of The Republic, *a dialogue in which Socrates is talking with Glaucon.*

For Plato, true knowledge is philosophic insight or awareness of the Good, not mere opinion or the knack of getting along in this world by remembering how things have usually worked in the past. To illustrate his idea that awareness of the Good is different from the ability to recognize the things of this shabby world, Plato (through his spokesman Socrates) resorts to an allegory: Men imprisoned in a cave see on a wall in front of them the shadows or images of objects that are really behind them, and they hear echoes, not real voices. (The shadows are caused by the light from a fire behind the objects, and the echoes by the cave's acoustical properties.) The prisoners, unable to perceive the real objects and the real voices, mistakenly think that the shadows and the echoes are real, and some of them grow highly adept at dealing with this illusory world. Were Plato writing today, he might have made the cave a movie theater: We see on the screen in front of us images caused by an object (film, passing in front of light) that is behind us. Moreover, the film itself is an illusory image, for it bears only the traces of a yet more real world—the world that was photographed—outside of the movie theater. And when we leave the theater to go into the real world, our eyes have become so accustomed to the illusory world that we at first blink with discomfort—just as Plato's freed prisoners do when they move out of the cave—at the real world of bright day, and we long for the familiar darkness. So too, Plato suggests, dwellers in ignorance may prefer the familiar shadows of their unenlightened world ("the world of becoming") to the bright world of the eternal Good ("the world of being") that education reveals.

We have just used the word "education." You will notice that the first sentence in the translation below (by Benjamin Jowett) says that the myth will show "how far our nature is enlightened or unenlightened." In the original Greek the words here translated enlightened *and* unenlightened *are* paideia *and* apaideusia*. No translation can fully catch the exact meanings of these elusive words. Depending on the context,* paideia *may be translated as* enlightenment, education, civilization, culture, knowledge of the good.

The Myth of the Cave

And now, I said, let me show in a figure how far our nature is enlightened or unenlightened—Behold! human beings living in an underground den, which has a mouth open toward the light and reaching all along the den; here they have been from their childhood, and have their legs and necks chained so that they cannot move, and can only see before them, being prevented by the chains from turning round their heads. Above and behind them a fire is blazing at a distance, and between the fire and the prisoners there is a raised way; and you will see, if you look, a low wall built along the way, like the screen which marionette players have in front of them, over which they show the puppets.

I see.

And do you see, I said, men passing along the wall carrying all sorts of vessels, and statues and figures of animals made of wood and stone and various materials, which appear over the wall? Some of them are talking, others silent.

You have shown me a strange image, and they are strange prisoners.

Like ourselves, I replied; and they see only their own shadows, or the   5
shadows of one another, which the fire throws on the opposite wall of the cave?

True, he said; how could they see anything but the shadows if they were never allowed to move their heads?

And of the objects which are being carried in like manner they would only see the shadows?

Yes, he said.

And if they were able to converse with one another, would they not suppose that they were naming what was actually before them?

Very true.   10

And suppose further that the prison had an echo which came from the other side, would they not be sure when one of the passersby spoke that the voice which they heard came from the passing shadow?

No question, he replied.

To them, I said, the truth would be literally nothing but the shadows of the images.

That is certain.

And now look again, and see what will naturally follow if the prison-   15
ers are released and disabused of their error. At first, when any of them is liberated and compelled suddenly to stand up and turn his neck round and walk and look toward the light, he will suffer sharp pains; the glare will distress him, and he will be unable to see the realities of which in his former state he had seen the shadows; and then conceive some one saying to him, that what he saw before was an illusion, but that now, when he is approaching nearer to being and his eye is turned toward more real existence, he has a clearer vision—what will be his reply? And you may

further imagine that his instructor is pointing to the objects as they pass and requiring him to name them—will he not be perplexed? Will he not fancy that the shadows which he formerly saw are truer than the objects which are now shown to him?

Far truer.

And if he is compelled to look straight at the light, will he not have a pain in his eyes which will make him turn away to take refuge in the objects of vision which he can see, and which he will conceive to be in reality clearer than the things which are now being shown to him?

True, he said.

And suppose once more, that he is reluctantly dragged up a steep and rugged ascent, and held fast until he is forced into the presence of the sun himself, is he not likely to be pained and irritated? When he approaches the light his eyes will be dazzled, and he will not be able to see anything at all of what are now called realities.

Not all in a moment, he said.   20

He will require to grow accustomed to the sight of the upper world. And first he will see the shadows best, next the reflections of men and other objects in the water, and then the objects themselves; then he will gaze upon the light of the moon and the stars and the spangled heaven; and he will see the sky and the stars by night better than the sun or the light of the sun by day?

Certainly.

Last of all he will be able to see the sun, and not mere reflections of him in the water, but he will see him in his own proper place, and not in another; and he will contemplate him as he is.

Certainly.

He will then proceed to argue that this is he who gives the season and   25
the years, and is the guardian of all that is in the visible world, and in a certain way the cause of all things which he and his fellows have been accustomed to behold?

Clearly, he said, he would first see the sun and then reason about him.

And when he remembered his old habitation, and the wisdom of the den and his fellow-prisoners, do you not suppose that he would felicitate himself on the change, and pity them?

Certainly, he would.

And if they were in the habit of conferring honors among themselves on those who were quickest to observe the passing shadows and to remark which of them went before, and which followed after, and which were together; and who were therefore best able to draw conclusions as to the future, do you think that he would care for such honors and glories, or envy the possessors of them? Would he not say with Homer,

Better to be the poor servant of a poor master,

and to endure anything, rather than think as they do and live after their manner?

Yes, he said, I think that he would rather suffer anything than entertain these false notions and live in this miserable manner. 30

Imagine once more, I said, such an one coming suddenly out of the sun to be replaced in his old situation; would he not be certain to have his eyes full of darkness?

To be sure, he said.

And if there were a contest, and he had to compete in measuring the shadows with the prisoners who had never moved out of the den, while his sight was still weak, and before his eyes had become steady (and the time which would be needed to acquire this new habit of sight might be very considerable), would he not be ridiculous? Men would say of him that up he went and down he came without his eyes; and that it was better not even to think of ascending; and if any one tried to loose another and lead him up to the light, let them only catch the offender, and they would put him to death.

No question, he said.

This entire allegory, I said, you may now append, dear Glaucon, to 35 the previous argument; the prison-house is the world of sight, the light of the fire is the sun, and you will not misapprehend me if you interpret the journey upwards to be the ascent of the soul into the intellectual world according to my poor belief, which, at your desire, I have expressed—whether rightly or wrongly God knows. But, whether true or false, my opinion is that in the world of knowledge the idea of good appears last of all, and is seen only with an effort; and, when seen, is also inferred to be the universal author of all things beautiful and right, parent of light and of the lord of light in this visible world, and the immediate source of reason and truth in the intellectual; and that this is the power upon which he who would act rationally either in public or private life must have his eye fixed.

I agree, he said, as far as I am able to understand you.

Moreover, I said, you must not wonder that those who attain to this beatific vision are unwilling to descend to human affairs; for their souls are ever hastening into the upper world where they desire to dwell; which desire of theirs is very natural, if our allegory may be trusted.

Yes, very natural.

And is there anything surprising in one who passes from divine contemplations to the evil state of man, misbehaving himself in a ridiculous manner; if, while his eyes are blinking and before he has become accustomed to the surrounding darkness, he is compelled to fight in courts of law, or in other places, about the images or the shadows of images of justice, and is endeavoring to meet the conceptions of those who have never yet seen absolute justice?

Anything but surprising, he replied. 40

Any one who has common sense will remember that the bewilderments of the eyes are of two kinds, and arise from two causes, either from coming out of the light or from going into the light, which is true of the mind's eye, quite as much as of the bodily eye; and he who remembers this when he sees any one whose vision is perplexed and weak, will not be too ready to laugh; he will first ask whether that soul of man has come out of the brighter life, and is unable to see because unaccustomed to the dark, or having turned from darkness to the day is dazzled by excess of light. And he will count the one happy in his condition and state of being, and he will pity the other; or, if he have a mind to laugh at the soul which comes from below into the light, there will be more reason in this than in the laugh which greets him who returns from above out of the light into the den.

That, he said, is a very just distinction.

But then, if I am right, certain professors of education must be wrong when they say that they can put a knowledge into the soul which was not there before, like sight into blind eyes.

They undoubtedly say this, he replied.

Whereas, our argument shows that the power and capacity of learn-   45
ing exists in the soul already; and that just as the eye was unable to turn from darkness to light without the whole body, so too the instrument of knowledge can only by the movement of the whole soul be turned from the world of becoming into that of being, and learn by degrees to endure the sight of being, and of the brightest and best of being, or in other words, of the good.

Very true.

And must there not be some art which will effect conversion in the easiest and quickest manner; not implanting the faculty of sight, for that exists already, but has been turned in the wrong direction, and is looking away from the truth?

Yes, he said, such an art may be presumed.

And whereas the other so-called virtues of the soul seem to be akin to bodily qualities, for even when they are not originally innate they can be implanted later by habit and exercise, the virtue of wisdom more than anything else contains a divine element which always remains, and by this conversion is rendered useful and profitable; or, on the other hand, hurtful and useless. Did you never observe the narrow intelligence flashing from the keen eye of a clever rogue—how eager he is, how clearly his paltry soul sees the way to his end; he is the reverse of blind, but his keen eyesight is forced into the service of evil, and he is mischievous in proportion to his cleverness?

Very true, he said.   50

But what if there had been a circumcision of such natures in the days of their youth; and they had been severed from those sensual pleasures, such as eating and drinking, which, like leaden weights, were attached to them at their birth, and which drag them down and turn the vision of their souls upon the things that are below—if, I say, they had been released from these impediments and turned in the opposite direction, the very same faculty in them would have seen the truth as keenly as they see what their eyes are turned to now.

Very likely.

Yes, I said; and there is another thing which is likely, or rather a necessary inference from what has preceded, that neither the uneducated and uninformed of the truth, nor yet those who never make an end of their education, will be able ministers of State; not the former, because they have no single aim of duty which is the rule of all their actions, private as well as public; nor the latter, because they will not act at all except upon compulsion, fancying that they are already dwelling apart in the islands of the blest.

Very true, he replied.

Then, I said, the business of us who are the founders of the State will be to compel the best minds to attain that knowledge which we have already shown to be the greatest of all—they must continue to ascend until they arrive at the good; but when they have ascended and seen enough we must not allow them to do as they do now. 55

What do you mean?

I mean that they remain in the upper world: but this must not be allowed; they must be made to descend again among the prisoners in the den, and partake of their labors and honors, whether they are worth having or not.

But is not this unjust? he said; ought we to give them a worse life, when they might have a better?

You have again forgotten, my friend, I said, the intention of the legislator, who did not aim at making any one class in the State happy above the rest; the happiness was to be in the whole State, and he held the citizens together by persuasion and necessity, making them benefactors of the State, and therefore benefactors of one another; to this end he created them, not to please themselves, but to be his instruments in binding up the State.

True, he said, I had forgotten. 60

Observe, Glaucon, that there will be no justice in compelling our philosophers to have a care and providence of others; we shall explain to them that in other States, men of their class are not obliged to share in the toils of politics: and this is reasonable, for they grow up at their own sweet will, and the government would rather not have them. Being self-taught, they cannot be expected to show any gratitude for a culture which they have never received. But we have brought you into the world to be rulers of the hive, kings of yourselves and of the other citizens, and have educated you far better and more perfectly than they have been educated, and you are better able to share in the double duty. Wherefore each of you, when his turn comes, must go down to the general underground abode, and get the habit of seeing in the dark. When you have acquired the habit, you will see ten thousand times better than the inhabitants of the den, and you will know what the several images are, and what they represent, because you have seen the beautiful and just and good in their truth. And thus our State which is also yours will be a reality, and not a dream only, and will be administered in a spirit unlike that of other States, in which men fight with one another about shadows only and are distracted in the struggle for power, which in their eyes is a great good. Whereas the truth is that the State in which the rulers are most reluctant to govern is always the best and most quietly governed, and the State in which they are most eager, the worst.

Quite true, he replied.

And will our pupils, when they hear this, refuse to take their turn at the toils of State, when they are allowed to spend the greater part of their time with one another in the heavenly light?

Impossible, he answered; for they are just men, and the commands which we impose upon them are just; there can be no doubt that every one of them will take office as a stern necessity, and not after the fashion of our present rulers of State.

Yes, my friend, I said; and there lies the point. You must contrive for your future rulers another and a better life than that of a ruler, and then you may have a well-ordered State; for only in the State which offers this, will they rule who are truly rich, not in silver and gold, but in virtue and wisdom, which are the true blessing of life. Whereas if they go to the administration of public affairs, poor and hungering after their own private advantage, thinking that hence they are to snatch the chief good, order there can never be; for they will be fighting about office, and the civil and domestic broils which thus arise will be the ruin of the rulers themselves and of the whole State.

Most true, he replied.

And the only life which looks down upon the life of political ambition is that of true philosophy. Do you know of any other?

Indeed, I do not, he said.

And those who govern ought not to be lovers of the task? For, if they are, there will be rival lovers, and they will fight.

No question.

Who then are those whom we shall compel to be guardians? Surely they will be the men who are wisest about affairs of State, and by whom the State is best administered, and who at the same time have other honors and another and a better life than that of politics?

They are the men, and I will choose them, he replied.

And now shall we consider in what way such guardians will be produced, and how they are to be brought from darkness to light—as some are said to have ascended from the world below to the gods?

By all means, he replied.

The process, I said, is not the turning over of an oyster-shell,[1] but the turning round of a soul passing from a day which is little better than

65

70

75

---

[1]An allusion to a game in which two parties fled or pursued according as an oyster shell that was thrown into the air fell with the dark or light side uppermost. (Translator's note)

night to the true day of being, that is, the ascent from below which we affirm to be true philosophy?

Quite so.

⟡ Joining the Conversation: Critical Thinking and Writing

1. Plato is not merely reporting one of Socrates conversations; he is teaching. What advantages does a dialogue have over a narrative or an essay as a way of teaching philosophy? How is the form of a dialogue especially suited to solving a problem?

2. If you don't know the etymology of the word *conversion*, look it up in a dictionary. How is the etymology appropriate to Plato's idea about education?

3. In paragraph 19, describing the prisoner as "reluctantly dragged" upward and "forced" to look at the sun, Socrates asks: "Is he not likely to be pained and irritated?" Can you recall experiencing pain and irritation while learning something you later were glad to have learned? Can you recall learning something new *without* experiencing pain and irritation?

4. "The State in which rulers are most reluctant to govern is always the best and most quietly governed, and the State in which they are most eager, the worst" (paragraph 61). What does Socrates mean? Using examples from contemporary politics, defend this proposition or argue against it.

5. Can you account for the power of this myth or fable? In our introductory comment (page 294), we tried to clarify the message by saying that a movie theater might serve as well as a cave. But, in fact, if the story were re-cast using a movie theater, would the emotional power be the same? Why or why not?

6. The metaphors of education as conversion and ascent are linked by the metaphor of light. Consider such expressions as "I see" (meaning "I understand") and "Let me give an illustration" (from the Latin *in* = in, and *lustrare* = to make bright). What other expressions about light are used metaphorically to describe intellectual comprehension?

Richard Rodriguez

Richard Rodriguez, the son of immigrants from Mexico, was born in San Francisco in 1944. He was educated at Stanford University, Columbia University, and the University of California, Berkeley, where he specialized in English literature of the Renaissance. In his book, Hunger of Memory: The Education of Richard Rodriguez *(1982), he reports how his progress in the Anglo world was accompanied by estrangement from the Spanish-speaking world. We print an excerpt from the book; the title of the excerpt is our own.*

Rodriguez is often seen and heard as a commentator on the NewsHour with Jim Lehrer.

Public and Private Language

Supporters of bilingual education today imply that students like me miss a great deal by not being taught in their family's language. What they seem not to recognize is that, as a socially disadvantaged child, I considered Spanish to be a private language. What I needed to learn in school was that I had the right—and the obligation—to speak the public language of *los gringos*. The odd truth is that my first-grade classmates could have become bilingual, in the conventional sense of that word, more easily than I. Had they been taught (as upper-middle-class children are often taught early) a second language like Spanish or French, they could have regarded it simply as that: another public language. In my case such bilingualism could not have been so quickly achieved. What I did not believe was that I could speak a single public language.

Without question, it would have pleased me to hear my teachers address me in Spanish when I entered the classroom. I would have felt much less afraid. I would have trusted them and responded with ease. But I would have delayed—for how long postponed?—having to learn the language of public society. I would have evaded—and for how long could I have afforded to delay?—learning the great lesson of school, that I had a public identity.

Fortunately, my teachers were unsentimental about their responsibility. What they understood was that I needed to speak a public language. So their voices would search me out, asking me questions. Each time I'd hear them, I'd look up in surprise to see a nun's face frowning at me. I'd mumble, not really meaning to answer. The nun would persist, "Richard, stand up. Don't look at the floor. Speak up. Speak to the entire class, not just to me!" But I couldn't believe that the English language was mine to use. (In part, I did not want to believe it.) I continued to mumble. I resisted the teacher's demands. (Did I somehow suspect that once I learned public language my pleasing family life would be changed?) Silent, waiting for the bell to sound, I remained dazed, diffident, afraid.

Because I wrongly imagined that English was intrinsically a public language and Spanish an intrinsically private one, I easily noted the difference between classroom language and the language of home. At school, words were directed to a general audience of listeners. ("Boys and girls.") Words were meaningfully ordered. And the point was not self-expression alone but to make oneself understood by many others. The teacher quizzed: "Boys and girls, why do we use that word in this sentence? Could we think of a better word to use there? Would the sentence change its meaning if the words were differently arranged? And wasn't there a better way of saying much the same thing?" (I couldn't say. I wouldn't try to say.)

Three months. Five. Half a year passed. Unsmiling, ever watchful, my teachers noted my silence. They began to connect my behavior with

5

the difficult progress my older sister and brother were making. Until one Saturday morning three nuns arrived at the house to talk to our parents. Stiffly, they sat on the blue living room sofa. From the doorway of another room, spying the visitors, I noted the incongruity—the clash of two worlds, the faces and voices of school intruding upon the familiar setting of home. I overheard one voice gently wondering, "Do your children speak only Spanish at home, Mrs. Rodriguez?" While another voice added, "That Richard especially seems so timid and shy."

That Rich-heard!

With great tact the visitors continued, "Is it possible for you and your husband to encourage your children to practice their English when they are home?" Of course, my parents complied. What would they not do for their children's well-being? And how could they have questioned the Church's authority which those women represented? In an instant, they agreed to give up the language (the sounds) that had revealed and accentuated our family's closeness. The moment after the visitors left, the change was observed. "*Ahora*, speak to us *en inglés*," my father and mother united to tell us.

At first, it seemed a kind of game. After dinner each night, the family gathered to practice "our" English. (It was still then *inglés*, a language foreign to us, so we felt drawn as strangers to it.) Laughing, we would try to define words we could not pronounce. We played with strange English sounds, often over-anglicizing our pronunciations. And we filled the smiling gaps of our sentences with familiar Spanish sounds. But that was cheating, somebody shouted. Everyone laughed. In school, meanwhile, like my brother and sister, I was required to attend a daily tutoring session. I needed a full year of special attention. I also needed my teachers to keep my attention from straying in class by calling out, *Rich-heard*—their English voices slowly prying loose my ties to my other name, its three notes. *Ri-car-do*. Most of all I needed to hear my mother and father speak to me in a moment of seriousness in broken—suddenly heartbreaking—English. The scene was inevitable: One Saturday morning I entered the kitchen where my parents were talking in Spanish. I did not realize that they were talking in Spanish however until, at the moment they saw me, I heard their voices change to speak English. Those *gringo* sounds they uttered startled me. Pushed me away. In that moment of trivial misunderstanding and profound insight, I felt my throat twisted by unsounded grief. I turned quickly and left the room. But I had no place to escape to with Spanish. (The spell was broken.) My brother and sisters were speaking English in another part of the house.

Again and again in the days following, increasingly angry, I was obliged to hear my mother and father: "Speak to us *en inglés*." (*Speak*). Only then did I determine to learn classroom English. Weeks after, it happened: One day in school I raised my hand to volunteer an answer. I spoke out in a loud voice. And I did not think it remarkable when the entire class understood. That day, I moved very far from the disadvantaged child I had been only days earlier. The belief, the calming assurance that I belonged in public, had at last taken hold.

Shortly after, I stopped hearing the high and loud sounds of *los gringos*.   10
A more and more confident speaker of English, I didn't trouble to listen to
how strangers sounded, speaking to me. And there simply were too many
English-speaking people in my day for me to hear American accents anymore. Conversations quickened. Listening to persons who sounded eccen-
trically pitched voices, I usually noted their sounds for an initial few
seconds before I concentrated on *what* they were saying. Conversations became content-full. Transparent. Hearing someone's *tone* of voice—angry or
questioning or sarcastic or happy or sad—I didn't distinguish it from the
words it expressed. Sound and word were thus tightly wedded. At the end
of a day, I was often bemused, always relieved, to realize how "silent,"
though crowded with words, my day in public had been. (This public silence measured and quickened the change in my life.)

At last, seven years old, I came to believe what had been technically
true since my birth: I was an American citizen.

But the special feeling of closeness at home was diminished by then.
Gone was the desperate, urgent, intense feeling of being at home: rare was
the experience of feeling myself individualized by family intimates. We
remained a loving family, but one greatly changed. No longer so close; no
longer bound tight by the pleasing and troubling knowledge of our public
separateness. Neither my older brother nor sister rushed home after school
anymore. Nor did I. When I arrived home there would often be neighborhood kids in the house. Or the house would be empty of sounds.

Following the dramatic Americanization of their children, even my parents grew more publicly confident. Especially my mother. She learned the
names of all the people on our block. And she decided we needed to have a
telephone installed in the house. My father continued to use the word *gringo*.
But it was no longer charged with the old bitterness or distrust. (Stripped of
any emotional content, the word simply became a name for those Americans
not of Hispanic descent.) Hearing him, sometimes, I wasn't sure if he was
pronouncing the Spanish word *gringo* or saying gringo in English.

Matching the silence I started hearing in public was a new quiet at
home. The family's quiet was partly due to the fact that, as we children
learned more and more English, we shared fewer and fewer words with
our parents. Sentences needed to be spoken slowly when a child addressed his mother or father. (Often the parent wouldn't understand.)
The child would need to repeat himself. (Still the parent misunderstood.)
The young voice, frustrated, would end up saying, "Never mind"—the
subject was closed. Dinners would be noisy with the clinking of knives
and forks against dishes. My mother would smile softly between her remarks; my father at the other end of the table would chew and chew at
his food, while he stared over the heads of his children.

My *mother!* My *father!* After English became my primary language,   15
I no longer knew what words to use in addressing my parents. The old
Spanish words (those tender accents of sound) I had used earlier—*mamá*
and *papá*—I couldn't use anymore. They would have been too painful
reminders of how much had changed in my life. On the other hand, the

words I heard neighborhood kids call *their* parents seemed equally unsatisfactory. *Mother* and *Father; Ma, Papa, Pa, Dad, Pop* (how I hated the all-American sound of that last word especially)—all these terms I felt were unsuitable, not really terms of address for *my* parents. As a result, I never used them at home. Whenever I'd speak to my parents, I would try to get their attention with eye contact alone. In public conversations, I'd refer to "my parents" or "my mother and father."

My mother and father, for their part, responded differently, as their children spoke to them less. She grew restless, seemed troubled and anxious at the scarcity of words exchanged in the house. It was she who would question me about my day when I came home from school. She smiled at small talk. She pried at the edges of my sentences to get me to say something more. (What?) She'd stopped her children's talking. By contrast, my father seemed reconciled to the new quiet. Though his English improved somewhat, he retired into silence. At dinner he spoke very little. One night his children and even his wife helplessly giggled at his garbled English pronunciation of the Catholic Grace before Meals. Thereafter he made his wife recite the prayer at the start of each meal, even on formal occasions, when there were guests in the house. Hers became the public voice of the family. On official business, it was she, not my father, one would usually hear on the phone or in stores, talking to strangers. His children grew so accustomed to his silence that, years later, they would speak routinely of his shyness. (My mother would often try to explain: Both his parents died when he was eight. He was raised by an uncle who treated him like little more than a menial servant. He was never encouraged to speak. He grew up alone. A man of few words.) But my father was not shy, I realized, when I'd watch him speaking Spanish with relatives. Using Spanish, he was quickly effusive. Especially when talking with other men, his voice would spark, flicker, flare alive with sounds. In Spanish, he expressed ideas and feelings he rarely revealed in English. With firm Spanish sounds, he conveyed confidence and authority English would never allow him.

The silence at home, however, was finally more than a literal silence. Fewer words passed between parent and child, but more profound was the silence that resulted from my inattention to sounds. At about the time I no longer bothered to listen with care to the sounds of English in public, I grew careless about listening to the sounds family members made when they spoke. Most of the time I heard someone speaking at home and didn't distinguish his sounds from the words people uttered in public. I didn't even pay much attention to my parents' accented and ungrammatical speech. At least not at home. Only when I was with them in public would I grow alert to their accents. Though, even then, their sounds caused me less and less concern. For I was increasingly confident of my own public identity.

I would have been happier about my public success had I not sometimes recalled what it had been like earlier, when my family had conveyed its intimacy through a set of conveniently private sounds. Sometimes in public, hearing a stranger, I'd hark back to my past. A Mexican farmworker approached me downtown to ask directions to somewhere. "Hijito . . . ?" he said. And his voice summoned deep longing. Another time, standing beside my mother in the visiting room of a Carmelite convent, before the dense screen which rendered the nuns shadowy figures, I heard several Spanish-speaking nuns—their busy, singsong overlapping voices—assure us that yes, yes, we were remembered, all our family was remembered in their prayers. (Their voices echoed faraway family sounds.) Another day, a dark-faced old woman—her hand light on my shoulder—steadied herself against me as she boarded a bus. She murmured something I couldn't quite comprehend. Her Spanish voice came near, like the face of a never-before-seen relative in the instant before I was kissed. Her voice, like so many of the Spanish voices I'd hear in public, recalled the golden age of my youth. Hearing Spanish then, I continued to be a careful, if sad, listener to sounds. Hearing a Spanish-speaking family walking behind me, I turned to look. I smiled for an instant, before my glance found the Hispanic-looking faces of strangers in the crowd going by.

 ## Joining the Conversation: Critical Thinking and Writing

1. We have called this selection from Rodriguez's *The Hunger of Memory* "Public and Private Language," and, indeed, the words occur often in the text. But, from reading these pages, how would you identify what is "public language" and what is "private"? What words and images would you associate with each?

2. In his first paragraph Rodriguez identifies himself as a "socially disadvantaged child." What does he mean?

3. At the end of his second paragraph Rodriguez identifies "the great lesson of school," that he "had a public identity." What does Rodriguez mean by his "public identity," and would you say that your elementary school also aided you in achieving one? Explain.

4. In his eleventh and twelfth paragraphs Rodriguez comes "to believe what had been technically true since [his] birth"—he was now an "American citizen." He seems to associate this truth with a change in his family relationships. Was there a period in your life when you felt such a change in your family—with or without a change in language? If so, how would you characterize it?

Maya Angelou

Maya Angelou, born in St. Louis, Missouri, in 1938, grew up in Arkansas and California. She studied music, dance, and drama (she had a role in the televised version of Alex Haley's Roots*), and she is now a professor of American studies at Wake Forest University. She has also worked as a cook, streetcar conductor, and waitress. In addition to writing books of poetry, she has written six autobiographical volumes.*

"Graduation" (editors' title) comes from her first autobiography, I Know Why the Caged Bird Sings *(1969).*

Graduation

The children in Stamps trembled visibly with anticipation. Some adults were excited too, but to be certain the whole young population had come down with graduation epidemic. Large classes were graduating from both the grammar school and the high school. Even those who were years removed from their own day of glorious release were anxious to help with preparations as a kind of dry run. The junior students who were moving into the vacating classes' chairs were tradition-bound to show their talents for leadership and management. They strutted through the school and around the campus exerting pressure on the lower grades. Their authority was so new that occasionally if they pressed a little too hard it had to be overlooked. After all, next term was coming, and it never hurt a sixth grader to have a play sister in the eighth grade, or a tenth-year student to be able to call a twelfth grader Bubba. So all was endured in a spirit of shared understanding. But the graduating classes themselves were the nobility. Like travelers with exotic destinations on their minds, the graduates were remarkably forgetful. They came to school without their books, or tablets or even pencils. Volunteers fell over themselves to secure replacements for the missing equipment. When accepted, the willing workers might or might not be thanked, and it was of no importance to the pregraduation rites. Even teachers were respectful of the now quiet and aging seniors, and tended to speak to them, if not as equals, as beings only slightly lower than themselves. After tests were returned and grades given, the student body, which acted like an extended family, knew who did well, who excelled, and what piteous ones had failed.

Unlike the white high school, Lafayette County Training School distinguished itself by having neither lawn, nor hedges, nor tennis court, nor climbing ivy. Its two buildings (main classrooms, the grade school and home economics) were set on a dirt hill with no fence to limit either its boundaries or those of bordering farms. There was a large expanse to the left of the school which was used alternately as a baseball diamond or a basketball court. Rusty hoops on the swaying poles represented the permanent recreational equipment, although bats and balls could be borrowed from the P.E. teacher if the borrower was qualified and if the diamond wasn't occupied.

Over this rocky area relieved by a few shady tall persimmon trees the graduating class walked. The girls often held hands and no longer bothered to speak to the lower students. There was a sadness about them, as if this old world was not their home and they were bound for higher ground. The boys, on the other hand, had become more friendly, more outgoing.

A decided change from the closed attitude they projected while studying for finals. Now they seemed not ready to give up the old school, the familiar paths and classrooms. Only a small percentage would be continuing on to college—one of the South's A & M (agricultural and mechanical) schools, which trained Negro youths to be carpenters, farmers, handymen, masons, maids, cooks and baby nurses. Their future rode heavily on their shoulders, and blinded them to the collective joy that had pervaded the lives of the boys and girls in the grammar school graduating class.

Parents who could afford it had ordered new shoes and ready-made clothes for themselves from Sears and Roebuck or Montgomery Ward. They also engaged the best seamstresses to make the floating graduating dresses and to cut down secondhand pants which would be pressed to a military slickness for the important event.

Oh, it was important, all right. Whitefolks would attend the ceremony, and two or three would speak of God and home, and the Southern way of life, and Mrs. Parsons, the principal's wife, would play the graduation march while the lower-grade graduates paraded down the aisles and took their seats below the platform. The high school seniors would wait in empty classrooms to make their dramatic entrance.

In the Store I was the person of the moment. The birthday girl. The center. Bailey had graduated the year before, although to do so he had had to forfeit all pleasures to make up for his time lost in Baton Rouge.

My class was wearing butter-yellow piqué dresses, and Momma launched out on mine. She smocked the yoke into tiny crisscrossing puckers, then shirred the rest of the bodice. Her dark fingers ducked in and out of the lemony cloth as she embroidered raised daisies around the hem. Before she considered herself finished she had added a crocheted cuff on the puff sleeves, and a pointy crocheted collar.

I was going to be lovely. A walking model of all the various styles of fine hand sewing and it didn't worry me that I was only twelve years old and merely graduating from the eighth grade. Besides, many teachers in Arkansas Negro schools had only that diploma and were licensed to impart wisdom.

The days had become longer and more noticeable. The faded beige of former times had been replaced with strong and sure colors. I began to see my classmates' clothes, their skin tones, and the dust that waved off pussy willows. Clouds that lazed across the sky were objects of great concern to me. Their shiftier shapes might have held a message that in my new happiness and with a little bit of time I'd soon decipher. During that period I looked at the arch of heaven so religiously my neck kept a steady ache. I had taken to smiling more often, and my jaws hurt from the unaccustomed activity. Between the two physical sore spots, I suppose I could have been uncomfortable, but that was not the case. As a member of the winning team (the graduating class of 1940) I had outdistanced unpleasant sensations by miles. I was headed for the freedom of open fields.

Youth and social approval allied themselves with me and we tram-   10
meled memories of slights and insults. The wind of our swift passage re-
modeled my features. Lost tears were pounded to mud and then to dust.
Years of withdrawal were brushed aside and left behind, as hanging
ropes of parasitic moss.

My work alone had awarded me a top place and I was going to be
one of the first called in the graduating ceremonies. On the classroom
blackboard, as well as on the bulletin board in the auditorium, there
were blue stars and white stars and red stars. No absences, no tardi-
nesses, and my academic work was among the best of the year. I could
say the preamble to the Constitution even faster than Bailey. We timed
ourselves often: "We the people of the United States in order to form a
more perfect union . . . " I had memorized the Presidents of the United
States from Washington to Roosevelt in chronological as well as alphabetical order.

My hair pleased me too. Gradually the black mass had lengthened
and thickened, so that it kept at last to its braided pattern, and I didn't
have to yank my scalp off when I tried to comb it.

Louise and I had rehearsed the exercises until we tired out ourselves.
Henry Reed was class valedictorian. He was a small, very black boy with
hooded eyes, a long, broad nose and an oddly shaped head. I had admired him for years because each term he and I vied for the best grades in
our class. Most often he bested me, but instead of being disappointed I
was pleased that we shared top places between us. Like many Southern
Black children, he lived with his grandmother, who was as strict as
Momma and as kind as she knew how to be. He was courteous, respectful
and soft-spoken to elders, but on the playground he chose to play the
roughest games. I admired him. Anyone, I reckoned, sufficiently afraid or
sufficiently dull could be polite. But to be able to operate at a top level
with both adults and children was admirable.

His valedictory speech was entitled "To Be or Not To Be." The rigid
tenth-grade teacher helped him to write it. He'd been working on the dramatic stresses for months.

The weeks until graduation were filled with heady activities. A group   15
of small children were to be presented in a play about buttercups and
daisies and bunny rabbits. They could be heard throughout the building
practicing their hops and their little songs that sounded like silver bells.
The older girls (non-graduates, of course) were assigned the task of making refreshments for the night's festivities. A tangy scent of ginger, cinna-
mon, nutmeg and chocolate wafted around the home economics building
as the budding cooks made samples for themselves and their teachers.

In every corner of the workshop, axes and saws split fresh timber as
the woodshop boys made sets and stage scenery. Only the graduates were
left out of the general bustle. We were free to sit in the library at the back
of the building or look in quite detachedly, naturally, on the measures being taken for our event.

Even the minister preached on graduation the Sunday before. His subject was, "Let your light so shine that men will see your good works and praise your Father, Who is in Heaven." Although the sermon was purported to be addressed to us, he used the occasion to speak to backsliders, gamblers, and general ne'er-do-wells. But since he had called our names at the beginning of the service we were mollified.

Among Negroes the tradition was to give presents to children going only from one grade to another. How much more important this was when the person was graduating at the top of the class. Uncle Willie and Momma had sent away for a Mickey Mouse watch like Bailey's. Louise gave me four embroidered handkerchiefs. (I gave her three crocheted doilies.) Mrs. Sneed, the minister's wife, made me an underskirt to wear for graduation, and nearly every customer gave me a nickel or maybe even a dime with the instruction "Keep on moving to higher ground," or some such encouragement.

Amazingly the great day finally dawned and I was out of bed before I knew it. I threw open the back door to see it more clearly, but Momma said, "Sister, come away from that door and put your robe on."

I hoped the memory of that morning would never leave me. Sunlight   20
was itself still young, and the day had none of the insistence maturity would bring it in a few hours. In my robe and barefoot in the backyard, under cover of going to see about my new beans, I gave myself up to the gentle warmth and thanked God that no matter what evil I had done in my life He had allowed me to live to see this day. Somewhere in my fatalism I had expected to die, accidentally, and never have the chance to walk up the stairs in the auditorium and gracefully receive my hard-earned diploma. Out of God's merciful bosom I had won reprieve.

Bailey came out in his robe and gave me a box wrapped in Christmas paper. He said he had saved his money for months to pay for it. It felt like a box of chocolates, but I knew Bailey wouldn't save money to buy candy when we had all we could want under our noses.

He was as proud of the gift as I. It was a soft-leather-bound copy of a collection of poems by Edgar Allan Poe, or, as Bailey and I called him, "Eap." I turned to "Annabel Lee" and we walked up and down the garden rows, the cool dirt between our toes, reciting the beautifully sad lines.

Momma made a Sunday breakfast although it was only Friday. After we finished the blessing, I opened my eyes to find the watch on my plate. It was a dream of a day. Everything went smoothly and to my credit I didn't have to be reminded or scolded for anything. Near evening I was too jittery to attend to chores, so Bailey volunteered to do all before his bath.

Days before, we had made a sign for the Store and as we turned out the lights Momma hung the cardboard over the doorknob. It read clearly: CLOSED. GRADUATION.

My dress fitted perfectly and everyone said that I looked like a sun-   25
beam in it. On the hill, going toward the school, Bailey walked behind

with Uncle Willie, who muttered, "Go on, Ju." He wanted him to walk ahead with us because it embarrassed him to have to walk so slowly. Bailey said he'd let the ladies walk together, and the men would bring up the rear. We all laughed, nicely.

Little children dashed by out of the dark like fireflies. Their crepe-paper dresses and butterfly wings were not made for running and we heard more than one rip, dryly, and the regretful "uh uh" that followed.

The school blazed without gaiety. The windows seemed cold and unfriendly from the lower hill. A sense of ill-fated timing crept over me, and if Momma hadn't reached for my hand I would have drifted back to Bailey and Uncle Willie, and possibly beyond. She made a few slow jokes about my feet getting cold, and tugged me along to the now-strange building.

Around the front steps, assurance came back. There were my fellow "greats," the graduating class. Hair brushed back, legs oiled, new dresses and pressed pleats, fresh pocket handkerchiefs and little hand-bags, all homesewn. Oh, we were up to snuff, all right. I joined my comrades and didn't even see my family go in to find seats in the crowded auditorium.

The school band struck up a march and all classes filed in as had been rehearsed. We stood in front of our seats, as assigned, and on a signal from the choir director, we sat. No sooner had this been accomplished than the band started to play the national anthem. We rose again and sang the song, after which we recited the pledge of allegiance. We remained standing for a brief minute before the choir director and the principal signaled to us, rather desperately I thought, to take our seats. The command was so unusual that our carefully rehearsed and smooth-running machine was thrown off. For a full minute we fumbled for our chairs and bumped into each other awkwardly. Habits change or solidify under pressure, so in our state of nervous tension we had been ready to follow our usual assembly pattern: the American National Anthem, then the pledge of allegiance, then the song every Black person I knew called the Negro National Anthem. All done in the same key, with the same passion and most often standing on the same foot.

Finding my seat at last, I was overcome with a presentiment of worse things to come. Something unrehearsed, unplanned, was going to happen, and we were going to be made to look bad. I distinctly remember being explicit in the choice of pronoun. It was "we," the graduating class, the unit, that concerned me then.

The principal welcomed "parents and friends" and asked the Baptist minister to lead us in prayer. His invocation was brief and punchy, and for a second I thought we were getting back on the high road to right action. When the principal came back to the dais, however, his voice had changed. Sounds always affected me profoundly and the principal's voice was one of my favorites. During assembly it melted and lowed weakly into the audience. It had not been in my plan to listen to him, but my curiosity was piqued and I straightened up to give him my attention.

30

He was talking about Booker T. Washington, our "late great leader," who said we can be as close as the fingers on the hand, etc. . . . Then he said a few vague things about friendship and the friendship of kindly people to those less fortunate than themselves. With that his voice nearly faded, thin, away. Like a river diminishing to a stream and then to a trickle. But he cleared his throat and said, "Our speaker tonight, who is also our friend, came from Texarkana to deliver the commencement address, but due to the irregularity of the train schedule, he's going to, as they say, 'speak and run.'" He said that we understood and wanted the man to know that we were most grateful for the time he was able to give us and then something about how we were willing always to adjust to another's program, and without more ado—"I give you Mr. Edward Donleavy."

Not one but two white men came through the door offstage. The shorter one walked to the speaker's platform, and the tall one moved over to the center seat and sat down. But that was our principal's seat, and already occupied. The dislodged gentleman bounced around for a long breath or two before the Baptist minister gave him his chair, then with more dignity than the situation deserved, the minister walked off the stage.

Donleavy looked at the audience once (on reflection, I'm sure that he wanted only to reassure himself that we were really there), adjusted his glasses and began to read from a sheaf of papers.

He was glad "to be here and to see the work going on just as it was in   35
the other schools."

At the first "Amen" from the audience I willed the offender to immediate death by choking on the word. But Amen's and Yes, sir's began to fall around the room like rain through a ragged umbrella.

He told us of the wonderful changes we children in Stamps had in store. The Central School (naturally, the white school was Central) had already been granted improvements that would be in use in the fall. A well-known artist was coming from Little Rock to teach art to them. They were going to have the newest microscopes and chemistry equipment for their laboratory. Mr. Donleavy didn't leave us long in the dark over who made these improvements available to Central High. Nor were we to be ignored in the general betterment scheme he had in mind.

He said that he had pointed out to people at a very high level that one of the first-line football tacklers at Arkansas Agricultural and Mechanical College had graduated from good old Lafayette County Training School. Here fewer Amen's were heard. Those few that did break through lay dully in the air with the heaviness of habit.

He went on to praise us. He went on to say how he had bragged that "one of the best basketball players at Fisk sank his first ball right here at Lafayette County Training School."

The white kids were going to have a chance to become Galileos and   40
Madame Curies and Edisons and Gauguins, and our boys (the girls weren't even in on it) would try to be Jesse Owenses and Joe Louises.

Owens and the Brown Bomber were great heroes in our world, but what school official in the white-goddom of Little Rock had the right to decide that those two men must be our only heroes? Who decided that for Henry Reed to become a scientist he had to work like George Washington Carver, as a bootblack, to buy a lousy microscope? Bailey was obviously always going to be too small to be an athlete, so which concrete angel glued to what county seat had decided that if my brother wanted to become a lawyer he had to first pay penance for his skin by picking cotton and hoeing corn and studying correspondence books at night for twenty years?

The man's dead words fell like bricks around the auditorium and too many settled in my belly. Constrained by hard-learned manners I couldn't look behind me, but to my left and right the proud graduating class of 1940 had dropped their heads. Every girl in my row had found something new to do with her handkerchief. Some folded the tiny squares into love knots, some into triangles, but most were wadding them, then pressing them flat on their yellow laps.

On the dais, the ancient tragedy was being replayed. Professor Parsons sat, a sculptor's reject, rigid. His large, heavy body seemed devoid of will or willingness, and his eyes said he was no longer with us. The other teachers examined the flag (which was draped stage right) or their notes, or the windows which opened on our now-famous playing diamond.

Graduation, the hush-hush magic time of frills and gifts and congratulations and diplomas, was finished for me before my name was called. The accomplishment was nothing. The meticulous maps, drawn in three colors of ink, learning and spelling decasyllabic words, memorizing the whole of *The Rape of Lucrece*—it was nothing. Donleavy had exposed us.

We were maids and farmers, handymen and washerwomen, and anything higher that we aspired to was farcical and presumptuous. Then I wished that Gabriel Prosser and Nat Turner had killed all white-folks in their beds and that Abraham Lincoln had been assassinated before the signing of the Emancipation Proclamation, and that Harriet Tubman had been killed by that blow on her head and Christopher Columbus had drowned in the *Santa Maria*.

It was awful to be Negro and have no control over my life. It was brutal to be young and already trained to sit quietly and listen to charges brought against my color and no chance of defense. We should all be dead. I thought I should like to see us all dead, one on top of the other. A pyramid of flesh with the whitefolks on the bottom, as the broad base, then the Indians with their silly tomahawks and teepees and wigwams and treaties, the Negroes with their mops and recipes and cotton sacks and spirituals sticking out of their mouths. The Dutch children should all stumble in their wooden shoes and break their necks. The French should choke to death on the Louisiana Purchase (1803) while silkworms ate all the Chinese with their stupid pigtails. As a species, we were an abomination. All of us.

45

Donleavy was running for election, and assured our parents that if he won we could count on having the only colored paved playing field in that part of Arkansas. Also—he never looked up to acknowledge the grunts of acceptance—also, we were bound to get some new equipment for the home economics building and the workshop.

He finished, and since there was no need to give any more than the most perfunctory thank-you's, he nodded to the men on the stage, and the tall white man who was never introduced joined him at the door. They left with the attitude that now they were off to something really important. (The graduation ceremonies at Lafayette County Training School had been a mere preliminary.)

The ugliness they left was palpable. An uninvited guest who wouldn't leave. The choir was summoned and sang a modern arrangement of "Onward, Christian Soldiers," with new words pertaining to graduates seeking their place in the world. But it didn't work. Elouise, the daughter of the Baptist minister, recited "Invictus," and I could have cried at the impertinence of "I am the master of my fate, I am the captain of my soul."

My name had lost its ring of familiarity and I had to be nudged to go and receive my diploma. All my preparations had fled. I neither marched up to the stage like a conquering Amazon, nor did I look in the audience for Bailey's nod of approval. Marguerite Johnson, I heard the name again, my honors were read, there were noises in the audience of appreciation, and I took my place on the stage as rehearsed.

I thought about colors I hated: ecru, puce, lavender, beige and black.

There was shuffling and rustling around me, then Henry Reed was giving his valedictory address, "To Be or Not to Be." Hadn't he heard the whitefolks? We couldn't *be*, so the question was a waste of time. Henry's voice came out clear and strong. I feared to look at him. Hadn't he got the message? There was no "nobler in the mind" for Negroes because the world didn't think we had minds, and they let us know it. "Outrageous fortune"? Now, that was a joke. When the ceremony was over I had to tell Henry Reed some things. That is, if I still cared. Not "rub," Henry, "erase." "Ah, there's the erase." Us.

Henry had been a good student in elocution. His voice rose on tides of promise and fell on waves of warnings. The English teacher had helped him to create a sermon winging through Hamlet's soliloquy. To be a man, a doer, a builder, a leader, or to be a tool, an unfunny joke, a crusher of funky toadstools. I marveled that Henry could go through with the speech as if we had a choice.

I had been listening and silently rebutting each sentence with my eyes closed; then there was a hush, which in an audience warns that something unplanned is happening. I looked up and saw Henry Reed, the conservative, the proper, the A student, turn his back to the audience and turn to us (the proud graduating class of 1940) and sing, nearly speaking,

50

Lift ev'ry voice and sing
Till earth and heaven ring
Ring with the harmonies of Liberty . . .

It was the poem written by James Weldon Johnson. It was the music   55
composed by J. Rosamond Johnson. It was the Negro National Anthem.
Out of habit we were singing it.

Our mothers and fathers stood in the dark hall and joined the hymn
of encouragement. A kindergarten teacher led the small children onto the
stage and the buttercups and daisies and bunny rabbits marked time and
tried to follow:

Stony the road we trod
Bitter the chastening rod
Felt in the days when hope, unborn, had died.
Yet with a steady beat
Have not our weary feet
Come to the place for which our fathers sighed?

Every child I knew had learned that song with his ABC's and along
with "Jesus Loves Me This I Know." But I personally had never heard it
before. Never heard the words, despite the thousands of times I had sung
them. Never thought they had anything to do with me.

On the other hand, the words of Patrick Henry had made such an impression on me that I had been able to stretch myself tall and trembling
and say, "I know not what course others may take, but as for me, give me
liberty or give me death."

And now I heard, really for the first time:

We have come over a way that with tears has been watered,
We have come, treading our path through the blood of the slaughtered.

While echoes of the song shivered in the air, Henry Reed bowed his   60
head, said "Thank you," and returned to his place in the line. The tears
that slipped down many faces were not wiped away in shame.

We were on top again. As always, again. We survived. The depths
had been icy and dark, but now a bright sun spoke to our souls. I was no
longer simply a member of the proud graduating class of 1940; I was a
proud member of the wonderful, beautiful Negro race.

Oh, Black known and unknown poets, how often have your auctioned pains sustained us? Who will compute the lonely nights made less
lonely by your songs, or the empty pots made less tragic by your tales?

If we were a people much given to revealing secrets, we might raise
monuments and sacrifice to the memories of our poets, but slavery cured
us of that weakness. It may be enough, however, to have it said that we
survive in exact relationship to the dedication of our poets (include
preachers, musicians and blues singers).

⟨⟨ Joining the Conversation:
Critical Thinking and Writing

1. In paragraph 1 notice such overstatements as "glorious release," "the gradu-ating classes themselves were the nobility," and "exotic destinations." Find further examples in the next few pages. What do you think is the function of this diction?

2. Characterize the writer as you perceive her through paragraph 28. Support your characterization with references to specific passages. Next, characterize her in paragraph 46, which begins. "It was awful to be Negro." Next, charac-terize her on the basis of the entire essay. Finally, in a sentence, try to de-scribe the change, telling the main attitudes or moods that she goes through.

3. How would you define *poets* as Angelou uses the word in the last sentence?

Neil Postman

Neil Postman (1931–2003) born in New York City in 1931, taught in elementary and secondary schools and later was a professor of communication arts and sciences at New York University.

Order in the Classroom

William O'Connor, who is unknown to me in a personal way, was once a member of the Boston School Committee, in which capacity he made the following remark: "We have no inferior education in our schools. What we have been getting is an inferior type of student."

The remark is easy to ridicule, and I have had some fun with it in the past. But there are a couple of senses in which it is perfectly sound.

In the first place, a classroom is a technique for the achievement of certain kinds of learning. It is a workable technique provided that both the teacher and the student have the skill and, particularly, the attitudes that are fundamental to it. Among these, from the student's point of view, are tolerance for delayed gratification, a certain measure of respect for and fear of authority, and a willingness to accommodate one's individual desires to the interests of group cohesion and purpose. These attitudes cannot be taught easily in school because they are a necessary component of the teaching situation itself. The problem is not unlike trying to find out how to spell a word by looking it up in the dictionary. If you do not know how a word is spelled, it is hard to look it up. In the same way, little can be taught in school unless these attitudes are present. And if they are not, to teach them is difficult.

Obviously, such attitudes must be learned during the years before a child starts school; that is, in the home. This is the real meaning of the phrase "preschool education." If a child is not made ready at home for the classroom experience, he or she usually cannot benefit from any normal school program. Just as important, the school is defenseless against such a child, who, typically, is a source of disorder in a situation that requires order. I raise this issue because education reform is impossible without order in the classroom. Without the attitudes that lead to order, the classroom is an entirely impotent technique. Therefore, one possible translation of Mr. O'Connor's remark is, "We have a useful technique for educating youth but too many of them have not been provided at home with the attitudes necessary for the technique to work."

In still another way Mr. O'Connor's remark makes plain sense. The electronic media, with their emphasis on visual imagery, immediacy, non-linearity, and fragmentation, do not give support to the attitudes that are fundamental to the classroom; that is, Mr. O'Connor's remark can be translated as, "We would not have an inferior education if it were the nineteenth century. Our problem is that we have been getting students who are products of the twentieth century." But there is nothing nonsensical about this, either. The nineteenth century had much to recommend it, and we certainly may be permitted to allow it to exert an influence on the twentieth. The classroom is a nineteenth-century invention, and we ought to prize what it has to offer. It is one of the few social organizations left to us in which sequence, social order, hierarchy, continuity, and deferred pleasure are important.

The problem of disorder in the classroom is created largely by two factors: a dissolving family structure, out of which come youngsters who are "unfit" for the presuppositions of a classroom; and a radically altered information environment, which undermines the foundation of school. The question, then, is, What should be done about the increasing tendency toward disorder in the classroom?

Liberal reformers, such as Kenneth Keniston, have answers, of a sort. Keniston argues that economic reforms should be made so that the integrity and authority of the family can be restored. He believes that poverty is the main cause of family dissolution, and that by improving the economic situation of families, we may kindle a sense of order and aspiration in the lives of children. Some of the reforms he suggests in his book *All Our Children* seem practical, although they are long-range and offer no immediate response to the problem of present disorder. Some Utopians, such as Ivan Illich, have offered other solutions; for example, dissolving the schools altogether, or so completely restructuring the school environment that its traditional assumptions are rendered irrelevant. To paraphrase

Karl Kraus's epigram about psychoanalysis, these proposals are the Utopian disease of which they consider themselves the cure.

One of the best answers comes from Dr. Howard Hurwitz, who is neither a liberal reformer nor a Utopian. It is a good solution, I believe, because it tries to respond to the needs not only of children who are unprepared for school because of parental failure but of children of all backgrounds who are being made strangers to the assumptions of school by the biases of the electronic media.

During the eleven years Dr. Hurwitz was principal at Long Island City High School, the average number of suspensions each year was three, while in many New York City high schools the average runs close to one hundred. Also, during his tenure, not one instance of an assault on a teacher was reported, and daily student attendance averaged better than 90 percent, which in the context of the New York City school scene represents a riot of devotion.

Although I consider some of Dr. Hurwitz's curriculum ideas uninspired and even wrong-headed, he understands a few things of overriding importance that many educators of more expansive imagination do not. The first is that educators must devote at least as much attention to the immediate consequences of disorder as to its abstract causes. Whatever the causes of disorder and alienation, the consequences are severe and, if not curbed, result in making the school impotent. At the risk of becoming a symbol of reaction, Hurwitz ran "a tight ship." He holds to the belief, for example, that a child's right to an education is terminated at the point where the child interferes with the right of other children to have one.

Dr. Hurwitz also understands that disorder expands proportionately to the tolerance for it, and that children of all kinds of home backgrounds can learn, in varying degrees, to function in situations where disorder is not tolerated at all. He does not believe that it is inevitably or only the children of the poor who are disorderly. In spite of what the "revisionist" education historians may say, poor people still regard school as an avenue of social and economic advancement for their children, and do not object in the least to its being an orderly and structured experience.

All this adds up to the common sense view that the school ought not to accommodate itself to disorder, or to the biases of other communication systems. The children of the poor are likely to continue to be with us. Some parents will fail to assume competent responsibility for the preschool education of their children. The media will increase the intensity of their fragmenting influence. Educators must live with these facts. But Dr. Hurwitz believes that as a technique for learning, the classroom can work if students are oriented toward its assumptions, not the other way around. William O'Connor, wherever he is, would probably agree. And so do I. The school is not an extension of the street, the movie theater, a rock concert, or a playground. And it is certainly not an extension of the psychiatric clinic. It is a special environment that requires the enforcement of certain

10

traditional rules of controlled group interaction. The school may be the only remaining public situation in which such rules have any meaning, and it would be a grave mistake to change those rules because some children find them hard or cannot function within them. Children who cannot ought to be removed from the environment in the interests of those who can.

Wholesale suspensions, however, are a symptom of disorder, not a cure for it. And what makes Hurwitz's school noteworthy is the small number of suspensions that have been necessary. This is not the result of his having "good" students or "bad" students. It is the result of his having created an unambiguous, rigorous, and serious attitude—a nineteenth-century attitude, if you will—toward what constitutes acceptable school behavior. In other words, Dr. Hurwitz's school turns out to be a place where children of all backgrounds—fit and unfit—can function, or can learn to function, and where the biases of our information environment are emphatically opposed.

At this point I should like to leave the particulars of Dr. Hurwitz's solution and, retaining their spirit, indicate some particulars of my own.

Let us start, for instance, with the idea of a dress code. A dress code   15 signifies that school is a special place in which special kinds of behavior are required. The way one dresses is an indication of an attitude toward a situation. And the way one is *expected* to dress indicates what that attitude ought to be. You would not wear dungarees and a T-shirt that says "Feel Me" when attending a church wedding. That would be considered an outrage against the tone and meaning of the situation. The school has every right and reason, I believe, to expect the same sort of consideration.

Those who are inclined to think this is a superficial point are probably forgetting that symbols not only reflect our feelings but to some extent create them. One's kneeling in church, for example, reflects a sense of reverence but also engenders reverence. If we want school to *feel* like a special place, we can find no better way to begin than by requiring students to dress in a manner befitting the seriousness of the enterprise and the institution. I should include teachers in this requirement. I know of one high school in which the principal has put forward a dress code of sorts for teachers. (He has not, apparently, had the courage to propose one for the students.) For males the requirement is merely a jacket and tie. One of his teachers bitterly complained to me that such a regulation infringed upon his civil rights. And yet, this teacher will accept without complaint the same regulation when it is enforced by an elegant restaurant. His complaint and his acquiescence tell a great deal about how he values schools and how he values restaurants.

I do not have in mind, for students, uniforms of the type sometimes worn in parochial schools. I am referring here to some reasonable standard of dress which would mark school as a place of dignity and seriousness. And I might add that I do not believe for one moment the argument that poor people would be unable to clothe their children properly if such a code were in force. Furthermore, I do not believe that poor people have advanced that argument. It is an argument that middle-class education critics have made on behalf of the poor.

Another argument advanced in behalf of the poor and oppressed is the students' right to their own language. I have never heard this argument come from parents whose children are not competent to use Standard English. It is an argument, once again, put forward by "liberal" education critics whose children *are* competent in Standard English but who in some curious way wish to express their solidarity with and charity for those who are less capable. It is a case of pure condescension, and I do not think teachers should be taken in by it. Like the mode of dress, the mode of language in school ought to be relatively formal and exemplary, and therefore markedly different from the custom in less rigorous places. It is particularly important that teachers should avoid trying to win their students' affection by adopting the language of youth. Such teachers frequently win only the contempt of their students, who sense that the language of teachers and the language of students ought to be different; that is to say, the world of adults is different from the world of children.

In this connection, it is worth saying that the modern conception of childhood is a product of the sixteenth century, as Philippe Aries has documented in his *Centuries of Childhood*. Prior to that century, children as young as six and seven were treated in all important respects as if they were adults. Their language, their dress, their legal status, their responsibilities, their labor, were much the same as those of adults. The concept of childhood as an identifiable stage in human growth began to develop in the sixteenth century and has continued into our own times. However, with the emergence of electronic media of communication, a reversal of this trend seems to be taking place. In a culture in which the distribution of information is almost wholly undifferentiated, age categories begin to disappear. Television, in itself, may bring an end to childhood. In truth, there is no such thing as "children's programming," at least not for children over the age of eight or nine. Everyone sees and hears the same things. We have already reached a point where crimes of youth are indistinguishable from those of adults; and we may soon reach a point where the punishments will be the same.

I raise this point because the school is one of our few remaining institutions based on firm distinctions between childhood and adulthood, and on the assumption that adults have something of value to teach the young. That is why teachers must avoid emulating in dress and speech the style of the young. It is also why the school ought to be a place for what we might call "manners education": the adults in school ought to be concerned with teaching youth a standard of civilized interaction.

Again those who are inclined to regard this as superficial may be underestimating the power of media such as television and radio to teach

20

how one is to conduct oneself in public. In a general sense, the media "unprepare" the young for behavior in groups. A young man who goes through the day with a radio affixed to his ear is learning to be indifferent to any shared sound. A young woman who can turn off a television program that does not suit her needs at the moment is learning impatience with any stimulus that is not responsive to her interests.

But school is not a radio station or a television program. It is a social situation requiring the subordination of one's own impulses and interests to those of the group. In a word, manners. As a rule, elementary school teachers will exert considerable effort in teaching manners. I believe they refer to this effort as "socializing the child." But it is astonishing how precipitously this effort is diminished at higher levels. It is certainly neglected in the high schools, and where it is not, there is usually an excessive concern for "bad habits," such as smoking, drinking, and in some nineteenth-century schools, swearing. But, as William James noted, our virtues are as habitual as our vices. Where is the attention given to the "Good morning" habit, to the "I beg your pardon" habit, to the "Please forgive the interruption" habit?

The most civilized high school class I have ever seen was one in which students and teacher said "Good morning" to each other and in which the students stood up when they had something to say. The teacher, moreover, thanked each student for any contribution made to the class, did not sit with his feet on the desk, and did not interrupt a student unless he had asked permission to do so. The students, in turn, did not interrupt each other, or chew gum, or read comic books when they were bored. To avoid being a burden to others when one is bored is the essence of civilized behavior.

Of this teacher, I might also say that he made no attempt to entertain his students or model his classroom along the lines of a TV program. He was concerned not only to teach his students manners but to teach them how to attend in a classroom, which is partly a matter of manners but also necessary to their intellectual development. One of the more serious difficulties teachers now face in the classroom results from the fact that their students suffer media-shortened attention spans and have become accustomed, also through intense media exposure, to novelty, variety, and entertainment. Some teachers have made desperate attempts to keep their students "tuned in" by fashioning their classes along the lines of *Sesame Street* or the *Tonight* show. They tell jokes. They change the pace. They show films, play records, and avoid *anything* that would take more than eight minutes. Although their motivation is understandable, this is what their students least need. However difficult it may be, the teacher must try to achieve student attention and even enthusiasm through the attraction of ideas, not razzmatazz. Those who think I am speaking here in favor of "dull" classes may themselves, through media exposure, have lost an understanding of the potential for excitement contained in an idea. The media (one prays) are not so powerful that they can obliterate in the young, particularly in the adolescent, what William James referred to as a "theoretic instinct," a need to know reasons, causes, abstract conceptions. Such an "instinct" can be seen in its earliest stages in what he calls the "sporadic metaphysical inquiries of children as to who made God, and why they have five fingers. . . ."

I trust that the reader is not misled by what I have been saying. As I   25
see it, nothing in any of the above leads to the conclusion that I favor a classroom that is authoritarian or coldhearted, or dominated by a teacher insensitive to students and how they learn. I merely want to affirm the importance of the classroom as a special place, aloof from the biases of the media; a place in which the uses of the intellect are given prominence in a setting of elevated language, civilized manners, and respect for social symbols.

Joining the Conversation: Critical Thinking and Writing

1. In paragraph 3, what does Postman mean by "tolerance for delayed gratification"? Two paragraphs later he uses an expression that is approximately synonymous with "delayed gratification." What is this expression?

2. Postman in part blames "the electronic media," because (he says in paragraph 5) they emphasize "fragmentation." Does he give any examples in his essay? Do you think you know what he means? And do you think he is right?

3. Who is Postman's audience? High school students? Parents and teachers? Professors of education? And who is Postman—that is, putting aside the biographical note on page 316, what sort of person does the author of the essay reveal himself to be? A frustrated high school teacher? A professor of education? An intelligent layperson? Does he seem to know what he is talking about?

4. In paragraph 10 we are told, with approval, that a principal named Dr. Howard Hurwitz "ran 'a tight ship.'" First, make sure that you know what the phrase means, and then write an essay of 500 words evaluating the degree of success of some instructor or administrator who ran a tight ship in your school. Your essay will, of course, have to give us a sense of what the instructor or administrator did, as well as your evaluation of the results of his or her teaching or administrating.

5. If you disagree with Postman on the value of a dress code, set forth your disagreement in a persuasive essay of 500 words.

6. Write an editorial—as an alumnus or alumna—for your high school newspaper, summarizing Postman's essay in a paragraph, and then comparing your school with Postman's idea of a good school, and, finally, evaluating your school and Postman's essay. You may, for example, conclude that, thank heavens, your school was nothing like Postman's ideal school.

Sara Bennett and Nancy Kalish

Sara Bennett and Nancy Kalish are the authors of The Case Against Homework: How Homework Is Hurting Our Children and What We Can Do About It *(2006).*

No More Teachers, Lots of Books

School is letting out for the summer, the final bell signaling the precious, unadulterated joy that comes with months of freedom stretching out ahead. But for many students that feeling will never come. Instead, summer these days often means more textbook reading, papers, exams and projects. It's called "vacation homework," an oxymoron that overburdens our children and sends many back to school burnt out and sick of learning.

Last summer, for example, students at one charter school in the Bronx were assigned 10 book reports, a thick math packet, a report on China including a written essay and a handmade doll in authentic costume and a daily log of their activities and the weather. Their parents say they are hoping this summer will be different, but who knows what drudgery will be assigned now that they've finished second grade?

An anomaly? Hardly.

Fifth and sixth graders in a Golden, Colo., public middle school are required to keep a journal on a different math topic each week this summer, read three books and complete a written and artistic report on two of them.

And what about high schoolers—just a little light reading to ease   5
teenage angst? One ninth grader we know was assigned a packet of materials on the Holocaust. Another must read a 656-page book on genocide, on top of three chapters of a science textbook followed by a 15-page take-home exam, prepare a 20-slide PowerPoint presentation and complete an English assignment involving three books and essays.

All parents want their children to be happy, healthy and competitive in a highly competitive world. But is year-round homework—or the nightly homework marathons during the school year, for that matter— the way to achieve it?

As adults know, a break from work is a necessary antidote for stress. We need what psychologists call "consolidation," the time away from a problem when newly learned material is absorbed. Often we return from a break to discover that the pieces have fallen into place. Too many of our children today are denied that consolidation time. And when parents are told that their children's skills will slip without summer homework, we have to wonder: if those skills are so fragile, what kind of education are they really getting?

In fact, there's serious doubt about whether homework has any benefit at all. Most studies have found little or no correlation between homework and achievement (meaning grades and test scores) in elementary school or middle school. According to Harris Cooper of Duke University, the nation's leading researcher on the subject, there is a clear correlation among high school students, but he warns that "overloading them with homework is not associated with higher grades."

Yet very few teachers have ever taken a course on homework or know what the research shows, and many told us homework assignments are an "afterthought."

Another claimed benefit of homework—instilling responsibility and self-discipline—is undermined when homework is so overwhelming that parents routinely have to help their children every step of the way. 10

In fact, most experts believe reading is the most important educational activity. Yet a poll released last week by Scholastic and Yankelovich found that the amount of time youngsters spend reading for fun declines sharply after age 8. The No. 1 reason given by parents: too much homework.

So, what's a parent to do? While it might be too late to challenge this summer's assignments, it's not too early to gather like-minded parents and get a head start on changing next year's policy. If your children just can't bear taking that Holocaust folder on vacation, give them permission not to read it and promise you'll take it up with teachers or school administrators in the fall. Encourage your children to read, play games, write stories and even experience a little boredom. It might just bring out their innate creativity.

In 2000, parents in Arlington, Va., banded together and took complaints about summer homework to the school board, spurring an overhaul of the district's policy. More parents around the country should stop complaining to each other and let school officials know that they won't stand by as large parts of our sons and daughters' childhoods are stolen for no good reason. Our children will grow up happier and healthier—and perhaps even have time to read a good book.

 Joining the Conversation:
Critical Thinking and Writing

1. In paragraph 1 Bennett and Kalish say that vacation homework sends many children "back to school burnt out and sick of learning." If you have been assigned vacation homework, does your experience confirm their assertion? Explain.

2. In paragraph 7 the authors say, "Often we return from a break to discover that the pieces have fallen into place." If you have had this experience, (1) describe the circumstances and (2) indicate why you do or do not think it provides evidence supporting Bennett and Kalish.

3. Bennett and Kalish say (paragraph 8), "In fact, there's serious doubt about whether homework has any benefit at all." In an essay of about 500 words set forth your ideas on this topic, offering evidence.

Suzy Maroon, Julia Collins, Elizabeth P. Ueland

The following letters were published in the New York Times *shortly after the Bennett and Kalish article appeared.*

Letters Responding to Sara Bennett and Nancy Kalish

To the Editor:

Sara Bennett and Nancy Kalish lament the ever-increasing barrage of summer schoolwork being assigned to children but do not mention what drives this trend.

It is precisely the "months of freedom stretching out ahead," an anachronism from the days when children were needed on farms.

At no other time in their lives will Americans enjoy such long vacations.

Indeed, as adults they will find their vacations among the shortest in the industrialized world.

Ms. Bennett and Ms. Kalish question whether students' skills can be so fragile that they will slip without summer work. Who knows?   5

But what has been proved definitively is that skills learned in school slip significantly during the summer break. And ask any athlete or musician what happens when he or she goes without practicing for three months.

All of which points to an obvious answer: Shorten the summer break! Extend the winter and spring breaks, and make them all what children really need: weeks, not months, of unencumbered freedom.

Suzy Maroon
Washington, June 19, 2006

To the Editor:

Kids are working hard over the summer whether they realize it or not—perfecting the undervalued art of relaxation and cultivating an imagination that is desperately needed in our ever-changing world.

Some homework is reasonable (I first encountered some of my favorite books as summer-reading homework), but the response assignments can wax to absurdity, and elementary school math packets still haunt my dreams.

Moderation is essential and creativity even more so. Kids are inventive by nature: give them options and artistic liberty, and they will develop in ways that are vital to life, even if you can't measure them on the SAT.

Julia Collins
Stratford, Conn., June 19, 2006

Letters to the editor by Suzy Maroon, Julia Collins, and Elizabeth P. Ueland, published in the *New York Times*, June 23, 2006. Reprinted by permission of the authors.

To the Editor:

I would like to counter the argument against "vacation homework."

First, American students spend a relatively shorter time in the class-room than their global counterparts. Second, during the school year, students are involved in a myriad of extracurricular activities, limiting their opportunity for reading great works of literature.

Finally, a comment that I frequently hear in the fall from my English students goes roughly like this: "If you hadn't assigned 'Anna Karenina,' I would have never read it. And I loved it."

Elizabeth P. Ueland
Philadelphia, June 19, 2006

 ### Joining the Conversation: Critical Thinking and Writing

1. Maroon argues from analogy: "And ask any athlete or musician what happens when he or she goes without practicing for three months." Are you convinced by this comparison? Why, or why not?

2. Do you agree with Collins that the summer is a time when youngsters are "perfecting the undervalued art of relaxation and cultivating an imagination that is desperately needed in our ever-changing world"? In 500 words set forth your reasoned response.

3. Write a 250 word response to Ueland, either arguing against her position or offering additional evidence supporting her position.

Robert Coles

Robert Coles is a psychiatrist and a professor at Harvard University. He is the author of many books, including Children of Crisis *(5 volumes, 1967–77), which won the Pulitzer Prize, and* The Spiritual Lives of Children *(1990). "On Raising Moral Children" is an excerpt from* The Moral Intelligence of Children, *published by Random House in 1997.*

On Raising Moral Children

The Child as Witness

I first heard the term "moral intelligence" many years ago, from Rustin McIntosh, a distinguished pediatrician who was teaching a group of us how to work with young patients who were quite ill. When we asked him to explain what he had in mind by that phrase, "moral intelligence," he did not respond with an elegantly precise definition. Rather, he told us about boys and girls he'd known and treated who had it—who were "good," who were kind, who thought about others, who extended themselves toward those others, who were "smart" that way. He told us stories of clinical moments he found unforgettable: a girl dying of leukemia who worried about the "burden" she'd put upon her terribly saddened mother; a boy who lost the effective use of his right arm due to an automobile injury, and who felt sorry less for himself than he did for his dad, who loved baseball, loved coaching his son and others in a neighborhood Little League team.

Moral intelligence isn't only acquired by memorization of rules and regulations, by dint of abstract classroom discussion or kitchen compliance. We grow morally as a consequence of learning how to be with others, how to behave in this world, a learning prompted by taking to heart what we have seen and heard. The child is an ever attentive witness of grownup morality.

Of course, some children don't explicitly tell us what they have witnessed, the sense they've made of us, our moral ways of being. It can be hard for our sons and daughters to stand up to us, their parents, and teachers, point things out that trouble them. I once realized this all too memorably when I was driving my nine-year-old son to the hospital. He had injured himself in an accident—he had disobeyed his mother and me by "playing" with some carpentry tools we had set aside in our garage. I was upset because he'd sustained a deep cut that obviously would require surgical attention and that he'd ignored our "rule." I raced with him to the hospital on a rainy morning, careless that my car was splashing pedestrians, and at one point, I ignored a yellow light, then a red light. Amidst this headlong rush to an emergency ward, my son said, "Dad, if we're not careful, we'll make more trouble on our way to getting out of trouble."

A boy was pointing out, tactfully, respectfully, and yes, a bit fearfully, a major irony—that this effort to get us out of "trouble" could lead to more trouble; and he was also giving me a reproving as well as an anxious look: Be careful, lest you hurt people on your all too hurried journey. I realized the ethical implications of my son's admonitory if not admonishing remark: There's something important at stake here, the lives of others. A boy had reached outside himself, thought of those others, no matter his own ordeal, with its justification of a heightened self-regard. That is what our children can offer us and what we can offer them—a chance to learn from them, even as we try to teach them.

Day One

"I think we start sending signals to our kids from Day One," said a 5 mother in one of my discussion groups. "My sister, Maisie, has a son who had a great appetite right from the beginning. They're going along fine—six months, seven months, and you know what? He'd be sitting in the bassinet or the high chair, and he'd gulp down that milk, and as he got bigger, and had a little more control, he started throwing the bottle away, throwing it on the floor. He knew what he was doing, he heard the 'bang', the 'thump', and he was obviously pleased with himself. A neighbor told my sister, 'He's just flexing his muscles, so let him do it—be glad he's like that.' But Maisie said no, no; she said she wasn't going to let her kid get the idea that he could behave like that: toss something away, when he was through with it, and see other people come running to clean up the mess he'd made! You know what she did? She didn't shout or get real tough with him; she just made sure she was there, right there, her hand ready, as the baby took his last bit of milk, and she took the bottle from him, while talking to him, or cleaning his face. In a while, the baby lost interest—she tested him a few times by not being so quick to ease the bottle away. Now, to my mind, my sister had started teaching her son right versus wrong—how he should behave, and what he shouldn't do, as early as it was, as young as the boy was."

Maisie had been smart enough to move in her mind from a boy who teased his mother, so she saw it, to an older child who had a similarly cavalier attitude toward his parents and others in authority. The parent has an opportunity to teach even a baby under one, and certainly a baby who is two or three, how to come to terms with wishes and yearnings, with times of disappointment and frustration that are part of love, of life. Some lucky babies have parents who show them love, and who love, in return—but do not become slaves to their child's demands, nor to their own nervous wish, natural for all of us, to give as much as we have, and as often as we can, to our sons and daughters. Other parents are less sure of themselves, or are lacking in self-restraint, and so let concern and affection deteriorate into an indulgence that can turn a child's head.

The Age of Conscience

In elementary school, maybe as never before or ever afterwards, the child becomes an intensely moral creature, quite interested in figuring out the reasons of this world—how and why things work, but also, how and why he or she should behave in various situations. "This is the age of conscience," Anna Freud once observed to me, and she went further: "This is the age that a child's conscience is built—or isn't; it is the time when a child's character is built and consolidated, or isn't." These are the years when a new world of knowledge and possibility arrives in the form of books, music, art, athletics, and, of course, the teachers and coaches who offer all that, the fellow students who share in the experiences. These are years of magic, of eager, lively searching on the part of children, whose parents and teachers are often hard put to keep up with them, as they try to understand things.

I once asked a six-year-old boy about his keen interest in telescopes. "When I look in it," he said, "it's like going on a long trip, and I'm far away, but I'm still here too." That child then took me on another kind of voyage, further into his mind and the thinking of other children than I had thought possible. "Those stars," he told me, "are moving fast, even if it looks like they're not moving one inch. A friend of mine said that God is keeping them from bumping into each other, but I told him, no, God isn't like that. He lets things happen—he doesn't keep interfering! He made everything, and then everything is on its own, and people too. In Sunday school, they say it's up to you, whether you'll be good or bad, and it's like that with the stars: they keep moving, and if they go off track, that's because something has gone wrong—it's an accident, it's not God falling asleep, or getting mad, something like that." He decided to complete his presentation: "Here it's different—there are people here. We're the star with people! That's why we could mess things up. The stars could hit each other—one star gets in the way of the other. That would be bad luck for both of them. But we could do something bad to this place, this star—and it would be as bad as if another star hit it, worse even!" A boy seemingly detoured by intellectual inclination from this planet's problems in favor of abiding interests in other planets was quite interested in addressing the biggest questions confronting all of us human beings—how our behavior might influence the very nature of existence.

Adolescence

Young people coming of age quite naturally command a good deal of our notice. They are understandably self-conscious, hence apt to call attention to themselves (while often claiming to want no such thing), and they bring us back to our own momentous time of adolescence—a second birth of sorts, only now accompanied by a blaze of self-awareness. Perhaps no other aspect of our life has prompted more writing on the part of our novelists, social scientists, journalists—it is as if these youths, in their habits, their interests, their language and dress, their music and politics, and not least, their developing sexuality, have a hold on us that is tied to our own memories.

Even if they have a good number of friends, many young people   10
have a loneliness that has to do with a self-imposed judgment of sorts: I am pushed and pulled by an array of urges, yearnings, worries, fears, that I can't share with anyone, really. This sense of utter difference makes for a certain moodiness well known among adolescents, who are, after all, constantly trying to figure out exactly how they ought to and might live.

I remember a young man of 15 who engaged in light banter, only to shut down, keep shaking his head, refuse to talk at all when his own life became the subject at hand. (He had stopped going to school, begun using large amounts of pot; he sat in his room for hours, listening to rock music.) After calling him, to myself, a host of psychiatric names—withdrawn, depressed, possibly psychotic—I asked him about his head-shaking behavior. I wondered whom he was thereby addressing. He did reply: "No one." I hesitated, gulped a bit as I took a chance: "Not yourself?" He looked right at me now in a sustained stare, for the first time. "Why do you say that?"

I decided not to answer the question in the manner that I was trained to reply—an account of what I had surmised about him, what I thought was happening inside him. Instead, with some unease, I heard myself saying this: "I've been there; I remember being there, when I felt I couldn't say a word to anyone." I can still remember those words, still remember feeling that I ought not have spoken them—a breach in "technique." The young man kept staring at me, didn't speak, at least through his mouth. When he took out his handkerchief and wiped his eyes, I realized they had begun to fill.

From there, we began a very gradual climb upward, step by step. As Anna Freud told me, "We are not miracle workers, who can say something, and—presto!—the trouble in a life has vanished. But I have noticed that in most of the adolescents that I see, in most of them a real effort at understanding . . . can go a long way."

To Parents and Teachers

Ralph Waldo Emerson once said, "Character is higher than intellect." Marian, a student of mine several years ago, much admired Emerson. She had arrived at Harvard from the Midwest and was trying hard to work her way through college by cleaning the rooms of her fellow students. Again and again she met classmates who had forgotten the meaning of please, of thank you, no matter their high SAT scores. They did not hesitate to be rude, even crude toward her. One day she was not so subtly propositioned by a young man she knew to be very bright. She quit her job, and was preparing to quit going to school. She came to see me full of anxiety and anger. "I've been taking all these philosophy courses," she said to me at one point, "and we talk about what's true, what's important, what's good. Well, how do you teach people to be good?"

Rather obviously, community service offers us all a chance to put our money where our mouths are. Books and classroom discussion, the skepticism of Marian notwithstanding, can be of help in this matter. But ultimately we must heed the advice of Henry James. When asked by his nephew what he ought to do in life, James replied, "Three things in human life are important. The first is to be kind. The second is to be kind. And the third is to be kind." The key to those words is the hortatory verb—the insistence that one find an existence that enables one to be kind. How to do so? By wading in, over and over, with that purpose in mind, with a willingness to sail on, tacking and tacking again, helped by those we aim to help, guided by our moral yearnings on behalf of others, on behalf of ourselves with others: a commitment to others that won't avoid squalls and periods of drift, a commitment that will become the heart of the journey itself.

15

◌ Joining the Conversation: Critical Thinking and Writing

1. Rustin McIntosh, from whom Coles first heard the term "moral intelligence," does not define it. Based on Cole's article, how would you define it? And how do children acquire it?

2. In his third and fourth paragraphs, Coles relates a personal anecdote. What is it, and what point is he making through it? What other anecdotes does he use, and why does he use them?

3. In his final paragraph, Coles uses a metaphor. What is it? Evaluate its effectiveness.

4. In a paragraph or two reveal through an anecdote a moral lesson.

Fan Shen

Fan Shen came to the United States from the People's Republic of China. A translator and writer, he also teaches at Rochester Community and Technical College, in Rochester, Minnesota.

The Classroom and the Wider Culture

Identity as a Key to Learning English Composition

One day in June 1975, when I walked into the aircraft factory where I was working as an electrician, I saw many large-letter posters on the walls and many people parading around the workshops shouting slogans like "Down with the word 'I'!" and "Trust in masses and the Party!" I then remembered that a new political campaign called "Against Individualism" was scheduled to begin that day. Ten years later, I got back my first English composition paper at the University of Nebraska–Lincoln. The professor's first comments were: "Why did you always use 'we' instead of 'I'?" and "Your paper would be stronger if you eliminated some sentences in the passive voice." The clashes between my Chinese background and the requirements of English composition had begun. At the center of this mental struggle, which has lasted several years and is still not completely over, is the prolonged, uphill battle to recapture "myself."

In this paper I will try to describe and explore this experience of reconciling my Chinese identity with an English identity dictated by the rules of English composition. I want to show how my cultural background shaped—and shapes—my approaches to my writing in English and how writing in English redefined—and redefines—my *ideological* and *logical* identities. By "ideological identity" I mean the system of values that I acquired (consciously and unconsciously) from my social and cultural background. And by "logical identity" I mean the natural (or Oriental) way I organize and express my thoughts in writing. Both had to be modified or redefined in learning English composition. Becoming aware of the process of redefinition of these different identities is a mode of learning that has helped me in my efforts to write in English, and, I hope, will be of help to teachers of English composition in this country. In presenting my case for this view, I will use examples from both my composition courses and literature courses, for I believe that writing papers for both kinds of courses contributed to the development of my "English identity." Although what I will describe is based on personal experience, many Chinese students whom I talked to said that they had had the same or similar experiences in their initial stages of learning to write in English.

Identity of the Self: Ideological and Cultural

Starting with the first English paper I wrote, I found that learning to compose in English is not an isolated classroom activity, but a social and cultural experience. The rules of English composition encapsulate values that are absent in, or sometimes contradictory to, the values of other societies (in my case, China). Therefore, learning the rules of English composition is, to a certain extent, learning the values of Anglo-American society. In writing classes in the United States I found that I had to reprogram my mind, to redefine some of the basic concepts and values that I had about myself, about society, and about the universe, values that had been imprinted and reinforced in my mind by my cultural background, and that had been part of me all my life.

Rule number one in English composition is: Be yourself. (More than one composition instructor has told me, "Just write what *you* think.") The values behind this rule, it seems to me, are based on the principle of protecting and promoting individuality (and private property) in this country. The instruction was probably crystal clear to students raised on these values, but, as a guideline of composition, it was not very clear or useful to me when I first heard it. First of all, the image or meaning that I attached to the word "I" or "myself" was, as I found out, different from that of my English teacher. In China, "I" is always subordinated to "We"—be it the working class, the Party, the country, or some other collective body. Both political pressure and literary tradition require that "I" be somewhat hidden or buried in writings and speeches; presenting the "self" too obviously would give people the impression of being disrespectful of the

Communist Party in political writings and boastful in scholarly writings. The word "I" has often been identified with another "bad" word, "individualism," which has become a synonym for selfishness in China. For a long time the words "self" and "individualism" have had negative connotations in my mind, and the negative force of the words naturally extended to the field of literary studies. As a result, even if I had brilliant ideas, the "I" in my papers always had to show some modesty by not competing with or trying to stand above the names of ancient and modern authoritative figures. Appealing to Mao or other Marxist authorities became the required way (as well as the most "forceful" or "persuasive" way) to prove one's point in written discourse. I remember that in China I had even committed what I can call "reversed plagiarism"—here, I suppose it would be called "forgery"—when I was in middle school: willfully attributing some of my thoughts to "experts" when I needed some arguments but could not find a suitable quotation from a literary or political "giant."

Now, in America, I had to learn to accept the words "I" and "self" as something glorious (as Whitman did), or at least something not to be ashamed of or embarrassed about. It was the first and probably biggest step I took into English composition and critical writing. Acting upon my professor's suggestion, I intentionally tried to show my "individuality" and to "glorify" "I" in my papers by using as many "I's" as possible— "I think," "I believe," "I see"—and deliberately cut out quotations from authorities. It was rather painful to hand in such "pompous" (I mean immodest) papers to my instructors. But to an extent it worked. After a while I became more comfortable with only "the shadow of myself." I felt more at ease to put down *my* thoughts without looking over my shoulder to worry about the attitudes of my teachers or the reactions of the Party secretaries, and to speak out as "bluntly" and "immodestly" as my American instructors demanded.

But writing many "I's" was only the beginning of the process of redefining myself. Speaking of redefining myself is, in an important sense, speaking of redefining the word "I." By such a redefinition I mean not only the change in how I envisioned myself, but also the change in how *I* perceived the world. The old "I" used to embody only one set of values, but now it had to embody multiple sets of values. To be truly "myself," which I knew was a key to my success in learning English composition, meant *not to be my Chinese self* at all. That is to say, when I write in English I have to wrestle with and abandon (at least temporarily) the whole system of ideology which previously defined me in myself. I had to forget Marxist doctrines (even though I do not see myself as a Marxist by choice) and the Party lines imprinted in my mind and familiarize myself with a system of capitalist/bourgeois values. I had to put aside an ideology of collectivism and adopt the values of individualism. In composition as well as in literature classes, I had to make a fundamental adjustment: If I used to examine society and literary materials through the microscopes of Marxist dialectical materialism and historical materialism, I now had to learn to look through the microscopes the other way around, i.e., to learn to look at and understand the world from the point of view of "idealism." (I must add here that there are American professors who use a Marxist approach in their teaching.)

The word "idealism," which affects my view of both myself and the universe, is loaded with social connotations, and can serve as a good example of how redefining a key word can be a pivotal part of redefining my ideological identity as a whole.

To me, idealism is the philosophical foundation of the dictum of English composition: "Be yourself." In order to write good English, I knew that I had to be myself, which actually meant not to be my Chinese self. It meant that I had to create an English self and be *that* self. And to be that English self, I felt, I had to understand and accept idealism the way a Westerner does. That is to say, I had to accept the way a Westerner sees himself in relation to the universe and society. On the one hand, I knew a lot about idealism. But on the other hand, I knew nothing about it. I mean I knew a lot about idealism through the propaganda and objections of its opponent, Marxism, but I knew little about it from its own point of view. When I thought of the word "materialism"—which is a major part of Marxism and in China has repeatedly been "shown" to be the absolute truth—there were always positive connotations, and words like "right," "true," etc., flashed in my mind. On the other hand, the word "idealism" always came to me with the dark connotations that surround words like "absurd," "illogical," "wrong," etc. In China "idealism" is depicted as a ferocious and ridiculous enemy of Marxist philosophy. Idealism, as the simplified definition imprinted in my mind had it, is the view that the material world does not exist; that all that exists is the mind and its ideas. It is just the opposite of Marxist dialectical materialism which sees the mind as a product of the material world. It is not too difficult to see that idealism, with its idea that mind is of primary importance, provides a philosophical foundation for the Western emphasis on the value of individual human minds, and hence individual human beings. Therefore, my final acceptance of myself as of primary importance—an importance that overshadowed that of authority figures in English composition—was, I decided, dependent on an acceptance of idealism.

My struggle with idealism came mainly from my efforts to understand and to write about works such as Coleridge's *Biographia Literaria* and Emerson's "Over-Soul." For a long time I was frustrated and puzzled by the idealism expressed by Coleridge and Emerson—given their ideas, such as "I think, therefore I am" (Coleridge obviously borrowed from Descartes) and "the transparent eyeball" (Emerson's view of himself)—because in my mind, drenched as it was in dialectical materialism, there was always a little voice whispering in my ear "You are, therefore you think." I could not see how human consciousness, which is not material, could create apples and trees. My intellectual conscience refused to let me believe that the human mind is the primary world and the material world secondary. Finally, I had to imagine that I was looking at a world with my head upside down. When I imagined that I was in a new body (born with the head upside down) it was easier to forget biases imprinted in my subconsciousness about idealism, the mind, and my former self. Starting from scratch, the new inverted self—which I called my "English Self" and into which I have transformed myself—could understand and *accept*, with ease, idealism as "the truth" and "himself" (i.e., my English Self) as the "creator" of the world.

Here is how I created my new "English Self." I played a "game" similar to ones played by mental therapists. First I made a list of (simplified) features about writing associated with my old identity (the Chinese Self), both ideological and logical, and then beside the first list I added a column of features about writing associated with my new identity (the English Self). After that I pictured myself getting out of my old identity, the timid, humble, modest Chinese "I," and creeping into my new identity (often in the form of a new skin or a mask), the confident, assertive, and aggressive English "I." The new "Self" helped me to remember and accept the different rules of Chinese and English composition and the values that underpin these rules. In a sense, creating an English Self is a way of reconciling my old cultural values with the new values required by English writing, without losing the former.

An interesting structural but not material parallel to my experiences in this regard has been well described by Min-zhan Lu in her important article, "From Silence to Words: Writing as Struggle" (*College English* 49 [April 1987]: 437–48). Min-zhan Lu talks about struggles between two selves, an open self and a secret self, and between two discourses, a mainstream Marxist discourse and a bourgeois discourse her parents wanted her to learn. But her struggle was different from mine. Her Chinese self was severely constrained and suppressed by mainstream cultural discourse, but never interfused with it. Her experiences, then, were not representative of those of the majority of the younger generation who, like me, were brought up on only one discourse. I came to English composition as a Chinese person, in the fullest sense of the term, with a Chinese identity already fully formed.

Identity of the Mind: Illogical and Alogical

In learning to write in English, besides wrestling with a different ideological system, I found that I had to wrestle with a logical system very different from the blueprint of logic at the back of my mind. By "logical system" I mean two things: the Chinese way of thinking I used to approach my theme or topic in written discourse, and the Chinese critical/logical way to develop a theme or topic. By English rules, the first is illogical, for it is the opposite of the English way of approaching a topic; the second is alogical (nonlogical), for it mainly uses mental pictures instead of words as a critical vehicle.

The Illogical Pattern. In English composition, an essential rule for the logical organization of a piece of writing is the use of a "topic sentence." In Chinese composition, "from surface to core" is an essential rule, a rule which means that one ought to reach a topic gradually and "systematically" instead of "abruptly."

The concept of a topic sentence, it seems to me, is symbolic of the values of a busy people in an industrialized society, rushing to get things done, hoping to attract and satisfy the busy reader very quickly. Thinking back, I realized that I did not fully understand the virtue of the concept until my life began to rush at the speed of everyone else's in this country. Chinese composition, on the other hand, seems to embody the values of a leisurely paced rural society whose inhabitants have the time to chew and taste a topic slowly. In Chinese composition, an introduction explaining how and why one chooses this topic is not only acceptable, but often regarded as necessary. It arouses the reader's interest in the topic little by little (and this is seen as a virtue of composition) and gives him/her a sense of refinement. The famous Robert B. Kaplan "noodles" contrasting a spiral Oriental thought process with a straight-line Western approach ("Cultural Thought Patterns in Inter-Cultural Education," *Readings on English as a Second Language*, ed. Kenneth Croft, 2nd ed., Winthrop, 1980, 403–10) may be too simplistic to capture the preferred pattern of writing in English, but I think they still express some truth about Oriental writing. A Chinese writer often clears the surrounding bushes before attacking the real target. This bush-clearing pattern in Chinese writing goes back two thousand years to Kong Fuzi (Confucius). Before doing anything, Kong says in his *Luen Yu (Analects)*, one first needs to call things by their proper names (expressed by his phrase "Zheng Ming"). In other words, before touching one's main thesis, one should first state the "conditions" of composition: how, why, and when the piece is being composed. All of this will serve as a proper foundation on which to build the "house" of the piece. In the two thousand years after Kong, this principle of composition was gradually formalized (especially through the formal essays required by imperial examinations) and became known as "Ba Gu," or the eightlegged essay. The logic of Chinese composition, exemplified by the eightlegged essay, is like the peeling of an onion: Layer after layer is removed until the reader finally arrives at the central point, the core.

Ba Gu still influences modern Chinese writing. Carolyn Matalene has   15
an excellent discussion of this logical (or illogical) structure and its influence on her Chinese students' efforts to write in English ("Contrastive Rhetoric: An American Writing Teacher in China," *College English* 47 [November 1985]: 789–808). A recent Chinese textbook for composition lists six essential steps (factors) for writing a narrative essay, steps to be taken in this order: time, place, character, event, cause, and consequence (*Yuwen Jichu Zhishi Liushi Jiang [Sixty Lessons on the Basics of the Chinese Language]*, ed. Beijing Research Institute of Education, Beijing Publishing

House, 1981, 525–609). Most Chinese students (including me) are taught to follow this sequence in composition.

The straightforward approach to composition in English seemed to me, at first, illogical. One could not jump to the topic. One had to walk step by step to reach the topic. In several of my early papers I found that the Chinese approach—the bush-clearing approach—persisted, and I had considerable difficulty writing (and in fact understanding) topic sentences. In what I deemed to be topic sentences, I grudgingly gave out themes. Today, those papers look to me like Chinese papers with forced or false English openings. For example, in a narrative paper on a trip to New York, I wrote the forced/false topic sentence, "A trip to New York in winter is boring." In the next few paragraphs, I talked about the weather, the people who went with me, and so on, before I talked about what I learned from the trip. My real thesis was that one could always learn something even on a boring trip.

The Alogical Pattern. In learning English composition, I found that there was yet another cultural blueprint affecting my logical thinking. I found from my early papers that very often I was unconsciously under the influence of a Chinese critical approach called the creation of "yijing," which is totally non-Western. The direct translation of the word "yijing" is: yi, "mind or consciousness," and jing, "environment." An ancient approach which has existed in China for many centuries and is still the subject of much discussion, yijing is a complicated concept that defies a universal definition. But most critics in China nowadays seem to agree on one point, that yijing is the critical approach that separates Chinese literature and criticism from Western literature and criticism. Roughly speaking, yijing is the process of creating a pictorial environment while reading a piece of literature. Many critics in China believe that yijing is a creative process of inducing oneself, while reading a piece of literature or looking at a piece of art, to create mental pictures, in order to reach a unity of nature, the author, and the reader. Therefore, it is by its very nature both creative and critical. According to the theory, this nonverbal, pictorial process leads directly to a higher ground of beauty and morality. Almost all critics in China agree that yijing is not a process of logical thinking—it is not a process of moving from the premises of an argument to its conclusion, which is the foundation of Western criticism. According to yijing, the process of criticizing a piece of art or literary work has to involve the process of creation on the reader's part. In yijing, verbal thoughts and pictorial thoughts are one. Thinking is conducted largely in pictures and then "transcribed" into words. (Ezra Pound once tried to capture the creative aspect of yijing in poems such as "In a Station of the Metro." He also tried to capture the critical aspect of it in his theory of imagism and vorticism, even though he did not know the term "yijing.") One characteristic of the yijing approach to criticism, therefore, is that it often includes a description of the created mental pictures on the part of the reader/critic and his/her mental attempt to bridge (unite) the literary work, the pictures, with ultimate beauty and peace.

In looking back at my critical papers for various classes, I discovered that I unconsciously used the approach of yijing, especially in some of my earlier papers when I seemed not yet to have been in the grip of Western logical critical approaches. I wrote, for instance, an essay entitled "Wordsworth's Sound and Imagination: The Snowdon Episode." In the major part of the essay I described the pictures that flashed in my mind while I was reading passages in Wordsworth's long poem, *The Prelude*.

> I saw three climbers (myself among them) winding up the mountain in silence "at the dead of night," absorbed in their "private thoughts." The sky was full of blocks of clouds of different colors, freely changing their shapes, like oily pigments disturbed in a bucket of water. All of a sudden, the moonlight broke the darkness "like a flash," lighting up the mountain tops. Under the "naked moon," the band saw a vast sea of mist and vapor, a silent ocean. Then the silence was abruptly broken, and we heard the "roaring of waters, torrents, streams/Innumerable, roaring with one voice" from a "blue chasm," a fracture in the vapor of the sea. It was a joyful revelation of divine truth to the human mind: the bright, "naked" moon sheds the light of "higher reasons" and "spiritual love" upon us; the vast ocean of mist looked like a thin curtain through which we vaguely saw the infinity of nature beyond; and the sounds of roaring waters coming out of the chasm of vapor cast us into the boundless spring of imagination from the depth of the human heart. Evoked by the divine light from above, the human spring of imagination is joined by the natural spring and becomes a sustaining source of energy, feeding "upon infinity" while transcending infinity at the same time.

Here I was describing my own experience more than Wordsworth's. The picture described by the poet is taken over and developed by the reader. The imagination of the author and the imagination of the reader are thus joined together. There was no "because" or "therefore" in the paper. There was little *logic*. And I thought it was (and it is) criticism. This seems to me a typical (but simplified) example of the yijing approach. (Incidentally, the instructor, a kind professor, found the paper interesting, though a bit "strange.")

In another paper of mine, "The Note of Life: Williams's 'The Orchestra'," I found myself describing my experiences of pictures of nature while reading William Carlos Williams's poem. "The Orchestra." I "painted" these fleeting pictures and described the feelings that seemed to lead me to an understanding of a harmony, a "common tone," between man and nature. A paragraph from that paper reads: 20

> The poem first struck me as a musical fairy tale. With rich musical sounds in my ear, I seemed to be walking in a solitary, dense forest on a spring morning. No sound from human society could be heard. I was now sitting under a giant pine tree, ready to hear the grand concert of Nature. With the sun slowly rising from the east, the cello (the creeping creek) and the clarinet (the rustling pine trees) started with a slow overture. Enthusiastically the violinists (the twittering birds) and the French horn (the mumbling cow) "interpose[d]

their voices," and the bass (bears) got in at the wrong time. The orchestra did not stop, they continued to play. The musicians of Nature do not always play in harmony. "Together, unattuned," they have to seek "a common tone" as they play along. The symphony of Nature is like the symphony of human life: both consist of random notes seeking a "common tone." For the symphony of life

> Love is that common tone
> shall raise his fiery head
> and sound his note.

Again, the logical pattern of this paper, the "pictorial criticism," is illogical to Western minds but "logical" to those acquainted with yijing. (Perhaps I should not even use the words "logical" and "think" because they are so conceptually tied up with "words" and with culturally-based conceptions, and therefore very misleading if not useless in a discussion of yijing. Maybe I should simply say that yijing is neither illogical nor logical, but alogical.)

I am not saying that such a pattern of "alogical" thinking is wrong— in fact some English instructors find it interesting and acceptable—but it is very non-Western. Since I was in this country to learn the English language and English literature, I had to abandon Chinese "pictorial logic," and to learn Western "verbal logic."

If I Had to Start Again

The change is profound: Through my understanding of new meanings of words like "individualism," "idealism," and "I," I began to accept the underlying concepts and values of American writing, and by learning to use "topic sentences" I began to accept a new logic. Thus, when I write papers in English, I am able to obey all the general rules of English composition. In doing this I feel that I am writing through, with, and because of a new identity. I welcome the change, for it has added a new dimension to me and to my view of the world. I am not saying that I have entirely lost my Chinese identity. In fact I feel that I will never lose it. Any time I write in Chinese, I resume my old identity, and obey the rules of Chinese composition such as "Make the 'I' modest," and "Beat around the bush before attacking the central topic." It is necessary for me to have such a Chinese identity in order to write authentic Chinese. (I have seen people who, after learning to write in English, use English logic and sentence patterning to write Chinese. They produce very awkward Chinese texts.) But when I write in English, I imagine myself slipping into a new "skin," and I let the "I" behave much more aggressively and knock the topic right on the head. Being conscious of these different identities has helped me to reconcile different systems of values and logic, and has played a pivotal role in my learning to compose in English.

Looking back, I realize that the process of learning to write in English is in fact a process of creating and defining a new identity and balancing it with the old identity. The process of learning English composition would have been easier if I had realized this earlier and consciously sought to compare the two different identities required by the two writing systems from two different cultures. It is fine and perhaps even necessary for American composition teachers to teach about topic sentences, paragraphs, the use of punctuation, documentation, and so on, but can anyone design exercises sensitive to the ideological and logical differences that students like me experience—and design them so they can be introduced at an early stage of an English composition class? As I pointed out earlier, the traditional advice "Just be yourself" is not clear and helpful to students from Korea, China, Vietnam, or India. From "Be yourself" we are likely to hear either "Forget your cultural habit of writing" or "Write as you would write in your own language." But neither of the two is what the instructor meant or what we want to do. It would be helpful if he or she pointed out the different cultural/ideological connotations of the word "I," the connotations that exist in a group-centered culture and an individual-centered culture. To sharpen the contrast, it might be useful to design papers on topics like "The Individual vs. The Group: China vs. America" or "Different 'I's' in Different Cultures."

Carolyn Matalene mentioned in her article (789) an incident concerning American businessmen who presented their Chinese hosts with gifts of cheddar cheese, not knowing that the Chinese generally do not like cheese. Liking cheddar cheese may not be essential to writing English prose, but being truly accustomed to the social norms that stand behind ideas such as the English "I" and the logical pattern of English composition—call it "compositional cheddar cheese"—is essential to writing in English. Matalene does not provide an "elixir" to help her Chinese students like English "compositional cheese," but rather recommends, as do I, that composition teachers not be afraid to give foreign students English "cheese," but to make sure to hand it out slowly, sympathetically, and fully realizing that it tastes very peculiar in the mouths of those used to a very different cuisine. 25

 ## Joining the Conversation: Critical Thinking and Writing

1. In his second paragraph Fan Shen says, "I will try to describe and explore this experience of reconciling my Chinese identity with an English identity." What does the article tell us is part of a "Chinese identity," and what is part of an "English identity"? How does your experience in answering this question account for the value of beginning his article with two narratives?

2. His article is based, primarily, on "personal experience." Is this part of his "English identity" or "Chinese identity"? Explain.

3. In paragraph 4 Fan Shen says, "Rule number one in English composition is: Be yourself." Whether you are from the United States or from another country, try to explain why "being yourself" is (or is not) difficult when you enter college writing. Why did Fan Shen find it difficult?

4. Does Fan Shen's explanation (paragraphs 13–15) of the value of the topic sentence in English help to explain it to you, or do you have some other account of it? Explain.

5. In his next-to-last paragraph Fan Shen suggests topics for instructors to assign to international students. One of the two, "Different 'I's'" in Different Cultures, strikes us as a good project to assign to native students as well as those from other cultures. We suggest here that you write a journal entry taking notes on the "different 'I's'" you have experienced before attending college and now. If it suits you to do this, divide your journal entry in two down the middle, taking notes on the "I" before and the "I" after.

David Gelernter

David Gelernter, a professor of computer science at Yale University, originally published this essay in the New Republic *in 1994.*

Unplugged

Over the last decade an estimated $2 billion has been spent on more than 2 million computers for America's classrooms. That's not surprising. We constantly hear from Washington that the schools are in trouble and that computers are a godsend. Within the education establishment, in poor as well as rich schools, the machines are awaited with nearly religious awe. An inner-city principal bragged to a teacher friend of mine recently that his school "has a computer in every classroom . . . despite being in a bad neighborhood!"

Computers should be in the schools. They have the potential to accomplish great things. With the right software, they could help make science tangible or teach neglected topics like art and music. They could help students form a concrete idea of society by displaying on screen a version of the city in which they live—a picture that tracks real life moment by moment.

In practice, however, computers make our worst educational nightmares come true. While we bemoan the decline of literacy, computers discount words in favor of pictures and pictures in favor of video. While we fret about the decreasing cogency of public debate, computers dismiss linear argument and promote fast, shallow romps across the information landscape. While we worry about basic skills, we allow into the classroom software that will do a student's arithmetic or correct his spelling.

David Gelernter, "Unplugged," the *New Republic*, September 19, 1994. Reprinted by permission.

Take multimedia. The idea of multimedia is to combine text, sound and pictures in a single package that you browse on screen. You don't just *read* Shakespeare; you watch actors performing, listen to songs, view Elizabethan buildings. What's wrong with that? By offering children candy-coated books, multimedia is guaranteed to sour them on unsweetened reading. It makes the printed page look even more boring than it used to look. Sure, books will be available in the classroom, too—but they'll have all the appeal of a dusty piano to a teen who has a Walkman handy.

So what if the little nippers don't read? If they're watching Olivier instead, what do they lose? The text, the written word along with all of its attendant pleasures. Besides, a book is more portable than a computer, has a higher-resolution display, can be written on and dog-eared and is comparatively dirt cheap.

Hypermedia, multimedia's comrade in the struggle for a brave new classroom, is just as troubling. It's a way of presenting documents on screen without imposing a linear start-to-finish order. Disembodied paragraphs are linked by theme; after reading one about the First World War, for example, you might be able to choose another about the technology of battleships, or the life of Woodrow Wilson, or hemlines in the '20s. This is another cute idea that is good in minor ways and terrible in major ones. Teaching children to understand the orderly unfolding of a plot or a logical argument is a crucial part of education. Authors don't merely agglomerate paragraphs; they work hard to make the narrative read a certain way, prove a particular point. To turn a book or a document into hypertext is to invite readers to ignore exactly what counts—the story.

The real problem, again, is the accentuation of already bad habits. Dynamiting documents into disjointed paragraphs is one more expression of the sorry fact that sustained argument is not our style. If you're a newspaper or magazine editor and your readership is dwindling, what's the solution? Shorter pieces. If you're a politician and you want to get elected, what do you need? Tasty sound bites. Logical presentation be damned.

Another software species, "allow me" programs, is not much better. These programs correct spelling and, by applying canned grammatical and stylistic rules, fix prose. In terms of promoting basic skills, though, they have all the virtues of a pocket calculator.

In Kentucky, as *The Wall Street Journal* recently reported, students in grades K–3 are mixed together regardless of age in a relaxed environment. It works great, the *Journal* says. Yes, scores on computation tests have dropped 10 percent at one school, but not to worry: "Drilling addition and subtraction in an age of calculators is a waste of time," the principal reassures us. Meanwhile, a Japanese educator informs University of Wisconsin mathematician Richard Akey that in his country, "calculators are not used in elementary or junior high school because the primary emphasis is on helping students develop their mental abilities." No wonder Japanese kids blow the pants off American kids in math. Do we really think "drilling addition and subtraction in an age of calculators is a waste of time"? If we do, then "drilling reading in an age of multimedia is a waste of time" can't be far behind.

Prose-correcting programs are also a little ghoulish, like asking a computer for tips on improving your personality. On the other hand, I ran this article through a spell-checker, so how can I ban the use of such programs in schools? Because to misspell is human; to have no idea of correct spelling is to be semiliterate.

There's no denying that computers have the potential to perform inspiring feats in the classroom. If we are ever to see that potential realized, however, we ought to agree on three conditions. First, there should be a completely new crop of children's software. Most of today's offerings show no imagination. There are hundreds of similar reading and geography and arithmetic programs, but almost nothing on electricity or physics or architecture. Also, they abuse the technical capacities of new media to glitz up old forms instead of creating new ones. Why not build a time-travel program that gives kids a feel for how history is structured by zooming you backward? A spectrum program that lets users twirl a frequency knob to see what happens?

Second, computers should be used only during recess or relaxation periods. Treat them as fillips, not as surrogate teachers. When I was in school in the '60s, we all loved educational films. When we saw a movie in class, everybody won: teachers didn't have to teach, and pupils didn't have to learn. I suspect that classroom computers are popular today for the same reasons.

Most important, educators should learn what parents and most teachers already know: you cannot teach a child anything unless you look him in the face. We should not forget what computers are. Like books—better in some ways, worse in others—they are devices that help children mobilize their own resources and learn for themselves. The computer's potential to do good is modestly greater than a book's in some areas. Its potential to do harm is vastly greater, across the board.

ꙅ Joining the Conversation: Critical Thinking and Writing

1. If you used computers in your elementary or secondary school, evaluate their contribution to your education. (This need not be an all-or-nothing issue; it may be that computers were useless in some courses, moderately useful in others, and highly useful in still others.)

2. One of Gelernter's complaints (paragraph 3) is that "computers discount words in favor of pictures and pictures in favor of video." Is this true—and if it is true, is it necessarily a bad thing? Explain.

3. Paragraph 9 touches on whether "drilling addition and subtraction in an age of calculators is a waste of time." Your views?

Amy Tan

Amy Tan was born in Oakland, California, in 1952, of Chinese immigrant parents. When she was eight years old, she won first prize among elementary students with an essay entitled, "What the Library Means to Me." In due time she attended Linfield College in Oregon, then transferred to San Jose State University where, while working two part-time jobs, she became an honors student and a President's Scholar. In 1973 she earned an M.A. in linguistics, also at San Jose, and she later enrolled as a doctoral student at the University of California, Berkeley, though she left this program after the murder of a close friend. For the next five years she worked as a language development consultant and a project director, and then she became a freelance business writer. In 1986 she published her first short story, and it was reprinted in Seventeen, *where it was noticed by an agent, who encouraged her to continue writing fiction. In 1989* The Joy Luck Club *was published. Other books include* The Kitchen God's Wife *(1991),* The Hundred Secret Senses *(1995), and* The Bonesetter's Daughter *(2001). She has also written two books for children,* The Moon Lady *(1992) and* SAGWA the Chinese Siamese Cat *(1994).*

In the Canon, for All the Wrong Reasons

Several years ago I learned that I had passed a new literary milestone. I had made it to the Halls of Education under the rubric of "Multicultural Literature," also known in many schools as "Required Reading."

Thanks to this development, I now meet students who proudly tell me they're doing their essays, term papers, or master's theses on me. By that they mean that they are analyzing not just my books but me—my grade-school achievements, youthful indiscretions, marital status, as well as the movies I watched as a child, the slings and arrows I suffered as a minority, and so forth—all of which, with the hindsight of classroom literary investigation, prove to contain many Chinese omens that made it inevitable that I would become a writer.

Once I read a master's thesis on feminist writings, which included examples from *The Joy Luck Club*. The student noted that I had often used the number four, something on the order of thirty-two or thirty-six times—in any case, a number divisible by four. She pointed out that there were four mothers, four daughters, four sections of the book, four stories per section. Furthermore, there were four sides to a mahjong table, four directions of the wind, four players. More important, she postulated, my use of the number four was a symbol for the four stages of psychological development, which corresponded in uncanny ways to the four stages of some type of Buddhist philosophy I had never heard of before. The student recalled that the story contained a character called Fourth Wife, symbolizing death, and a four-year-old girl with a feisty spirit, symbolizing regeneration.

In short, her literary sleuthing went on to reveal a mystical and rather Byzantine puzzle, which, once explained, proved to be completely brilliant and precisely logical. She wrote me a letter and asked if her analysis had been correct. How I longed to say "absolutely."

The truth is, if there are symbols in my work they exist largely by accident or through someone else's interpretive design. If I wrote of "an orange moon rising on a dark night," I would more likely ask myself later if the image was a cliché, not whether it was a symbol for the feminine force rising in anger, as one master's thesis postulated. To plant symbols like that, you need a plan, good organizational skills, and a prescient understanding of the story you are about to write. Sadly, I lack those traits.

All this is by way of saying that I don't claim my use of the number four to be a brilliant symbolic device. In fact, now that it's been pointed out to me in rather astonishing ways, I consider my overuse of the number to be a flaw.

Reviewers and students have enlightened me about not only how I write but why I write. Apparently, I am driven to capture the immigrant experience, to demystify Chinese culture, to point out the differences between Chinese and American culture, even to pave the way for other Asian American writers.

If only I were that noble. Contrary to what is assumed by some students, reporters, and community organizations wishing to bestow honors on me, I am not an expert on China, Chinese culture, mahjong, the psychology of mothers and daughters, generation gaps, immigration, illegal aliens, assimilation, acculturation, racial tension, Tiananmen Square, the Most Favored Nation trade agreements, human rights, Pacific Rim economics, the purported one million missing baby girls of China, the future of Hong Kong after 1997, or, I am sorry to say, Chinese cooking. Certainly I have personal opinions on many of these topics, but by no means do my sentiments and my world of make-believe make me an expert.

So I am alarmed when reviewers and educators assume that my very personal, specific, and fictional stories are meant to be representative down to the nth detail not just of Chinese Americans but, sometimes, of all Asian culture. Is Jane Smiley's *A Thousand Acres* supposed to be taken as representative of all of American culture? If so, in what ways? Are all American fathers tyrannical? Do all American sisters betray one another? Are all American conscientious objectors flaky in love relationships?

Over the years my editor has received hundreds of permissions requests from publishers of college textbooks and multicultural anthologies, all of them wishing to reprint my work for "educational purposes." One publisher wanted to include an excerpt from *The Joy Luck Club*, a scene in which a Chinese woman invites her non-Chinese boyfriend to her parents' house for dinner. The boyfriend brings a bottle of wine as a gift and commits a number of social gaffes at the dinner table. Students were supposed to read this excerpt, then answer the following question: "If you are invited to a Chinese family's house for dinner, should you bring a bottle of wine?"

In many respects, I am proud to be on the reading lists for courses such as Ethnic Studies, Asian American Studies, Asian American Literature, Asian American History, Women's Literature, Feminist Studies, Feminist Writers of Color, and so forth. What writer wouldn't want her work to be read? I also take a certain perverse glee in imagining countless students, sleepless at three in the morning, trying to read *The Joy Luck Club* for the next day's midterm. Yet I'm also not altogether comfortable about my book's status as required reading.

Let me relate a conversation I had with a professor at a school in southern California. He told me he uses my books in his literature class but he makes it a point to lambast those passages that depict China as backward or unattractive. He objects to any descriptions that have to do with spitting, filth, poverty, or superstitions. I asked him if China in the 1930s and 1940s was free of these elements. He said, No, such descriptions are true; but he still believes it is "the obligation of the writer of ethnic literature to create positive, progressive images."

I secretly shuddered and thought, Oh well, that's southern California for you. But then, a short time later, I met a student from UC Berkeley, a school that I myself attended. The student was standing in line at a book signing. When his turn came, he swaggered up to me, then took two steps back and said in a loud voice, "Don't you think you have a responsibility to write about Chinese men as positive role models?"

In the past, I've tried to ignore the potshots. A *Washington Post* reporter once asked me what I thought of another Asian American writer calling me something on the order of "a running dog whore sucking on the tit of the imperialist white pigs."

"Well," I said, "you can't please everyone, can you?" I pointed out that   15
readers are free to interpret a book as they please, and that they are free to appreciate or not appreciate the result. Besides, reacting to your critics makes a writer look defensive, petulant, and like an all-around bad sport.

But lately I've started thinking it's wrong to take such a laissez-faire attitude. Lately I've come to think that I must say something, not so much to defend myself and my work but to express my hopes for American literature, for what it has the potential to become in the twenty-first century—that is, a truly American literature, democratic in the way it includes many colorful voices.

Until recently, I didn't think it was important for writers to express their private intentions in order for their work to be appreciated; I believed that any analysis of my intentions belonged behind the closed doors of literature classes. But I've come to realize that the study of literature does have its effect on how books are being read, and thus on what might be read, published, and written in the future. For that reason, I do believe writers today must talk about their intentions—if for no other reason than to serve as an antidote to what others say our intentions should be.

For the record, I don't write to dig a hole and fill it with symbols. I don't write stories as ethnic themes. I don't write to represent life in general. And I certainly don't write because I have answers. If I knew everything there is to know about mothers and daughters, Chinese and Americans, I wouldn't have any stories left to imagine. If I had to write about only positive role models, I wouldn't have enough imagination left to finish the first story. If I knew what to do about immigration, I would be a sociologist or a politician and not a long-winded storyteller.

So why do I write?

Because my childhood disturbed me, pained me, made me ask foolish questions. And the questions still echo. Why does my mother always talk about killing herself? Why did my father and brother have to die? If I die, can I be reborn into a happy family? Those early obsessions led to a belief that writing could be my salvation, providing me with the sort of freedom and danger, satisfaction and discomfort, truth and contradiction I can't find in anything else in life.

20

I write to discover the past for myself. I don't write to change the future for others. And if others are moved by my work—if they love their mothers more, scold their daughters less, or divorce their husbands who were not positive role models—I'm often surprised, usually grateful to hear from kind readers. But I don't take either credit or blame for changing their lives for better or for worse.

Writing, for me, is an act of faith, a hope that I will discover what I mean by "truth." I also think of reading as an act of faith, a hope that I will discover something remarkable about ordinary life, about myself. And if the writer and the reader discover the same thing, if they have that connection, the act of faith has resulted in an act of magic. To me, that's the mystery and the wonder of both life and fiction—the connection between two individuals who discover in the end that they are more the same than they are different.

And if that doesn't happen, it's nobody's fault. There are still plenty of other books on the shelf. Choose what you like.

Joining the Conversation: Critical Thinking and Writing

1. In paragraph 11 Tan mentions that her books are "required reading" in various courses. What qualities, in your view, should a book of fiction have if it is to be required reading?

2. In paragraph 21 Tan says she doesn't expect her books to influence her readers. Have you ever read a work that has indeed shaped your thoughts or actions in even the slightest degree? If so, explain. If not, explain why you read anything, other than to kill time.

3. The patterns that critics see, Tan says in her first six paragraphs, are not present or, if present, are accidental. Are you convinced, or do you think (1) she may be speaking tongue-in-cheek, or (2) she may not be aware of how her unconscious mind works? In an essay of 250 words indicate why you do or do not accept at face value her words on this point.

4. Tan says (paragraph 15) that "readers are free to interpret a book as they please." She goes on, however, in paragraph 16 to indicate that she no longer holds this "laissez-faire" attitude. Do you believe that your interpretation of a work should coincide with the author's? In an essay of 250 words, explain why, or why not.

5. In paragraph 18 Tan says she cannot write a story with only "positive role models." Can you think of a work of literature that includes a character from a minority group who is not a "positive" role model? (Many people believe that Shylock in Shakespeare's *The Merchant of Venice* is such an example.) If you are familiar with such a work, do you think that members of the minority group are right to find the depiction offensive? Should such a work not be taught in high school, and perhaps not even in college? Explain, in an essay of 500 words.

Wu-tsu Fa-yen

Wu-tsu Fa-yen (1025–1104) was a Chinese Zen Buddhist priest. More exactly, he was a Ch'an priest: Zen is Japanese for the Chinese Ch'an.

The practitioner of Zen (to use the more common name) seeks satori, "enlightenment" or "awakening." The awakening is from a world of blind strivings (including those of reason and of morality). The awakened being, free from a sense of the self in opposition to all other things, perceives the unity of all things. Wu-tsu belonged to the branch of Zen that uses "shock therapy, the purpose of which is to jolt the student out of his analytical and conceptual way of thinking and lead him back to his natural and spontaneous faculty" (Kenneth Ch'en, Buddhism in China [1964, rptd. 1972], p. 359).

The title of this story, from The Sayings of Goso Hōyen, *is the editors'.*

Zen and the Art of Burglary

If people ask me what Zen is like, I will say that it is like learning the art of burglary. The son of a burglar saw his father growing older and thought, "If he is unable to carry on his profession, who will be the breadwinner of the family, except myself? I must learn the trade." He intimated the idea to his father, who approved of it.

One night the father took the son to a big house, broke through the fence, entered the house, and, opening one of the large chests, told the son to go in and pick out the clothing. As soon as the son got into it, the father dropped the lid and securely applied the lock. The father now came out to the courtyard and loudly knocked at the door, waking up the whole family; then he quietly slipped away by the hole in the fence. The residents got excited and lighted candles, but they found that the burglar had already gone.

Daisetz T Suzuki, *Zen and Japanese Culture.* Copyright © 1959 by Bollingen Foundation, Inc., 1987 renewed Princeton University Press. Reprinted by permission of Princeton University Press.

The son, who remained all the time securely confined in the chest, thought of his cruel father. He was greatly mortified, then a fine idea flashed upon him. He made a noise like the gnawing of a rat. The family told the maid to take a candle and examine the chest. When the lid was unlocked, out came the prisoner, who blew out the light, pushed away the maid, and fled. The people ran after him. Noticing a well by the road, he picked up a large stone and threw it into the water. The pursuers all gathered around the well trying to find the burglar drowning himself in the dark hole.

In the meantime he went safely back to his father's house. He blamed his father deeply for his narrow escape. Said the father, "Be not offended, my son. Just tell me how you got out of it." When the son told him all about his adventures, the father remarked, "There you are, you have learned the art."

Joining the Conversation: Critical Thinking and Writing

1. What assumptions about knowledge did the father make? Can you think of any of your own experiences that substantiate these assumptions?

2. Is there anything you have studied or are studying to which Zen pedagogical methods would be applicable? If so, explain by setting forth a sample lesson.

A Casebook on What Colleges Should Teach

Stanley Fish

Stanley Fish, born in 1938, taught for many years at Johns Hopkins University and at Duke University before serving as dean of the College of Liberal Arts and Sciences at the University of Illinois, Chicago. He is one of the most influential literary critics in the United States, but he is also widely known for his essays on a variety of academic and legal issues. Among his books are Self-Consuming Artifacts *(1970),* The Trouble with Principle *(1999).*

Why We Built the Ivory Tower

After nearly five decades in academia, and five and a half years as a dean at a public university, I exit with a three-part piece of wisdom for those who work in higher education: do your job; don't try to do someone else's job, as you are unlikely to be qualified; and don't let anyone else do your job. In other words, don't confuse your academic obligations with the obligation to save the world; that's not your job as an academic; and don't surrender your academic obligations to the agenda of any non-academic constituency—parents, legislators, trustees or donors. In short, don't cross the boundary between academic work and partisan advocacy, whether the advocacy is yours or someone else's.

Marx famously said that our job is not to interpret the world, but to change it. In the academy, however, it is exactly the reverse: our jobs is not to change the world, but to interpret it. While academic labors might in some instances play a role in real-world politics—if, say, the Supreme Court cites your book on the way to a decision—it should not be the design or aim of academics to play that role.

While academics in general will agree that a university should not dance to the tune of external constituencies, they will most likely resist the injunction to police the boundary between academic work and political work. They will resist because they simply don't believe in the boundary—they believe that all activities are inherently political, and an injunction to avoid politics is meaningless and futile.

Now there is some truth to that, but it is not a truth that goes very far. And it certainly doesn't go where those who proclaim it would want it to go. It is true that no form of work—including even the work of, say, natural science—stands apart from the political, social and economic concerns that underlie the structures and practices of a society. This does not mean, however, that there is no difference between academic labors and partisan labors, or that there is no difference between, for example, analyzing the history of welfare reform—a history that would necessarily include opinions pro and con—and urging students to go out and work for welfare reform or for its reversal.

Analyzing welfare reform in an academic context is a political action in the sense that any conclusion a scholar might reach will be one another scholar might dispute. (That, after all, is what political means: subject to dispute.) But such a dispute between scholars will not be political in the everyday sense of the word, because each side will represent different academic approaches, not different partisan agendas.

My point is not that academics should refrain from being political in an absolute sense—that is impossible—but that they should engage in politics appropriate to the enterprise they signed onto. And that means arguing about (and voting on) things like curriculum, department leadership, the direction of research, the content and manner of teaching, establishing standards—everything that is relevant to the responsibilities we take on when we accept a paycheck. These responsibilities include meeting classes, keeping up in the discipline, assigning and correcting papers, opening up new areas of scholarship, and so on.

This is a long list, but there are many in academia who would add to it the larger (or so they would say) tasks of "forming character" and "fashioning citizens." A few years ago the presidents of nearly 500 universities issued a declaration on the "Civic Responsibility of Higher Education." It called for colleges and universities to take responsibility for helping students "realize the values and skills of our democratic society."

Derek Bok, the former president of Harvard and one of the forces behind the declaration, has urged his colleagues to "consider civic responsibility as an explicit and important aim of college education." In January, some 1,300 administrators met in Washington under the auspices of the Association of American Colleges and Universities to take up this topic: "What practices provide students with the knowledge and commitments to be socially responsible citizens?" That's not a bad question, but the answers to it should not be the content of a college or university course.

No doubt, the practices of responsible citizenship and moral behavior should be encouraged in our young adults—but it's not the business of the university to do so, except when the morality in question is the morality that penalizes cheating, plagiarizing and shoddy teaching, and the desired citizenship is defined not by the demands of democracy, but by the demands of the academy.

This is so not because these practices are political, but because they are the political tasks that belong properly to other institutions. Universities could engage in moral and civic education only by deciding in advance which of the competing views of morality and citizenship is the right one, and then devoting academic resources and energy to the task of realizing it. But that task would deform (by replacing) the true task of academic work: the search for truth and the dissemination of it through teaching.

The idea that universities should be in the business of forming character and fashioning citizens is often supported by the claim that academic work should not be hermetically sealed or kept separate from the realm of values. But the search for truth is its own value, and fidelity to it mandates the accompanying values of responsibility in pedagogy and scholarship.

Performing academic work responsibly and at the highest level is a job big enough for any scholar and for any institution. And, as I look around, it does not seem to me that we academics do that job so well that we can now take it upon ourselves to do everyone else's job too. We should look to the practices in our own shop, narrowly conceived, before we set out to alter the entire world by forming moral character, or fashioning democratic citizens, or combating globalization, or embracing globalization, or anything else.

One would like to think that even the exaggerated sense of virtue that is so much a part of the academic mentality has its limits. If we aim low and stick to the tasks we are paid to perform, we might actually get something done.

10

Joining the Conversation:
Critical Thinking and Writing

1. What do you make of the term "Ivory Tower"? If someone is said to "live in an Ivory Tower" is that a favorable or unfavorable remark? What does living in an Ivory Tower imply? What does Fish appear to mean or imply when he uses the term?

2. In his second paragraph Fish says, speaking of instructors but probably he also includes students in their role as students, "Our job is not to change the world, but to interpret it." Do you agree? Explain.

3. In his seventh paragraph Fish insistently argues that college instructors should not be concerned with "forming character" or "fashioning citizens." Do you agree? Explain.

4. Fish's final paragraph runs thus:

> One would like to think that even the exaggerated sense of virtue that is so much a part of the academic mentality has its limits. If we aim low and stick to the tasks we are paid to perform, we might actually get something done.

First, have you seen evidence of "the exaggerated sense of virtue that is so much a part of the academic mentality"? If so, in a paragraph or two report the evidence. Second, in your view, exactly what "tasks" are college and university faculty members "paid to perform"? Do you have any sense of whether they adequately perform these tasks? Explain.

5. In an essay of 250–500 words explain why you would or would not want to take a course in composition or in literature with Professor Fish.

6. Read Dave Eggers's "Serve or Fail" (page 355), and then imagine what Eggers might say about Fish's essay. In an essay of 250 words set forth your imagined response.

Rachel Milbauer

Rachel Milbauer wrote this essay in a first-year course in composition. It is used with the author's permission.

Coercive Thinking

In English 101 we have read essays on a variety of controversial topics, including "Should the States Endorse Gambling in the Form of Lotteries?," "Should The United States Pay Reparations to the Descendants of Slaves?" and "Should Abortion Be Legal?" It is in connection with this last topic that I write a note of protest.

We have been asked not only to read several essays on each side of the controversy, but also to write "the best argument you can write on each side of the issue." Prof. Holmes has explained that by having to write "the best argument" that we can, on each side, we will (a) clearly see the reasons held by people on the other side, and (b) also see, perhaps for the first time, the reasons that underlie our own beliefs. In making this assignment, Prof. Holmes said that by having to think about a view that we oppose, and having to put that view into words that our opponents might agree are a fair statement of their views, we will be fair to them, and we will be helping ourselves. He quoted the statesman Edmund Burke, who said, "He that wrestles with us strengthens our nerves, and sharpens our skill. Our antagonist is our helper." The professor said that we often do not really understand our own views until we have honestly faced the opposing views, and that when we state these opposing views as clearly and as forcefully as we can, we perhaps for the first time really understand our own views.

I can see that for some issues this idea makes sense. Let's say that I oppose timed tests in my math course. If I try to think hard about the arguments in *favor* of timed tests, I might possibly see their merit and I might change my own position, or, on the other hand, I might for the first time realize that I not only *hold* a position but now I really know *why* it is the right position, or at least why this position makes more sense to me than the opposing position. But, as I said, "I can see that for some issues" this position makes sense. Where it does *not* make sense, I believe is where strong moral and perhaps religious convictions are at stake. It happens that my religious teachings strongly disapprove of abortion, and I find that although I can read—but with a lot of anger—arguments favoring abortion, I cannot bring myself to put onto paper arguments in its favor.

Yes, I understand that the instructor is asking us to write these arguments as a kind of intellectual exercise, an exercise that perhaps will cause us to change our minds—and surely a college education ought to help a student to develop an open mind—or, if we don't change our minds on this issue, the exercise will supposedly help us to understand our own position, help us to see that it really *is* a strong and well-thought-out position. But consider this comparison: Suppose an instructor required us to see a pornographic movie—just as a sort of exercise, a way of perhaps opening our minds—and required us to write (again, as an exercise in thinking) a defense of it.

I think that most people—students, parents, professors, lawyers, 5 judges—would agree that students should not have to view material that they regard as morally objectionable, and most people would also agree that students should not have to write—even as an intellectual exercise—a defense of such material. Well, for me, arguments on behalf of abortion are truly comparable to this. Let me say, very clearly, that I am *not* saying that the pros and cons of abortion cannot be taught in college. This issue, and other highly sensitive moral/religious issues such as gay marriage, can be taught—in courses that students *elect* to take.

I can easily imagine a course entitled "Current Moral Issues" that addresses both of these topics (abortion and pornography), as well as (for instance) gay marriage and polygamy. I can even imagine a film course that showed pornographic movies, and discussed them from both a film-criticism and a moral point of view. But all such courses would be elective courses, not required courses. Students who took such courses would know what they were getting into, or they could drop the courses once they saw what was going to be discussed. But a required course, such as our Composition course, is another thing. We *must* take it. And because we must take it, I believe that instructors should be aware that some of us have strong feelings, rooted in deep beliefs, that make it very difficult for us to read arguments on certain topics, and make it virtually impossible for us to write arguments—even as an intellectual exercise—advocating certain positions.

I don't think I can make a convincing argument to those who take the other view. They probably will talk about open-mindedness, and maybe about academic freedom. But let me propose a thought-experiment. I recall reading an art historian who was writing about the power of certain pictures. This art historian mentioned that if we took a photograph of a beloved relative—let's say a photograph of our spouse or our child—and we were given a knife and we were told to gouge out the eyes in the photograph, we would refuse to follow the instructions. Almost surely everyone would agree that a professor has no right to require such an action in class, even if the idea is (for instance) to make us really feel the power of pictures, or perhaps to help us to overcome a sort of superstitious belief that pictures have a sort of magic. Professors should help us to think independently, but they should not require us to engage in actions that violate our sensibilities and our beliefs.

Now, this is only a comparison, but for me to have to write an essay advocating abortion—even as an exercise that is supposed in the end to help to strengthen my present belief—is repulsive to me. Perhaps the professors who are so eager to talk about open-mindedness should themselves be a little more open-minded, should understand that students may have sensibilities that ought not be violated.

◎ Joining the Conversation:
Critical Thinking and Writing

1. Do you agree with the writer's position? Explain your answer, and, if possible, refer to examples from your own experiences as a student.

2. Do you think that Milbauer's argument is an effective one? Point to the features of her essay that make the argument effective, or else that need to be revised in order for it to be made more effective.

3. Construct an argument in which you seek to refute Milbauer's position. What is your thesis? What is your evidence to support it?

4. In class discussions and in assignments, should a teacher challenge the views of students? Is there a point when a teacher should stop—when he or she should (as the saying goes) "back off" from challenging a student? Give specific examples, which could arise from your own experiences or which you imagine could occur.

5. Milbauer argues that teachers should be open-minded. Describe a teacher of your own who impressed you as being open-minded. Be as specific as you can about why this was the case. Next, describe a teacher who was not open-minded—do *not* name the instructor—and, again, explain carefully what it was that led you to this conclusion.

Dave Eggers

Dave Eggers, the founder of 826 Valencia, a nonprofit learning center, and the editor of McSweeney's, *is also an author, most notably of* A Heartbreaking Work of Staggering Genius *(2000).*

Serve or Fail

About now, most recent college graduates, a mere week or two beyond their last final, are giving themselves a nice respite. Maybe they're on a beach, maybe they're on a road trip, maybe they're in their rooms, painting their toenails black with a Q-tip and shoe polish. Does it matter? What's important is that they have some time off.

Do they deserve the time off? Well, yes and no. Yes, because finals week is stressful and sleep-deprived and possibly involves trucker-style stimulants. No, because a good deal of the four years of college is spent playing foosball.

I went to a large state school—the University of Illinois—and during my time there, I became one of the best two or three foosball players in the Land of Lincoln. I learned to pass deftly between my rigid players, to play the corners, to strike the ball like a cobra would strike something a cobra would want to strike. I also mastered the dart game called Cricket, and the billiards contest called Nine-ball. I became expert at whiffle ball, at backyard archery, and at a sport we invented that involved one person tossing roasted chickens from a balcony to a group of us waiting below. We got to eat the parts that didn't land on the patio.

The point is that college is too long—it should be three years—and that even with a full course load and part-time jobs (I had my share) there are many hours in the days and weeks that need killing. And because most of us, as students, saw our hours as in need of killing—as opposed to thinking about giving a few of these hours to our communities in one

way or another—colleges should consider instituting a service requirement for graduation.

I volunteered a few times in Urbana-Champaign—at a Y.M.C.A. and   5
at a home for senior citizens—and in both cases it was much too easy to
quit. I thought the senior home smelled odd, so I left, and though the
Y.M.C.A. was a perfect fit, I could have used nudging to continue—nudging
the university might have provided. Just as parents and schools need to
foster in young people a "reading habit"—a love of reading that becomes a
need, almost an addiction—colleges are best-poised to create in their students a lifelong commitment to volunteering even a few hours a month.

Some colleges, and many high schools, have such a thing in place, and
last year Michael R. Veon, a Democratic member of Pennsylvania's House of
Representatives, introduced a bill that would require the more than 90,000
students at 14 state-run universities to perform 25 hours of community service annually. That comes out to more than two million volunteer hours a year.

College students are, for the most part, uniquely suited to have time
for and to benefit from getting involved and addressing the needs of
those around them. Unlike high school students, they're less programmed,
less boxed-in by family and after-school obligations. They're also more
mature, and better able to handle a wide range of tasks. Finally, they're at
a stage where exposure to service—and to the people whose lives nonprofit service organizations touch—would have a profound effect on
them. Meeting a World War II veteran who needs meals brought to
him would be educational for the deliverer of that meal, I would think.
A college history major might learn something by tutoring a local middle
school class that's studying the Underground Railroad. A connection
would be forged; a potential career might be discovered.

A service requirement won't work everywhere. It probably wouldn't
be feasible, for example, for community college students, who tend to be
transient and who generally have considerable family and work demands. But exempt community colleges and you would still have almost
10 million college students enrolled in four-year colleges in the United
States. If you exempted a third of them for various reasons, that would
leave more than 6 million able-bodied young people at the ready. Even
with a modest 10-hour-a-year requirement (the equivalent of two mornings a year) America would gain 60 million volunteer hours to invigorate
the nation's nonprofit organizations, churches, job corps, conservation
groups and college outreach programs.

And with some flexibility, it wouldn't have to be too onerous.
Colleges could give credit for service. That is, at the beginning of each
year, a student could opt for service, and in return he or she might get
credits equal to one class period. Perhaps every 25 hours of service could
be traded for one class credit, with a maximum of three credits a year.
What a student would learn from working in a shelter for the victims of
domestic abuse would surely equal or surpass his or her time spent in
racquetball class—at my college worth one full unit.

Alternatively, colleges could limit the service requirement to a student's junior year—a time when the students are settled and have more hours and stability in their schedules. Turning the junior year into a year when volunteering figures prominently could also help colleges bridge the chasm that usually stands between the academic world and the one that lies beyond it.

When Gov. Gray Davis of California proposed a service requirement in 1999, an editorial in The Daily Californian, the student newspaper at the University of California at Berkeley, opposed the plan: "Forced philanthropy will be as much an oxymoron in action as it is in terms. Who would want to receive community service from someone who is forced to serve? Is forced community service in California not generally reserved for criminals and delinquents?"

First of all, that's putting forth a pretty dim view of the soul of the average student. What, is the unwilling college volunteer going to *throw food* at visitors to the soup kitchen? Volunteering is by nature transformative—reluctant participants become quick converts every day, once they meet those who need their help.

Second, college is largely about fulfilling requirements, isn't it? Students have to complete this much work in the sciences, that much work in the arts. Incoming freshmen accept a tacit contract, submitting to the wisdom of the college's founders and shapers, who decide which experiences are necessary to create a well-rounded scholar, one ready to make a contribution to the world. But while colleges give their students the intellectual tools for life beyond campus, they largely ignore the part about how they might contribute to the world. That is, until the commencement speech, at which time all the "go forth's" and "be helpful's" happen.

But what if such a sentiment happened on the student's first day? What if graduating seniors already knew full well how to balance jobs, studies, family and volunteer work in the surrounding community? What if campuses were full of under-served high school students meeting with their college tutors? What if the tired and clogged veins of thousands of towns and cities had the energy of millions of college students coursing through them? What if the student who might have become a foosball power—and I say this knowing how much those skills have enhanced my life and those who had the good fortune to have watched me—became instead a lifelong volunteer? That might be pretty good for everybody.

Joining the Conversation: Critical Thinking and Writing

1. Eggers argues that colleges should consider instituting a service requirement for graduation. How does he support his argument? What kinds of evidence does he offer?

2. Overall, do you find Eggers's argument reasonable? Would a service requirement work in your college? Why, or why not?

3. Characterize the tone of Eggers's opening paragraph. Where else do you observe this tone? How does the tone serve (or undermine) the argument he offers?

4. Read (or reread) Stanley Fish's essay "Why We Built the Ivory Tower (page 349)." What do you imagine Fish's response to Eggers's argument would be? Where in Fish's essay do you find your evidence?

Patrick Allitt

Patrick Allitt, a professor of American history at Emory University, is the author of I'm a Teacher, You're a Student: A Semester in the University Classroom *(2005). We reprint an essay that first appeared in 2006 in the* Chronicle Review *section of the* Chronicle of Higher Education, *a weekly publication read chiefly by college teachers and administrators.*

Should Undergraduates Specialize?

I was a college freshman 32 years ago, in 1974. My daughter, Frances, is about to become a college freshman this fall. I went to the University of Oxford in England. She's going to Emory University in America, and her experience is going to be completely different. There are some obvious outward contrasts. I was a shabby pseudo-hippie with a tangle of crazy hair and no decent clothes. She's well dressed, groomed, and presentable. I had a fountain pen and a record player. She has a computer and an iPod.

The ideas and justifications surrounding these two college adventures differ sharply. I was a product of the British meritocratic system which, after World War II, had nationalized higher education. The governing idea was that intelligent people were a national asset and that the nation was investing wisely by educating them, no matter their social origins.

Every student's tuition was paid in full, and every student was given, in addition, a grant to cover living expenses, board and lodging. Only very wealthy Britons had to pay more than a token sum toward their children's college education. My three years at Oxford cost my parents a total of about $400. In those days, however, only a very small minority of British kids went to any kind of college. Most dropped out of school on the day of their 16th birthday, breathed a great sigh of relief, and never thought about education again.

The only criterion for British university admission then was academic. Oxford and Cambridge held their own entrance exams, interviewed

Patrick Allitt, "Should Undergraduates Specialize?" published in the *Chronicle of Higher Education*, June 16, 2006. Reprinted by permission of the author.

students who wrote good answers, and chose the best of the interviewees. My class at Hertford College, Oxford, consisted of 90 students, all of them academic achievers.

Right from the start, each of us studied, or "read," only one discipline; mine was history. Half my friends read in other academic disciplines: physics, biochemistry, English, French, and so on. The other half read in vocational disciplines like medicine, law, and engineering. Central to the entire system was early specialization. Even the broadest curriculum choice, PPE (Philosophy, Politics, and Economics), consisted of just three elements.

Learning was organized through the tutorial system. Every week I and one other student met our tutor. He had assigned a paper the previous week, and we had spent the time reading widely in the relevant literature. One of us read his paper aloud to begin the tutorial, then the tutor rubbished it and told us, in blistering detail, what we should have written, and how we should have interpreted the readings. The tutors didn't show any delicate concern for our feelings.

Frances, by contrast, is entering a decentralized system. Here the assumption is that the person who gets the education is going to be its chief beneficiary and that, accordingly, she should bear the cost. As a member of the great American middle class, she belongs to a generation whose parents have been fretting about the cost of higher education from the moment they beheld their newborns. Paying your way through Emory or its sisters in the American college big leagues is almost certain to cost more than $150,000. It's also a system in which half or more of her generation of 18-year-olds enroll in some kind of postsecondary institution; she'll be one of literally millions of freshmen this fall.

Criteria for admission are diverse. Doing well in high school is still a terrific idea, and, bless her heart, Frances has. But ever since seventh grade her teachers and counselors have nudged her to perform community service, play music and competitive sports, act, publish poems, edit magazines, do internships in hospitals, and in a dozen other ways be extracurricular to give her an edge in college applications. Being a legacy or (as in her case) the child of a professor certainly helps.

She will study the liberal arts. In practice that means a couple of science classes, a bit of math, a language, a social-science-methods course, a spot of history, some "health" (such as "Principles of Physical Education," which is the Emory meaning of PPE), something in the performing arts, and then the nine or 10 courses of a typical major. None of those courses will be vocational, but ideally they'll make her a well-rounded individual—mature, informed, and tolerant.

She will take classes containing from six to 100 students. Occasionally she'll have to write a paper, but she'll rarely have to read one aloud to her teacher. She'll be in discussion groups with professors and teaching assistants, all of whom have been trained in sensitivity and diversity. Counselors, tutors, and an array of considerate "campus life" helpers will surround her. After four years, she'll probably have to select a graduate school to pursue her vocation, buckling down there to more years of toil.

How do the two systems compare in the eyes of someone who has seen plenty of each? The great virtue of the British system, particularly the early specialization, was that it enabled us to learn one discipline really well, to become far more deeply engaged with it than was possible for our American counterparts. It gave a marvelous opportunity to students who already knew where they were going to pursue their ambitions without distraction. As an undergraduate, I was already studying historical theory and the philosophy of history, which here is deferred to graduate school.

Its great and equal drawback was that it forced some students to choose too soon, before they were ready. An old girlfriend thought she wanted to be a psychologist but decided after a year that it had been a terrible idea, and had to petition to switch into French, which detained her at college a year longer than the rest of us. The system assumed freshmen were grown-ups who knew their own minds. Anyone familiar with a crowd of 17- and 18-year-olds knows that assumption is not always dependable.

The great virtue of the American system is its breadth. How impressed I was, as a TA at Berkeley, to have undergraduates in my very first history discussion group mention a relevant insight from Freud that they had picked up in "Psych," or refer to Laffer Curves that they'd studied in "Econ." They made me feel a trifle narrow and parochial.

Then they handed in their papers and wrote their finals, and my feelings of inadequacy disappeared. The great American drawbacks revealed themselves: The students' writing was awful, and their knowledge utterly superficial. Their breadth was the breadth of rivers an inch deep. The experience also drove home to me the truth, verified hundreds of times since, that the study of history is simply far too difficult for most students.

There are pros and cons to both systems. Surely it's possible, now, to combine the merits of each rather than putting up with their weaknesses. I think more American colleges should offer the chance to specialize right from the outset to those students who want it. Bright young physicists who want only to study physics should be free to do so, without laboring through courses in art history that seem to them a waste of valuable time.

In the same way, students who already have a clear vocational objective at the age of 18 should be able to pursue it at top schools. My own experience showed that most law and medical students at Oxford *wanted* to get busy in preparation for the careers they had chosen, and were glad to be able to do so. (Incidentally, it didn't make them philistines; they enjoyed literature and read widely in other disciplines, just as I read plenty of great novels and a little science, even though I didn't take classes in those areas.)

15

At the same time, the vast American system can maintain the liberal-arts option for those who prefer it and don't yet have a clear sense of direction. Students with the right frame of mind thrive on studying diverse subjects until they're ready, sometimes at age 20 or older, to make a stronger commitment. But let's get rid of the idea that liberal arts is for everyone. America's commitment to equality and to universal education is noble and invigorating. But it shouldn't mean that one size fits all.

ℛ Joining the Conversation: Critical Thinking and Writing

1. When you first read Allitt's title, what was your response? After you read the article, did your response to the title change or remain the same?

2. Do you think that Allitt's first sentence is effective? Explain your answer. What about the first paragraph?

3. What is the most significant difference between the education that Allitt received and the one that his daughter Frances will soon receive at Emory University?

4. Allitt states that "there are pros and cons to both systems." In his view, what are they? Can you think of others?

5. Does Allitt consider an issue that you think about yourself? Are there other issues, bearing on your own education, that you believe are more important than this one?

Carol Geary Schneider and Ellis M. West

Letters Responding to Patrick Allitt

To the Editor:

Patrick Allitt is right to question whether common frameworks guiding American undergraduate education have outlived their usefulness ("Should Undergraduates Specialize?," *The Chronicle Review*, June 16). The alternatives he proposes, however—specialization for those who know what they want to study and liberal arts for the less focused—are both decidedly inadequate for today's students.

Letters to the editor by Carol Geary Schneider and Ellis M. West, published in the *Chronicle of Higher Education*, August 4, 2006. Reprinted by permission of the authors.

In a volatile, globally interdependent, and fast-changing world, everyone will need more liberal education, not less. But we need a new approach to the design of undergraduate liberal education, a design that takes full account of the needs of an innovation-fueled economy and an increasingly complex and globally interconnected society.

Today's college students should not be presented with a false choice between either vocational preparation or liberal-arts education defined as nonvocational personal development. It is time to embrace a far more purposeful approach to college that sets clear expectations for all students, cultivates the achievement of a set of essential skills and capacities, and enables every student to place his or her interests—including career aspirations—in the broader context of a complex and fast-changing world.

Students certainly should have every opportunity to pursue their interests in depth, and this pursuit can begin as early as the first year of college. But while doing so, they should also be working to develop strong intellectual and practical skills that can be transferred to new settings when the students or their fields move, as they surely will, in new and unexpected directions. Students should develop the ability to communicate clearly; to think through the ethical, civic, and intercultural issues relevant to their interests; and to locate those interests in a wide-ranging understanding of the world in which they live.

To prepare students well both for productive work and responsible   5
citizenship in a complex world, we need a new vision for liberal education that emphasizes inquiry and integration and transferability to learning, rather than narrow depth or shallow breadth.

Carol Geary Schneider
President
Association of American Colleges and Universities
Washington

To the Editor:

Breadth or depth? Patrick Allitt, using the British system as a model, makes a case for allowing some college students—those "who already have a clear vocational objective at the age of 18"—to start studying their chosen vocation, like law or medicine, at the beginning of their time in college. They would also be excused from having to take general-education courses such as "art history that seem to them a waste of valuable time." The traditional liberal-arts option—a breadth of courses—would be available to (but presumably not required of) only those students "who prefer it and don't yet have a clear sense of [vocational] direction."

Allitt's case, however, is fundamentally flawed because it is based on a false assumption—that the primary, if not sole, purpose of higher education is to train students in and for a particular vocation. If that were its purpose, then of course early specialization would make sense.... Allitt overlooks at least two other purposes of education that in America have been more important than vocational training and that have justified a broad, liberal-arts education.

The first of these purposes is to enable students to get their act together. In other words, a liberal-arts education has traditionally provided students an opportunity to decide what kind of persons they want to be—not just what kind of work they want to do. It forces them to confront the "big questions," as the Teagle Foundation likes to phrase it (see W. Robert Connor's "The Right Time and Place for Big Questions," *The Chronicle Review*, June 9), questions having to do with the purpose or meaning of their lives, including the moral values to which they should adhere.

The second traditional purpose of a liberal-arts education is closely related to the first—to prepare students to be good citizens in a free and democratic society. At a minimum, this means teaching them to be concerned about the public good, to respect the dignity and worth of all persons, and to be informed about our political system and public issues.

Other purposes of a liberal-arts education, such as cultivating a love of beauty, could also be mentioned. In short, as Aristotle argued centuries ago, because humans are spiritual, moral, political, and aesthetic beings, not just producers of goods and services, they should be encouraged, if not required, to study subjects that will help to make them genuinely happy.

Granted, more and more liberal-arts colleges seem to be less and less committed to those goals. Fewer courses are required for a degree; general-education requirements seem to be justified only to give as many departments as possible a piece of the action; and faculty members are concerned mainly with their own disciplines and areas of research and not with the overall education of their students. De facto specialization seems to be the name of the game.

Given this reality, perhaps Allitt can be excused for overlooking the traditional purposes of a higher education. I can only hope that Emory University, where his daughter will be a first-year student in the fall and which is one of my alma maters, has not forsaken these purposes.

Ellis M. West
Professor of Political Science
University of Richmond
Richmond, Va.

 Joining the Conversation:
Critical Thinking and Writing

1. With what do you agree and with what do you disagree in Schneider's letter? Put your reasoned responses in the form of a letter of 250 to 500 words to Schneider.

2. Imagine that Allitt wrote a letter of 250 to 500 words to West. Now write the letter.

Caitlin Petre

Caitlin Petre, a recent college graduate who is now a resident of New York City, published this essay in Newsweek *in 2006.*

The Lessons I Didn't Learn in College

To think there was once a time when I thought nailing the interview was the hardest part of getting a job. I recently applied to be a cocktail waitress at an upscale bowling alley in Manhattan. After a brief interview, the manager congratulated me, saying I'd be a great fit. It was only a momentary victory. She produced a sheaf of papers, and my stomach turned flips. I knew what was coming—the dreaded W-4. I'd filled them out before, for various summer jobs, but I'd always been exempted from taxes because I was a full-time student. Now that I had graduated from college, this was the first W-4 I had to complete fully.

The manager watched as I hesitated. "Are you having trouble?" she asked as I squinted at the tiny print. "Oh, no, I'm fine." I stared at the form, trying to figure out how many allowances to claim—or what an allowance was, for that matter. I didn't want to admit that I was stumped, so finally I just took a guess.

Later I asked my friends to shed some light on the matter, but none of them knew any more than I did. Instead, they advised me to do what they did: make it up and hope for the best. So much for being a well-educated college graduate.

Having taken seminars on government, I could hold forth on the relationship between taxation and the federal deficit but was clueless about filling out a basic tax form. I'd graduated with a B.A. in philosophy in May, and had decided against going straight to graduate school. But while countless newspapers claimed that the job market for graduates was the best it had been in years, I had no idea how to take advantage of it. I couldn't imagine myself in an entry-level administrative position staring at a spreadsheet for eight hours a day—partly because it sounded dull, but also because in college I had never learned how to use spreadsheet programs. Cocktail waitressing seemed like a good way to make ends meet.

My friends and I are graduates of Wesleyan, Barnard, Stanford and Yale. We've earned 3.9 GPAs and won academic awards. Yet none of us   5

---

knows what a Roth IRA is or can master a basic tax form. And heaven help us when April comes and we have to file tax returns.

My friends and I are incredibly lucky to have gotten the educations we have. But there's a discrepancy between what we learn in school and what we need to know for work, and there must be some way for universities to bridge this gap. They might, for example, offer classes in personal finance as part of the economics department. How about a class on renting an apartment? Granted, it might be hard to lure students to such mundane offerings, but the students who don't go will wish they had.

College students are graduating with greater debt than ever before, yet we haven't learned how to manage our money. We can wing it for only so long before employers start wising up to our real-world incompetence. In fact, they already are: a study released last month showed that hundreds of employers have found their college-graduate hires to be "woefully unprepared" for the job market.

All this raises a disturbing question: when I spent a ton of time and money on my fancy degree, what exactly was I buying? The ability to think, some might say. OK, fine, that's important. Still, my résumé would look odd if it read, "Skills: proficient in French, word processing, thinking." The thinking I did in college seems to be of limited utility in the "real world." The fact that I wrote a 30-page critical analysis of the function of shame in society did nothing to ease the sting when I spilled beer on a customer at the bowling alley.

That's not the only time I've found my education incompatible with real life. I had trouble getting used to my new uniform, which consists of a supershort '50s-style bowling skirt, boots and fishnet stockings. As I changed into it for the first time, I had a vision of the feminist philosophers I had read in college hovering over me, shaking their heads disapprovingly.

But it wasn't long before I began to see that the short skirt played a   10
role in boosting my tips—a definite plus now that I was trying to rent an apartment, feed myself and buy the occasional book or new toothbrush.

So which to live by: the philosophers or the skirt? I'm trying to fashion some combination, one that allows me to retain my principles without having to file for bankruptcy. After all, the last thing I want is to be confronted with more confusing government paperwork.

Joining the Conversation:
Critical Thinking and Writing

1. In paragraph 5 Petre says that she and her friends are college graduates but "none of us knows what a Roth IRA is or can master a basic tax form." Do you assume that the colleges are at fault for Petre's and her friends' ignorance on these matters? Should instruction in such matters be required? Be available—for college credit—but not required? Or what?

2. In paragraph 7 Petre says that college students "haven't learned how to manage [their] money." If this statement is true, whose fault is it? The students? Their families? The colleges?

3. In paragraph 8 Petre asks herself about the money she spent on her degree: "What exactly was I buying?" What are you buying at college? Is "buying" too commercial a word, or is it the most accurate word?

4. If you found this essay interesting, try to account for some of the strategies Petre uses. For example, what tone does she adopt? How heavily does she rely on concrete examples? How does she manage to talk a good deal about herself and yet not sound overly self-centered?

Langston Hughes

Langston Hughes (1902–1967) was born in Joplin, Missouri. He lived part of his youth in Mexico, spent a year at Columbia University, served as a merchant seaman, and worked in a Paris nightclub. After returning to the United States, he showed some of his poems to Dr. Alain Locke, a strong advocate of African American literature. Hughes went on to publish poetry, fiction, plays, essays, and biographies.

Theme for English B

The instructor said,

> *Go home and write*
> *a page tonight!*
> *And let that page come out of you—*
> *Then, it will be true.*   5

I wonder if it's that simple?

I am twenty-two, colored, born in Winston-Salem.
I went to school there, then Durham, then here
to his college on the hill above Harlem.
I am the only colored student in my class.   10
The steps from the hill lead down into Harlem,
through a park, then I cross St. Nicholas,
Eighth Avenue, Seventh, and I come to the Y,
the Harlem Branch Y, where I take the elevator
up to my room, sit down, and write this page: 15

It's not easy to know what is true for you or me
at twenty-two, my age. But I guess I'm what
I feel and see and hear, Harlem, I hear you:
hear you, hear me—we two—you, me, talk on this page.
(I hear New York, too.) Me—who?   20

Well, I like to eat, sleep, drink, and be in love.
I like to work, read, learn, and understand life.
I like a pipe for a Christmas present,
or records—Bessie,[1] bop, or Bach.
I guess being colored doesn't make me *not* like   25
the same things other folks like who are other races.

So will my page be colored that I write?
Being me, it will not be white.
But it will be
a part of you, instructor.   30

You are white—
yet a part of me, as I am a part of you.
That's American.
Sometimes perhaps you don't want to be a part of me.
Nor do I often want to be a part of you.   35
But we are, that's true!
As I learn from you,
I guess you learn from me—
although you're older—and white—
and somewhat more free.   40

This is my page for English B.

 ## Joining the Conversation:
Critical Thinking and Writing

1. Look up all of the references to places, persons, and things in this poem. What does this knowledge contribute to your understanding of the poem?

2. The instructor's advice sounds good. Why, then, does the speaker question it? Do you agree with the speaker, or do you think he is being oversensitive?

3. Does Hughes present an argument in this poem? If you believe he does *not*, explain. If you believe he does, summarize the argument in your own words. What is the difference, if any, between presenting this argument in a poem and presenting it in prose?

[1]*Bessie*: Bessie Smith (1898?–1937), African American blues singer.

4. A student said to us that when she first read "Theme for English B," it struck her as an "angry" poem. Is there evidence in the text that supports her response? Can you locate evidence that suggests her response might be mistaken or incomplete? If you had to sum up the poem in a single word, what would this word be?

5. In your high school courses, were you always accepted as an equal? What about in your college courses? Explain, perhaps with the help of a specific story or anecdote or two.

6. What does the speaker mean when he says, "That's American"? Do you agree with his claim? In a paragraph, define what it means to be "American." Do you find this to be a hard task or an easy one?

A Casebook on Testing and Grading

Paul Goodman

Paul Goodman (1911–72) received his bachelor's degree from City College in New York and his Ph.D. from the University of Chicago. He taught in several colleges and universities, and he was a prolific writer on literature, politics, and education. Goodman's view that students were victims of a corrupt society made him especially popular on campuses—even in the 1960s when students tended to distrust anyone over thirty. "A Proposal to Abolish Grading" (editors' title) is an extract from Compulsory Mis-Education and the Community of Scholars *(1966).*

A Proposal to Abolish Grading

Let half a dozen of the prestigious Universities—Chicago, Stanford, the Ivy League—abolish grading, and use testing only and entirely for pedagogic purposes as teachers see fit.

Anyone who knows the frantic temper of the present schools will understand the transvaluation of values that would be effected by this modest innovation. For most of the students, the competitive grade has come to be the essence. The naïve teacher points to the beauty of the subject and the ingenuity of the research; the shrewd student asks if he is responsible for that on the final exam.

Let me at once dispose of an objection whose unanimity is quite fascinating. I think that the great majority of professors agree that grading hinders teaching and creates a bad spirit, going as far as cheating and plagiarizing.

Paul Goodman, "A Proposal to Abolish Grading," *Compulsory Mis-Education,* Horizon Press, 1964. Reprinted by permission.

I have before me the collection of essays, *Examining in Harvard College,* and this is the consensus. It is uniformly asserted, however, that the grading is inevitable; for how else will the graduate schools, the foundations, the corporations *know* whom to accept, reward, hire? How will the talent scouts know whom to tap?

By testing the applicants, of course, according to the specific task-requirements of the inducting institution, just as applicants for the Civil Service or for licenses in medicine, law, and architecture are tested. Why should Harvard professors do the testing *for* corporations and graduate-schools?

The objection is ludicrous. Dean Whitla, of the Harvard Office of Tests, points out that the scholastic-aptitude and achievement tests used for *admission* to Harvard are a super-excellent index for all-around Harvard performance, better than high-school grades or particular Harvard course-grades. Presumably, these college-entrance tests are tailored for what Harvard and similar institutions want. By the same logic, would not an employer do far better to apply his own job-aptitude test rather than to rely on the vagaries of Harvard sectionmen. Indeed, I doubt that many employers bother to look at such grades; they are more likely to be interested merely in the fact of a Harvard diploma, whatever that connotes to them. The grades have most of their weight with the graduate schools— here, as elsewhere, the system runs mainly for its own sake.

It is really necessary to remind our academics of the ancient history of Examination. In the medieval university, the whole point of the gruelling trial of the candidate was whether or not to accept him as a peer. His disputation and lecture for the Master's was just that, a masterpiece to enter the guild. It was not to make comparative evaluations. It was not to weed out and select for an extra-mural licensor or employer. It was certainly not to pit one young fellow against another in an ugly competition. My philosophic impression is that the medievals thought they knew what a good job of work was and that we are competitive because we do not know. But the more status is achieved by largely irrelevant competitive evaluation, the less will we ever know.

(Of course, our American examinations never did have this purely guild orientation, just as our faculties have rarely had absolute autonomy; the examining was to satisfy Overseers, Elders, distant Regents—and they as paternal superiors have always doted on giving grades, rather than accepting peers. But I submit that this set-up itself makes it impossible for the student to *become* a master, to *have* grown up, and to commence on his own. He will always be making A or B for some overseer. And in the present atmosphere, he will always be climbing on his friend's neck.)

Perhaps the chief objectors to abolishing grading would be the students and their parents. The parents should be simply disregarded; their anxiety has done enough damage already. For the students, it seems to me that a primary duty of the university is to deprive them of their props, their dependence on extrinsic valuation and motivation, and to force them to confront the difficult enterprise itself and finally lose themselves in it.

A miserable effect of grading is to nullify the various uses of testing. Testing, for both student and teacher, is a means of structuring, and also of finding out what is blank or wrong and what has been assimilated and can be taken for granted. Review—including high-pressure review—is a means of bringing together the fragments, so that there are flashes of synoptic insight.

There are several good reasons for testing, and kinds of test. But if the aim is to discover weakness, what is the point of down-grading and punishing it, and thereby inviting the student to conceal his weakness, by faking and bulling, if not cheating? The natural conclusion of synthesis is the insight itself, not a grade for having had it. For the important purpose of placement, if one can establish in the student the belief that one is testing *not* to grade and make invidious comparisons but for his own advantage, the student should normally seek his own level, where he is challenged and yet capable, rather than trying to get by. If the student dares to accept himself as he is, a teacher's grade is a crude instrument compared with a student's self-awareness. But it is rare in our universities that students are encouraged to notice objectively their vast confusion. Unlike Socrates, our teachers rely on power-drives rather than shame and ingenuous idealism.

Many students are lazy, so teachers try to goad or threaten them by grading. In the long run this must do more harm than good. Laziness is a character-defense. It may be a way of avoiding learning, in order to protect the conceit that one is already perfect (deeper, the despair that one *never* can). It may be a way of avoiding just the risk of failing and being down-graded. Sometimes it is a way of politely saying, "I won't." But since it is the authoritarian grown-up demands that have created such attitudes in the first place, why repeat the trauma? There comes a time when we must treat people as adult, laziness and all. It is one thing courageously to fire a do-nothing out of your class; it is quite another thing to evaluate him with a lordly F.

Most important of all, it is often obvious that balking in doing the work, especially among bright young people who get to great universities, means exactly what it says: The work does not suit me, not this subject, or not at this time, or not in this school, or not in school altogether. The student might not be bookish; he might be school-tired; perhaps his development ought now to take another direction. Yet unfortunately, if such a student is intelligent and is not sure of himself, he *can* be bullied into passing, and this obscures everything. My hunch is that I am describing a common situation. What a grim waste of young life and teacherly effort! Such a student will retain nothing of what he has "passed" in. Sometimes he must get mononucleosis to tell his story and be believed.

And ironically, the converse is also probably commonly true. A student flunks and is mechanically weeded out, who is really ready and eager to learn in a scholastic setting, but he has not quite caught on. A good teacher can recognize the situation, but the computer wreaks its will.

 ## Joining the Conversation: Critical Thinking and Writing

1. In his opening paragraph Goodman limits his suggestion about grading and testing to "half a dozen of the prestigious Universities." Does he offer any reason for this limitation? Can you?

2. In paragraph 3 Goodman says that "the great majority of professors agree that grading hinders teaching." What evidence does he offer to support this claim? What arguments might be made that grading assists teaching? Should Goodman have made them?

3. As a student, have grades helped you to learn, or have grades hindered you? Explain.

4. If you have been a student in an ungraded course, describe the course and evaluate the experience.

Diane Ravitch

Diane Ravitch has taught history and education at Teachers College, Columbia University, and has served as Assistant Secretary of Education. Her book Left Back: A Century of Failed School Reforms *was published in 2000. The following essay was originally published in* Time *(September 11, 2000).*

In Defense of Testing

No one wants to be tested. We would all like to get a driver's license without answering questions about right of way or showing that we can parallel park a car. Many future lawyers and doctors probably wish they could join their profession without taking an exam.

But tests and standards are a necessary fact of life. They protect us—most of the time—from inept drivers, hazardous products, and shoddy professionals. In schools too, exams play a constructive role. They tell public officials whether new school programs are making a difference and where new investments are likely to pay off. They tell teachers what their students have learned—and have not. They tell parents how their children are doing compared with others their age. They encourage students to exert more effort.

It is important to recall that for most of this century, educators used intelligence tests to decide which children should get a high-quality education. The point of IQ testing was to find out how much children were capable of learning rather than to test what they had actually learned. Based on IQ scores, millions of children were assigned to dumbed-down programs instead of solid courses in science, math, history, literature, and foreign languages.

This history reminds us that tests should be used to improve education, not ration it. Every child should have access to a high-quality education. Students should have full opportunity to learn what will be tested; otherwise their test scores will merely reflect whether they come from an educated family.

In the past few years, we have seen the enormous benefits that flow   5
to disadvantaged students because of the information provided by state tests. Those who fall behind are now getting extra instruction in after-school classes and summer programs. In their efforts to improve student performance, states are increasing teachers' salaries, testing new teachers, and insisting on better teacher education.

Good tests should include a mix of essay, problem-solving, short-answer, and even some multiple-choice questions. On math quizzes, students should be able to show how they arrived at their answer. The tests widely used today often rely too much on multiple-choice questions, which encourage guessing rather than thinking. Also, they frequently ignore the importance of knowledge. Today's history tests, for example, seldom expect the student to know any history—sometimes derided as "mere facts"—but only to be able to read charts, graphs, and cartoons.

Performance in education means the mastery of both knowledge and skills. This is why it is reasonable to test teachers to make sure they know their subject matter, as well as how to teach it to young children. And this is why it is reasonable to assess whether students are ready to advance to the next grade or graduate from high school. To promote students who cannot read or do math is no favor to them. It is like pushing them into a deep pool before they have learned to swim. If students need extra time and help, they should get it, but they won't unless we first carefully assess what they have learned.

Joining the Conversation: Critical Thinking and Writing

1. In paragraph 2 Ravitch says of tests that "they tell teachers what their students have learned—and have not." Thinking back on tests you took in school, to what extent do you agree with Ravitch's assertion? Do you agree with her claim that tests "encourage students to exert more effort"? Is that true of you?

2. In paragraph 4 Ravitch seems to link testing to her assertion that "every child should have access to a high-quality education." Do you believe that testing and improving education are linked? Explain.

3. In paragraph 6 Ravitch says that history tests "seldom expect the student to know any history." What history courses did you take in high school? To what extent did the tests you took support Ravitch's claim?

4. In paragraph 7 Ravitch asserts that "it is reasonable to test teachers to make sure they know their subject matter, as well as how to teach it to young children." In your schools were teachers ever tested? If not, do you think that testing your teachers would have led to improvement in your education? What measures other than testing are there to assess the competence of teachers?

Joy Alonso

Until her retirement in 2004, Joy Alonso taught Spanish language and literature in high schools, community colleges, and four-year colleges. Her experience is therefore unusually varied. We reprint a talk that she gave at Tufts University in 2004.

Two Cheers for Examinations

First, I must say that my title is borrowed from E. M. Forster's collection of essays. I am speaking about an academic topic, to an audience of students and teachers, and I don't want to be accused of plagiarism.

Second, I want to tell a joke, a joke that I believe is highly relevant to our topic, "The Role of Examinations in College Courses." A father visited the college where he had been a student, and where his daughter was now a student. They happened to encounter an instructor who some twenty years earlier had taught the father and who last year had taught the daughter. The father said, sincerely, that he had greatly enjoyed the course and that his daughter had raved to him about the course, but he confessed that he was greatly disappointed in one respect. "The questions on the examination you gave to my daughter's class were exactly the same as the ones you gave to my class twenty years ago." "Ah, yes," the professor explained, "the questions are the same, but we have changed the answers."

A joke, but with a good deal of truth in it. No one can doubt the truth with reference to courses in the sciences. I have heard that a distinguished professor at a medical school begins his lectures by telling his students,

"Half of what we are teaching you will, in twenty years, be disproved. The trouble is, we don't know which half." But even in the humanities and in the social sciences it is evident, at least to those who have been teaching the subjects for a couple of decades, that things change, that new knowledge makes us look differently at the works and issues that we studied when we were students.

What are the purposes of examinations? I think most people will agree that examinations have a dual purpose: to test or measure achievement, and to stimulate learning. The first purpose serves the interests of those who want to evaluate the student, perhaps for honors within the college, for admission to a graduate or professional school, or for employment. This purpose, this business of measuring students, may even serve the students themselves or their parents, who are interested in knowing how things seem to be going, where the students stand. I take this last point seriously; many students need reassurance that they are doing just fine. I suppose I should also mention, while speaking about tests as an instrument of measuring, that tests measure the *teachers* too; they measure how well we have taught. But this is not relevant to our topic today, which is the pros and cons of tests in two- and four-year colleges.

The second purpose of a test is to stimulate learning. On the most obvious level, a vocabulary quiz or a quiz on a reading assignment forces the student to do the necessary work before the quiz. The usual metaphor is that such a test is a police measure, a device that forces the student to obey the law, in this case to master (at least to some degree) the assigned work. I don't think this is a bad thing. Yes, it would be better if all students at all times eagerly turned to their studies without any sort of compulsion, but none of us is cut from this sort of cloth. We all have lots of pressures on us, and inevitably we neglect some things—even things that we want to do—unless deadlines are imposed. A quiz tomorrow morning is a sort of deadline, a deadline that makes busy students turn for an hour or two to the assigned reading.

But when I say that tests stimulate learning, I am also thinking of something larger than this. Quizzes tend to test only details—the meanings of certain words, the uses of the subjunctive, the dates of certain events, and so forth. Midterm examinations and especially final examinations help a student to see how details may connect. In studying for examinations, a student begins to see not just the trees but the forest. The student has perhaps taken a quiz that established whether he or she had read the assigned novel—Who did what to whom?—but not until the student prepares for the final examination does the student achieve an overview, partly by reviewing notes and readings, partly by trying to anticipate examination questions, perhaps by discussing the course with fellow-students in a study group, and in any case by thinking about what the course adds up to. And finally, when the student actually faces the questions on the exam and responds thoughtfully to them, he or she is likely to experience a gratifying sense of accomplishment, an intellectual high.

5

I won't go so far as to say that students like examinations, but I will claim that many students experience a sense of exhilaration when the ordeal is over, when, so to speak, the initiation rite is completed and they justifiably feel that they have achieved something, they know things (at least for the moment) that they hadn't known they knew. They have met the challenge, risen to the occasion, learned (among other things) that they can do pretty well when it comes to the test—and the effort was worthwhile. Perhaps here I should say that in most of my courses, where there were several assigned papers and a midterm examination, I assured students that the final examination would count heavily if they did well, but if their grade on the final was notably lower than the average of their papers and midterm, it would count only as one unit in computing the average. I believe this system encouraged students to take the final seriously, but it protected the very rare student whose final examination was for some unfathomable reason far below his or her earlier work.

Why did I regularly put more emphasis on the final examination than on papers on topics that the students select? I did indeed assign several papers, of varying lengths, in my literature courses, but papers usually are on a relatively limited topic, rarely allowing for more than a comparison of two works. Students can write excellent papers on how the Elizabethans may have regarded the ghost in *Hamlet*, or how a director today might stage the scenes with the ghost, or they might write on, say, Shakespeare's use of prose in *Hamlet*: "Why does Hamlet sometimes speak verse, and sometimes prose?" And does Hamlet's prose differ from other prose in the play? These are worthy topics; students will learn a great deal about the play by working on them—but even the student who in a course in Shakespeare's Tragedies has written three such essays will not achieve an overview of the topic such as is afforded by studying for a final examination.

The title of my talk is "Two Cheers for Examinations." Why not three cheers? Because I know that there are drawbacks to examinations. Examinations can indeed deal with trivia, they can be badly conceived and thus can cause needless anxiety in the students who struggle to make sense out of poorly-written or poorly-focused questions.

Most damaging of all, perhaps, is the fact that professors are human beings and therefore they will sometimes grade examinations unfairly. Probably very few instructors are knowingly unfair, but an instructor who grades a paper at 8:00 p.m. is not quite the same person when he or she is grading at midnight. My own practice—an effort to guard against the unfairness that may be inherent in reading dozens of papers, one after the other, was to grade the first question on all the papers, then, when I had graded all of the responses to the first question, I turned to the second, and so on, in an effort to make certain that no student had the bad luck of being the first to be graded, when I might be more demanding, and no student had the bad luck to be the last to be graded, when I may have run out of patience. Still, even this system could not insure that I was fair to those papers that were barely legible.

10

I confess that I often found grading examination to be a tedious job, but I must also add that the examinations were often a learning-experience for me as well as for the students. How and why? In preparing the questions for the examination I had to think about the course as a whole, and I tried to construct questions that would help students to make connections, to go beyond the details of each day's assignment. And in reading the essays, I learned something about my failures, *my* failures, not the students'; some of the responses let me see where I had not been clear, or perhaps even where I had been misleading. On the whole, however, after reading all of the essays I felt pretty good, I felt something of the satisfaction that I hope students felt after they finished writing their examinations. It's been a lot of effort, thought, but it was worth it.

As for me, now that I am retired, well, I am preparing for my Final Examination.

Joining the Conversation: Critical Thinking and Writing

1. Alonso does not discuss take-home examinations. What are the advantages (if any) and disadvantages (if any) of this form of examination?

2. In your view, what are the advantages (if any) and disadvantages (if any) of timed examinations (i.e., of in-class examinations that run for a specific number of minutes)?

3. If you were in the audience when Alonso gave her talk, what two questions might you raise during the discussion period that followed the talk?

Work and Play

Short Views

Work and play are words used to describe the same thing under differing conditions.

    Mark Twain

The Battle of Waterloo was won on the playing fields of Eton.

    Attributed to the Duke of Wellington

Personally, I have nothing against work, particularly when performed, quietly and unobtrusively, by someone else. I just don't happen to think it's an appropriate subject for an "ethic."

    Barbara Ehrenreich

My young men shall never work. Men who work cannot dream, and wisdom comes in dreams.

    Smohalla, of the Nez Perce

Everyone who is prosperous or successful must have dreamed of something. It is not because he is a good worker that he is prosperous, but because he dreamed.

    Lost Star, of the Maricopa

The possible quantity of play depends on the possible quantity of pay.

    John Ruskin

Winning is not the most important thing; it's everything.

    Vince Lombardi

Serious sport has nothing to do with fair play. It is bound up with hatred, jealousy, boastfulness, disregard of all rules and sadistic pleasure in witnessing violence: in other words, it is war minus the shooting.

    George Orwell

The maturity of man—that means to have reacquired the seriousness that one has as a child at play.
> *Friedrich Nietzsche*

I see great things in baseball. It's our game—the American game.
It will take our people out-of-doors, fill them with oxygen, give
them a larger physical stoicism. Tend to relieve us from being a
nervous, dyspeptic set. Repair these losses, and be a blessing to us.
> *Walt Whitman*

[Baseball is] great because it has no clock. You can play forever.
You can't kill that clock or run a few plays up the middle as you
can do in the other sports.

    It's great because it is a sport of rigid, complex rules, but every
field is unique. No park is the same, and no other sport can make
that claim.

    It's great because you can do things in foul territory; you can
win a game, you can lose a game, outside the field.

    It's great because it not only follows the rhythms of the seasons
but it is as much about loss as it is about winning. The greatest
baseball players fail seven times out of ten.

    It's great because you can't go to your best player every time as
you can in other sports. Even Babe Ruth came up only once every
nine times.
> *Ken Burns*

The boys throw stones at the frogs in sport, but the frogs die not
in sport but in earnest.
> *Bion*

Bertrand Russell

Bertrand Russell (1872–1970) was educated at Trinity College, Cambridge. He published his first book, The Study of German Social Democracy, *in 1896; subsequent books on mathematics and on philosophy quickly established his international reputation. His pacifist opposition to World War I cost him his appointment at Trinity College and won him a prison sentence of six months. While serving this sentence he wrote his* Introduction to Mathematical Philosophy. *In 1940 an appointment to teach at the College of the City of New York was withdrawn because of his unorthodox moral views. But he was not always treated shabbily; he won numerous awards, including (in 1950) a Nobel Prize. After World War II, he devoted most of his energy to warning the world about the dangers of nuclear war.*

In reading the first sentence of the essay that we reprint, you should know that the essay comes from the book The Conquest of Happiness, *published in 1930.*

Work

Whether work should be placed among the causes of happiness or among the causes of unhappiness may perhaps be regarded as a doubtful question. There is certainly much work which is exceedingly irksome, and an excess of work is always very painful. I think, however, that, provided work is not excessive in amount, even the dullest work is to most people less painful than idleness. There are in work all grades, from mere relief of tedium up to the profoundest delights, according to the nature of the work and the abilities of the worker. Most of the work that most people have to do is not in itself interesting, but even such work has certain great advantages. To begin with, it fills a good many hours of the day without the need of deciding what one shall do. Most people, when they are left free to fill their own time according to their own choice, are at a loss to think of anything sufficiently pleasant to be worth doing. And whatever they decide on, they are troubled by the feeling that something else would have been pleasanter. To be able to fill leisure intelligently is the last product of civilization, and at present very few people have reached this level. Moreover the exercise of choice is in itself tiresome. Except to people with unusual initiative it is positively agreeable to be told what to do at each hour of the day, provided the orders are not too unpleasant. Most of the idle rich suffer unspeakable boredom as the price of their freedom from drudgery. At times, they may find relief by hunting big game in Africa, or by flying round the world, but the number of such sensations is limited, especially after youth is past. Accordingly the more intelligent rich men work nearly as hard as if they were poor, while rich women for the most part keep themselves busy with innumerable trifles of whose earth-shaking importance they are firmly persuaded.

Work therefore is desirable, first and foremost, as a preventive of boredom, for the boredom that a man feels when he is doing necessary though uninteresting work is as nothing in comparison with the boredom that he feels when he has nothing to do with his days. With this advantage of work another is associated, namely that it makes holidays much more delicious when they come. Provided a man does not have to work so hard as to impair his vigor, he is likely to find far more zest in his free time than an idle man could possibly find.

The second advantage of most paid work and of some unpaid work is that it gives chances of success and opportunities for ambition. In most work success is measured by income, and while our capitalistic society continues, this is inevitable. It is only where the best work is concerned that this measure ceases to be the natural one to apply. The desire that men feel to increase their income is quite as much a desire for success as for the extra comforts that a higher income can procure. However dull work may be, it becomes bearable if it is a means of building up a reputation, whether in the world at large or only in one's own circle. Continuity of purpose is one of the most essential ingredients of happiness in the long run, and for most men this comes chiefly through their work. In this respect those women whose lives are occupied with housework are much less fortunate than men, or than women who work outside the home. The domesticated wife does not receive wages, has no means of bettering herself, is taken for granted by her husband (who sees practically nothing of what she does), and is valued by him not for her housework but for quite other qualities. Of course this does not apply to those women who are sufficiently well-to-do to make beautiful houses and beautiful gardens and become the envy of their neighbors; but such women are comparatively few, and for the great majority housework cannot bring as much satisfaction as work of other kinds brings to men and to professional women.

The satisfaction of killing time and of affording some outlet, however modest, for ambition, belongs to most work, and is sufficient to make even a man whose work is dull happier on the average than a man who has no work at all. But when work is interesting, it is capable of giving satisfaction of a far higher order than mere relief from tedium. The kinds of work in which there is some interest may be arranged in a hierarchy. I shall begin with those which are only mildly interesting and end with those that are worthy to absorb the whole energies of a great man.

Two chief elements make work interesting; first, the exercise of skill,   5
and second, construction.

Every man who has acquired some unusual skill enjoys exercising it until it has become a matter of course, or until he can no longer improve himself. This motive to activity begins in early childhood: a boy who can stand on his head becomes reluctant to stand on his feet. A great deal of work gives the same pleasure that is to be derived from games of skill. The work of a lawyer or a politician must contain in a more delectable form a great deal of the same pleasure that is to be derived from playing bridge.

Here of course there is not only the exercise of skill but the outwitting of a skilled opponent. Even where this competitive element is absent, however, the performance of difficult feats is agreeable. A man who can do stunts in an aeroplane finds the pleasure so great that for the sake of it he is willing to risk his life. I imagine that an able surgeon, in spite of the painful circumstances in which his work is done, derives satisfaction from the exquisite precision of his operations. The same kind of pleasure, though in a less intense form, is to be derived from a great deal of work of a humbler kind. All skilled work can be pleasurable, provided the skill required is either variable or capable of indefinite improvement. If these conditions are absent, it will cease to be interesting when a man has acquired his maximum skill. A man who runs three-mile races will cease to find pleasure in this occupation when he passes the age at which he can beat his own previous record. Fortunately there is a very considerable amount of work in which new circumstances call for new skill and a man can go on improving, at any rate until he has reached middle age. In some kinds of skilled work, such as politics, for example, it seems that men are at their best between sixty and seventy, the reason being that in such occupations a wide experience of other men is essential. For this reason successful politicians are apt to be happier at the age of seventy than any other men of equal age. Their only competitors in this respect are the men who are the heads of big businesses.

There is, however, another element possessed by the best work, which is even more important as a source of happiness than is the exercise of skill. This is the element of constructiveness. In some work, though by no means in most, something is built up which remains as a monument when the work is completed. We may distinguish construction from destruction by the following criterion. In construction the initial state of affairs is comparatively haphazard, while the final state of affairs embodies a purpose: in destruction the reverse is the case; the initial state of affairs embodies a purpose, while the final state of affairs is haphazard, that is to say, all that is intended by the destroyer is to produce a state of affairs which does not embody a certain purpose. This criterion applies in the most literal and obvious case, namely the construction and destruction of buildings. In constructing a building a previously made plan is carried out, whereas in destroying it no one decides exactly how the materials are to lie when the demolition is complete. Destruction is of course necessary very often as a preliminary to subsequent construction; in that case it is part of a whole which is constructive. But not infrequently a man will engage in activities of which the purpose is destructive without regard to any construction that may come after. Frequently he will conceal this from himself by the belief that he is only sweeping away in order to build afresh, but it is generally possible to unmask this pretense, when it is a pretense, by asking him what the subsequent construction is to be. On this subject it will be found that he will speak vaguely and without enthusiasm, whereas on the preliminary destruction he has spoken precisely and with zest. This applies to not a few revolutionaries and militarists and other apostles of violence. They are actuated, usually without their own knowledge, by hatred: the destruction of what they hate is their real purpose, and they are comparatively indifferent to the question what is to come after it. Now I cannot deny that in the work of destruction as in the work of construction there may be joy. It is a fiercer joy, perhaps at moments more intense, but it is less profoundly satisfying, since the result is one in which little satisfaction is to be found. You kill your enemy, and when he is dead your occupation is gone, and the satisfaction that you derive from victory quickly fades. The work of construction, on the other hand, when completed is delightful to contemplate, and moreover is never so fully completed that there is nothing further to do about it. The most satisfactory purposes are those that lead on indefinitely from one success to another without ever coming to a dead end; and in this respect it will be found that construction is a greater source of happiness than destruction. Perhaps it would be more correct to say that those who find satisfaction in construction find in it greater satisfaction than the lovers of destruction can find in destruction, for if once you have become filled with hate you will not easily derive from construction the pleasure which another man would derive from it.

At the same time few things are so likely to cure the habit of hatred as the opportunity to do constructive work of an important kind.

The satisfaction to be derived from success in a great constructive enterprise is one of the most massive that life has to offer, although unfortunately in its highest forms it is open only to men of exceptional ability. Nothing can rob a man of the happiness of successful achievement in an important piece of work, unless it be the proof that after all his work was bad. There are many forms of such satisfaction. The man who by a scheme of irrigation has caused the wilderness to blossom like the rose enjoys it in one of its most tangible forms. The creation of an organization may be a work of supreme importance. So is the work of those few statesmen who have devoted their lives to producing order out of chaos, of whom Lenin is the supreme type in our day. The most obvious examples are artists and men of science. Shakespeare says of his verse: "So long as men can breathe, or eyes can see, so long lives this." And it cannot be doubted that the thought consoled him for misfortune. In his sonnets he maintains that the thought of his friend reconciled him to life, but I cannot help suspecting that the sonnets he wrote to his friend were even more effective for this purpose than the friend himself. Great artists and great men of science do work which is in itself delightful; while they are doing it, it secures them the respect of those whose respect is worth having, which gives them the most fundamental kind of power, namely power over men's thoughts and feelings. They have also the most solid reasons for thinking well of themselves. This combination of fortunate circumstances ought, one would think, to be enough to make any man happy. Nevertheless it is not so. Michelangelo, for example, was a profoundly unhappy man, and maintained (not, I am sure, with truth) that he would not have troubled to produce works of art if he had not had to pay the debts of his impecunious relations. The power to produce great art is very often, though by no means always, associated with a temperamental unhappiness, so great that but for the joy which the artist derives from his work, he would be driven to suicide. We cannot, therefore, maintain that even the greatest work must make a man happy; we can only maintain that it must make him less unhappy. Men of science, however, are far less often temperamentally unhappy than artists are, and in the main the men who do great work in science are happy men, whose happiness is derived primarily from their work.

One of the causes of unhappiness among intellectuals in the present day is that so many of them, especially those whose skill is literary, find no opportunity for the independent exercise of their talents, but have to hire themselves out to rich corporations directed by Philistines, who insist upon their producing what they themselves regard as pernicious nonsense. If you were to inquire among journalists in either England or America whether they believed in the policy of the newspaper for which they worked, you would find, I believe, that only a small minority do so; the rest, for the sake of a livelihood, prostitute their skill to purposes which they believe to be harmful. Such work cannot bring any real satisfaction, and in the course of reconciling himself to the doing of it, a man has to make himself so cynical that he can no longer derive whole-hearted satisfaction from anything whatever. I cannot condemn men who undertake work of this sort, since starvation is too serious an alternative, but I think that where it is possible to do work that is satisfactory to a man's constructive impulses without entirely starving, he will be well advised from the point of view of his own happiness if he chooses it in preference to work much more highly paid but not seeming to him worth doing on its own account. Without self-respect genuine happiness is scarcely possible. And the man who is ashamed of his work can hardly achieve self-respect.

The satisfaction of constructive work, though it may, as things are, be the privilege of a minority, can nevertheless be the privilege of a quite large minority. Any man who is his own master in his work can feel it; so can any man whose work appears to him useful and requires considerable skill. The production of satisfactory children is a difficult constructive work capable of affording profound satisfaction. Any woman who has achieved this can feel that as a result of her labor the world contains something of value which it would not otherwise contain.

Human beings differ profoundly in regard to the tendency to regard their lives as a whole. To some men it is natural to do so, and essential to happiness to be able to do so with some satisfaction. To others life is a series of detached incidents without directed movement and without unity. I think the former sort are more likely to achieve happiness than the latter, since they will gradually build up those circumstances from which they can derive contentment and self-respect, whereas the others will be blown about by the winds of circumstances now this way, now that, without ever arriving at any haven. The habit of viewing life as a whole is an

10

essential part both of wisdom and of true morality, and is one of the things which ought to be encouraged in education. Consistent purpose is not enough to make life happy, but it is an almost indispensable condition of a happy life. And consistent purpose embodies itself mainly in work.

 ## Joining the Conversation: Critical Thinking and Writing

1. Russell says (paragraph 3): "The desire that men feel to increase their income is quite as much a desire for success as for the extra comforts that a higher income can procure." In its context, what does *success* mean? In your experience, do Russell's words ring true? Why or why not?

2. In paragraphs 7–11 Russell develops a contrast between what he calls "destructive" and "constructive" work. Is the contrast clarified by the examples he offers? What examples from your own experience or knowledge can you add?

3. In paragraph 10 Russell speaks of workers who "prostitute their skill to purposes which they believe to be harmful." What work does he use as an example here? What other examples can you offer? Imagine yourself doing work that you do not respect or that you even find "harmful." Then imagine being offered work that you do respect but at a much lower salary. How helpful would you find Russell's advice? What would you do? (Specific examples of work that you respect and work that you don't respect will help you to form a clear idea of the choice and a clear argument to support it.)

4. What new point does Russell introduce in his last paragraph? How well does this last paragraph work as a conclusion?

5. Russell is generally admired for his exceptionally clear prose. List some of the devices that make for clarity in this essay.

6. Through most of his essay, Russell writes as if only men were engaged in work. What references to women working do you find? From these references and from the predominant references to men, would you describe Russell as sexist? Why or why not?

7. Compare Russell with Gloria Steinem (page 389) on the value of work.

Mike Rose

Mike Rose, the son of impoverished immigrants, received degrees from Loyola University and the University of California, Los Angeles. Now a professor in the Graduate School of Education and Information Studies at UCLA, Rose is the author of numerous books, including Writer's Block: The Cognitive Dimension *(1984),* Lives on the Boundary: The Struggles and Achievements of America's Underprepared *(1989), and* Possible Lives: The Promise of Public Education in America *(1995). We reprint an essay drawn from* The Mind at Work: Valuing the Intelligence of the American Worker *(2005).*

Brains as Well as Brawn

I am watching a carpenter install a set of sliding French doors in a tight wall space. He stands back, surveying the frame, imagining the pieces as he will assemble them.

What angle is required to create a threshold that will shed water? Where might the sliding panels catch or snag? How must the casings be remade to match the woodwork in the rest of the room? And how can he put it all together fast enough and smart enough to make his labor pay?

This isn't the usual stuff of a Labor Day tribute. Our typical tributes spotlight the economic contribution that the labor force has made to the country, the value of the work ethic. But what about the intelligence of the laborer—the thought, the creativity, the craft it takes to do work, any work, well.

Over the last six years, I've been studying the thinking involved in what is often dismissed as manual labor, exploring the way knowledge is gained and used strategically on job sites, in trade schools and in businesses such as beauty salons and restaurants, auto factories and welding shops. And I've been struck by the intellectual demands of what I saw.

Consider what a good waitress or waiter has to do in a busy restaurant: 5
remember orders and monitor them, attend to an ever-changing environment, juggle the flow of work, make decisions on the fly. Or the carpenter: To build a cabinet, a staircase or a pitched roof requires complex mathematical calculations, a high level of precision. The hairstylist's practice is a mix of scissors technique, knowledge of biology, aesthetic judgment and communication skills. The mechanic, electrician and plumber are trouble-shooters and problem-solvers. Even the routinized factory floor calls for working smart. Yet we persist in dividing labor into the work of the hand and the work of the mind.

Distinctions between blue collar and white collar do exist. White-collar work, for example, often requires a large investment of money and time in formal schooling. And, on average, white-collar work leads to higher occupational status and income, more autonomy and less physical risk. But these distinctions carry with them unfair assumptions about the intelligence of the people who do physical work. Those assumptions have a long history, from portrayals of 18th century mechanics as illiterate and incapable of participating in government to the autoworkers I heard labeled by one supervisor as "a bunch of dummies."

Such beliefs are intensified in our high-tech era. Listen to the language we use: Work involving electronic media and symbolic analysis is "neck up" while old-style manufacturing or service work is "neck down."

If society labels whole categories of people, identified by their occupations, as less intelligent, then social separations are reinforced and divisions

Mike Rose, "Extol Brains as Well as Brawn of the Blue Collar." Originally published in the *Los Angeles Times*, September 6, 2004. Reprinted by permission of the author. Mike Rose is the author of *The Mind at Work: Valuing the Intelligence of the American Worker* (Penguin, 2005).

constrict the kind of civic life we can create or imagine. And if society ignores the intelligence behind the craft, it mistakes prejudice for fact.

Many Labor Day tributes will render the muscled arm, sleeve rolled tight. How many also will celebrate the link between hand and brain? It would be fitting, on this day especially, to have a truer, richer sense of all that is involved in the wide range of work that surrounds and sustains us. We need to honor the brains as well as the brawn of American labor.

Joining the Conversation: Critical Thinking and Writing

1. Do you like Rose's title? Explain why or why not.

2. A student we know said she found Rose's first two paragraphs "confusing." Why might she have responded in this way? Do you agree with her?

3. What point about "manual labor" is Rose making here?

4. Look up the word "intelligence" in a good dictionary. What are the main meanings of this word? Is there anything in this dictionary definition that surprises you, something you had not known before?

5. What kinds of manual labor have you performed? Did all of them require brains as well as brawn? Some more than others? Did any require little or no brains at all?

Gloria Steinem

Gloria Steinem was born in Toledo in 1934 and educated at Smith College. An active figure in politics, civil rights affairs, and feminist issues, she was a co-founder of the Women's Action Alliance and a co-founder and editor of Ms. *magazine. We reprint an essay from one of her books,* Outrageous Acts and Everyday Rebellions *(1983).*

The Importance of Work

Toward the end of the 1970s, *The Wall Street Journal* devoted an eight-part, front-page series to "the working woman"—that is, the influx of women into the paid-labor force—as the greatest change in American life since the Industrial Revolution.

Many women readers greeted both the news and the definition with cynicism. After all, women have always worked. If all the productive work

---

of human maintenance that women do in the home were valued at its replacement cost, the gross national product of the United States would go up by 26 percent. It's just that we are now more likely than ever before to leave our poorly rewarded, low-security, high-risk job of homemaking (though we're still trying to explain that it's a perfectly good one and that the problem is male society's refusal both to do it and to give it an economic value) for more secure, independent, and better-paid jobs outside the home.

Obviously, the real work revolution won't come until all productive work is rewarded—including child rearing and other jobs done in the home—and men are integrated into so-called women's work as well as vice versa. But the radical change being touted by the *Journal* and other media is one part of that long integration process: the unprecedented flood of women into salaried jobs, that is, into the labor force as it has been male-defined and previously occupied by men. We are already more than 41 percent of it—the highest proportion in history. Given the fact that women also make up a whopping 69 percent of the "discouraged labor force" (that is, people who need jobs but don't get counted in the unemployment statistics because they've given up looking), plus an official female unemployment rate that is substantially higher than men's, it's clear that we could expand to become fully half of the national work force by 1990.

Faced with this determination of women to find a little independence and to be paid and honored for our work, experts have rushed to ask: "Why?" It's a question rarely directed at male workers. Their basic motivations of survival and personal satisfaction are taken for granted. Indeed, men are regarded as "odd" and therefore subjects for sociological study and journalistic reports only when they *don't* have work, even if they are rich and don't need jobs or are poor and can't find them. Nonetheless, pollsters and sociologists have gone to great expense to prove that women work outside the home because of dire financial need, or if we persist despite the presence of a wage-earning male, out of some desire to buy "little extras" for our families, or even out of good old-fashioned penis envy.

Job interviewers and even our own families may still ask salaried women the big "Why?" If we have small children at home or are in some job regarded as "men's work," the incidence of such questions increases. Condescending or accusatory versions of "What's a nice girl like you doing in a place like this?" have not disappeared from the workplace.

How do we answer these assumptions that we are "working" out of some pressing or peculiar need? Do we feel okay about arguing that it's as natural for us to have salaried jobs as for our husbands—whether or not we have young children at home? Can we enjoy strong career ambitions without worrying about being thought "unfeminine"? When we confront men's growing resentment of women competing in the work force (often in the form of such guilt-producing accusations as "You're taking men's jobs away" or "You're damaging your children"), do we simply state that a decent job is a basic human right for everybody?

5

I'm afraid the answer is often no. As individuals and as a movement, we tend to retreat into some version of a tactically questionable defense: "Womenworkbecausewehaveto." The phrase has become one word, one key on the typewriter—an economic form of the socially "feminine" stance of passivity and self-sacrifice. Under attack, we still tend to present ourselves as creatures of economic necessity and familial devotion. "Womenworkbecausewehaveto" has become the easiest thing to say.

Like most truisms, this one is easy to prove with statistics. Economic need *is* the most consistent work motive—for women as well as men. In 1976, for instance, 43 percent of all women in the paid-labor force were single, widowed, separated, or divorced, and working to support themselves and their dependents. An additional 21 percent were married to men who had earned less than ten thousand dollars in the previous year, the minimum then required to support a family of four. In fact, if you take men's pensions, stocks, real estate, and various forms of accumulated wealth into account, a good statistical case can be made that there are more women who "have" to work (that is, who have neither the accumulated wealth, nor husbands whose work or wealth can support them for the rest of their lives) than there are men with the same need. If we were going to ask one group "Do you really need this job?" we should ask men.

But the first weakness of the whole "have to work" defense is its deceptiveness. Anyone who has ever experienced dehumanized life on welfare or any other confidence-shaking dependency knows that a paid job may be preferable to the dole, even when the hand-out is coming from a family member. Yet the will and self-confidence to work on one's own can diminish as dependency and fear increase. That may explain why— contrary to the "have to" rationale—wives of men who earn less than three thousand dollars a year are actually *less* likely to be employed than wives whose husbands make ten thousand dollars a year or more.

Furthermore, the greatest proportion of employed wives is found among families with a total household income of twenty-five to fifty thousand dollars a year. This is the statistical underpinning used by some sociologists to prove that women's work is mainly important for boosting families into the middle or upper middle class. Thus, women's incomes are largely used for buying "luxuries" and "little extras": a neat double-whammy that renders us secondary within our families, and makes our jobs expendable in hard times. We may even go along with this interpretation (at least, up to the point of getting fired so a male can have our job). It preserves a husbandly ego-need to be seen as the primary breadwinner, and still allows us a safe "feminine" excuse for working.

But there are often rewards that we're not confessing. As noted in *The Two-Career Couple,* by Francine and Douglas Hall: "Women who hold jobs by choice, even blue-collar routine jobs, are more satisfied with their lives than are the full-time housewives."

In addition to personal satisfaction, there is also society's need for all its members' talents. Suppose that jobs were given out on only a "have to work" basis to both women and men—one job per household. It would be unthinkable to lose the unique abilities of, for instance, Eleanor Holmes Norton, the distinguished chair of the Equal Employment Opportunity Commission. But would we then be forced to question the important work of her husband, Edward Norton, who is also a distinguished lawyer? Since men earn more than twice as much as women on the average, the wife in most households would be more likely to give up her job. Does that mean the nation could do as well without millions of its nurses, teachers, and secretaries? Or that the rare man who earns less than his wife should give up his job?

It was this kind of waste of human talents on a society-wide scale that traumatized millions of unemployed or underemployed Americans during the Depression. Then, a one-job-per-household rule seemed somewhat justified, yet the concept was used to displace women workers only, create intolerable dependencies, and waste female talent that the country needed. That Depression experience, plus the energy and example of women who were finally allowed to work during the manpower shortage created by World War II, led Congress to reinterpret the meaning of the country's full-employment goal in its Economic Act of 1946. Full employment was officially defined as "the employment of those who want to work, without regard to whether their employment is, by some definition, necessary. This goal applies equally to men and to women." Since bad economic times are again creating a resentment of employed women—as well as creating more need for women to be employed—we need such a goal more than ever. Women are again being caught in a tragic double bind: We are required to be strong and then punished for our strength.

Clearly, anything less than government and popular commitment to this 1946 definition of full employment will leave the less powerful groups, whoever they may be, in danger. Almost as important as the financial penalty paid by the powerless is the suffering that comes from being shut out of paid and recognized work. Without it, we lose much of our self-respect and our ability to prove that we are alive by making some difference in the world. That's just as true for the suburban woman as it is for the unemployed steel worker.

But it won't be easy to give up the passive defense of "weworkbecausewehaveto."   15

When a woman who is struggling to support her children and grandchildren on welfare sees her neighbor working as a waitress, even though that neighbor's husband has a job, she may feel resentful; and the waitress (of course, not the waitress's husband) may feel guilty. Yet unless we establish the obligation to provide a job for everyone who is willing and able to work, that welfare woman may herself be penalized by policies that give out only one public-service job per household. She and her daughter will have to make a painful and divisive decision about which of them gets that precious job, and the whole household will have to survive on only one salary.

A job as a human right is a principle that applies to men as well as women. But women have more cause to fight for it. The phenomenon of the "working woman" has been held responsible for everything from an increase in male impotence (which turned out, incidentally, to be attributable to medication for high blood pressure) to the rising cost of steak (which was due to high energy costs and beef import restrictions, not women's refusal to prepare the cheaper, slower-cooking cuts). Unless we see a job as part of every citizen's right to autonomy and personal fulfillment, we will continue to be vulnerable to someone else's idea of what "need" is, and whose "need" counts the most.

In many ways, women who do not have to work for simple survival, but who choose to do so nonetheless, are on the frontier of asserting this right for all women. Those with well-to-do husbands are dangerously easy for us to resent and put down. It's easier still to resent women from families of inherited wealth, even though men generally control and benefit from that wealth. (There is no Rockefeller Sisters Fund, no J. P. Morgan & Daughters, and sons-in-law may be the ones who really sleep their way to power.) But to prevent a woman whose husband or father is wealthy from earning her own living, and from gaining the self-confidence that comes with that ability, is to keep her needful of that unearned power and less willing to disperse it. Moreover, it is to lose forever her unique talents.

Perhaps modern feminists have been guilty of a kind of reverse snobbism that keeps us from reaching out to the wives and daughters of wealthy men; yet it was exactly such women who refused the restrictions of class and financed the first wave of feminist revolution.

For most of us, however, "womenworkbecausewehaveto" is just true enough to be seductive as a personal defense.   20

If we use it without also staking out the larger human right to a job, however, we will never achieve that right. And we will always be subject to the false argument that independence for women is a luxury affordable only in good economic times. Alternatives to layoffs will not be explored, acceptable unemployment will always be used to frighten those with jobs into accepting low wages, and we will never remedy the real cost, both to families and to the country, of dependent women and a massive loss of talent.

Worst of all, we may never learn to find productive, honored work as a natural part of ourselves and as one of life's basic pleasures.

Joining the Conversation: Critical Thinking and Writing

1. In paragraph 2 Steinem characterizes homemaking as a "poorly rewarded, low-security, high-risk job." How might she justify each of these descriptions of homemaking? Do you agree that homemaking is rightly classified as a job? If so, do you agree with her description of it?

2. Restate in your own words Steinem's explanation (paragraph 9) of why "wives of men who earn *less* than three thousand dollars a year are actually *less* likely to be employed than wives whose husbands make ten thousand

dollars a year or more." The salary figures are, of course, out of date. Is the point nevertheless still valid? Explain.

3. To whom does Steinem appear to address her remarks? Cite evidence for your answer. In your opinion, is this audience likely to find her argument persuasive? Would a different audience find it more or less persuasive? Explain.

4. In addition to arguments, what persuasive devices does Steinem use? How, for example, does she persuade you that she speaks with authority? What other authorities does she cite? How would you characterize her diction and tone, for instance in paragraph 18? (On diction, see page 652; on tone, see pages 16–17 and 657.)

5. Steinem suggests two reasons for working: "personal satisfaction" and "society's need for all its members' talents." Suppose that you had no financial need to work. Do you imagine that you would choose to work in order to gain "personal satisfaction"? Or, again if you had no need to work, would you assume that you are morally obligated to contribute to society by engaging in paid work?

6. Summarize, in a paragraph of about 100 to 150 words, Steinem's argument that it is entirely proper for wealthy women to work for pay. In the course of your paragraph, you may quote briefly from the essay.

7. Compare Steinem with Bertrand Russell (page 382) on the value of work.

Felice N. Schwartz

Felice N. Schwartz is founder and president of Catalyst, a not-for-profit organization that works with corporations to foster the career development of women.

In 1989 Schwartz published in the Harvard Business Review *an article that was widely interpreted as advising women to limit their expectations of advancement if they entered the business world. The controversy was reported in the newspapers, and Schwartz took the opportunity to reach a mass audience by writing an essay—printed below—for the* New York Times.

The "Mommy Track" Isn't Anti-Woman

"The cost of employing women in business is greater than the cost of employing men."

This sentence, the first of my recent article in the *Harvard Business Review*, has provoked an extraordinary debate, now labeled by others "the Mommy track." The purpose of the article was to urge employers to

Felice N. Schwartz, "The 'Mommy Track' Isn't Anti-Woman," *New York Times*, March 22, 1989. Used with permission of Catalyst.

create policies that help mothers balance career and family responsibilities, and to eliminate barriers to female productivity and advancement.

But two fears have emerged in the debate. One is that, by raising the issue that it costs more to employ women, we will not be hired and promoted. The other is the fear that if working mothers are offered a variety of career paths, including a part-time option, all women will be left with the primary responsibility for child care.

Acknowledging that there are costs associated with employing women will not lead companies to put women in dead-end jobs. Time taken from work for childbearing, recovery and child care, as well the counterproductive attitudes and practices women face in a male-dominated workplace, do take their toll on women's productivity. But in our competitive marketplace, the costs of employing women pale beside the payoffs.

Current "baby-bust" demographics compel companies to employ   5
women at every level, no matter what the cost. Why? Women comprise half the talent and competence in the country. The idea that companies are looking for excuses to send women home again is untrue. Companies are looking for solutions, not excuses.

Over and over, corporate leaders tell me that their most pressing concern is not why but *how* to respond cost-effectively to the needs of women. Some take bold steps to provide women with the flexibility and family supports they need; others implement ground-breaking programs to remove barriers to women's leadership. The farsighted do both.

Their programs address the needs of women as individuals. There can be no one career "track" to which women, or men, can be expected to adhere throughout their lives. Few can know from the start to what degree they will be committed to career or to family. Raising the issue of the costs of employing women motivates companies to find solutions that work for individuals with diverse and sometimes changing goals and needs.

The second fear voiced in this debate is that making alternative career paths available to women may freeze them in the role of primary caretakers of children.

Today, men are more involved in their children's upbringing, from fixing breakfast to picking up kids at school—enriching our children's lives. But despite increased sharing of parental responsibilities, women remain at the center of family life. According to a recent study, 54 percent of married women who work full-time said child care was their responsibility—contrasted with two percent of surveyed men.

The danger of charting our direction on the basis of wishful thinking   10
is clear. Whether or not men play a greater role in child rearing, companies must reduce the family-related stresses on working women. The flexibility companies provide for women now will be a model in the very near future for men—thus women will not be forced to continue to take primary responsibility for child care. Giving men flexibility will benefit companies in many ways, including greater women's productivity.

What I advocate is that companies create options that allow employees to set their own pace, strive for the top, find satisfaction at the mid-level or cut back for a period of time—not to be penalized for wanting to make a substantial commitment to family. Achievement should not be a function of whether an employee has children. Success is the reward of talent, hard work and commitment.

What benefits women benefits companies. In reducing the cost of employing women—by clearing obstacles to their advancement and providing family benefits—companies create an environment in which all can succeed. But employers will not be motivated to reduce the costs if it remains taboo to discuss them. Only by putting the facts on the table will employers and women—and men—be able to form a partnership in addressing the issues.

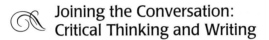

Joining the Conversation:
Critical Thinking and Writing

Read the following letters, and then answer the questions on page 400.

Pat Schroeder, Lois Brenner, Hope Dellon, Anita M. Harris, Peg McAulay Byrd

The following letters were published in the New York Times *shortly after Schwartz's article appeared.*

Letters Responding to Felice N. Schwartz

To the Editor:

Felice N. Schwartz might have had the best of intentions when she wrote "Management Women and the New Facts of Life" for the *Harvard Business Review* and reiterated her thesis in "The 'Mommy Track' Isn't Anti-Woman" (Op-Ed, March 22). Her arguments, however, are hardly supported by her scholarship, which relies on unidentified studies at

Letters to the Editor by Pat Schroeder, Lois Brenner, Hope Dellon, Anita M. Harris, and Peg McAulay Byrd, published (respectively) in the *New York Times*, March 27, 19, 24, 12 and 20, 1989. Used by permission of the authors.

unnamed corporations about undefined "turnover" rates, assertions that begin with phrases like "we know" and "what we know to be true," and an undocumented assumption that women in business cost more.

The linchpin of Ms. Schwartz's thesis is an unidentified study at a single multinational corporation where the turnover rate for female managers was allegedly two and a half times that for male managers. Ms. Schwartz does not say whether the actual rates were an insignificant 1 percent for men and 2.5 percent for women, a significant 40 percent for men and 100 percent for women or something between. Moreover, she fails to explore the reasons for the difference. These might include poor personnel policies, like rigid relocation demands or a lack of parental leave, better job opportunities at other corporations or downturns in the company's fortunes that prompted more recently hired female managers to seek greener pastures.

Ms. Schwartz cites a second unidentified study (apparently of all female employees, not just managers) at another unnamed company, where "half of the women who take maternity leave return to their jobs late or not at all." That is, half returned as scheduled, and an unspecified number did not return, but for unexplained reasons.

Singling out turnover rates among female employees, whether clerks or managers, is a dubious approach. The days of an employee's spending 50 years with a single employer and retiring with a gold watch and a handshake are over. (Indeed, thanks to the buyout, merger and acquisition mania of the 1980s, the days of a company's lasting even a few years under the same ownership, management or even the same name, are diminishing.)

A January 1983 Bureau of Labor Statistics job-tenure survey that represented 54 million male and 42 million female workers reported that fewer that 10 percent of workers of either sex had been with their current employers 25 years or more. Of the 14 million male and 9.5 million female managers and executives covered by the survey, the median tenure was 6.6 years for males and 4.7 years for females.   5

The survey also showed that 60 percent of the male managers and executives and 74 percent of their female counterparts had the same employer for 9 years or less. Only 11 percent of the males and 3 percent of the females had the same employer for 25 years or more.

In short, few men or women remain with one employer for their entire careers, and women's somewhat lower managerial tenures might be explained partly by women's having only recently entered the executive ranks in significant numbers.

If Ms. Schwartz's scholarship is suspect, her two-track career model (future mommies in this corner, future nonmommies in that corner) is quaint—indeed Victorian—in view of what businesses are doing for men and women.

Impelled by the changing American work force and striving to remain competitive, corporations like U S West, I.B.M., A.T. & T., Time Inc., Corning Glass, Quaker Oats and Merck have concluded that productivity and family obligations are not mutually exclusive, that the almighty dollar and the family are not enemies. To accommodate these new realities companies have instituted such employment practices as parental leave, flexible and part-time schedules, sabbaticals, child care, telecommuting and job sharing.

But workers are not the only beneficiaries of these new practices.   10
Employers are finding that meeting the needs of employees makes companies more productive and more competitive.

Pat Schroeder
Member of Congress, 1st Dist., Colo.
Washington, March 27, 1989

The writer of the following letter heads the family law department of a law firm and is co-author of *Getting Your Share: A Woman's Guide to Successful Divorce Strategies* (1989).

To the Editor:

Corporations may welcome Felice Schwartz's discovery of the "career and family" woman and "her willingness to accept lower pay and little advancement in return for a flexible schedule" (news story, March 8), but such women should consider the recent history of divorce laws before agreeing to this definition.

Although the law says marriage is an economic partnership that values child rearing and other domestic contributions as well as earning power, the reality is that when a marriage ends, women are not adequately compensated for having devoted themselves to their families at the expense of pursuing their career development.

If young women are going to be doubly penalized this way for choosing "the mommy track," they would do well to look closely at the experience of a generation of middle-aged women who have been left divorced and financially derailed by that choice.

Lois Brenner
New York, March 19, 1989

To the Editor:

Felice N. Schwartz, in her attempt to persuade us that "The 'Mommy Track' Isn't Anti-Woman" (Op-Ed, March 22), cites an intriguing statistic. According to a recent study, she says, 54 percent of married women working full-time regard child care as their responsibility, whereas only 2 percent of men say the same.

Does this mean that 46 percent of women in these circumstances see child care as a shared responsibility—presumably because men are sharing in the work? While not a majority, such a figure would be a significant enough minority to lend force to the argument for the importance of making businesses more responsive to the needs of both mothers and fathers—and, perhaps more compellingly, to the needs of the nation's children.

While Ms. Schwartz's assurance that "current 'baby-bust' demographics compel companies to employ women at every level" may be true, it is also true that few mothers have reached the top.

The idea of tracks has always had its limitations—whether in junior high school or in the corporate world. But if we must have such tracks in business, the chances of discrimination are surely much less for a "parent track" than for a "mommy track." Corporations may or may not believe that they can get along without mothers in high places, but they must realize that they cannot function without parents.

Hope Dellon
New York, March 24, 1989

The writer of the following letter is the author of *Broken Patterns: Professional Women and the Quest for a New Feminine Identity* (1995).

To the Editor:

Another problem with Felice Schwartz's proposal to track working women according to the likelihood they will want to raise children is that it is impossible to tell ahead of time which women are which.

In interviewing highly successful career women in predominantly male fields, I found that some women who as late as age 34 said adamantly that they did not want children had, by 40, had them. One executive who had had her tubes tied at 29, with the idea that she wanted a career and no children was, at 35, about to be married; she wanted desperately to have the ligation reversed and was seriously contemplating a completely different line of work.

Women who in their 20's had expected to quit work to have families found themselves in their 30's still single or divorced and enjoying their careers. Most women, married or single, with or without children, expressed ambivalence both about children and about their careers.

The problem is not that women don't know what they want, but that women, like men, grow and change along the life cycle. Stereotyping women early on into mothers and nonmothers would hamper their ability to develop fully both as individuals and as productive employees.

Even worse, it would perpetuate a cycle in which generations of women have been depreciated, divided and weakened through a paradoxical message that says women are inferior if they—and unless they—compete in terms that are set by and for men.

Anita M. Harris
Cambridge, Mass., March 13, 1989

5

To the Editor:

While I mostly agree with your response to "Management Women and the New Facts of Life" (editorial, March 13), your perspective does not include or explore the profoundly different attitudes men and women have toward money, which is, after all, why people work. There has been a spate of surveys highlighting these different attitudes.

Men see money as a means to power, heightening their visibility for selection for leadership within society. Looked at this way, the insatiable appetite for money, frequently bordering on greed, makes sense, albeit an insane sense. Capital accumulation is seen as primarily a male activity.

Women, on the other hand, see money as a means of power to purchase. Money purchases food, clothing, shelter or the means of nurturing. This idea too has its insane side, giving rise to gross materialism. Excessive spending is seen as a female trait.

Both these traits cross gender, but a greater number fall within a male-female perspective.

Women cannot satisfy their primary need, nurturing family and society, with the same single-minded directness that men can bring to their primary need of territory (capital accumulation). The marketplace, a male invention, reflects this bias, presenting women with unnatural choices, creating for them a practical as well as psychological disadvantage.   5

We must force the news media to include differing economic attitudes in covering the brave woman who daily deals with the multifaceted pressures of family life and living up to her potential as described by others.

Peg McAulay Byrd
Madison, N.J., March 20, 1989

 ## Joining the Conversation:
Critical Thinking and Writing

1. In paragraph 5 Schwartz says that "'baby-bust' demographics compel companies to employ women at every level, no matter what the cost." Exactly what does she mean?

2. In paragraph 9 Schwartz says, "Today, men are more involved in their children's upbringing. . . ." One often hears comparable statements, but are they true? How would one verify such a statement? In any case, if *you* have any reason to agree or disagree with the statement, express the grounds. To what extent do you think men *ought* to be involved in child-rearing?

3. Schwartz begins her final paragraph by asserting, "What benefits women benefits companies." What evidence or arguments does she offer to support this claim? Or do you think the point is self-evident and needs no support?

4. List the three most cogent arguments the letter-writers make against Schwartz's position.

5. Imagine that you are Schwartz. Write a letter to the *New York Times* in which you reply to one of the letters.

Virginia Woolf

Virginia Woolf (1882–1941) was born in London into an upper-middle-class literary family. In 1912 she married a writer, and with him she founded the Hogarth Press, whose important publications included not only books by T. S. Eliot, but also her own novels.
 This essay was originally a talk delivered in 1931 to the Women's Service League.

Professions for Women

When your secretary invited me to come here, she told me that your Society is concerned with the employment of women and she suggested that I might tell you something about my own professional experiences. It is true I am a woman; it is true I am employed, but what professional experiences have I had? It is difficult to say. My profession is literature; and in that profession there are fewer experiences for women than in any other, with the exception of the stage—fewer, I mean, that are peculiar to women. For the road was cut many years ago—by Fanny Burney, by Aphra Behn, by Harriet Martineau, by Jane Austen, by George Eliot—many famous women, and many more unknown and forgotten, have been before me, making the path smooth, and regulating my steps. Thus, when I came to write, there were very few material obstacles in my way. Writing was a reputable and harmless occupation. The family peace was not broken by the scratching of a pen. No demand was made upon the family purse. For ten and sixpence one can buy paper enough to write all the plays of Shakespeare—if one has a mind that way. Pianos and models, Paris, Vienna and Berlin, masters and mistresses, are not needed by a writer. The cheapness of writing paper is, of course, the reason why women have succeeded as writers before they have succeeded in the other professions.

But to tell you my story—it is a simple one. You have only got to figure to yourselves a girl in a bedroom with a pen in her hand. She had only to move that pen from left to right—from ten o'clock to one. Then it occurred to her to do what is simple and cheap enough after all—to slip a few of those pages into an envelope, fix a penny stamp in the corner, and drop the envelope in the red box at the corner. It was thus that I became a journalist; and my effort was rewarded on the first day of the following month—a very glorious day it was for me—by a letter from an editor containing a check for one pound ten shillings and sixpence. But to show you how little I deserve to be called a professional woman, how little I know of the struggles and difficulties of such lives, I have to admit that instead of spending that sum upon bread and butter, rent, shoes and stockings, or butcher's bills, I went out and bought a cat—a beautiful cat, a Persian cat, which very soon involved me in bitter disputes with my neighbors.

What could be easier than to write articles and to buy Persian cats with the profits? But wait a moment. Articles have to be about something. Mine, I seem to remember, was about a novel by a famous man. And while I was writing this review, I discovered that if I were going to review books I should need to do battle with a certain phantom. And the phantom was a woman, and when I came to know her better I called her after the heroine of a famous poem, The Angel in the House. It was she who used to come between me and my paper when I was writing reviews. It was she who bothered me and wasted my time and so tormented me that at last I killed her. You who come of a younger and happier generation may not have heard of her—you may not know what I mean by the Angel in the House. I will describe her as shortly as I can. She was intensely sympathetic. She was immensely charming. She was utterly unselfish. She excelled in the difficult arts of family life. She sacrificed herself daily. If there was chicken, she took the leg; if there was a draught she sat in it— in short she was so constituted that she never had a mind or a wish of her own but preferred to sympathize always with the minds and wishes of others. Above all—I need not say it—she was pure. Her purity was supposed to be her chief beauty—her blushes, her great grace. In those days—the last of Queen Victoria—every house had its Angel. And when I came to write I encountered her with the very first words. The shadow of her wings fell on my page; I heard the rustling of her skirts in the room. Directly, that is to say, I took my pen in hand to review that novel by a famous man, she slipped behind me and whispered: "My dear, you are a young woman. You are writing about a book that has been written by a man. Be sympathetic; be tender; flatter; deceive; use all the arts and wiles of our sex. Never let anybody guess that you have a mind of your own. Above all, be pure." And she made as if to guide my pen. I now record the one act for which I take some credit to myself, though the credit rightly belongs to some excellent ancestors of mine who left me a certain sum of money—shall we say five hundred pounds a year?—so that it was not necessary for me to depend solely on charm for my living. I turned upon her and caught her by the throat. I did my best to kill her. My excuse, if I were to be had up in a court of law, would be that I acted in self-defense. Had I not killed her she would have killed me. She would have plucked the heart out of my writing. For, as I found, directly I put pen to paper, you cannot review even a novel without having a mind of your own, without expressing what you think to be the truth about human relations, morality, sex. And all these questions, according to the Angel in the House, cannot be dealt with freely and openly by women; they must charm, they must conciliate, they must—to put it bluntly—tell lies if they are to succeed. Thus, whenever I felt the shadow of her wing or the radiance of her halo upon my page, I took up the inkpot and flung it at her. She died hard. Her fictitious nature was of great assistance to her. It is far harder to kill a phantom than a reality. She was always creeping back when I thought I had dispatched her. Though I flatter myself that I killed her in the end, the struggle was severe; it took much time that had better have been spent upon learning Greek grammar; or in roaming the world in search of adventures. But it was a real experience; it was an experience that was bound to befall all women writers at that time. Killing the Angel in the House was part of the occupation of a woman writer.

But to continue my story. The Angel was dead; what then remained? You may say that what remained was a simple and common object—a young woman in a bedroom with an inkpot. In other words, now that she had rid herself of falsehood, that young woman had only to be herself. Ah, but what is "herself"? I mean, what is a woman? I assure you, I do not know. I do not believe that you know. I do not believe that anybody can know until she has expressed herself in all the arts and professions open to human skill. That indeed is one of the reasons why I have come here—out of respect for you, who are in process of showing us by your experiments what a woman is, who are in process of providing us, by your failures and successes, with that extremely important piece of information.

But to continue the story of my professional experiences. I made one pound ten and six by my first review; and I bought a Persian cat with the proceeds. Then I grew ambitious. A Persian cat is all very well, I said; but a Persian cat is not enough. I must have a motor car. And it was thus that I became a novelist—for it is a very strange thing that people will give you a motor car if you will tell them a story. It is a still stranger thing that there is nothing so delightful in the world as telling stories. It is far pleasanter than writing reviews of famous novels. And yet, if I am to obey your secretary and tell you my professional experiences as a novelist, I must tell you about a very strange experience that befell me as a novelist. And to understand it you must try first to imagine a novelist's state of mind. I hope I am not giving away professional secrets if I say that a novelist's chief desire is to be as unconscious as possible. He has to induce in himself a state of perpetual lethargy. He wants life to proceed with the utmost quiet and regularity. He wants to see the same faces, to read the same books, to do the same things day after day, month after month, while he is writing, so that nothing may break the illusion in which he is living—so that nothing may disturb or disquiet the mysterious nosings about, feelings round, darts, dashes and sudden discoveries of that very shy and illusive spirit, the imagination. I suspect that this state is the same both for men and women. Be that as it may, I want you to imagine me writing a novel in a state of trance. I want you to figure to yourselves a girl sitting with a pen in her hand, which for minutes, and indeed for hours, she never dips into the inkpot. The image that comes to my mind when I think of this girl is the image of a fisherman lying sunk in dreams on the verge of a deep lake with a rod held out over the water. She was letting her imagination sweep unchecked round every rock and cranny of the world that lies submerged in the depths of our unconscious being. Now came the experience, the experience that I believe to be far commoner with women writers than with men. The line raced through the girl's fingers. Her imagination had rushed away. It had sought the pools, the depths, the dark places where the largest fish slumber. And then there was a smash. There was an explosion. There was foam and confusion. The imagination had dashed itself against something hard. The girl was roused from her dream. She was indeed in a state of the most acute and difficult distress. To speak without figure she had thought of something, something about the body, about the passions which it was unfitting for her as a woman to say. Men, her reason told her, would be shocked. The consciousness of what men will say of a woman who speaks the truth about her passions had roused her from her artist's state of unconsciousness. She could write no more. The trance was over. Her imagination could work no longer. This I believe to be a very common experience with women writers—they are impeded by the extreme conventionality of the other sex. For though men sensibly allow themselves great freedom in these respects, I doubt that they realize or can control the extreme severity with which they condemn such freedom in women.

These then were two very genuine experiences of my own. These were two of the adventures of my professional life. The first—killing the Angel in the House—I think I solved. She died. But the second, telling the truth about my own experiences as a body, I do not think I solved. I doubt that any woman has solved it yet. The obstacles against her are still immensely powerful—and yet they are very difficult to define. Outwardly, what is simpler than to write books? Outwardly, what obstacles are there for a woman rather than for a man? Inwardly, I think the case is very different; she has still many ghosts to fight, many prejudices to overcome. Indeed it will be a long time still, I think, before a woman can sit down to write a book without finding a phantom to be slain, a rock to be dashed against. And if this is so in literature, the freest of all professions for women, how is it in the new professions which you are now for the first time entering?

Those are the questions that I should like, had I time, to ask you. And indeed, if I have laid stress upon these professional experiences of mine, it is because I believe that they are, though in different forms, yours also. Even when the path is nominally open—when there is nothing to prevent a woman from being a doctor, a lawyer, a civil servant—there are many phantoms and obstacles, as I believe, looming in her way. To discuss and define them is I think of great value and importance; for thus only can the labor be shared, the difficulties be solved. But besides this, it is necessary also to discuss the ends and the aims for which we are fighting, for which we are doing battle with these formidable obstacles. Those aims cannot be taken for granted; they must be perpetually questioned and examined. The whole position, as I see it—here in this hall surrounded by women practising for the first time in history I know not how many different professions—is one of extraordinary interest and importance. You have won rooms of your own in the house hitherto exclusively owned by men. You are able, though not without great labor and effort, to pay the rent. You are earning your five hundred pounds a year. But this freedom is only a beginning; the room is your own, but it is still bare. It has to be furnished; it has to be decorated; it has to be shared. How are you going to furnish it, how are you going to decorate it? With whom are you going to share it, and upon what terms? These, I think, are questions of the utmost importance and interest. For the first time in history you are able to ask them; for the first time you are able to decide for yourselves what the answers should be. Willingly would I stay and discuss those questions and answers—but not tonight. My time is up; and I must cease.

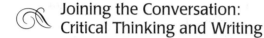 Joining the Conversation: Critical Thinking and Writing

1. How would you characterize Woolf's tone, especially her attitude toward her subject and herself, in the first paragraph?

2. What do you think Woolf means when she says (paragraph 3): "It is far harder to kill a phantom than a reality"?

3. Woolf conjectures (paragraph 6) that she has not solved the problem of "telling the truth about my own experiences as a body." Is there any reason to believe that today a woman has more difficulty than a man in telling the truth about the experiences of the body?

4. In paragraph 7, Woolf suggests that phantoms as well as obstacles impede women from becoming doctors and lawyers. What might some of these phantoms be?

5. This speech is highly metaphoric. What is the meaning of the metaphor of "rooms" in the final paragraph? What does Woolf mean when she says: "The room is your own, but it is still bare. . . . With whom are you going to share it, and upon what terms?"

6. Evaluate the last two sentences. Are they too abrupt and mechanical? Or do they provide a fitting conclusion to the speech?

Henry Louis Gates Jr.

Henry Louis Gates Jr., born in West Virginia in 1950, holds degrees from Yale University and Clare College in Cambridge, England. Returning to the United States, Gates quickly established a reputation as a leading scholar of African American literature. He is now chair of Harvard University's program in African American Studies, and he is also the director of the W. E. B. Du Bois Institute.

We reprint an essay that originally appeared in Sports Illustrated.

Delusions of Grandeur

Standing at the bar of an all-black VFW post in my home-town of Piedmont, W.Va., I offered five dollars to anyone who could tell me how many African-American professional athletes were at work today. There are 35 million African-Americans, I said.

"Ten million!" yelled one intrepid soul, too far into his cups.

"No way . . . more like 500,000," said another.

"You mean *all* professional sports," someone interjected, "including golf and tennis, but not counting the brothers from Puerto Rico?" Everyone laughed.

"Fifty thousand, minimum," was another guess.   5

Here are the facts:

There are 1,200 black professional athletes in the U.S.

There are 12 times more black lawyers than black athletes.

There are 2½ times more black dentists than black athletes.

There are 15 times more black doctors than black athletes.   10

Nobody in my local VFW believed these statistics; in fact, few people would believe them if they weren't reading them in the pages of *Sports Illustrated*. In spite of these statistics, too many African-American youngsters still believe that they have a much better chance of becoming another Magic Johnson or Michael Jordan than they do of matching the achievements of Baltimore Mayor Kurt Schmoke or neurosurgeon Dr. Benjamin Carson, both of whom, like Johnson and Jordan, are black.

In reality, an African-American youngster has about as much chance of becoming a professional athlete as he or she does of winning the lottery. The tragedy for our people, however, is that few of us accept that truth.

Let me confess that I love sports. Like most black people of my generation—I'm 40—I was raised to revere the great black athletic heroes, and I never tired of listening to the stories of triumph and defeat that, for blacks, amount to a collective epic much like those of the ancient Greeks: Joe Louis's demolition of Max Schmeling; Satchel Paige's dazzling repertoire of pitches; Jesse Owens's in-your-face performance in Hitler's 1936 Olympics; Willie Mays's over-the-shoulder basket catch; Jackie Robinson's quiet strength when assaulted by racist taunts; and a thousand other grand tales.

Nevertheless, the blind pursuit of attainment in sports is having a devastating effect on our people. Imbued with a belief that our principal avenue to fame and profit is through sport, and seduced by a win-at-any-cost system that corrupts even elementary school students, far too many black kids treat basketball courts and football fields as if they were classrooms in an alternative school system. "O.K., I flunked English," a young athlete will say. "But I got an A plus in slam-dunking."

The failure of our public schools to educate athletes is part and parcel 15
of the schools' failure to educate almost everyone. A recent survey of the
Philadelphia school system, for example, stated that "more than half of all
students in the third, fifth and eighth grades cannot perform minimum
math and language tasks." One in four middle school students in that city
fails to pass to the next grade each year. It is a sad truth that such statistics
are repeated in cities throughout the nation. Young athletes—particularly
young black athletes—are especially ill-served. Many of them are function-
ally illiterate, yet they are passed along from year to year for the greater
glory of good old Hometown High. We should not be surprised to learn,
then, that only 26.6% of black athletes at the collegiate level earn their degrees. For every successful educated black professional athlete, there are
thousands of dead and wounded. Yet young blacks continue to aspire to careers as athletes, and it's no wonder why; when the University of North
Carolina recently commissioned a sculptor to create archetypes of its student body, guess which ethnic group was selected to represent athletes?

Those relatively few black athletes who do make it in the professional
ranks must be prevailed upon to play a significant role in the education of
all of our young people, athlete and nonathlete alike. While some have done
so, many others have shirked their social obligations: to earmark small
percentages of their incomes for the United Negro College Fund; to appear
on television for educational purposes rather than merely to sell sneakers;
to let children know the message that becoming a lawyer, a teacher or a
doctor does more good for our people than winning the Super Bowl; and
to form productive liaisons with educators to help forge solutions to the
many ills that beset the black community. These are merely a few modest
proposals.

A similar burden falls upon successful blacks in all walks of life. Each
of us must strive to make our young people understand the realities. Tell
them to cheer Bo Jackson but to emulate novelist Toni Morrison or busi-
nessman Reginald Lewis or historian John Hope Franklin or Spelman
College president Johnetta Cole—the list is long.

Of course, society as a whole bears responsibility as well. Until colleges stop using young blacks as cannon fodder in the big-business wars
of so-called nonprofessional sports, until training a young black's mind
becomes as important as training his or her body, we will continue to perpetuate a system akin to that of the Roman gladiators, sacrificing a class
of people for the entertainment of the mob.

Joining the Conversation: Critical Thinking and Writing

1. Strictly speaking, the first five paragraphs are not necessary to Gates's argu-
    ment. Why do you suppose he included them? Evaluate his strategy for
    opening the essay.

2. In his next-to-last paragraph Gates says that "successful blacks in all walks of life" have a special obligation. In his last paragraph he widens his vision, saying that "society as a whole bears responsibility as well." Two questions:

   (a) In what ways is society responsible?

   (b) How effective do you think the final paragraph is, and why? (Consider especially the comparison to gladiatorial games.)

3. In paragraph 13 Gates mentions Joe Louis, Satchel Paige, Jesse Owens, Willie Mays, and Jackie Robinson. Do a little research on one of these men and write a short paragraph explaining Gates's reference to him. For instance, *when* did Joe Louis defeat Max Schmeling (and who *was* Schmeling)—in what year, in what round, and with what sorts of punches?

Marie Winn

Marie Winn, born in Czechoslovakia (now the Czech Republic) in 1936, came to New York when she was still a child. She later attended Radcliffe College and received her degree from Columbia University. Our selection comes from Children without Childhood *(1983), a book based in part on interviews with hundreds of children and parents.*

The End of Play

Of all the changes that have altered the topography of childhood, the most dramatic has been the disappearance of childhood play. Whereas a decade or two ago children were easily distinguished from the adult world by the very nature of their play, today children's occupations do not differ greatly from adult diversions.

Infants and toddlers, to be sure, continue to follow certain timeless patterns of manipulation and exploration; adolescents, too, have not changed their free-time habits so very much, turning as they ever have towards adult pastimes and amusements in their drive for autonomy, self-mastery, and sexual discovery. It is among the ranks of school-age children, those six-to-twelve-year-olds who once avidly filled their free moments with childhood play, that the greatest change is evident. In the place of traditional, sometimes ancient childhood games that were still popular a generation ago, in the place of fantasy and make-believe play— "You be the mommy and I'll be the daddy"—doll play or toy-soldier play, jump-rope play, ball-bouncing play, today's children have substituted television viewing and, most recently, video games.

Many parents have misgivings about the influence of television. They sense that a steady and time-consuming exposure to passive entertainment might damage the ability to play imaginatively and resourcefully, or prevent this ability from developing in the first place. A mother of two school-age children recalls: "When I was growing up, we used to go out into the vacant lots and make up week-long dramas and sagas. This was during third, fourth, fifth grades. But my own kids have never done that sort of thing, and somehow it bothers me. I wish we had cut down on the TV years ago, and maybe the kids would have learned how to play."

The testimony of parents who eliminate television for periods of time strengthens the connection between children's television watching and changed play patterns. Many parents discover that when their children don't have television to fill their free time, they resort to the old kinds of imaginative, traditional "children's play." Moreover, these parents often observe that under such circumstances "they begin to seem more like children" or "they act more childlike." Clearly, a part of the definition of childhood, in adults' minds, resides in the nature of children's play.

Children themselves sometimes recognize the link between play and   5
their own special definition as children. In an interview about children's books with four ten-year-old girls, one of them said: "I read this story about a girl my age growing up twenty years ago—you know, in 1960 or so,—and she seemed so much younger than me in her behavior. Like she might be playing with dolls, or playing all sorts of children's games, or jump-roping or something." The other girls all agreed that they had noticed a similar discrepancy between themselves and fictional children in books of the past: those children seemed more like children. "So what do *you* do in your spare time, if you don't play with dolls or play make-believe games or jump rope or do things kids did twenty years ago?" they were asked. They laughed and answered, "We watch TV."

But perhaps other societal factors have caused children to give up play. Children's greater exposure to adult realities, their knowledge of adult sexuality, for instance, might make them more sophisticated, less likely to play like children. Evidence from the counterculture communes of the sixties and seventies adds weight to the argument that it is television above all that has eliminated children's play. Studies of children raised in a variety of such communes, all television-free, showed the little communards continuing to fill their time with those forms of play that have all but vanished from the lives of conventionally reared American children. And yet these counterculture kids were casually exposed to all sorts of adult matters—drug taking, sexual intercourse. Indeed, they sometimes incorporated these matters into their play: "We're mating," a pair of six-year-olds told a reporter to explain their curious bumps and grinds. Nevertheless, to all observers the commune children preserved a distinctly childlike and even innocent demeanor, an impression that was produced mainly by the fact that they spent most of their time playing. Their play defined them as belonging to a special world of childhood.

Not all children have lost the desire to engage in the old-style childhood play. But so long as the most popular, most dominant members of the peer group, who are often the most socially precocious, are "beyond" playing, then a common desire to conform makes it harder for those children who still have the drive to play to go ahead and do so. Parents often report that their children seem ashamed of previously common forms of play and hide their involvement with such play from their peers. "My fifth-grader still plays with dolls," a mother tells, "but she keeps them hidden in the basement where nobody will see them." This social check on the play instinct serves to hasten the end of childhood for even the least advanced children.

What seems to have replaced play in the lives of great numbers of preadolescents these days, starting as early as fourth grade, is a burgeoning interest in boy-girl interactions—"going out" or "going together." These activities do not necessarily involve going anywhere or doing anything sexual, but nevertheless are the first stage of a sexual process that used to commence at puberty or even later. Those more sophisticated children who are already involved in such manifestly unchildlike interest make plain their low opinion of their peers who still *play*. "Some of the kids in the class are real weird," a fifth-grade boy states. "They're not interested in going out, just in trucks and stuff, or games pretending they're monsters. Some of them don't even *try* to be cool."

Video Games versus Marbles

Is there really any great difference, one might ask, between that gang of kids playing video games by the hour at their local candy store these days and those small fry who used to hang around together spending equal amounts of time playing marbles? It is easy to see a similarity between the two activities: each requires a certain amount of manual dexterity, each is almost as much fun to watch as to play, each is simple and yet challenging enough for that middle-childhood age group for whom time can be so oppressive if unfilled.

One significant difference between the modern pre-teen fad of video games and the once popular but now almost extinct pastime of marbles is economic: playing video games costs twenty-five cents for approximately three minutes of play; playing marbles, after a small initial investment, is free. The children who frequent video-game machines require a considerable outlay of quarters to subsidize their fun; two, three, or four dollars is not an unusual expenditure for an eight- or nine-year-old spending an hour or two with his friends playing Asteroids or Pac-Man or Space Invaders. For most of the children the money comes from their weekly allowance. Some augment this amount by enterprising commercial ventures—trading and selling comic books, or doing chores around the house for extra money.

But what difference does it make *where* the money comes from? Why should that make video games any less satisfactory as an amusement for

10

children? In fact, having to pay for the entertainment, whatever the source of the money, and having its duration limited by one's financial resources changes the nature of the game, in a subtle way diminishing the satisfactions it offers. Money and time become intertwined, as they so often are in the adult world and as, in the past, they almost never were in the child's world. For the child playing marbles, meanwhile, time has a far more carefree quality, bounded only by the requirements to be home by suppertime or by dark.

But the video-game-playing child has an additional burden—a burden of choice, of knowing that the money used for playing Pac-Man could have been saved for Christmas, could have been used to buy something tangible, perhaps something "worthwhile," as his parents might say, rather than being "wasted" on video games. There is a certain sense of adultness that spending money imparts, a feeling of being a consumer, which distinguishes a game with a price from its counterparts among the traditional childhood games children once played at no cost.

There are other differences as well. Unlike child-initiated and child-organized games such as marbles, video games are adult-created mechanisms not entirely within the child's control, and thus less likely to impart a sense of mastery and fulfillment. The coin may get jammed, the machine may go haywire, the little blobs may stop eating the funny little dots. Then the child must go to the storekeeper to complain, to get his money back. He may be "ripped off" and simply lose his quarter, much as his parents are when they buy a faulty appliance. This possibility of disaster gives the child's play a certain weight that marbles never imposed on its lighthearted players.

Even if a child has a video game at home requiring no coin outlay, the play it provides is less than optimal. The noise level of the machine is high—too high, usually, for the child to conduct a conversation easily with another child. And yet, according to its enthusiasts, this very noisiness is a part of the game's attraction. The loud whizzes, crashes, and whirrs of the video-game machine "blow the mind" and create an excitement that is quite apart from the excitement generated simply by trying to win a game. A traditional childhood game such as marbles, on the other hand, has little built-in stimulation; the excitement of playing is generated entirely by the players' own actions. And while the pace of a game of marbles is close to the child's natural physiological rhythms, the frenzied activities of video games serve to "rev up" the child in an artificial way, almost in the way a stimulant or an amphetamine might. Meanwhile the perceptual impact of a video game is similar to that of watching television—the action, after all, takes place on a television screen—causing the eye to defocus slightly and creating a certain alteration in the child's natural state of consciousness.

Parents' instinctive reaction to their children's involvement with video games provides another clue to the difference between this contemporary form of play and the more traditional pastimes such as marbles. While

15

parents, indeed most adults, derive open pleasure from watching children at play, most parents today are not delighted to watch their kids flicking away at the Pac-Man machine. This does not seem to them to be real play. As a mother of two school-age children anxiously explains, "We used to do real childhood sorts of things when I was a kid. We'd build forts and put on crazy plays and make up new languages, and just generally we *played*. But today my kids don't play that way at all. They like video games and of course they still go in for sports outdoors. They go roller skating and ice skating and skiing and all. But they don't seem to really *play*."

Some of this feeling may represent a certain nostalgia for the past and the old generation's resistance to the different ways of the new. But it is more likely that most adults have an instinctive understanding of the importance of play in their own childhood. This feeling stokes their fears that their children are being deprived of something irreplaceable when they flip the levers on the video machines to manipulate the electronic images rather than flick their fingers to send a marble shooting towards another marble.

Play Deprivation

In addition to television's influence, some parents and teachers ascribe children's diminished drive to play to recent changes in the school curriculum, especially in the early grades.

"Kindergarten, traditionally a playful port of entry into formal school, is becoming more academic, with children being taught specific skills, taking tests, and occasionally even having homework," begins a report on new directions in early childhood education. Since 1970, according to the United States census, the proportion of three- and four-year-olds enrolled in school has risen dramatically, from 20.5 percent to 36.7 percent in 1980, and these nursery schools have largely joined the push towards academic acceleration in the early grades. Moreover, middle-class nursery schools in recent years have introduced substantial doses of academic material into their daily programs, often using those particular devices originally intended to help culturally deprived preschoolers in compensatory programs such as Headstart to catch up with their middle-class peers. Indeed, some of the increased focus on academic skills in nursery schools and kindergartens is related to the widespread popularity among young children and their parents of *Sesame Street*, a program originally intended to help deprived children attain academic skills, but universally watched by middle-class toddlers as well.

Parents of the *Sesame Street* generation often demand a "serious," skill-centered program for their preschoolers in school, afraid that the old-fashioned, play-centered curriculum will bore their alphabet-spouting, number-chanting four- and five-year-olds. A few parents, especially those whose children have not attended television classes or nursery school, complain of the high-powered pace of kindergarten these days. A father whose five-year-old daughter attends a public kindergarten declares: "There's a lot more pressure put on little kids these days than when we were kids, that's for sure. My daughter never went to nursery school and never watched *Sesame,* and she had a lot of trouble when she entered kindergarten this fall. By October, just a month and a half into the program, she was already flunking. The teacher told us our daughter couldn't keep up with the other kids. And believe me, she's a bright kid! All the other kids were getting gold stars and smiley faces for their work, and every day Emily would come home in tears because she didn't get a gold star. Remember when we were in kindergarten? We were *children* then. We were allowed just to play!"

A kindergarten teacher confirms the trend towards early academic pressure. "We're expected by the dictates of the school system to push a lot of curriculum," she explains. "Kids in our kindergarten can't sit around playing with blocks any more. We've just managed to squeeze in one hour of free play a week, on Fridays."

The diminished emphasis on fantasy and play and imaginative activities in early childhood education and the increased focus on early academic-skill acquisition have helped to change childhood from a play-centered time of life to one more closely resembling the style of adulthood: purposeful, success-centered, competitive. The likelihood is that these preschool "workers" will not metamorphose back into players when they move on to grade school. This decline in play is surely one of the reasons why so many teachers today comment that their third- or fourth-graders act like tired businessmen instead of like children.

What might be the consequences of this change in children's play? Children's propensity to engage in that extraordinary series of behaviors characterized as "play" is perhaps the single great dividing line between childhood and adulthood, and has probably been so throughout history. The make-believe games anthropologists have recorded of children in primitive societies around the world attest to the universality of play and to the uniqueness of this activity to the immature members of each society. But in those societies, and probably in Western society before the middle or late eighteenth century, there was always a certain similarity between children's play and adult work. The child's imaginative play took the form of imitation of various aspects of adult life, culminating in the gradual transformation of the child's play from make-believe work to *real* work. At this point, in primitive societies or in our own society of the past, the child took her or his place in the adult work world and the distinctions between adulthood and childhood virtually vanished. But in today's technologically advanced society there is no place for the child in the adult work world. There are not enough jobs, even of the most menial kind, to go around for adults, much less for children. The child must continue to be dependent on adults for many years while gaining the knowledge and skills necessary to become a working member of society.

This is not a new situation for children. For centuries children have endured a prolonged period of dependence long after the helplessness of early childhood is over. But until recent years children remained childlike

20

and playful far longer than they do today. Kept isolated from the adult world as a result of deliberate secrecy and protectiveness, they continued to find pleasure in socially sanctioned childish activities until the imperatives of adolescence led them to strike out for independence and self-sufficiency.

Today, however, with children's inclusion in the adult world both through the instrument of television and as a result of a deliberately preparatory, integrative style of child rearing, the old forms of play no longer seem to provide children with enough excitement and stimulation. What then are these so-called children to do for fulfillment if their desire to play has been vitiated and yet their entry into the working world of adulthood must be delayed for many years? The answer is precisely to get involved in those areas that cause contemporary parents so much distress: addictive television viewing during the school years followed, in adolescence or even before, by a search for similar oblivion via alcohol and drugs; exploration of the world of sensuality and sexuality before achieving the emotional maturity necessary for altruistic relationships.

Psychiatrists have observed among children in recent years a marked   25
increase in the occurrence of depression, a state long considered antithetical to the nature of childhood. Perhaps this phenomenon is at least somewhat connected with the current sense of uselessness and alienation that children feel, a sense that play may once upon a time have kept in abeyance.

Joining the Conversation: Critical Thinking and Writing

1. In a sentence or two sum up Winn's thesis.

2. When you were a child, what did you do in your "spare time"? Judging from your own experience, is Winn's first paragraph true, or at least roughly true?

3. Assuming that children today do indeed spend many hours watching television and playing video games, is it true that these activities "do not differ greatly from adult diversions"? To test Winn's assertion, list the diversions of adults and of children that you know of from your own experience. Are the two lists indeed strikingly similar? Or do the lists reveal important differences? Explain.

4. Winn's argument is largely composed of a series of comparisons between the play of children before and after access to TV; between traditional and contemporary kindergarten; between childhood in "primitive" (and our own preindustrial) society and in technologically advanced societies. List the points she makes to develop each of these comparisons. How well does each comparison support her thesis?

5. Winn obviously prefers that children play by making up stories rather than by watching television. What reasons can be given to prefer making up stories, or reading stories in a book, to watching stories on television? In

this section of her book, Winn does not mention being read to by an adult as an activity of childhood. Draw your own comparison between traditional bedtime story-reading and night-time TV-watching. Would such a comparison have strengthened or weakened Winn's argument?

6. Speaking of video games (paragraph 11), Winn argues that "having to pay for the entertainment . . . changes the nature of the game, in a subtle way diminishing the satisfactions it offers." Can one reply that having to pay helps a child to appreciate the value of money? In short, can it be argued that paying for one's pleasure is a way of becoming mature?

W. H. Auden

W[ystan] H[ugh] Auden (1907–1973) was born and educated in England. In 1939 he came to the United States and later became an American citizen, but in 1972 he returned to England to live. Auden established his reputation chiefly with his poetry, but he also wrote plays, libretti, and essays, all bearing the stamp of his highly original mind.

The Unknown Citizen

(To JS/O7/M/378 This Marble Monument Is Erected by the State)

He was found by the Bureau of Statistics to be
One against whom there was no official complaint,
And all the reports on his conduct agree
That, in the modern sense of an old-fashioned word, he was a saint,
For in everything he did he served the Greater Community.   5
Except for the War till the day he retired
He worked in a factory and never got fired,
But satisfied his employers, Fudge Motors Inc.
Yet he wasn't a scab or odd in his views,
For his Union reports that he paid his dues,   10
(Our report on his Union shows it was sound)
And our Social Psychology workers found
That he was popular with his mates and liked a drink.
The press are convinced that he bought a paper every day
And that his reactions to advertisements were normal in
      every way.   15
Policies taken out in his name prove that he was fully insured,
And his Health-card shows he was once in hospital but left it cured.

Both Producers Research and High-Grade Living declare
He was fully sensible to the advantages of the Installment Plan
And had everything necessary to the Modern Man,   20
A phonograph, radio, a car and a frigidaire.
Our researchers into Public Opinion are content
That he held the proper opinions for the time of year;
When there was peace, he was for peace; when there was war, he
    went.
He was married and added five children to the population,   25
Which our Eugenist says was the right number for a parent of his
    generation,
And our teachers report that he never interfered with their
    education.
Was he free? Was he happy? The question is absurd:
Had anything been wrong, we should certainly have heard.

⚓ Joining the Conversation: Critical Thinking and Writing

1. Who is the speaker, and on what occasion is he supposed to be speaking?

2. What do the words "The Unknown Citizen" suggest to you?

3. How does Auden suggest that he doesn't share the attitudes of the speaker and is, in fact, satirizing them? What else does he satirize?

4. If Auden were writing the poem today, what might he substitute for "Installment Plan" in line 19 and the items listed in line 21?

5. Explicate, i.e. "unfold," explain, the last two lines.

6. Write a tribute to The Unknown Student or The Unknown Professor or Politician or Professional Athlete or some other object of your well-deserved scorn.

A Casebook on Poker

Jeremy Marks

Jeremy Marks wrote "The Power of Poker" (at the request of the editors of The Little, Brown Reader) *when he was a first-year student at Pennsylvania State University. He plans to major in either finance or accounting and, in his words "to aspire one day to work on Wall Street as a stock broker or a financial analyst for an investment firm." At Penn State, he devotes his time to his studies, to hosting a radio show, and, of course, to playing poker.*

The Power of Poker

The popularity of poker has grown exponentially in the last ten years. Whether it's the World Series of Poker, online poker, or the basic home game, no one can deny that poker has become one of the most popular activities in American colleges. However, along with the rise in popularity, there has also been a rise in the number of its critics. Various organizations, from Gamblers Anonymous to simple community groups, have done their best to claim that poker is nothing but an unhealthy vice. As a college student who has been playing poker since I was a first-year student in high school, I have seen the negative effects that poker can have on players. I have seen college students drop out of class because online poker has consumed their lives, and I have seen students lose every penny in their bank account because they cannot control their compulsive gambling. However, from what I have seen, these cases are in the minority, and there are many benefits to playing poker that are ignored or are simply unseen by the general public. Before I go into the positives of poker though, here is a question to think about: If poker is such a terrible thing, why has its popularity continued to rise at such an astonishing rate? In the five years that I have been playing poker I have developed many new habits, the most important being my ability to strategize and to think quickly. Not only can poker help players develop their abilities to think and to strategize, but it can also improve their money management skills. And for me playing poker helped deter me from making potentially harmful decisions.

When I began playing poker, I consistently lost, and I couldn't figure out why. After reading *Super Systems 2* by professional Doyle Brunson and watching the World Series of Poker and the United States Poker Championship, I realized that if you want to be successful in poker you needed to be able to think on your feet, strategize well, and ultimately make good decisions. The great thing about poker is that there are so many intricacies; the opportunities to use good strategy to gain an advantage over your opponent are endless. Strategy can be employed before the flop, when you can raise and try to push people out before the flop or just call the blind with a huge hand, or during a hand, where you can try to make your opponent believe you are strong when you are weak, or seem weak when you are strong. In addition, you need to trust your judgment, and to develop confidence in every decision you make. As I began to play multiple times per week and gained more experience, I developed winning strategies, for example raising heavily before the flop, and following that up with more heavy bets and putting the pressure on my opponent. Aggressive moves similar to this helped turn around my losing ways, and I began to start winning. Not only did the development of strategy help me at the poker table, but I began to see it help me in the classroom as well. When I would write a

Jeremy Marks, "The Power of Poker." Reprinted by permission of the author.

paper or present a project, rather than just talk or write aimlessly, I would try to get inside the head of my teacher and try to think about what he or she wanted to think or hear. I believe that the strategies I developed at the poker table, mainly being able to get into the head of my opponent (or in terms of schoolwork, my teacher) helped me excel in the classroom.

A common misconception about poker players is that they have poor money management skills. True, as I've said, there are some who cannot manage their money, but intelligent poker players are always conscious of their bankroll. In order to make the most effective bet, or to get the desired result you want in a hand, you need to know how much money you have, how much your opponent has, and the amount in the pot. Also, smart poker players never play in a game which they cannot afford. I know that poker has helped me become more conscious of my money, and has helped me to stay within my means. Helping me become more conscious of my money was important, but the largest impact poker has had on me is that it helped distract me from negative influences.

My dad often told me that he supported my poker playing because he felt it gave me an engaging pastime and it kept me away from damaging activities, such as taking drugs. When I entered high school, which was around the same time I began to play, many people I knew, and even some of my friends, had been experimenting with drugs. Being an athlete, I knew that drugs would harm my body, but I also think that because I enjoyed playing poker so much I never felt influenced by peer pressure to use drugs or that I was missing out on anything. Poker is a game in which you constantly need to be attentive and on your toes if you want to excel; if you are under the influence of drugs, your state of mind will be altered and you will not do well at the poker table. The people I played poker with had also made the same decisions as I, and because of poker, many of my now closest friends never got involved in drugs. I don't think enough can be said about abstaining from drugs, and for the people who criticize poker, I would use this specific example to attest as to how beneficial poker can be on a young adult.

For all these reasons, people who are quick to frown upon poker should take a closer look. They might then realize that the power of poker can help young adults away from the table, and can possibly help them make some of the most important decisions of their lives. I am glad that I got caught up in the poker craze, and if poker can help others the same way it has me, I hope its popularity will never cease to grow.

5

Joining the Conversation: Critical Thinking and Writing

1. According to Marks, what are the advantages of playing poker? In your opinion, do all of these advantages also apply to playing poker online? Explain.

2. If you have played poker, would you agree that poker can increase a student's "abilities to think and to strategize"? In particular, Marks says poker has helped him to get into the minds of teachers. Has poker helped you (or anyone whom you know) to develop this skill? Or do you think that whatever skill in poker a player may develop is nontransferable? Explain.

3. In paragraph 1, Marks poses this question: "If poker is such a terrible thing, why has its popularity continued to rise at such an astonishing rate?" How might you answer this question?

4. In paragraph 2, which discusses strategies, Marks writes of "the flop" and "the blind." Do you know what these terms mean? If so, explain them to someone who doesn't. Would it have been a useful strategy for Marks to have explained these terms?

5. Marks begins paragraph 4 with his dad's support of his poker playing. Do you find this a persuasive detail? Explain.

6. One reader of this essay thought that Marks appears to regard his teachers as opponents. Do you agree with this interpretation or not? Explain. Do you regard teachers as your opponents? Explain.

7. Can you think of any arguments against playing poker that Marks fails to discuss? If so, do you think he should have included them? Why, or why not?

8. Do you know of any student who has been harmed by poker? If so, do you think the college is in some degree responsible? Explain.

Lauren Patrizi

Lauren Patrizi wrote this essay in 2005, when she was a junior at Loyola University in Chicago. She had become addicted to online poker during her sophomore year.

My College Addiction

I am an addict. And I'm not alone. There is a new addiction plaguing college campuses: online gambling.

Sure, it might not seem as pernicious as other troubling hallmarks of the college experience like binge drinking or unprotected sex. But at least colleges have taken major steps towards educating students to prevent these practices. Condom distribution and hazing prohibitions are measures many universities have taken. But online gambling only takes a credit card or debit card and an Internet connection. Which puts pretty much every college student at risk.

Lauren Patrizi, "My College Addiction." Originally appeared on CampusProgress.org. Reprinted by permission of The Center for American Progress.

Poker has grown increasingly popular over the last few years. Even ESPN covers the World Series of Poker, which is an annual poker tournament in Las Vegas. Celebrities like Sarah Jessica Parker and Ben Affleck can be seen on television playing the game. Who ever thought watching other people play cards would be so entertaining? Natural consumers of popular culture, college students are buying in to the poker phenomenon. And online gambling institutions are listening.

My 2 a.m. pre-econ exam late-night binge is what I call the "gambling me." The reason I don't connect it directly to myself is because I never knew I was capable of an addiction. I've never smoked or done drugs and only drink socially. I was the last person in the entire world that I thought could become addicted to anything.

After watching a poker tournament on television I thought that the game looked entertaining. I decided to go online and see if I could play. I really had no clue that you could even access real money tournaments, I just thought I could find the poker equivalent of those minesweeper games that come on your computer. At 19 years old, I did not believe I would be able to access any real gambling programs. However, the process was seamless. What was once a $20 bet "just for fun" became hundreds and then well over a thousand dollars of debt.

College students are picking up on the craze in large numbers, and corporations have been taking notice. Party Poker, one of the largest and best known online gambling institutions, has begun advertising on facebook.com. In the ad, college students are hugging each other with the

5

tagline, "Just wanna have fun?" The ad also offers a $50 dollar sign-up bonus to students on Facebook. No company offers that kind of money unless they know they will make it all back and then some. Another site, Absolute Poker, has ads proclaiming, "College Students: Win Your Tuition."

The trend has Ed Looney, the director of the New Jersey Council on Compulsive Gambling, concerned. Looney said, "I've been doing this for 35 years, and I've never seen anything like this Texas Hold 'Em rage. When crack cocaine came out, the phenomenon was similar."

Others, including Senator Charles Schumer of New York, are troubled by the fact that, in practice, there is no age limitation on online gambling because there is no true age identification process. As Senator Schumer said, "These online gambling sites think they have really hit the jackpot by targeting kids." One study found that out of 37 randomly selected online gambling sites, a minor was able to register, play, and pay at 30 of them.

How many college students are actually logging on and playing for cash? The numbers seem to be growing quickly, although firm data is hard to come by. However, there are several indicators that would suggest it is a serious problem. In 2003 online gambling reported $5.5 billion in earnings, which rose from $4.1 billion in 2002. Senator Schumer stated that the problem was so serious that, "Unless we take the necessary steps to eliminate online gambling, more and more of America's young people will be returning from college holding a receipt of outstanding debt, instead of a diploma." According to the Annenberg Public Policy Center at the University of Pennsylvania in 2004, 11.4% of in-school male youth reported betting on cards at least once a week. In 2003 only 6.2% had reported the same activity. That makes for an 84% increase within one year.

But do college students gamble more than the regular population? According to the Journal of Gambling Studies, which issued a report on college gambling, 1.6% of the general population has engaged in pathological gambling with an additional 3.85% having experienced gambling related problems at sub-clinical levels. College students are at greater risk, with 5% reporting pathological gambling and over 9% reporting sub-clinical gambling related problems. Keith Whyte, director of the National Council on Problem Gambling, told the Associated Press, "We believe college gambling is on the increase and gambling on poker has certainly surged. We know that the students were always risk-takers; it is a definition of youth. But we believe kids are now betting more money on more intensive types of gambling."

10

In one case that briefly captivated national attention about student gambling in June 2003, a student at the University of Wisconsin murdered three roommates because he owed them thousands in gambling debts. The trio had helped him place bets with an offshore gambling company. He had lost $15,000 through gambling and withdrawn $72,000 from his bank account to support his habit before he committed the murders.

For me, online gambling has a specific appeal that other forms of gambling do not—anonymity. I never found casinos particularly attractive, but staying up all hours on my computer was something I already did and online gambling was just another way to keep me awake and procrastinating. With an unpaid internship, my financial outlook was bleak at best. The thought of an easy couple of hundred dollars was extremely appealing and was what kept me coming back. Most college students are in debt—on average about $10,000 dollars worth. With tuitions increasing, available grant money decreasing, and minimum wage retail jobs not exactly paying our way, gambling as a path out of debt or into a bit of pocket money seems pretty attractive.

And as opposed to actual gambling at an actual brick and mortar casino, financial transactions seem much less "real" over the computer, allowing players to more easily deny the kind of financial troubles they have gotten themselves into. It is easy to hide. Not a single person knew about my problem until I told my mother in desperation. Yet, I gambled for hours and hours on my computer. It was a totally solitary addiction.

I know a lot of people have a problem with government intervening to regulate private activities like gambling. But the government has a significant interest in protecting the individual lives and well-being of its citizens. What can be done? Well, some universities are starting to prevent and treat gambling addiction. More should be taking the simple measure of blocking Internet gambling sites from university servers. Visa has changed its policies, preventing users from placing online bets with its credit cards.

On a political level, both states and the federal government are starting to take note of the issue. The House passed the Unlawful Internet Gambling Funding Prohibition Act (HR 2143) in hopes of blocking credit card and debit card companies from permitting the flow of dollars to the illegal gambling sites. However, this measure is currently stalled in the Senate. Democratic Assemblywoman from New Jersey Joan Voss controversially proposed charging a fee to television programs such as Celebrity Poker in order to provide education to counter addiction in students. In October 2001, anti-Internet gambling provisions were included in the Financial Anti-Terrorism Act that would ban Internet gambling sites from accessing U.S. financial service systems, ostensibly to prevent the flow of money to and from terrorist organizations.

No state explicitly allows online betting and three states, Nevada, Louisiana, and my state of Illinois, have banned online casinos. Attorneys General in New York, Wisconsin, Minnesota and Missouri have already used their existing laws to shut down the few online gambling sites based in the United States. Now, essentially all online gambling sites, even if owned by Americans, are physically located off-shore, many in the Caribbean precisely so they can avoid American laws and regulations. (Sometimes "physically located off-shore" can mean one server or a post office box in Antigua.) Because these gambling sites are all located off-shore, no one really knows how large the online gambling industry is.

The appropriate corrective for online gambling addiction is up for debate, but I think the government needs to go to greater measures to protect its citizens, especially its young ones, on this issue. I just wish I had

15

talked about it sooner. I had pretty much everything to lose—college funds, credit card payments, a debt-free life. I am not even entirely sure how much I have spent over the last six months and I really don't want to know. After a last, desperate $50 bet to try to cut my losses, I knew that I needed to stop. I finally told my family and backed away from the computer.

 Joining the Conversation:
Critical Thinking and Writing

1. In paragraph 2 Patrizi says she is a poker "addict," and in paragraph 3 she compares the dangers of poker to those of binge drinking and unprotected sex. Do college administrators have the responsibility to protect students from poker? From online gambling? From binge drinking? From unprotected sex? Why, or why not?

2. In paragraph 9 Patrizi says that according to an Annenberg study, in 2003 only 6.2% of students bet on cards at least once a week, but in 2004, 11.4% bet, "for an 84% increase within one year." But suppose someone put it this way: In 2003, 6.2% bet, and in 2004, 11.4% bet, *for an increase of 5.2%* (rather than Patrizi's increase of 84%). What is going on with the statistics?

3. Why did Patrizi find online poker more appealing than other forms of gambling? And why, do you suppose, does Marks prefer playing poker at a table with classmates? If you play poker, or any other game, do you play online? Why, or why not?

4. In paragraph 14 Patrizi grants that "a lot of people have a problem with government intervening to regulate private activities like gambling." She goes on, however, to say that "the government has a significant interest in protecting the individual lives and well-being of its citizens." What is your view on this issue, specifically with reference to gambling?

Chris Berger

Christopher Berger, a native of New York but brought up in England, graduated with honors from Princeton University in 2006, with a major in history. While at Princeton he wrote a biweekly column exploring topics relevant to college students. We reprint one of those columns. Berger now works in New York on Wall Street.

Gen Y: The Poker Generation

I guarantee that if you went around and randomly asked 20 Princeton students what Doyle Brunson, Pocket Rockets and "the flop" have in common, everyone would know. My generation has definitely

Chris Berger, "Gen Y: The Poker Generation." Originally published in the *Daily Princetonian*, March 28, 2005. Reprinted by permission of the author and the Daily Princetonian.

cast itself as the poker generation. From watching Chris Moneymaker on the ESPN televised World Series of Poker, to Matt Damon's over-quoted "Sorry John, I don't remember," Texas hold-em has, seemingly overnight, become one of the most popular collegiate pastimes. In the past few years, poker has risen from the dead of antiquated smoke-filled pool halls to become indisputably "cool."

Poker is cool in the way Paul Newman is in *The Sting* when he takes down Robert Shaw, or cool in the way George Clooney holds his pocket aces in *Oceans 11*. Poker is cool in the way you get to wear sunglasses inside and use expressions like "full house" and "Fifth Street," and cool in the way an expensive chip or a crisp ace feels between your fingers. I am terrible at poker, and yet I can't seem to get enough of it. I can't shuffle, I can't bluff, I bet big when I have no business still being in the hand, and yet every time I hear of a poker game I jump at the chance to lose $20. I am always glued to the "Rounders" philosophy of "you can't win what you don't put in the middle." Poker is a smart, exciting, skillful, frustrating and addictive game, and fast becoming a national collegiate phenomenon.

But is the "cool factor" becoming a problem? Are the dangers of gambling, the evil lurking behind the smooth soundtracks and trendy catchphrases, a real problem for college-age students? A *New York Times* article published on March 14, titled "Ante Up at Dear Old Princeton: Online Poker Is a Campus Draw," unflatteringly chronicled the extreme gambling of a handful of Princeton seniors, and the amazing success of 22-year-old senior Michael Sandberg, who says that since September he has won $120,000, including $30,000 in Atlantic City and $90,000 playing at PartyPoker.com (the online casino regulated by the government of Gibraltar). The *Times* described Sandberg as an extreme example of the "gambling revolution on the nation's college campuses . . . one spurred by televised poker championships and a proliferation of Web sites that offer online poker games." The article pointed out that this poker addiction has spread through campuses across the country, citing enormously popular games at Columbia, U-Penn and the University of North Carolina.

While Princeton has no explicit rules about gambling on campus—except the New Jersey State law that forbids online gambling—and has not as yet taken steps to address it, Hilary Herbold, the associate dean of undergraduate students, was quoted as saying that "this is something we, the administration, need to sit down and decide if there should be a uniform policy about it." While the administration has been known to break up group games at the Street,[1] and has a policy of treating students with gambling problems, it has for the most part kept its nose out of this

---

[1] **the street** Prospect Avenue, near the Princeton campus, where the university's ten "eating clubs" are. The clubs have a semi-official status. [Editors' note]

faction of the Princeton social subculture. While last year students took it into their own hands to curb the surge in gambling when Tower[2] banned poker games that involved "large exchanges of money," the grapevine still speaks of legendary poker games that start in the afternoon and creep into morning, seeing hundreds, and even thousands, of dollars pass across expensive felt tables.

This is one of those situations in which the administration would be   5
best advised to keep its distance and trust the student body to play the game with the innocent intentions of passing time with friends. While there will always be the Michael Sandbergs who choose poker at the Mirage over graduate school after Princeton, the majority of the student body plays poker with the same philosophy that it would a pickup basketball game. While the easy accessibility of online gambling has certainly begun to tempt the eager gambling voice in the head of many a casual poker player, the overwhelming majority of the student body, I have faith, is smart enough to understand when they simply can't afford to keep playing. It would be a dark day in my life if I were to make that fateful phone call to my father explaining how I had just gone on "tilt" and emptied out my/his bank account to satisfy my gambling addiction. Princeton poker games and online gambling aren't going anywhere, and my advice for the administration would be to keep its distance; I plan on getting good grades and going to grad school, but for right now I'm going all in on my Jack, nine suited.

Joining the Conversation: Critical Thinking and Writing

1. Analyze the style of the second paragraph. What are its chief characteristics? How does Berger's style help to advance his argument?

2. In paragraph 4 Berger quotes a Princeton University dean as saying that the administration needs to "sit down and decide if there should be a uniform policy" about gambling on campus. What is Berger's position on establishing a university policy? What are his reasons? How does his position contrast with Patrizi's (see page 419)?

3. Imagine that you are an administrator at a college. What's your position on this issue? Why?

4. Compare the essays written by Marks, Patrizi, and Berger. Which do you find the most readable, and why?

---

[2] **Tower** One of the eating clubs. [Editors' note]

CHAPTER 11

Messages

Born Kicking, Graffiti on Billboard, London
Jill Posener, 1983

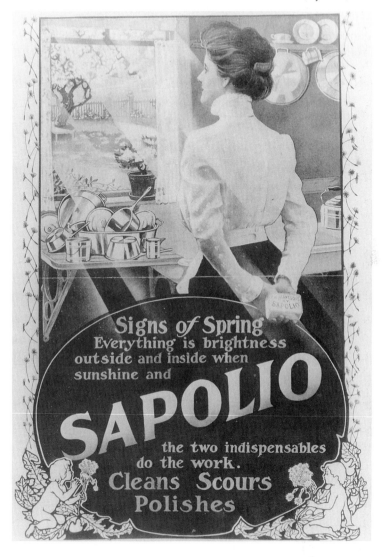

Short Views

Men . . . employ speech only to conceal their thoughts.
  Voltaire

We must be as clear as our natural reticence allows us to be.
  Marianne Moore

To change your language you must change your life.
  Derek Walcott

I personally think we developed language because of our deep inner need to complain.
  Jane Wagner

If you saw a bullet hit a bird, and he told you he wasn't shot, you might weep at his courtesy, but you would certainly doubt his word.
  Emily Dickinson

While I am thinking about metaphor, a flock of purple finches arrives on the lawn. Since I haven't seen these birds for some years, I am only fairly sure of their being in fact purple finches, so I get down Peterson's Field Guide and read his description: "Male: About size of House Sparrow, rosy-red, brightest on head and rump." That checks quite well, but his next remark—"a sparrow dipped in raspberry juice," is decisive: it fits. I look out the window again, and now I know that I am seeing purple finches.
  Howard Nemerov

We will understand the world, and preserve ourselves and our values in it, only insofar as we have a language that is alert and responsive to it, and careful of it. I mean that literally. When we give our plows such brand names as "Sod Blaster," we are imposing on their use conceptual limits which raise the likelihood that they will be used destructively. When we speak of man's "war against nature," or of a "peace offensive," we are accepting the limitations of a metaphor that suggests, and even proposes, violent solutions. When students ask for the right of "participatory input" at the meetings of a faculty organization, they are thinking of democratic process, but they are speaking of a convocation of robots, and are thus devaluing the very traditions that they invoke.

Wendell Berry

Sticks and stones may break my bones, but words will never hurt me.

Anonymous

Language both reflects and shapes society. The textbook on American government that consistently uses male pronouns for the president, even when not referring to a specific individual (e.g., "a president may cast his veto"), reflects the fact that all our presidents have so far been men. But it also shapes a society in which the idea of a female president somehow "doesn't sound right."

Rosalie Maggio

The search is for the just word, the happy phrase, that will give expression to the thought, but somehow the thought itself is transfigured by the phrase when found.

Benjamin Cardozo

"Wild and Free." An American dream-phrase loosing images; a long-maned stallion racing across the grasslands, a V of Canada Geese high and honking, a squirrel chattering and leaping limb to limb overhead in an oak. It also sounds like an ad for a Harley-Davidson. Both words, profoundly political and sensitive as they are, have become consumer baubles.

Gary Snyder

It is no insult to the recent, but already cherished, institution of the blogosphere to say that blogs cannot do everything well. Right now, and for the foreseeable future, the blogosphere is the friend of information but the enemy of thought.

Alan Jacobs

There can be too much communication between people.

Ann Beattie

Abraham Lincoln

Abraham Lincoln (1809–1965), sixteenth president of the United States, is not usually thought of as a writer, but his published speeches and writings comprise about 1,078,000 words, the equivalent of about four thousand pages of double-spaced typing. They were all composed without the assistance of a speech writer.

The Gettysburg campaign—a series of battles fought near Gettysburg in southeastern Pennsylvania—took place in June and July of 1863. Each side lost something like twenty-three thousand men. The battle is regarded as a turning point in the Civil War, but the Confederate army escaped and the war continued until April 1865.

On November 19, 1863, Lincoln delivered a short speech (printed below) at the dedication of a national cemetery on the battlefield at Gettysburg.

Address at the Dedication of the Gettysburg National Cemetery

Four score and seven years ago our fathers brought forth on this continent, a new nation, conceived in Liberty, and dedicated to the proposition that all men are created equal.

Now we are engaged in a great civil war, testing whether that nation, or any nation so conceived and so dedicated, can long endure. We are met on a great battlefield of that war. We have come to dedicate a portion of that field as a final resting-place for those who here gave their lives that that nation might live. It is altogether fitting and proper that we should do this.

But, in a larger sense, we cannot dedicate—we cannot consecrate—we cannot hallow—this ground. The brave men, living and dead, who struggled here have consecrated it, far above our poor power to add or detract. The world will little note, nor long remember, what we say here, but it can never forget what they did here. It is for us the living, rather, to be dedicated here to the unfinished work which they who fought here have thus far so nobly advanced. It is rather for us to be here dedicated to the great task remaining before us—that from these honored dead we take increased devotion to that cause for which they gave the last full measure of devotion; that we here highly resolve that these dead shall not have died in vain; that this nation, under God, shall have a new birth of freedom; and that government of the people, by the people, for the people, shall not perish from the earth.

Gilbert Highet

Gilbert Highet (1906–1978) was born in Glasgow, Scotland, and was educated at Glasgow University and at Oxford University. In 1937 he came to the United States, and in 1951 he was naturalized. Until his retirement in 1972 he taught Latin, Greek, and comparative literature at Columbia University. In addition to writing scholarly studies of classical authors, he wrote several general and more popular books.

The Gettysburg Address

Fourscore and seven years ago. . . .

These five words stand at the entrance to the best-known monument of American prose, one of the finest utterances in the entire language, and surely one of the greatest speeches in all history. Greatness is like granite: it is molded in fire, and it lasts for many centuries.

Fourscore and seven years ago. . . . It is strange to think that President Lincoln was looking back to the 4th of July 1776, and that he and his speech are now further removed from us than he himself was from George Washington and the Declaration of Independence. Fourscore and seven years before the Gettysburg Address, a small group of patriots signed the Declaration. Fourscore and seven years after the Gettysburg Address, it was the year 1950, and that date is already receding rapidly into our troubled, adventurous, and valiant past.

Inadequately prepared and at first scarcely realized in its full importance, the dedication of the graveyard at Gettysburg was one of the supreme moments of American history. The battle itself had been a turning point of the war. On the 4th of July 1863, General Meade repelled Lee's invasion of Pennsylvania. Although he did not follow up his victory, he had broken one of the most formidable aggressive enterprises of the Confederate armies. Losses were heavy on both sides. Thousands of dead were left on the field, and thousands of wounded died in the hot days following the battle. At first, their burial was more or less haphazard; but thoughtful men gradually came to feel that an adequate burying place and memorial were required. These were established by an interstate commission that autumn, and the finest speaker in the North was invited to dedicate them. This was the scholar and statesman Edward Everett of Harvard. He made a good speech—which is still extant: not at all academic, it is full of close strategic analysis and deep historical understanding.

Lincoln was not invited to speak, at first. Although people knew him as an effective debater, they were not sure whether he was capable of making a serious speech on such a solemn occasion. But one of the impressive

5

things about Lincoln's career is that he constantly strove to *grow*. He was anxious to appear on that occasion and to say something worthy of it. (Also, it has been suggested, he was anxious to remove the impression that he did not know how to behave properly—an impression which had been strengthened by a shocking story about his clowning on the battlefield of Antietam the previous year.) Therefore when he was invited he took considerable care with his speech. He drafted rather more than half of it in the White House before leaving, finished it in the hotel at Gettysburg the night before the ceremony (not in the train, as sometimes reported), and wrote a fair copy next morning.

There are many accounts of the day itself, 19 November 1863. There are many descriptions of Lincoln, all showing the same curious blend of grandeur and awkwardness, or lack of dignity, or—it would be best to call it humility. In the procession he rode horseback: a tall lean man in a high plug hat, straddling a short horse, with his feet too near the ground. He arrived before the chief speaker, and had to wait patiently for half an hour or more. His own speech came right at the end of a long and exhausting ceremony, lasted less than three minutes, and made little impression on the audience. In part this was because they were tired, in part because (as eyewitnesses said) he ended almost before they knew he had begun, and in part because he did not speak the Address, but read it, very slowly, in a thin high voice, with a marked Kentucky accent, pronouncing "to" as "toe" and dropping his final R's.

Some people of course were alert enough to be impressed. Everett congratulated him at once. But most of the newspapers paid little attention to the speech, and some sneered at it. The *Patriot and Union* of Harrisburg wrote, "We pass over the silly remarks of the President; for the credit of the nation we are willing . . . that they shall no more be repeated or thought of"; and the London *Times* said, "The ceremony was rendered ludicrous by some of the sallies of that poor President Lincoln," calling his remarks "dull and commonplace." The first commendation of the Address came in a single sentence of the Chicago *Tribune*, and the first discriminating and detailed praise of it appeared in the Springfield *Republican*, the Providence *Journal*, and the Philadelphia *Bulletin*. However, three weeks after the ceremony and then again the following spring, the editor of *Harper's Weekly* published a sincere and thorough eulogy of the Address, and soon it was attaining recognition as a masterpiece.

At the time, Lincoln could not care much about the reception of his words. He was exhausted and ill. In the train back to Washington, he lay down with a wet towel on his head. He had caught smallpox. At that moment he was incubating it, and he was stricken down soon after he reentered the White House. Fortunately it was a mild attack, and it evoked one of his best jokes: he told his visitors, "At last I have something I can give to everybody."

He had more than that to give to everybody. He was a unique person, far greater than most people realize until they read his life with care. The wisdom of his policy, the sources of his statesmanship—these were things too complex to be discussed in a brief essay. But we can say something about the Gettysburg Address as a work of art.[1]

A work of art. Yes: for Lincoln was a literary artist, trained both by others and by himself. The textbooks he used as a boy were full of difficult exercises and skillful devices in formal rhetoric, stressing the qualities he practiced in his own speaking: antithesis, parallelism, and verbal harmony. Then he read and reread many admirable models of thought and expression: the King James Bible, the essays of Bacon, the best plays of Shakespeare. His favorites were *Hamlet, Lear, Macbeth, Richard III*, and *Henry VIII*, which he had read dozens of times. He loved reading aloud, too, and spent hours reading poetry to his friends. (He told his partner Herndon that he preferred getting the sense of any document by reading it aloud.) Therefore his serious speeches are important parts of the long and noble classical tradition of oratory which begins in Greece, runs through Rome to the modern world, and is still capable (if we do not neglect it) of producing masterpieces.

The first proof of this is that the Gettysburg Address is full of quotations—or rather of adaptations—which give it strength. It is partly religious, partly (in the highest sense) political: therefore it is interwoven with memories of the Bible and memories of American history. The first and the last words are Biblical cadences. Normally Lincoln did not say "fourscore" when he meant eighty; but on this solemn occasion he recalled the important dates in the Bible—such as the age of Abraham when his first son was born to him, and he was "fourscore and six years old." Similarly, he did not say there was a chance that democracy might die out: he recalled the somber phrasing in the Book of Job—where Bildad speaks of the destruction of one who shall vanish without a trace, and says that "his branch shall be cut off; his remembrance shall perish from the earth." Then again, the famous description of our State as "government of the people, by the people, for the people" was adumbrated by Daniel Webster in 1830 (he spoke of "the people's government, made for the people, made by the people, and answerable to the people") and then elaborated in 1854 by the abolitionist Theodore Parker (as "government of all the people, by all the people, for all the people"). There is good reason to think that Lincoln took the important phrase "under God" (which he interpolated at the last moment) from Weems, the biographer of Washington; and we know that it had been used at least once by Washington himself.

Analyzing the Address further, we find that it is based on a highly imaginative theme, or group of themes. The subject is—how can we put it

10

[1]For further reference, see W. E. Barton, *Lincoln at Gettysburg* (Indianapolis: Bobbs-Merrill, 1930); R. P. Basler, "Abraham Lincoln's Rhetoric." *American Literature* 11 (1939–40), 167–82; and L. E. Robinson, *Abraham Lincoln as a Man of Letters* (Chicago, 1918).

so as not to disfigure it?—the subject is the kinship of life and death, that mysterious linkage which we see sometimes as the physical succession of birth and death in our world, sometimes as the contrast, which is perhaps a unity, between death and immortality. The first sentence is concerned with birth:

> Our *fathers brought forth a new* nation, *conceived* in liberty.

The final phrase but one expresses the hope that

> this nation, under God, shall have a *new birth* of freedom.

And that last phrase of all speaks of continuing life as the triumph over death. Again and again throughout the speech, this mystical contrast and kinship reappear: "those who *gave their lives* that that nation might *live,*" "the brave men *living and dead,*" and so in the central assertion that the dead have already consecrated their own burial place, while "it is for us, the *living,* rather to be dedicated . . . to the great task remaining." The Gettysburg Address is a prose poem; it belongs to the same world as the great elegies, and the adagios of Beethoven.

Its structure, however, is that of a skillfully contrived speech. The oratorical pattern is perfectly clear. Lincoln describes the occasion, dedicates the ground, and then draws a larger conclusion by calling on his hearers to dedicate themselves to the preservation of the Union. But within that, we can trace his constant use of at least two important rhetorical devices.

The first of these is *antithesis*: opposition, contrast. The speech is full   15
of it. Listen:

The world will little	*note*		
nor long	*remember*	what	*we say* here
but it can never	*forget*	what	*they did* here

And so in nearly every sentence: "brave men, *living* and *dead*"; "to *add* or *detract*." There is the antithesis of the Founding Fathers and men of Lincoln's own time:

> Our *fathers brought forth* a new nation . . .
>
> now *we* are testing whether that nation . . . can *long endure.*

And there is the more terrible antithesis of those who have already died and those who still live to do their duty. Now, antithesis is the figure of contrast and conflict. Lincoln was speaking in the midst of a great civil war.

The other important pattern is different. It is technically called *tricolon*—the division of an idea into three harmonious parts, usually of increasing power. The most famous phrase of the Address is a tricolon:

> government of the people
> > by the people
> > for the people.

The most solemn sentence is a tricolon:

> we cannot dedicate
> we cannot consecrate
> we cannot hallow   this ground.

And above all, the last sentence (which has sometimes been criticized as too complex) is essentially two parallel phrases, with a tricolon growing out of the second and then producing another tricolon: a trunk, three branches, and a cluster of flowers. Lincoln says that it is for his hearers to be dedicated to the great task remaining before them. Then he goes on. 20

> that from these honored dead

—apparently he means "in such a way that from these honored dead"—

> we take increased devotion to that cause.

Next, he restates this more briefly:

> that we here highly resolve . . .

And now the actual resolution follows, in three parts of growing intensity:

> that these dead shall not have died in vain

> that this nation, under God, shall have a new birth of freedom

and that (one more tricolon)

> government of the people
> > by the people
> > for the people
> shall not perish from the earth.

Now, the tricolon is the figure which, through division, emphasizes basic harmony and unity. Lincoln used antithesis because he was speaking to a people at war. He used the tricolon because he was hoping, planning, praying for peace.

No one thinks that when he was drafting the Gettysburg Address, Lincoln deliberately looked up these quotations and consciously chose these particular patterns of thought. No, he chose the theme. From its development and from the emotional tone of the entire occasion, all the rest followed, or grew—by that marvelous process of choice and rejection which is essential to artistic creation. It does not spoil such a work of art to analyze it as closely as we have done; it is altogether fitting and proper that we should do this: for it helps us to penetrate more deeply into the rich meaning of the Gettysburg Address, and it allows us the very rare privilege of watching the workings of a great man's mind.

25

 ## Joining the Conversation: Critical Thinking and Writing

1. At the start of his essay, after quoting the opening words of Lincoln's speech, Highet uses a metaphor and a simile: He says that the words "stand at the entrance to the best-known monument," and that "greatness is like granite: it is molded in fire, and it lasts for many centuries." Are these figures of speech effective? Why or why not? How are the two figures related to each other?

2. Analyze the structure of Highet's essay.

3. This essay was a talk given on the radio, presumably to a large general public. Find passages in the essay that suggest oral delivery to an unspecialized audience. How would you describe Highet's tone?

4. It has been suggested that "government of the people, by the people" is redundant; a government *of* the people, it is argued, must be the same as a government *by* the people. Did Lincoln repeat himself merely to get a triad: "of the people, by the people, for the people"? If so, is this a fault? Or can it be argued that "government of the people" really means "government over the people"? If so, what does the entire expression mean?

5. Highet claims that Lincoln was not only a great statesman, but also a literary artist. According to Highet, what was Lincoln's training as a literary artist? Highet implies that such training is still available. To what extent has it been available to you? Traditionally, studying "admirable models of thought and expression," including poetry, was an important part of writing instruction, but it is less common now. Should such study be included in writing courses? Why, or why not?

6. In paragraph 11 Highet points out that "the Gettysburg Address is full of quotations—or rather of adaptations," and he analyzes several examples of Lincoln's adaptations of sources. How is such adaptation different from plagiarism? Or is it?

Elizabeth Cady Stanton

Elizabeth Cady Stanton (1815–1902), born into a prosperous conservative family in Johnstown, New York, became one of the most radical advocates of women's rights in the nineteenth century. In 1840 she married Henry Brewster Stanton, an ardent abolitionist lecturer. In the same year, at the World Anti-Slavery Convention in England—which refused to seat the women delegates—she met Lucretia Mott, and the two women resolved to organize a convention to discuss women's rights. Not until 1848, however, did the convention materialize. Of the three hundred or so people who attended the Seneca Falls convention, sixty-eight women and thirty-two men signed the Declaration of Sentiments, *but the press on the whole was unfavorable. Not until 1920, with the passage of the Nineteenth Amendment, did women gain the right to vote. (For further details about her life and times, see Stanton's* Eighty Years & More: Reminiscences 1815–1897.)

Declaration of Sentiments and Resolutions

When, in the course of human events, it becomes necessary for one portion of the family of man to assume among the people of the earth a position different from that which they have hitherto occupied, but one to which the laws of nature and of nature's God entitle them, a decent respect to the opinions of mankind requires that they should declare the causes that impel them to such a course.

We hold these truths to be self-evident: that all men and women are created equal; that they are endowed by their Creator with certain inalienable rights; that among these are life, liberty, and the pursuit of happiness; that to secure these rights governments are instituted, deriving their just powers from the consent of the governed. Whenever any form of government becomes destructive of these ends, it is the right of those who suffer from it to refuse allegiance to it, and to insist upon the institution of a new government, laying its foundation on such principles, and organizing its powers in such form, as to them shall seem most likely to effect their safety and happiness. Prudence, indeed, will dictate that governments long established should not be changed for light and transient causes; and accordingly all experience hath shown that mankind are more disposed to suffer, while evils are sufferable, than to right themselves by abolishing the forms to which they were accustomed. But when a long train of abuses and usurpations, pursuing invariably the same object, evinces a design to reduce them under absolute despotism, it is their duty to throw off such government, and to provide new guards for their future security. Such has been the patient sufferance of the women under this government, and such is now the necessity which constrains them to demand the equal station to which they are entitled.

The history of mankind is a history of repeated injuries and usurpations on the part of man toward woman, having in direct object the establishment of an absolute tyranny over her. To prove this, let facts be submitted to a candid world.

He has never permitted her to exercise her inalienable right to the elective franchise.

He has compelled her to submit to laws, in the formation of which she had no voice.

He has withheld from her rights which are given to the most ignorant and degraded men—both natives and foreigners.

Having deprived her of this first right of a citizen, the elective franchise, thereby leaving her without representation in the halls of legislation, he has oppressed her on all sides.

He has made her, if married, in the eye of the law, civilly dead.

He has taken from her all right in property, even to the wages she earns.

He has made her, morally, an irresponsible being, as she can commit many crimes with impunity, provided they be done in the presence of her husband. In the covenant of marriage, she is compelled to promise obedience to her husband, he becoming to all intents and purposes, her master—the law giving him power to deprive her of her liberty, and to administer chastisement.

He has so framed the laws of divorce, as to what shall be the proper causes, and in case of separation, to whom the guardianship of the children shall be given, as to be wholly regardless of the happiness of women—the law, in all cases, going upon a false supposition of the supremacy of man, and giving all power into his hands.

After depriving her of all rights as a married woman, if single, and the owner of property, he has taxed her to support a government which recognizes her only when her property can be made profitable to it.

He has monopolized nearly all the profitable employments, and from those she is permitted to follow, she receives but a scanty remuneration. He closes against her all the avenues to wealth and distinction which he considers most honorable to himself. As a teacher of theology, medicine, or law, she is not known.

He has denied her the facilities for obtaining a thorough education, all colleges being closed against her.

He allows her in Church, as well as State, but a subordinate position, claiming Apostolic authority for her exclusion from the ministry, and, with some exceptions, from any public participation in the affairs of the Church.

He has created a false public sentiment by giving to the world a different code of morals for men and women, by which moral delinquencies which exclude women from society, are not only tolerated, but deemed of little account in man.

He has usurped the prerogative of Jehovah himself, claiming it as his right to assign for her a sphere of action, when that belongs to her conscience and to her God.

He has endeavored, in every way that he could, to destroy her confidence in her own powers, to lessen her self-respect, and to make her willing to lead a dependent and abject life.

Now, in view of this entire disfranchisement of one-half the people of this country, their social and religious degradation—in view of the unjust laws above mentioned, and because women do feel themselves aggrieved, oppressed, and fraudulently deprived of their most sacred rights, we insist that they have immediate admission to all the rights and privileges which belong to them as citizens of the United States.

In entering upon the great work before us, we anticipate no small 20
amount of misconception, misrepresentation, and ridicule; but we shall use every instrumentality within our power to effect our object. We shall employ agents, circulate tracts, petition the State and National legislatures, and endeavor to enlist the pulpit and the press in our behalf. We hope this Convention will be followed by a series of Conventions embracing every part of the country.

[The following resolutions were discussed by Lucretia Mott, Thomas and Mary Ann McClintock, Amy Post, Catharine A. F. Stebbins, and others, and were adopted:]

Whereas, The great precept of nature is conceded to be, that "man shall pursue his own true and substantial happiness." Blackstone in his Commentaries remarks, that this law of Nature being coeval with mankind, and dictated by God himself, is of course superior in obligation to any other. It is binding over all the globe, in all countries, and at all times; no human laws are of any validity if contrary to this, and such of them as are valid, derive all their force, and all their validity, and all their authority, mediately and immediately, from this original; therefore,

Resolved, That such laws as conflict, in any way, with the true and substantial happiness of woman, are contrary to the great precept of nature and of no validity, for this is "superior in obligation to any other."

Resolved, That all laws which prevent woman from occupying such a station in a society as her conscience shall dictate, or which place her in a position inferior to that of man, are contrary to the great precept of nature, and therefore of no force or authority.

Resolved, That woman is man's equal—was intended to be so by the Creator, and the highest good of the race demands that she should be recognized as such.

Resolved, That the women of this country ought to be enlightened in regard to the laws under which they live, that they may no longer publish their 25
degradation by declaring themselves satisfied with their present position, nor their ignorance, by asserting that they have all the rights they want.

Resolved, That inasmuch as man, while claiming for himself intellectual superiority, does accord to woman moral superiority, it is preeminently his duty to encourage her to speak and teach, as she has an opportunity, in all religious assemblies.

Resolved, That the same amount of virtue, delicacy, and refinement of behavior that is required of woman in the social state, should also be required of man, and the same transgressions should be visited with equal severity on both man and woman.

Resolved, That the objection of indelicacy and impropriety, which is so often brought against woman when she addresses a public audience, comes with a very ill-grace from those who encourage, by their attendance, her appearance on the stage, in the concert, or in feats of the circus.

Resolved, That woman has too long rested satisfied in the circumscribed limits which corrupt customs and a perverted application of the Scriptures have marked out for her, and that it is time she should move in the enlarged sphere which her great Creator has assigned her.

Resolved, That it is the duty of the women of this country to secure to themselves their sacred right to the elective franchise.   30

Resolved, That the equality of human rights results necessarily from the fact of the identity of the race in capabilities and responsibilities.

Resolved, therefore, That, being invested by the Creator with the same capabilities, and the same consciousness of responsibility for their exercise, it is demonstrably the right and duty of woman, equally with man, to promote every righteous cause by every righteous means; and especially in regard to the great subjects of morals and religion, it is self-evidently her right to participate with her brother in teaching them, both in private and in public, by writing and by speaking, by any instrumentalities proper to be used, and in any assemblies proper to be held; and this being a self-evident truth growing out of the divinely implanted principles of human nature, any custom or authorities adverse to it, whether modern or wearing the hoary sanction of antiquity, is to be regarded as a self-evident falsehood, and at war with mankind.

[At the last session Lucretia Mott offered and spoke to the following resolution:]

Resolved, That the speedy success of our cause depends upon the zealous and untiring efforts of both men and women, for the overthrow of the monopoly of the pulpit, and for the securing to woman an equal participation with men in the various trades, professions, and commerce.

Joining the Conversation: Critical Thinking and Writing

1. Stanton echoes the Declaration of Independence because she wishes to associate her ideas and the movement she supports with a document and a movement that her readers esteem. And of course she must have believed that if readers esteem the Declaration of Independence, they must grant the justice of her goals. Does her strategy work, or does it backfire by making her essay seem strained?

2. The Declaration claims that women have "the same capabilities" as men (paragraph 32). Yet in 1848 Stanton and the others at Seneca Falls knew, or should

have known, that history recorded no example of an outstanding woman philosopher to compare with Plato or Kant, a great composer to compare with Beethoven or Chopin, a scientist to compare with Galileo or Newton, or a creative mathematician to compare with Euclid or Descartes. Do these facts contradict the Declaration's claim? If not, why not? How else but by different intellectual capabilities do you think such facts are to be explained?

3. Stanton's Declaration is more than 150 years old. Have all of the issues she raised been satisfactorily resolved? If not, which ones remain?

4. In our society, children have very few rights. For instance, a child cannot decide to drop out of elementary school or high school, and a child cannot decide to leave his or her parents in order to reside with some other family that he or she finds more compatible. Whatever your view of children's rights, compose the best Declaration of the Rights of Children that you can.

Robin Lakoff

Robin Lakoff was born in 1943 and educated at Radcliffe College and Harvard University. A professor of linguistics at the University of California at Berkeley, she has been especially interested in the language that women use. The essay that we give here was first published in Ms. *magazine in 1974.*

You Are What You Say

Women's language is that pleasant (dainty?), euphemistic never-aggressive way of talking we learned as little girls. Cultural bias was built into the language we were allowed to speak, the subjects we were allowed to speak about, and the ways we were spoken of. Having learned our linguistic lesson well, we go out in the world, only to discover that we are communicative cripples—damned if we do, and damned if we don't.

If we refuse to talk "like a lady," we are ridiculed and criticized for being unfeminine. ("She thinks like a man" is, at best, a left-handed compliment.) If we do learn all the fuzzy-headed, unassertive language of our sex, we are ridiculed for being unable to think clearly, unable to take part in a serious discussion, and therefore unfit to hold a position of power.

It doesn't take much of this for a woman to begin feeling she deserves such treatment because of inadequacies in her own intelligence and education.

Robin Lakoff, "You Are What You Say" from *Ms.*, July 1974. Reprinted by permission of the author.

"Women's language" shows up in all levels of English. For example, women are encouraged and allowed to make far more precise discriminations in naming colors than men do. Words like *mauve, beige, ecru, aquamarine, lavender,* and so on, are unremarkable in a woman's active vocabulary, but largely absent from that of most men. I know of no evidence suggesting that women actually *see* a wider range of colors than men do. It is simply that fine discriminations of this sort are relevant to women's vocabularies, but not to men's; to men, who control most of the interesting affairs of the world, such distinctions are trivial—irrelevant.

In the area of syntax, we find similar gender-related peculiarities of   5
speech. There is one construction, in particular, that women use conversationally far more than men: the tag question. A tag is midway between an outright statement and a yes-no question; it is less assertive than the former, but more confident than the latter.

A *flat statement* indicates confidence in the speaker's knowledge and is fairly certain to be believed; a *question* indicates a lack of knowledge on some point and implies that the gap in the speaker's knowledge can and will be remedied by an answer. For example, if, at a Little League game, I have had my glasses off, I can legitimately ask someone else: "Was the player out at third?" A *tag question*, being intermediate between statement and question, is used when the speaker is stating a claim, but lacks full confidence in the truth of that claim. So if I say, "Is Joan here?" I will probably not be surprised if my respondent answers "no"; but if I say, "Joan is here, isn't she?" instead, chances are I am already biased in favor of a positive answer, wanting only confirmation. I still want a response, but I have enough knowledge (or think I have) to predict that response. A tag question, then, might be thought of as a statement that doesn't demand to be believed by anyone but the speaker, a way of giving leeway, of not forcing the addressee to go along with the views of the speaker.

Another common use of the tag question is in small talk when the speaker is trying to elicit conversation: "Sure is hot here, isn't it?"

But in discussing personal feelings or opinions, only the speaker normally has any way of knowing the correct answer. Sentences such as "I have a headache, don't I?" are clearly ridiculous. But there are other examples where it is the speaker's opinions, rather than perceptions, for which corroboration is sought, as in "The situation in Southeast Asia is terrible, isn't it?"

While there are, of course, other possible interpretations of a sentence like this, one possibility is that the speaker has a particular answer in mind—"yes" or "no"—but is reluctant to state it baldly. This sort of tag question is much more apt to be used by women than by men in conversation. Why is this the case?

The tag question allows a speaker to avoid commitment, and thereby   10
avoid conflict with the addressee. The problem is that, by so doing, speakers may also give the impression of not really being sure of themselves, or looking to the addressee for confirmation of their views. This

uncertainty is reinforced in more subliminal ways, too. There is a peculiar sentence-intonation pattern, used almost exclusively by women, as far as I know, which changes a declarative answer into a question. The effect of using the rising inflection typical of a yes-no question is to imply that the speaker is seeking confirmation, even though the speaker is clearly the only one who has the requisite information, which is why the question was put to her in the first place:

(Q) When will dinner be ready?
(A) Oh . . . around six o'clock. . . ?

It is as though the second speaker was saying, "Six o'clock—if that's okay with you, if you agree." The person being addressed is put in the position of having to provide confirmation. One likely consequence of this sort of speech pattern in a woman is that, often unbeknownst to herself, the speaker builds a reputation of tentativeness, and others will refrain from taking her seriously or trusting her with any real responsibilities, since she "can't make up her mind," and "isn't sure of herself."

Such idiosyncrasies may explain why women's language sounds much more "polite" than men's. It is polite to leave a decision open, not impose your mind, or views, or claims, on anyone else. So a tag question is a kind of polite statement, in that it does not force agreement or belief on the addressee. In the same way a request is a polite command, in that it does not force obedience on the addressee, but rather suggests something be done as a favor to the speaker. A clearly stated order implies a threat of certain consequences if it is not followed, and—even more impolite—implies that the speaker is in a superior position and able to enforce the order. By couching wishes in the form of a request, on the other hand, a speaker implies that if the request is not carried out, only the speaker will suffer; noncompliance cannot harm the addressee. So the decision is really left up to the addressee. The distinction becomes clear in these examples:

Close the door.

Please close the door.

Will you close the door?

Will you please close the door?

Won't you close the door?

In the same ways as words and speech patterns used *by* women undermine their image, those used to *describe* women make matters even worse. Often a word may be used of both men and women (and perhaps of things as well); but when it is applied to women, it assumes a special meaning that, by implication rather than outright assertion, is derogatory to women as a group.

The use of euphemisms has this effect. A euphemism is a substitute for a word that has acquired a bad connotation by association with something unpleasant or embarrassing. But almost as soon as the new word comes into common usage, it takes on the same old bad connotations, since feelings about the things or people referred to are not altered by a change of name; thus new euphemisms must be constantly found.

There is one euphemism for *woman* still very much alive. The word, of course, is *lady*. *Lady* has a masculine counterpart, namely *gentleman*, occasionally shortened to *gent*. But for some reason *lady* is very much commoner than *gent(leman)*.

The decision to use *lady* rather than *woman*, or vice versa, may considerably alter the sense of a sentence, as the following examples show:

a. A woman (lady) I know is a dean at Berkeley.
b. A woman (lady) I know makes amazing things out of shoelaces and old boxes.

The use of *lady* in (a) imparts a frivolous, or nonserious, tone to the sentence: the matter under discussion is not one of great moment. Similarly, in (b), using *lady* here would suggest that the speaker considered the "amazing things" not to be serious art, but merely a hobby or an aberration. If *woman* is used, she might be a serious sculptor. To say *lady doctor* is very condescending, since no one ever says *gentleman doctor* or even *man doctor*. For example, mention in the San Francisco *Chronicle* of January 31, 1972, of Madalyn Murray O'Hair as the *lady atheist* reduces her position to that of scatterbrained eccentric. Even *woman atheist* is scarcely defensible: sex is irrelevant to her philosophical position.

Many women argue that, on the other hand, *lady* carries with it overtones recalling the age of chivalry: conferring exalted stature on the person so referred to. This makes the term seem polite at first, but we must also remember that these implications are perilous: they suggest that a "lady" is helpless, and cannot do things by herself.

Lady can also be used to infer frivolousness, as in titles of organizations. Those that have a serious purpose (not merely that of enabling "the ladies" to spend time with one another) cannot use the word *lady* in their titles, but less serious ones may. Compare the *Ladies' Auxiliary* of a men's group, or the *Thursday Evening Ladies' Browning and Garden Society* with *Ladies' Liberation* or *Ladies' Strike for Peace*.

What is curious about this split is that *lady* is in origin a euphemism—a substitute that puts a better face on something people find uncomfortable—for *woman*. What kind of euphemism is it that subtly denigrates the people to whom it refers? Perhaps *lady* functions as a euphemism for *woman* because it does not contain the sexual implications present in *woman*: it is not "embarrassing" in that way. If this is so, we may expect that, in the future, *lady* will replace woman as the primary word for the human female, since *woman* will have become too blatantly sexual. That this distinction is already made in some contexts at least is shown in the following examples, where you can try replacing *woman* with *lady*:

15

20

a. She's only twelve, but she's already a woman.
b. After ten years in jail, Harry wanted to find a woman.
c. She's my woman, see, so don't mess around with her.

Another common substitute for *woman* is *girl*. One seldom hears a man past the age of adolescence referred to as a boy, save in expressions like "going out with the boys," which are meant to suggest an air of adolescent frivolity and irresponsibility. But women of all ages are "girls": one can have a man—not a boy—Friday, but only a girl—never a woman or even a lady—Friday; women have girlfriends, but men do not—in a nonsexual sense—have boyfriends. It may be that this use of *girl* is euphemistic in the same way the use of *lady* is: in stressing the idea of immaturity, it removes the sexual connotations lurking in *woman*. *Girl* brings to mind irresponsibility: you don't send a girl to do a woman's errand (or even, for that matter, a boy's errand). She is a person who is both too immature and too far from real life to be entrusted with responsibilities or with decisions of any serious or important nature.

Now let's take a pair of words which, in terms of the possible relationships in an earlier society, were simple male-female equivalents, analogous to *bull: cow*. Suppose we find that, for independent reasons, society has changed in such a way that the original meanings now are irrelevant. Yet the words have not been discarded, but have acquired new meanings, metaphorically related to their original senses. But suppose these new metaphorical uses are no longer parallel to each other. By seeing where the parallelism breaks down, we discover something about the different roles played by men and women in this culture. One good example of such a divergence through time is found in the pair, *master: mistress*. Once used with reference to one's power over servants, these words have become unusable today in their original master-servant sense as the relationship has become less prevalent in our society. But the words are still common.

Unless used with reference to animals, *master* now generally refers to a man who has acquired consummate ability in some field, normally nonsexual. But its feminine counterpart cannot be used this way. It is practically restricted to its sexual sense of "paramour." We start out with two terms, both roughly paraphrasable as "one who has power over another." But the masculine form, once one person is no longer able to have absolute power over another, becomes usable metaphorically in the sense of "having power over *something*." *Master* requires as its object only the name of some activity, something inanimate and abstract. But *mistress* requires a masculine noun in the possessive to precede it. One cannot say: "Rhonda is a mistress." One must be *someone's* mistress. A man is defined by what he does, a woman by her sexuality, that is, in terms of one particular aspect of her relationship to men. It is one thing to be an *old master* like Hans Holbein,[1] and another to be an *old mistress*.

[1]German painter of the sixteenth century.

The same is true of the words *spinster* and *bachelor*—gender words for "one who is not married." The resemblance ends with the definition. While *bachelor* is a neuter term, often used as a compliment, *spinster* normally is used pejoratively, with connotations of prissiness, fussiness, and so on. To be a bachelor implies that one has a choice of marrying or not, and this is what makes the idea of a bachelor existence attractive, in the popular literature. He has been pursued and has successfully eluded his pursuers. But a spinster is one who has not been pursued, or at least not seriously. She is old, unwanted goods. The metaphorical connotations of *bachelor* generally suggest sexual freedom; of *spinster*, puritanism or celibacy.

These examples could be multiplied. It is generally considered a *faux pas*, in society, to congratulate a woman on her engagement, while it is correct to congratulate her fiancé. Why is this? The reason seems to be that it is impolite to remind people of things that may be uncomfortable to them. To congratulate a woman on her engagement is really to say, "Thank goodness! You had a close call!" For the man, on the other hand, there was no such danger. His choosing to marry is viewed as a good thing, but not something essential.

The linguistic double standard holds throughout the life of the relationship. After marriage, bachelor and spinster become man and wife, not man and woman. The woman whose husband dies remains "John's widow"; John, however, is never "Mary's widower."

Finally, why is it that salesclerks and others are so quick to call women customers "dear," "honey," and other terms of endearment they really have no business using? A male customer would never put up with it. But women, like children, are supposed to enjoy these endearments, rather than being offended by them.

In more ways than one, it's time to speak up.

 ## Joining the Conversation: Critical Thinking and Writing

1. Lakoff's first example of "women's language" (paragraph 4) has to do with colors. She says that women are more likely than men to use such words as *mauve, beige,* and *lavender* not because women see a wider range of colors but because men, "who control most of the interesting affairs of the world," regard distinctions of color as trivial and presumably leave them to the women. How adequate does this explanation seem to you?

2. For a day or so, try to notice if Lakoff's suggestion is correct that women are more inclined than men to use "tag questions" and to use a "rising inflection" with a declarative sentence. Jot down examples you hear, and write an essay of about 500 words, either supporting or refuting Lakoff's suggestion.

3. While you are eavesdropping, you might notice, too, whether or not in mixed company women talk more than men. Many men assume that "women talk a lot," but is it true? If, for instance, you spend an evening with

an adult male and female couple, try to form an impression about which of the two does more of the talking. Of course this is too small a sample to allow for a generalization; still, it is worth thinking about. If you are at a meeting—perhaps a meeting of a committee with men and women—again try to see whether the males or the females do most of the talking. Try also to see whether one sex interrupts the other more often than the other way around. And try to make some sense out of your findings.

4. In paragraph 12 Lakoff says, "Women's language sounds much more 'polite' than men's," and she implies that this politeness is a way of seeming weak. Do you associate politeness with weakness?

5. The essay originally appeared in *Ms.*, a feminist magazine, rather than in an academic journal devoted to language or to sociology. Why do you suppose Lakoff chose *Ms.*? What would you say her purpose was in writing and publishing the essay?

6. This essay was first published in 1974. Do you think it is dated? You might begin by asking yourself if women today use "women's language."

Barbara Lawrence

Barbara Lawrence was born in Hanover, New Hampshire, and educated at Connecticut College and New York University. She teaches at the State University of New York, at Old Westbury. This essay first appeared in the New York Times.

Four-Letter Words Can Hurt You

Why should any words be called obscene? Don't they all describe natural human functions? Am I trying to tell them, my students demand, that the "strong, earthy, gut-honest"—or, if they are fans of Norman Mailer, the "rich, liberating, existential"—language they use to describe sexual activity isn't preferable to "phony-sounding, middle-class words like 'intercourse' and 'copulate'?" "Cop You Late!" they say with fancy inflections and gagging grimaces. "Now, what is *that* supposed to mean?"

Well, what is it supposed to mean? And why indeed should one group of words describing human functions and human organs be acceptable in ordinary conversation and another, describing presumably the same organs and functions, be tabooed—so much so, in fact, that some of these words still cannot appear in print in many parts of the English-speaking world?

The argument that these taboos exist only because of "sexual hangups" (middle-class, middle-age, feminist), or even that they are a result of class oppression (the contempt of the Norman conquerors for the language of their Anglo-Saxon serfs), ignores a much more likely explanation, it seems to me, and that is the sources and functions of the words themselves.

The best known of the tabooed sexual verbs, for example, comes from the German *ficken*, meaning "to strike"; combined, according to Partridge's etymological dictionary *Origins*, with the Latin sexual verb *futuere*; associated in turn with the Latin *fustis*, "a staff or cudgel"; the Celtic *buc*, "a point, hence to pierce"; the Irish *bot*, "the male member"; the Latin *battuere*, "to beat"; the Gaelic *batair*, "a cudgeller"; the Early Irish *bualaim*, "I strike"; and so forth. It is one of what etymologists sometimes call "the sadistic group of words for the man's part in copulation."

The brutality of this word, then, and its equivalents ("screw," "bang," etc.), is not an illusion of the middle class or a crotchet of Women's Liberation. In their origins and imagery these words carry undeniably painful, if not sadistic, implications, the object of which is almost always female. Consider, for example, what a "screw" actually does to the wood it penetrates; what a painful, even mutilating, activity this kind of analogy suggests. "Screw" is particularly interesting in this context, since the noun, according to Partridge, comes from words meaning "groove," "nut," "ditch," "breeding sow," "scrofula" and "swelling," while the verb, besides its explicit imagery, has antecedent associations to "write on," "scratch," "scarify," and so forth—a revealing fusion of a mechanical or painful action with an obviously denigrated object.

Not all obscene words, of course, are as implicitly sadistic or denigrating to women as these, but all that I know seem to serve a similar purpose: to reduce the human organism (especially the female organism) and human functions (especially sexual and procreative) to their least organic, most mechanical dimension; to substitute a trivializing or deforming resemblance for the complex human reality of what is being described.

Tabooed male descriptives, when they are not openly denigrating to women, often serve to divorce a male organ or function from any significant interaction with the female. Take the word "testes," for example, suggesting "witnesses" (from the Latin *testis*) to the sexual and procreative strengths of the male organ; and the obscene counterpart of this word, which suggests little more than a mechanical shape. Or compare almost any of the "rich," "liberating" sexual verbs, so fashionable today among male writers, with that much-derided Latin word "copulate" ("to bind or join together") or even that Anglo-Saxon phrase (which seems to have had no trouble surviving the Norman Conquest) "make love."

How arrogantly self-involved the tabooed words seem in comparison to either of the other terms, and how contemptuous of the female partner. Understandably so, of course, if she is only a "skirt," a "broad," a "chick,"

5

a "pussycat" or a "piece." If she is, in other words, no more than her skirt, or what her skirt conceals; no more than a breeder, or the broadest part of her; no more than a piece of a human being or a "piece of tail."

The most severely tabooed of all the female descriptives, incidentally, are those like a "piece of tail," which suggest (either explicitly or through antecedents) that there is no significant difference between the female channel through which we are all conceived and born and the anal outlet common to both sexes—a distinction that pornographers have always enjoyed obscuring.

This effort to deny women their biological identity, their individuality, their humanness, is such an important aspect of obscene language that one can only marvel at how seldom, in an era preoccupied with definitions of obscenity, this fact is brought to our attention. One problem, of course, is that many of the people in the best position to do this (critics, teachers, writers) are so reluctant today to admit that they are angered or shocked by obscenity. Bored, maybe, unimpressed, aesthetically displeased, but—no matter how brutal or denigrating the material—never angered, never shocked.

And yet how eloquently angered, how piously shocked many of these same people become if denigrating language is used about any minority group other than women; if the obscenities are racial or ethnic, that is, rather than sexual. Words like "coon," "kike," "spic," "wop," after all, deform identity, deny individuality and humanness in almost exactly the same way that sexual vulgarisms and obscenities do.

No one that I know, least of all my students, would fail to question the values of a society whose literature and entertainment rested heavily on racial or ethnic pejoratives. Are the values of a society whose literature and entertainment rest as heavily as ours on sexual pejoratives any less questionable?

Joining the Conversation: Critical Thinking and Writing

1. In addition to giving evidence to support her view, what persuasive devices (such as irony, analogy) does Lawrence use? (On irony, see page 654; on analogy, see page 651.)

2. Not all authorities agree with all of Lawrence's etymologies. Is her argument, therefore, weakened?

3. Examine your own use or nonuse of four-letter words. How and when did you learn to use them or to avoid using them? If you have reasons to avoid them other than the ones Lawrence provides, what are they? If you do use such words, under what circumstances are you likely to use them? Will Lawrence's analysis persuade you to avoid them altogether? Why or why not?

Edward T. Hall

Edward T. Hall, born in Missouri in 1914, was for many years a professor of anthropology at Northwestern University.

Hall is especially concerned with "proxemics," a word derived from the Latin proximus, "nearest." Proxemics is the study of people's responses to spatial relationships—for example, their ways of marking out their territory in public places and their responses to what they consider to be crowding. In these pages from his book The Hidden Dimension *(1966), Hall suggests that Arabs and Westerners must understand the proxemic customs of each other's culture; without such understanding, other communications between them are likely to be misunderstood.*

Proxemics in the Arab World

In spite of over two thousand years of contact, Westerners and Arabs still do not understand each other. Proxemic research reveals some insights into this difficulty. Americans in the Middle East are immediately struck by two conflicting sensations. In public they are compressed and overwhelmed by smells, crowding, and high noise levels; in Arab homes Americans are apt to rattle around, feeling exposed and often somewhat inadequate because of too much space! (The Arab houses and apartments of the middle and upper classes which Americans stationed abroad commonly occupy are much larger than the dwellings such Americans usually inhabit.) Both the high sensory stimulation which is experienced in public places and the basic insecurity which comes from being in a dwelling that is too large provide Americans with an introduction to the sensory world of the Arab.

Behavior in Public

Pushing and shoving in public places is characteristic of Middle Eastern culture. Yet it is not entirely what Americans think it is (being pushy and rude) but stems from a different set of assumptions concerning not only the relations between people but how one experiences the body as well. Paradoxically, Arabs consider northern Europeans and Americans pushy, too. This was very puzzling to me when I started investigating these two views. How could Americans who stand aside and avoid touching be considered pushy? I used to ask Arabs to explain this paradox. None of my subjects was able to tell me specifically what particulars of American behavior were responsible, yet they all agreed that the impression was widespread among Arabs. After repeated unsuccessful attempts to gain insight into the cognitive world of the Arab on this particular point, I filed it away as a question that only time would answer. When the answer came, it was because of a seemingly inconsequential annoyance.

While waiting for a friend in a Washington, D.C., hotel lobby and wanting to be both visible and alone, I had seated myself in a solitary chair outside the normal stream of traffic. In such a setting most Americans follow a rule, which is all the more binding because we seldom think about it, that can be stated as follows: as soon as a person stops or is seated in a public place, there balloons around him a small sphere of privacy which is considered inviolate. The size of the sphere varies with the degree of crowding, the age, sex, and the importance of the person, as well as the general surroundings. Anyone who enters this zone and stays there is intruding. In fact, a stranger who intrudes, even for a specific purpose, acknowledges the fact that he has intruded by beginning his request with "Pardon me, but can you tell me. . . ?"

To continue, as I waited in the deserted lobby, a stranger walked up to where I was sitting and stood close enough so that not only could I easily touch him but I could even hear him breathing. In addition, the dark mass of his body filled the peripheral field of vision on my left side. If the lobby had been crowded with people, I would have understood his behavior, but in an empty lobby his presence made me exceedingly uncomfortable. Feeling annoyed by this intrusion, I moved my body in such a way as to communicate annoyance. Strangely enough, instead of moving away, my actions seemed only to encourage him, because he moved even closer. In spite of the temptation to escape the annoyance, I put aside thoughts of abandoning my post, thinking, "To hell with it. Why should I move? I was here first and I'm not going to let this fellow drive me out even if he is a boor." Fortunately, a group of people soon arrived whom my tormentor immediately joined. Their mannerisms explained his behavior, for I knew from both speech and gestures that they were Arabs. I had not been able to make this crucial identification by looking at my subject when he was alone because he wasn't talking and he was wearing American clothes.

In describing the scene later to an Arab colleague, two contrasting   5
patterns emerged. My concept and my feelings about my own circle of privacy in a "public" place immediately struck my Arab friend as strange and puzzling. He said, "After all, it's a public place, isn't it?" Pursuing this line of inquiry, I found that an Arab thought I had no rights whatsoever by virtue of occupying a given spot; neither my place nor my body was inviolate! For the Arab, there is no such thing as an intrusion in public. Public means public. With this insight, a great range of Arab behavior that had been puzzling, annoying, and sometimes even frightening began to make sense. I learned, for example, that if *A* is standing on a street corner and *B* wants his spot, *B* is within his rights if he does what he can to make *A* uncomfortable enough to move. In Beirut only the hardy sit in the last row in a movie theater, because there are usually standees who want seats and who push and shove and make such a nuisance that most people give up and leave. Seen in this light, the Arab who "intruded" on my space in the hotel lobby had apparently selected it for the very reason I

had: it was a good place to watch two doors and the elevator. My show of annoyance, instead of driving him away, had only encouraged him. He thought he was about to get me to move.

Another silent source of friction between Americans and Arabs is in an area that Americans treat very informally—the manners and rights of the road. In general, in the United States we tend to defer to the vehicle that is bigger, more powerful, faster, and heavily laden. While a pedestrian walking along a road may feel annoyed he will not think it unusual to step aside for a fast-moving automobile. He knows that because he is moving he does not have the right to the space around him that he has when he is standing still (as I was in the hotel lobby). It appears that the reverse is true with the Arabs who apparently *take on rights to space as they move*. For someone else to move into a space an Arab is also moving into is a violation of his rights. It is infuriating to an Arab to have someone else cut in front of him on the highway. It is the American's cavalier treatment of moving space that makes the Arab call him aggressive and pushy.

Concepts of Privacy

The experience described above and many others suggested to me that Arabs might actually have a wholly contrasting set of assumptions concerning the body and the rights associated with it. Certainly the Arab tendency to shove and push each other in public and to feel and pinch women in public conveyances would not be tolerated by Westerners. It appeared to me that they must not have any concept of a private zone outside the body. This proved to be precisely the case.

In the Western world, the person is synonymous with an individual inside a skin. And in northern Europe generally, the skin and even the clothes may be inviolate. You need permission to touch either if you are a stranger. This rule applies in some parts of France, where the mere touching of another person during an argument used to be legally defined as assault. For the Arab the location of the person in relation to the body is quite different. The person exists somewhere down inside the body. The ego is not completely hidden, however, because it can be reached very easily with an insult. It is protected from touch but not from words. The dissociation of the body and the ego may explain why the public amputation of a thief's hand is tolerated as standard punishment in Saudi Arabia. It also sheds light on why an Arab employer living in a modern apartment can provide his servant with a room that is a box-like cubicle approximately 5 by 10 by 4 feet in size that is not only hung from the ceiling to conserve floor space but has an opening so that the servant can be spied on.

As one might suspect, deep orientations toward the self such as the one just described are also reflected in the language. This was brought to my attention one afternoon when an Arab colleague who is the author of an Arab-English dictionary arrived in my office and threw himself into a chair in a state of obvious exhaustion. When I asked him what had been going on, he said: "I have spent the entire afternoon trying to find the Arab equivalent of the English word 'rape.' There is no such word in Arabic. All my sources, both written and spoken, can come up with no more than an approximation, such as 'He took her against her will.' There is nothing in Arabic approaching your meaning as it is expressed in that one word."

Differing concepts of the placement of the ego in relation to the body are not easily grasped. Once an idea like this is accepted, however, it is possible to understand many other facets of Arab life that would otherwise be difficult to explain. One of these is the high population density of Arab cities like Cairo, Beirut, and Damascus. According to the animal studies described [elsewhere], the Arabs should be living in a perpetual behavioral sink. While it is probable that Arabs are suffering from population pressures, it is also just as possible that continued pressure from the desert has resulted in a cultural adaptation to high density which takes the form described above. Tucking the ego down inside the body shell not only would permit higher population densities but would explain why it is that Arab communications are stepped up as much as they are when compared to northern European communication patterns. Not only is the sheer noise level much higher, but the piercing look of the eyes, the touch of the hands, and the mutual bathing in the warm moist breath during conversation represent stepped-up sensory inputs to a level which many Europeans find unbearably intense.

The Arab dream is for lots of space in the home, which unfortunately many Arabs cannot afford. Yet when he has space, it is very different from what one finds in most American homes. Arab spaces inside their upper middle-class homes are tremendous by our standards. They avoid partitions because Arabs *do not like to be alone*. The form of the home is such as to hold the family together inside a single protective shell, because Arabs are deeply involved with each other. Their personalities are intermingled and take nourishment from each other like the roots and soil. If one is not with people and actively involved in some way, one is deprived of life. An old Arab saying reflects this value: "Paradise without people should not be entered because it is Hell." Therefore, Arabs in the United States often feel socially and sensorially deprived and long to be back where there is human warmth and contact.

Since there is no physical privacy as we know it in the Arab family, not even a word for privacy, one could expect that the Arabs might use some other means to be alone. Their way to be alone is to stop talking. Like the English, an Arab who shuts himself off in this way is not indicating that anything is wrong or that he is withdrawing, only that he wants to be alone with his own thoughts or does not want to be intruded upon. One subject said that her father would come and go for days at a time without saying a word, and no one in the family thought anything of it. Yet for this very reason, an Arab exchange student visiting a Kansas farm failed to pick up the cue that his American hosts were mad at him when they gave him the "silent treatment." He only discovered something was wrong when they took him to town and tried forcibly to put him on a bus to Washington, D.C., the headquarters of the exchange program responsible for his presence in the U.S.

Arab Personal Distances

Like everyone else in the world, Arabs are unable to formulate specific rules for their informal behavior patterns. In fact, they often deny that there are any rules, and they are made anxious by suggestions that such is the case. Therefore, in order to determine how the Arab sets distances, I investigated the use of each sense separately. Gradually, definite and distinctive behavioral patterns began to emerge.

Olfaction occupies a prominent place in the Arab life. Not only is it one of the distance-setting mechanisms, but it is a vital part of a complex system of behavior. Arabs consistently breathe on people when they talk. However, this habit is more than a matter of different manners. To the Arab good smells are pleasing and a way of being involved with each other. To smell one's friend is not only nice but desirable, for to deny him your breath is to act ashamed. Americans, on the other hand, trained as they are not to breathe in people's faces, automatically communicate shame in trying to be polite. Who would expect that when our highest diplomats are putting on their best manners they are also communicating shame? Yet this is what occurs constantly, because diplomacy is not only "eyeball to eyeball" but breath to breath.

By stressing olfaction, Arabs do not try to eliminate all the body's odors, only to enhance them and use them in building human relationships. Nor are they self-conscious about telling others when they don't like the way they smell. A man leaving his house in the morning may be told by his uncle, "Habib, your stomach is sour and your breath doesn't smell too good. Better not talk too close to people today." Smell is even considered in the choice of a mate. When couples are being matched for marriage, the man's go-between will sometimes ask to smell the girl, who may be turned down if she doesn't "smell nice." Arabs recognize that smell and disposition may be linked.

In a word, the olfactory boundary performs two roles in Arab life. It enfolds those who want to relate and separates those who don't. The Arab finds it essential to stay inside the olfactory zone as a means of keeping tab on changes in emotion. What is more, he may feel crowded as soon as he smells something unpleasant. While not much is known about "olfactory crowding," this may prove to be as significant as any other variable in the crowding complex because it is tied directly to the body chemistry and hence to the state of health and emotions. It is not surprising, therefore, that the olfactory boundary constitutes for the Arabs an informal distance-setting mechanism in contrast to the visual mechanisms of the Westerner.

Facing and Not Facing

One of my earliest discoveries in the field of intercultural communication was that the position of the bodies of people in conversation varies with the culture. Even so, it used to puzzle me that a special Arab friend seemed unable to walk and talk at the same time. After years in the United States, he could not bring himself to stroll along, facing forward while talking. Our progress would be arrested while he edged ahead, cutting slightly in front of me and turning sideways so we could see each other. Once in this position, he would stop. His behavior was explained when I learned that for the Arabs to view the other person peripherally is regarded as impolite, and to sit or stand back-to-back is considered very rude. You must be involved when interacting with Arabs who are friends.

One mistaken American notion is that Arabs conduct all conversations at close distance. This is not the case at all. On social occasions, they may sit on opposite sides of the room and talk across the room to each other. They are, however, apt to take offense when Americans use what are to them ambiguous distances, such as the four- to seven-foot social-consultative distance. They frequently complain that Americans are cold or aloof or "don't care." This was what an elderly Arab diplomat in an American hospital thought when the American nurses used "professional" distance. He had the feeling that he was being ignored, that they might not take good care of him. Another Arab subject remarked, referring to American behavior, "What's the matter? Do I smell bad? Or are they afraid of me?"

Arabs who interact with Americans report experiencing a certain flatness traceable in part to a very different use of the eyes in private and in public as well as between friends and strangers. Even though it is rude for a guest to walk around the Arab home eying things, Arabs look at each other in ways which seem hostile or challenging to the American. One Arab informant said that he was in constant hot water with Americans because of the way he looked at them without the slightest intention of offending. In fact, he had on several occasions barely avoided fights with American men who apparently thought their masculinity was being challenged because of the way he was looking at them. As noted earlier, Arabs look each other in the eye when talking with an intensity that makes most Americans highly uncomfortable.

Involvement

As the reader must gather by now, Arabs are involved with each other on many different levels simultaneously. Privacy in a public place is foreign to them. Business transactions in the bazaar, for example, are not just between buyer and seller, but are participated in by everyone. Anyone who is standing around may join in. If a grownup sees a boy breaking a window, he must stop him even if he doesn't know him. Involvement and participation   20 are expressed in other ways as well. If two men are fighting, the crowd must intervene. On the political level, *to fail to intervene* when trouble is brewing is to take sides, which is what our State Department always seems to be doing. Given the fact that few people in the world today are even remotely aware of the cultural mold that forms their thoughts, it is normal for Arabs to view *our* behavior as though it stemmed from *their* own hidden set of assumptions.

Feelings about Enclosed Spaces

In the course of my interviews with Arabs the term "tomb" kept cropping up in conjunction with enclosed space. In a word, Arabs don't mind being crowded by people but hate to be hemmed in by walls. They show a much greater overt sensitivity to architectural crowding than we do. Enclosed space must meet at least three requirements that I know of if it is to satisfy the Arabs: there must be plenty of unobstructed space in which to move around (possibly as much as a thousand square feet); very high ceilings—so high in fact that they do not normally impinge on the visual field; and, in addition, there must be an unobstructed view. It was spaces such as these in which the Americans referred to earlier felt so uncomfortable. One sees the Arab's need for a view expressed in many ways, even negatively, for to cut off a neighbor's view is one of the most effective ways of spiting him. In Beirut one can see what is known locally as the "spite house." It is nothing more than a thick, fourstory wall, built at the end of a long fight between neighbors, on a narrow strip of land, for the express purpose of denying a view of the Mediterranean to any house built on the land behind. According to one of my informants, there is also a house on a small plot of land between Beirut and Damascus which is completely surrounded by a neighbor's wall built high enough to cut off the view from all windows!

Boundaries

Proxemic patterns tell us other things about Arab culture. For example, the whole concept of the boundary as an abstraction is almost impossible to pin down. In one sense, there are no boundaries. "Edges" of towns, yes, but permanent boundaries out in the country (hidden lines), no. In the course of my work with Arab subjects I had a difficult time translating our concept of a boundary into terms which could be equated with theirs. In order to clarify the distinctions between the two very different definitions, I thought it might be helpful to pinpoint acts which constituted trespass. To date, I have been unable to discover anything even remotely resembling our own legal concept of trespass.

Arab behavior in regard to their own real estate is apparently an extension of, and therefore consistent with, their approach to the body. My subjects simply failed to respond whenever trespass was mentioned. They didn't seem to understand what I meant by this term. This may be explained by the fact that they organize relationships with each other according to closed social systems rather than spatially. For thousands of years Moslems, Marinites, Druses, and Jews have lived in their own villages, each with strong kin affiliations. Their hierarchy of loyalties is: first to one's self, then to kinsman, townsman, or tribesman, coreligionist and/or countryman. Anyone not in these categories is a stranger. Strangers and enemies are very closely linked, if not synonymous, in Arab thought. Trespass in this context is a matter of who you are, rather than a piece of land or a space with a boundary that can be denied to anyone and everyone, friend and foe alike.

In summary, proxemic patterns differ. By examining them it is possible to reveal hidden cultural frames that determine the structure of a given people's perceptual world. Perceiving the world differently leads to differential definitions of what constitutes crowded living, different interpersonal relations, and a different approach to both local and international politics.

 ## Joining the Conversation: Critical Thinking and Writing

1. According to Hall, why do Arabs think Americans are pushy? And, again according to Hall, why do Arabs not consider themselves pushy?

2. Explain what Hall means by "cognitive world" (paragraph 2); by "ego" (paragraph 10); by "behavioral sink" (in the same paragraph). Then explain, for the benefit of someone who does not understand the terms, how you know what Hall means by each.

3. In paragraph 9 Hall points out that there is no Arabic equivalent of the English word *rape*. Can you provide an example of a similar gap in English or in another language? Does a cultural difference account for the linguistic difference?

4. In paragraph 3 Hall says of a rule that it "is all the more binding because we seldom think about it." Is this generally true of rules? What examples or counterexamples support your view?

Deborah Tannen

Deborah Tannen holds a Ph.D. in linguistics from the University of California, Berkeley, and is University Professor of linguistics at Georgetown University. She is the author of scholarly articles and books as well as of popular articles in such magazines as New York *and* Vogue. *We reprint a chapter from one of her books,* That's Not What I Meant!

The Workings of Conversational Style

The Meaning Is the Metamessage

You're sitting at a bar—or in a coffee shop or at a party—and suddenly you feel lonely. You wonder, "What do all these people find to talk about that's so important?" Usually the answer is, Nothing. Nothing that's so important. But people don't wait until they have something important to say in order to talk.

Very little of what is said is important for the information expressed in the words. But that doesn't mean that the talk isn't important. It's crucially important, as a way of showing that we are involved with each other, and how we feel about being involved. Our talk is saying something about our relationship.

Information conveyed by the meanings of words is the message. What is communicated about relationships—attitudes toward each other, the occasion, and what we are saying—is the metamessage. And it's metamessages that we react to most strongly. If someone says, "I'm not angry," and his jaw is set hard and his words seem to be squeezed out in a hiss, you won't believe the message that he's not angry; you'll believe the metamessage conveyed by the way he said it—that he is. Comments like "It's not what you said but the way you said it" or "Why did you say it like that?" or "Obviously it's not nothing; something's wrong" are responses to metamessages of talk.

Many of us dismiss talk that does not convey important information as worthless—meaningless small talk if it's a social setting or "empty rhetoric" if it's public. Such admonitions as "Skip the small talk," "Get to the point," or "Why don't you say what you mean?" may seem to be reasonable. But they are reasonable only if information is all that counts. This attitude toward talk ignores the fact that people are emotionally involved with each other and that talking is the major way we establish, maintain, monitor, and adjust our relationships.

Whereas words convey information, how we speak those words—how loud, how fast, with what intonation and emphasis—communicates what we think we're doing when we speak: teasing, flirting, explaining, or chastising; whether we're feeling friendly, angry, or quizzical; whether we want to get closer or back off. In other words, how we say what we say communicates social meanings.

5

Although we continually respond to social meaning in conversation, we have a hard time talking about it because it does not reside in the dictionary definitions of words, and most of us have unwavering faith in the gospel according to the dictionary. It is always difficult to talk about—even to see or think about—forces and processes for which we have no

---

names, even if we feel their impact. Linguistics provides terms that describe the processes of communication and therefore make it possible to see, talk, and think about them.

This chapter introduces some of the linguistic terms that give names to concepts that are crucial for understanding communication—and therefore relationships. In addition to the concept of metamessages—underlying it, in a sense—there are universal human needs that motivate communication: the needs to be connected to others and to be left alone. Trying to honor these conflicting needs puts us in a double bind. The linguistic concept of politeness accounts for the way we serve these needs and react to the double bind—through metamessages in our talk.

Involvement and Independence

The philosopher Schopenhauer gave an often-quoted example of porcupines trying to get through a cold winter. They huddle together for warmth, but their sharp quills prick each other, so they pull away. But then they get cold. They have to keep adjusting their closeness and distance to keep from freezing and from getting pricked by their fellow porcupines—the source of both comfort and pain.

We need to get close to each other to have a sense of community, to feel we're not alone in the world. But we need to keep our distance from each other to preserve our independence, so others don't impose on or engulf us. This duality reflects the human condition. We are individual and social creatures. We need other people to survive, but we want to survive as individuals.

Another way to look at this duality is that we are all the same—and all different. There is comfort in being understood and pain in the impossibility of being understood completely. But there is also comfort in being different—special and unique—and pain in being the same as everyone else, just another cog on the wheel.

10

Valuing Involvement and Independence

We all keep balancing the needs for involvement and independence, but individuals as well as cultures place different relative values on these needs and have different ways of expressing those values. America as a nation has glorified individuality, especially for men. This is in stark contrast to people in many parts of the world outside Western Europe, who more often glorify involvement in family and clan, for women and men.

The independent pioneers—and later our image of them—have served us well. The glorification of independence served the general progress of the nation as (traditionally male) individuals have been willing to leave their hometowns—the comfort of the familiar and familial—to find opportunity, get the best education, travel, work wherever they could find the best jobs or wherever their jobs sent them. The yearning for involvement enticed (traditionally female) individuals to join them.

The values of the group are reflected in personal values. Many Americans, especially (but not only) American men, place more emphasis on their need for independence and less on their need for social involvement. This often entails paying less attention to the metamessage level of talk— the level that comments on relationships—focusing instead on the information level. The attitude may go as far as the conviction that only the information level really counts—or is really there. It is then a logical conclusion that talk not rich in information should be dispensed with. Thus, many daughters and sons of all ages, calling their parents, find that their fathers want to exchange whatever information is needed and then hang up, but their mothers want to chat, to "keep in touch."

American men's information-focused approach to talk has shaped the American way of doing business. Most Americans think it's best to "get down to brass tacks" as soon as possible, and not "waste time" in small talk (social talk) or "beating around the bush." But this doesn't work very well in business dealings with Greek, Japanese, or Arab counterparts for whom "small talk" is necessary to establish the social relationship that must provide the foundation for conducting business.

Another expression of this difference—one that costs American 15 tourists huge amounts of money—is our inability to understand the logic behind bargaining. If the African, Indian, Arab, South American, or Mediterranean seller wants to sell a product, and the tourist wants to buy it, why not set a fair price and let the sale proceed? Because the sale is only one part of the interaction. Just as important, if not more so, is the interaction that goes on during the bargaining: an artful way for buyer and seller to reaffirm their recognition that they're dealing with—and that they are—humans, not machines.

Believing that only the information level of communication is important and real also lets men down when it comes to maintaining personal relationships. From day to day, there often isn't any significant news to talk about. Women are negatively stereotyped as frivolously talking at length without conveying significant information. Yet their ability to keep talking to each other makes it possible for them to maintain close friendships. *Washington Post* columnist Richard Cohen observed that he and the other men he knows don't really have friends in the sense that women have them. This may be at least partly because they don't talk to each other if they can't think of some substantive topic to talk about. As a result, many men find themselves without personal contacts when they retire.

The Double Bind

No matter what relative value we place on involvement and independence, and how we express these values, people, like porcupines, are always balancing the conflicting needs for both. But the porcupine metaphor is a little misleading because it suggests a sequence: alternately drawing close and pulling back. Our needs for involvement and independence—to be connected and to be separate—are not sequential but simultaneous. We must serve both needs at once in all we say.

And that is why we find ourselves in a double bind. Anything we say to show we're involved with others is in itself a threat to our (and their) individuality. And anything we say to show we're keeping our distance from others is in itself a threat to our (and their) need for involvement. It's not just a conflict—feeling torn between two alternatives—or ambivalence—feeling two ways about one thing. It's a double bind because whatever we do to serve one need necessarily violates the other. And we can't step out of the circle. If we try to withdraw by not communicating, we hit the force field of our need for involvement and are hurled back in.

Because of this double bind, communication will never be perfect; we cannot reach stasis. We have no choice but to keep trying to balance independence and involvement, freedom and safety, the familiar and the strange—continually making adjustments as we list to one side or the other. The way we make these adjustments in our talk can be understood as politeness phenomena.

Information and Politeness in Talk

A language philosopher, H. P. Grice, codified the rules by which conversation would be constructed if information were its only point:

20

Say as much as necessary and no more.

Tell the truth.

Be relevant.

Be clear.

These make perfect sense—until we start to listen to and think about real conversations. For one thing, all the seeming absolutes underlying these injunctions are really relative. How much is necessary? Which truth? What is relevant? What is clear?

But even if we could agree on these values, we wouldn't want simply to blurt out what we mean, because we're juggling the needs for involvement and independence. If what we mean shows involvement, we want to temper it to show we're not imposing. If what we mean shows distance, we want to temper it with involvement to show we're not rejecting. If we state what we want to believe, others may not agree or may not want the same thing, so our statement could introduce disharmony; therefore we prefer to get an idea of what others want or think, or how they feel about what we want or think, before we commit ourselves to—maybe even before we make up our minds about—what we mean.

This broad concept of the social goals we serve when we talk is called "politeness" by linguists and anthropologists—not the pinky-in-the-air idea of politeness, but a deeper sense of trying to take into account the effect of what we say on other people.

Linguist Robin Lakoff devised another set of rules that describe the motivations behind politeness—that is, how we adjust what we say to take into account its effects on others. Here they are as Lakoff presents them:

1. Don't impose; keep your distance.
2. Give options; let the other person have a say.
3. Be friendly; maintain camaraderie.

Following Rule 3, Be friendly, makes others comfortable by serving their need for involvement. Following Rule 1, Don't impose, makes others comfortable by serving their need for independence. Rule 2, Give options, falls between Rules 1 and 3. People differ with respect to which rules they tend to apply, and when, and how.

To see how these rules work, let's consider a fairly trivial but common conversation. If you offer me something to drink, I may say, "No, thanks," even though I am thirsty. In some societies this is expected; you insist, and I give in after about the third offer. This is polite in the sense of Rule 1, Don't impose. If you expect this form of politeness and I accept on the first offer, you will think I'm too forward—or dying of thirst. If you don't expect this form of politeness, and I use it, you will take my refusal at face value—and I might indeed die of thirst while waiting for you to ask again.

I may also say, in response to your offer, "I'll have whatever you're having." This is polite in the sense of Rule 2, Give options: I'm letting you decide what to give me. If I do this, but you expect me to refuse the first offer, you may still think I'm pushy. But if you expect Rule 3, Be friendly, you may think me wishy-washy. Don't I know what I want? 25

Exercising Rule 3-style politeness, Be friendly, I might respond to your offer of something to drink by saying, "Yes, thanks, some apple juice, please." In fact, if this is my style of politeness, I might not wait for you to offer at all, but ask right off, "Have you got anything to drink?," or even head straight for your kitchen, throw open the refrigerator door, and call out, "Got any juice?"

If you and I both feel this is appropriate, my doing it will reinforce our rapport because we both subscribe to the rule of breaking rules; not having to follow the more formal rule sends a metamessage: "We are such good friends, we don't have to stand on ceremony." But if you don't subscribe to this brand of politeness, or don't want to get that chummy with me, you will be offended by my way of being friendly. If we have only recently met, that could be the beginning of the end of our friendship.

Of course, these aren't actually rules, but senses we have of the "natural" way to speak. We don't think of ourselves as following rules, or even (except in formal situations) of being polite. We simply talk in ways that seem obviously appropriate at the time they pop out of our mouths— seemingly self-evident ways of being a good person.

Yet our use of these "rules" is not unconscious. If asked about why we said one thing or another in this way or that, we are likely to explain that we spoke the way we did "to be nice" or "friendly" or "considerate." These are commonsense terms for what linguists refer to, collectively, as politeness—ways of taking into account the effect on others of what we say.

The rules, or senses, of politeness are not mutually exclusive. We don't choose one and ignore the others. Rather we balance them all to be appropriately friendly without imposing, to keep appropriate distance without appearing aloof.

Negotiating the offer of a drink is a fairly trivial matter, though the importance of such fleeting conversations should not be underestimated. The way we talk in countless such daily encounters is part of what constitutes our image of ourselves, and it is on the basis of such encounters that we form our impressions of each other. They have a powerful cumulative effect on our personal and interactive lives.

Furthermore, the process of balancing these conflicting senses of politeness—serving involvement and independence—is the basis for the most consequential of interactions as well as the most trivial. Let's consider the linguistic means we have of serving these needs—and their inherent indeterminacy, which means they can easily let us down.

The Two-Edged Sword of Politeness

Sue was planning to visit Amy in a distant city, but shortly before she was supposed to arrive, Sue called and canceled. Although Amy felt disappointed, she tried to be understanding. Being polite by not imposing, and respecting Sue's need for independence, Amy said it was really okay if Sue didn't come. Sue was very depressed at that time, and she got more depressed. She took Amy's considerateness—a sign of caring, respecting Sue's independence—as indifference—not caring at all, a lack of involvement. Amy later felt partly responsible for Sue's depression because she hadn't insisted that Sue visit. This confusion was easy to fall into and hard to climb out of because ways of showing caring and indifference are inherently ambiguous.

You can be nice to someone either by showing your involvement or by not imposing. And you can be mean by refusing to show involvement—cutting her off—or by imposing—being "inconsiderate." You can show someone you're angry by shouting at her—imposing—or refusing to talk to her at all: the silent activity called snubbing.

You can be kind by saying something or by saying nothing. For example, if someone has suffered a misfortune—failed an exam, lost a job, or contracted a disease—you may show sympathy by expressing your concern in words or by deliberately not mentioning it to avoid causing pain by bringing it up. If everyone takes the latter approach, silence becomes a chamber in which the ill, the bereaved, and the unemployed are isolated.

If you choose to avoid mentioning a misfortune, you run the risk of seeming to have forgotten, or of not caring. You may try to circumvent that interpretation by casting a knowing glance, making an indirect reference, or softening the impact with euphemisms ("your situation"), hedges and hesitations ("your . . . um . . . well . . . er . . . you know"), or apologies ("I hope you don't mind my mentioning this"). But meaningful glances and verbal hedging can themselves offend by sending the metamessage "This is too terrible to mention" or "Your condition is shameful." A person thus shielded may feel like shouting, "Why don't you just say it!?"

An American couple visited the husband's brother in Germany, where he was living with a German girlfriend. One evening during dinner, the girlfriend asked the brother where he had taken his American guests that day. Upon hearing that he had taken them to the concentration camp at Dachau, she exclaimed in revulsion that that was an awful place to take them; why would he do such a stupid thing? The brother cut off her exclamations by whispering to her while glancing at the American woman. His girlfriend immediately stopped complaining and nodded in understanding, also casting glances at the American, who was not appreciative of their discretion. Instead, she was offended by the assumption that being Jewish is cause for whispering and furtive glances.

Any attempt to soften the impact of what is said can have the opposite effect. For example, a writer recalled the impression that a colleague had written something extremely critical about the manuscript of her book. Preparing to revise the manuscript, she returned to his comments and was surprised to see that the criticism was very mild indeed. The guilty word was the one that preceded the comment, not the comment itself. By beginning the sentence with "Frankly," her colleague sent a metamessage: "Steel yourself. This is going to hurt a lot."

Such layers of meaning are always at work in conversation; anything you say or don't say sends metamessages that become part of the meaning of the conversation.

Mixed Metamessages at Home

Parental love puts relative emphasis on involvement, but as children   40
grow up, most parents give more and more signs of love by respecting their independence. Usually this comes too late for the children's tastes. The teenager who resents being told to put on a sweater or eat breakfast interprets the parent's sign of involvement as an imposition. Although this isn't in the message, the teenager hears a metamessage to the effect "You're still a child who needs to be told how to take care of yourself."

Partners in intimate relationships often differ about how they balance involvement and independence. There are those who show love by making sure the other eats right, dresses warmly, or doesn't drive alone at night. There are others who feel this is imposing and treating them like children.

And there are those who feel that their partners don't care about them because they aren't concerned with what they eat, wear, or do. What may be meant as a show of respect for their independence is taken as lack of involvement—which it also might be.

Maxwell wants to be left alone, and Samantha wants attention. So she gives him attention, and he leaves her alone. The adage "Do unto others as you would have others do unto you" may be the source of a lot of anguish and misunderstanding if the doer and the done unto have different styles.

Samantha and Maxwell might feel differently if the other acted differently. He may want to be left alone precisely because she gives him so much attention, and she may want attention precisely because he leaves her alone. With a doting spouse she might find herself craving to be left alone, and with an independent spouse, he might find himself craving attention. It's important to remember that others' ways of talking to you are partly a reaction to your style, just as your style with them is partly a reaction to their style—with you.

The ways we show our involvement and considerateness in talk seem self-evidently appropriate. And in interpreting what others say, we assume they mean what we would mean if we said the same thing in the same way. If we don't think about differences in conversational style, we see no reason to question this. Nor do we question whether what we perceive as considerate or inconsiderate, loving or not, was *intended* to be so.

In trying to come to an understanding with someone who has misinterpreted our intentions, we often end up in a deadlock, reduced to childlike insistence:

"You said so."

"I said no such thing!"

"You did! I heard you!"

"Don't tell me what I said."

In fact, both parties may be sincere—and both may be right. He recalls what he meant, and she recalls what she heard. But what he intended was not what she understood—which was what she would have meant if she had said what he said in the way he said it.

These paradoxical metamessages are recursive and potentially confusing in all conversations. In a series of conversations between the same people, each encounter bears the burdens as well as the fruits of earlier ones. The fruits of ongoing relationships are an ever-increasing sense of understanding based on less and less talk. This is one of the great joys of intimate conversations. But the burdens include the incremental confusion and disappointment of past misunderstandings, and hardening conviction of the other's irrationality or ill will.

45

The benefits of repeated communication need no explanation; all our conventional wisdom about "getting to know each other," "working it out," and "speaking the same language" gives us ways to talk about and understand that happy situation. But we need some help—and some terms and concepts—to understand why communicating over time doesn't always result in understanding each other better, and why sometimes it begins to seem that one or the other is speaking in tongues.

Mixed Metamessages across Cultures

The danger of misinterpretation is greatest, of course, among speakers who actually speak different native tongues, or come from different cultural backgrounds, because cultural difference necessarily implies different assumptions about natural and obvious ways to be polite.

Anthropologist Thomas Kochman gives the example of a white office worker who appeared with a bandaged arm and felt rejected because her black fellow worker didn't mention it. The (doubly) wounded worker assumed that her silent colleague didn't notice or didn't care. But the co-worker was purposely not calling attention to something her colleague might not want to talk about. She let her decide whether or not to mention it: being considerate by not imposing. Kochman says, based on his research, that these differences reflect recognizable black and white styles.

An American woman visiting England was repeatedly offended— even, on bad days, enraged—when Britishers ignored her in settings in which she thought they should pay attention. For example, she was sitting at a booth in a railroad-station cafeteria. A couple began to settle into the opposite seat in the same booth. They unloaded their luggage; they laid their coats on the seat; he asked what she would like to eat and went off to get it; she slid into the booth facing the American. And throughout all this, they showed no sign of having noticed that someone was already sitting in the booth.

When the British woman lit up a cigarette, the American had a concrete object for her anger. She began ostentatiously looking around for another table to move to. Of course there was none; that's why the British couple had sat in her booth in the first place. The smoker immediately crushed out her cigarette and apologized. This showed that she had noticed that someone else was sitting in the booth, and that she was not inclined to disturb her. But then she went back to pretending the American wasn't there, a ruse in which her husband collaborated when he returned with their food and they ate it.

To the American, politeness requires talk between strangers forced to share a booth in a cafeteria, if only a fleeting "Do you mind if I sit down?" or a conventional "Is anyone sitting here?" even if it's obvious no one is. The omission of such talk seemed to her like dreadful rudeness. The American couldn't see that another system of politeness was at work. (She

50

could see nothing but red.) By not acknowledging her presence, the British couple freed her from the obligation to acknowledge theirs. The American expected a show of involvement; they were being polite by not imposing.

An American man who had lived for years in Japan explained a similar politeness ethic. He lived, as many Japanese do, in frightfully close quarters—a tiny room separated from neighboring rooms by paper-thin walls. In this case the walls were literally made of paper. In order to preserve privacy in this most unprivate situation, his Japanese neighbors simply acted as if no one else lived there. They never showed signs of having overheard conversations, and if, while walking down the hall, they caught a neighbor with the door open, they steadfastly glued their gaze ahead as if they were alone in a desert. The American confessed to feeling what I believe most Americans would feel if a next-door neighbor passed within a few feet without acknowledging their presence—snubbed. But he realized that the intention was not rudeness by omitting to show involvement, but politeness by not imposing.

The fate of the earth depends on cross-cultural communication. Nations must reach agreements, and agreements are made by individual representatives of nations sitting down and talking to each other—public analogues of private conversations. The processes are the same, and so are the pitfalls. Only the possible consequences are more extreme.

We Need the Eggs

Despite the fact that talking to each other frequently fails to yield the understanding we seek, we keep at it, just as nations keep trying to negotiate and reach agreement. Woody Allen knows why, and tells, in his film *Annie Hall*, which ends with a joke that is heard in a voice-over: 55

> This guy goes to a psychiatrist and says, "Doc my brother's crazy. He thinks he's a chicken." And the doctor says, "Well, why don't you turn him in?" And the guy says, "I would, but I need the eggs." Well, I guess that's pretty much how I feel about relationships.

Even though intimate as well as fleeting conversations don't yield the perfect communication we crave—and we can see from past experience and from the analysis presented here that they can't—we still keep hoping and trying because we need the eggs of involvement and independence. The communication chicken can't give us these golden eggs because of the double bind: Closeness threatens our lives as individuals, and our real differences as individuals threaten our needs to be connected to other people.

But because we can't step out of the situation—the human situation— we keep trying to balance these needs. We do it by not saying exactly what we mean in our messages, while at the same time negotiating what we mean in metamessages. Metamessages depend for their meaning on subtle linguistic signals and devices.

Notes

[The page references have been changed to accord with pages in *The Little, Brown Reader*, 11th ed., and the bibliographic citations have been amplified where necessary.]

pp. 460, 462. The terms *metamessage* and *double bind* are found in Gregory Bateson, *Steps to an Ecology of Mind* (1972). For Bateson, a double bind entailed contradictory orders at different levels: the message and metamessage conflict. I use the term, as do other linguists (for example, Scollon, "The Rhythmic Integration of Ordinary Talk," in *Analyzing Discourse: Text and Talk*, Deborah Tannen, ed. [1981]), simply to describe the state of receiving contradictory orders without being able to step out of the situation.

p. 461. I am grateful to Pamela Gerloff for bringing to my attention Bettelheim's reference (in *Surviving* [1979]) to Schopenhauer's porcupine metaphor.

p. 461. Mary Catherine Bateson, *With a Daughter's Eye: A Memoir of Margaret Mead and Gregory Bateson* (1984), discusses G. Bateson's idea that living systems (biological processes as well as human interaction) never achieve a static state of balance, but achieve balance only as a series of adjustments within a range.

p. 463. For his conversational maxims, see H. P. Grice, "Logic and Conservation," rptd. in *Syntax and Semantics*, vol. 3, *Speech Acts*, eds. Peter Cole and Jerry Morgan (1975).

p. 464. Lakoff's original statement of the rules of politeness is in Lakoff, "The Logic of Politeness, or Minding Your P's and Q's," *Papers from the Ninth Regional Meeting of the Chicago Linguistics Society* (1973). She also presents this system in the context of discussing male/female differences (Lakoff, *Language and Woman's Place* [1975]). Penelope Brown and Stephen Levinson, "Universals in Language Usage: Politeness Phenomena," in *Questions and Politeness*, ed. Esther Goody (1978), provide an extended and formalized discussion of politeness phenomena.

p. 468. Thomas Kochman presents an extended analysis of *Black and White Styles in Conflict* (1981).

p. 469. The quotation from *Annie Hall* is taken from the screenplay by Woody Allen and Marshall Brickman in *Four Films of Woody Allen* (NY: Random House, 1982).

Joining the Conversation: Critical Thinking and Writing

1. Tannen begins this chapter using the second person ("You're sitting at a bar—or in a coffee shop or at a party—and suddenly you feel lonely. You wonder . . ."), a usage often prohibited in high school English classes and textbooks. How well do you think it works here? Try to make the same point without using the second person. *Have* you made the same point? What has been left out?

2. How does Tannen define *metamessages*? The word will not appear in most dictionaries, but we can probably guess what it means, even without Tannen's explanation. What does *meta* usually mean as a prefix to a word? (Most dictionaries do define *meta* as a prefix.)

3. Why, according to Tannen, has the word *metamessages* been invented? What other linguistic terms does she introduce, and what do they mean?

4. What is the example of porcupines introduced to explain? Why do you suppose it is easier to remember the example than to remember what it explains?

5. In paragraph 11 Tannen says "individuals as well as cultures place different relative values" on the "needs for involvement and independence." In the same paragraph and in the next several paragraphs, she says that Americans glorify independence and she offers a historical explanation of the glorification of independence and other values that flow from it. What does she assume here about "Americans," American culture, and American history?

6. In paragraph 16 Tannen contrasts women talking to women and men talking to men. What does she *assume* here, in addition to what she says, about the differences? On the whole, do you agree with her about women's talk and men's talk?

7. In paragraphs 47–53 Tannen talks about misinterpretations between persons of different cultural backgrounds. If possible, provide an example from your own experience.

8. Write an essay or a journal entry analyzing an encounter that illustrates the "double bind," a "politeness phenomenon," or "mixed metamessages," as Tannen defines these terms and situations. Or summarize this chapter in 750 words.

James B. Twitchell

James B. Twitchell teaches English and advertising at the University of Florida. He is the author of several books, including Carnival Culture: The Trashing of Taste in America *(1992) and* Twenty Ads That Shook the World: The Century's Most Groundbreaking Advertising and How It Changed Us All *(2000). The following essay comes from* Twenty Ads.

The Marlboro Man: The Perfect Campaign

Although advertising agencies love giving themselves prizes, there has been no award for the perfect campaign. If there were, Marlboro would win. Suffice it to say that this brand went from selling less than one quarter of one percent of the American market in the early 1950s to being the most popular in the entire world in just twenty years. Every fourth cigarette smoked is a Marlboro. Leo Burnett's brilliant campaign made Marlboro the most valuable brand in the world.

First, let's dispense with the politics of the product. We all know that cigarettes are the most dangerous legal product in the world. They kill more people each year than do guns. And yes, it is dreadful that the myth of independence is used to sell addiction. But never forget as well that it is exactly this danger that animates the Marlboro Man. He came into being just as smoking became problematic and, ironically, as long as anxiety exists, so will he.

And, second, cigarettes, like domestic beer and bottled water, build deep affiliations that have absolutely nothing to do with taste. As David Ogilvy said, "Give people a taste of Old Crow and *tell* them it's Old Crow. Then give them another taste of Old Crow, *but tell them it's Jack Daniels*. Ask them which they prefer. They'll think the two drinks are quite different. *They are tasting images*" (Ogilvy 1985, 87).

In fact, it was the cigarette companies that found this out first. In the 1920s they blindfolded brand-dedicated smokers and put them into dark rooms. Then they gave them Luckies, Pall Malls, Chesterfields, and Camels, as well as European smokes, and asked the smokers to identify "their own brand"—the one they were sure they knew. By now we all know the results. Taste has basically little or nothing to do with why people choose specific brands of cigarettes.

Just as we drink the label, we smoke the advertising. So what's so smokable, so tasty, about this ad?   5

First, everything fits around the dominant image. The heading and the logotype fall naturally in place. Product name mediates between visual and verbal. Let's start with the name, *Marlboro*. Like so many cigarette brand names, it is English and elegant and, like its counterpart Winston, deceptively vague. Like the joke about how there's gotta be a pony in there somewhere, there's gotta be prestige in here somewhere. (Oddly enough, Marlboro was first created in Victorian England, then transported to the States as a cigarette for women.) The ersatz PM crest at the apex of the "red roof" chevron on the package hints of a bloodline, and the Latin motto "Veni, Vidi, Vici"[1] (!) conveys ancient warrior strength. Clearly, the power is now both in the pack and in the buckaroo.

The buckaroo is, of course, the eponymous Marlboro Man. He is what we have for royalty, distilled manhood. (Alas, the Winston man barely exists. What little of him there is is opinionated, urbane, self-assured—and needs to tell you so.) The Marlboro Man needs to tell you nothing. He carries no scepter, no gun. He never even speaks. Doesn't need to. The

---

[1]**Veni, Vidi, Vici** Latin: I came, I saw, I conquered (Julius Caesar's announcement of a victory). (Editors' note)

difference between Marlboro and Winston is the difference between myth and reality. Winston needed to break the rules publicly to be independent ("Winston tastes good *like* a cigarette should"); the Marlboro Man has already been there, done that. Little wonder the Viceroy man ("a thinking man's filter, a smoking man's taste") couldn't even make the cut.

Generating prestige *and* independence is a crucial aspect of cigarette selling. If you are targeting those who are just entering the consumption community, and if the act of consumption is dangerous, then you do not need to stress rebellion—that's a given. What you need to announce is initiation into the pack.

When R.J. Reynolds tested Marlboro on focus groups, they found that it was not rugged machismo that was alluring to young Marlboro smokers, but separation from restraints (the tattoo) *and* a sense of belonging (Marlboro Country). This "secret" RJR report, now available on the World Wide Web, is one reason why the "I'd walk a mile for a Camel" man was subsumed into the more personable, intelligent, and independent "Cool Joe" Camel.

Let's face it, the Camel man was downright stupid. In the most repeated of his ill-fated "walk a mile" ads he is shown carrying a tire (instead of rolling it) across the desert (with no canteen), wearing no shade-providing hat. That he seemingly forgot the spare tire is as stupid as his choosing to smoke. Little wonder Cool Joe pushed him aside. A camel seems intelligent in comparison.

The Marlboro Man's transformation was less traumatic, but no less meaningful. In fact, it is a reversal of the most popular tabloid story of the 1950s. It was to be, as David Ogilvy would say, one of the "riskiest decisions ever made" and one "which few advertisers would take." Here's the cultural context on a thumbnail and what Philip Morris did about it:

On February 13, 1953, George Jorgenson went to Denmark and returned as Christine. The idea that one could change one's sex was profoundly unsettling to American culture. Once back at home, she uttered the perhaps apocryphal testament to his journey: "Men are wary of me and I'm wary of the ones who aren't."

At almost the same time, another repositioning was occurring. Now, as any modern ten-year-old can tell you, objects have sexual characteristics, too. Philip Morris had a female cigarette, Marlboro, that wouldn't sell. So they sent her up to Chicago to be regendered by Leo Burnett. Miss Marlboro was a "sissy smoke . . . a tea room smoke," Burnett said. Although she had been in and out of production for most of the century, in her most recent incarnation she had a red filter tip (called the "beauty tip," to hide lipstick stains) and a long-running theme: "Mild as May." Men wouldn't touch her, nor would many women.

In December 1954, Burnett took Miss Marlboro out to his gentleman's farm south of Chicago and invited some of his agency cohorts over to

10

brainstorm. Something had to be done to put some hair on her chest, to change her out of pinafores and into cowboy chaps, anything to get her out of the suffocating tea room.

"What is the most masculine figure in America?" Burnett asked. "Cab   15
driver, sailor, marine, pilot, race car driver" came the replies. Then someone simply said, "Cowboy." Bingo! Copywriter Draper Daniels filled in the blank: this smoke "Delivers the Goods on Flavor."

But these admen were not thinking of a real cowboy, not some dirty, spitting, toothless, smelly wrangler. They were city boys who knew cowboys in bronzes and oils by Frederic Remington, or in oils and watercolors by Charles Russell, or in the purple prose of Owen Wister's *The Virginian* or in the pulp of Zane Grey's countless novels. Philip Morris and Leo Burnett now love to tell you that the Marlboro Man was always a "real cowboy." Just don't remind them that almost half of the real cowpunchers were black or Mexican.

No matter, Leo Burnett had just the image in mind. He remembered seeing one C. H. Long, a thirty-nine-year-old foreman at the JA Ranch in the Texas panhandle, a place described as "320,000 acres of nothing much," who had been heroically photographed by Leonard McCombe for a cover of *Life* magazine in 1949. In other words, this Marlboro cowboy was a real/reel cowboy, something like what Matt Dillon, played by James Arness, was on television. A slightly roughed-up, *High Noon* Gary Cooper, a lite-spaghetti Clint Eastwood.

To get to this image, the Leo Burnett Company tried out all manner of windblown wranglers, some professional models, some not. Then, in 1963, just as the health concerns about lung cancer really took hold, they discovered Carl "Big-un" Bradley at the 6666 Ranch in Guthrie, Texas. Carl was the first real cowboy they used, and from then on the Marlboro Men were honest-to-God cowboys, rodeo riders, and stuntmen.

One look at him and you know: no Ralph Lauren jeans, no 401(k) plans, no wine spritzers, nothing with little ducks all over it, just independence, pure and simple. He doesn't concern himself with the Surgeon General. He's his own sheriff. To make sure he stayed that way, all background was airbrushed out. Later he got a grubstake in Marlboro Country.

Even today the Philip Morris Company receives letters from all over   20
the world, mostly at the beginning of the summer, from travelers wishing to know how to get to Marlboro Country.

But there's more to the ad than the free-ranging cowboy. That package with the insignia, built truck-tough as a flip-top *box*, was a badge. With its hearty red, white, and black lettering, the smoker pinned it to his chest on the average of twenty-three times a day. This *vade mecum*[2] of a package was designed by Frank Gianninoto and carefully tested through consumer surveys by Elmo Roper & Associates and the Color Research

---

[2]**vade mecum** Latin: "come with me" (Editors' note)

Institute. Now the *Veni, Vidi, Vici* starts making sense. With this package you are the decorated conqueror. You burn bridges, bust broncos, confront stuff like lung cancer.

Sure, the girlie filter was there for the women (incidentally, the famous Marlboro red came from the lipstick red of the original "beauty filter"), but it was battled by the box, the medallion—the manliness of it all.

Should you still not be convinced, there was always the brand, the literal brand—the tattoo. Remember, this was the 1950s, when tattoos were not a fashion accessory, but an unambiguous sign of antisocial "otherness." But this brand was not on the biceps to signify Charles Atlas manliness; rather it was on the back of the smoking hand, or on the wrist. A strange place for a tattoo, to be sure, but appropriate.

Although research departments may cringe to hear this, the tattoo was not the result of motivational research showing that the image would be super macho. Leo Burnett supposedly thought the tattoo would "say to many men that here is a successful man who used to work with his hands," while "to many women, we believe it will suggest a romantic past."

But there is another story that also may be true. Alas, it doesn't emphasize virility and romance but the bugaboo of interpretation, namely, happenstance. It seems someone at the agency had scribbled on the hand of the *Life* magazine cowboy that there was no copyright clearance for this particular image. The agency sent this image in a paste-up to Philip Morris and then made another version from another cowboy photo to avoid copyright problems. It, too, went to the client. Back came the reaction: "Where's the tattoo on the second cowboy?" Perplexed agency people dug up the original photo and saw the warning scribbled across the wrist (McGuire 1989, 23).

No matter what the story, the tattoo stuck, not because of any massive testing but because everyone knew the branding itself was compelling. You are what you smoke.

When a campaign "works," every part seems compelling. In fact, in great ads, as in great works of art, the sum of the parts is always more than the whole. The visual and verbal rhetoric is so strong that they seem to have always been in place. They seem indestructible. In truth, however, often the greatest act of creativity is knowing when to leave well enough alone. "I have learned that any fool can write a bad ad," Burnett says in one of his pithy *100 Leo's*, "but that it takes a real genius to keep his hands off a good one" (Burnett 1995, 53).

Most of the tinkering with this campaign has been by the government. For instance, many people thought that by removing the Marlboro Man from television in the early 1970s the feds would send him into the sunset. No such luck. You can take down all the billboards and remove him from magazines. "Just a little dab" of this rhetoric "will do ya."

When Philip Morris attempted to introduce brand extension—Marlboro Light—after all the advertising bans were in place, all they did was unsaddle

25

the cowboy and foreground the horse. Now that even mentioning the cigarette by name is becoming taboo, they are mining the original campaign by making Marlboro Country into Marlboro Unlimited and selling lots of logo'd stuff to smokers, calling it Gear Without Limits. By selling annually some 20 million T-shirts, caps, jackets, and other items bearing Marlboro logos, Philip Morris was, for a time, the nation's third-largest mail-order house.

This attempt to get around the fear of legal restrictions on advertising is called "sell-through," and you see it happening with almost all the major cigarette and beer brands. So Smokin' Joe, the super-cool Camel musician, appears on a host of nontobacco products like clothing, beach towels, baseball caps, while at the same time he also appears on the hit list of the FTC as a public nuisance. 30

And so what is Gear Without Limits for people who want to go to the Land That Knows No Limits? Well, what about products from the Marlboro Country Store like Snake River Fishing Gear ("An outfit made to go where the cold rivers run"), the Marlboro Folding Mountain Bike, a Mountain Lantern in Marlboro red, and the Marlboro Country Cookbook (complete with their green salsa recipe for couch cowpokes). Marlboro has so captured the iconography of cowboydom that they now have ads in mass-circulation magazines consisting *only* of recipes for such grub as Huevos Rancheros, Barkeeper's Burger, and Whiskey Beef Sandwiches.

My favorite Marlboro ad, however, is an English one in which a Harleyesque motorcycle is set out in the bleak Western plains. The only color in the bleached scene is on the bike's gas tank—Marlboro red. In art lingo, this trope is called *metonymy*.

Metonymy transfers meaning because the host image, the Marlboro cowboy, is imbedded so deep not just in American culture but in world culture that we close the circuit. Ironically, slow learners are helped by the appearance of the warning box telling you that smoking is dangerous! The Marlboro Man may indeed be Dracula to his foes, but he is still the perfect icon of adolescent independence.

Ironically, the greatest danger faced by the Marlboro Man is not from lawmen armed with scientific studies, but from some wiseguy MBA in Manhattan who will try to earn his spurs by tinkering with the campaign. This almost happened on April 22, 1993, as Michael Miles, CEO of Philip Morris, thought he could play chicken with the generics who were rustling his customers. Overnight, Miles cut the price of Marlboro by sixty cents a pack.

But the only critter he scared was the stock market, which lopped 23 percent off the price of PM stock in a single day. This day, still called "Marlboro Friday," will live in infamy as it seemed for a moment that other advertisers might follow. The whole point of branding is to make sure the consumer *pays* for the advertising by thinking that the 35

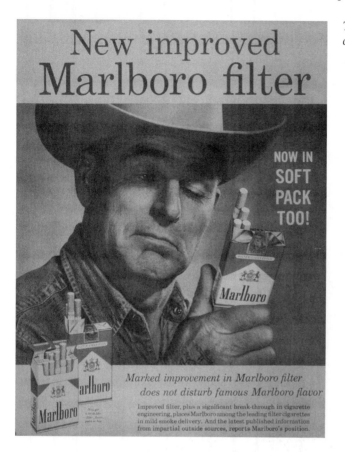

The Marlboro Man of the 1950s

interchangeable product is unique. He knows this when he pays a premium for it. When *Forbes* magazine (February 2, 1987) offered Marlboro smokers their chosen brand in a generic brown box at half the price, only 21 percent were interested. Just as the price of Marlboro is what economists call "inelastic," so is the advertising. Michael Miles lost his job and the company lost $13 billion in shareholder equity, but marketers learned a lesson: you don't fool with Mother Nature or a great campaign.

Works Cited

Burnett, Leo. *100 Leo's: The Wit and Wisdom of Leo Burnett.* Lincolnwood, Ill.: NTC Business Books, 1995.

McGuide, John M. "How the Marlboro Cowboy Acquired His Tattoo." *St. Louis Post-Dispatch*, November 12, 1989.

Ogilvy, David. *On Advertising.* New York: Vintage, 1985.

The Marlboro Woman of the 1940s

Joining the Conversation: Critical Thinking and Writing

1. Reread the first two sentences of this essay. Does Twitchell prove the claim that he makes?

2. Did anything in this essay surprise you? Before you read it, were you familiar with the Marlboro Man? If so, in what contexts? If not, why do you think this is the case?

3. Early on, Twitchell contends that smokers and drinkers in fact cannot tell the difference between their favorite brand and other brands. Did you believe this before you read Twitchell's essay? Do you believe it now? Could you tell the difference between your favorite brand of soft drink and other brands?

4. If you are a smoker, what brand do you smoke? How much influence, do you suppose, has advertising had on your choice? If you are not a smoker, think of a product you use (e.g., jeans, underwear, sneakers) and, again, evaluate the effect of advertising on your choice.

5. What is Twitchell's conclusion about the importance of the Marlboro Man's tattoo? Do you have a tattoo? What made you decide to get one, or perhaps more than one? If you do not have a tattoo, do you think that you might get one at some point? And what would that tattoo be?

6. Reread the essay, noting the devices Twitchell uses to persuade. Then write a paragraph listing and analyzing these devices, providing examples for your reader.

7. The following sentences may puzzle some readers. Choose one, and explain it.

   (a) [The Marlboro Man] came into being just as smoking became problematic and, ironically, as long as anxiety exists, so will he. (paragraph 2)
   (b) The ersatz PM crest at the apex of the "red roof" chevron on the package hints of a bloodline, and the Latin motto "Vini, Vidi, Vici" (!) conveys ancient warrior strength. (paragraph 6)
   (c) The Marlboro Man may indeed be Dracula to his foes, but he is still the perfect icon of adolescent independence. (paragraph 33)

Eric Schlosser

Eric Schlosser, born in 1959, is an investigative journalist who has published in such journals as the Atlantic Monthly, Rolling Stone, *the* New Yorker, *and the* Nation. *We reprint a selection from his best-selling book,* Fast Food Nation *(2001), an exposé of the fast-food industry.*

Kid Kustomers

Twenty-five years ago, only a handful of American companies directed their marketing at children—Disney, McDonald's, candy makers, toy makers, manufacturers of breakfast cereal. Today children are being targeted by phone companies, oil companies, and automobile companies, as well as clothing stores and restaurant chains. The explosion in children's advertising occurred during the 1980s. Many working parents, feeling guilty about spending less time with their kids, started spending more money on them. One marketing expert has called the 1980s "the decade of the child consumer." After largely ignoring children for years, Madison Avenue began to scrutinize and pursue them. Major ad agencies now have children's divisions, and a variety of marketing firms focus solely on kids. These groups tend to have sweet-sounding names: Small Talk, Kid Connection, Kid2Kid, the Gepetto Group, Just Kids, Inc. At least three industry publications—*Youth Market Alert, Selling to Kids,* and *Marketing to Kids Report*—cover the latest ad campaigns and market research. The growth in children's advertising has been driven by efforts to increase not just current, but also future, consumption. Hoping that nostalgic childhood memories of a brand will lead to a lifetime of purchases, companies now plan "cradle-to-grave" advertising strategies. They have come to believe what Ray Kroc and Walt Disney realized long ago—a person's "brand loyalty" may begin as early as the age of two. Indeed, market research has found that children often recognize a brand logo before they can recognize their own name.

The discontinued Joe Camel ad campaign, which used a hip cartoon character to sell cigarettes, showed how easily children can be influenced by the right corporate mascot. A 1991 study published in the *Journal of the American Medical Association* found that nearly all of America's six-year-olds could identify Joe Camel, who was just as familiar to them as Mickey Mouse. Another study found that one-third of the cigarettes illegally sold to minors were Camels. More recently, a marketing firm conducted a survey in shopping malls across the country, asking children to describe their favorite TV ads. According to the CME KidCom Ad Traction Study II, released at the 1999 Kids' Marketing Conference in San Antonio, Texas, the Taco Bell commercials featuring a talking chihuahua were the most popular fast food ads. The kids in the survey also liked Pepsi and Nike commercials, but their favorite television ad was for Budweiser.

The bulk of the advertising directed at children today has an immediate goal. "It's not just getting kids to whine," one marketer explained in *Selling to Kids*, "it's giving them a specific reason to ask for the product." Years ago sociologist Vance Packard described children as "surrogate salesmen" who had to persuade other people, usually their parents, to buy what they wanted. Marketers now use different terms to explain the intended response to their ads—such as "leverage," "the nudge factor," "pester power." The aim of most children's advertising is straightforward: get kids to nag their parents and nag them well.

James U. McNeal, a professor of marketing at Texas A&M University, is considered America's leading authority on marketing to children. In his book *Kids As Customers* (1992), McNeal provides marketers with a thorough analysis of "children's requesting styles and appeals." He classifies juvenile nagging tactics into seven major categories. A *pleading* nag is one accompanied by repetitions of words like "please" or "mom, mom, mom." A *persistent* nag involves constant requests for the coveted product and may include the phrase "I'm gonna ask just one more time." *Forceful* nags are extremely pushy and may include subtle threats, like "Well, then, I'll go and ask Dad." *Demonstrative* nags are the most high-risk, often characterized by full-blown tantrums in public places, breath-holding, tears, a refusal to leave the store. *Sugar-coated* nags promise affection in return for a purchase and may rely on seemingly heartfelt declarations like "You're the best dad in the world." *Threatening* nags are youthful forms of blackmail, vows of eternal hatred and of running away if something isn't bought. *Pity* nags claim the child will be heartbroken, teased, or socially stunted if the parent refuses to buy a certain item. "All of these appeals and styles may be used in combination," McNeal's research has discovered, "but kids tend to stick to one or two of each that prove most effective . . . for their own parents."

McNeal never advocates turning children into screaming, breath-holding monsters. He has been studying "Kid Kustomers" for more than thirty years and believes in a more traditional marketing approach. "The key is getting children to see a firm . . . in much the same way as [they see] mom or dad, grandma or grandpa," McNeal argues. "Likewise, if a company can ally itself with universal values such as patriotism, national defense, and good health, it is likely to nurture belief in it among children."

Before trying to affect children's behavior, advertisers have to learn about their tastes. Today's market researchers not only conduct surveys of children in shopping malls, they also organize focus groups for kids as young as two or three. They analyze children's artwork, hire children to run focus groups, stage slumber parties and then question children into the night. They send cultural anthropologists into homes, stores, fast food restaurants, and other places where kids like to gather, quietly and surreptitiously observing the behavior of prospective customers. They study the academic literature on child development, seeking insights from the work of theorists such as Erik Erikson and Jean Piaget. They study the fantasy lives of young children, then apply the findings in advertisements and product designs.

Dan S. Acuff—the president of Youth Market System Consulting and the author of *What Kids Buy and Why* (1997)—stresses the importance of dream research. Studies suggest that until the age of six, roughly 80 percent of children's dreams are about animals. Rounded, soft creatures like Barney, Disney's animated characters, and the Teletubbies therefore have an obvious appeal to young children. The Character Lab, a division of Youth Market System Consulting, uses a proprietary technique called Character Appeal Quadrant Analysis to help companies develop new mascots. The technique purports to create imaginary characters who perfectly fit the targeted age group's level of cognitive and neurological development.

Children's clubs have for years been considered an effective means of targeting ads and collecting demographic information; the clubs appeal to a child's fundamental need for status and belonging. Disney's Mickey Mouse Club, formed in 1930, was one of the trailblazers. During the 1980s and 1990s, children's clubs proliferated, as corporations used them to solicit the names, addresses, zip codes, and personal comments of young customers. "Marketing messages sent through a club not only can be personalized," James McNeal advises, "they can be tailored for a certain age or geographical group." A well-designed and well-run children's club can be extremely good for business. According to one Burger King executive, the creation of a Burger King Kids Club in 1991 increased the sales of children's meals as much as 300 percent.

The Internet has become another powerful tool for assembling data about children. In 1998 a federal investigation of Web sites aimed at children found that 89 percent requested personal information from kids; only 1 percent required that children obtain parental approval before supplying the information. A character on the McDonald's Web site told children that Ronald McDonald was "the ultimate authority in everything." The site encouraged kids to send Ronald an e-mail revealing their favorite menu item at McDonald's, their favorite book, their favorite sports team—and their name. Fast food Web sites no longer ask children to provide personal information without first gaining parental approval; to do so is now a violation of federal law, thanks to the Children's Online Privacy Protection Act, which took effect in April of 2000.

Despite the growing importance of the Internet, television remains the primary medium for children's advertising. The effects of these TV ads have long been a subject of controversy. In 1978, the Federal Trade Commission (FTC) tried to ban all television ads directed at children seven years old or younger. Many studies had found that young children often could not tell the difference between television programming and television advertising. They also could not comprehend the real purpose of commercials and trusted that advertising claims were true. Michael Pertschuk, the head of the FTC, argued that children need to be shielded from advertising that preys upon their immaturity. "They cannot protect themselves," he said, "against adults who exploit their present-mindedness." 10

The FTC's proposed ban was supported by the American Academy of Pediatrics, the National Congress of Parents and Teachers, the Consumers Union, and the Child Welfare League, among others. But it was attacked by the National Association of Broadcasters, the Toy Manufacturers of America, and the Association of National Advertisers. The industry groups lobbied Congress to prevent any restrictions on children's ads and sued in federal court to block Pertschuk from participating in future FTC meetings on the subject. In April of 1981, three months after the inauguration of President Ronald Reagan, an FTC staff report argued that a ban on ads aimed at children would be impractical, effectively killing the proposal. "We are delighted by the FTC's reasonable recommendation," said the head of the National Association of Broadcasters.

The Saturday-morning children's ads that caused angry debates twenty years ago now seem almost quaint. Far from being banned, TV advertising aimed at kids is now broadcast twenty-four hours a day, closed-captioned and in stereo. Nickelodeon, the Disney Channel, the Cartoon Network, and the other children's cable networks are now responsible for about 80 percent of all television viewing by kids. None of these networks existed before 1979. The typical American child now spends about twenty-one hours a week watching television—roughly one and a half months of TV every year. That does not include the time children spend in front of a screen watching videos, playing video games, or using the computer. Outside of school, the typical American child spends more time watching television than doing any other activity except sleeping. During the course of a year, he or she watches more than thirty thousand TV commercials. Even the nation's youngest children are watching a great deal of television. About one-quarter of American children between the ages of two and five have a TV in their room.

Notes

[The page references have been changed to accord with pages in *The Little, Brown Reader*, 11th ed., and the bibliographic citations have been amplified where necessary.]

p. 480. *"the decade of the child consumer":* McNeal, *Kids as Customers,* p. 6.

as early as the age of two: Cited in "Brand Aware," *Children's Business,* June 2000.

children often recognize a brand logo: See "Brand Consciousness," *IFF on Kids: Kid Focus,* no. 3.

a 1991 study . . . found: Paul Fischer et al., "Brand Logo Recognition by Children Aged 3 to 6 Years: Mickey Mouse and Old Joe the Camel," *Journal of the American Medical Association,* December 11, 1991.

Another study found: See Judann Dagnoli, "JAMA Lights New Fire Under Camel's Ads," *Advertising Age,* December 16, 1991.

the CME KidCom Ad Traction Study II: Cited in "Market Research Ages 6–17: Talking Chihuahua Strikes Chord with Kids," *Selling to Kids,* February 3, 1999.

"It's not just getting kids to whine": Quoted in "Market Research: The Old Nagging Game Can Pay off for Marketers," *Selling to Kids,* April 15, 1998.

Vance Packard described children as "surrogate salesmen": See Boas and Chain, *Big Mac,* p. 127; Vance Packard, *The Hidden Persuaders* (New York: D. McKay, 1957), pp. 158–61.

"children's requesting styles and appeals": McNeal, *Kids as Customers,* pp. 72–75.

p. 481. *"Kid Kustomers":* Ibid., p. 4.

"The key is getting children to see a firm": Ibid., p. 98.

learn about their tastes: For a sense of the techniques now being used by marketers, see Tom McGee, "Getting Inside Kids' Heads," *American Demographics,* January 1997.

roughly 80 percent of children's dreams: Cited in Acuff, *What Kids Buy and Why,* pp. 45–46.

"Marketing messages sent through a club": McNeal, *Kids As Customers,* p. 175.

increased the sales of children's meals: Cited in Karen Benezra, "Keeping Burger King on a Roll," *Brandweek,* January 15, 1996.

p. 482. *a federal investigation of Web sites aimed at children:* Cited in "Children's Online Privacy Proposed Rule Issued by FTC," press release, Federal Trade Commission, April 20, 1999.

p. 486. *"the ultimate authority in everything":* Quoted in "Is Your Kid Caught Up in the Web?" *Consumer Reports,* May 1997.

The site encouraged kids: See Matthew McAllester, "Life in Cyberspace: What's McDonald's Doing with Kids' E-mail Responses?" *Newsday,* July 20, 1997.

"They cannot protect themselves": Quoted in Linda E. Demkovich, "Pulling the Sweet Tooth of Children's TV Advertising," *National Journal,* January 7, 1978.

"We are delighted by the FTC's reasonable recommendation": Quoted in A. O. Sulzberger, Jr., "FTC Staff Urges End to Child-TV Ad Study," *New York Times,* April 3, 1981.

about 80 percent of all television viewing by kids: Cited in Steve McClellan and Richard Tedesco, "Children's TV Market May Be Played Out," *Broadcasting & Cable,* March 1, 1999.

about twenty-one hours a week: Cited in "Policy Statement: Media Education," American Academy of Pediatrics, August 1999.

more time watching television than doing: Cited in "Policy Statement: Children, Adolescents, and Television," American Academy of Pediatrics, October 1995.

p. 483. *more than thirty thousand TV commercials:* Cited in Mary C. Martin, "Children's Understanding of the Intent of Advertising: A Meta-Analysis," *Journal of Public Policy & Marketing,* Fall 1997.

one-quarter of American children: Cited in Lisa Jennings, "Baby, Hand Me the Remote," *Scripps Howard News Service,* October 13, 1999.

 ## Joining the Conversation:
Critical Thinking and Writing

1. In his opening paragraph, Schlosser asserts that advertising aimed at small children attempts "to increase not just current, but also future, consumption." Explain the reasoning of the advertising companies here. Does Schlosser provide evidence that supports their reasoning? Explain.

2. Let's assume that everything Schlosser says is true. Do you regard as unethical some or all of the practices he describes? Ethical but deplorable? Good business, and thoroughly in the spirit of free enterprise? Or what?

3. Have you acquired any "brand loyalty" derived from children's advertising? If so, what are the products you are "loyal" to? When were you first exposed to the commercials, and what was memorable about them?

4. Do you think that parents should attempt to limit small children's exposure to advertising aimed at them? Or do you believe that such exposure is harmless? Explain.

5. A writing assignment: Watch a TV program for children and observe the ads. Choose one ad that you find particularly effective (whether you

approve of it or not). Then write a two or three paragraph essay in which you first describe the ad in detail, and then analyze its effectiveness. (On page 124 we offer advice for writing about an advertisement. Our topic there is ads in print, but you might nevertheless find the discussion useful.)

Stevie Smith

Stevie Smith (1902–1971) was born Florence Margaret Smith in England. Her first book was a novel, published in 1936, but she is best known for her several volumes of poetry.

Not Waving but Drowning

Nobody heard him, the dead man,
But still he lay moaning:
I was much further out than you thought
And not waving but drowning.

Poor chap, he always loved larking   5
And now he's dead
It must have been too cold for him his heart gave way,
They said.

Oh, no no no, it was too cold always
(Still the dead one lay moaning)   10
I was much too far out all my life
And not waving but drowning.

 Joining the Conversation:
Critical Thinking and Writing

1. The first line, "Nobody heard him, the dead man," is, of course, literally true. Dead men do not speak. In what other ways is it true?

2. Who are "they" whose voices we hear in the second stanza? What does the punctuation—or lack of it—in line 7 tell us of their feelings for the dead man? What effect is produced by the brevity of line 6? Of line 8?

3. In the last stanza, does the man reproach himself, or others, or simply bemoan his fate? What was the cause of his death?

A Casebook on Virtual Worlds

Brent Staples

Brent Staples, born in 1951, holds a Ph.D. in psychology from the University of Chicago. He taught briefly, then turned to journalism, and now is on the editorial board of the New York Times. *We reprint an essay that appeared in this paper in 2004.*

What Adolescents Miss When We Let Them Grow Up in Cyberspace

My 10th-grade heartthrob was the daughter of a fearsome steel-worker who struck terror into the hearts of 15-year-old boys. He made it his business to answer the telephone—and so always knew who was calling—and grumbled in the background when the conversation went on too long. Unable to make time by phone, the boy either gave up or appeared at the front door. This meant submitting to the intense scrutiny that the girl's father soon became known for.

He greeted me with a crushing handshake, then leaned in close in a transparent attempt to find out whether I was one of those *bad* boys who smoked. He retired to the den during the visit, but cruised by the living room now and then to let me know he was watching. He let up after some weeks, but only after getting across what he expected of a boy who spent time with his daughter and how upset he'd be if I disappointed him.

This was my first sustained encounter with an adult outside my family who needed to be convinced of my worth as a person. This, of course, is a crucial part of growing up. Faced with same challenge today, however, I would probably pass on meeting the girl's father—and outflank him on the Internet.

Thanks to e-mail, online chat rooms and instant messages—which permit private, real-time conservations—adolescents have at last succeeded in shielding their social lives from adult scrutiny. But this comes at a cost: teenagers nowadays are both more connected to the world at large than ever, and more cut off from the social encounters that have historically prepared young people for the move into adulthood.

The Internet was billed as a revolutionary way to enrich our social lives and expand our civic connections. This seems to have worked well for elderly people and others who were isolated before they got access to the World Wide Web. But a growing body of research is showing that   5 heavy use of the Net can actually isolate younger socially connected people who unwittingly allow time online to replace face-to-face interactions with their families and friends.

Online shopping, checking e-mail and Web surfing—mainly solitary activities—have turned out to be more isolating than watching television, which friends and family often do in groups. Researchers have found that the time spent in direct contact with family members drops by as much as half for every hour we use the Net at home.

This should come as no surprise to the two-career couples who have seen their domestic lives taken over by e-mail and wireless tethers that keep people working around the clock. But a startling body of research from the Human-Computer Interaction Institute at Carnegie Mellon has shown that heavy Internet use can have stunting effect outside the home as well.

Studies show that gregarious, well-connected people actually lost friends, and experienced symptoms of loneliness and depression, after joining discussion groups and other activities. People who communicated with disembodied strangers online found the experience empty and emotionally frustrating but were nonetheless seduced by the novelty of the new medium. As Prof. Robert Kraut, a Carnegie Mellon researcher, told me recently, such people allowed low-quality relationships developed in virtual reality to replace higher-quality relationships in the real world.

No group has embraced this socially impoverishing trade-off more enthusiastically than adolescents, many of whom spend most of their free hours cruising the Net in sunless rooms. This hermetic existence has left many of these teenagers with nonexistent social skills—a point widely noted in stories about the computer geeks who rose to prominence in the early days of Silicon Valley.

Adolescents are drawn to cyberspace for different reasons than adults. 10 As the writer Michael Lewis observed in his book "Next: The Future Just Happened," children see the Net as a transformational device that lets them discard quotidian identities for more glamorous ones. Mr. Lewis illustrated the point with Marcus Arnold, who, as a 15-year-old, adopted a pseudonym a few years ago and posed as a 25-year-old legal expert for an Internet information service. Marcus did not feel the least bit guilty, and wasn't deterred, when real-world lawyers discovered his secret and accused him of being a fraud. When asked whether he had actually read the law, Marcus responded that he found books "boring," leaving us to conclude that he had learned all he needed to know from his family's big-screen TV.

Marcus is a child of the Net, where everyone has a pseudonym, telling a story makes it true, and adolescents create older, cooler, more socially powerful selves any time they wish. The ability to slip easily into a new, false self is tailor-made for emotionally fragile adolescents, who can consider a bout of acne or a few excess pounds an unbearable tragedy.

But teenagers who spend much of their lives hunched over computer screens miss the socializing, the real-world experience that would allow them to leave adolescence behind and grow into adulthood. These vital experiences, like much else, are simply not available in a virtual form.

✑ Joining the Conversation: Critical Thinking and Writing

1. Staples might have begun this article with the fourth paragraph. What does the argument gain through an account of his own experience in the first three paragraphs?

2. What is his argument? Try to restate it in a sentence or two and then evaluate it.

3. Do you think that parents should restrict their children's use of the Internet, or supervise it? Has reading this article affected your decision? Explain.

Jeremy Rifkin

Born in Denver, Colorado, in 1945, Jeremy Rifkin is a graduate of the Wharton School of the University of Pennsylvania and of the Fletcher School of Law and Diplomacy at Tufts University. Rifkin is the author of numerous books including The End of Work *(1995),* The Biotech Century *(1998), and* The Age of Access *(2001), and he is president of the Foundation on Economic Trends, a nonprofit organization that examines the impact of trends in science and technology on the environment and on society.*

Virtual Companionship

Over the past 20 years or so, we have preoccupied ourselves with developing ingenious new ways of communicating with each other. Our cellphones, personal computers, Blackberries, text messaging, e-mail, and the Internet connect 25 percent of the human race in a speed of light global village. At the same time that we are connecting the central nervous system of our species in a single, electronic embrace, the human vocabulary is plummeting all over the world, making it more difficult to express ourselves and participate in a meaningful way with our fellow human beings. It appears that we are all communicating more, but saying less.

According to a national survey conducted by the US Department of Education, English literacy among college graduates has declined dramatically in the past 10 years. Only 31 percent of college graduates today are proficient in English literacy, compared with 40 percent just a decade ago. Grover J. Whitehurst, the director of the DOE Institute responsible for overseeing The National Assessment of Adult Literacy, said that he

---

Jeremy Rifkin, "Virtual Companionship." Originally published in the *Boston Globe*, October 10, 2006. Jeremy Rifkin is the author of *The Age of Access* and President of the Foundation on Economic Trends in Washington, D.C. Reprinted by permission of the author.

believes that literacy is declining as a result of the increase in television viewing and surfing the Internet.

Worse, it seems the more connected we are in our electronically mediated landscapes, the lonelier we find ourselves. A study conducted by the Kaiser Family Fund showed that American children now spend an average of 6.5 hours per day watching television, surfing the Internet, text messaging, and playing with video games and other electronic media.

More worrisome, the study found that most children interact with electronic media alone. For example, older children spend up to 95 percent of their time watching television alone, while children between the ages of 2 and 7 watch television alone more than 81 percent of the time. Our children are seeping further into virtual worlds and losing the emotional attachments that come with face to face real time participation with their fellow human beings. Nor are American youngsters an anomaly. Children in other high-tech countries are following close on the heels of their American peers. This new human condition can best be described as the "high-tech blues."

Are future generations to be forever lonely? No, say the technological   5
optimists. Engineers at some of the leading technology centers are feverishly working on the next generation of technological marvels to address our lonesome high-tech existence. The field is called "affective computing" and the goal is to create technology that can express emotion, interpret and respond to the emotions of their human handlers, and even establish a sense of intimacy with their human companions. Built-in cameras allow the computers to detect even subtle changes in facial expressions, which are then processed in real time, allowing the computer to recognize the emotional state of the person. Researchers at the Massachusetts Institute of Technology have even developed an "affective wearable computer" that picks up different emotional states and subtle change of emotion by detecting changes in heart-rate, breathing, skin conductivity, temperature, pulse, and muscle activity.

Rosalind Picard, one of the pioneer researchers in the field of "affective computing," reports on an amazing study done at the MIT Media Lab. A computerized virtual person named "Laura" plays the role of an exercise adviser, helping real-life subjects increase their physical activity levels. Laura is capable of conversing with her subjects and is able to use hand gestures, eye gaze behavior, posture shifts, head-nods, and facial expressions. Laura, like any good exercise trainer, provides her subjects with feedback on their performance, helps them improve on their regimen, and gives empathetic verbal and facial feedback, cued to the appropriate emotional state of her human companions.

The reactions of the subjects are revealing. Compared with subjects interacting with a "nonrelational" computer interface, a number of the subjects—but not all—working with Laura reported an emotional rapport similar with what one might expect with a real-life trainer. One subject in the study remarked, "I feel Laura, in her own unique way, is genuinely concerned about my welfare." Another said, "I feel like Laura . . . likes me." A third subject confided, "Laura and I trust each other." Here is a typical response: "I like talking to Laura, especially those little conversations, about school, weather, interests, etc. She is very caring . . . I found myself looking forward to these fresh chats that pop up every now and then. They make Laura so much more like a real person." To be fair, there were skeptics as well. One subject said, "Personally, I detest Laura."

Other experiments conducted at Stanford University report similarly positive results with empathetic embodied computer agents interacting with subjects, leading researchers to conclude that "embodied computer agents are indeed social actors in the truest sense of the word 'social,' capable of forming relationships with users comparable to those found in the world of human-human interactions."

Frankly, it's hard to know whether to laugh off such technological pretensions as sadly pathological or whether to be truly frightened. There is no doubt that a growing number of young people find themselves enmeshed in virtual worlds where make believe substitutes for real-life experience. With "affective computing" looming on the horizon, the truly lonely can look forward to interacting with silicon companions, emotionally programmed to empathize and even care, to be a friend, and an intimate confidant.

Progress? Surely we can do better.   10

🖋 Joining the Conversation: Critical Thinking and Writing

1. In the first paragraph Rifkin claims that "the human vocabulary is plummeting all over the world, making it more difficult to express ourselves and participate in a meaningful way with our fellow human beings." What does he mean?

2. In paragraph 2 Rifkin refers to a study that says that "only 31 percent of college graduates today are proficient in English literacy, compared with 40 percent just a decade ago." Rifkin does not tell us how the study defined "literacy." How do you define it? Given your definition, do you consider yourself "proficient in English literacy"? Explain.

3. In paragraph 3 Rifkin reports that American children now are "lonelier" because they "spend an average of 6.5 hours per day watching television, surfing the Internet, text messaging, and playing with video games and other electronic media." Suppose someone said to Rifkin, "For *real* loneliness, for *real* isolation, nothing beats reading a book. Reading is really a solitary pleasure. Why don't you complain about the kids who like to read?" What reply do you think Rifkin might make?

4. In paragraph 4, Rifkin says that the "new human condition can best be described as 'high-tech blues.'" What does he mean? And what is "affective computing"? Of what "technological marvels" does it now consist?

5. In paragraph 9, speaking about such developments as "Laura," Rifkin says, "Frankly, it's hard to know whether to laugh off such technological pretensions as sadly pathological or whether to be truly frightened." Your reaction to these technological developments?

Kay S. Hymowitz

Kay S. Hymowitz, born in 1948, holds degrees from Brandeis University, Tufts University, and Columbia University. Among her publications are Ready or Not: Why Treating Our Children as Small Adults Endangers Their Future and Ours *(1999) and* Liberation's Children *(2001). We reprint an essay that originally appeared in the* Wall Street Journal *in 2006.*

Big Mother Is Watching

Some years ago my older daughter, then a senior in college, listened to me fret about rumors of drinking at the parties her ninth-grade sister was begging to go to. "They're so young to deal with this sort of thing," I worried. "Mom," she began in a knowing tone, "What do you think was going on when I went to parties in the ninth grade?"

I lingered for a moment over the disconnect between this young woman standing before me, a premed student, an Organization Kid who would sooner live on bread and water than turn in a late paper, and the image of her 14-year-old self chugging a Budweiser. Then, I struggled with two contradictory responses. First, discomfiture; I had been naïve, a mental status that we been-there-done-that boomer parents find pretty embarrassing. How could I have been so out of it? And second: relief. Thank God I didn't know. If I had, I would have had to transform my parenting approach from trust-but-verify (check-in phone calls to friends' parents, "so how did the movie end again?" sort of questions, etc.) to all-out war.

This incident and my response came to mind when I read recently about the burgeoning market in parental surveillance devices. There's a gizmo that parents can plug in beneath their SUV's dashboard; when your 16-year-old daughter drives to her new boyfriend's house, it records the vehicle's speed, or any sudden stops or swerves it may have made—as well as the location of said house. There are Global Positioning Systems that you can attach to your children's cellphones; they beep your cell if your son wanders beyond his allowed haunts or notify you by email that your tween is at the mall rather than her tutoring session.

And then there are the popular Internet spy programs like eBlaster or IM Einstein that let you monitor your kid's computer activities. The more sophisticated models send an email to your work account with the content of your son or daughter's emails or Instant Messages; one of them can even show you a screen snapshot of online conversations.

Orwellian as this high-tech snooping sounds, frightening reports of   5
abducted children, not to mention drinking parties for kids still in braces, suggest that there's a reasonable argument in its favor. A few generations ago when neighborhoods were more stable and mothers were home during the day to survey them, parents could feel pretty confident that there were familiar adult eyes watching over their kids even when they were out of parental range. Moreover, childhood had well-defined boundaries that pretty much everyone, including the corner merchant and Hollywood mediacrats, respected.

But as mothers went to work, neighborhoods emptied and the public meaning of childhood splintered, children's lives became both more anonymous and more threatened. Suddenly strangers with suspect motives were everywhere—sometimes in your own home. The Nannycam, a camera that can be secreted into the kitchen smoke alarm, for instance, to watch over babysitters, was perhaps the first of the surveillance devices to deal with the new conditions of childhood, followed quickly by the V-chip. Now with the Internet, the dangers have been globalized as online predators and porn Web sites whisper their enticements to every wired third-grader. Little wonder some parents are tempted by what one parent quoted in a Los Angeles Times article on the GPS systems, called "another set of eyes."

Still, there's a lot more behind Big Mother and Father spyware than protecting children from the dangers of an anonymous and treacherous 21st-century world. The truth is that today's parents worry about their kids' most mundane activities in a way that would baffle the legendarily meddling mothers and fathers of the 1950s. They are practitioners of what British sociologist Frank Furedi calls "paranoid parenting."

This, after all, is the generation of parents that has made bike helmets and car seats a matter of state interest and has banned such perilous pastimes as tag and dodgeball from school playgrounds. An increasing number of parents seem to be trying to control their kids' lives even after they move away from home. College administrators are now complaining about a cadre of "helicopter parents" who hassle deans with phone calls if their little one doesn't like her roommate or Chemistry grade. With a population of parents like these, Sprint's Family Locator service is bound to turn a hefty profit—even if parents have to rely on their 14-year-old, as in the case of a Kansas family described in the *Los Angeles Times*, to program the blasted thing.

Now, the obvious danger of such devices is that they raise paranoid parenting to an even more extreme level, thereby further depriving children of the chance to test their capacity for independence. Anthropologists tell us that traditional Japanese families often discouraged their babies from taking their first steps in an effort to keep them tied to their mothers. The custom makes a kind of sense in a culture that prizes group identity and interdependence above all. But Americans celebrate their children's first steps; they have always prided themselves on their self-sufficiency, which is a precondition for success in our society. The problem is that children who grow up knowing their parents keep track of them 24/7 fail to internalize the common sense and limit-setting that can only emerge from the experience of making independent judgments.

The more subtle, but equally important, objection to spyware is that it isn't good for parents either. By making snooping relatively impersonal, these technologies prompt mothers and fathers to bypass important moral questions about their relationship with their children. If it's all right to scrutinize your daughter's text messages, then it should be OK to read her diary. If it's all right to electronically monitor her driving, then it should be equally kosher to get in to your own car and follow her. Yet there are good reasons most sane adults would balk at these low-tech invasions of their children's privacy.

Equally pernicious, by making spying seem less intrusive, technology discourages parents from taking the periodic measurements of their child's maturity that are essential to guiding their development. Your 11-year-old son wants to take a public bus for the first time: Absent a GPS phone, you think about his judgment, how he handles money, how alert he is to his surroundings. With GPS, parents are trying to make an end-run around careful, and admittedly difficult, deliberation.

The fact is that raising children to become independent adults means years of worrying. Kids make stupid decisions. Terrible things can happen. How do you know when to let your toddler climb the steps on her own? Your 7-year-old walk to school? Your 12-year-old have free access to the Internet? Your 14-year-old go to a party where you suspect beer will be on the menu? No matter how much technology you buy, at some point your kids will be in a place you don't want them to be and do something you don't want them to do. Just remember, someday when they are older, they will probably tell you all about it—and you will breathe a sigh of relief.

10

Joining the Conversation: Critical Thinking and Writing

1. Hymowitz introduces her essay with an account of a conversation she had with her daughter "some years ago." After reading the essay, evaluate the narrative as an introduction.

2. How does the title "Big Mother Is Watching" prepare readers for Hymowitz's argument? Does the title echo something else you have read?

3. What is Hymowitz's argument? How does she support it? Does she sufficiently acknowledge opinions counter to her own?

4. What is your own view of parental surveillance devices? Did reading "Big Mother Is Watching" change or strengthen your own view? Explain.

5. Imagine an issue you might have had with your parents or with your children. Would you be pleased to find an article by Hymowitz arguing on behalf of your position? Why, or why not?

George F. Will

George F. Will, a syndicated columnist whose writing appears in more than 400 newspapers, was born in Champaign, Illinois, in 1941, and educated at Trinity College (Hartford Connecticut), University of Oxford, and Princeton University. Will has served as the Washington, D.C., editor of the National Review, *and he now writes a regular column for* Newsweek.

You Bloggin' to Me?

Time magazine asked a large number of people to name the Person of the Year. They were in a populist mood and named the largest possible number of Persons of the Year: Everybody.

Of course. The most capacious modern entitlement is not to Social Security but to self-esteem. So *Time*'s cover features a mirror-like panel. The reader—but why bother to read the magazine when merely gazing at its cover gives immediate and intense gratification?—can gaze at the reflection of his or her favorite person. Narcissism is news? Evidently.

To the person looking at his reflection, *Time*'s cover announces: "You control the Information Age." By "control" *Time* means only that everyone is created equal—equally entitled to create content for the World Wide Web, which is controlled by neither law nor taste.

Richard Stengel, *Time*'s managing editor, says, "Thomas Paine was in effect the first blogger" and "Ben Franklin was essentially loading his persona into the MySpace of the 18th century, 'Poor Richard's Almanack.' "

Not exactly.

Franklin's extraordinary persona informed what he wrote but was not the subject of what he wrote. Paine was perhaps history's most consequential pamphleteer. There are expected to be 100 million bloggers worldwide by the middle of 2007, which is why none will be like Franklin or Paine. Both were geniuses; genius is scarce. Both had a revolutionary civic purpose, which they accomplished by amazing exertions. Most bloggers have the private purpose of expressing themselves, for their own satisfaction. There is nothing wrong with that, but nothing demanding or especially admirable, either.

According to the Pew Internet & American Life Project, 76 percent of bloggers say one reason they blog is to document and share their personal experiences. And 37 percent—soon, 37 million—say the primary topic of their blog is "my life and experiences." George III would have preferred dealing with 100 million bloggers rather than one Paine.

Stengel says that bloggers and the people who upload videos onto YouTube (65,000 new videos a day; 100 million watched daily) are

5

George F. Will, "You Bloggin' Me?" (original title: "Full Steam Ahead") published in the *Washington Post*, December 21, 2006. Copyright © 2006, The Washington Post Writers Group. Reprinted with permission.

bringing "events" to us in ways that are often more "authentic" than the services of traditional media. But authenticity can be easy and of no inherent value.

Time's Lev Grossman writes that "an explosion of productivity and innovation" is under way as "millions of minds that would otherwise have drowned in obscurity" become participants in "the global intellectual economy." Grossman continues:

"Who actually sits down after a long day at work and says, I'm not   10 going to watch 'Lost' tonight. I'm going to turn on my computer and make a movie starring my pet iguana? I'm going to mash up 50 Cent's vocals with Queen's instrumentals? I'm going to blog about my state of mind or the state of the union or the *steak-fries* at the new bistro down the street? Who has that time and that energy and that passion?

"The answer is, you do. And for seizing the reins of the global media, for founding and framing the new digital democracy, for working for nothing and beating the pros at their own game, *Time*'s Person of the Year is you."

There are, however, essentially no reins on the Web— few means of control and direction. That is good, but vitiates the idea that the Web's chaos of entertainment, solipsism and occasional intellectual seriousness and civic engagement is anything like a polity (a "digital democracy"). *Time*'s bow to the amateurs who are, it strangely suggests, no longer obscure, and in the same game that *Time* is in, is refuted by a glance—which is all an adult will want—at YouTube's most popular videos.

Time includes an unenthralled essay by NBC's Brian Williams, who believes that raptures over the Web's egalitarianism arise from the same impulse that causes today's youth soccer programs to award trophies to any child who shows up: "The danger just might be that we miss the next great book or the next great idea, or that we will fail to meet the next great challenge . . . because we are too busy celebrating ourselves and listening to the same tune we already know by heart."

The fact that Stengel included Williams' essay proves that Stengel's *Time* has what 99.9 percent of the Web's content lacks: seriousness.

ᘓ Joining the Conversation: Critical Thinking and Writing

1. Will quotes the managing editor of *Time* as saying that "Thomas Paine was in effect the first blogger." Who was Paine, and does it make sense to say that he was a blogger? Why, or why not? Will also says that "George III would have preferred dealing with 100 million bloggers rather than one Paine." What does he mean, and what is his point?

2. What is Will's attitude toward blogging? What is your evidence?

3. Are you a blogger? If so, why? If not, why not?

Rob Nixon

Rob Nixon, a professor of English at the University of Wisconsin at Madison, published this essay in the Chronicle of Higher Education *in 2000.*

Please Don't E-Mail Me about This Article

It's Saturday morning, and I've sought refuge in my favorite place to write: a café a few blocks from home. Ten years ago, I would have found the infant mewling, the bleats of laughter, the cup clatter, and the chatter way too distracting. But these days, I find them easy to screen out. I relish the mental solitude I can achieve here against a backdrop of buzzing human sociability. But what I value most is the sanctuary the café offers from the supreme distraction of our age: the silent and unceasing cacophony of e-mail.

To judge from the testimony of friends and colleagues, the volume of e-mail we process daily has reached some kind of crisis point. More and more, the medium has become both utterly integral and a major source of exhaustion and disquiet. I don't know any academics who feel they would become better teachers or intellectuals if they received and sent more e-mail. I hasten to add that I can't claim to speak from the thick of the phenomenon. I am just a regular 25-to-30-e-mails-a-day guy. They arrive from colleagues, electronic mailing lists, administrators, students, ex-students, publishers, friends, family, and solicitous strangers (some wonderful, others out-and-out crackpots).

But even that moderate amount makes me rail against the merciless immediacy of e-mail, and feel as if I am constantly treading water. How, I wonder, do deans and chairs survive the e-mail tsunamis (80, 90 messages a day?) that crash down on them unceasingly?

Sometimes, one gets an inkling of the frustration at the top. A dean at my university sent a mass mailing accompanied by this appeal: "Do not reply to this e-mail. Please do not say yes, do not say no. Just come if you can"—thus sparing some administrative assistant carpal-tunnel syndrome from punching the delete button all the way to the hospital.

The distribution of my online affections has undergone a radical reversal. A decade ago, I found the Internet laborious, insubstantial, unenticing. 5

E-mail, on the other hand, charmed me totally. I adored the frisson, the serendipity, the quick-flaring intimacy. I remember reading W. H. Auden's line—"Now he is scattered among a hundred cities"—and thinking he had

Rob Nixon, "Please Don't E-mail Me about This Article," *Chronicle of Higher Education,* September 29, 2000. Reprinted by permission of the author.

no idea just how scattered identity would become. Or how exhilarating that could feel.

However, my romance with e-mail is now on the rocks. E-mail must rank as one of the most time-devouring timesavers of all time. Too often it makes nothing happen—fast. I don't say this out of some Luddite sensibility: I'd make a very feeble Luddite. I've come to delight in the Internet at large, which appeals to both the hunter-gatherer and the pastoralist browser in me. My research and teaching alike are unthinkable without it. Unlike e-mail, the Internet doesn't insistently demand responses. It seems less controlling, less of an imposition, and more of a resource. Once upon a time e-mail looked as if it would become an invigorating part of university life. By now, however, it has come to feel like a Sisyphean labor akin to hauling out the garbage or shoveling snow.

E-mail has become efficient to the point of counterefficiency, threatening to overwhelm the primary activities—teaching, reading, writing, and thinking—that we once hoped it might help sustain. The best teaching and writing require some professional space within which to give the illusion of inefficiency. It is in this space that we are most likely to be surprised by new ideas or to discover compelling ways to give fresh life to old ones. E-mail's demands for metronomic efficiency threatens such expanses of "idle" creativity.

At the heart of the problem is e-mail's paradoxical status. It is and isn't writing. You bend over the same computer, tapping the same keys, straining the same muscles you use to write your lectures, your articles, your books. But what you're composing is mostly ephemeral: It's not writing but meta-writing. A reply to a reply to a reply. The challenge is how to keep a technology with a rodentlike reproductive rate supplementary, not something that overruns our days.

Going to the café is one of my coping strategies. There my computer is reduced to a one-dimensional technology temporarily severed from interactive temptations and distractions. But such trips are a rare luxury. More often, I impose on myself a kind of inverted curfew: I try never to check e-mail before 4 P.M. Like many people, I experience my best energy in the mornings. I try to reserve that dream-inflected, caffeine-charged creativity for the activities that matter most: writing, teaching, reading, and one-on-one meetings with students. It's all too easy to go online first thing (and then again, and again) and scatter a day's worth of concentration within an hour or two of breakfast.

Certainly, e-mail can have a lingering seductiveness. Not least because it appears to resolve a central, often painful tension in the life of anyone who writes. As the editor Betsy Lerner puts it in her new book, *The Forest for the Trees*, "the great paradox of the writer's life is how much time he spends alone trying to connect with other people." We feel that paradox most acutely when we're writing books. But even composing lectures demands deferred connection. E-mail seems to resolve the paradox by transforming

10

writing into a quick feedback loop. This is writing on the no-solitude, no-sweat, no-deferral plan.

To move from that mode of expectation back to real writing takes energy and discipline. Writing is hardest when you set out. It usually takes me an hour or two, after my first faltering starts, to enter "the zone." Historically, writers have used all kinds of ingenious and desperate acts to try to kick start the process—like John McPhee's strapping himself into his chair with a seat belt. I've made the mistake often enough of using e-mail to kick start me. In my experience, it warms you up for nothing but dispersion; the real writing is less likely to get done.

These days the buzz—and the money that follows the buzz—is all about connection. However, if we don't force ourselves into regular periods of disconnectedness, our students will be shortchanged. Academics have less time than ever to read and write. That's why intervals of withdrawal remain essential to our jobs as educators. Our task is to redeem information and yeast it, through research, reflection, and passion, into communicable knowledge. "Only connect," E. M. Forster exhorted his readers 90 years ago, in what became a celebrated liberal mantra. But connecting has become the easy part. Disconnection (in order to connect more deeply later) now requires the greater discipline and resourcefulness.

I wish e-mail were routed through some other apparatus than a computer—like, say, the DustBuster. That would have two primary advantages. First, we wouldn't be as prone to equate writing proper with e-mail, writing's easy surrogate. Second, we wouldn't have two physically unhealthy activities compressed into one posture. It's bad enough that writing locks us into a computer stoop. Now we must assume the same stance to absorb the ephemeral communications that used to pass through the telephone. No wonder our deltoid, trapezius, and infraspinatus muscles go into revolt.

I have friends (retirees, artists, writers) who lead more isolated lives   15
than I do, without a matrix of institutional responsibilities. I'm talking about the 5-or-6-e-mails-a-day folk, for whom the medium can still feel like something of a pastime. Often they'll send me letter-length dispatches: long, witty, eloquent, and intimate. I feel the need, the desire, to respond in kind. But mostly I'm e-mailed out and can't endure more time filling up boxes on my computer screen. I watch with horror as my friends' long missives sink into the sedimentary layers of unanswered e-mail, turning into the digital equivalent of anthracite. These days, I'm more likely to respond by picking up the telephone.

This summer, I spent a month at an artists' colony in New Hampshire. The setup there was my idea of e-mail heaven. Thirty artists shared a single phone link. You had to pack up your computer and hike half a mile to the main residence to plug into it. What I adored was the sheer inconvenience of it all. Going online became a conscious choice, not a facile reflex that could derail your train of thought. I checked my e-mail every three days or so. In between, I could build up a head of steam, without the temptation of logging on for an incidental glance and finding, an hour later, that I was still inside e-mail's thrall and that the writing zone had fled.

The colony experience reminded me that I don't want e-mail to disappear. I just need periods in my life when it is less relentless and less convenient.

In moderation, e-mail is a boon. And yes, it can save time. But we'd do well to recall the Buddha's response on being told that a sprinter had shaved 0.1 seconds off the 100-meter record. "What," the Buddha inquired, "did she do with the time she saved?" To which I'd add: Write more e-mail?

Joining the Conversation: Critical Thinking and Writing

1. What is Nixon's point?

2. Does he believe that e-mail has some value?

3. Why does he protest so vigorously against e-mail?

4. Does Nixon propose a solution?

5. If he does propose a solution, do you find this solution convincing?

CHAPTER 12

Law and Order

Flower Power
Bernie Boston, 1967

The Problem We All Live With
Norman Rockwell, 1964

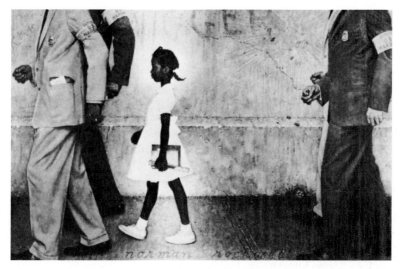

Short Views

The trouble for the thief is not how to steal the chief's bugle, but where to blow it.
African Proverb

Whoever desires to found a state and give it laws, must start with assuming that all men are bad and ever ready to display their vicious nature, whenever they may find occasion for it.
Niccolò Machiavelli

It is questionable whether, when we break a murderer on the wheel, we aren't lapsing into precisely the mistake of the child who hits the chair he bumps into.
G. C. Lichtenberg

If a man were permitted to make all the ballads, he need not care who should make the laws of a nation.
Andrew Fletcher

Nature has given women so much power that the law has very wisely given them very little.
Samuel Johnson

One law for the ox and the ass is oppression.
William Blake

The law, in its majestic equality, forbids the rich as well as the poor to sleep under bridges, to beg in the streets, and to steal bread.
Anatole France

Decency, security and liberty alike demand that government officials shall be subjected to the same rules of conduct that are commands to the citizen. In a government of laws, existence of the government will be imperilled if it fails to observe the law scrupulously. Our Government is the potent, the omnipresent teacher. For good or for ill, it teaches the whole people by its example. Crime is contagious. If the Government becomes a lawbreaker, it breeds contempt for law; it invites every man to become a law unto himself; it invites anarchy. To declare that in the administration of the criminal law the end justifies the means—to declare that the Government may commit crimes in order to secure the conviction of a private criminal—would bring terrible retribution. Against that pernicious doctrine this Court should resolutely set its face.

> *Louis D. Brandeis*

The trouble about fighting for human freedom is that you have to spend much of your life defending sons of bitches; for oppressive laws are always aimed at them originally, and oppression must be stopped in the beginning if it is to be stopped at all.

> *H. L. Mencken*

What the framework of our Constitution can do is organize the way by which we argue about our future. All of its elaborate machinery—its separation of powers and checks and balances and federalist principles and Bill of Rights—are designed to force us into a conversation, a "deliberative democracy" in which all citizens are required to engage in a process of testing their ideas against an external reality, persuading others of their point of view, and building shifting alliances of consent.

> *Barack Obama*

Censorship upholds the dignity of the profession, know what I mean?

> *Mae West*

Thomas Jefferson

Thomas Jefferson (1743–1826), governor of Virginia and the third president of the United States, devoted most of his adult life, until his retirement, to the service of Virginia and of the nation. The spirit and the wording of the Declaration are almost entirely Jefferson's.

The Declaration of Independence

In CONGRESS, July 4, 1776.
The Unanimous Declaration of the Thirteen United States of America.

When in the Course of human events, it becomes necessary for one people to dissolve the political bands which have connected them with another, and to assume among the powers of the earth, the separate and equal station to which the Laws of Nature and of Nature's God entitle them, a decent respect to the opinions of mankind requires that they should declare the causes which impel them to the separation.

We hold these truths to be self-evident, that all men are created equal, that they are endowed by their Creator with certain unalienable Rights, that among these are Life, Liberty and the pursuit of Happiness.

That to secure these rights, Governments are instituted among Men, deriving their just powers from the consent of the governed.

That whenever any Form of Government becomes destructive of these ends, it is the Right of the People to alter or to abolish it, and to institute new Government, laying its foundation on such principles and organizing its powers in such form, as to them shall seem most likely to effect their Safety and Happiness. Prudence, indeed, will dictate that Governments long established should not be changed for light and transient causes; and accordingly all experience hath shewn, that mankind are more disposed to suffer, while evils are sufferable, than to right themselves by abolishing the forms to which they are accustomed. But when a long train of abuses and usurpations, pursuing invariably the same Object evinces a design to reduce them under absolute Despotism, it is their right, it is their duty, to throw off such Government, and to provide new Guards for their future security.

Such has been the patient sufferance of these Colonies; and such is now the necessity which constrains them to alter their former Systems of Government. The history of the present King of Great Britain is a history of repeated injuries and usurpations, all having in direct object the establishment of an absolute Tyranny over these States. To prove this, let Facts be submitted to a candid world.

He has refused his Assent to Laws, the most wholesome and necessary for the public good.

He has forbidden his Governors to pass Laws of immediate and pressing importance, unless suspended in their operation till his Assent should be obtained; and when so suspended, he has utterly neglected to attend to them.

He has refused to pass other Laws for the accommodation of large districts of people, unless those people would relinquish the right of Representation in the Legislature, a right inestimable to them and formidable to tyrants only.

He has called together legislative bodies at places unusual, uncomfortable, and distant from the depository of their public Records, for the sole purpose of fatiguing them into compliance with his measures.

He has dissolved Representative Houses repeatedly, for opposing with manly firmness his invasions on the rights of people.

He has refused for a long time, after such dissolutions, to cause others to be elected; whereby the Legislative powers, incapable of Annihilation, have returned to the People at large for their exercise; the State remaining in the mean time exposed to all the dangers of invasion from without, and convulsions within.

He has endeavoured to prevent the population of these States; for that purpose obstructing the Laws for Naturalization of Foreigners; refusing to pass others to encourage their migrations hither, and raising the conditions of new Appropriations of Lands.

He has obstructed the Administration of Justice, by refusing his Assent to Laws for establishing Judiciary powers.

He has made Judges dependent on his Will alone, for the tenure of their offices, and the amount and payment of their salaries.

He has erected a multitude of New Offices, and sent hither swarms of Officers to harass our people, and eat out their substance.

He has kept among us, in times of peace, Standing Armies without the Consent of our legislatures.

He has affected to render the Military independent of and superior to the Civil power.

He has combined with others to subject us to a jurisdiction foreign to our constitution, and unacknowledged by our laws; giving his Assent to their Acts of pretended Legislation:

For Quartering large bodies of armed troops among us:

For Protecting them, by a mock Trial, from punishment for any Murders which they should commit on the Inhabitants of these States:

For cutting off our Trade with all parts of the world:

For imposing Taxes on us without our Consent:

For depriving us in many cases, of the benefits of Trial by Jury:

For transporting us beyond Seas to be tried for pretended offences:

For abolishing the free System of English Laws in a neighbouring Province, establishing therein an Arbitrary government, and enlarging its Boundaries so as to render it at once an example and fit instrument for introducing the same absolute rule into these Colonies:

For taking away our Charters, abolishing our most valuable Laws, and altering fundamentally the Forms of our Governments:

For suspending our own Legislatures, and declaring themselves invested with power to legislate for us in all cases whatsoever.

He has abdicated Government here, by declaring us out of his Protection and waging War against us:

He has plundered our seas, ravaged our Coasts, burnt our towns, and destroyed the lives of our people.

He is at this time transporting large Armies of foreign Mercenaries to compleat the works of death, desolation and tyranny, already begun with circumstances of Cruelty & perfidy scarcely paralleled in the most barbarous ages, and totally unworthy the Head of a civilized nation.   30

He has constrained our fellow Citizens taken Captive on the high Seas to bear Arms against their Country, to become the executioners of their friends and Brethren, or to fall themselves by their Hands.

He has excited domestic insurrections amongst us, and has endeavoured to bring on the inhabitants of our frontiers, the merciless Indian Savages, whose known rule of warfare, is an undistinguished destruction of all ages, sexes and conditions. In every stage of these Oppressions We have Petitioned for Redress in the most humble terms: Our repeated Petitions have been answered only by repeated injury. A Prince, whose character is thus marked by every act which may define a Tyrant, is unfit to be the ruler of a free people. Nor have We been wanting in attentions to our British brethren. We have warned them from time to time of attempts by their legislature to extend an unwarrantable jurisdiction over us. We have reminded them of the circumstances of our emigration and settlement here. We have appealed to their native justice and magnanimity, and we have conjured them by the ties of our common kindred to disavow these usurpations, which, would inevitably interrupt our connections and correspondence. They too have been deaf to the voice of justice and of consanguinity. We must, therefore, acquiesce in the necessity, which denounces our Separation, and hold them, as we hold the rest of mankind, Enemies in War, in Peace Friends.

We, THEREFORE, the Representatives of the UNITED STATES OF AMERICA, in General Congress Assembled, appealing to the Supreme Judge of the world for the rectitude of our intentions, do, in the Name and by Authority of the good People of these Colonies, solemnly publish and declare, That these United Colonies are, and of Right ought to be FREE AND INDEPENDENT STATES; that they are Absolved from all Allegiance to the British Crown, and that all political connection between them and the State of Great Britain, is and ought to be totally dissolved; and that as Free and Independent States, they have full Power to levy War, conclude Peace, contract Alliances, establish Commerce, and to do all other Acts and Things which Independent States may of right do.

And for the support of this Declaration, with a firm reliance on the protection of divine Providence, we mutually pledge to each other our Lives, our Fortunes and our sacred Honor.

✑ Joining the Conversation: Critical Thinking and Writing

1. What audience is being addressed in the Declaration of Independence? Cite passages in the text that support your answer.

2. The Library of Congress has the original manuscript of the rough draft of the Declaration. This manuscript itself includes revisions that are indicated below, but it was later further revised. We print the first part of the second paragraph of the draft and, after it, the corresponding part of the final version. Try to account for the changes within the draft, and from the revised draft to the final version.

> *self evident,*
> We hold these truths to be ~~sacred & undeniable,~~ that all men are
> *they are endowed by their creator*
> created equal ~~& independent,~~ that ~~from that equal creation they~~
> ~~derive equal rights some of which are in rights~~ *with*
> *rights; that these*
> inherent & inalienable among ~~which~~ are ~~the preservation of~~ life,
> liberty, & the pursuit of happiness.

> We hold these Truths to be self-evident, that all men are created
> equal, that they are endowed by their Creator with certain
> unalienable Rights, that among these are Life, Liberty and the
> pursuit of Happiness.

   In a paragraph evaluate the changes. Try to put yourself into Jefferson's mind and see if you can sense why Jefferson made the changes.

3. In a paragraph define *happiness*, and then in a second paragraph explain why, in your opinion, Jefferson spoke of "the pursuit of happiness" rather than of "happiness."

4. In "We Have No 'Right to Happiness'" (page 22) C. S. Lewis discusses the meaning of "the pursuit of happiness" in the Declaration and a current misinterpretation of the phrase. How does he explain and define the phrase? How does his interpretation differ from what he considers an erroneous interpretation?

5. What assumptions lie behind the numerous specific reasons that are given to justify the rebellion? Set forth the gist of the argument of the Declaration using the form of reasoning known as a *syllogism*, which consists of a major premise (such as "All men are mortal"), a minor premise ("Socrates is a man"), and a conclusion ("Therefore, Socrates is mortal"). For a brief discussion of syllogisms, see page 87 (deduction).

6. In a paragraph argue that the assertion that "all Men are created equal" is nonsense, or, on the other hand, that it makes sense.

7. If every person has an unalienable right to life, how can capital punishment be reconciled with the Declaration of Independence? You need not
in fact be a supporter of capital punishment; simply offer the best defense
you can think of, in an effort to make it harmonious with the Declaration.

Martin Luther King Jr.

*Martin Luther King Jr. (1929–1968), clergyman and civil rights leader, achieved national fame in
1955–1956 when he led the boycott against segregated bus lines in Montgomery, Alabama. His
policy of passive resistance succeeded in Montgomery, and King then organized the Southern
Christian Leadership Conference in order to extend his efforts. In 1964 he was awarded the Nobel
Peace Prize, but he continued to encounter strong opposition. On April 4, 1968, while in
Memphis to support striking sanitation workers, he was shot and killed.*

Nonviolent Resistance

Oppressed people deal with their oppression in three characteristic
ways. One way is acquiescence: the oppressed resign themselves to their
doom. They tacitly adjust themselves to oppression, and thereby become
conditioned to it. In every movement toward freedom some of the oppressed prefer to remain oppressed. Almost 2800 years ago Moses set out
to lead the children of Israel from the slavery of Egypt to the freedom of the
promised land. He soon discovered that slaves do not always welcome
their deliverers. They become accustomed to being slaves. They would
rather bear those ills they have, as Shakespeare pointed out, than flee to
others that they know not of. They prefer the "fleshpots of Egypt" to the or-
deals of emancipation.

There is such a thing as the freedom of exhaustion. Some people are
so worn down by the yoke of oppression that they give up. A few years
ago in the slum areas of Atlanta, a Negro guitarist used to sing almost
daily: "Ben down so long that down don't bother me." This is the type
of negative freedom and resignation that often engulfs the life of the
oppressed.

But this is not the way out. To accept passively an unjust system is to
cooperate with that system; thereby the oppressed become as evil as the
oppressor. Noncooperation with evil is as much a moral obligation as is
cooperation with good. The oppressed must never allow the conscience
of the oppressor to slumber. Religion reminds every man that he is his
brother's keeper. To accept injustice or segregation passively is to say to
the oppressor that his actions are morally right. It is a way of allowing his
conscience to fall asleep. At this moment the oppressed fails to be his
brother's keeper. So acquiescence—while often the easier way—is not the

moral way. It is the way of the coward. The Negro cannot win the respect of his oppressor by acquiescing; he merely increases the oppressor's arrogance and contempt. Acquiescence is interpreted as proof of the Negro's inferiority. The Negro cannot win the respect of the white people of the South or the peoples of the world if he is willing to sell the future of his children for his personal and immediate comfort and safety.

A second way that oppressed people sometimes deal with oppression is to resort to physical violence and corroding hatred. Violence often brings about momentary results. Nations have frequently won their independence in battle. But in spite of temporary victories, violence never brings permanent peace. It solves no social problem; it merely creates new and more complicated ones.

Violence as a way of achieving racial justice is both impractical and immoral. It is impractical because it is a descending spiral ending in destruction for all. The old law of an eye for an eye leaves everybody blind. It is immoral because it seeks to humiliate the opponent rather than win his understanding; it seeks to annihilate rather than to convert. Violence is immoral because it thrives on hatred rather than love. It destroys community and makes brotherhood impossible. It leaves society in monologue rather than dialogue. Violence ends by defeating itself. It creates bitterness in the survivors and brutality in the destroyers. A voice echoes through time saying to every potential Peter, "Put up your sword." History is cluttered with the wreckage of nations that failed to follow his command.

If the American Negro and other victims of oppression succumb to the temptation of using violence in the struggle for freedom, future generations will be the recipients of a desolate night of bitterness, and our chief legacy to them will be an endless reign of meaningless chaos. Violence is not the way.

The third way open to oppressed people in their quest for freedom is the way of nonviolent resistance. Like the synthesis in Hegelian philosophy, the principle of nonviolent resistance seeks to reconcile the truths of two opposites—acquiescence and violence—while avoiding the extremes and immoralities of both. The nonviolent resister agrees with the person who acquiesces that one should not be physically aggressive toward his opponent; but he balances the equation by agreeing with the person of violence that evil must be resisted. He avoids the nonresistance of the former and the violent resistance of the latter. With nonviolent resistance, no individual or group need submit to any wrong, nor need anyone resort to violence in order to right a wrong.

It seems to me that this is the method that must guide the actions of the Negro in the present crisis in race relations. Through nonviolent resistance the Negro will be able to rise to the noble height of opposing the unjust system while loving the perpetrators of the system. The Negro must work passionately and unrelentingly for full stature as a citizen, but he must not use inferior methods to gain it. He must never come to terms with falsehood, malice, hate, or destruction.

Nonviolent resistance makes it possible for the Negro to remain in the South and struggle for his rights. The Negro's problem will not be solved by running away. He cannot listen to the glib suggestion of those who would urge him to migrate en masse to other sections of the country. By grasping his great opportunity in the South he can make a lasting contribution to the moral strength of the nation and set a sublime example of courage for generations yet unborn.

By nonviolent resistance, the Negro can also enlist all men of good   10
will in his struggle for equality. The problem is not a purely racial one, with Negroes set against whites. In the end, it is not a struggle between people at all, but a tension between justice and injustice. Nonviolent resistance is not aimed against oppressors but against oppression. Under its banner consciences, not racial groups, are enlisted.

If the Negro is to achieve the goal of integration, he must organize himself into a militant and nonviolent mass movement. All three elements are indispensable. The movement for equality and justice can only be a success if it has both a mass and militant character; the barriers to be overcome require both. Nonviolence is an imperative in order to bring about ultimate community.

A mass movement of militant quality that is not at the same time committed to nonviolence tends to generate conflict, which in turn breeds anarchy. The support of the participants and the sympathy of the uncommitted are both inhibited by the threat that bloodshed will engulf the community. This reaction in turn encourages the opposition to threaten and resort to force. When, however, the mass movement repudiates violence while moving resolutely toward its goal, its opponents are revealed as the instigators and practitioners of violence if it occurs. Then public support is magnetically attracted to the advocates of nonviolence, while those who employ violence are literally disarmed by overwhelming sentiment against their stand.

Only through a nonviolent approach can the fears of the white community be mitigated. A guilt-ridden white minority lives in fear that if the Negro should ever attain power, he would act without restraint or pity to revenge the injustices and brutality of the years. It is something like a parent who continually mistreats a son. One day that parent raises his hand to strike the son, only to discover that the son is now as tall as he is. The parent is suddenly afraid—fearful that the son will use his new physical power to repay his parent for all the blows of the past.

The Negro, once a helpless child, has now grown up politically, culturally, and economically. Many white men fear retaliation. The job of the Negro is to show them that they have nothing to fear, that the Negro understands and forgives and is ready to forget the past. He must convince the white man that all he seeks is justice, *for both himself and the white man*. A mass movement exercising nonviolence is an object lesson in power under discipline, a demonstration to the white community that if such a movement attained a degree of strength, it would use its power creatively and not vengefully.

Nonviolence can touch men where the law cannot reach them. When the law regulates behavior it plays an indirect part in molding public sentiment. The enforcement of the law is itself a form of peaceful persuasion. But the law needs help. The courts can order desegregation of the public schools. But what can be done to mitigate the fears, to disperse the hatred, violence, and irrationality gathered around school integration, to take the initiative out of the hands of racial demagogues, to release respect for the law? In the end, for laws to be obeyed, men must believe they are right.

Here nonviolence comes in as the ultimate form of persuasion. It is the method which seeks to implement the just law by appealing to the conscience of the great decent majority who through blindness, fear, pride, or irrationality have allowed their consciences to sleep.

The nonviolent resisters can summarize their message in the following simple terms: We will take direct action against injustice without waiting for other agencies to act. We will not obey unjust laws or submit to unjust practices. We will do this peacefully, openly, cheerfully because our aim is to persuade. We adopt the means of nonviolence because our end is a community at peace with itself. We will try to persuade with our words, but if our words fail, we will try to persuade with our acts. We will always be willing to talk and seek fair compromise, but we are ready to suffer when necessary and even risk our lives to become witnesses to the truth as we see it.

The way of nonviolence means a willingness to suffer and sacrifice. It may mean going to jail. If such is the case the resister must be willing to fill the jail houses of the South. It may even mean physical death. But if physical death is the price that a man must pay to free his children and his white brethren from a permanent death of the spirit, then nothing could be more redemptive.

Joining the Conversation: Critical Thinking and Writing

1. In the first paragraph, the passage about Moses and the children of Israel is not strictly necessary; the essential idea of the paragraph is stated in the previous sentence. Why, then, does King add this material? And why the quotation from Shakespeare?

2. Pick out two or three sentences that seem to you to be especially effective and analyze the sources of their power. You can choose either isolated sentences or (because King often effectively links sentences with repetition of words or of constructions) consecutive ones.

3. In a paragraph set forth your understanding of what nonviolent resistance is. Use whatever examples from your own experience or reading you find

useful. In a second paragraph, explain how Maya Angelou's "Graduation" (page 307) offers an example of nonviolent resistance.

Martin Luther King Jr.

Martin Luther King Jr. (1929–1968), clergyman and civil rights leader, achieved national fame in 1955–1956 when he led the boycott against segregated bus lines in Montgomery, Alabama. His policy of passive resistance succeeded in Montgomery, and King then organized the Southern Christian Leadership Conference in order to extend his efforts. In 1963 Dr. King was arrested in Birmingham, Alabama, for participating in a march for which no parade permit had been issued by the city officials. In jail he wrote a response to a letter that eight local clergymen had published in a newspaper. In 1964 he was awarded the Nobel Peace Prize, but he continued to encounter strong opposition. On April 4, 1968, while in Memphis to support striking sanitation workers, he was shot and killed.

Note: *We begin, not with King's letter, but with the newspaper piece by eight clergymen entitled "A Call for Unity," so that you can see the context of King's response.*

[Letter by Eight Local Clergymen]

A Call for Unity

April 12, 1963

We the undersigned clergymen are among those who, in January, issued "An Appeal for Law and Order and Common Sense," in dealing with racial problems in Alabama. We expressed understanding that honest convictions in racial matters could properly be pursued in the courts, but urged that decisions of those courts should in the meantime be peacefully obeyed.

Since that time there had been some evidence of increased forbearance and a willingness to face facts. Responsible citizens have undertaken to work on various problems which cause racial friction and unrest. In Birmingham, recent public events have given indication that we all have opportunity for a new constructive and realistic approach to racial problems.

However, we are now confronted by a series of demonstrations by some of our Negro citizens, directed and led in part by outsiders. We recognize the natural impatience of people who feel that their hopes are slow in being realized. But we are convinced that these demonstrations are unwise and untimely.

We agree rather with certain local Negro leadership which has called for honest and open negotiation of racial issues in our area. And we believe this kind of facing of issues can best be accomplished by citizens of our own metropolitan area, white and Negro, meeting with their knowledge and experience of the local situation. All of us need to face that responsibility and find proper channels for its accomplishment.

Just as we formerly pointed out that "hatred and violence have no sanction in our religious and political traditions," we also point out that such actions as incite to hatred and violence, however technically peaceful those actions may be, have not contributed to the resolution of our local problems. We do not believe that these days of new hope are days when extreme measures are justified in Birmingham.

We commend the community as a whole, and the local news media and law enforcement officials in particular, on the calm manner in which these demonstrations have been handled. We urge the public to continue to show restraint should the demonstrations continue, and the law enforcement officials to remain calm and continue to protect our city from violence.

We further strongly urge our own Negro community to withdraw support from these demonstrations, and to unite locally in working peacefully for a better Birmingham. When rights are consistently denied, a cause should be pressed in the courts and in negotiations among local leaders, and not in the streets. We appeal to both our white and Negro citizenry to observe the principles of law and order and common sense.

C.C.J. Carpenter, D.D., L.L.D., Bishop of Alabama; Joseph A. Durick, D.D., Auxiliary Bishop, Diocese of Mobile-Birmingham; Rabbi Milton L. Grafman, Temple Emanu-El, Birmingham, Alabama; Bishop Paul Hardin, Bishop of the Alabama–West Florida Conference of the Methodist Church; Bishop Nolan B. Harmon, Bishop of the North Alabama Conference of the Methodist Church; George M. Murray, D.D., L.L.D., Bishop Coadjutor, Episcopal Diocese of Alabama; Edward V. Ramage, Moderator, Synod of the Alabama Presbyterian Church in the United States; Earl Stallings, Pastor, First Baptist Church, Birmingham, Alabama.

Letter from Birmingham Jail

In Response to "A Call for Unity"

April 16, 1963

My Dear Fellow Clergymen:

While confined here in the Birmingham city jail, I came across your recent statement calling my present activities "unwise and untimely."[1] Seldom do I pause to answer criticism of my work and ideas. If I sought to answer all the criticisms that cross my desk, my secretaries would have little time for anything other than such correspondence in the course of

---

[1]This response to a published statement by eight fellow clergymen from Alabama (Bishop C.C.J. Carpenter, Bishop Joseph A. Durick, Rabbi Milton L. Grafman, Bishop Paul Hardin, Bishop Nolan B. Harmon, the Reverend George M. Murray, the Reverend Edward V. Ramage, and the Reverend Earl Stallings) was composed under somewhat constricting circumstances. Begun on the margins of the newspaper in which the statement appeared while I was in jail, the letter was continued on scraps of writing paper supplied by a friendly Negro trusty, and concluded on a pad my attorneys were eventually permitted to leave me. Although the text remains in substance unaltered, I have indulged in the author's prerogative of polishing it for publication. [King's note]

the day, and I would have no time for constructive work. But since I feel that you are men of genuine good will and that your criticisms are sincerely set forth, I want to try to answer your statement in what I hope will be patient and reasonable terms.

I think I should indicate why I am here in Birmingham, since you have been influenced by the view which argues against "outsiders coming in." I have the honor of serving as president of the Southern Christian Leadership Conference, an organization operating in every southern state, with headquarters in Atlanta, Georgia. We have some eighty-five affiliated organizations across the South, and one of them is the Alabama Christian Movement for Human Rights. Frequently we share staff, educational, and financial resources with our affiliates. Several months ago the affiliate here in Birmingham asked us to be on call to engage in a nonviolent direct-action program if such were deemed necessary. We readily consented, and when the hour came we lived up to our promise. So I, along with several members of my staff, am here because I was invited here. I am here because I have organizational ties here.

But more basically, I am in Birmingham because injustice is here. Just as the prophets of the eighth century B.C. left their villages and carried their "thus saith the Lord" far beyond the boundaries of their home towns, and just as the Apostle Paul left his village of Tarsus and carried the gospel of Jesus Christ to the far corners of the Greco-Roman world, so am I compelled to carry the gospel of freedom beyond my own home town. Like Paul, I must constantly respond to the Macedonian call for aid.

Moreover, I am cognizant of the interrelatedness of all communities and states. I cannot sit idly by in Atlanta and not be concerned about what happens in Birmingham. Injustice anywhere is a threat to justice everywhere. We are caught in an inescapable network of mutuality; tied in a single garment of destiny. Whatever affects one directly, affects all indirectly. Never again can we afford to live with the narrow, provincial "outside agitator" idea. Anyone who lives inside the United States can never be considered an outsider anywhere within its bounds.

You deplore the demonstrations taking place in Birmingham. But your   5
statement, I am sorry to say, fails to express a similar concern for the conditions that brought about the demonstrations. I am sure that none of you would want to rest content with the superficial kind of social analysis that deals merely with effects and does not grapple with underlying causes. It is unfortunate that demonstrations are taking place in Birmingham, but it is even more unfortunate that the city's white power structure left the Negro community with no alternative.

In any nonviolent campaign there are four basic steps: collection of the facts to determine whether injustices exist; negotiation; self-purification; and direct action. We have gone through all these steps in Birmingham. There can be no gainsaying the fact that racial injustice engulfs this community. Birmingham is probably the most thoroughly segregated city in the United States. Its ugly record of brutality is widely known. Negroes have experienced grossly unjust treatment in the courts. There have been more unsolved bombings of Negro homes and churches in Birmingham than in any other city in the nation. These are the hard, brutal facts of the case. On the basis of these conditions, Negro leaders sought to negotiate with the city fathers. But the latter consistently refused to engage in good-faith negotiation.

Then, last September, came the opportunity to talk with leaders of Birmingham's economic community. In the course of the negotiations, certain promises were made by the merchants—for example, to remove the stores' humiliating racial signs. On the basis of these promises, the Reverend Fred Shuttlesworth and the leaders of the Alabama Christian Movement for Human Rights agreed to a moratorium on all demonstrations. As the weeks and months went by, we realized that we were the victims of a broken promise. A few signs, briefly removed, returned; the others remained.

As in so many past experiences, our hopes had been blasted, and the shadow of deep disappointment settled upon us. We had no alternative except to prepare for direct action, whereby we would present our very bodies as a means of laying our case before the conscience of the local and the national community. Mindful of the difficulties involved, we decided to undertake a process of self-purification. We began a series of workshops on nonviolence, and we repeatedly asked ourselves: "Are you able to accept blows without retaliating?" "Are you able to endure the ordeal of jail?" We decided to schedule our direct-action program for the Easter season, realizing that except for Christmas, this is the main shopping period of the year. Knowing that a strong economic-withdrawal program would be the by-product of direct action, we felt that this would be the best time to bring pressure to bear on the merchants for the needed change.

Then it occurred to us that Birmingham's mayoralty election was coming up in March, and we speedily decided to postpone action until after election day. When we discovered that the Commissioner of Public Safety, Eugene "Bull" Connor, had piled up enough votes to be in the run-off, we decided again to postpone action until the day after the run-off so that the demonstrations could not be used to cloud the issues. Like many others, we waited to see Mr. Connor defeated, and to this end we endured postponement after postponement. Having aided in this community need, we felt that our direct-action program could be delayed no longer.

You may well ask: "Why direct action? Why sit-ins, marches, and so forth? Isn't negotiation a better path?" You are quite right in calling for negotiation. Indeed, this is the very purpose of direct action. Nonviolent direct action seeks to create such a crisis and foster such a tension that a community which has constantly refused to negotiate is forced to confront the issue. It seeks so to dramatize the issue that it can no longer be ignored. My citing the creation of tension as part of the work of the nonviolent resister may sound rather shocking. But I must confess that I am not afraid of the word "tension." I have earnestly opposed violent tension, but

10

there is a type of constructive, nonviolent tension which is necessary for growth. Just as Socrates felt that it was necessary to create a tension in the mind so that individuals could rise from the bondage of myths and half-truths to the unfettered realm of creative analysis and objective appraisal, so must we see the need for nonviolent gadflies to create the kind of tension in society that will help men rise from the dark depths of prejudice and racism to the majestic heights of understanding and brotherhood.

The purpose of our direct-action program is to create a situation so crisis-packed that it will inevitably open the door to negotiation. I therefore concur with you in your call for negotiation. Too long has our beloved Southland been bogged down in a tragic effort to live in monologue rather than dialogue.

One of the basic points in your statement is that the action that I and my associates have taken in Birmingham is untimely. Some have asked: "Why didn't you give the new city administration time to act?" The only answer that I can give to this query is that the new Birmingham administration must be prodded about as much as the outgoing one, before it will act. We are sadly mistaken if we feel that the election of Albert Boutwell as mayor will bring the millennium to Birmingham. While Mr. Boutwell is a much more gentle person than Mr. Connor, they are both segregationists, dedicated to maintenance of the status quo. I have hope that Mr. Boutwell will be reasonable enough to see the futility of massive resistance to desegregation. But he will not see this without pressure from devotees of civil rights. My friends, I must say to you that we have not made a single gain in civil rights without determined legal and nonviolent pressure. Lamentably, it is an historical fact that privileged groups seldom give up their privileges voluntarily. Individuals may see the moral light and voluntarily give up their unjust posture; but as Reinhold Niebuhr[2] has reminded us, groups tend to be more immoral than individuals.

We know through painful experience that freedom is never voluntarily given by the oppressor; it must be demanded by the oppressed. Frankly, I have yet to engage in a direct-action campaign that was "well timed" in the view of those who have not suffered unduly from the disease of segregation. For years now I have heard the word "Wait!" It rings in the ear of every Negro with piercing familiarity. This "Wait" has almost always meant "Never." We must come to see, with one of our distinguished jurists, that "justice too long delayed is justice denied."[3]

We have waited for more than 340 years for our constitutional and God-given rights. The nations of Asia and Africa are moving with jetlike

---

[2]**Reinhold Niebuhr** (1892–1971) Minister, political activist, author, and professor of applied Christianity at Union Theological Seminary. (This and the following notes are the editors'.)
[3]**Justice . . . denied** A quotation attributed to William E. Gladstone (1809–1898), British statesman and prime minister.

speed toward gaining political independence, but we still creep at horse-and-buggy pace toward gaining a cup of coffee at a lunch counter. Perhaps it is easy for those who have never felt the stinging darts of segregation to say, "Wait." But when you have seen vicious mobs lynch your mothers and fathers at will and drown your sisters and brothers at whim; when you have seen hate-filled policemen curse, kick, and even kill your black brothers and sisters; when you see the vast majority of your twenty million Negro brothers smothering in an airtight cage of poverty in the midst of an affluent society; when you suddenly find your tongue twisted and your speech stammering as you seek to explain to your six-year-old daughter why she can't go to the public amusement park that has just been advertised on television, and see tears welling up in her eyes when she is told that Funtown is closed to colored children, and see ominous clouds of inferiority beginning to form in her little mental sky, and see her beginning to distort her personality by developing an unconscious bitterness toward white people; when you have to concoct an answer for a five-year-old son who is asking: "Daddy, why do white people treat colored people so mean?"; when you take a cross-country drive and find it necessary to sleep night after night in the uncomfortable corners of your automobile because no motel will accept you; when you are humiliated day in and day out by nagging signs reading "white" and "colored"; when your first name becomes "nigger," your middle name becomes "boy" (however old you are) and your last name becomes "John," and your wife and mother are never given the respected title "Mrs."; when you are harried by day and haunted by night by the fact that you are a Negro, living constantly at tiptoe stance, never quite knowing what to expect next, and are plagued with inner fears and outer resentments; when you are forever fighting a degenerating sense of "nobodiness"—then you will understand why we find it difficult to wait. There comes a time when the cup of endurance runs over, and men are no longer willing to be plunged into the abyss of despair. I hope, sirs, you can understand our legitimate and unavoidable impatience.

You express a great deal of anxiety over our willingness to break laws. 15 This is certainly a legitimate concern. Since we so diligently urge people to obey the Supreme Court's decision of 1954 outlawing segregation in the public schools, at first glance it may seem rather paradoxical for us consciously to break laws. One may well ask: "How can you advocate breaking some laws and obeying others?" The answer lies in the fact that there are two types of laws: just and unjust. I would be the first to advocate obeying just laws. One has not only a legal but a moral responsibility to obey just laws. Conversely, one has a moral responsibility to disobey unjust laws. I would agree with St. Augustine that "an unjust law is no law at all."

Now, what is the difference between the two? How does one determine whether a law is just or unjust? A just law is a man-made code that squares with the moral law or the law of God. An unjust law is a code that is out of harmony with the moral law. To put it in the terms of St. Thomas Aquinas: An unjust law is a human law that is not rooted in eternal law and natural law. Any law that uplifts human personality is just. Any law that degrades human personality is unjust. All segregation statutes are unjust because segregation distorts the soul and damages the personality. It gives the segregator a false sense of superiority and the segregated a false sense of inferiority. Segregation, to use the terminology of the Jewish philosopher Martin Buber, substitutes an "I-it" relationship for an "I-thou" relationship and ends up relegating persons to the status of things. Hence segregation is not only politically, economically, and socio-logically unsound, it is morally wrong and sinful. Paul Tillich[4] has said that sin is separation. Is not segregation an existential expression of man's tragic separation, his awful estrangement, his terrible sinfulness? Thus it is that I can urge men to obey the 1954 decision of the Supreme Court, for it is morally right; and I can urge them to disobey segregation ordinances, for they are morally wrong.

Let us consider a more concrete example of just and unjust laws. An unjust law is a code that a numerical or power majority group compels a minority group to obey but does not make binding on itself. This is *difference* made legal. By the same token, a just law is a code that a major-ity compels a minority to follow and that it is willing to follow itself. This is *sameness* made legal.

Let me give another explanation. A law is unjust if it is inflicted on a minority that, as a result of being denied the right to vote, had no part in enacting or devising the law. Who can say that the legislature of Alabama which set up that state's segregation laws was democratically elected? Throughout Alabama all sorts of devious methods are used to prevent Negroes from becoming registered voters, and there are some counties in which, even though Negroes constitute a majority of the population, not a single Negro is registered. Can any law enacted under such circum-stances be considered democratically structured?

Sometimes a law is just on its face and unjust in its application. For instance, I have been arrested on a charge of parading without a permit. Now, there is nothing wrong in having an ordinance which requires a permit for a parade. But such an ordinance becomes unjust when it is used to maintain segregation and to deny citizens the First Amendment privilege of peaceful assembly and protest.

I hope you are able to see the distinction I am trying to point out. In no sense do I advocate evading or defying the law, as would the rabid segregationist. That would lead to anarchy. One who breaks an unjust law must do so openly, lovingly, and with a willingness to accept the penalty.

20

---

[4]**Paul Tillich** Tillich (1886–1965), born in Germany, taught theology at several German uni-versities, but in 1933 he was dismissed from his post at the University of Frankfurt because of his opposition to the Nazi regime. At the invitation of Reinhold Niebuhr, he came to the United States and taught at Union Theological Seminary.

I submit that an individual who breaks a law that conscience tells him is unjust, and who willingly accepts the penalty of imprisonment in order to arouse the conscience of the community over its injustice, is in reality expressing the highest respect for law.

Of course, there is nothing new about this kind of civil disobedience. It was evidenced sublimely in the refusal of Shadrach, Meshach, and Abednego to obey the laws of Nebuchadnezzar, on the ground that a higher moral law was at stake. It was practiced superbly by the early Christians, who were willing to face hungry lions and the excruciating pain of chopping blocks rather than submit to certain unjust laws of the Roman Empire. To a degree, academic freedom is a reality today because Socrates practiced civil disobedience. In our own nation, the Boston Tea Party represented a massive act of civil disobedience.

We should never forget that everything Adolf Hitler did in Germany was "legal" and everything the Hungarian freedom fighters did in Hungary was "illegal." It was "illegal" to aid and comfort a Jew in Hitler's Germany. Even so, I am sure that, had I lived in Germany at the time, I would have aided and comforted my Jewish brothers. If today I lived in a Communist country where certain principles dear to the Christian faith are suppressed, I would openly advocate disobeying that country's anti-religious laws.

I must make two honest confessions to you, my Christian and Jewish brothers. First, I must confess that over the past few years I have been gravely disappointed with the white moderate. I have almost reached the regrettable conclusion that the Negro's great stumbling block in his stride toward freedom is not the White Citizen's Counciler or the Ku Klux Klanner, but the white moderate, who is more devoted to "order" than to justice; who prefers a negative peace which is the absence of tension to a positive peace which is the presence of justice; who constantly says: "I agree with you in the goal you seek, but I cannot agree with your methods or direct action"; who paternalistically believes he can set the timetable for another man's freedom; who lives by a mythical concept of time and who constantly advises the Negro to wait for a "more convenient season." Shallow understanding from people of good will is more frustrating than absolute misunderstanding from people of ill will. Lukewarm acceptance is much more bewildering than outright rejection.

I had hoped that the white moderate would understand that law and order exist for the purpose of establishing justice and that when they fail in this purpose they become the dangerously structured dams that block the flow of social progress. I had hoped that the white moderate would understand that the present tension in the South is a necessary phase of the transition from an obnoxious negative peace, in which the Negro passively accepted his unjust plight, to a substantive and positive peace, in which all men will respect the dignity and worth of human personality. Actually, we who engage in nonviolent direct action are not the creators of tension. We merely bring to the surface the hidden tension that is already alive. We bring it out in the open, where it can be seen and dealt with. Like a boil that can never be cured so long as it is covered up but must be opened with all its ugliness to the natural medicines of air and light, injustice must be exposed, with all the tension its exposure creates, to the light of human conscience and the air of national opinion before it can be cured.

In your statement you assert that our actions, even though peaceful,   25
must be condemned because they precipitate violence. But is this a logical assertion? Isn't this like condemning a robbed man because his possession of money precipitated the evil act of robbery? Isn't this like condemning Socrates because his unswerving commitment to truth and his philosophical inquiries precipitated the act by the misguided populace in which they made him drink hemlock? Isn't this like condemning Jesus because his unique God-consciousness and never-ceasing devotion to God's will precipitated the evil act of crucifixion? We must come to see that, as the federal courts have consistently affirmed, it is wrong to urge an individual to cease his efforts to gain his basic constitutional rights because the quest may precipitate violence. Society must protect the robbed and punish the robber.

I had also hoped that the white moderate would reject the myth concerning time in relation to the struggle for freedom. I have just received a letter from a white brother in Texas. He writes: "All Christians know that the colored people will receive equal rights eventually, but it is possible that you are in too great a religious hurry. It has taken Christianity almost two thousand years to accomplish what it has. The teachings of Christ take time to come to earth." Such an attitude stems from a tragic misconception of time, from the strangely irrational notion that there is something in the very flow of time that will inevitably cure all ills. Actually, time itself is neutral; it can be used either destructively or constructively. More and more I feel that the people of ill will have used time much more effectively than have the people of good will. We will have to repent in this generation not merely for the hateful words and actions of the bad people but for the appalling silence of the good people. Human progress never rolls in on wheels of inevitability; it comes through the tireless efforts of men willing to be co-workers with God, and without this hard work, time itself becomes an ally of the forces of social stagnation. We must use time creatively, in the knowledge that the time is always ripe to do right. Now is the time to make real the promise of democracy and transform our pending national elegy into a creative psalm of brotherhood. Now is the time to lift our national policy from the quicksand of racial injustice to the solid rock of human dignity.

You speak of our activity in Birmingham as extreme. At first I was rather disappointed that fellow clergymen would see my nonviolent efforts as those of an extremist. I began thinking about the fact that I stand in the middle of two opposing forces in the Negro community. One is a force of complacency, made up in part of Negroes who, as a result of long years of oppression, are so drained of self-respect and a sense of "somebodiness" that they have adjusted to segregation; and in part of a few middle-class Negroes who, because of a degree of academic and economic security and because in some ways they profit by segregation, have become insensitive to the problems of the masses. The other force is one of bitterness and hatred, and it comes perilously close to advocating violence. It is expressed in the various black nationalist groups that are springing up across the nation, the largest and best-known being Elijah Muhammad's Muslim movement. Nourished by the Negro's frustration over the continued existence of racial discrimination, this movement is made up of people who have lost faith in America, who have absolutely repudiated Christianity, and who have concluded that the white man is an incorrigible "devil."

I have tried to stand between these two forces, saying that we need emulate neither the "do-nothingism" of the complacent nor the hatred and despair of the black nationalist. For there is the more excellent way of love and nonviolent protest. I am grateful to God that, through the influence of the Negro church, the way of nonviolence became an integral part of our struggle.

If this philosophy had not emerged, by now many streets of the South should, I am convinced, be flowing with blood. And I am further convinced that if our white brothers dismiss as "rabble-rousers" and "outside agitators" those of us who employ nonviolent direct action, and if they refuse to support our nonviolent efforts, millions of Negroes will, out of frustration and despair, seek solace and security in black-nationalist ideologies—a development that would inevitably lead to a frightening racial nightmare.

Oppressed people cannot remain oppressed forever. The yearning for   30
freedom eventually manifests itself, and that is what has happened to the American Negro. Something within has reminded him of his birthright of freedom, and something without has reminded him that it can be gained. Consciously or unconsciously, he has been caught up by the *Zeitgeist*,[5] and with his black brothers of Africa and his brown and yellow brothers of Asia, South America, and the Caribbean, the United States Negro is moving with a sense of great urgency toward the promised land of racial justice. If one recognizes this vital urge that has engulfed the Negro community, one should readily understand why public demonstrations are taking place. The Negro has many pent-up resentments and latent frustrations, and he must release them. So let him march; let him make prayer pilgrimages to the city hall; let him go on freedom rides—and try to understand why he must do so. If his repressed emotions are not released in nonviolent ways, they will seek expression through violence; this is not a threat but a fact of history. So I have not said to my people: "Get rid of your discontent." Rather, I have tried to say that this normal and healthy discontent can be channeled into the creative outlet of nonviolent direct action. And now this approach is being termed extremist.

[5]***Zeitgeist*** German for "spirit of the age"

But though I was initially disappointed at being categorized as an extremist, as I continued to think about the matter I gradually gained a measure of satisfaction from the label. Was not Jesus an extremist for love: "Love your enemies, bless them that curse you, do good to them that hate you, and pray for them which despitefully use you, and persecute you." Was not Amos an extremist for justice: "Let justice roll down like waters and righteousness like an ever-flowing stream." Was not Paul an extremist for the Christian gospel: "I bear in my body the marks of the Lord Jesus." Was not Martin Luther an extremist: "Here I stand; I cannot do otherwise, so help me God." And John Bunyan: "I will stay in jail to the end of my days before I make a butchery of my conscience." And Abraham Lincoln: "This nation cannot survive half slave and half free." And Thomas Jefferson: "We hold these truths to be self-evident, that all men are created equal. . . . " So the question is not whether we will be extremists, but what kind of extremists we will be. Will we be extremists for hate or for love? Will we be extremists for the preservation of injustice or for the extension of justice? In that dramatic scene on Calvary's hill three men were crucified. We must never forget that all three were crucified for the same crime—the crime of extremism. Two were extremists for immorality, and thus fell below their environment. The other, Jesus Christ, was an extremist for love, truth, and goodness, and thereby rose above his environment. Perhaps the South, the nation, and the world are in dire need of creative extremists.

I had hoped that the white moderate would see this need. Perhaps I was too optimistic; perhaps I expected too much. I suppose I should have realized that few members of the oppressor race can understand the deep groans and passionate yearnings of the oppressed race, and still fewer have the vision to see that injustice must be rooted out by strong, persistent, and determined action. I am thankful, however, that some of our white brothers in the South have grasped the meaning of this social revolution and committed themselves to it. They are still all too few in quantity, but they are big in quality. Some—such as Ralph McGill, Lillian Smith, Harry Golden, James McBride Dabbs, Ann Braden, and Sarah Patton Boyle—have written about our struggle in eloquent and prophetic terms. Others have marched with us down nameless streets of the South. They have languished in filthy, roach-infested jails, suffering the abuse and brutality of policemen who view them as "dirty nigger-lovers." Unlike so many of their moderate brothers and sisters, they have recognized the urgency of the moment and sensed the need for powerful "action" antidotes to combat the disease of segregation.

Let me take note of my other major disappointment. I have been so greatly disappointed with the white church and its leadership. Of course, there are some notable exceptions. I am not unmindful of the fact that each of you has taken some significant stands on this issue. I commend you, Reverend Stallings, for your Christian stand on this past Sunday, in welcoming Negroes to your worship service on a nonsegregated basis.

I commend the Catholic leaders of this state for integrating Spring Hill College several years ago.

But despite these notable exceptions, I must honestly reiterate that I have been disappointed with the church. I do not say this as one of those negative critics who can always find something wrong with the church. I say this as a minister of the gospel, who loves the church; who was nurtured in its bosom; who has been sustained by its spiritual blessings and who will remain true to it as long as the cord of life shall lengthen.

When I was suddenly catapulted into the leadership of the bus protest in Montgomery, Alabama, a few years ago, I felt we would be supported by the white church. I felt that the white ministers, priests, and rabbis of the South would be among our strongest allies. Instead, some have been outright opponents, refusing to understand the freedom movement and misrepresenting its leaders; all too many others have been more cautious than courageous and have remained silent behind the anesthetizing security of stained-glass windows.

35

In spite of my shattered dreams, I came to Birmingham with the hope that the white religious leadership of this community would see the justice of our cause and, with deep moral concern, would serve as the channel through which our just grievances could reach the power structure. I had hoped that each of you would understand. But again I have been disappointed.

I have heard numerous southern religious leaders admonish their worshipers to comply with a desegregation decision because it is the law, but I have longed to hear white ministers declare: "Follow this decree because integration is morally right and because the Negro is your brother." In the midst of blatant injustices inflicted upon the Negro, I have watched white churchmen stand on the sideline and mouth pious irrelevancies and sanctimonious trivialities. In the midst of a mighty struggle to rid our nation of racial and economic injustice, I have heard many ministers say: "Those are social issues, with which the gospel has no real concern." And I have watched many churches commit themselves to a completely otherworldly religion which makes a strange, unbiblical distinction between body and soul, between the sacred and the secular.

I have traveled the length and breadth of Alabama, Mississippi, and all the other southern states. On sweltering summer days and crisp autumn mornings I have looked at the South's beautiful churches with their lofty spires pointing heavenward. I have beheld the impressive outlines of her massive religious-education buildings. Over and over I have found myself saying: "What kind of people worship here? Who is their God? Where were their voices when the lips of Governor Barnett dripped with words of interposition and nullification? Where were they when Governor Wallace gave a clarion call for defiance and hatred? Where were their voices of support when bruised and weary Negro men and women decided to rise from the dark dungeons of complacency to the bright hills of creative protest?"

Yes, these questions are still in my mind. In deep disappointment I have wept over the laxity of the church. But be assured that my tears have been tears of love. There can be no deep disappointment where there is not deep love. Yes, I love the church. How could I do otherwise? I am in the rather unique position of being the son, the grandson, and the great-grandson of preachers. Yes, I see the church as the body of Christ. But, Oh! How we have blemished and scarred that body through social neglect and through fear of being nonconformists.

There was a time when the church was very powerful—in the time   40 when the early Christians rejoiced at being deemed worthy to suffer for what they believed. In those days the church was not merely a thermometer that recorded the ideas and principles of popular opinion; it was a thermostat that transformed the mores of society. Whenever the early Christians entered a town, the people in power became disturbed and immediately sought to convict the Christians for being "disturbers of the peace" and "outside agitators." But the Christians pressed on, in the conviction that they were "a colony of heaven," called to obey God rather than man. Small in number, they were big in commitment. They were too God-intoxicated to be "astronomically intimidated." By their effort and example they brought an end to such ancient evils as infanticide and gladiatorial contests.

Things are different now. So often the contemporary church is a weak, ineffectual voice with an uncertain sound. So often it is an archdefender of the status quo. Far from being disturbed by the presence of the church, the power structure of the average community is consoled by the church's silent—and often even vocal—sanction of things as they are.

But the judgment of God is upon the church as never before. If today's church does not recapture the sacrificial spirit of the early church, it will lose its authenticity, forfeit the loyalty of millions, and be dismissed as an irrelevant social club with no meaning for the twentieth century. Every day I meet young people whose disappointment with the church has turned into outright disgust.

Perhaps I have once again been too optimistic. Is organized religion too inextricably bound to the status quo to save our nation and the world? Perhaps I must turn my faith to the inner spiritual church, the church within the church, as the true *ekklesia* and the hope of the world. But again I am thankful to God that some noble souls from the ranks of organized religion have broken loose from the paralyzing chains of conformity and joined us as active partners in the struggle for freedom. They have left their secure congregations and walked the streets of Albany, Georgia, with us. They have gone down the highways of the South on tortuous rides for freedom. Yes, they have gone to jail with us. Some have been dismissed from their churches, have lost the support of their bishops and fellow ministers. But they have acted in the faith that right defeated is stronger than evil triumphant. Their witness has been the spiritual salt that has preserved the true meaning of the gospel in these troubled times. They have carved a tunnel of hope through the dark mountain of disappointment.

I hope the church as a whole will meet the challenge of this decisive hour. But even if the church does not come to the aid of justice, I have no despair about the future. I have no fear about the outcome of our struggle in Birmingham, even if our motives are at present misunderstood. We will reach the goal of freedom in Birmingham and all over the nation, because the goal of America is freedom. Abused and scorned though we may be, our destiny is tied up with America's destiny. Before the pilgrims landed at Plymouth, we were here. Before the pen of Jefferson etched the majestic words of the Declaration of Independence across the pages of history, we were here. For more than two centuries our forebears labored in this country without wages; they made cotton king; they built the homes of their masters while suffering gross injustice and shameful humiliation—and yet out of a bottomless vitality they continue to thrive and develop. If the inexpressible cruelties of slavery could not stop us, the opposition we now face will surely fail. We will win our freedom because the sacred heritage of our nation and the eternal will of God are embodied in our echoing demands.

Before closing I feel impelled to mention one other point in your state- 45
ment that has troubled me profoundly. You warmly commended the Birmingham police force for keeping "order" and "preventing violence." I doubt that you would have so warmly commended the police force if you had seen its dogs sinking their teeth into unarmed, nonviolent Negroes. I doubt that you would so quickly commend the policemen if you were to observe their ugly and inhumane treatment of Negroes here in the city jail; if you were to watch them push and curse old Negro women and young Negro girls; if you were to see them slap and kick old Negro men and young boys; if you were to observe them, as they did on two occasions, refuse to give us food because we wanted to sing our grace together. I cannot join you in your praise of the Birmingham police department.

It is true that the police have exercised a degree of discipline in handling the demonstrators. In this sense they have conducted themselves rather "nonviolently" in public. But for what purpose? To preserve the evil system of segregation. Over the past few years I have consistently preached that nonviolence demands that the means we use must be as pure as the ends we seek. I have tried to make clear that it is wrong to use immoral means to attain moral ends. But now I must affirm that it is just as wrong, or perhaps even more so, to use moral means to preserve immoral ends. Perhaps Mr. Connor and his policemen have been rather nonviolent in public, as was Chief Pritchett in Albany, Georgia, but they have used the moral means of nonviolence to maintain the immoral end of racial injustice. As T. S. Eliot has said: "The last temptation is the greatest treason: To do the right deed for the wrong reason."

I wish you had commended the Negro sit-inners and demonstrators of Birmingham for their sublime courage, their willingness to suffer, and their amazing discipline in the midst of great provocation. One day the South will recognize its real heroes. They will be the James Merediths, with the noble sense of purpose that enables them to face jeering and hostile mobs, and with the agonizing loneliness that characterizes the life of the pioneer. They will be old, oppressed, battered Negro women, symbolized in a seventy-two-year-old woman in Montgomery, Alabama, who rose up with a sense of dignity and with her people decided not to ride segregated buses, and who responded with ungrammatical profundity to one who inquired about her weariness: "My feets is tired, but my soul is at rest." They will be the young high school and college students, the young ministers of the gospel and a host of their elders, courageously and nonviolently sitting in at lunch counters and willingly going to jail for conscience's sake. One day the South will know that when these disinherited children of God sat down at lunch counters, they were in reality standing up for what is best in the American dream and for the most sacred values in our Judaeo-Christian heritage, thereby bringing our nation back to those great wells of democracy which were dug deep by the founding fathers in their formulation of the Constitution and the Declaration of Independence.

Never before have I written so long a letter. I'm afraid it is much too long to take your precious time. I can assure you that it would have been much shorter if I had been writing from a comfortable desk, but what else can one do when he is alone in a narrow jail cell, other than write long letters, think long thoughts, and pray long prayers?

If I have said anything in this letter that overstates the truth and indicates an unreasonable impatience, I beg you to forgive me. If I have said anything that understates the truth and indicates my having a patience that allows me to settle for anything less than brotherhood, I beg God to forgive me.

I hope this letter finds you strong in the faith. I also hope that circumstances will soon make it possible for me to meet each of you, not as an integrationist or a civil-rights leader but as a fellow clergyman and a Christian brother. Let us all hope that the dark clouds of racial prejudice will soon pass away and the deep fog of misunderstanding will be lifted from our fear-drenched communities, and in some not too distant tomorrow the radiant stars of love and brotherhood will shine over our great nation with all their scintillating beauty.

50

Yours for the cause of Peace and Brotherhood,
Martin Luther King Jr.

 ## Joining the Conversation:
Critical Thinking and Writing

1. In his first five paragraphs how does King assure his audience that he is not a meddlesome intruder but a man of goodwill?

2. In paragraph 3 King refers to Hebrew prophets and to the Apostle Paul, and later (paragraph 10) to Socrates. What is the point of these references?

3. In paragraph 11 what does King mean when he says that "our beloved Southland" has long tried to "live in monologue rather than dialogue"?

4. King begins paragraph 23 with "I must make two honest confessions to you, my Christian and Jewish brothers." What would have been gained or lost if he had used this paragraph as his opening?

5. King's last three paragraphs do not advance his argument. What do they do?

6. Why does King advocate breaking unjust laws "openly, lovingly" (paragraph 20)? What does he mean by these words? What other motives or attitudes do these words rule out?

7. Construct two definitions of *civil disobedience*, and explain whether and to what extent it is easier (or harder) to justify civil disobedience, depending on how you have defined the expression.

8. If you feel that you wish to respond to King's letter on some point, write a letter nominally addressed to King. You may, if you wish, adopt the persona of one of the eight clergymen whom King initially addressed.

9. King writes (paragraph 46) that "nonviolence demands that the means we use must be as pure as the ends we seek." How do you think King would evaluate the following acts of civil disobedience:

   (a) occupying a college administration building in order to protest the administration's unsatisfactory response to a racial incident on campus, or in order to protest the failure of the administration to hire minority persons as staff and faculty;

   (b) sailing on a collision course with a whaling ship to protest against whaling;

   (c) trespassing on an abortion clinic to protest abortion?

   Set down your answer in an essay of 500 words.

Cathy Booth Thomas

Cathy Booth Thomas, drawing on reporting by Hilary Hylton of Austin, wrote this article for Time *magazine, June 11, 2001.*

A New Scarlet Letter

Gabriel Trevino did a bad, bad thing. Three years ago, at age 31, he fondled the 14-year-old daughter of a friend. For this "slipup," as he calls it, he pleaded no contest and took five years' probation rather than risk a two-to-20-year prison term. Now he thinks prison would have been preferable. These days, people drive by his modest bungalow house, then back up to read the 18-in. by 24-in. sign posted by the little white birdhouse, DANGER, it says. REGISTERED SEX OFFENDER LIVES HERE.

Sitting by the front window in his darkened living room in Corpus Christi, Texas, last week, Trevino was at once defiant and near tears as he talked about this public mortification. "I made my mistake, and I'm paying for it," he said. But, he wondered, why should his wife and two stepdaughters pay too? "I can't even go out and cut my yard. I just stay in the house . . . I was doing good in therapy. How is this helping me?"

The answer is simple, says state District Judge J. Manuel Bañales, who on May 18 ordered Trevino and 13 other "high-risk" sex offenders on probation to post the signs in their yards. "It will keep people like you, sir, honest," he told Trevino last week after denying a request to rescind the order. "Your neighbors will watch you and make sure you're not taking another child into your home." Hours later, Bañales ordered yet another sex offender—No. 15—to put up a sign on release from jail.

In the past decade, all 50 states have passed so-called Megan's laws, requiring sex offenders to alert the community to their presence. Twenty-eight states run Internet sites listing such criminals. In the mid-1990s, judges in Texas, Louisiana, Florida and Oregon began ordering individual sex offenders to post signs outside their homes. But Bañales—who also mandated bumper stickers and even temporary placards for traveling in someone else's car—drew national attention by applying his ruling to so many at one time. His move sparked a debate on the rights of these offenders and the merits of public shaming. "We don't brand people in America," argues Gerald Rogen, president of the Coastal Bend Criminal Defense Lawyers Association. "And we damn sure don't punish the offender's family as well as the offender."

Bañales' judgment, however, was in keeping with a 1999 Texas law—signed by then Governor George W. Bush—permitting judges to impose public punishment for some crimes. Drunk drivers in the state, for instance, are sometimes made to stand at busy intersections with signs identifying their transgression. Whether more conventional public notifications have worked as a deterrent is unclear. A Washington State study found that such policies didn't keep sex offenders from committing more crimes, though they did help police find and arrest recidivists more quickly.

Bañales' extreme version of notification is having immediate consequences for the Corpus Christi 15, as landlords evict them and bosses fire them. One man attempted suicide after Bañales' ruling. The families also worry about vigilantes. "I'm scared for my mother's life and myself," says Trevino's stepdaughter Ann, 20. Lawyers for the 15 are considering filing a joint challenge or separate ones in the 13th Court of Appeals, arguing that the signs violate the right to privacy and constitute "cruel and unusual punishment."

Judge Bañales is unmoved. From a list of nearly 300 adult sex offenders, he chose 14 of the 15 by working with probation officers and a polygrapher to pinpoint those who had multiple victims, were not showing progress in therapy or had failed to show empathy for their victims. Even in court last week, for instance, Trevino persisted in questioning the judge on why a 14-year-old could be tried for murder, but could not consent to sex.

Though Bañales, a Democrat, has been accused of issuing his order to win popularity at the polls next year—his is an elected judgeship—his cheering section includes probation officers who already see a sobering effect on new probationers. "It's definitely a deterrent now," says Iris Davila, probation supervisor in the Nueces County Community Supervision and Correction Department. "Other offenders are saying to us, 'We'll do whatever it takes not to have signs.'"

Joining the Conversation: Critical Thinking and Writing

1. To what does the title of the article refer? How appropriate or relevant do you find the reference?

2. Describe the tone of the first sentence. Would you have advised Thomas to revise the sentence, or keep it? Explain.

3. How did Judge Bañales choose the sex offenders who were then ordered to put signs in their yards?

4. If you lived in Judge Bañales's district would you be part of what the last paragraph calls his "cheering section"? Explain.

5. In paragraph 7, Thomas reports, as a sign that Gabriel Trevino has failed to show empathy for his victim, that "Trevino persisted in questioning the judge on why a 14-year-old could be tried for murder, but could not consent to sex." Do you think it was improper of Trevino to ask this question? If the question were asked of you, what would your answer be?

6. Several legislators in California have proposed that people who have drunk-driving records be required to use license plates that say "DUI" [driving under the influence]. Your view? In your answer, consider at least the following issues:

   (a) Should offenders be put to shame?

   (b) If so, what is the purpose of shaming them? To make them suffer? To rehabilitate them? To safeguard others? To deter others from criminal activity?

7. A sheriff in Arizona, believing that offenders should be subjected to humiliation, requires prisoners to wear striped uniforms and to serve in chain-gangs trimming grass along highways. Your view?

Chesa Boudin

Chesa Boudin—his first name is Swahili for "dancing feet"—is the son of Kathy Boudin and David Gilbert, both of whom were members of a violent group in the 1960s called the Weather Underground. In 1981, when Boudin was fourteen months old, his parents were convicted and imprisoned for their part in the robbery of a Brink's armored truck in which a guard and two police officers were shot to death. As a child, Boudin was afflicted with epilepsy and dyslexia, and he was given to tantrums. In adolescence, however, he managed to overcome these difficulties, was admitted to Yale University, and in his senior year was awarded a Rhodes scholarship. In 2003, after twenty-five years in prison, his mother was paroled, but his father in effect is not eligible for parole. Boudin has become a spokesman for children whose parents are imprisoned.

Making Time Count

Both of my biological parents have been confined in New York State maximum security prisons since I was 14 months old. My father is serving 75 years to life, and my mother was recently paroled from her sentence of 20 years to life. My parents were in jail for the roles they played in the 1981 Brinks Robbery in Nyack, New York, that left three men dead. Their participation in the crime was limited. They drove a getaway car that waited a mile from the tragically bungled robbery. The people who carried out the robbery, members of the Black Liberation Army, killed a security guard named Peter Paige, fled to where my parents were waiting and got into my parents' van. When the van was pulled over by the police, the people from the robbery shot and killed police officers Waverly Brown and Edward O'Grady. Although neither of my parents was armed nor hurt anyone, they helped cause a horrendous loss to the families of the murdered men, and to an entire community.

The crime was reported on the front page of *The New York Times* and has received continuous media attention to this day. This is presumably a result of my parents' active membership in the radical anti-Vietnam War group known as the Weather Underground. In many ways, this crime was born out of the radical anti-war, anti-imperialist struggles of the 1960s and 1970s. Of course, this chapter went terribly wrong.

When my parents were arrested, I was still breastfeeding. After their arrest I went to live with friends of theirs, who already had two sons, and became part of this new family. Despite staying in close contact with my biological parents through visits, letters and phone calls, I endured the trauma of having had them taken away. In the aftermath of the sentencing, I was so angry that I did not speak for months. I suffered from learning disabilities and developed a violent temper, developmental problems not uncommon for children whose parents are behind bars.

Chesa Boudin is a graduate of Yale University and a Rhodes Scholar. He is a writer and an activist. Used by permission.

One of the early problems I faced was the basic dilemma of language. How would I think of and address my two sets of parents? As a child, I just did what felt natural. I called my adoptive mom "Mom" and my mom in jail "Kathy." Luckily my new brothers and I called our shared father by his first name, since he worked at our daycare center where all the children just called him Bill. But even today, these issues are still complicated for me. I want to acknowledge my adoptive parents and their role in my life, but I don't want to distance myself from my biological parents or erase what we share. This made even the simple phone greeting difficult. Yet phone calls were one of the primary ways I maintained contact with my incarcerated parents. New York state prisoners are not allowed to receive phone calls but can make collect calls to a limited list of pre-approved numbers. Although my parents' access to phones varied, they were usually able to call a couple of times a week. Initially, they asked typical questions—"How was your day?", "What did you learn in school today?"—but these questions never generated much of a conversation. I found it boring to just report to them about past activities; what I wanted was to be doing something with them, right then. So I asked them to tell me adventure stories. Though they came in short segments (phone calls were limited to only 20 minutes), the stories gave me something to look forward to and became my way to maintain a relationship with my parents.

These calls were not always easy. Once, when I was four years old, I burst into tears after getting off the phone with my biological mother. My adoptive parents asked what was wrong, and through my tears I cried, "If only I could've talked. If only I could've talked, I would have told them not to go." I felt that at 14 months it was my job to tell my parents not to participate in a crime—and that, more generally, I should have done something differently. I never knew exactly when they would be able to call, and even when we tried to plan a call time in advance, unpredictable events in the prison could force them to miss calls. On those days, I was left at the phone, sad and confused. And the worst part of our phone relationship was that I could never call them. At times when I was feeling down and wanted nothing more than to talk to my biological parents, I had to hope they would be able to make it to a phone that day.

Still, despite the limitations of prison life, my parents were both determined to have a relationship with me and came up with creative ways to show their love. One of the simplest things they did was write letters, lots of letters. As a child, I received a letter from one or both of my parents almost every day. A letter from my dad might have been as simple as a picture of a butterfly torn out of a *National Geographic* and pasted onto brightly colored construction paper with a note on the other side saying, "I love you." As I got older, the letters began to include more sophisticated descriptions of their lives in prison, current events and, of course, the necessary logistical planning needed to stay in touch and

5

arrange visits. I always looked forward to receiving those letters, stamped in block letters with the name of my parents' prisons. Every summer I received far more mail than any of my bunkmates at sleep-away camp.

My parents also used letters to help me in school. Entering the third grade, I had already fallen far behind my classmates in basic reading and writing skills. Because my biological parents could not teach me to read in person, they decided to have a letter-writing contest. Each of us had to write a certain number of letters a week, and if over six months I wrote enough letters, I would win the contest. Needless to say, I won. That year I went on to read more books than anyone in my class, winning our class "bookworm" competition.

My mom's prison also had a program called "story corner" that helped the inmates record cassette tapes for their children. Kathy would send tapes of her singing songs, reading adventure books and telling the story of my birth. Whenever I really needed to hear her voice—and couldn't reach for the phone—I could pop one of those tapes into the cassette player and listen as she told me how much she loved me.

While letters, phone calls and such were important in developing and maintaining our relationship from prison, by far the most significant time I have spent interacting with my incarcerated parents is in the visiting room. As a child, I depended on family and friends to make these visits possible. My mom's prison was located just one hour outside of New York City, but my father was moved to several different prisons throughout upstate New York. (This is one reason I was able to see my mom more than twice as often as my dad.) Because their prisons were always several hundred miles apart, I always made separate trips to visit each of them. The last time my parents saw each other was in 1983.

Usually, I would arrange to skip a day of school in Chicago and fly east to visit one of my parents for several days in a row. Visiting hours are from 9 A.M. to 3:30 P.M., so a three-day trip would allow us, at most, 20 hours together. I visited often enough that my parents rarely looked different from one visit to the next, but I probably did. When I was in the midst of my growth spurt, my mom and I came up with a way to track it. Her prison allowed us to pay for Polaroid pictures on visits. So for several years, on each visit we took a picture of us standing back to back. Once I was finally a full head taller than she is, Kathy put all of the pictures together in a long frame and gave it to me as a present.

That is the happy side. And I looked forward to our visits. But they were stressful. First, there's the visiting room itself. Although the visiting room is the place where children can directly interact with their incarcerated parents, some prisons do not even allow contact visits. Those that do frequently do not have a child-friendly learning environment. The difference between my mom's and my dad's prisons illustrates both the dismal norm and what is possible in its place.

Great Meadows Correctional Facility, where my dad spent the better part of a decade during my childhood, is a prison without a family-friendly visiting room. The room has cold, gray cinder block walls and long, wide tables that run the length of the room. The tables separate inmates from visitors, making contact virtually impossible. After stretching across the table for a hug at the beginning of the visit, I had to spend the remaining time in a plastic chair across from my father. As a child of nine years old, I could not possibly sit still and have a conversation for hours on end. I wanted to play games, sit on my dad's lap and listen to him read to me. There were never any toys, games or activities. Nor was I permitted to bring any with me. There was nothing for kids to do.

On the other hand, Bedford Hills Correctional Facility, where my mom was incarcerated for the entirety of her sentence, is one of the best prisons in the country—and the visiting room shows it. It includes a carpeted and cheerfully painted "children's center," with games, toys, blocks, paper and pens, pillows, books—the basics of what's needed for normal mother-child interaction. There is also an outdoor patio connected to the visiting room. One winter day, the patio became available and my mother and I were able to spend time in the snow for the first time. We built a snowman. The snow was the perfect consistency, and we used toys from the children's center for eyes, ears, a mouth and a nose. We were both so excited to be outside together that we hardly noticed the cold snow on our bare hands, or the chill of the winter air.

My mom helped her prison develop a "Teen Time" program to supplement the nursery and parenting classes. This program brings together a group of teenagers whose mothers are incarcerated in Bedford Hills and provides them with activities, trips, a peer support network and college counseling. Meanwhile, the mothers of these teenagers also work together as a group to become better parents and to meet the particular challenges of raising adolescents.

Unfortunately, when it comes to visiting rooms and the treatment   15
of mothers, Bedford Hills is unique. Nearly ten percent of women entering prison are pregnant, but Bedford Hills is one of only a handful of women's prisons in the country that has a nursery. The nursery allows these young mothers to spend the first 12 months with their children. They can breast-feed and use that time to build a mother-child bond. (In prisons without a nursery, new mothers have to say goodbye to their newborn almost immediately after giving birth—in handcuffs.) Bedford Hills also has a range of parenting classes to teach prisoners everything from basic parenting skills to child custody law. These programs are almost never available for men, though for most children with parents in prison it is the father who is incarcerated. These men need to gain access to parenting classes so that they can learn to take better responsibility for their families both from prison and once they get out. Parenting classes have the potential to help an entire

generation of children growing up without their parents, and to reduce recidivism rates by helping prisoners make a smooth transition into family life once they are released.

Although nothing like "Teen Time" is available in my father's prison, he does have access to the Family Reunion program, or trailer visits. A couple of times a year, trailer visits give us a chance to spend about 48 hours together in a small two-bedroom home within the prison. I bring all the food and we are allowed to cook our own meals, go outside and play, read books, have pillow fights and so on. For those 48 hours it almost feels normal. Almost.

The one kitchen knife is chained to the sink. The 50-foot cement wall and miles of barbed wire surrounding us are never out of sight. The heavily armed guards in watch-towers with flood lights interrupt us every few hours to make sure my dad is still there—apparently, that dull kitchen knife, if we ever got it unchained, might cut right through that steel-reinforced cement wall. Still, if it were not for the trailer visits, I cannot imagine that I would have much of a relationship with my dad at all. He will not be eligible for parole until 2056, when he will be 112 years old.

Unfortunately, only a handful of states give their prisoners access to trailer visits. Even then, only long-term inmates are allowed to have them, and there is always a waiting list for the next available visiting date. Trailer visits, and the invaluable family bonding time they provide, offer an incentive for good behavior and dramatically lower recidivism rates. It is a shame they are not more widely available.

No matter what type of visit, whether with Kathy or my father David, the goodbye is the most painful part. This is especially true after a visit in the Great Meadows visiting room. Being forced to say goodbye, to turn your back on a loved one, is never easy. The click of each steel gate resonates in my ear and deep within my gut. Sometimes it seems that all that separates us is the translucent ink stamped on my hand on the way in. But as I clear the final steel gate and walk through the 50-foot cement wall—while my dad undergoes the standard, post-visit strip search—I cannot help but remember that there is a whole world separating us.

One thing my parents did that helped me forgive them and grapple with my own problems was simply be honest. Too many families lie to kids about where their parents are. I have seen parents in prison tell their kids they are not in jail but in a high security hospital or dog training school and all sorts of other fantastic lies. Rather than sheltering kids, this betrayal of trust teaches children to feel that there is something to be ashamed of. The dynamic that developed with my parents helped me to never feel ashamed. All the way through school, my entire class always knew about my parents. By telling people that my parents are in prison (instead of hiding it), I am able to educate those around me about the prison system in general, and how to talk to me about it in a sensitive

20

way. As a result, I have largely been spared the social stigma that so many kids with parents in prison face.

This honesty was just one of the advantages I have had compared to most kids growing up with parents in prison. I was always part of a stable family and had a large, extended support network. In spite of the considerable cost and effort it takes to make each visit possible, I have always been able to visit my parents as often as I have wanted. When my adoptive family moved from New York to Chicago, I was only six years old. For each visit to a New York prison, someone had to pay for the plane ticket, take me to the airport, pick me up from the airport, give me a place to stay in New York, take me to the prison, pick me up from the prison and so on. It quite literally took a village of loving, dedicated family and friends.

My biological parents' devotion has also been extraordinary. As much as I appreciate their letters, for example, I haven't written back since I won that writing contest in the third grade. It isn't that I don't care or that I am trying to be mean; I just don't like writing letters. Still, even without ever getting responses to their letters, my parents have never stopped writing them.

Most children are not so lucky. I met a childhood friend named Tony in the prison visiting room while we were both visiting our incarcerated mothers. Tony was born in Guyana and came to the United States with his parents when he was four. By the time he turned nine, his parents were both sentenced to long prison terms under New York state's Rockefeller drug laws—his mother in the same prison as Kathy; his father in the same prison as David. He grew up with his strict grandmother and often felt as though he did not have any parents.

After years of friendship, we fell out of touch. It was not until heading off for my freshman year at Yale University that I caught up with Tony: he was incarcerated in Great Meadows Correctional Facility, with my dad. After serving his five-year sentence, Tony was immediately transferred to INS custody (his grandmother never thought to have him naturalized). Tony spent 18 months in overcrowded INS jails and was deported to Guyana—where he has not been since he was four—the week before my mom was granted parole. His life might have turned out differently if his mother and father, nonviolent offenders, had been able to help raise him themselves.

Joining the Conversation: Critical Thinking and Writing

1. Boudin says that after his parents were sentenced, he "developed a violent temper." Do you perceive any anger in the tone of his essay? How would you characterize his tone?

2. What was the importance of the letters that Boudin and his biological parents exchanged? Did it surprise you to learn that Boudin stopped writing back?

3. Do you write and receive letters yourself? Does a letter feel special to you? More so than an e-mail? Why is that?

4. Why does Boudin conclude with the story about his friend Tony? If he had asked you to comment on a draft of his essay, would you have advised him to keep this story as is, revise it, or cut it altogether? Please explain.

5. Do you know anyone who is, or has been, in prison? Have you ever been inside a prison; if so, what was the experience like for you? Do you agree with a statement made recently by a leading educator: "Every teenager in America should spend a night in jail?" Why would he say that? Does this idea sound like a good one to you?

Derek Bok

Derek Bok was born in 1930 in Bryn Mawr, Pennsylvania, and was educated at Stanford University and Harvard University, where he received a law degree. He taught law at Harvard, served as dean of the law school, and held the office of president of Harvard from 1971 to 1991. The essay here was published in a Boston newspaper, prompted by the display of Confederate flags hung from the window of a dormitory room.

Protecting Freedom of Expression on the Campus

For several years, universities have been struggling with the problem of trying to reconcile the rights of free speech with the desire to avoid racial tension. In recent weeks, such a controversy has sprung up at Harvard. Two students hung Confederate flags in public view, upsetting students who equate the Confederacy with slavery. A third student tried to protest the flags by displaying a swastika.

These incidents have provoked much discussion and disagreement. Some students have urged that Harvard require the removal of symbols that offend many members of the community. Others reply that such symbols are a form of free speech and should be protected.

Different universities have resolved similar conflicts in different ways. Some have enacted codes to protect their communities from forms of speech that are deemed to be insensitive to the feelings of other groups. Some have refused to impose such restrictions.

Derek Bok, "Protecting Freedom of Expression on the Campus" from the *Boston Globe*, March 25, 1991. Reprinted by permission of the author.

It is important to distinguish between the appropriateness of such communications and their status under the First Amendment. The fact that speech is protected by the First Amendment does not necessarily mean that it is right, proper, or civil. I am sure that the vast majority of Harvard students believe that hanging a Confederate flag in public view—or displaying a swastika in response—is insensitive and unwise because any satisfaction it gives to the students who display these symbols is far outweighed by the discomfort it causes to many others.

I share this view and regret that the students involved saw fit to 5 behave in this fashion. Whether or not they merely wished to manifest their pride in the South—or to demonstrate the insensitivity of hanging Confederate flags by mounting another offensive symbol in return—they must have known that they would upset many fellow students and ignore the decent regard for the feelings of others so essential to building and preserving a strong and harmonious community.

To disapprove of a particular form of communication, however, is not enough to justify prohibiting it. We are faced with a clear example of the conflict between our commitment to free speech and our desire to foster a community founded on mutual respect. Our society has wrestled with this problem for many years. Interpreting the First Amendment, the Supreme Court has clearly struck the balance in favor of free speech.

While communities do have the right to regulate speech in order to uphold aesthetic standards (avoiding defacement of buildings) or to protect the public from disturbing noise, rules of this kind must be applied across the board and cannot be enforced selectively to prohibit certain kinds of messages but not others.

Under the Supreme Court's rulings, as I read them, the display of swastikas or Confederate flags clearly falls within the protection of the free-speech clause of the First Amendment and cannot be forbidden simply because it offends the feelings of many members of the community. These rulings apply to all agencies of government, including public universities.

Although it is unclear to what extent the First Amendment is enforceable against private institutions, I have difficulty understanding why a university such as Harvard should have less free speech than the surrounding society—or than a public university.

One reason why the power of censorship is so dangerous is that it is 10 extremely difficult to decide when a particular communication is offensive enough to warrant prohibition or to weigh the degree of offensiveness against the potential value of the communication. If we begin to forbid flags, it is only a short step to prohibiting offensive speakers.

I suspect that no community will become humane and caring by restricting what its members can say. The worst offenders will simply find other ways to irritate and insult.

In addition, once we start to declare certain things "offensive," with all the excitement and attention that will follow, I fear that much ingenuity will be exerted trying to test the limits, much time will be expended trying to draw tenuous distinctions, and the resulting publicity will eventually attract more attention to the offensive material than would ever have occurred otherwise.

Rather than prohibit such communications, with all the resulting risks, it would be better to ignore them, since students would then have little reason to create such displays and would soon abandon them. If this response is not possible—and one can understand why—the wisest course is to speak with those who perform insensitive acts and try to help them understand the effects of their actions on others.

Appropriate officials and faculty members should take the lead, as the Harvard House Masters have already done in this case. In talking with students, they should seek to educate and persuade, rather than resort to ridicule or intimidation, recognizing that only persuasion is likely to produce a lasting, beneficial effect. Through such effects, I believe that we act in the manner most consistent with our ideals as an educational institution and most calculated to help us create a truly understanding, supportive community.

 ## Joining the Conversation: Critical Thinking and Writing

1. In paragraph 8 Bok argues that "the display of swastikas or Confederate flags clearly falls within the protection of the free-speech clause of the First Amendment and cannot be forbidden simply because it offends the feelings of many members of the community." Suppose someone replied thus: "The display of swastikas or of Confederate flags—symbols loaded with meaning—is, to a Jew or an African-American, at least equivalent to a slap in the face. Such a display is, in short, an act of violence." What would you reply, and how would you support your response?

2. Do you find Bok persuasive? Support your answer with evidence about the points of his argument and his techniques of argument.

3. What rules, if any, does your school have concerning limitations of speech? What rules, if any, would you propose?

George Orwell

George Orwell (1903–1950), an Englishman, adopted this name; he was born Eric Blair, in India. He was educated at Eton, in England, but in 1921 he went to Burma (now Myanmar), where he served for five years as a police officer. He then returned to Europe, doing odd jobs while writing novels and stories. In 1936 he fought in the Spanish Civil War on the side of the Republicans, an experience reported in Homage to Catalonia *(1938). His last years were spent writing in England.*

Shooting an Elephant

In Moulmein, in Lower Burma, I was hated by large numbers of people—the only time in my life that I have been important enough for this to happen to me. I was sub-divisional police officer of the town, and in an aimless, petty kind of way anti-European feeling was very bitter. No one had the guts to raise a riot, but if a European woman went through the bazaars alone somebody would probably spit betel juice over her dress. As a police officer I was an obvious target and was baited whenever it seemed safe to do so. When a nimble Burman tripped me up on the football field and the referee (another Burman) looked the other way, the crowd yelled with hideous laughter. This happened more than once. In the end the sneering yellow faces of young men that met me everywhere, the insults hooted after me when I was at a safe distance, got badly on my nerves. The young Buddhist priests were the worst of all. There were several thousands of them in the town and none of them seemed to have anything to do except stand on street corners and jeer at Europeans.

All this was perplexing and upsetting. For at that time I had already made up my mind that imperialism was an evil thing and the sooner I chucked up my job and got out of it the better. Theoretically—and secretly, of course—I was all for the Burmese and all against their oppressors, the British. As for the job I was doing, I hated it more bitterly than I can perhaps make clear. In a job like that you see the dirty work of the Empire at close quarters. The wretched prisoners huddling in the stinking cages of the lockups, the grey, cowed faces of the long-term convicts, the scarred buttocks of the men who had been flogged with bamboos—all these oppressed me with an intolerable sense of guilt. But I could get nothing into perspective. I was young and ill-educated and I had had to think out my problems in the utter silence that is imposed on every Englishman in the East. I did not even know that the British Empire is dying, still less did I know that it is a great deal better than the younger empires that are going to supplant it. All I knew was that I was stuck between my hatred of the empire I served and my rage against the evil-spirited little beasts who tried to make my job impossible. With one part of my mind I thought of the British Raj as an unbreakable tyranny, as something clamped down, in *saecula saeculorum*,[1] upon the will of prostrate

---

[1]*Saecula saeculorum* Latin, "For world without end." In the next paragraph *in terrorem* is Latin for "as a warning." (Editors' note)

---

peoples; with another part I thought that the greatest joy in the world would be to drive a bayonet into a Buddhist priest's guts. Feelings like these are the normal by-products of imperialism; ask any Anglo-Indian official, if you can catch him off duty.

One day something happened which in a roundabout way was enlightening. It was a tiny incident in itself, but it gave me a better glimpse than I had had before of the real nature of imperialism—the real motives for which despotic governments act. Early one morning the sub-inspector at a police station at the other end of the town rang me up on the 'phone and said that an elephant was ravaging the bazaar. Would I please come and do something about it? I did not know what I could do, but I wanted to see what was happening and I got onto a pony and started out. I took my rifle, an old .44 Winchester and much too small to kill an elephant, but I thought the noise might be useful *in terrorem*. Various Burmans stopped me on the way and told me about the elephant's doings. It was not, of course, a wild elephant, but a tame one which had gone "must." It had been chained up, as tame elephants always are when their attack of "must" is due, but on the previous night it had broken its chain and escaped. Its mahout, the only person who could manage it when it was in that state, had set out in pursuit, but had taken the wrong direction and was now twelve hours' journey away, and in the morning the elephant had suddenly reappeared in the town. The Burmese population had no weapons and were quite helpless against it. It had already destroyed somebody's bamboo hut, killed a cow and raided some fruit-stalls and devoured the stock; also it had met the municipal rubbish van and, when the driver jumped out and took to his heels, had turned the van over and inflicted violences upon it.

The Burmese sub-inspector and some Indian constables were waiting for me in the quarter where the elephant had been seen. It was a very poor quarter, a labyrinth of squalid bamboo huts, thatched with palmleaf, winding all over a steep hillside. I remember that it was a cloudy, stuffy morning at the beginning of the rains. We began questioning the people as to where the elephant had gone and, as usual, failed to get any definite information. That is invariably the case in the East; a story always sounds clear enough at a distance, but the nearer you get to the scene of events the vaguer it becomes. Some of the people said that the elephant had gone in one direction, some said that he had gone in another, some professed not even to have heard of any elephant. I had almost made up my mind that the whole story was a pack of lies, when we heard yells a little distance away. There was a loud, scandalized cry of "Go away, child! Go away this instant!" and an old woman with a switch in her hand came round the corner of a hut, violently shooing away a crowd of naked children. Some more women followed, clicking their tongues and exclaiming; evidently there was something that the children ought not to have seen. I rounded the hut and saw a man's dead body sprawling in the mud. He was an Indian, a black Dravidian coolie, almost naked, and he could not have been dead many minutes. The people said that the elephant had come suddenly upon him round the corner of the hut, caught him with its trunk, put its foot on his back and ground him into the earth. This was the rainy season and the ground was soft, and his face had scored a trench a foot deep and a couple of yards long. He was lying on his belly with arms crucified and head sharply twisted to one side. His face was coated with mud, the eyes wide open, the teeth bared and grinning with an expression of unendurable agony. (Never tell me, by the way, that the dead look peaceful. Most of the corpses I have seen look devilish.) The friction of the great beast's foot had stripped the skin from his back as neatly as one skins a rabbit. As soon as I saw the dead man I sent an orderly to a friend's house nearby to borrow an elephant rifle. I had already sent back the pony, not wanting it to go mad with fright and throw me if it smelt the elephant.

The orderly came back in a few minutes with a rifle and five cartridges, and meanwhile some Burmans had arrived and told us that the elephant was in the paddy fields below, only a few hundred yards away. As I started forward practically the whole population of the quarter flocked out of the houses and followed me. They had seen the rifle and were all shouting excitedly that I was going to shoot the elephant. They had not shown much interest in the elephant when he was merely ravaging their homes, but it was different now that he was going to be shot. It was a bit of fun to them, as it would be to an English crowd; besides they wanted the meat. It made me vaguely uneasy. I had no intention of shooting the elephant—I had merely sent for the rifle to defend myself if necessary—and it is always unnerving to have a crowd following you. I marched down the hill, looking and feeling a fool, with the rifle over my shoulder and an ever-growing army of people jostling at my heels. At the bottom, when you got away from the huts, there was a metalled road and beyond that a miry waste of paddy fields a thousand yards across, not yet ploughed but soggy from the first rains and dotted with coarse grass. The elephant was standing eight yards from the road, his left side towards us. He took not the slightest notice of the crowd's approach. He was tearing up bunches of grass, beating them against his knees to clean them and stuffing them into his mouth. 5

I had halted on the road. As soon as I saw the elephant I knew with perfect certainty that I ought not to shoot him. It is a serious matter to shoot a working elephant—it is comparable to destroying a huge and costly piece of machinery—and obviously one ought not to do it if it can possibly be avoided. And at that distance, peacefully eating, the elephant looked no more dangerous than a cow. I thought then and I think now that his attack of "must" was already passing off; in which case he would merely wander harmlessly about until the mahout came back and caught him. Moreover, I did not in the least want to shoot him. I decided that I would watch him for a little while to make sure that he did not turn savage again, and then go home.

But at that moment I glanced round at the crowd that had followed me. It was an immense crowd, two thousand at the least and growing every minute. It blocked the road for a long distance on either side. I looked at the sea of yellow faces above the garish clothes—faces all happy and excited over this bit of fun, all certain that the elephant was going to be shot. They were watching me as they would watch a conjurer about to perform a trick. They did not like me, but with the magical rifle in my hands I was momentarily worth watching. And suddenly I realized that I should have to shoot the elephant after all. The people expected it of me and I had got to do it; I could feel their two thousand wills pressing me forward, irresistibly. And it was at this moment, as I stood there with the rifle in my hands, that I first grasped the hollowness, the futility of the white man's dominion in the East. Here was I, the white man with his gun, standing in front of the unarmed native crowd—seemingly the leading actor of the piece; but in reality I was only an absurd puppet pushed to and fro by the will of those yellow faces behind. I perceived in this moment that when the white man turns tyrant it is his own freedom that he destroys. He becomes a sort of hollow, posing dummy, the conventionalized figure of a sahib. For it is the condition of his rule that he shall spend his life in trying to impress the "natives," and so in every crisis he has got to do what the "natives" expect of him. He wears a mask, and his face grows to fit it. I had got to shoot the elephant. I had committed myself to doing it when I sent for the rifle. A sahib has got to act like a sahib; he has got to appear resolute, to know his own mind and do definite things. To come all that way, rifle in hand, with two thousand people marching at my heels, and then to trail feebly away, having done nothing—no, that was impossible. The crowd would laugh at me. And my whole life, every white man's life in the East, was one long struggle not to be laughed at.

But I did not want to shoot the elephant. I watched him beating his bunch of grass against his knees, with that preoccupied grandmotherly air that elephants have. It seemed to me that it would be murder to shoot him. At that age I was not squeamish about killing animals, but I had never shot an elephant and never wanted to. (Somehow it always seems worse to kill a *large* animal.) Besides, there was the beast's owner to be considered. Alive, the elephant was worth at least a hundred pounds; dead, he would only be worth the value of his tusks, five pounds, possibly. But I had got to act quickly. I turned to some experienced-looking Burmans who had been there when we arrived, and asked them how the elephant had been behaving. They all said the same thing: he took no notice of you if you left him alone, but he might charge if you went too close to him.

It was perfectly clear to me what I ought to do. I ought to walk up to within, say, twenty-five yards of the elephant and test his behavior. If he charged, I could shoot; if he took no notice of me, it would be safe to leave him until the mahout came back. But also I knew that I was going to do no such thing. I was a poor shot with a rifle and the ground was soft mud into which one would sink at every step. If the elephant charged and

I missed him, I should have about as much chance as a toad under a steam-roller. But even then I was not thinking particularly of my own skin, only of the watchful yellow faces behind. For at that moment, with the crowd watching me, I was not afraid in the ordinary sense, as I would have been if I had been alone. A white man mustn't be frightened in front of "natives"; and so, in general, he isn't frightened. The sole thought in my mind was that if anything went wrong those two thousand Burmans would see me pursued, caught, trampled on and reduced to a grinning corpse like that Indian up the hill. And if that happened it was quite probable that some of them would laugh. That would never do. There was only one alternative. I shoved the cartridges into the magazine and lay down on the road to get a better aim.

The crowd grew very still, and a deep, low, happy sigh, as of people who see the theatre curtain go up at last breathed from innumerable throats. They were going to have their bit of fun after all. The rifle was a beautiful German thing with cross-hair sights. I did not then know that in shooting an elephant one would shoot to cut an imaginary bar running from ear-hole to ear-hole. I ought, therefore, as the elephant was sideways on, to have aimed straight at his ear-hole; actually I aimed several inches in front of this, thinking the brain would be further forward. 10

When I pulled the trigger I did not hear the bang or feel the kick—one never does when a shot goes home—but I heard the devilish roar of glee that went up from the crowd. In that instant, in too short a time, one would have thought, even for the bullet to get there, a mysterious, terrible change had come over the elephant. He neither stirred nor fell, but every line of his body had altered. He looked suddenly stricken, shrunken, immensely old, as though the frightful impact of the bullet had paralysed him without knocking him down. At last, after what seemed a long time—it might have been five seconds, I dare say—he sagged flabbily to his knees. His mouth slobbered. An enormous senility seemed to have settled upon him. One could have imagined him thousands of years old. I fired again into the same spot. At the second shot he did not collapse but climbed with desperate slowness to his feet and stood weakly upright, with legs sagging and head dropping. I fired a third time. That was the shot that did for him. You could see the agony of it jolt his whole body and knock the last remnant of strength from his legs. But in falling he seemed for a moment to rise, for as his hind legs collapsed beneath him he seemed to tower upward like a huge rock toppling, his trunk reaching skywards like a tree. He trumpeted, for the first and only time. And then down he came, his belly towards me, with a crash that seemed to shake the ground even where I lay.

I got up. The Burmans were already racing past me across the mud. It was obvious that the elephant would never rise again, but he was not dead. He was breathing very rhythmically with long rattling gasps, his great mound of a side painfully rising and falling. His mouth was wide open. I could see far down into caverns of pale pink throat. I waited a long time for him to die, but his breathing did not weaken. Finally I fired my two remaining shots into the spot where I thought his heart must be. The thick blood welled out of him like red velvet, but still he did not die. His body did not even jerk when the shots hit him, the tortured breathing continued without a pause. He was dying, very slowly and in great agony, but in some world remote from me where not even a bullet could damage him further. I felt I had got to put an end to that dreadful noise. It seemed dreadful to see the great beast lying there, powerless to move and yet powerless to die, and not even to be able to finish him. I sent back for my small rifle and poured shot after shot into his heart and down his throat. They seemed to make no impression. The tortured gasps continued as steadily as the ticking of a clock.

In the end I could not stand it any longer and went away. I heard later that it took him half an hour to die. Burmans were bringing dahs and baskets even before I left, and I was told they had stripped his body almost to the bones by the afternoon.

Afterwards, of course, there were endless discussions about the shooting of the elephant. The owner was furious, but he was only an Indian and could do nothing. Besides, legally I had done the right thing, for a mad elephant has to be killed, like a mad dog, if its owner fails to control it. Among the Europeans opinion was divided. The older men said I was right, the younger men said it was a damn shame to shoot an elephant for killing a coolie, because an elephant was worth more than any damn Coringhee coolie. And afterwards I was very glad that the coolie had been killed; it put me legally in the right and it gave me a sufficient pretext for shooting the elephant. I often wondered whether any of the others grasped that I had done it solely to avoid looking a fool.

Joining the Conversation: Critical Thinking and Writing

1. How does Orwell characterize himself at the time of the events he describes? What evidence in the essay suggests that he wrote it some years later?

2. Orwell says the incident was "enlightening." What does he mean? Picking up this clue, state in a sentence or two the thesis or main point of the essay.

3. Compare Orwell's description of the dead coolie (in the fourth paragraph) with his description of the elephant's death (in the eleventh and twelfth paragraphs). Why does Orwell devote more space to the death of the elephant?

4. How would you describe the tone of the last paragraph, particularly of the last two sentences? Do you find the paragraph an effective conclusion to the essay? Explain.

John (?)

The following story, "The Woman Taken in Adultery," appears in several places in various early manuscripts of the New Testament, for instance in the Gospel according to Luke, after 21:38, in the Gospel according to John, after 7:36, and, in other manuscripts of John, after 7:53. The most famous English translation of the Bible, the King James Version (1611), gives it at John 8:3–11, and so it is commonly regarded as belonging to John. But most biblical scholars agree that the language of this short story differs notably from the language of the rest of this Gospel, and that it is not in any manuscript of John before the sixth century is further evidence that it was not originally part of this Gospel.

The Gospel according to John was apparently compiled in the late first century. John 21:20–24 says the author, or "the disciple which testifieth of these things," is "the disciple whom Jesus loved, . . . which also leaned on his breast at supper, and said, 'Lord, which is he that betrayeth thee?'" Since the second century the book has traditionally been ascribed to John, one of the inner circle of twelve disciples.

The Woman Taken in Adultery

Jesus went unto the mount of Olives. And early in the morning he came again into the temple, and all the people came unto him; and he sat down, and taught them.

And the scribes and Pharisees[1] brought unto him a woman taken in adultery; and when they had set her in the midst, they say unto him, "Master, this woman was taken in adultery, in the very act. Now Moses in the law commanded us that such should be stoned: but what sayest thou?" This they said, tempting him, that they might have to accuse him. But Jesus stooped down, and with his finger wrote on the ground, as though he heard them not. So when they continued asking him, he lifted up himself, and said unto them, "He that is without sin among you, let him first cast a stone at her." And again he stooped down, and wrote on the ground. And they which heard it, being convicted by their own conscience, went out one by one, beginning at the eldest, even unto the last: and Jesus was left alone, and the woman standing in the midst.

When Jesus had lifted up himself, and saw none but the woman, he said unto her, "Woman, where are those thine accusers? Hath no man condemned thee?" She said, "No man, Lord." And Jesus said unto her, "Neither do I condemn thee; go, and sin no more."

Joining the Conversation:
Critical Thinking and Writing

1. Do you interpret the episode of "The Woman Taken in Adultery" to say that crime should go unpunished? Or that adultery is not a crime? Or that a judge cannot punish a crime if he himself is guilty of it? Or what?

---

[1]**scribes and Pharisees** The scribes were specialists who copied and interpreted the Hebrew law; the Pharisees were members of a sect that emphasized strict adherence to the Mosaic law. (Editors' note)

2. We read that Jesus wrote with his finger on the ground but we are not told what Jesus wrote. How relevant do you find Jesus' action to the story? Explain.

3. This story is widely quoted and alluded to. Why, in your opinion, has the story such broad appeal?

A Casebook on Torture

Michael Levin

Michael Levin, educated at Michigan State University and Columbia University, has taught philosophy at Columbia and now at City College of the City University of New York. Levin has written numerous papers for professional journals and a book entitled Metaphysics and the Mind-Body Problem *(1979). The following essay is intended for a general audience.*

The Case for Torture

It is generally assumed that torture is impermissible, a throwback to a more brutal age. Enlightened societies reject it outright, and regimes suspected of using it risk the wrath of the United States.

I believe this attitude is unwise. There are situations in which torture is not merely permissible but morally mandatory. Moreover, these situations are moving from the realm of imagination to fact.

Death: Suppose a terrorist has hidden an atomic bomb on Manhattan Island which will detonate at noon on July 4 unless . . . (here follow the usual demands for money and release of his friends from jail). Suppose, further, that he is caught at 10 A.M. of the fateful day, but—preferring death to failure—won't disclose where the bomb is. What do we do? If we follow due process—wait for his lawyer, arraign him—millions of people will die. If the only way to save those lives is to subject the terrorist to the most excruciating possible pain, what grounds can there be for not doing so? I suggest there are none. In any case, I ask you to face the question with an open mind.

Torturing the terrorist is unconstitutional? Probably. But millions of lives surely outweigh constitutionality. Torture is barbaric? Mass murder is far more barbaric. Indeed, letting millions of innocents die in deference

---

Michael Levin, "The Case for Torture," *Newsweek*, June 7, 1982. Reprinted by permission of the author.

to one who flaunts his guilt is moral cowardice, an unwillingness to dirty one's hands. If *you* caught the terrorist, could you sleep nights knowing that millions died because you couldn't bring yourself to apply the electrodes?

Once you concede that torture is justified in extreme cases, you have admitted that the decision to use torture is a matter of balancing innocent lives against the means needed to save them. You must now face more realistic cases involving more modest numbers. Someone plants a bomb on a jumbo jet. He alone can disarm it, and his demands cannot be met (or if they can, we refuse to set a precedent by yielding to his threats). Surely we can, we must, do anything to the extortionist to save the passengers. How can we tell 300, or 100, or 10 people who never asked to be put in danger, "I'm sorry, you'll have to die in agony, we just couldn't bring ourselves to . . . "

Here are the results of an informal poll about a third, hypothetical, case. Suppose a terrorist group kidnapped a newborn baby from a hospital. I asked four mothers if they would approve of torturing kidnappers if that were necessary to get their own newborns back. All said yes, the most "liberal" adding that she would like to administer it herself.

I am not advocating torture as punishment. Punishment is addressed to deeds irrevocably past. Rather, I am advocating torture as an acceptable measure for preventing future evils. So understood, it is far less objectionable than many extant punishments. Opponents of the death penalty, for example, are forever insisting that executing a murderer will not bring back his victim (as if the purpose of capital punishment were supposed to be resurrection, not deterrence or retribution). But torture, in the cases described, is intended not to bring anyone back but to keep innocents from being dispatched. The most powerful argument against using torture as a punishment or to secure confessions is that such practices disregard the rights of the individual. Well, if the individual is all that important—and he is—it is correspondingly important to protect the rights of individuals threatened by terrorists. If life is so valuable that it must never be taken, the lives of the innocents must be saved even at the price of hurting the one who endangers them.

Better precedents for torture are assassination and pre-emptive attack. No Allied leader would have flinched at assassinating Hitler, had that been possible. (The Allies did assassinate Heydrich.) Americans would be angered to learn that Roosevelt could have had Hitler killed in 1943—thereby shortening the war and saving millions of lives—but refused on moral grounds. Similarly, if nation *A* learns that nation *B* is about to launch an unprovoked attack, *A* has a right to save itself by destroying *B*'s military capability first. In the same way, if the police can by torture save those who would otherwise die at the hands of kidnappers or terrorists, they must.

Idealism: There is an important difference between terrorists and their victims that should mute talk of the terrorists' "rights." The terrorist's victims are at risk unintentionally, not having asked to be endangered.

5

But the terrorist knowingly initiated his actions. Unlike his victims, he volunteered for the risks of his deed. By threatening to kill for profit or idealism, he renounces civilized standards, and he can have no complaint if civilization tries to thwart him by whatever means necessary.

Just as torture is justified only to save lives (not extort confessions   10 or recantations) it is justifiably administered only to those *known* to hold innocent lives in their hands. Ah, but how can the authorities ever be sure they have the right malefactor? Isn't there a danger of error and abuse? Won't We turn into Them?

Questions like these are disingenuous in a world in which terrorists proclaim themselves and perform for television. The name of their game is public recognition. After all, you can't very well intimidate a government into releasing your freedom fighters unless you announce that it is your group that has seized its embassy. "Clear guilt" is difficult to define, but when 40 million people see a group of masked gunmen seize an airplane on the evening news, there is not much question about who the perpetrators are. There will be hard cases where the situation is murkier. Nonetheless, a line demarcating the legitimate use of torture can be drawn. Torture only the obviously guilty, and only for the sake of saving innocents, and the line between Us and Them will remain clear.

There is little danger that the Western democracies will lose their way if they choose to inflict pain as one way of preserving order. Paralysis in the face of evil is the greater danger. Someday soon a terrorist will threaten tens of thousands of lives, and torture will be the only way to save them. We had better start thinking about this.

 ## Joining the Conversation:
Critical Thinking and Writing

1. At the beginning of his essay, Levin presents a number of examples designed to show that torture is sometimes acceptable. Do you agree with his interpretation of these examples?

2. In paragraph 11, Levin contends: "Torture only the obviously guilty, and only for the sake of saving innocents, and the line between Us and Them will remain clear." Imagine that you are taking the other side in a debate with Levin: How would you reply to his claim?

3. How would you evaluate Levin's essay as a piece of writing? Is his argument clearly stated? Does he support it effectively? Is it convincing, or if not, why not?

4. Whether or not you agree with Levin, can you imagine being the torturer yourself? Or do you think that this job should be performed by someone else? What might be the circumstances that would lead you to feel that torture would be justified?

5. Is it one thing to present an argument like Levin's in an essay, and another to put Levin's ideas into practice? Do you believe that Levin's ideas could ever be put into practice in the United States? Is that fortunate or unfortunate, in your view?

Philip B. Heymann

Philip B. Heymann, a former U.S. deputy attorney general in the Clinton administration, is a professor at Harvard Law School. His most recent publications include Preserving Liberty in an Age of Terror *(with Juliette Kayyem, 2005), and* Terrorism, Freedom, and Security *(2003). The following essay was published in the* Boston Globe *in 2002 and represents Heymann's position in his ongoing debate with Alan Dershowitz about the authorization of torture. Dershowitz's response appears on pages 553–555.*

Torture Should Not Be Authorized

Authorizing torture is a bad and dangerous idea that can easily be made to sound plausible. There is a subtle fallacy embedded in the traditional "ticking bomb" argument for torture to save lives.

That argument goes like this. First, I can imagine dangers so dire that I might torture or kill guilty or innocent persons if I was quite sure that was necessary and sufficient to prevent those dangers. Second, very many feel this way, although differing in the circumstances and the certainty level they would want. Therefore, the "ticking bomb" argument concludes, everyone wants a system for authorizing torture or murder; we need only debate the circumstances and the level of certainty.

This conclusion, leading to abandonment of one of the few worldwide legal prohibitions, leaves out the fact that I do not have faith in the authorizing system for finding the required circumstances with any certainty because the costs of errors are born by the suspect tortured, not by those who decide to torture him. The conclusion also ignores the high probability that the practice of torture will spread unwisely if acceptance of torture with the approval of judges is substituted for a flat, worldwide prohibition.

The use of torture would increase sharply if there were "torture warrants." Any law enforcement or intelligence official who tortures

Philip B. Heymann, "Torture Should Not Be Authorized" published in the *Boston Globe*, February 16, 2002. Reprinted by permission of the author.

a prisoner in the United States now is very likely to be prosecuted and imprisoned.

Punches may be thrown, but anything we think of as "torture" is considered an inexcusable practice. That revulsion will disappear if we make torture acceptable and legal whenever a judge accepts the judgment of intelligence officials that: (1) there is a bomb; (2) the suspect knows where it is; (3) torture will get the truth, not a false story, out of him before the bomb explodes; (4) the bomb won't be moved in the meantime. Every individual who believes in his heart, however recklessly, that those conditions (or others he thinks are just as compelling) are met will think there is nothing seriously wrong with torture. 5

Professor Alan Dershowitz wants to bet that judges will say "no" in a high enough percentage of cases of "ticking bombs" that whatever moral force their refusal has will offset the legitimating and demoralizing effects of authorizing occasional torture. It's a bad bet.

Judges have deferred to the last several thousand requests for national security wiretaps and they would defer here. The basis of their decisions, information revealing secret "sources and methods" of intelligence gathering, would not be public. And if the judge refused, overrode the judgment of agents who thought lives would be lost without torture, and denied a warrant, why would that decision be more likely to be accepted and followed by agents desperate to save lives than the flat ban on torture we now have?

How many false positives do you want to accept? You would get six false positives out of ten occasions of torture even in the extraordinarily unlikely event that the intelligence officers convince the judge that they were really 80 percent sure of each of the above four predictions.

And even if you would tolerate this number of false positives if torture were in fact the only way to get the needed information to defuse the bomb, there are frequently other promising ways (such as emergency searches or stimulating conversations over tapped phones) that will be abandoned or discounted if torture is available.

Finally, if we approve torture in one set of circumstances, isn't every country then free to define its own exceptions, applicable to Americans as well as its own citizens? Fear of that led us to accept the Geneva Convention prohibiting torture of a prisoner of war, although obtaining his information might save dozens of American lives. 10

As to preventing terrorism, torture is an equally bad idea. Torture is a prescription for losing a war for support of our beliefs in the hope of reducing the casualties from relatively small battles.

Dershowitz misunderstands my argument. I do not accept torture either "off the books" with a wink at the secret discretion of the torturers or on the open authority of the judges from whom they might seek authorization. I predict so many types of harms to so many people and to the nation from any system that authorizes torture, either secretly or openly, that I would prohibit it.

The overall, longer-term cost of any system authorizing torture, openly or tacitly, would far outweigh its occasional, short-term benefits.

Joining the Conversation: Critical Thinking and Writing

1. Do you think that Heymann's first sentence is effective? Explain why or why not.

2. What is the "ticking bomb" argument to which Heymann refers? What is his assessment of it? Do you agree?

3. What does Heymann mean by "false positives"?

4. When you finished Heymann's essay, were you convinced by it? What is his strongest point? His weakest?

5. Imagine that you have been chosen to present a rebuttal to Heymann. What would be the first sentence of the rebuttal? What would be the most important point you would want to convey to your audience?

Alan M. Dershowitz

Alan Dershowitz is a professor of law at Harvard University, where he has taught since 1964. His most recent publications include Preemption: A Knife that Cuts Both Ways *(2006),* The Case for Peace *(2005), and* America on Trial: Inside the Legal Battles that Transformed Our Nation—From the Salem Witches to the Guantanamo Detainees *(2004).*

Yes, It Should Be "On the Books"

Professor Philip Heymann and I share a common goal: to eliminate torture from the world, or at the very least to reduce it to an absolute minimum. The real disagreement between us seems to be over whether the use of torture, under these extreme circumstances, would be worse if done in secret without being incorporated into our legal system—or worse if it required a torture warrant to be issued by a judge. This is truly a choice of evils, with no perfect resolution. However, I insist that any extraordinary steps contemplated by a democracy must be done "on the books." Of course there is the risk of false positives and ever expanding criteria. But these evils would exist whether torture was conducted off or

Alan M. Dershowitz, "Yes, It Should Be 'On the Books' " published in the *Boston Globe*, February 16, 2002. Reprinted by permission of the author.

on the books. A carefully designed judicial procedure is more likely to reduce the amount of torture actually conducted, by creating accountability and leaving a public record of every warrant sought and granted.

The legal historian John Langbein has shown that there was far more torture in Medieval France than England because in France the practice was left to the discretion of local officials, whereas in England it required an extraordinary warrant, which was rarely granted. Heymann suggests that "any law enforcement and intelligence official who tortures a prisoner in the United States now is very likely to be prosecuted and imprisoned." I believe that a police officer who tortured and successfully prevented a terrorist attack would not be prosecuted, and if he were, he would be acquitted.

Indeed, in a case decided in 1984, the Court of Appeals for the 11th circuit commended police officers who tortured a kidnapper into disclosing the location of his victim. Although there was no evidence that the victim's life was in imminent danger, the court described the offending police officers as "a group of concerned officers acting in a reasonable manner to obtain information in order to protect another individual from bodily harm or death." Elsewhere in the opinion, they described the "reasonable manner" as including "choking him until he revealed where [the victim] was being held." These police officers were not prosecuted. Under my proposal, no torture warrant could have been granted in such a case.

Our nation has had extensive experience with "off the book" actions. President Nixon authorized an off the book "plumbers" operation to break into homes and offices. President Reagan authorized an off the book foreign policy that culminated in the Iran-Contra debacle. President[s] Eisenhower and Kennedy apparently authorized off the book attempts to assassinate Fidel Castro. The road to tyranny is paved by executive officials authorizing actions which they deem necessary to national security, without subjecting these actions to the check and balance of legislative approval, judicial imprimatur, and public accountability. We are a nation of laws, and if the rule of law means anything, it means that no action regardless of how unpalatable, must ever be taken outside of the rule of law. If the action is to be taken, it must be deemed lawful. If it cannot be deemed lawful it should not be taken.

Unless we are prepared to authorize the issuance of a torture warrant in the case of the ticking bomb, we should not torture, even if that means that innocent people may die. If we want to prevent the death of hundreds of innocent people by subjecting one guilty person to nonlethal pain, then we must find a way to justify this exception to the otherwise blanket prohibition against torture. All the evils of torture would be multiplied if we were to accept the way of the hypocrite, by proclaiming loudly that we are against it but subtly winking an eye of approval when it is done.

Hypocrisy, too, is contagious. Several years ago, an Israeli prime minister reprimanded security officials for bringing him "unwanted information of misdeeds by Shin Bet" (the Israeli FBI). A wise professor commented on this action in the following words: "That strategy is extremely dangerous to democratic values, because it is designed to prevent oversight and to deny accountability to the public."

That wise professor was Philip Heymann.

Joining the Conversation: Critical Thinking and Writing

1. Why does Dershowitz say that we face "a choice of evils"?

2. What does Dershowitz mean by the phrase "on the books"? Why does he put this phrase in quotes? Later, he says, "off the book." What does he mean by that?

3. Do you think it is acceptable to torture a person if it is suspected that he or she might have knowledge of a terrorist plot?

4. How would Dershowitz reply to a foreign government that declares, "You say you can torture our citizens if you believe they possess important information. We claim the right to do the same thing to your citizens"?

CHAPTER 13

Consuming Desires

American Gothic
Grant Wood, 1930

Just what is it that makes today's homes so different, so appealing?
Richard Hamilton, 1956

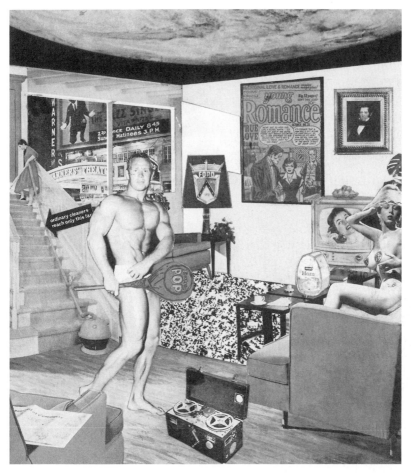

Short Views

Heaven is not as high as the desires of the human heart.
>   *Chinese Proverb*

Desire without knowledge is not good, and one who moves too hurriedly misses the way.
>   *Hebrew Bible, Proverbs 19.2*

He who desires but acts not, breeds pestilence.
>   *William Blake*

Living is more a question of what one spends than what one makes.
>   *Marcel Duchamp*

You are what you eat.
>   *Anonymous*

The great secret of vegetarianism is never to eat vegetables.
>   *George Bernard Shaw*

Coffee drunk out of wine glasses is really miserable stuff, as is meat cut at the table with a pair of scissors.
>   *G. C. Lichtenberg*

I can't help thinking that the decline in table manners has something to do with fast food. There are no rules of etiquette for eating a Big Mac and a side of fries. The whole idea of fast food is to get eating out of the way as quickly as possible so you can get to something else. It's difficult to have respect for a fast food cheeseburger. And if you don't have respect for what you're eating how can you have any respect for yourself or the people you are eating with?
>   *Diane White*

Eat, drink, and be merry, for tomorrow we die.
        Anonymous

Long before I am near enough to talk to you on the street, in a meeting, or at a party, you announce your sex, age and class to me through what you are wearing—and very possibly give me important information (or misinformation) as to your occupation, origin, personality, opinions, tastes, sexual desires and current mood. . . . By the time we meet and converse we have already spoken to each other in an older and more universal tongue.
        Alison Lurie

Skin, if it is attractive, can be part of the design.
        Rudi Gernreich

If I had to say which was telling the truth about society, a speech by a Minister of Housing or the actual buildings put up in his time, I should believe the buildings.
        Kenneth Clark

A house is a machine for living.
        Le Corbusier

I like a man who likes to see a fine barn as well as a good tragedy.
        Ralph Waldo Emerson

Michael Ableman

Michael Ableman, of the Center for Ecoliteracy, is a farmer, author, and photographer. His most recent book is Fields of Plenty: A Farmer's Journey in Search of Real Food and the People Who Grow It *(2005). We reprint an essay from a series called "Thinking Outside the Lunchbox," published in 2005 by the Center for Ecoliteracy.*

Feeding Our Future

Lunchtime at Goleta Valley Junior High starts at 12:07. Within 28 minutes, 700 students have to be "fed" before returning to classes. The scene is pandemonium. Students are either standing in lines, clustered in small bands, or racing around as if lost. The lunch tables are folded and stacked with their accompanying chairs; students eat outside while standing up (a food fight a couple years ago resulted in the administration's removing any opportunity for students to sit down and eat together).

The cool stainless tubular slides that once carried plastic trays of hot food dished out by hair-netted women in starched white uniforms remain. But no milk machines squirt columns of regular or chocolate milk; no bottom-heated tables keep mashed potatoes or lasagna warm; no fish-cakes wait in stacks; no coleslaw sits at the ready; no clam chowder simmers, ready to be ladled into waiting bowls.

The heating table's large pans are now filled with prepackaged barbecued beef sandwiches and cheeseburgers prepared at anonymous kitchens, miles away, with ingredients from U.S. government commodities programs. On the wall a faded sign reads, "Fruits and vegetables are always in season. Whether they're fresh, frozen, canned, or dried, they all count." The cardboard "No pizza today" sign brings audible sighs of disappointment.

A salad bar graces one corner of the room, laden with shredded iceberg lettuce, grated cheese, pickles, peppers, yogurt, granola, peanuts, and apple and orange pieces. Another station is stacked with Italian subs, ham sandwiches, and celery pieces with containers of peanut butter. With a pair of plastic tongs, the lady in charge of the salad bar makes a futile attempt to conceal the brown lettuce leaves. She asks if I'm an inspector, then apologizes for the condition of the lettuce. She tells me that it's the last day before the break and that they're trying to "get rid of" the old product.

The longest lines of students lead to two wire mesh-covered windows   5
outside the building, where attendants dispense nachos—orange gooey imitation cheese squirted from a machine onto chips. Every purchased

item is placed in a thick cardboard tray. I watch as students pay for their food, then immediately toss the trays, foil wrappers, napkins, and cans into rapidly filling trash barrels.

Just a few blocks away, in the fertile fields of Fairview Gardens, a small community farm, long rows of asparagus poke their heads out of sandy soil, crimson strawberries dot a nearby field, and multicolored lettuces stand up straight and tall. Peach, plum, apricot, and nectarine trees have just shed their pink and white flower petals, revealing branches loaded with small fruit. In neighboring fields, the last of the mandarin oranges hang like orange beacons, and the first avocados cluster from huge grandfather trees in the "cathedral" orchard that dominates the land.

The farm is often referred to as "the little farm that could" for its unprecedented diversity of products and as a model of urban agriculture and public education. It has operated since 1895, holding out against the tide of development, withstanding a range of threats to its existence, and now permanently preserved under an agricultural conservation easement.

In the large field along Fairview Avenue, the main thoroughfare used by most students going to and from the school, carrots, beets, spinach, onions, broccoli, artichokes, and snap and English peas provide food for the burgeoning suburban population that now inhabits this once agricultural valley. In the surrounding neighborhood, fields containing some of the richest and deepest topsoil on the West Coast now yield housing developments, shopping centers, and clogged roadways.

It takes about 10 minutes to walk from Goleta Valley Junior High to Fairview Gardens farm, about four minutes by bicycle, and about one minute by car. This stunning twelve-and-a-half-acre outdoor classroom is open to the public. Thousands of people come each year to enjoy a different kind of educational experience, starting with soil and moving through a range of food crops and animals. Hundreds of students from the school have toured the farm. The farm helped the school to start a garden and has done assembly presentations about food and farming. But while those experiences are well received, the ideas and inspiration they engender stop at the cafeteria door. As founder and executive director of the Center for Urban Agriculture at Fairview Gardens, I've tried to interest the school in replacing some of the highly processed, distantly grown items that its cafeteria serves. I've offered the alternative of fresh, organic food grown by the school's neighbor down the street, but have never been able to generate interest.

Recently, the school district spent $150,000 on a computer system to   10
manage the inflow of anonymous food from distant sources. But it doesn't require a computer to figure out that young people need whole food— food that tastes better because it's grown in living soil and harvested locally, food that makes clear the relationship between human health and the health of the Earth. It doesn't require a computer to tell us that by feeding young people the best, not just the cheapest, we are in effect feeding and nourishing our own future.

Why shouldn't students be eating the sweet French carrots, the Clementine mandarins, the year-round salad greens, the radishes and beets and avocados that grow so near the school? How difficult would it be to replace nachos with real corn on the cob? How much more time and expense would be required to serve farm-fresh eggs, or ripe strawberries, or bean or vegetable soups and stew produced with real local ingredients? How difficult would it be to spend less on hardware and more on providing professional development so that cafeteria staff can help students make connections between the food they eat and the farms where it's grown?

Imagine if students could plant, harvest, and cultivate the very foods that later appear in their lunch at the cafeteria. Shouldn't all 700 students at Goleta Valley Junior High be required, as part of their education, to develop a relationship with the farm in order to understand the connections between soil life and their own life—between taste and health?

For more than 20 years I have hosted local students on the farm, walking and grazing from the fields with them, allowing them to settle into a different rhythm for an hour or two. I always take a few moments to get to know them, to ask a few simple questions before we begin; How many of you live on farms, how many have ever visited one, what did you eat for breakfast? Over the years I have seen a dramatic shift in young people's responses and in their relationship to food and the land.

It used to be that a handful in every group lived on farms; most had at least visited one. Their breakfast might have included an egg or a piece of fruit or bread, or even some whole grain. Now it is rare to find a kid who lives on a farm, or has even visited one. Many have not had breakfast, and those who have often tell me that it consisted of a granola bar, a corn dog, or even a can of Coke. It is not just kids' answers that tell me that something has changed. When young people come to the farm, I look at each of them, study them the way I do the farm's soil and plants and trees, try to get a feel for how they are doing. These days, many are overweight; they seem to lack focus and have difficulty being still. Our task with our young visitors is different now, our goals very basic. We want to provide them with something real to eat—a fresh carrot or strawberry—and an hour or two outside of the walls of the classroom, a chance to slow down and an opportunity to touch the Earth for just one moment and to be calmed and settled by it. Change, I have to remind myself, comes slowly and incrementally.

Joining the Conversation: Critical Thinking and Writing

1. Do you think Ableman is a good writer? Cite and comment on passages from the essay to support your view.

2. Describe how this essay is organized.

3. What is Ableman's main point? Is this point new to you, or is it familiar?

4. A student said that she liked Ableman's essay but wished that he had omitted the references in it to himself. She thinks that the essay would have been more effective that way. Why would she say that? Do you agree or disagree? Explain.

5. Describe what you typically eat for breakfast, lunch, and dinner. Be as specific as you can. How do you think that Ableman would respond to your food choices? What would be your response to him?

David Gerard Hogan

David Gerard Hogan, a historian of food, is the author of Sell 'Em by the Sack *(1997), an account of the first (pre-McDonald) promoter of fast-food hamburger. He is also the author of* The Creation of American Food *(1999). We print part of an essay that originally appeared in* Encyclopedia of Food and Culture *(2003).*

Fast Food

Criticism of Fast Food

Despite the widespread popularity of fast food in modern American culture, critics abound. Since the 1930s, articles and books have condemned the industry, exposing allegedly poor sanitary conditions, unhealthy food products, related environmental problems, and unfair working conditions. Whether it warrants the attention or not, the fast-food industry is still regularly cited for exploiting young workers, polluting, and contributing to obesity and other serious health problems among American consumers. American beef consumption, and more specifically the fast-food hamburger industry, is often blamed for the burning of the Amazon rain forests to make way for more grazing lands for beef cattle. Early foes of fast food cited the deplorable filth of many hamburger stands, in addition to claiming that the beef ground for their sandwiches was either spoiled, diseased, or simply of low quality. In fact, many critics maintained that much of the meat used in fast-food hamburgers came from horse carcasses. The high fat content of fast food was also controversial. Despite deceptive industry claims about the high quality and the health benefits of their products, in the 1920s and 1930s concerned nutritionists

From *Encyclopedia of Food and Culture*, Volume 3, edited by Solomon H. Katz and William Woys Weaver, 2003. Reprinted with permission of Gale, a division of Thomson Learning.

warned the public about the medical dangers of regular burger consumption. This distrust and criticism of fast food continue today, extending even further to include dire warnings about the industry's use of genetically modified and antibiotic-laden beef products. Most major chains have responded to recent attacks by prominently posting calorie and nutritional charts in their restaurants, advertising fresh ingredients, and offering alternatives to their fried foods. Despite a few more health-conscious items on the menu, fast-food chains now aggressively advertise the concept that bigger is better, offering large "super-size" or "biggie" portions of french fries, soft drinks, and milkshakes. Critics point to this marketing emphasis as a reason for an excessive and greatly increasing per-capita caloric intake among fast-food consumers, resulting in fast-growing rates of obesity in the United States.

Increased litter is another problem that critics have blamed on the fast-food industry. Selling their products in paper wrappings and paper bags, early outlets created a source of litter that had not previously existed. Wrappers strewn about city streets, especially those close to fast-food restaurants, brought harsh criticism, and often inspired new local ordinances to address the problem. Some municipalities actually forced chains to clean up litter that was imprinted with their logos, but such sanctions were rare. Fast-food wrappers became part of the urban, and later suburban, landscape. Since bags and wrappers were crucial in the delivery of fast food, the industry as a whole continued to use disposable packaging, superficially assuaging public criticism by providing outside trash receptacles for the discarded paper. Years later, environmentalists again attacked the industry for excessive packaging litter, criticizing both the volume and the content of the refuse. By the early 1970s, the harshest criticisms focused more on the synthetic materials used in packaging, and less on the carelessly discarded paper. Critics derided the industry's use of styrofoam sandwich containers and soda cups, claiming that these products were not sufficiently biodegradable and were clogging landfills. Facing mounting opposition from a growing environmental movement, most of the major chains returned to packaging food in paper wrappings or small cardboard boxes.

Labor activists have criticized fast-food chains' tendency to employ inexpensive teenage workers. Usually offering the lowest possible wages, with no health or retirement benefits, these restaurants often find it difficult hiring adults for stressful, fast-paced jobs. Many critics claim that the industry preys on teenagers, who will work for less pay and are less likely to organize. Though these accusations may have merit, the industry's reliance on teenage labor also has inherent liabilities, such as a high employee turnover rate, which result in substantial recruiting and training costs. Companies have countered criticism about their use of teenage workers with the rationale that they offer young people entry-level work experience, teaching them: both skills and responsibility.

Despite the relentless attacks, hundreds of millions of hungry customers eat fast food daily. The media constantly remind American consumers about its supposed evils. Most are conscious of the health risks from fatty, greasy meals; most realize that they are being served by a poorly paid young worker; and if they choose to ponder it, most are aware that the excessive packaging causes millions of tons of trash each year. But they continue to purchase and eat fast food on a regular basis. Fast food remains central to the American diet because it is inexpensive, quick, convenient, and predictable, and because it tastes good. Even more important, Americans eat fast food because it is now a cultural norm. As American culture homogenized and became distinctively "American" in the second half of the twentieth century, fast food, and especially the hamburger, emerged as the primary American ethnic food. Just as the Chinese eat rice and Mexicans eat tamales, Americans eat burgers.

And fast food has grown even beyond being just a distinctive ethnic   5
food. Since the 1960s, the concept has extended far beyond the food itself, with the term becoming a common descriptor for other quick-service operations, even a metaphor for many of the negative aspects of mainstream American life. Theorists and pundits sometimes use the term "fast food" to denigrate American habits, institutions, and values, referring to them as elements of a "fast-food society." In fact, "fast-food" has become a frequently used adjective, implying not only ready availability but also superficiality, mass-produced standardization, lack of authenticity, or just poor quality.

In the last two decades of the twentieth century, fast food gained additional economic and cultural significance, becoming a popular American export to nations around the world. Some detractors claim that it is even deliberately used by the United States, as a tool of cultural imperialism. The appearance of a McDonald's or Kentucky Fried Chicken restaurant on the streets of a foreign city signals to many the demise of indigenous culture, replacing another country's traditional practices and values with American materialism. In fact, the rapid spread of American fast food is probably not an organized conspiracy, rather more the result of aggressive corporate marketing strategies. Consumers in other countries are willing and able to buy fast-food products, so chains are quick to accommodate demand. Thought of around the world as "American food," fast food continues its rapid international growth.

Joining the Conversation: Critical Thinking and Writing

1. How would you define fast food?

2. What fast foods, if any, do you consume? What criticisms of fast food does Hogan list? To what extent do you share these criticisms?

3. In his last paragraph, Hogan writes: "Some detractors claim that it [fast food] is even deliberately used by the United States, as a tool of cultural imperialism." What does Hogan mean here? To what extent do you find this claim reasonable?

4. How would you classify Hogan's essay? Is it expository? Or is it, in part, an argument? Explain your answer. It might be helpful to compare Hogan's essay with Donna Maurer's (p. 581) to answer this question.

Janna Malamud Smith

Janna Malamud Smith, born in 1952 in Oregon, spent her childhood in Vermont and Boston. A psychoanalyst and writer, her books include My Father Is a Book *(2006), a study of her father, Bernard Malamud, short story writer and novelist.*

My Son, My Compass

We stopped eating red meat in our house. Our younger, teenage son convinced us that it was something we had to do. He read aloud from books, shocked us with disgusting descriptions, and explained the ethical, practical, and ecological issues. He ordered large pictures of skinned cows' heads from People for the Ethical Treatment of Animals, found a friend willing to accompany him, and picketed a Burger King. He expounded on the inhumanity of mass meat production.

Weren't we big on humane? The square peg of our practices didn't fit into the round hole of our proffered worldview, the one we'd been belaboring him with since birth: "Pat the bunny," not "Eat the bunny." We felt cornered; for us, his force was startling. The cute, bottle-fed, nuzzling calf we'd kept warm near the stove was back—a grown bull busting its horns right through our screen door without slowing.

Not that we were philosophically opposed to his propositions; we were simply accustomed to eating cows, pigs, and sheep. In fact, we really enjoyed red meat: roasted spring lamb marinated with garlic and mustard à la Julia Child (bless her carnivorous soul); large grilled hamburgers with ketchup and sour pickles. My husband and I had long fancied ourselves gourmands and had spent years together preparing exacting recipes from French cookbooks. (You try convincing a pharmacist that the saltpeter—read: gunpowder ingredient—you wish to buy will be used to preserve a duck.) We were proud of our sense of culinary adventure.

Janna Malamud Smith, "My Son, My Compass." Originally published in *Organic Style* magazine, November, 2004. Copyright © 2004 by Janna Malamud Smith. Reprinted by permission of Miriam Altshuler Literary Agency, on behalf of Janna Malamud Smith.

Until you have raised a child, it is hard to comprehend how unsettling it is the first time you take moral direction from him. I'm not talking about instruction, such as how to skip tracks on the CD player or turn on the new computer. The feeling I describe is more fundamental. There is something about the momentous emotional occasion of giving birth to—or adopting—a child that creates a sweeping, elaborate frieze. You become the heroic protector holding off the attacking centaurs. However sturdy your fragile infant grows, you are still on that pediment: carved in stone, directing his view, your whole body and soul curved around him.

But somehow, in the middle of this tale, our boy departed from our story line. All at once, he led, and shouted to us to follow. He declared himself, voice trembling, a vegan, knowing we did not approve. He renounced not just meat, but fish, milk, cheese, eggs, honey, and leather products. He bought cloth sneakers and made a wallet out of duct tape. He started reading food labels, spotting hidden by-products such as ground-up cow udder in jars of tomato sauce.

I was beside myself—on one hand, feeling hassled by his assertions; on the other, fearful of his becoming malnourished or being put on some FBI domestic terrorism list. I felt I had fallen down a rabbit hole and landed in a world dominated by a tyrannical zealot who believed tempeh was food. He suffered, I said to my husband, from a left-wing, overprivileged-child eating disorder.

Or did he? I wondered, lying in bed, sleepless, worrying about protein deficiency. Could he be right? Or partly right? "Human beings have always eaten meat," I had challenged him. "Our bodies need animal protein."

"Mom, people needed any food they could get in the past. We don't. We have plenty of vegetable proteins, and vitamins and supplements. Half the water used in this country goes for raising beef. And think of all the animal waste running into the rivers. It's not right. It's not right to bring animals into the world in crowded cages where they never walk or see daylight; to treat living creatures as if they were nothing more than industrial objects."

Trying to come to terms with my split feelings, I thought about a lecture on aging I'd heard by George Vaillant, a Harvard professor who studied adaptation. For decades, he had tracked and repeatedly interviewed hundreds of men, seeking to decipher who fared well or badly across time, and why. One trait the successful fellows held in common was that they allowed themselves to learn from their children.

"Easy for him to say," I grumbled. Yet, in spite of my grouchiness, the penny dropped. The years had repositioned me. At 12, I attended my first rally with Martin Luther King Jr. I marched against the Vietnam war and for women's rights. But time had reset the stage. At 50, mine had become the outdated worldview in need of reform. Not only was I being called upon to loosen my protective grip on my charge, I needed to reconsider my position in the universe. Like a skilled karate artist, our son took the very premises we'd espoused to him and pushed them further, until we toppled.

So ours is now a household, and a menu, in transition. My husband and I still eat fish and, occasionally, fowl, but our boy's efforts have fundamentally altered out thinking, and our diets. Most nights we cook vegan dishes. No tempeh yet, but red lentil soup; pinto bean, onion, salsa, and brown-rice burritos; baked winter squash stuffed with apples, raisins, and walnuts; pasta with spinach, sun-dried tomatoes, and artichokes. A fresh cornucopia.

I scan vegan cookbooks for recipes offering flavor and enough nutrition to appease the bones of a growing teenager. Some taste delicious. Others don't. Some evenings, walking around my neighborhood, the smell of meat grilling starts me hallucinating about flank steak marinated in garlic, soy sauce, and grated orange peel, seared medium rare, sliced on the bias, nicely salted. My husband and I sometimes whisper conspiratorially about sneaking away to, say, Italy for a delicate slice of prosciutto wrapped around a bit of perfectly ripened melon.

But the truth is, in spite of an occasional longing, I feel healthy consuming less animal protein—lighter, closer to the earth, in tune with an older Mediterranean diet. And I enjoy with my family a peaceable sense that by eating lower on the food chain, we're doing the right thing for the environment, and for livestock. It's gratifying to let a compelling argument alter your behavior. It gives you hope. If you can change, the world can. Every so often, I still annoy our son by lecturing him about some esoteric peril of vegan nutrition I've discovered on the Web. Every so often, he annoys me by proselytizing: "Couldn't you please stop eating dead birds, Mom?" But mostly, we are all quietly satisfied to discover our family making its way together, finding our footing through two transitions: red meat to legumes, and sons to men.

Joining the Conversation:
Critical Thinking and Writing

1. Why, according to Smith, did her son become a vegan? What was Smith's initial reaction?

2. At the time Smith wrote her essay, how had the family's eating habits changed, and how did Smith feel about the change?

3. Describe and then evaluate Smith's style, beginning with the title of her essay. Did you find any humorous passages? Any passages you found unclear? Be sure to include them in your description and analysis.

4. In her last paragraph, Smith writes "It's gratifying to let a compelling argument alter your behaviour." In your own family, was there ever an occasion

when a "compelling argument" by a child altered the behavior of the adults? If so, write a brief account (500 words) explaining what happened, and why.

5. Smith also claims that the change in her family's behavior satisfies her because "It gives you hope. If you can change, the world can." Do you agree? Write a brief essay (500 words) summarizing Smith's argument and explaining why you agree with Smith on this point, or not.

Jacob Alexander

In the following research essay, Jacob Alexander, a Tufts University undergraduate, uses the APA form of in-text citations, which are clarified by a list headed "References."

Jacob Alexander

Professor Louis

Writing 1B: Environmental Issues

May 2, 2004

Nitrite: Preservative or Carcinogen?

Abstract

Sodium nitrite, added to cured meats and smoked fish as a color fixative, can combine in meat and in the stomach to form a powerful carcinogen. Some argue that restrictions placed in recent years by the FDA on nitrite use have significantly reduced the health threat nitrite poses; however, recent research suggests that it may still be a significant cancer cause. The public must remain cautious about nitrite consumption.

Nitrite: Preservative or Carcinogen?

According to Julie Miller Jones, a professor of food and nutrition and the author of Food Safety, "average Americans eat their weight in food additives every year" (cited in Murphy, 1996, p. 140). There are approximately fifteen thousand additives currently in use (National Cancer Institute Fact Sheet [NCI], 1996); many of them are known to be dangerous. Of these, nitrites may be among the most hazardous of all.

In this country, ham, bacon, corned beef, salami, bologna, lox, and other cold cuts and smoked fish almost invariably contain sodium nitrite. In fact, one-third of the federally inspected meat and fish we consume--more than seven billion pounds of it every year--contains this chemical (Jacobson, 1987, p. 169).

Just how dangerous are nitrites, and why--if they really <u>are</u> dangerous--does the food industry still use them? Both questions are difficult to answer. Some experts say that nitrites protect consumers from botulism, a deadly disease that can be caused by spoiled food, and that "the benefits of nitrite additives outweigh the risks" (Edlefsen & Brewer, no date). Others argue that the dangers nitrites once posed have been significantly reduced--even eliminated--by restrictions placed on their use by the Food and Drug Administration. Nevertheless, the evidence has long suggested that nitrites are linked to stomach cancer; recent research has linked nitrites to leukemia and brain tumors as well (Warrick, 1994; Legator & Daniel, 1995). Perhaps the only certain conclusions one can reach are that the effects of nitrite on the human body are still to some degree uncertain--and that to protect themselves, consumers must be cautious and informed.

That nitrite is a poison has been clear for almost three decades. In 1974, Jacqueline Verrett, who worked for the FDA for fifteen years, and Jean Carper reported on several instances of people poisoned by accidental overdoses of nitrites in cured meats:

> In Buffalo, New York, six persons were hospitalized with "cardiovascular collapse" after they ate blood sausage which contained excessive amounts of nitrites . . . In New Jersey, two persons died and many others were critically poisoned after eating fish illegally loaded with nitrites. In New Orleans, ten youngsters between the ages of one and a half and five became seriously ill . . . after eating wieners or bologna

overnitrited by a local meat-processing firm; one wiener that was obtained later from the plant was found to contain a whopping 6,570 parts per million. In Florida, a three-year-old boy died after eating hot dogs with three times greater nitrite concentration than the government allows. (pp. 138–39)

The chemical has the unusual and difficult-to-replace quality of keeping meat a fresh-looking pink throughout the cooking, curing, and storage process (Assembly of Life Science, 1982, p. 3). The nitrous acid from the nitrite combines with the hemoglobin in the blood of the meat, fixing its red color so that the meat does not turn the tired brown or gray natural to cured meats.

Unfortunately, it does much the same thing in humans. Although most of the nitrite passes through the body unchanged, a small amount is released into the bloodstream. This combines with the hemoglobin in the blood to form a pigment called methemoglobin, which cannot carry oxygen. If enough oxygen is incapacitated, a person dies. The allowable amount of nitrite in a quarter pound of meat has the potential to incapacitate between 1.4 and 5.7 percent of the hemoglobin in an average-sized adult (Verrett & Carper, 1974, pp. 138–39). One of the problems with nitrite poisoning is that infants under a year, because of the quantity and makeup of their blood, are especially susceptible to it.

If the consumer of nitrite isn't acutely poisoned (and granted, such poisonings are rare), his or her blood soon returns to normal and this particular danger passes: the chemical, however, has long-term effects, as research conducted in the 1970's clearly established. Nitrite can cause headaches in people who are especially sensitive to it, an upsetting symptom considering that in rats who ate it regularly for a period of time it has produced lasting "epileptic like" changes in the brain--abnormalities which showed up when the rats were fed only a little more than an American fond of cured meats might eat (Wellford, 1973, p. 173).

Experiments with chickens, cattle, sheep, and rats have shown that nitrite, when administered for several days, inhibits the ability of the liver to store vitamin A and carotene (Hunter, 1972, p. 90). And finally, Nobel laureate Joshua Lederberg points out that, in microorganisms, nitrite enters the DNA. "If it does the same thing in humans," he says, "it will cause mutant genes." Geneticist Bruce Ames adds, "If out of one million people, one person's genes are mutant, that's a serious problem. . . . If we're filling ourselves now with mutant genes, they're going to be around for generations" (cited in Zwerdling, 1971, pp. 34–35).

By far the most alarming characteristic of nitrite, however, is that in test tubes, in meats themselves, in animal stomachs, and in human stomachs--wherever a mildly acidic solution is present--it can combine with amines to form nitrosamines. And nitrosamines are carcinogens. Even the food industry and the agencies responsible for allowing the use of nitrite in foods admit that nitrosamines cause cancer. Edlefsen and Brewer, writing recently for the National Food Safety Database, note that "over 90 percent of the more than 300 known nitrosamines in foods have been shown to cause cancer in laboratory animals." They continue: "No case of human cancer has been shown to result from exposure to nitrosamines," but they acknowledge that "indirect evidence indicates that humans would be susceptible" (no date).

It is important to note that nitrite alone, when fed to rats on an otherwise controlled diet, does not induce cancer. It must first combine with amines to form nitrosamines. Considering, however, that the human stomach has the kind of acidic solution in which amines and nitrites readily combine, and considering as well that amines are present in beer, wine, cereals, tea, fish, cigarette smoke, and a long list of drugs including antihistamines, tranquilizers, and even oral contraceptives, it is hardly surprising to find that nitrosamaines have been found in human stomachs.

When animals are fed amines in combination with nitrite, they developed cancer with a statistical consistency that is frightening, even to scientists. Verrett and Carper report that after feeding animals 250 parts per million (ppm) of nitrites and amines, William Lijinsky, a scientist at Oak Ridge National Laboratory,

> found malignant tumors in 100 percent of the test animals within six months. . . . "Unheard of," he says. . . . "You'd usually expect to find 50 percent at the most. And the cancers are all over the place--in the brain, lung, pancreas, stomach liver, adrenals, intestines. We open up the animals and they are a bloody mess." [He] believes that nitrosamines, because of their incredible versatility in inciting cancer, may be the key to an explanation for the mass production of cancer in seemingly dissimilar populations. In other words, nitrosamines may be a common factor in cancer that has been haunting us all these years. (1974, p. 136)

Verrett and Carper (1974, pp. 43–46) list still more damning evidence. Nitrosamines have caused cancer in rats, hamsters, mice, guinea pigs, dogs, and monkeys. It has been proven that nitrosamines of over a hundred kinds cause cancer. Nitrosamines have been shown to pass through the placenta from the mother to cause cancer in the offspring. Even the lowest levels of nitrosamines ever tested have produced cancer in animals. When animals are fed nitrite and amines separately over a period of time, they develop cancers of the same kind and at the same frequency as animals fed the corresponding nitrosamines already formed.

To address these problems (and in response to intense public concern), in 1978, the FDA ruled that a reducing agent, such as ascorbic acid, must be added to products containing nitrite; the reducing agent inhibits the formation of nitrosamines (Edlefsen & Brewer, no date). And in the last two decades, at least, the furor over nitrite seems as a consequence to have abated. In fact, a 1997 article published by the

International Food Information Council Foundation (a group primarily sponsored by the food industry, according to information provided by its Website), celebrates nitrite as a "naturally-derived" substance that, according to the American Academy of Science, has never been found to cause cancer. On the contrary, the anonymous author states, nitrite does many good things for consumers; it may even help to fight cancer: "it safeguards cured meats against the most deadly foodborne bacterium known to man" and helps with "promoting blood clotting, healing wounds and burns and boosting immune function to kill tumor cells."

Other experts are less certain that reducing agents have entirely solved the nitrosamine problem. The Consumer's Dictionary of Food Additives notes that one common agent, sodium ascorbate, which is added to the brine in which bacon is cured, "offers only a partial barrier because ascorbate is soluble in fatty tissues" (Winter, 1994, p. 282). But in the wake of several studies it is unclear that "inhibiting" the formation of nitrosamines actually makes nitrites safe to consume.

The Los Angeles Times reports that one of these studies, conducted by John Peters, an epidemiologist at USC, found that "children who eat more than 12 hot dogs per month have nine times the normal risk of developing childhood leukemia" (Warrick, 1994). Interestingly, the study was focused not on nitrites, but rather on electromagnetic fields. "Dietary exposure to processed or cured meats was part of a little side questionnaire to our study on electromagnetic fields." Peters said. "We were as surprised as anyone by the hot dogs findings. . . . It was the biggest risk for anything we saw in the study--about four times the risk for EMF's" (cited in Warrick, 1994).

In another of these recent studies, hot dogs were linked to brain tumors: researchers found that "children born to mothers who ate at least one hot dog per week while pregnant have twice the risk of developing brain tumors, as do children whose fathers ate too many hot dogs before conception" (Warrick, 1994). Dr. M. Legator and Amanda Daniel comment that "these studies confirm thirty years worth of scientific research on the cancer causing properties of preserved meats and fish" (1995).

The question, then, is why nitrite continues to be used in so much of the meat Americans consume. Although nitrite adds a small amount to flavor, it is used primarily for cosmetic purposes. Food producers are of course also quick to point out that nitrite keeps people safe from botulinum in cured meats, an argument to which the public may be particularly susceptible because of a number of recent and serious food scares. Nevertheless, some evidence suggests that the protection nitrite offers is both unnecessary and ineffective.

Michael Jacobson explains the preservative action of nitrite:

> Nitrite makes botulinum spores sensitive to heat. When foods are treated with nitrite and then heated, any botulinum spores that may be present are killed. In the absence of nitrite, spores can be inactivated only at temperatures that ruin the meat products. . . . Nitrite's preservative action is particularly important in foods that are not cooked after they leave the factory, such as ham, because these offer an oxygen-free environment, the kind in which botulinum can grow. The toxin does not pose a danger in foods that are always well cooked, such as bacon, because the toxin would be destroyed in cooking.
>
> Laboratory studies demonstrate clearly that nitrite can kill botulinum, but whether it actually does in commercially processed meat has been called into question. Frequently, the levels used may be too low to do anything but contribute to the color. (1987, p. 165)

Bratwurst and breakfast sausage are manufactured now without nitrite because they don't need to be colored pink; bacon is always cooked thoroughly enough to kill off any botulinum spores present. Certainly there are other ways of dealing with botulism. High or low temperature prevents botulism. What nitrite undoubtedly does lower, however, is the level of care and sanitation necessary in handling meat.

Clearly, the use of nitrite adds immeasurably to the profit-making potential of the meat industry, but why does the federal government allow this health hazard in our food? In the first place, nitrite and nitrate have been used for so long that it is hard for lawmakers to get past their instinctive reaction. "But that's the way we've always done it." Indeed, the Romans used saltpeter, a nitrate, to keep meat and, as early as 1899, scientists discovered that the nitrate breaks down into nitrite and that it is the nitrite which actually preserves the red color in meats (Jacobson, 1987, pp. 164–65). Thus, by the time the U.S. Department of Agriculture and the Food and Drug Administration got into the business of regulating food, they tended to accept nitrite and nitrate as givens.

A second reason for the inadequacy of regulation is that government mechanisms for protecting the consumer are full of curious loopholes. In 1958 Congress passed the Food Additive Amendment, including the Delaney Clause, which clearly states that additives should be banned if they induce cancer in laboratory animals. Unfortunately, however, the amendment does not apply to additives that were in use before it was passed, so, since nitrite and nitrate had already been in use for a long time, they were automatically included on the list of chemicals "Generally Recognized as Safe." To complicate matters further, nitrite in meat is regulated by the USDA, while nitrite in fish is under the jurisdiction of the FDA. And these agencies generally leave it to industry--the profit-maker--to establish whether or not an additive is safe. The final irony in this list of governmental errors is that the FDA depends heavily, for "independent" research and advice, on the food committees of the National Academy of Sciences, which Daniel Zwerdling claims are "like a Who's Who of the food and chemical industry" (1971, p. 34). (This, of course, is the organization cited in the anonymous web posting quoted above, the organization that holds that "nitrite levels in cured meat have not been linked to the development of human cancers.")

Clearly, consumers need to be informed; clearly, it is unwise to count on government agencies for protection against the dangers food additives may pose. Some experts continue to argue that nitrite is safe enough; Edelfson and Brewer, for example, cite a 1992 study by J. M. Jones that suggests that drinking beer exposes a consumer to more nitrite than does eating bacon--and that new car interiors are a significant source of nitrite as well.[1] Others recommend caution. One expert advises: "If you must eat nitrite-laced meats, include a food or drink high in vitamin C at the same time--for example, orange juice, grapefruit juice, cranberry juice, or lettuce" (Winter, 1994, p. 282). And, in fact, a study by a committee organized by the National Academy of Science strongly implies (Assembly, 1982, p. 12) that the government should develop a safe alternative to nitrites.

In the meantime, the chemical additive industry doesn't seem very worried that alternatives, such as biopreservatives, will pose a threat to its profits. An industry publication, "Chemical Marketing Reporter," recently reassured its readers by announcing that "around 82.5 million pounds of preservatives, valued at $133 million, were consumed in the US in 1991." The report also stated that "though the trend toward phasing out controversial preservatives like sulfites, nitrates and nitrites continues, natural substitutes remain expensive and often less than effective, making biopreservatives a distant threat" (Tollefson, 1995).

References

Assembly of Life Science. (1982). Alternatives to the current use of nitrite in food. Washington, DC: National Academy Press.

---

[1]Presumably the exposure here results from contact, not ingestion.

Edlefsen, M., & Brewer, M. S. (n.d.). The national food safety database. Nitrates/Nitrites. Retrieved May 6, 2004, from http://www.foodsafety.org/il/il1089.html

Hunter, B. T. (1972). Fact/book on food additives and your health. New Canaan, CT: Keats.

International Food Information Council Foundation. (1997). Nitrite: keeping food safe. Food Insight. Retrieved July 15, 2004, from http://ific.org/proactive/newsroom/release.vtml?id=18036

Jacobson, M. F. (1987). Eater's digest. Washington, DC: Center for Science in the Public Interest.

Legator, M., & Daniel, A. (1995). Reproductive systems can be harmed by toxic exposure. Galveston County Daily News. Retrieved May 6, 2004, from http://www.utmb.edu/toxics/newsp.htm#canen

Murphy, K. (1996, May 6). Do food additives subtract from health? Business Week, p. 140. Retrieved July 30, 1998, from LexisNexis.

National Cancer Institute (1996, June). NCI fact sheet. Food additives. Retrieved May 4, 2004, from http://nisc8a.uponn.edu/pdghtml/6/eng/600037.html

Tollefson, C. (1995. May 29). Stability preserved; preservatives; food additives '95. Chemical Marketing Reporter 247 (22) SR28. Retrieved May 6, 2004, from LexisNexis.

Verrett, J., & Carper, J. (1974). Eating may be hazardous to your health. New York: Simon and Schuster.

Warrick, P. (1994, June 8). A frank discussion. Los Angeles Times, El. Retrieved May 6, 2004, from LexisNexis.

Welford, H. (1973). Sowing the wind; a report from Ralph Nader's Center for Study of Responsible Law on food safety and the chemical harvest. New York: Bantam.

Winter, R. (1994). A consumer's dictionary of food additives (Updated 4th ed.). New York. Crown.

Zwerdling, D. (1971, June). Food pollution. Ramparts, 9(11), 31–37, 53–54.

Joining the Conversation:
Critical Thinking and Writing

1. Alexander begins his essay with a quotation. Do you think that was a good idea? Explain.

2. What is Alexander's thesis? Where in his essay do you find it stated or implied?

3. Why, considering the hazards of using nitrite to cure meat, does the food industry continue to use it? Where in his essay does Alexander offer answers to this question?

4. Do you consume hot dogs or other foods cured with nitrite? If so, has reading Alexander's essay given you food for thought?

Donna Maurer

Donna Maurer, author of Vegetarianism: Movement or Moment *(2002), has co-edited several books on food and nutrition. We reprint material that she contributed to* Encyclopedia of Food and Culture, *ed. Solomon H. Katz (2003).*

Vegetarianism

Varieties of Vegetarianism

A wide range of dietary practices falls under the rubric of "vegetarianism." People who practice the strictest version, veganism, do not use any animal products or by-products. They do not eat meat, poultry, or seafood, nor do they wear leather or wool. They avoid foods that contain such animal by-products as whey and gelatin and do not use products that have been tested on animals.

Other vegetarians limit their avoidances to food. For example, ovo-lacto vegetarians consume eggs and dairy products but not meat, poultry, and seafood. Ovo vegetarians do not consume dairy products, and lacto vegetarians consume dairy products but not eggs. Semivegetarians occasionally consume some or all animal products and may or may not consider themselves vegetarians. Studies suggest that semivegetarians outnumber "true" vegetarians by about four to one.

From *Encyclopedia of Food and Culture*, Volume 3, edited by Solomon H. Katz and William Woys Weaver, 2003. Reprinted with permission of Gale, a division of Thomson Learning.

These terms define the various types of vegetarians by what they do not consume. Consequently, many vegetarians are concerned that non-vegetarians view vegetarian diets as primarily prohibitive and restrictive. They emphasize that following a vegetarian diet often leads people to consume a wider variety of foods than many meat eaters do, as vegetarians often include a wider range of fruits, vegetables, grains, and legumes in their diets.

•   •   •

Characteristics of Contemporary Vegetarians

While vegetarians probably exhibit more differences than similarities, researchers have discerned several patterns regarding their social backgrounds and statuses. Vegetarians tend to come from predominantly middle-class backgrounds, and a substantially smaller percentage comes from lower social classes. This can be explained by the fact that people who have less money view meat as desirable and associate it with upward social mobility. Therefore, when they have discretionary income, they are likely to use it to purchase meat products. In North America meat is often associated with success and social status. People are only likely to reject meat once they have the opportunity to consume as much as they want.

Gender is another patterned feature of vegetarians in North America. Studies have consistently found that about 70 percent of all vegetarians are female. Several explanations are possible. First, the foods embraced by vegetarian diets are those already symbolically linked with feminine attributes, that is, foods that are light, low-fat, and not bloody (as people often equate blood with strength). For many people meat and masculinity are inextricably linked; therefore it is easier for women than for men to escape cultural expectations. In addition, women tend to be more concerned with weight loss, and many pursue a vegetarian diet as the means to that end. Finally, some researchers hold that women are more likely than men to hold a compassionate attitude toward animals, leading them to have more concern about killing animals for food. All of these factors contribute to the reality that women are more likely than men to become vegetarians.

Studies have suggested that vegetarians may share a variety of other characteristics as well. For example, while vegetarians are less likely than the general population to follow a conventional religion, they are more likely to describe themselves as spiritual and to practice some form of yoga or meditation. They are more likely to describe themselves as "liberal" and less likely to adhere to traditional values that embrace upholding the existing social order. They are also less likely than the general population to smoke cigarettes and drink alcohol. Yet it is important to point out that vegetarians are more different than similar in their social backgrounds, political beliefs, and health practices.

Reasons for Vegetarianism

People become vegetarians for a variety of reasons, including personal health, a concern for the treatment of farm animals and the environment, spiritual beliefs, and sometimes simply a physical disgust toward meat. Most commonly North Americans follow a gradual path toward vegetarianism that starts with a health motivation. They perceive that a vegetarian diet will give them more energy, will help them lose weight, or will assuage a health condition, such as heart disease or cancer. Other people become vegetarians out of a concern for the rights of animals or a belief that meat production causes devastating effects to the environment. Some grew up with or adopted a religion (for example, Hinduism, Jainism, Seventh Day Adventism) that encourages or requires a vegetarian diet. Still others are concerned with world hunger and take the view that many more people can be fed on a vegetarian diet than on a meat-based one.

People tend to first stop eating the foods they view as the most offensive or unhealthy. For most gradual vegetarians this is red meat. The typical path for a new vegetarian is to stop eating red meat first, then poultry, and then fish. Some move to further prohibitions by adopting a vegan lifestyle as they eliminate eggs, dairy products, and other animal by-products. As people progress along the vegetarian "path," they tend to adopt new reasons to support their lifestyle practices. Most commonly people begin with a health motivation and gradually become concerned with the humane treatment of animals and protecting the environment, and many develop a disgust response to meat products.

Joining the Conversation: Critical Thinking and Writing

1. How would you define vegetarianism? Do all vegetarians observe similar practices? If not, what is the range of vegetarian practices? If you do not know the answers to these questions, what sources might you use to retrieve reliable explanations?

2. Why, according to Maurer, do people become vegetarians?

3. A writing exercise (2 paragraphs): If you are a vegetarian, what do you consume (or refuse to consume) and what were your reasons for becoming vegetarian? If you are not a vegetarian, interview one or two vegetarians, and then explain their practices and their reasons.

Paul Goldberger

Paul Goldberger, formerly the architecture critic for the New York Times, *has contributed articles to various magazines, and is the author of many books about architecture.*

Quick! Before It Crumbles!

An Architecture Critic Looks at Cookie Architecture

Sugar Wafer (Nabisco)

There is no attempt to imitate the ancient forms of traditional, individually baked cookies here—this is a modern cookie through and through. Its simple rectangular form, clean and pure, just reeks of mass production and modern technological methods. The two wafers, held together by the sugar-cream filling, appear to float, and the Nabisco trademark, stamped repeatedly across the top, confirms that this is a machine-age object. Clearly the Sugar Wafer is the Mies van der Rohe of cookies.

Fig Newton (Nabisco)

This, too, is a sandwich but different in every way from the Sugar Wafer. Here the imagery is more traditional, more sensual even; a rounded form of cookie dough arcs over the fig concoction inside, and the whole is soft and pliable. Like all good pieces of design, it has an appropriate form for its use, since the insides of Fig Newtons can ooze and would not be held in place by a more rigid form. The thing could have had a somewhat different shape, but the rounded top is a comfortable, familiar image, and it's easy to hold. Not a revolutionary object but an intelligent one.

Milano (Pepperidge Farm)

This long, chocolate-filled cookie summons up contradictory associations. Its rounded ends suggest both the traditional image of stodgy ladyfingers and the curves of Art Deco, while the subtle yet forceful "V" embossed onto the surface creates an abstract image of force and movement. The "V" is the kind of ornament that wishes to appear modern without really being modern, which would have meant banning ornament altogether. That romantic symbolism of the modern was an Art Deco characteristic, of course; come to think of it the Milano is rather Art Deco in spirit.

Mallomar (Nabisco)

This marshmallow, chocolate and cracker combination is the ultimate sensual cookie—indeed, its resemblance to the female breast has been cited so often as to sound rather trite. But the cookie's imagery need not be read so literally—the voluptuousness of the form, which with its nipped waist rather resembles the New Orleans Superdome, is enough. Like all good pieces of design, the form of the cookie is primarily derived from functional needs, but with just enough distinction to make it instantly identifiable. The result is a cultural icon—the cookie equivalent, surely, of the Coke bottle.

Lorna Doone (Nabisco)

Like the Las Vegas casino that is overwhelmed by its sign, image is all in the Lorna Doone. It is a plain, simple cookie (of shortbread, in fact), but a cookie like all other cookies—except for its sign. The Lorna Doone logo, a four-pointed star with the cookie's name and a pair of fleur-de-lis-like decorations, covers the entire surface of the cookie in low relief. Cleverly, the designers of this cookie have placed the logo so that the points of the star align with the corners of the square, forcing one to pivot the cookie forty-five degrees, so that its shape appears instead to be a diamond. It is a superb example of the ordinary made extraordinary.

Oatmeal Peanut Sandwich (Sunshine)

If the Sugar Wafer is the Mies van der Rohe of cookies, this is the Robert Venturi—not pretentiously modern but, rather, eager to prove its ordinariness, its lack of real design, and in so zealous a way that it ends up looking far dowdier than a *really* ordinary cookie like your basic gingersnap. The Oatmeal Peanut Sandwich is frumpy, like a plump matron in a flower-print dress, or an old piece of linoleum. But it is frumpy in an intentional way and not by accident—one senses that the designers of this cookie knew the Venturi principle that the average user of architecture (read eater of cookies) is far more comfortable with plain, ordinary forms that do not require him to adjust radically any of his perceptions.

⟪ Joining the Conversation:
Critical Thinking and Writing

1. How seriously do you take these descriptions? Do they have any point, or are they sheer fooling around?

2. Explain, to someone who does not understand them, the references, in context, to Mies van der Rohe, Art Deco, the New Orleans Superdome, and Robert Venturi. If you had to do some research, explain what sources you used and how you located the sources. What difficulties, if any, did you encounter?

3. Explain Goldberger's final sentence on "Mallomar"; "The result is a cultural icon—the cookie equivalent, surely, of the Coke bottle."

4. Write a similar description of some cookie not discussed by Goldberger. Or write a description, along these lines, of a McDonald's hamburger, a BLT, and a hero sandwich. Other possibilities: a pizza, a bagel, and a taco.

Peter Singer and Jim Mason

Peter Singer, a professor of bio-ethics at Princeton University, became internationally known in 1973 with an essay on animal liberation. In his writings about animals Singer argues that if a creature can suffer, it deserves consideration. He has not argued—so far as we know—that human beings ought not to eat animals but he has argued that, given the horrific treatment of animals in farms and slaughterhouses, a vegetarian diet is a reasonable solution.

Jim Mason grew up on a family farm in Missouri. With Peter Singer he is the coauthor of Animal Factories *(1980) and the author of* Why We Are Destroying the Planet and Each Other *(1997).*

We reprint below an extract from a new book by Singer and Mason, The Way We Eat: Why Our Food Choices Matter *(2006). The authors introduce three families and examine their food choices. One of these families consists of Jake Hilliard (age 36), her husband, and their two small children, who live in Mabelvale, Arkansas. Jake does most of the family shopping at a Wal-Mart Supercenter because, she explains, it is hard to beat their prices and she can get everything at one stop.*

Wal-Mart: Everyday Low Prices—At What Cost?

If Jake's chicken is an iconic American food, the place she buys it is equally characteristic of America today. Wal-Mart is the biggest everything—world's largest grocer, world's largest retailer, world's largest corporation.

Short of being a nation, nothing gets bigger than that. (If Wal-Mart were a nation, it would have a bigger economy than 80 percent of the world's countries.) Each week, 138 million people go to one of Wal-Mart's 5,000 stores in the United States and nine other countries, giving the corporation annual sales of more than $300 billion. With a global workforce of 1.6 million, it is the largest private employer in the United States, as well as in Mexico and Canada. The ethics of what we eat encompasses not only how our food is produced, but also how our food is sold. If so many people do it, can there be anything wrong with shopping at Wal-Mart?

One reason for concern about Wal-Mart is simply its size. Wal-Mart already has 11 percent of all U.S. grocery store sales, and according to Merrill Lynch analyst Daniel Berry, by 2013 that figure is likely to rise to 21 percent.[1] Being the biggest buyer of food gives Wal-Mart a lot of clout over how the food it buys is produced. Do we really want a single corporation to have so great a sway over that? The answer might depend on how the corporation behaves.

No corporation as big as Wal-Mart can avoid criticism, and Wal-Mart gets so much flak that it has set up a "war room" to fight back.[2] So let's focus our discussion on something that Wal-Mart does not deny, and indeed boasts of: the way it seeks to drive down costs in order to provide "everyday low prices." As Wal-Mart CEO Lee Scott said to CNBC's David Faber when discussing Wal-Mart's approach to its suppliers, "The idea is that we say—we sit down with you and say, 'How do we take cost out of doing business with you.'"[3] As a result, according to a UBS-Warburg study, Wal-Mart has grocery prices 17 to 20 percent lower than other supermarkets. Our question is: In constantly striving to reduce costs, has Wal-Mart breached any ethical limits?

Low prices are a good thing. If customers like Jake pay less for their food at Wal-Mart than they would at another store, they have more money to spend on meeting their other needs, or, if they are so inclined, to increase their contributions to good causes. Low food prices are particularly good for the poor, who spend a higher proportion of their income on food than the rich. People living in poor areas often have few places to buy fresh food, and the stores they do have charge higher prices than stores in more affluent neighborhoods. When a Wal-Mart moves in—and Wal-Mart's stores are disproportionately located in the poorer parts of the country—that changes, and the poor can save significant sums.[4]

[1]Jennifer Waters, "Wal-Mart Grocery Share Seen Doubling," *CBS MarketWatch*, June 24, 2004, cited from RetailWire Discussions, www.retailwire.com/Discussions/Sngl_Discussion.cfm/9953.
[2]Michael Barbaro, "A New Weapon for Wal-Mart: A War Room," *New York Times*, November 1, 2005.
[3]John Dicker, *The United States of Wal-Mart*, Tarcher/Penguin, New York, 2005, p. 122.
[4]Pankaj Ghemawat and Ken Mark, "The Price Is Right," *New York Times*, August 3, 2005.

The positive value of a store with low prices can, however, turn negative [5] if the low prices are achieved by passing costs onto others. In 2004, Wal-Mart's spokesperson Mona Williams told *Forbes* that a full-time store assistant takes home around $18,000 annually. Some think this estimate is generous, but assuming that it is accurate, it still means that if the employee is the only income earner in a family of four, the family is living below the poverty line. According to documents released as part of a gender-discrimination suit against Wal-Mart, researchers found that the average non-salaried Wal-Mart associate in California gets nearly $2,000 in public welfare benefits each year, including health care, food stamps, and subsidized housing. If all California's retailers lowered their wages and benefits to Wal-Mart's level, that would pass an additional burden of $400 million to the state.[5] In 2005 Wal-Mart acknowledged that nearly half of the children of its employees either have no health insurance or are on Medicaid. Wal-Mart itself admits that for the national labor force as a whole, that figure is only one-third. M. Susan Chambers, a senior Wal-Mart executive who led the investigation that produced this finding, admits that she was "startled" by the discovery. Wal-Mart's critics would not have been. Wal-Mart subsequently announced that it would improve the health care benefits it offers its workers.[6]

Nevertheless, Wal-Mart says "it doesn't make sense to say that we cost taxpayers money" and then cites the substantial amounts of federal, state, and local taxes the corporation pays, including sales taxes.[7] But that's no answer to the charge. If Wal-Mart were replaced by stores that paid better wages and gave better health benefits, consumers would still buy food. So the various taxes Wal-Mart now pays would be paid by the corporations or family-owned businesses that sold the food Wal-Mart now sells—and their better-paid workers, instead of needing assistance from taxpayers, would pay taxes themselves.

Wal-Mart's impact on wages and benefits was most clearly shown in 2002 when it announced plans to open 40 Supercenters in California over the next three years. California was then a stronghold for Safeway, Albertsons, and Kroger, three of the largest grocery chains in the country. In contrast to Wal-Mart, which has succeeded in keeping unions out of its U.S. stores, these three chains have unionized workforces, and their workers were paid about 50 percent more than workers at Wal-Mart and had much better health insurance programs. The big three chains believed, with some justification, that these costs would be a fatal handicap in the coming battle to defend their market share against Wal-Mart. They therefore demanded that their workers accept a new contract that contained no wage increases and would require workers to contribute substantially to their health insurance. In effect, the workers were being asked to take a pay cut. The result

[5]John Dicker, *The United States of Wal-Mart*, Tarcher/Penguin, New York, 2005, p. 86.
[6]Michael Barbaro, "Wal-Mart to Expand Health Plan for Workers," *New York Times*, October 24, 2005; Reed Abelson, "Wal-Mart's Health Care Struggle Is Corporate America's Too," *New York Times*, October 29, 2005.
[7]"Wal-Mart Sets the Record Straight" www.walmartfacts.com/newsdesk/article.aspx?id=1091

was the biggest strike in California's history, but against their employers' fear of Wal-Mart, even 70,000 united workers could gain little. After 20 weeks on strike, they agreed to take a contract with reduced benefits. Wal-Mart, or the threat of it, was forcing wages and benefits down.

Wal-Mart applies a similar strategy of cost-reduction to its suppliers. Gib Carey is a partner with Bain & Co., a management consultant firm that has Wal-Mart suppliers among its clients. For many suppliers, Carey says, maintaining their business with Wal-Mart becomes indispensable, but it isn't easy to do so. "Year after year," Carey says, "for any product that is the same as what you sold them last year, Wal-Mart will say, 'Here's the price you gave me last year. Here's what I can get a competitor's product for. Here's what I can get a private-label version for. I want to see a better value that I can bring to my shopper this year. Or else I'm going to use that shelf space differently.' " As business writer Charles Fishman sums it up, "The Wal-Mart squeeze means vendors have to be as relentless and as microscopic as Wal-Mart is at managing their own costs. They need, in fact, to turn themselves into shadow versions of Wal-Mart itself."[8] As a result, suppliers of American-made goods often have to look for cheaper goods made in countries with lower wage costs. If they don't, Wal-Mart will go to a Chinese manufacturer and cut them out entirely. Wal-Mart acknowledges that it bought $18 billion worth of goods from China last year.

Is it wrong to buy goods from China if they can be made more cheaply there than in the U.S.? We don't think so. People in China, Bangladesh, and Indonesia need work too, and since they are, in general, poorer than Americans, they probably need it even more than Americans do. So we are not going to chastise Wal-Mart for buying goods made abroad. The issue is, rather, whether in countries with deep poverty and endemic corruption, the unremitting drive to reduce costs can stop short of sweatshop conditions that include hazards to workers' health, child labor, and debt bondage that verges on forced labor.

In this area, Wal-Mart acknowledges past mistakes. A 1993 *Dateline* exposé showed that clothes sold in Wal-Mart stores under a "Made in the USA" banner were actually made in Bangladesh, and, worse still, were made by child labor. Four years later it emerged that a Wal-Mart line of clothing brand-named Kathie Lee, after ABC morning show cohost Kathie Lee Gifford, was also made by factories that used child labor. Now, however, Wal-Mart insists that it has strict supplier standards that absolutely forbid the employment of anyone younger than 14. Yet Wal-Mart's standards still allow workers to be pushed very hard. Employees may be made to work for 72 hours in a six-day week—that's 12 hours a day, for six days solid—and to work for 14 hours in a single day.[9]

10

---

[8]Charles Fishman, "The Wal-Mart You Don't Know," *Fast Company*, December 2003, www.fastcompany.com/magazine/77/walmart.html; the quote from Gib Carey is also from this article.
[9]Wal-Mart Stores, Inc., "Standards for Suppliers," www.walmartstores.com/Files/Supplier Standards-June2005.pdf

In the minds of Wal-Mart's critics, however, the problem is more one of enforcement than of the standards Wal-Mart espouses. Some corporations, like Gap, allow independent organizations to inspect the foreign factories of its suppliers. Wal-Mart prefers to use only inspectors it hires. Their impartiality can be questioned.

Wal-Mart is a member of the Food Marketing Institute and as such has been taking part in the discussions that this Institute and the National Council of Chain Restaurants have been holding to set standards for animal welfare. As we saw when looking at McDonald's, the move to set standards was triggered by measures taken first by McDonald's and then matched by other chain restaurants. In many areas of animal production, the FMI/NCCR standards do little more than describe existing factory farm practices, although in a few places they tinker with some of the details, to the modest benefit of the animals. For example, they adopt wholesale most of the National Chicken Council's Animal Welfare Guidelines, which, as we have seen, give chickens a space allowance the size of a standard sheet of typing paper, permit their beaks to be seared off, and allow the breeder birds to be kept half-starved. They also allow catchers to pick up the birds by one leg and dangle five live chickens from each hand.[10] Regrettably, as we have already seen, there is a tension between strong animal welfare policies and "everyday low prices." We'll learn more about that in Part II, when we consider the animal welfare standards being set by Whole Foods Market, a food retailer at the other end of the spectrum from Wal-Mart.

In his book *The United States of Wal-Mart*, John Dicker writes that the success of Wal-Mart says something about us: "The cult of low prices has become so ingrained in the consumer culture that deep discounts are no longer novelties. They are entitlements."[11] Bargain-seeking seems to be such a basic aspect of human nature that to question it can appear quixotic. But at Wal-Mart, the bargains hide costs to taxpayers, the community, animals, and the environment. That is why, despite the undoubted benefits of Wal-Mart's low prices, a very large ethical questionmark hangs over buying our food at Wal-Mart.

Joining the Conversation: Critical Thinking and Writing

1. Do you think Singer and Mason are fair? Support your response by citing a few sentences or passages from their essay.

2. In paragraph 6 the authors say that Wal-Mart does not adequately answer the charge that it costs taxpayers money. Your view? (Reread paragraphs 5 and 6 carefully.)

---

[10]Food Marketing Institute, "Status FMI-NCCR Animal Welfare Guidelines, Updated May 2005," www.fmi.org/animal_welfare/guideline_status_chart_May_2005.pdf
[11]John Dicker, *The United States of Wal-Mart*, Tarcher/Penguin, New York, 2005, p. 213.

3. Judging from this essay, do you think Wal-Mart's practices are ethical? Ethical but ungenerous? Unethical? Good business? Or what?

4. In paragraph 9 the authors ask, "Is it wrong to buy goods from China if they can be made more cheaply there than in the U.S?" Their answer to the question—based on a reason that perhaps surprised you—is "We don't think so." Your answer? And your reasons? By the way, what do you think of *their* reason why it is not wrong to buy goods that are made cheaply abroad?

5. In their final paragraph the authors use the word "quixotic." If you don't know the meaning of the word, check a dictionary. Do you think Singer and Mason are quixotic? Explain.

6. Singer is a professor. If he taught at your institution, would you be eager to take a course with him? Explain.

Sheldon Richman

Sheldon Richman, a libertarian, is the editor of The Freeman, *published by the Foundation for Economic Education, and the author of several books, including* Why We Must Abolish the Income Tax.

The *Chutzpah* of Wal-Mart's Critics

When critics attack a big, successful corporation no matter what it does, maybe it's the critics who have the problem. Wal-Mart pleases tens of millions of customers every day and provides desirable jobs to thousands of workers. The company is a blessing particularly to the "working families" whom the politicians and social activists love to champion with words. Yet these same politicians and activists have a bottomless bag of charges against Wal-Mart. In their eyes nothing the corporation does is right.

Consider this: Wal-Mart is the biggest corporate donor in the country. The Foundation Center says the Wal-Mart Foundation is second to none in contributing money to charitable causes, with annual donations totaling $120 million. If for no other reason, you'd think this would win some plaudits from Wal-Mart's critics—and you'd be wrong.

According to the National Committee for Responsive Philanthropy (NCRP), Wal-Mart's efforts hardly qualify as charity at all. "Unfortunately, their philanthropy is more about corporate advertising than it is about helping nonprofits or communities." That's how NCRP deputy director Jeffrey Krehely sees it. Anyone surprised?

Sheldon Richman, "The *Chutzpah* of Wal-Mart's Critics." Posted on The Future of Freedom Foundation website, August 12, 2005. Reprinted by permission of The Future of Freedom Foundation.

It seems that Wal-Mart's giving is too locally oriented. Store managers pick the beneficiaries. Now this is a funny sort of criticism, since Wal-Mart is routinely accused of destroying communities. Yet Wal-Mart gives lots of small donations of the Little League, Girl Scouts, United Way, literacy programs, teacher recognition, police and fire departments, and the Children's Miracle Network, an alliance of children's hospitals. How cynical! says the NCRP. It's all geared to make the company look good! Why isn't it contributing to international causes?

Whatever happened to "think globally, act locally"? Smell some   5
hypocrisy here?

Wal-Mart has also been criticized for giving money to 261 women's clinics, some of which don't approve of abortion, and for giving money to the Sons of Confederate Veterans, which, while condemning racism, supports use of the Confederate Battle Flag.

But this issue is not about whom Wal-Mart gives money to or how much. One can make a case that corporations shouldn't engage in philanthropy at all. A corporation is owned by its shareholders, who buy stock to increase their wealth. Corporate money given away is money that cannot be paid in dividends or used to improve the company, which in turn would raise the stock price. Thus, donated money is diverted from shareholders, employees, and customers, who are perfectly capable of giving to charity if they choose.

On the other hand, charity can create goodwill, which is good for shareholders and employees. At any rate, if shareholders think the company diverts too much money from the business, they can sell their stock and invest elsewhere. Obviously that isn't happening.

The real issue here is the chutzpah of Wal-Mart's critics. The NCRP supports the estate tax, opposes income-tax cuts, and favors government intervention in private economic affairs. Thus, ironically, if the NCRP and its ilk had their way, Wal-Mart would have far less money to contribute. As Ayn Rand wrote in *The Fountainhead*, "Men have been taught that the highest virtue is not to achieve, but to give. Yet one cannot give that which has not been created. Creation comes before distribution—or there will be nothing to distribute. The need of the creator comes before the need of any possible beneficiary. Yet we are taught to admire the second-hander who dispenses gifts he has not produced above the man who made the gifts possible. We praise an act of charity. We shrug at an act of achievement."

The criticism of Wal-Mart amounts to people telling other people   10
who satisfy countless consumers every day what to do with their money.

 ## Joining the Conversation:
Critical Thinking and Writing

1. Exactly what is *chutzpah*? (Check a dictionary if you are in doubt.) Why is Richman's title better than—or worse than—a title with some synonym that you might substitute for *chutzpah*?

2. Does Richman's first paragraph provide an effective opening? Why, or why not?

3. What is your response to paragraph 6? Do you find the actions that Richman specifies objectionable? Why, or why not?

4. What is Richman's thesis? Does he offer enough evidence to support it? Be specific.

5. In paragraph 7 Richman quotes Ayn Rand. Do you find the quotation effective? (Note that our question is *not* "Do you agree with Rand"; rather, it concerns Richman's use of the quotation.)

6. Evaluate paragraph 10 as a concluding paragraph.

7. If you have read Singer and Mason (page 587), do you believe that they exhibit the *chutzpah* that Richman attributes to Wal-Mart's critics? Explain.

Jonathan Swift

Jonathan Swift (1667–1745) was born in Ireland of an English family. He was ordained in the Church of Ireland in 1694, and in 1714 he became dean of St. Patrick's Cathedral, Dublin. He wrote abundantly on political and religious topics, often motivated (in his own words) by "savage indignation." It is ironic that Gulliver's Travels, *the masterpiece by this master of irony, is most widely thought of as a book for children.*

From the middle of the sixteenth century, the English regulated the Irish economy so that it would enrich England. Heavy taxes and other repressive legislation impoverished Ireland, and in 1728, the year before Swift wrote "A Modest Proposal," Ireland was further weakened by a severe famine. Swift, deeply moved by the injustice, the stupidity, and the suffering that he found in Ireland, adopts the disguise or persona of an economist and offers an ironic suggestion on how Irish families may improve their conditions.

A Modest Proposal

For Preventing the Children of Poor People in Ireland from Being a Burden to Their Parents or Country, and for Making Them Beneficial to the Public

It is a melancholy object to those who walk through this great town or travel in the country, when they see the streets, the roads, and cabin doors, crowded with beggars of the female sex, followed by three, four, or six children, all in rags and importuning every passenger for an alms. These mothers, instead of being able to work for their honest livelihood, are forced to employ all their time in strolling to beg sustenance for their helpless infants: who as they grow up either turn thieves for want of work, or leave their dear native country to fight for the pretender in Spain, or sell themselves to the Barbadoes.

I think it is agreed by all parties that this prodigious number of children in the arms, or on the backs, or at the heels of their mothers, and frequently of their fathers, is in the present deplorable state of the kingdom a very great additional grievance; and, therefore, whoever could find out a fair, cheap, and easy method of making these children sound, useful members of the commonwealth, would deserve so well of the public as to have his statue set up for a preserver of the nation.

But my intention is very far from being confined to provide only for the children of professed beggars; it is of a much greater extent, and shall take in the whole number of infants at a certain age who are born of parents in effect as little able to support them as those who demand our charity in the streets.

As to my own part, having turned my thoughts for many years upon this important subject, and maturely weighed the several schemes of our projectors, I have always found them grossly mistaken in their computation. It is true, a child just dropped from its dam may be supported by her milk for a solar year, with little other nourishment; at most not above the value of 2s.,[1] which the mother may certainly get, or the value in scraps, by her lawful occupation of begging; and it is exactly at one year old that I propose to provide for them in such a manner as instead of being a charge upon their parents or the parish, or wanting food and raiment for the rest of their lives, they shall on the contrary contribute to the feeding, and partly to the clothing, of many thousands.

There is likewise another great advantage in my scheme, that it will prevent those voluntary abortions, and that horrid practice of women murdering their bastard children, alas! too frequent among us! sacrificing the poor innocent babes I doubt more to avoid the expense than the shame, which would move tears and pity in the most savage and inhuman breast.

The number of souls in this kingdom being usually reckoned one million and a half, of these I calculate there may be about 200,000 couple whose wives are breeders; from which number I subtract 30,000 couple who are able to maintain their own children (although I apprehend there cannot be so many, under the present distress of the kingdom); but this being granted, there will remain 170,000 breeders. I again subtract 50,000 for those women who miscarry, or whose children die by accident or disease within the year. There only remain 120,000 children of poor parents annually born. The question therefore is, how this number shall be reared and provided for? which, as I have already said, under the present situation of affairs, is utterly impossible by all the methods hitherto proposed. For we can neither employ them in handicraft or agriculture; we neither build houses (I mean in the country) nor cultivate land; they can very seldom pick up a livelihood by stealing, till they arrive at six years

5

---

[1]**2s** Two shillings. Later in the essay, "£" and "1" stand for pounds and "d" for pence. (Editors' note)

old, except where they are of towardly parts; although I confess they learn the rudiments much earlier; during which time they can, however, be properly looked upon only as probationers; as I have been informed by a principal gentleman in the country of Cavan, who protested to me that he never knew above one or two instances under the age of six, even in a part of the kingdom so renowned for the quickest proficiency in that art.

I am assured by our merchants, that a boy or a girl before twelve years old is no saleable commodity; and even when they come to this age they will not yield above 3l. or 3l. 2s. 6d. at most on the exchange; which cannot turn to account either to the parents or kingdom, the charge of nutriment and rags having been at least four times that value.

I shall now therefore humbly propose my own thoughts, which I hope will not be liable to the least objection.

I have been assured by a very knowing American of my acquaintance in London, that a young healthy child well nursed is at a year old a most delicious, nourishing, and wholesome food, whether stewed, roasted, baked, or broiled; and I make no doubt that it will equally serve in a fricassee or a ragout.

I do therefore humbly offer it to public consideration that of the 120,000 children already computed, 20,000 may be reserved for breed, whereof only one-fourth part to be males; which is more than we allow to sheep, black cattle, or swine; and my reason is, that these children are seldom the fruits of marriage, a circumstance not much regarded by our savages; therefore one male will be sufficient to serve four females. That the remaining 100,000 may, at a year old, be offered in sale to the persons of quality and fortune through the kingdom; always advising the mother to let them suck plentifully in the last month, so as to render them plump and fat for a good table. A child will make two dishes at an entertainment for friends; and when the family dines alone, the fore or hind quarter will make a reasonable dish, and seasoned with a little pepper or salt will be very good boiled on the fourth day, especially in winter.

I have reckoned upon a medium that a child just born will weigh 12 pounds, and in a solar year, if tolerably nursed, will increase to 28 pounds.

I grant this food will be somewhat dear, and therefore very proper for landlords, who, as they have already devoured most of the parents, seem to have the best title to the children.

Infant's flesh will be in season throughout the year, but more plentiful in March, and a little before and after: for we are told by a grave author, an eminent French physician, that fish being a prolific diet, there are more children born in Roman Catholic countries about nine months after Lent than at any other season; therefore, reckoning a year after Lent, the markets will be more glutted than usual, because the number of popish infants is at least three to one in this kingdom: and therefore it will have one other collateral advantage, by lessening the number of papists among us.

I have already computed the charge of nursing a beggar's child (in which list I reckon all cottagers, laborers, and four-fifths of the farmers) to be about 2s. per annum, rags included; and I believe no gentleman would repine to give 10s. for the carcass of a good fat child, which, as I have said, will make four dishes of excellent nutritive meat, when he has only some particular friend or his own family to dine with him. Thus the squire will learn to be a good landlord, and grow popular among the tenants; the mother will have 8s. net profit, and be fit for work till she produces another child.

Those who are more thrifty (as I must confess the times require) may flay the carcass; the skin of which artificially dressed will make admirable gloves for ladies, and summer boots for fine gentlemen.

15

As to our city of Dublin, shambles may be appointed for this purpose in the most convenient parts of it, and butchers we may be assured will not be wanting: although I rather recommend buying the children alive, and dressing them hot from the knife as we do roasting pigs.

A very worthy person, a true lover of his country, and whose virtues I highly esteem, was lately pleased in discoursing on this matter to offer a refinement upon my scheme. He said that many gentlemen of this kingdom, having of late destroyed their deer, he conceived that the want of venison might be well supplied by the bodies of young lads and maidens, not exceeding fourteen years of age nor under twelve; so great a number of both sexes in every country being now ready to starve for want of work and service; and these to be disposed of by their parents, if alive, or otherwise by their nearest relations. But with due deference to so excellent a friend and so deserving a patriot, I cannot be altogether in his sentiments; for as to the males, my American acquaintance assured me from frequent experience that their flesh was generally tough and lean, like that of our schoolboys by continual exercise, and their taste disagreeable; and to fatten them would not answer the charge. Then as to the females, it would, I think, with humble submission be a loss to the public, because they soon would become breeders themselves: and besides, it is not improbable that some scrupulous people might be apt to censure such a practice (although indeed very unjustly), as a little bordering upon cruelty; which, I confess, has always been with me the strongest objection against any project, how well soever intended.

But in order to justify my friend, he confessed that this expedient was put into his head by the famous Psalmanazar, a native of the island Formosa, who came from thence to London about twenty years ago: and in conversation told my friend, that in his country when any young person happened to be put to death, the executioner sold the carcass to persons of quality as a prime dainty; and that in his time the body of a plump girl of fifteen, who was crucified for an attempt to poison the emperor, was sold to his imperial majesty's prime minister of state, and other great mandarins of the court, in joints from the gibbet, at 400 crowns. Neither indeed can I deny, that if the same use were made of several plump young girls in this town, who without one single groat to their fortunes cannot stir abroad without a chair, and appear at the playhouse and assemblies in foreign fineries which they never will pay for, the kingdom would not be the worse.

Some persons of a desponding spirit are in great concern about that vast number of poor people, who are aged, diseased, or maimed, and I have been desired to employ my thoughts what course may be taken to ease the nation of so grievous an encumbrance. But I am not in the least pain upon that matter, because it is very well known that they are every day dying and rotting by cold and famine, and filth and vermin, as fast as can be reasonably expected. And as to the young laborers, they are now in as hopeful a condition: they cannot get work, and consequently pine away for want of nourishment, to a degree that if at any time they are accidentally hired to common labor, they have not strength to perform it; and thus the country and themselves are happily delivered from the evils to come.

I have too long digressed, and therefore shall return to my subject. I think the advantages by the proposal which I have made are obvious and many, as well as of the highest importance. 20

For first, as I have already observed, it would greatly lessen the number of papists, with whom we are yearly overrun, being the principal breeders of the nation as well as our most dangerous enemies; and who stay at home on purpose to deliver the kingdom to the Pretender, hoping to take their advantage by the absence of so many good Protestants, who have chosen rather to leave their country than stay at home and pay tithes against their conscience to an Episcopal curate.

Secondly, The poor tenants will have something valuable of their own, which by law may be made liable to distress and help to pay their landlord's rent, their corn and cattle being already seized, and money a thing unknown.

Thirdly, Whereas the maintenance of 100,000 children from two years old and upward, cannot be computed at less than 10s, a-piece per annum, the nation's stock will be thereby increased £50,000 per annum, beside the profit of a new dish introduced to the tables of all gentlemen of fortune in the kingdom who have any refinement in taste. And the money will circulate among ourselves, the goods being entirely of our own growth and manufacture.

Fourthly, The constant breeders beside the gain of 8s. sterling per annum by the sale of their children, will be rid of the charge of maintaining them after the first year.

Fifthly, This food would likewise bring great custom to taverns, where the vintners will certainly be so prudent as to procure the best receipts for dressing it to perfection, and consequently have their houses frequented by all the fine gentlemen, who justly value themselves upon their knowledge in good eating; and a skilful cook who understands how to oblige his guests, will contrive to make it as expensive as they please. 25

Sixthly, This would be a great inducement to marriage, which all wise nations have either encouraged by rewards or enforced by laws and penalties. It would increase the care and tenderness of mothers toward their children, when they were sure of a settlement for life to the poor babes, provided in some sort by the public, to their annual profit instead of expense. We should see an honest emulation among the married women, which of them would bring the fattest child to the market. Men would become as fond of their wives during the time of their pregnancy as they are now of their mares in foal, their cows in calf, their sows when they are ready to farrow; nor offer to beat or kick them (as is too frequent a practice) for fear of a miscarriage.

Many other advantages might be enumerated. For instance, the addition of some thousand carcasses in our exportation of barreled beef, the propagation of swine's flesh, and improvement in the art of making good bacon, so much wanted among us by the great destruction of pigs, too frequent at our table; which are no way comparable in taste or magnificence to a well-grown, fat, yearling child, which roasted whole will make a considerable figure at a lord mayor's feast or any other public entertainment. But this and many others I omit, being studious of brevity.

Supposing that 1,000 families in this city would be constant customers for infants' flesh, besides others who might have it at merry-meetings, particularly at weddings and christenings, I compute that Dublin would take off annually about 20,000 carcasses; and the rest of the kingdom (where probably they will be sold somewhat cheaper) the remaining 80,000.

I can think of no one objection that will possibly be raised against this proposal, unless it should be urged that the number of people will be thereby much lessened in the kingdom. This I freely own, and it was indeed one principal design in offering it to the world. I desire the reader will observe, that I calculate my remedy for this one individual kingdom of Ireland and for no other that ever was, is, or I think ever can be upon earth. Therefore let no man talk to me of other expedients: of taxing our absentees at 5s. a pound: of using neither clothes nor household furniture except what is of our own growth and manufacture: of utterly rejecting the materials and instruments that promote foreign luxury: of curing the expensiveness of pride, vanity, idleness, and gaming in our women: of introducing a vein of parsimony, prudence, and temperance: of learning to love our country, in the want of which we differ even from Laplanders and the inhabitants of Topinamboo: of quitting our animosities and factions, nor acting any longer like the Jews, who were murdering one another at the very moment their city was taken: of being a little cautious not to sell our country and conscience for nothing: of teaching landlords to have at least one degree of mercy toward their tenants: lastly, of putting a spirit of honesty, industry, and skill into our shopkeepers; who, if a resolution could now be taken to buy only our native goods, would immediately unite to cheat and exact upon us in the price, the measure, and the goodness, nor could ever yet be brought to make one fair proposal of just dealing, though often and earnestly invited to it.

Therefore, I repeat, let no man talk to me of these and the like expedients, till he has at least some glimpse of hope that there will be ever some
hearty and sincere attempt to put them in practice.

But as to myself, having been wearied out for many years with offering vain, idle, visionary thoughts, and at length utterly despairing of success, I fortunately fell upon this proposal; which, as it is wholly new, so it
has something solid and real, of no expense and little trouble, full in our
own power, and whereby we can incur no danger in disobliging England.
For this kind of commodity will not bear exportation, the flesh being of
too tender a consistence to admit a long continuance in salt, although perhaps I could name a country which would be glad to eat up our whole
nation without it.

After all, I am not so violently bent upon my own opinion as to reject any offer proposed by wise men, which shall be found equally innocent, cheap, easy, and effectual. But before something of that kind shall
be advanced in contradiction to my scheme, and offering a better, I desire the author or authors will be pleased maturely to consider two
points. First, as things now stand, how they will be able to find food and
raiment for 100,000 useless mouths and backs. And secondly, there being a round million of creatures in human figure throughout this kingdom, whose subsistence put into a common stock would leave them in
debt 200,000,000 pounds sterling, adding those who are beggars by profession to the bulk of farmers, cottagers, and laborers, with the wives and
children who are beggars in effect; I desire those politicians who dislike
my overture, and may perhaps be so bold as to attempt an answer, that
they will first ask the parents of these mortals, whether they would not at
this day think it a great happiness to have been sold for food at a year old
in the manner I prescribe, and thereby have avoided such a perpetual
scene of misfortunes as they have since gone through by the oppression
of landlords, the impossibility of paying rent without money or trade, the
want of common sustenance, with neither house nor clothes to cover
them from the inclemencies of the weather, and the most inevitable
prospect of entailing the like or greater miseries upon their breed for ever.

I profess, in the sincerity of my heart, that I have not the least personal interest in endeavoring to promote this necessary work, having no
other motive than the public good of my country, by advancing our
trade, providing for infants, relieving the poor, and giving some pleasure
to the rich. I have no children by which I can propose to get a single penny;
the youngest being nine years old, and my wife past child-bearing.

⟋ Joining the Conversation: Critical Thinking and Writing

1. Characterize the pamphleteer (not Swift but his persona) who offers his "modest proposal." What sort of man does he think he is? What sort of man do we regard him as? Support your assertions with evidence.

2. In the first paragraph, the speaker says that the sight of mothers begging Is "melancholy." In this paragraph what assumption does the speaker make about women that in part gives rise to this melancholy? Now that you are familiar with the entire essay, explain Swift's strategy in his first paragraph.

3. Explain the function of the "other expedients" (listed in paragraph 29).

4. How might you argue that although this satire is primarily ferocious, it also contains some playful touches? What specific passages might support your argument?

James Wright

James Wright (1927–1980) was born in Martins Ferry, Ohio, which provided him with the locale for many of his poems. He is often thought of as a poet of the Midwest, but (as in the example that we give) his poems move beyond the scenery. Wright was educated at Kenyon College in Ohio and at the University of Washington. He wrote several books of poetry and published many translations of European and Latin American poetry.

Lying in a Hammock at William Duffy's Farm in Pine Island, Minnesota

Over my head, I see the bronze butterfly,
Asleep on the black trunk,
Blowing like a leaf in green shadow.
Down the ravine behind the empty house,
The cowbells follow one another   5
Into the distances of the afternoon.
To my right,

James Wright, "Lying in a Hammock at William Duffy's Farm in Pine Island, Minnesota" from *The Branch Will Not Break*. Copyright © 1963 Wesleyan University Press. Reprinted by permission.

In a field of sunlight between two pines,
The droppings of last year's horses
Blaze up into golden stones.   10
I lean back, as the evening darkens and comes on.
A chicken hawk floats over, looking for home.
I have wasted my life.

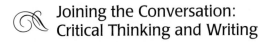

Joining the Conversation: Critical Thinking and Writing

1. How important is it that the poet is "lying in a hammock"? That he is at some place other than his own home?

2. Do you take the last line as a severe self-criticism, or as a joking remark, or as something in between, or what?

3. Write an imitation of Wright's poem, placing yourself somewhere specific, your eye taking in the surroundings. End with a Judgment or concluding comment, as Wright does. Try to imitate the sentence structure as well as the form of Wright's poem. Here is an imitation written by a student at Wellesley College:

> Near my side, I feel his strong body,
> Asleep on the blue sheet,
> Smiling like a babe in soft blankets,
> Behind the house, past the blooming garden,
> The children chase one another
> Through the haziness of the morning.
> In the yard,
> In a pool of shadow behind high hedges,
> The hummings of late summer's honeybees
> Sound among the yellow flowers.
> I stand up, as the morning brightens and comes on.
> A wild goose cries somewhere, looking for the path.
> I have enjoyed my life.

CHAPTER 14

Body and Soul

Lifted Lotus
Ken Gray

Short Views

Man can embody truth but he cannot know it.
> *W. B. Yeats*

Anatomy is destiny.
> *Napoleon*

If anything is sacred, the human body is sacred.
> *Walt Whitman*

Man consists of two parts, his mind and his body, only the body
has more fun.
> *Woody Allen*

It is a sign of a dull nature to occupy oneself deeply in matters that
concern the body; for instance, to be over much occupied about exercise, about eating and drinking, about easing oneself, about sexual intercourse.
> *Epictetus*

It is much more difficult to live with one's body than with one's
soul. One's body is so much more exacting: What it won't have it
won't have, and nothing can make bitter into sweet.
> *D. H. Lawrence*

A sound mind in a sound body, is a short but full definition of a
happy state in this world. He that has these two, has little more to
wish for; and he that wants either of them, will be little the better
for anything else.
> *John Locke*

This soul, or life within us, by no means agrees with the life outside us. If one has the courage to ask her what she thinks, she is
always saying the very opposite to what other people say.
> *Virginia Woolf*

The Soul unto itself
Is an imperial friend—
Or the most agonizing Spy—
An Enemy—could send—
> *Emily Dickinson*

We are bound to our bodies like an oyster to its shell.
　　Plato

Body: The material substance of an animal, opposed to the immaterial soul. Soul: The immaterial and immortal substance of man.
　　Samuel Johnson

Men cannot be broken if their tormentors cannot invade and violate their souls. . . . The soul that is within me no man can degrade.
　　Frederick Douglass

Soul is like electricity—we don't know what it is, but it's a force
that can light a room.
　　Ray Charles

The abdomen is the reason why man does not easily take himself
for a God.
　　Friedrich Nietzsche

Those who see any difference between soul and body have neither.
　　Oscar Wilde

However broken down is the spirit's shrine, the spirit is there all
the same.
　　Nigerian Proverb

What shall it profit a man, if he shall gain the whole world, and
lose his own soul?
　　Jesus

Anonymous

The following story is told of two nineteenth-century Japanese Zen monks. It may or may not be historically true.

Muddy Road

Two monks, Tanzan and Ekido, were once traveling together down a muddy road. A heavy rain was still falling.

Coming around a bend, they met a lovely girl in a silk kimono and sash, unable to cross the intersection.

"Come on, girl," said Tanzan at once. Lifting her in his arms, he carried her over the mud.

Ekido did not speak again until that night when they reached a lodging temple. Then he no longer could restrain himself. "We monks don't go near females," he told Tanzan, "especially not young and lovely ones. It is dangerous. Why did you do that?"

"I left the girl there," said Tanzan. "Are you still carrying her?"

 Joining the Conversation:
Critical Thinking and Writing

1. The storyteller reports that after several hours Ekido "no longer could restrain himself." What emotion(s) has Ekido been experiencing? Why?

2. Is this story of interest only to persons interested in Zen Buddhism, or does it speak to a wider audience? Explain.

Henry David Thoreau

Henry David Thoreau (1817–1862) was born in Concord, Massachusetts, where he spent most of his life ("I have travelled a good deal in Concord"). He taught and lectured, but chiefly he observed, thought, and wrote. From July 4, 1845, to September 6, 1847, he lived near Concord in a cabin at Walden Pond, an experience recorded in Walden *(1854).*

We reprint part of the first chapter of Walden.

Economy

The mass of men lead lives of quiet desperation. What is called resignation is confirmed desperation. From the desperate city you go into the desperate country, and have to console yourself with the bravery of

From Paul Reps, "Muddy Road," *Zen Flesh, Zen Bones,* Charles E. Tuttle Co., Inc. of Boston, Massachusetts, and Tokyo, Japan.

minks and muskrats. A stereotyped but unconscious despair is concealed even under what are called the games and amusements of mankind. There is no play in them, for this comes after work. But it is a characteristic of wisdom not to do desperate things.

When we consider what, to use the words of the catechism, is the chief end of man, and what are the true necessaries and means of life, it appears as if men had deliberately chosen the common mode of living because they preferred it to any other. Yet they honestly think there is no choice left. But alert and healthy natures remember that the sun rose clear. It is never too late to give up our prejudices. No way of thinking or doing, however ancient, can be trusted without proof. What everybody echoes or in silence passes by as true to-day may turn out to be falsehood to-morrow, mere smoke of opinion, which some had trusted for a cloud that would sprinkle fertilizing rain on their fields. What old people say you cannot do you try and find that you can. Old deeds for old people, and new deeds for new. Old people did not know enough once, perchance, to fetch fresh fuel to keep the fire a-going; new people put a little dry wood under a pot, and are whirled round the globe with the speed of birds, in a way to kill old people, as the phrase is. Age is no better, hardly so well, qualified for an instructor as youth, for it has not profited so much as it has lost. One may almost doubt if the wisest man has learned anything of absolute value by living. Practically, the old have no very important advice to give the young, their own experience has been so partial, and their lives have been such miserable failures, for private reasons, as they must believe; and it may be that they have some faith left which belies that experience, and they are only less young than they were. I have lived some thirty years on this planet, and I have yet to hear the first syllable of valuable or even earnest advice from my seniors. They have told me nothing, and probably cannot tell me anything to the purpose. Here is life, an experiment to a great extent untried by me; but it does not avail me that they have tried it. If I have any experience which I think valuable, I am sure to reflect that this my Mentors said nothing about.

One farmer says to me, "You cannot live on vegetable food solely, for it furnishes nothing to make bones with;" and so he religiously devotes a part of his day to supplying his system with the raw material of bones; walking all the while he talks behind his oxen, which, with vegetable-made bones, jerk him and his lumbering plough along in spite of every obstacle. Some things are really necessaries of life in some circles, the most helpless and diseased, which in others are luxuries merely, and in others still are entirely unknown.

The whole ground of human life seems to some to have been gone over by their predecessors, both the heights and the valleys, and all things to have been cared for. According to Evelyn, "the wise Solomon prescribed ordinances for the very distances of trees; and the Roman prætors have decided how often you may go into your neighbor's land to gather the acorns which fall on it without trespass, and what share belongs to that neighbor." Hippocrates has even left directions how we should cut our nails; that is, even with the ends of the fingers, neither shorter nor longer. Undoubtedly the very tedium and ennui which presume to have exhausted the variety and the joys of life are as old as Adam. But man's capacities have never been measured; nor are we to judge of what he can do by any precedents, so little has been tried. Whatever have been thy failures hitherto, "be not afflicted, my child, for who shall assign to thee what thou hast left undone?"

We might try our lives by a thousand simple tests; as, for instance, that the same sun which ripens my beans illumines at once a system of earths like ours. If I had remembered this it would have prevented some mistakes. This was not the light in which I hoed them. The stars are the apexes of what wonderful triangles! What distant and different beings in the various mansions of the universe are contemplating the same one at the same moment! Nature and human life are as various as our several constitutions. Who shall say what prospect life offers to another? Could a greater miracle take place than for us to look through each other's eyes for an instant? We should live in all the ages of the world in an hour; ay, in all the worlds of the ages. History, Poetry, Mythology!—I know of no reading of another's experience so startling and informing as this would be.

The greater part of what my neighbors call good I believe in my soul to be bad, and if I repent of anything, it is very likely to be my good behavior. What demon possessed me that I behaved so well? You may say the wisest thing you can, old man—you who have lived seventy years, not without honor of a kind,—I hear an irresistible voice which invites me away from all that. One generation abandons the enterprises of another like stranded vessels.

I think that we may safely trust a good deal more than we do. We may waive just so much care of ourselves as we honestly bestow elsewhere. Nature is as well adapted to our weakness as to our strength. The incessant anxiety and strain of some is a well-nigh incurable form of disease. We are made to exaggerate the importance of what work we do; and yet how much is not done by us! or, what if we had been taken sick? How vigilant we are! determined not to live by faith if we can avoid it; all the day long on the alert, at night we unwillingly say our prayers and commit ourselves to uncertainties. So thoroughly and sincerely are we compelled to live, reverencing our life, and denying the possibility of change. This is the only way, we say; but there are as many ways as there can be drawn radii from one centre. All change is a miracle to contemplate; but it is a miracle which is taking place every instant. Confucius said, "To know that we know what we know, and that we do not know what we do not know, that is true knowledge." When one man has reduced a fact of the imagination to be a fact to his understanding, I foresee that all men will at length establish their lives on that basis.

5

Let us consider for a moment what most of the trouble and anxiety which I have referred to is about, and how much it is necessary that we be troubled, or at least careful. It would be some advantage to live a primitive and frontier life, though in the midst of an outward civilization, if only to learn what are the gross necessaries of life and what methods have been taken to obtain them; or even to look over the old day-books of the merchants, to see what it was that men most commonly bought at the stores, what they stored, that is, what are the grossest groceries. For the improvements of ages have had but little influence on the essential laws of man's existence; as our skeletons, probably, are not to be distinguished from those of our ancestors.

By the words, *necessary of life*, I mean whatever, of all that man obtains by his own exertions, has been from the first, or from long use has become, so important to human life that few, if any, whether from savageness, or poverty, or philosophy, ever attempt to do without it. To many creatures there is in this sense but one necessary of life. Food. To the bison of the prairie it is a few inches of palatable grass, with water to drink; unless he seeks the Shelter of the forest or the mountain's shadow. None of the brute creation requires more than Food and Shelter. The necessaries of life for man in this climate may, accurately enough, be distributed under the several heads of Food, Shelter, Clothing, and Fuel; for not till we have secured these are we prepared to entertain the true problems of life with freedom and a prospect of success. Man has invented, not only houses, but clothes and cooked food; and possibly from the accidental discovery of the warmth of fire, and the consequent use of it, at first a luxury, arose the present necessity to sit by it. We observe cats and dogs acquiring the same second nature. By proper Shelter and Clothing we legitimately retain our own internal heat; but with an excess of these, or of Fuel, that is, with an external heat greater than our own internal, may not cookery properly be said to begin? Darwin, the naturalist, says of the inhabitants of Tierra del Fuego, that while his own party, who were well clothed and sitting close to a fire, were far from too warm, these naked savages, who were farther off, were observed, to his great surprise, "to be steaming with perspiration at undergoing such a roasting." So, we are told, the New Hollander goes naked with impunity, while the European shivers in his clothes. Is it impossible to combine the hardiness of these savages with the intellectualness of the civilized man? According to Liebig, man's body is a stove, and food the fuel which keeps up the internal combustion in the lungs. In cold weather we eat more, in warm less. The animal heat is the result of a slow combustion, and disease and death take place when this is too rapid; or for want of fuel, or from some defect in the draught, the fire goes out. Of course the vital heat is not to be confounded with fire; but so much for analogy. It appears, therefore, from the above list, that the expression, *animal life*, is nearly synonymous with the expression, *animal heat*; for while Food may be regarded as the Fuel which keeps up the fire within us,—and Fuel serves only to prepare that Food or to increase the warmth of our bodies by addition from without—Shelter and Clothing also serve only to retain the *heat* thus generated and absorbed.

The grand necessity, then, for our bodies, is to keep warm, to keep the vital heat in us. What pains we accordingly take, not only with our Food, and Clothing, and Shelter, but with our beds, which are our night-clothes, robbing the nests and breasts of birds to prepare this shelter within a shelter, as the mole has its bed of grass and leaves at the end of its burrow! The poor man is wont to complain that this is a cold world; and to cold, no less physical than social, we refer directly a great part of our ails. The summer, in some climates, makes possible to man a sort of Elysian life. Fuel, except to cook his Food, is then unnecessary; the sun is his fire, and many of the fruits are sufficiently cooked by its rays; while Food generally is more various, and more easily obtained, and Clothing and Shelter are wholly or half unnecessary. At the present day, and in this country, as I find by my own experience, a few implements, a knife, an axe, a spade, a wheelbarrow, etc.; and for the studious, lamplight, stationery, and access to a few books, rank next to necessaries, and can all be obtained at a trifling cost. Yet some, not wise, go to the other side of the globe, to barbarous and unhealthy regions, and devote themselves to trade for ten or twenty years, in order that they may live—that is, keep comfortably warm,—and die in New England at last. The luxuriously rich are not simply kept comfortably warm, but unnaturally hot; as I implied before, they are cooked, of course *à la mode*.

Most of the luxuries, and many of the so-called comforts of life, are not only not indispensable, but positive hindrances to the elevation of mankind. With respect to luxuries and comforts, the wisest have ever lived a more simple and meagre life than the poor. The ancient philosophers, Chinese, Hindoo, Persian, and Greek, were a class than which none has been poorer in outward riches, none so rich in inward. We know not much about them. It is remarkable that *we* know so much of them as we do. The same is true of the more modern reformers and benefactors of their race. None can be an impartial or wise observer of human life but from the vantage ground of what *we* should call voluntary poverty. Of a life of luxury the fruit is luxury, whether in agriculture, or commerce, or literature, or art. There are nowadays professors of philosophy, but not philosophers. Yet it is admirable to profess because it was once admirable to live. To be a philosopher is not merely to have subtle thoughts, nor even to found a school, but so to love wisdom as to live accordingly to its dictates, a life of simplicity, independence, magnanimity, and trust. It is to solve some of the problems of life, not only theoretically, but practically. The success of great scholars and thinkers is commonly a courtier-like success, not kingly, not manly. They make shift to live merely by conformity, practically as their fathers did, and are in no sense the progenitors of a nobler race of men. But why do men degenerate ever? What makes families run out? What is the nature of the luxury which enervates and destroys nations? Are we sure that there is none of it in our own lives? The

10

philosopher is in advance of his age even in the outward form of his life. He is not fed, sheltered, clothed, warmed, like his contemporaries. How can a man be a philosopher and not maintain his vital heat by better methods than other men?

When a man is warmed by the several modes which I have described, what does he want next? Surely not more warmth of the same kind, as more and richer food, larger and more splendid houses, finer and more abundant clothing, more numerous incessant and hotter fires, and the like. When he has obtained those things which are necessary to life, there is another alternative than to obtain the superfluities; and that is, to adventure on life now, his vacation from humbler toil having commenced. The soil, it appears, is suited to the seed, for it has sent its radicle downward, and it may now send its shoot upward also with confidence. Why has man rooted himself thus firmly in the earth, but that he may rise in the same proportion into the heavens above?—for the nobler plants are valued for the fruit they bear at last in the air and light, far from the ground, and are not treated like the humbler esculents, which, though they may be biennials, are cultivated only till they have perfected their root, and often cut down at top for this purpose, so that most would not know them in their flowering season.

I do not mean to prescribe rules to strong and valiant natures, who will mind their own affairs whether in heaven or hell, and perchance build more magnificently and spend more lavishly than the richest, without ever impoverishing themselves, not knowing how they live,—if, indeed, there are any such, as has been dreamed; nor to those who find their encouragement and inspiration in precisely the present condition of things, and cherish it with the fondness and enthusiasms of lovers,—and, to some extent, I reckon myself in this number; I do not speak to those who are well employed, in whatever circumstances, and they know whether they are well employed or not;—but mainly to the mass of men who are discontented, and idly complaining of the hardness of their lot or of the times, when they might improve them. There are some who complain most energetically and inconsolably of any, because they are, as they say, doing their duty. I also have in my mind that seemingly wealthy, but most terribly impoverished class of all, who have accumulated dross, but know not how to use it, or get rid of it, and thus have forged their own golden or silver fetters.

As for Clothing, to come at once to the practical part of the question, perhaps we are led oftener by the love of novelty and a regard for the opinions of men, in procuring it, than by a true utility. Let him who has work to do recollect that the object of clothing is, first, to retain the vital heat, and secondly, in this state of society, to cover nakedness, and he may judge how much of any necessary or important work may be accomplished without adding to his wardrobe. Kings and queens who wear a suit but once, though made by some tailor or dressmaker to their majesties, cannot know the comfort of wearing a suit that fits. They are no better than wooden horses to hang the clean clothes on. Every day our garments become more assimilated to ourselves, receiving the impress of the wearer's character, until we hesitate to lay them aside, without such delay and medical appliances and some such solemnity even as our bodies. No man ever stood the lower in my estimation for having a patch in his clothes; yet I am sure that there is greater anxiety, commonly, to have fashionable, or at least clean and unpatched clothes, then to have a sound conscience. But even if the rent is not mended, perhaps the worst vice betrayed is improvidence. I sometimes try my acquaintances by such tests as this,—Who could wear a patch, or two extra seams only, over the knee? Most behave as if they believed that their prospects for life would be ruined if they should do it. It would be easier for them to hobble to town with a broken leg than with a broken pantaloon. Often if an accident happens to a gentleman's legs, they can be mended; but if a similar accident happens to the legs of his pantaloons, there is no help for it; for he considers, not what is truly respectable, but what is respected. We know but few men, a great many coats and breeches. Dress a scarecrow in your last shift, you standing shiftless by, who would not soonest salute the scarecrow? Passing a cornfield the other day, close by a hat and coat on a stake, I recognized the owner of the farm. He was only a little more weather-beaten than when I saw him last. I have heard of a dog that barked at every stranger who approached his master's premises with clothes on, but was easily quieted by a naked thief. It is an interesting question how far men would retain their relative rank if they were divested of their clothes. Could you, in such a case, tell surely of any company of civilized men which belonged to the most respected class? When Madam Pfeiffer, in her adventurous travels round the world, from east to west, had got so near home as Asiatic Russia, she says that she felt the necessity of wearing other than a travelling dress, when she went to meet the authorities, for she "was now in a civilized country, where . . . people are judged of by their clothes." Even in our democratic New England towns the accidental possession of wealth, and its manifestation in dress and equipage alone, obtain for the possessor almost universal respect. But they who yield such respect, numerous as they are, are so far heathen, and need to have a missionary sent to them. Besides, clothes introduced sewing, a kind of work which you may call endless; a woman's dress, at least, is never done.

A man who has at length found something to do will not need to get a new suit to do it in; for him the old will do, that has lain dusty in the garret for an indeterminate period. Old shoes will serve a hero longer than they have served his valet,—if a hero ever has a valet,—bare feet are older than shoes, and he can make them do. Only they who go to soirées and legislative halls must have new coats, coats to change as often as the man changes in them. But if my jacket and trousers, my hat and shoes, are fit to worship God in, they will do; will they not? Who ever saw his old

15

clothes,—his old coat, actually worn out, resolved into its primitive elements, so that it was not a deed of charity to bestow it on some poor boy, by him perchance to be bestowed on some poorer still, or shall we say richer, who could do with less? I say, beware of all enterprises that require new clothes, and not rather a new wearer of clothes. If there is not a new man, how can the new clothes be made to fit? If you have any enterprise before you, try it in your old clothes. All men want, not something to *do with*, but something to *do*, or rather something to *be*. Perhaps we should never procure a new suit, however ragged or dirty the old, until we have so conducted, so enterprised or sailed in some way, that we feel like new men in the old, and that to retain it would be like keeping new wine in old bottles. Our moulting season, like that of the fowls, must be a crisis in our lives. The loon retires to solitary ponds to spend it. Thus also the snake casts its slough, and the caterpillar its wormy coat, by an internal industry and expansion; for clothes are but our outmost cuticle and mortal coil. Otherwise we shall be found sailing under false colors, and be inevitably cashiered at last by our own opinion, as well as that of mankind.

We don garment after garment, as if we grew like exogenous plants by addition without. Our outside and often thin and fanciful clothes are our epidermis, or false skin, which partakes not of our life, and may be stripped off here and there without fatal injury; our thicker garments, constantly worn, are our cellular integument, or cortex; but our shirts are our liber,[1] or true bark, which cannot be removed without girdling and so destroying the man. I believe that all races at some seasons wear something equivalent to the shirt. It is desirable that a man be clad so simply that he can lay his hands on himself in the dark, and that he live in all respects so compactly and preparedly, that, if an enemy take the town, he can, like the old philosopher, walk out the gate empty-handed without anxiety. While one thick garment is, for most purposes, as good as three thin ones, and cheap clothing can be obtained at prices really to suit customers; while a thick coat can be bought for five dollars, which will last as many years, thick pantaloons for two dollars, cowhide boots for a dollar and a half a pair, a summer hat for a quarter of a dollar, and a winter cap for sixty-two and a half cents, or a better be made at home at a nominal cost, where is he so poor that, clad in such a suit, *of his own earning*, there will not be found wise men to do him reverence?

When I ask for a garment of a particular form, my tailoress tells me gravely, "They do not make them so now," not emphasizing the "They" at all, as if she quoted an authority as impersonal as the Fates, and I find it difficult to get made what I want, simply because she cannot believe that I mean what I say, that I am so rash. When I hear this oracular sentence, I am for a moment absorbed in thought, emphasizing to myself each

---

[1]**Liber** Latin for "bark" (Editors' note)

word separately that I may come at the meaning of it, that I may find out by what degree of consanguinity *They* are related to *me*, and what authority they may have in an affair which affects me so nearly; and finally, I am inclined to answer her with equal mystery, and without any more emphasis of the "they"—"It is true, they did not make them so recently, but they do now." Of what use this measuring of me if she does not measure my character, but only the breadth of my shoulders, as it were a peg to hang the coat on? We worship not the Graces, nor the Parcæ, but Fashion. She spins and weaves and cuts with full authority. The head monkey at Paris puts on a traveller's cap, and all the monkeys in America do the same. I sometimes despair of getting anything quite simple and honest done in this world by the help of men. They would have to be passed through a powerful press first, to squeeze their old notions out of them, so that they would not soon get upon their legs again; and then there would be some one in the company with a maggot in his head, hatched from an egg deposited there nobody knows when, for not even fire kills these things, and you would have lost your labor. Nevertheless, we will not forget that some Egyptian wheat was handed down to us by a mummy.

On the whole, I think that it cannot be maintained that dressing has in this or any country risen to the dignity of an art. At present men make shift to wear what they can get. Like shipwrecked sailors, they put on what they can find on the beach, and at a little distance, whether of space or time, laugh at each other's masquerade. Every generation laughs at the old fashions, but follows religiously the new. We are amused at beholding the costume of Henry VIII., or Queen Elizabeth, as much as if it was that of the King and Queen of the Cannibal Islands. All costume off a man is pitiful or grotesque. It is only the serious eye peering from and the sincere life passed within it which restrain laughter and consecrate the costume of any people. Let Harlequin be taken with a fit of the colic and his trappings will have to serve that mood too. When the soldier is hit by a cannon ball rags are as becoming as purple.

The childish and savage taste of men and women for new patterns keeps how many shaking and squinting through kaleidoscopes that they may discover the particular figure which this generation requires today. The manufacturers have learned that this taste is merely whimsical. Of two patterns which differ only by a few threads more or less of a particular color, the one will be sold readily, the other lie on the shelf, though it frequently happens that after the lapse of a season the latter becomes the most fashionable. Comparatively, tattooing is not the hideous custom which it is called. It is not barbarous merely because the printing is skin-deep and unalterable.

I cannot believe that our factory system is the best mode by which men   20
may get clothing. The condition of the operatives is becoming every day more like that of the English; and it cannot be wondered at, since, as far as I have heard or observed, the principal object is, not that mankind may be well and honestly clad, but, unquestionably, that the corporations may be

enriched. In the long run men hit only what they aim at. Therefore, though they should fail immediately, they had better aim at something high.

As for a Shelter, I will not deny that this is now a necessary of life, though there are instances of men having done without it for long periods in colder countries than this. Samuel Laing says that "the Laplander in his skin dress, and in a skin bag which he puts over his head and shoulders, will sleep night after night on the snow . . . in a degree of cold which would extinguish the life of one exposed to it in any woollen clothing." He had seen them asleep thus. Yet he adds, "They are not hardier than other people." But, probably, man did not live long on the earth without discovering the convenience which there is in a house, the domestic comforts, which phrase may have originally signified the satisfactions of the house more than of the family; though these must be extremely partial and occasional in those climates where the house is associated in our thoughts with winter or the rainy season chiefly, and two thirds of the year, except for a parasol, is unnecessary. In our climate, in the summer, it was formerly almost solely a covering at night. In the Indian gazettes a wigwam was the symbol of a day's march, and a row of them cut or painted on the bark of a tree signified that so many times they had camped. Man was not made so large limbed and robust but that he must seek to narrow his world, and wall in a space such as fitted him. He was at first bare and out of doors; but though this was pleasant enough in serene and warm weather, by daylight, the rainy season and the winter, to say nothing of the torrid sun, would perhaps have nipped his race in the bud if he had not made haste to clothe himself with the shelter of a house. Adam and Eve, according to the fable, wore the bower before other clothes. Man wanted a home, a place of warmth, or comfort, first of physical warmth, then the warmth of the affections.

We may imagine a time when, in the infancy of the human race, some enterprising mortal crept into a hollow in a rock for shelter. Every child begins the world again, to some extent, and loves to stay out doors, even in wet and cold. It plays house, as well as horse, having an instinct for it. Who does not remember the interest with which, when young, he looked at shelving rocks, or any approach to a cave? It was the natural yearning of that portion of our most primitive ancestor which still survived in us. From the cave we have advanced to roofs of palm leaves, of bark and boughs, of linen woven and stretched, of grass and straw, of boards and shingles, of stones and tiles. At last, we know not what it is to live in the open air, and our lives are domestic in more senses than we think. From the hearth the field is a great distance. It would be well, perhaps, if we were to spend more of our days and nights without any obstruction between us and the celestial bodies, if the poet did not speak so much from under a roof, or the saint dwell there so long. Birds do not sing in caves, nor do doves cherish their innocence in dovecots.

However, if one designs to construct a dwelling house, it behooves him to exercise a little Yankee shrewdness, lest after all he finds himself in a workhouse, a labyrinth without a clue, a museum, an almshouse, a prison, or a splendid mausoleum instead. Consider first how slight a shelter is absolutely necessary. I have seen Penobscot Indians, in this town, living in tents of thin cotton cloth, while the snow was nearly a foot deep around them, and I thought that they would be glad to have it deeper to keep out the wind. Formerly, when how to get my living honestly, with freedom left for my proper pursuits, was a question which vexed me even more than it does now, for unfortunately I am become somewhat callous, I used to see a large box by the railroad, six feet long by three wide, in which the laborers locked up their tools at night; and it suggested to me that every man who was hard pushed might get such a one for a dollar, and, having bored a few auger holes in it, to admit the air at least get into it when it rained and at night, and hook down the lid, and so have freedom in his love, and in his soul be free. This did not appear the worst, nor by any means a despicable alternative. You could sit up as late as you pleased, and, whenever you got up, go abroad without any landlord or house-lord dogging you for rent. Many a man is harassed to death to pay the rent of a larger and more luxurious box who would not have frozen to death in such a box as this. I am far from jesting. Economy is a subject which admits of being treated with levity, but it cannot so be disposed of. A comfortable house for a rude and hardy race, that lived mostly out of doors, was once made here almost entirely of such materials as Nature furnished ready to their hands. Gookin, who was superintendent of the Indians subject to the Massachusetts Colony, writing in 1674, says, "The best of their houses are covered very neatly, tight and warm, with barks of trees, slipped from their bodies at those seasons when the sap is up, and made into great flakes, with pressure of weighty timber, when they are green. . . . The meaner sort are covered with mats which they make of a kind of bulrush, and are also indifferently tight and warm, but not so good as the former. . . . Some I have seen, sixty or a hundred feet long and thirty feet broad. . . . I have often lodged in their wigwams, and found them as warm as the best English houses." He adds that they were commonly carpeted and lined within with well-wrought embroidered mats, and were furnished with various utensils. The Indians had advanced so far as to regulate the effect of the wind by a mat suspended over the hole in the roof and moved by a string. Such a lodge was in the first instance constructed in a day or two at most, and taken down and put up in a few hours; and every family owned one, or its apartment in one.

In the savage state every family owns a shelter as good as the best, and sufficient for its coarser and simpler wants; but I think that I speak within bounds when I say that, though the birds of the air have their nests, and the foxes their holes, and the savages their wigwams, in modern civilized society not more than one half the families own a shelter. In the large towns and cities, where civilization especially prevails, the number of those who own a shelter is a very small fraction of the whole. The rest pay an annual tax for this outside garment of all, become indispensable summer and winter, which would buy a village of Indian wigwams, but now helps to keep them poor as long as they live. I do not mean to insist here on the disadvantage of hiring compared with owning, but it is evident that the savage owns his shelter because it costs so little, while the civilized man hires his commonly because he cannot afford to own it; nor can he, in the long run, any better afford to hire. But, answers one, by merely paying this tax the poor civilized man secures an abode which is a palace compared with the savage's. An annual rent of from twenty-five to a hundred dollars (these are the country rates) entitles him to the benefit of the improvements of centuries, spacious apartments, clean paint and paper, Rumford fireplace, back plastering, Venetian blinds, copper pump, spring lock, a commodious cellar, and many other things. But how happens it that he who is said to enjoy these things is so commonly a *poor* civilized man, while the savage, who has them not, is rich as a savage? If it is asserted that civilization is a real advance in the condition of man,—and I think that it is, though only the wise improve their advantages,—it must be shown that it has produced better dwellings without making them more costly; and the cost of a thing is the amount of what I will call life which is required to be exchanged for it, immediately or in the long run. An average house in this neighborhood costs perhaps eight hundred dollars, and to lay up this sum will take from ten to fifteen years of the laborer's life, even if he is not encumbered with a family,—estimating the pecuniary value of every man's labor at one dollar a day, for if some receive more, others receive less;—so that he must have spent more than half his life commonly before *his* wigwam will be earned. If we suppose him to pay a rent instead, this is but a doubtful choice of evils. Would the savage have been wise to exchange his wigwam for a palace on these terms?

 ## Joining the Conversation: Critical Thinking and Writing

1. What, according to Thoreau (paragraphs 11–20), are the legitimate functions of clothing? What other functions does he reject, or fail to consider?

2. In paragraph 20, beginning "I cannot believe," Thoreau criticizes the factory system. Is the criticism mild or severe? Explain. Point out some of the earlier passages in which he touches on the relation of clothes to a faulty economic system.

3. List or briefly set forth Thoreau's assumptions (paragraphs 21–24) about architecture.

4. In paragraph 24 Thoreau says: "The cost of a thing is the amount of what I will call life which is required to be exchanged for it, immediately or in the

long run." The definition of cost is interesting, but no less so than the definition implicit in "what I will call life." Of what other definitions of cost are you aware? Do they also involve an implicit definition of what Thoreau calls life?

5. Many of Thoreau's sentences mean both what they say literally and something more; often, like proverbs, they express abstract or general truths in concrete, homely language. How might these sentences (from paragraph 14–18) be interpreted?

    (a) We know but few men, a great many coats and breeches.
    (b) Dress a scarecrow in your last shift, you standing shiftless by, who would not soonest salute the scarecrow?
    (c) If you have any enterprise before you, try it in your old clothes.
    (d) Every generation laughs at the old fashions, but follows religiously the new.
    (e) When the soldier is hit by a cannon ball rags are as becoming as purple.

Natalie Angier

Natalie Angier was born in New York in 1958. In college, at the University of Michigan and Barnard College, she studied English, physics, and astronomy, and formed the ambition of writing for nonspecialists about literary and scientific matters. At the age of 22 she was hired by Time Inc. as a member of the staff of a new magazine, Discover, where she wrote about biology for four years. She has also worked as a science writer for Time magazine, and has taught at New York University's Graduate Program in Science and Environmental Reporting. In 1990 she began writing on science-related subjects for the New York Times, and the next year she won a Pulitzer prize for her reporting. Angier's most recent books are Women, an Intimate Geography (1999), The Best American Science and Nature Writing (2002) and The Canon: A Whirligig Tour of the Beautiful Business of Science (2007).

The Sandbox: Bully for You— Why Push Comes to Shove

Some people are just fair game for being picked on and put down: lawyers, politicians, journalists, mothers-in-law and, now, bullies. These days, everybody is ganging up on bullies, blaming them for all that ails us.

Bullies and their taunting, arrogant ways are said to have been the driving force behind the student shootings at Columbine and Santana High Schools. Young bullies supposedly grow into sociopaths, angry drunks, wife abusers or maybe mayors of major East Coast cities.

The victims of bullying are portrayed as emotionally disfigured for life, unable to shake the feeling that they are unlovable wimps, or that everybody is out to get them.

The news bristles with reports that bullies abound. Recently, in one of the largest studies ever of child development, researchers at the National Institutes of Health reported that about a quarter of all middle-school children were either perpetrators or victims (or in some cases, both) of serious and chronic bullying, behavior that included threats, ridicule, name calling, punching, slapping, jeering and sneering.

Another highly contentious study suggested that too much time in   5
day care may predispose a child to bullying: youngsters who spent more than 30 hours a week away from mommy had a 17 percent chance of ending up as garden-variety bullies and troublemakers, compared to only 6 percent of children who spent less than 10 hours a week in day care.

Everywhere, legislators are struggling to beat each other to the punch in demanding that schools stamp out bad behavior. In Colorado, for example, home to Columbine High School, Gov. Bill Owens has just signed legislation requiring all state school districts to develop anti-bullying programs to prevent bullying.

In a similar spirit, the familiar phys-ed game of dodgeball—also known as killerball, prison ball or bombardment—is taking a hit lately, as school authorities nationwide have moved to ban the game on the theory that it fosters hyperaggression and gives the class klutzes an inferiority complex.

Yet even as quick-fix programs with names like "Taking the Bully by the Horns" proliferate across the academic and electronic universe, experts in aggressive behavior warn that there is no easy way to stamp out bullying among children. Short of raising kids in isolation chambers, they say, bullying behaviors can never be eliminated entirely from the sustained hazing ritual otherwise known as growing up.

"Can we get rid of bullying altogether? I don't think so," said Richard J. Hazler, a professor of counselor education at Ohio University in Athens. "We can't eliminate all growing pains, either. It's tough learning to make your way in this world."

Philip C. Rodkin, an assistant professor of educational psychology at   10
the University of Illinois at Urbana-Champaign, pointed out that, despite all the attention being paid to the subject, the root causes of bullying remain a mystery. "This is not a trivial problem," he said. "Bullies have always been with us, and we're only beginning to ask why."

Some researchers say that, despite the hype and handwringing, there is no epidemic of bullying in schools, and in fact the incidence of serious bullying has very likely declined over the years.

"It certainly was a problem when I was in boarding school, but that was ages ago," said Richard Dawkins, a professor at Oxford University who has studied the evolution of aggressive and selfish behavior. "I believe there is far less bullying now, though there probably will always be a bit."

As an example of how bad it used to be, Professor Dawkins cited a passage from the British poet John Betjeman's 1960 autobiographical poem, "Summoned by Bells."

> Twelve to one:
> What chance had Angus? They surrounded him,
> Pulled off his coat and trousers, socks and shoes
> And, wretched in his shirt, they hoisted him
> Into the huge waste paper basket; then
> Poured ink and treacle on his head. With ropes

They strung the basket up among the beams
And as he soared I only saw his eyes
Look through the slats at us who watched below.

As Frans de Waal, a primatologist at Emory University, sees it, one of the problems in the standard approach to bully analysis is that researchers tend to ignore the subtle dynamics between a bully and the object of a bully's scorn—the scapegoat. "Some individuals may have bully characteristics, and others may have scapegoat characteristics," he said. "The two things need to be studied together, but because personality research is generally done from an individual perspective, they rarely are."

Dr. de Waal has observed that bullying behavior is quite common among most species of monkeys and apes, and that many animals at or near the top of the hierarchy will harass, charge, snap and howl at their subordinates for no other reason than because they can. But at least as striking as the presence of simian bullies, Dr. de Waal said, are the resident scapegoats, the low-ranking individuals who seem to be chosen for the role by other members of the group. Whenever a group is under strain, or when its hierarchy is in doubt, the higher-ranking primates start taking it out on the scapegoat, with the result that any time the beleaguered monkey ventures from its corner, it gets beaten up.

"This is not just a way to release frustration," said Dr. de Waal. "The scapegoat also gives the high-ranking individuals in the group a common enemy, a unifier. By uniting against the scapegoat in moments of tension, it creates a bond."

And while primate research can never be applied directly to human affairs, even when those humans are swinging from monkey bars, bully experts admit that children in groups will often encourage, or at least not discourage, a bully's nasty acts against an underling. In one study of how peers contribute to bullying, researchers from York University studied videotapes of 53 episodes of bullying among elementary school students on the school playground. The researchers found that 54 percent of the time, onlookers stood by passively as the bully picked on the victim, an inactive form of activity that the researchers said ended up reinforcing the bully's behavior. And 21 percent of the time, some of the onlookers joined in on the taunting. Only in 25 percent of the cases did a child attempt to step in and help the victim or call a teacher to help.

But as researchers lately have discovered, many bullies in fact are quite popular. "Some kids may be goaders, cheering the bully on because they want to be accepted," said Laura Hess Olson, an assistant professor of child development at Purdue University in West Lafayette, Ind. "Or they may just stand by and do nothing because they're afraid they might be targeted next." Whatever the case, she added, "We have to realize that everybody is a player in creating the atmosphere in which bullying occurs."

Another point worth noting, said Dr. Olson, is that the old stereotype of the bully as an antisocial and unpopular misfit is false. In one study of

15

third- to fifth-graders in two East Coast schools, she and her colleagues found that, while the students described by their peers and teachers as friendly, outgoing and self-confident were the most popular, the boys known to be bullies were the second-most popular group, way beyond the perceived wimps, eggheads and teacher's pets.

"There are a fair amount of kids in a classroom who think that bullies are cool," said Dr. Rodkin, "especially when they're attractive and athletic."   20

Adding to the challenge of curbing bullies is the fact that, as researchers have learned, many students blame victims of bullying for bringing their troubles on themselves by sulking or whimpering or walking around with their head hanging low. A sizable number of students agree with the premise that bullying can help "toughen" people and teach which behaviors are laudable and which are risible to the group.

In this scenario, then, bullies are neither born nor made, but instead have bulliness thrust upon them. The group needs its whipcracking rulemeister, just as an army boot camp needs its snarling, abusive sergeant if the soft-bellied newcomers are ever to get into fighting trim.

Indeed, it's hard to see how bullying behavior in schools can be eliminated when bullying behavior among adults is not only common but often applauded—at least if it results in wild success. J. P. Morgan, for example, was thought by many of his colleagues and subordinates to be, in the words of Robert M. LaFollette, the Wisconsin progressive, "a beefy, red-faced thick-necked financial bully, drunk with wealth and power." Yet he was also lionized in his day, described by officials at Harvard University as a "prince among merchants," a man of "skill, wisdom and courage." Hey, he was the richest guy in the world, wasn't he?

It's perhaps a bit of delicious paradox that, at a time when the nation is seized with concern over school bullying, the international community views with alarm the recent moves by the United States to scuttle the Kyoto global warming treaty and to promote the construction of a space-based nuclear missile shield. To the rest of the world, it seems, America is the biggest bully of them all.

 ## Joining the Conversation: Critical Thinking and Writing

1. How would you describe the tone of Angier's first sentence? Do you find it attractive?

2. When you were in school, were you the victim of bullying, or a bully, or both? Did you observe bullying going on around you? If so, what were your responses to bullying? (Your answer to any of these questions might provide an excellent topic for an essay of 500 words. Remember to ask yourself: Who? What? When? Where? And—most important—why?)

3. Do you agree or disagree with the premise offered in paragraph 21 "that bullying can help 'toughen' people and teach which behaviors are laudable and which are risible to the group"? On what do you base your answer? Personal or observed experience? Reasoning? Reading? or What? Set forth your answer in an essay of 500 words.

4. In one paragraph evaluate Angier's last paragraph as a conclusion to her article. Support your evaluation with evidence.

Robert Santos

Robert Santos, a highly decorated veteran of the Vietnam War, was a platoon leader with an airborne division in 1967–1968. He recounted his story to Al Santolini, who published it in Everything We Had: An Oral History of the Vietnam War by Thirty-Three American Soldiers Who Fought It *(1981). After Santos returned from Vietnam, he became a lawyer.*

My Men

I was drafted in March 1966. It wasn't my intention to go into combat, but to go to Officer Candidate School, and quit a month before OCS ended. It wouldn't be held against me and I'd have less than a year left. But the way it worked out, a friend did that ahead of me and he went to 'Nam, anyway. So I decided that based on what I had seen and my own feelings about myself, I should complete OCS.

I went over to 'Nam with two other guys as part of an advance party for the 101st Airborne, mainly to handle logistics and to make sure all the equipment was there. The rumors were that advance parties were being wiped out. When my company got there, they were under the impression that I had already died, which was a really weird feeling, to meet the company commander, who I didn't get along with, and the first words out of his mouth are "I thought you were dead." My response was "Too bad, huh?"

The 101st were mostly West Point officers. I was the first guy to come there from OCS, and was not well received. They had a camaraderie. Most of the lieutenants out of West Point graduated from the same class. They graduated through Airborne school, Ranger school, and all came there as a unit.

We were part of the Hue liberation force in the Tet offensive. The North Vietnamese Army had taken the city. So the Marine Corps, the South Vietnamese, the 101st and the 1st Cavalry went in from different angles to liberate the city.

I was twenty-one. But I was young in terms of commanding men in   5
combat. I didn't know anything. I was the kind of lieutenant that they'd
say, "Oh, shit, here's another green lieutenant." That's what I was. You
don't know what to do, your mind races over the training you've taken in
how to deal with these kinds of situations. I was naïve and really took
what they said at face value.

We operated for maybe two weeks with only minor contact. I was
working the whole time, spreading the platoon out, doing it right. I was
lead platoon on our way into Hue. We came past the paddies, the trees,
came around the green. I looked up and saw an NVA flag flying over the
next open space. I couldn't believe it. I just . . . I guess I just freaked. I got
on the horn right away and called the CO. I was stuttering and stammering: "I see it. I see the flag! I . . . My God, they're finally there."

All I knew at that point was "My God! I'm scared shitless. Holy shit.
This is the real thing." I never expected to see a flag. I expected to get shot
at. But they were so brazen. They were there. Dug in. The CO said, "Move
out." I've heard that before: "Follow me." But I was in the bottom of the
infantry. He didn't say "Follow me," he said "Move out." I said, "Now I
know what 'Follow me' means—Lieutenant says 'Follow me.'" And
that's what we did.

The strange thing about war, there's always humor. Prior to that,
when I was walking around I was your typical "asshole lieutenant."
Everyplace I walked something got caught. You know, guys could walk
right through a bush. My helmet would fall off, my pack would get
snagged. And although no one ever told me, I had a reputation as the
wait-a-minute-lieutenant. "Hold up, hold up, the lieutenant's caught."
Here you're trying to lead men in combat and be a tough guy. Most of the
guys were bigger than me. I weighed like 130 pounds. And really, always
getting snagged was embarrassing.

I remember walking through the rice paddies that opened up and the
small stream and the green on both sides. We were walking down the
right side, near the trail, and there was another company on my left flank.
All of a sudden all hell opened up. You have to understand, I've never
been a Boy Scout, I've never been a Cub Scout. The closest I came to that
was going to my sister's Campfire Girl meetings. I grew up in New York
City and Long Island. Watched a lot of movies and read a lot of books.
I never fired a weapon. I never got into fights with my buddies. My RTO[1]
was from East Wenatchee, Washington. Grew up a hunter. They opened
up fire and Wes started going down. You make a connection real quick
that someone's being shot and someone's getting hurt.

The first thing I did was yell, "Follow me," and I turned to the right   10
to run for cover. There was a bamboo thicket. I couldn't walk through a
jungle, an open field, without tripping. Somehow I made a hole through

---
[1]**RTO** Radio telephone operator (Editor's note).

those bushes that everyone in the platoon could go through side by side. Got on the other side—my hat was on my head, my rifle was in my hands, I'd lost nothing. There were guys from another platoon that didn't know what they were doing. Everyone was running around crazy.

I said, "Come with me. Follow me." And I didn't know what I was doing. I knew I was supposed to go toward the enemy. I was trained not to stand still. Don't stand in the killing zone. Don't get shot. Move. So I moved, and as I ran forward I heard these noises. Kind of like *ping, ping*—no idea what that noise was. I finally jumped down behind this mound of dirt that turned out to be a grave, which I didn't know at that time. So I jumped behind this mound of dirt with my RTO and we're all kind of hid behind this stuff. I said, "Just climb up, tell them we're in place and we're hooked up with the left flank and the enemy is in front of us." And I started playing the game. I got up and ran around yelling "Move this machine gun over here" and "Do this over there." I mean, all this noise is going past me. I still didn't know what this noise was. *Ping.* Just a little weird, something new. I finally got back after running around, sat down next to the RTO, and he said, "What the fuck are you doing?" I said, "What do you mean?" He said, "Don't you know what's going on?" I said, "Yeah, goddamnit. I know what's going on. Who do you think I am? He says, "Don't you know what that noise is?" I said no. He said, "That's the bullets going over your head." I never knew it. I mean, If I'd known it I probably would've just buried myself and hid. But I didn't know it. I just didn't know it.

The NVA were in the thicket. There was a stream between us and them, and they were dug in on the opposite side. And they nailed us. They had us pinned down all over the place. Everything that day was done by the book. Just incredible. I don't know how I survived that day, because lieutenants had a very short life expectancy and the reason is because they're jerks and they run out and do stupid stuff by the book. That day we took our first casualties in our platoon. Sergeant Berringer, I think his name was, next to me got shot in the arm. And I remember the training again. Here you were a medic. Look for the bullet's exit. So I found the exit and patched him up with his bandage. Then I realized that there's also an entrance. So I took my bandage out. This is a mistake. You're not supposed to take out your bandage and patch someone else up. But I had to do it. I turned around and called the medic, but he was all freaked out. The bullet that went through Berringer's arm killed the guy next to him. It was a very traumatic day for all of us.

I had told that guy's squad leader that morning, "Tell him to stay behind with the gear and the chopper will bring him forward later." But he wanted to go out. To this day I still think you can tell ahead of time when someone's going to die. Whether they know it or not, I'm convinced that I can tell. It's not something deliberate. Kind of a blankness comes over their face. It's not like they're already dead. It's like a distance and a softness to their features.

But he died and it was a really bad day. We found out how heavy a dead guy could be. The biggest guy in our platoon couldn't pick him up and carry him. So I picked him up, took about three steps, and I couldn't go much farther. But by that time the big guy realized that he could pick him up—it was just mental. We were freaked. And eventually we got out of that mess.

From that first time we made contact we proceeded to keep sweeping   15 in toward the city. The way the 101st operated, we sometimes moved as a battalion, but generally the company split off and we did that whole anvil/hammer bit. So although you were working in the battalion operation, you were functioning as a company and sometimes as small a unit as a platoon.

I think it's funny how you can rationalize everything while you're there. Everything is justifiable in terms of survival, which is unfortunate. I can criticize people today, like at law school when I went there, for being so competitive, so survival-oriented. They were called "gunners," would do things just to make sure they got a better grade. Seems to me today's perception of how unimportant that all is . . . Whereas you go back there and you're justifying killing someone. I'm not sure which one's worse— whether it's unimportant or the means by which you compete. It's really crazy. But we would chase them every day, they'd shoot at us and we'd shoot at them, never making contact. And then every day, almost like clockwork, in the late afternoon they'd stop and make a stand and we'd fight. Went on for months, literally for months. Even after the city was retaken, they still operated in the area.

We overran a base camp on the way into Hue. We called it a base camp, but it probably wasn't but a staging area—there were packs just like ours lined up on the ground. It's a really freaky thing to think you're chasing someone and then to suddenly show up and there they are taking a break for exercise or going inside a barracks for a class—I don't know what they did. But psychologically it really shook us because shit, they're just as disciplined and efficient as we are. They're so confident they can just walk away and leave their stuff like it was a field exercise, training. Maybe it was. Maybe that's what I was to them. But this time we were using live fire. We opened up their packs and they had sets of civilian clothes, military clothes, personal effects. I really wondered if they were at war, except to know that we fought with them every day.

North Vietnamese, that's all I fought. I went into Hue and saw the civilian bodies lined up. I know I didn't kill them. Americans don't shoot people from a distance and then line the bodies up. So when you walk in and find them lined up there on their stomachs with their hands tied behind their backs, you know it was the NVA who did that. I know no Americans did that because we were the first ones to enter that portion of the village. They killed the water buffalo, everything.

It was civil war and we were in there and they were killing us as we killed them. I mean, the poor victims who had relatives in the North and relatives in the South . . . The only equivalent I can imagine was I was sent to the Detroit riots with the 101st before I went to 'Nam. Coming back, my biggest fear was going to Fort Dix, because even though I wanted to be close to home, I didn't want to be stuck on riot duty. I said, "I'll be damned if I come all the way back here from Vietnam to go on riot duty and have someone throw a bottle or a brick and split my head open." What's your reaction going to be? Pull that trigger? Shoot my own countrymen?

Patriotism is just loyalty to friends, people, families . . . I didn't even know those guys in Vietnam until I got there, and it wouldn't have mattered if you came to my platoon tomorrow—if we got hit, I would go out and try to save your ass just as I would've done for anyone else I'd been with for a month, two months, three months. Instant bonding.

20

One thing I did find out after I went to Hue and came back, which I didn't know at the time because of the cultural gap, was the significance of the pine trees in the middle of the jungle. Every time someone died that was relatively famous, they'd plant a pine tree in his honor so his spirit would live on. I had a teacher who was Vietnamese when I went to school after getting out of the service. His father was a poet laureate of Hue who had a tree planted for him. I never had the heart to tell the teacher, who was a friend, that I used to sling a poncho on those trees. I mean, I thought it was a great place to sleep because the pine needles were nice and it was always clean. I didn't make the connection that there was something special about the area. We used the needles to help start our fires. Dig little holes in the hedges around it—dig in. Sacrilege. In some sense his father's spirit gave me shelter, which is kind of ironic.

It was really a break for us to go to the rice hovels because we hadn't cooked for so many months. A little boy came out and wanted some C-rations. When they want C-rations, you know they're hurting, the food's just terrible. He was going to share his dinner with us and he brought out some fish. The hottest damn thing I ever had. I can still to this day remember them being fuming hot. We shared our food and we asked him where he lived. He pointed to this house in the clearing. He said he was there with his sister, and we said, "Well, why doesn't your sister come out and join us for dinner?" And he said, "She can't. The VC will see her with us, they'll kill her." We said, "What about you? They'll see you." He said it didn't matter because they know he's getting food.

So it's just like everything else: you leave and they're back, and people have to live with that. They have to deal with the fact that we're going to be gone and leave them behind. But what struck me that day when I was looking at that kid—and I didn't know how old he was, but he had to be under ten—was that all his life he knew war. And then when we're gone he's going to know that Americans may have come through and raped his sister. The VC may have raped his sister because she allowed the Americans to do this. And if the Americans had conceivably seen her with the VC, they would've . . . the whole thing was just . . . it was certainly a statement. It was a tragedy and it was so horrifying. I tried to think of what I would be like if this took place in my hometown. This may have been a turning point in my life, at least in the terms of the war.

Joining the Conversation: Critical Thinking and Writing

1. In his opening paragraph, how does Santos explain his decision to "complete OCS?" What is your response to this explanation?

2. The author includes some coarse language in this piece. Does such language offend you? Do you think that Santos could have been just as effective if he had left out these words?

3. How does Santos describe his first experience of combat? How would you characterize his tone and point of view as he narrates this scene?

4. Does Santos suggest how he perceived the North Vietnamese, the "other side" he was fighting against? What do military manuals mean when they say, "Make sure you know the enemy"?

5. Do you know anyone who served in the military in the Vietnam War or in any of America's more recent wars in Iraq and Afghanistan? Have you talked with them about their experiences?

6. One lawmaker recently proposed that every young person in America should spend one or two years in the military in some capacity or other, with no possibility of deferment. Do you believe that this is a good idea? What would be your strongest argument in favor of it? And what would be your strongest argument against it?

Plato

Plato (427–347 B.C.) in his dialogues often uses the Athenian philosopher Socrates as a mouthpiece for ideas that scholars believe are Platonic, but in the dialogue called Crito *he probably was fairly careful to represent Socrates' own ideas.*

In 399 B.C. Socrates was convicted of impiety and was sentenced to death. Behind the charge of impiety was another, that Socrates had "corrupted the young." It seems clear, however, that the trial was a way of getting rid of a man considered by some to be a troublesome questioner of conventional opinions.

About a month intervened between the trial and Socrates' death because the law prohibited execution until a sacred ship had returned to Athens. Socrates could easily have escaped from prison but made no effort to leave, as we see in this dialogue reporting his decision to abide by the unjust decision of a duly constituted group of jurors.

Crito

(Scene: A room in the State prison at Athens in the year 399 B.C. The time is half an hour before dawn, and the room would be almost dark but for the light of a little oil lamp. There is a pallet bed against the back wall. At the head of it a small table supports the lamp; near the foot of it Crito is sitting patiently on a stool. He is an old

man, kindly, practical, simple-minded; at present he is suffering from acute emotional strain. On the bed lies Socrates asleep. He stirs, yawns, opens his eyes and sees Crito.)

Socrates: Here already, Crito? Surely it is still early?

Crito: Indeed it is.

Socrates: About what time?

Crito: Just before dawn.

Socrates: I wonder that the warder paid any attention to you.

Crito: He is used to me now, Socrates, because I come here so often; besides, he is under some small obligation to me.

Socrates: Have you only just come, or have you been here for long?

Crito: Fairly long.

Socrates: Then why didn't you wake me at once, instead of sitting by my bed so quietly?

Crito: I wouldn't dream of such a thing, Socrates. I only wish I were not so sleepless and depressed myself. I have been wondering at you, because I saw how comfortably you were sleeping; and I deliberately didn't wake you because I wanted you to go on being as comfortable as you could. I have often felt before in the course of my life how fortunate you are in your disposition, but I feel it more than ever how in your present misfortune when I see how easily and placidly you put up with it.

Socrates: Well, really, Crito, it would be hardly suitable for a man of my age to resent having to die.

Crito: Other people just as old as you are get involved in these misfortunes, Socrates, but their age doesn't keep them from resenting it when they find themselves in your position.

Socrates: Quite true. But tell me, why have you come so early?

Crito: Because I bring bad news, Socrates; not so bad from your point of view, I suppose, but it will be very hard to bear for me and your other friends, and I think that I shall find it hardest of all.

Socrates: Why, what is this news? Has the boat come in from Delos—the boat which ends my reprieve when it arrives?[1]

Crito: It hasn't actually come in yet, but I expect that it will be here today, judging from the report of some people who have just arrived from Sunium and left it there. It's quite clear from their account that it will be here today; and so by tomorrow, Socrates, you will have to—to end your life.

Socrates: Well, Crito, I hope that it may be for the best; if the gods will it so, so be it. All the same, I don't think it will arrive today.

Crito: What makes you think that?

Socrates: I will try to explain. I think I am right in saying that I have to die on the day after the boat arrives?

---

[1]**Delos . . . arrives** Ordinarily execution was immediately carried out, but the day before Socrates' trial was the first day of an annual ceremony that involved sending a ship to Delos. When the ship was absent—in this case for about a month—executions could not be performed. As Crito goes on to say, Socrates could easily escape, and indeed he could have left the country before being tried. (All notes are the editors'.)

Crito: That's what the authorities say, at any rate.   20

Socrates: Then I don't think it will arrive on this day that is just begin-ning, but on the day after. I am going by a dream that I had in the night, only a little while ago. It looks as though you were right not to wake me up.

Crito: Why, what was the dream about?

Socrates: I thought I saw a gloriously beautiful woman dressed in white robes, who came up to me and addressed me in these words: "Socrates, to the pleasant land of Phthia on the third day thou shalt come."

Crito: Your dream makes no sense, Socrates.

Socrates: To my mind, Crito, it is perfectly clear.   25

Crito: Too clear, apparently. But look here, Socrates, it is still not too late to take my advice and escape. Your death means a double calamity for me. I shall not only lose a friend whom I can never pos-sibly replace, but besides a great many people who don't know you and me very well will be sure to think that I let you down, because I could have saved you if I had been willing to spend the money; and what could be more contemptible than to get a name for thinking more of money than of your friends? Most people will never believe that it was you who refused to leave this place although we tried our hardest to per-suade you.

Socrates: But my dear Crito, why should we pay so much attention to what "most people" think? The really reasonable people, who have more claim to be considered, will believe that the facts are exactly as they are.

Crito: You can see for yourself, Socrates, that one has to think of pop-ular opinion as well. Your present position is quite enough to show that the capacity of ordinary people for causing trouble is not confined to petty annoyances, but has hardly any limits if you once get a bad name with them.

Socrates: I only wish that ordinary people *had* unlimited capacity for doing harm; then they might have an unlimited power for doing good; which would be a splendid thing, if it were so. Actually they have neither. They cannot make a man wise or stupid; they simply act at random.

Crito: Have it that way if you like; but tell me this, Socrates. I hope   30 that you aren't worrying about the possible effects on me and the rest of your friends, and thinking that if you escape we shall have trouble with informers for having helped you to get away, and have to forfeit all our property or pay an enormous fine, or even incur some further punish-ment? If any idea like that is troubling you, you can dismiss it altogether. We are quite entitled to run that risk in saving you, and even worse, if necessary. Take my advice, and be reasonable.

Socrates: All that you say is very much in my mind, Crito, and a great deal more besides.

Crito: Very well, then, don't let it distress you. I know some people who are willing to rescue you from here and get you out of the country for quite a moderate sum. And then surely you realize how cheap these informers are to buy off; we shan't need much money to settle them; and

I think you've got enough of my money for yourself already. And then even supposing that in your anxiety for my safety you feel that you oughtn't to spend my money, there are these foreign gentlemen staying in Athens who are quite willing to spend theirs. One of them, Simmias of Thebes, has actually brought the money with him for this very purpose; and Cebes and a number of others are quite ready to do the same. So as I say, you mustn't let any fears on these grounds make you slacken your efforts to escape; and you mustn't feel any misgivings about what you said at your trial, that you wouldn't know what to do with yourself if you left this country. Wherever you go, there are plenty of places where you will find a welcome; and if you choose to go to Thessaly, I have friends there who will make much of you and give you complete protection, so that no one in Thessaly can interfere with you.

Besides, Socrates, I don't even feel that it is right for you to try to do what you are doing, throwing away your life when you might save it. You are doing your best to treat yourself in exactly the same way as your enemies would, or rather did, when they wanted to ruin you. What is more, it seems to me that you are letting your sons down too. You have it in your power to finish their bringing up and education, and instead of that you are proposing to go off and desert them, and so far as you are concerned they will have to take their chance. And what sort of chance are they likely to get? The sort of thing that usually happens to orphans when they lose their parents. Either one ought not to have children at all, or one ought to see their upbringing and education through to the end. It strikes me that you are taking the line of least resistance, whereas you ought to make the choice of a good man and a brave one, considering that you profess to have made goodness your object all through life. Really, I am ashamed, both on your account and on ours your friends'; it will look as though we had played something like a coward's part all through this affair of yours. First, there was the way you came into court when it was quite unnecessary—that was the first act; than there was the conduct of the defense—that was the second; and finally, to complete the farce, we get this situation, which makes it appear that we have let you slip out of our hands through some lack of courage and enterprise on our part, because we didn't save you, and you didn't save yourself, when it would have been quite possible and practicable, if we had been any use at all.

There, Socrates; if you aren't careful, besides the suffering there will be all this disgrace for you and us to bear. Come, make up your mind. Really it's too late for that now; you ought to have it made up already. There is no alternative; the whole thing must be carried through during this coming night. If we lose any more time, it can't be done, it will be too late. I appeal to you, Socrates, on every ground; take my advice and please don't be unreasonable!

Socrates: My dear Crito, I appreciate your warm feelings very much— 35 that is, assuming that they have some justification; if not, the stronger they are, the harder they will be to deal with. Very well, then; we must consider whether we ought to follow your advice or not. You know that this is not a new idea of mine; it has always been my nature never to accept advice from any of my friends unless reflection shows that it is the best course that reason offers. I cannot abandon the principles which I used to hold in the past simply because this accident has happened to me; they seem to me to be much as they were, and I respect and regard the same principles now as before. So unless we can find better principles on this occasion, you can be quite sure that I shall not agree with you; not even if the power of the people conjures up fresh hordes of bogies to terrify our childish minds, by subjecting us to chains and executions and confiscations of our property.

Well, then, how can we consider the question most reasonably? Suppose that we begin by reverting to this view which you hold about people's opinions. Was it always right to argue that some opinions should be taken seriously but not others? Or was it always wrong? Perhaps it was right before the question of my death arose, but now we can see clearly that it was a mistaken persistence in a point of view which was really irresponsible nonsense. I should like very much to inquire into this problem, Crito, with your help, and to see whether the argument will appear in any different light to me now that I am in this position, or whether it will remain the same; and whether we shall dismiss it or accept it.

Serious thinkers, I believe, have always held some such view as the one which I mentioned just now: that some of the opinions which people entertain should be respected, and others should not. Now I ask you, Crito, don't you think that this is a sound principle?—You are safe from the prospect of dying tomorrow, in all human probability; and you are not likely to have your judgment upset by this impending calamity. Consider, then; don't you think that this is a sound enough principle, that one should not regard all the opinions that people hold, but only some and not others? What do you say? Isn't that a fair statement?

Crito: Yes, it is.

Socrates: In other words, one should regard the good ones and not the bad?

Crito: Yes.

Socrates: The opinions of the wise being good, and the opinions of the foolish bad?

Crito: Naturally.

Socrates: To pass on, then: What do you think of the sort of illustration that I used to employ? When a man is in training, and taking it seriously, does he pay attention to all praise and criticism and opinion indiscriminately, or only when it comes from the one qualified person, the actual doctor or trainer?

Crito: Only when it comes from the one qualified person.

Socrates: Then he should be afraid of the criticism and welcome the praise of the one qualified person, but not those of the general public.

Crito: Obviously.

Socrates: So he ought to regulate his actions and exercises and eating and drinking by the judgment of his instructor, who has expert knowledge, rather than by the opinions of the rest of the public.

Crito: Yes, that is so.

Socrates: Very well. Now if he disobeys the one man and disregards his opinion and commendations, and pays attention to the advice of the many who have no expert knowledge, surely he will suffer some bad effect?

Crito: Certainly.

Socrates: And what is this bad effect? Where is it produced?—I mean, in what part of the disobedient person?

Crito: His body, obviously; that is what suffers.

Socrates: Very good. Well now, tell me, Crito—we don't want to go through all the examples one by one—does this apply as a general rule, and above all to the sort of actions which we are trying to decide about: just and unjust, honorable and dishonorable, good and bad? Ought we to be guided and intimidated by the opinion of the many or by that of the one—assuming that there is someone with expert knowledge? Is it true that we ought to respect and fear this person more than all the rest put together; and that if we do not follow his guidance we shall spoil and mutilate that part of us which, as we used to say, is improved by right conduct and destroyed by wrong? Or is this all nonsense?

Crito: No, I think it is true, Socrates.

Socrates: Then consider the next step. There is a part of us which is improved by healthy actions and ruined by unhealthy ones. If we spoil it by taking the advice of nonexperts, will life be worth living when this part is once ruined? The part I mean is the body; do you accept this?

Crito: Yes.

Socrates: Well, is life worth living with a body which is worn out and ruined by health?

Crito: Certainly not.

Socrates: What about the part of us which is mutilated by wrong actions and benefited by right ones? Is life worth living with this part ruined? Or do we believe that this part of us, whatever it may be, in which right and wrong operate, is of less importance than the body?

Crito: Certainly not.

Socrates: It is really more precious?

Crito: Much more.

Socrates: In that case, my dear fellow, what we ought to consider is not so much what people in general will say about us but how we stand with the expert in right and wrong, the one authority, who represents the actual truth. So in the first place your proposition is not correct when you say that we should consider popular opinion in questions of what is right and honorable and good, or the opposite. Of course one might object "All the same, the people have the power to put us to death."

50

55

60

Crito: No doubt about that! Quite true, Socrates; it is a possible objection.

Socrates: But so far as I can see, my dear fellow, the argument which we have just been through is quite unaffected by it. At the same time I should like you to consider whether we are still satisfied on this point: that the really important thing is not to live, but to live well.

Crito: Why, yes.

Socrates: And that to live well means the same thing as to live honorably or rightly?

Crito: Yes.

Socrates: Then in the light of this agreement we must consider whether or not it is right for me to try to get away without an official discharge. If it turns out to be right, we must make the attempt; if not, we must let it drop. As for the considerations you raise about expense and reputation and bringing up children, I am afraid, Crito, that they represent the reflections of the ordinary public, who put people to death, and would bring them back to life if they could, with equal indifference to reason. Our real duty, I fancy, since the argument leads that way, is to consider one question only, the one which we raised just now: Shall we be acting rightly in paying money and showing gratitude to these people who are going to rescue me, and in escaping or arranging the escape ourselves, or shall we really be acting wrongly in doing all this? If it becomes clear that such conduct is wrong, I cannot help thinking that the question whether we are sure to die, or to suffer any other ill effect for that matter, if we stand our ground and take no action, ought not to weigh with us at all in comparison with the risk of doing what is wrong.

Crito: I agree with what you say, Socrates; but I wish you would consider what we ought to *do*.

Socrates: Let us look at it together, my dear fellow; and if you can challenge any of my arguments, do so and I will listen to you; but if you can't, be a good fellow and stop telling me over and over again that I ought to leave this place without official permission. I am very anxious to obtain your approval before I adopt the course which I have in mind; I don't want to act against your convictions. Now give your attention to the starting point of this inquiry—I hope that you will be satisfied with my way of stating it—and try to answer my questions to the best of your judgment.

Crito: Well, I will try.

Socrates: Do we say that one must never willingly do wrong, or does it depend upon circumstance? Is it true, as we have often agreed before, that there is no sense in which wrongdoing is good or honorable? Or have we jettisoned all our former convictions in these last few days? Can you and I at our age, Crito, have spent all these years in serious discussions without realizing that we were no better than a pair of children? Surely the truth is just what we have always said. Whatever the popular view is, and whether the alternative is pleasanter than the present one or even

65

70

harder to bear, the fact remains that to do wrong is in every sense bad and dishonorable for the person who does it. Is that our view, or not?

Crito: Yes, it is.

Socrates: Then in no circumstances must one do wrong.   75

Crito: No.

Socrates: In that case one must not even do wrong when one is wronged, which most people regard as the natural course.

Crito: Apparently not.

Socrates: Tell me another thing, Crito: Ought one to do injuries or not?

Crito: Surely not, Socrates.   80

Socrates: And tell me: Is it right to do an injury in retaliation, as most people believe, or not?

Crito: No, never.

Socrates: Because, I suppose, there is no difference between injuring people and wronging them.

Crito: Exactly.

Socrates: So one ought not to return a wrong or an injury to any per-   85
son, whatever the provocation is. Now be careful, Crito, that in making these single admissions you do not end by admitting something contrary to your real beliefs. I know that there are and always will be few people who think like this; and consequently between those who do think so and those who do not there can be no agreement on principle; they must always feel contempt when they observe one another's decisions. I want even you to consider very carefully whether you share my views and agree with me, and whether we can proceed with our discussion from the established hypothesis that it is never right to do a wrong or return a wrong or defend one's self against injury by retaliation; or whether you dissociate yourself from any share in this view as a basis for discussion. I have held it for a long time, and still hold it; but if you have formed any other opinion, say so and tell me what it is. If, on the other hand, you stand by what we have said, listen to my next point.

Crito: Yes, I stand by it and agree with you. Go on.

Socrates: Well, here is my next point, or rather question. Ought one to fulfill all one's agreements, provided that they are right, or break them?

Crito: One ought to fulfill them.

Socrates: Then consider the logical consequence. If we leave this place without first persuading the State to let us go, are we or are we not doing an injury, and doing it in a quarter where it is least justifiable? Are we or are we not abiding by our just agreements?

Crito: I can't answer your question, Socrates; I am not clear in my mind.   90

Socrates: Look at it in this way. Suppose that while we were preparing to run away from here (or however one should describe it) the Laws and Constitution of Athens were to come and confront us and ask this question: "Now, Socrates, what are you proposing to do? Can you deny that by this act which you are contemplating you intend, so far as you have the power, to destroy us, the Laws, and the whole State as well? Do you imagine that a

city can continue to exist and not be turned upside down, if the legal judgments which are pronounced in it have no force but are nullified and destroyed by private persons?"—how shall we answer this question, Crito,
and others of the same kind? There is much that could be said, especially
by a professional advocate, to protest against the invalidation of this law
which enacts that judgments once pronounced shall be binding. Shall we
say "Yes, I do intend to destroy the laws, because the State wronged me by
passing a faulty judgment at my trial"? Is this to be our answer, or what?

Crito: What you have just said, by all means, Socrates.

Socrates: Then what if supposing the Laws say, "Was there provision for
this in the agreement between you and us, Socrates? Or did you undertake
to abide by whatever judgments the State pronounced?" If we expressed
surprise at such language, they would probably say: "Never mind our language, Socrates, but answer our questions; after all, you are accustomed to
the method of question and answer. Come now, what charge do you bring
against us and the State, that you are trying to destroy us? Did we not give
you life in the first place? Was it not through us that your father married
your mother and begot you? Tell us, have you any complaint against those
of us Laws that deal with marriage?" "No, none," I should say. "Well, have
you any against the laws which deal with children's upbringing and education, such as you had yourself? Are you not grateful to those of us Laws
which were instituted for this end, for requiring your father to give you a
cultural and physical education?" "Yes," I should say. "Very good. Then
since you have been born and brought up and educated, can you deny, in
the first place, that you were our child and servant, both you and your ancestors? And if this is so, do you imagine that what is right for us is equally
right for you, and that whatever we try to do to you, you are justified in retaliating? You did not have equality of rights with your father, or your employer (supposing that you had had one), to enable you to retaliate; you
were not allowed to answer back when you were scolded or to hit back
when you were beaten, or to do a great many other things of the same kind.
Do you expect to have such license against your country and its laws that if
we try to put you to death in the belief that it is right to do so, you on your
part will try your hardest to destroy your country and us its Laws in return?
And will you, the true devotee of goodness, claim that you are justified in
doing so? Are you so wise as to have forgotten that compared with your
mother and father and all the rest of your ancestors your country is something far more precious, more venerable, more sacred, and held in greater
honor both among gods and among all reasonable men? Do you not realize
that you are even more bound to respect and placate the anger of your country than your father's anger? That if you cannot persuade your country you
must do whatever it orders, and patiently submit to any punishment that it
imposes, whether it be flogging or imprisonment? And if it leads you out to
war, to be wounded or killed, you must comply, and it is right that you
should do so; you must not give way or retreat or abandon your position.
Both in war and in the law courts and everywhere else you must do
whatever your city and your country commands, or else persuade it in

accordance with universal justice; but violence is a sin even against your parents, and it is a far greater sin against your country"—What shall we say to this, Crito?—that what the Laws say is true, or not?

Crito: Yes, I think so.

Socrates: "Consider, then, Socrates," the Laws would probably con- 95 tinue, "whether it is also true for us to say that what you are now trying to do to us is not right. Although we have brought you into the world and reared you and educated you, and given you and all your fellow citizens a share in all the good things at our disposal, nevertheless by the very fact of granting our permission we openly proclaim this principle: that any Athenian, on attaining to manhood and seeing for himself the political organization of the State and us its Laws, is permitted, if he is not satisfied with us, to take his property and go away wherever he likes. If any of you chooses to go to one of our colonies, supposing that he should not be satisfied with us and the State, or to emigrate to any other country, not one of us Laws hinders or prevents him from going away wherever he likes, without any loss of property. On the other hand, if any one of you stands his ground when he can see how we administer justice and the rest of our public organization, we hold that by so doing he had in fact undertaken to do anything that we tell him; and we maintain that anyone who disobeys is guilty of doing wrong on three separate counts: first because we are his parents, and secondly because we are his guardians; and thirdly because, after promising obedience, he is neither obeying us nor persuading us to change our decision if we are at fault in any way; and although all our orders are in the form of proposals, not of savage commands, and we give him the choice of either persuading us or doing what we say, he is actually doing neither. These are the charges, Socrates, to which we say that you will be liable if you do what you are contemplating; and you will not be the least culpable of your fellow countrymen, but one of the most guilty." If I said "Why do you say that?" they would no doubt pounce upon me with perfect justice and point out that there are very few people in Athens who have entered into this agreement with them as explicitly as I have. They would say "Socrates, we have substantial evidence that you are satisfied with us and with the State. You would not have been so exceptionally reluctant to cross the borders of your country if you had not been exceptionally attached to it. You have never left the city to attend a festival or for any other purpose, except on some military expedition; you have never traveled abroad as other people do, and you have never felt the impulse to acquaint yourself with another country or constitution; you have been content with us and with our city. You have definitely chosen us, and undertaken to observe us in all your activities as a citizen; and as the crowning proof that you are satisfied with our city, you have begotten children in it. Furthermore, even at the time of your trial you could have proposed the penalty of banishment, if you had chosen to do so; that is, you could have done then with the sanction of the State what you are now trying to do without it. But whereas at that time you made a noble show of indifference if you had to die, and in fact preferred death, as you said, to banishment, now you show no respect for your earlier professions, and no regard for us, the Laws, whom you are trying to destroy; you are behaving like the lowest type of menial, trying to run away in spite of the contracts and undertakings by which you agreed to live as a member of our State. Now first answer this question: Are we or are we not speaking the truth when we say that you have undertaken, in deed if not in word, to live your life as a citizen in obedience to us?" What are we to say to that, Crito? Are we not bound to admit it?

Crito: We cannot help it, Socrates.

Socrates: "It is a fact, then," they would say, "that you are breaking covenants and undertakings made with us, although you made them under no compulsion or misunderstanding, and were not compelled to decide in a limited time; you had seventy years in which you could have left the country, if you were not satisfied with us or felt that the agreements were unfair. You did not choose Sparta or Crete—your favorite models of good government— or any other Greek or foreign state; you could not have absented yourself from the city less if you had been lame or blind or decrepit in some other way. It is quite obvious that you stand by yourself above all other Athenians in your affection for this city and for us its Laws;—who would care for a city without laws? And now, after all this, are you not going to stand by your agreement? Yes, you are, Socrates, if you will take our advice; and then you will at least escape being laughed at for leaving the city.

"We invite you to consider what good you will do to yourself or your friends if you commit this breach of faith and stain your conscience. It is fairly obvious that the risk of being banished and either losing their citizenship or having their property confiscated will extend to your friends as well. As for yourself, if you go to one of the neighboring states, such as Thebes or Megara, which are both well governed, you will enter them as an enemy to their constitution[2] and all good patriots will eye you with suspicion as a destroyer of law and order. Incidentally you will confirm the opinion of the jurors who tried you that they gave a correct verdict; a destroyer of laws might very well be supposed to have a destructive influence upon young and foolish human beings. Do you intend, then, to avoid well governed states and the higher forms of human society? And if you do, will life be worth living? Or will you approach these people and have the impudence to converse with them? What arguments will you use, Socrates? The same which you used here, that goodness and integrity, institutions and laws, are the most precious possessions of mankind? Do you not think that Socrates and everything about him will appear in a disreputable light? You certainly ought to think so. But perhaps you will retire from this part of the world and go to Crito's friends in Thessaly? That is the home of indiscipline and laxity, and no doubt they would enjoy hearing the amusing story of how you managed to run away from prison by arraying yourself in some costume or putting on a shepherd's smock or some other conventional runaway's disguise, and altering your personal appearance. And will no one comment on the fact that an old man of your age, probably with

[2]**as an enemy to their constitution** As a lawbreaker.

only a short time left to live, should dare to cling so greedily to life, at the price of violating the most stringent laws? Perhaps not, if you avoid irritating anyone. Otherwise, Socrates, you will hear a good many humiliating comments. So you will live as the toady and slave of all the populace, literally 'roistering in Thessaly' as though you had left this country for Thessaly to attend a banquet there; and where will your discussions about goodness and uprightness be then, we should like to know? But of course you want to live for your children's sake, so that you may be able to bring them up and educate them. Indeed! by first taking them off to Thessaly and making foreigners of them, so that they may have that additional enjoyment? Or if that is not your intention, supposing that they are brought up here with you still alive, will they be better cared for and educated without you, because of course your friends will look after them? Will they look after your children if you go away to Thessaly, and not if you go away to the next world? Surely if those who profess to be your friends are worth anything, you must believe that they would care for them.

"No, Socrates; be advised by us your guardians, and do not think more of your children or of your life or of anything else than you think of what is right; so that when you enter the next world you may have all this to plead in your defense before the authorities there. It seems clear that if you do this thing, neither you nor any of your friends will be the better for it or be more upright or have a cleaner conscience here in this world, nor will it be better for you when you reach the next. As it is, you will leave this place, when you do, as the victim of a wrong done not by us, the Laws, but by your fellow men. But if you leave in that dishonorable way, returning wrong for wrong and evil for evil, breaking your agreements and covenants with us, and injuring those whom you least ought to injure—yourself, your friends, your country, and us—then you will have to face our anger in your lifetime, and in that place beyond when the laws of the other world know that you have tried, so far as you could, to destroy even us their brothers, they will not receive you with a kindly welcome. Do not take Crito's advice, but follow ours."

That, my dear friend Crito, I do assure you, is what I seem to hear them saying, just as a mystic seems to hear the strains of music; and the sound of their arguments rings so loudly in my head that I cannot hear the other side. I warn you that, as my opinion stands at present, it will be useless to urge a different view. However, if you think that you will do any good by it, say what you like.

Crito: No, Socrates, I have nothing to say.

Socrates: Then give it up, Crito, and let us follow this course, since God points out the way.

Joining the Conversation: Critical Thinking and Writing

1. Socrates argues that because throughout his life he lived in Athens, in effect he established a compact with the city to live by its laws and must therefore

now accept the judgment—however mistaken—of a duly constituted court. How convincing is this argument? Suppose this argument were omitted. Would Socrates' conclusion be affected?

2. Socrates argues that just as in matters of caring for the body we heed only experts and not the multitude, so in moral matters we should heed the expert, not the multitude. How convincing is this analogy between bodily health and moral goodness? Socrates sometimes compared himself to an athletic coach, saying he trained people to think. Judging from the dialogue, how did he train a student to think?

3. The personified figure of the laws does not add much to the essential argument. Why, then, is the passage included?

4. The ancient Chinese teacher Confucius asked one of his pupils, "Do you think of me as a man who knows about things as the result of wide study?" When the pupil replied "Yes," Confucius disagreed: "I have one thing, and upon it all the rest is rooted." Exactly what did Confucius mean? In an essay of 500 words explain what Socrates would have said, if he had been asked the question.

T. S. Eliot

T. S. Eliot

Thomas Stearns Eliot (1888–1965) was born into a New England family that had moved to St. Louis. He attended a preparatory school in Massachusetts, then graduated from Harvard and did further study in literature and philosophy in France, Germany, and England. In 1914 he began working for Lloyd's Bank in London, and three years later he published his first book of poems (it included "Prufrock"). In 1925 he joined a publishing firm, and in 1927 he became a British citizen and a member of the Church of England. Much of his later poetry, unlike "The Love Song of J. Alfred Prufrock," is highly religious. In 1948 Eliot received the Nobel Prize for Literature.

The Love Song of J. Alfred Prufrock

S'io credesse che mia risposta fosse
A persona che mai tornasse al mondo,
Questa fiamma staria senza piu scosse.
Ma perciocche giammai di questo fondo
Non torno vivo alcun. s'i' odo il vero,
Senza tema d'infama ti rispondo.[1]

Let us go then, you and I,
When the evening is spread out against the sky
Like a patient etherized upon a table;
Let us go, through certain half-deserted streets,
The muttering retreats   5
Of restless nights in one-night cheap hotels
And sawdust restaurants with oyster-shells:
Streets that follow like a tedious argument
Of insidious intent
To lead you to an overwhelming question . . .   10
Oh, do not ask, "What is it?"
Let us go and make our visit.

In the room the women come and go
Talking of Michelangelo.

The yellow fog that rubs its back upon the window-panes,   15
The yellow smoke that rubs its muzzle on the window-panes
Licked its tongue into the corners of the evening,
Lingered upon the pools that stand in drains,
Let fall upon its back the soot that falls from chimneys,
Slipped by the terrace, made a sudden leap,   20
And seeing that it was a soft October night,
Curled once about the house, and fell asleep.

And indeed there will be time
For the yellow smoke that slides along the street,
Rubbing its back upon the window-panes;   25
There will be time, there will be time
To prepare a face to meet the faces that you meet;
There will be time to murder and create,

----

[1]In Dante's *Inferno* XXVII:61–66, a damned soul who had sought absolution before committing a crime addresses Dante, thinking that his words will never reach the Earth: "If I believed that my answer were to a person who could ever return to the world, this flame would no longer quiver. But because no one ever returned from this depth, if what I hear is true without fear of infamy, I answer you."

And time for all the works and days[2] of hands
That lift and drop a question on your plate;   30
Time for you and time for me,
And time yet for a hundred indecisions,
And for a hundred visions and revisions,
Before the taking of a toast and tea.
In the room the women come and go   35
Talking of Michelangelo.

And indeed there will be time
To wonder, "Do I dare?" and, "Do I dare?"
Time to turn back and descend the stair,
With a bald spot in the middle of my hair—   40
[They will say: "How his hair is growing thin!"]
My morning coat, my collar mounting firmly to the chin,
My necktie rich and modest, but asserted by a simple pin—
[They will say: "But how his arms and legs are thin!"]
Do I dare   45
Disturb the universe?
In a minute there is time
For decisions and revisions which a minute will reverse.

For I have known them all already, known them all:—
Have known the evenings, mornings, afternoons,   50
I have measured out my life with coffee spoons;
I know the voices dying with a dying fall[3]
Beneath the music from a farther room.
    So how should I presume?

And I have known the eyes already, known them all—   55
The eyes that fix you in a formulated phrase,
And when I am formulated, sprawling on a pin,
When I am pinned and wriggling on the wall,
Then how should I begin
To spit out all the butt-ends of my days and ways?   60
    And how should I presume?

And I have known the arms already, known them all—
Arms that are braceleted and white and bare
[But in the lamplight, downed with light brown hair!]

Is it perfume from a dress   65
That makes me so digress?

[2]**works and days** "Works and Days" is the title of a poem on farm life by Hesiod (eighth century B.C.).
[3]**dying fall** This line echoes Shakespeare's *Twelfth Night* 1.1.4.

Arms that lie along a table, or wrap about a shawl.
  And should I then presume?
  And how should I begin?

            . . .

Shall I say, I have gone at dusk through narrow streets   70
And watched the smoke that rises from the pipes
Of lonely men in shirt-sleeves, leaning out of windows? . . .

I should have been a pair of ragged claws
Scuttling across the floors of silent seas.

            . . .

And the afternoon, the evening, sleeps so peacefully!   75
Smoothed by long fingers,
Asleep . . . tired . . . or it malingers,
Stretched on the floor, here beside you and me.
Should I, after tea and cakes and ices,
Have the strength to force the moment to its crisis?   80
But though I have wept and fasted, wept and prayed,
Though I have seen my head [grown slightly bald]
  brought in upon a platter,[4]
I am no prophet—and here's no great matter;
And I have seen the moment of my greatness flicker,
And I have seen the eternal Footman hold my coat, and snicker,   85
And in short, I was afraid.

And would it have been worth it, after all,
After the cups, the marmalade, the tea,
Among the porcelain, among some talk of you and me,
Would it have been worth while,   90
To have bitten off the matter with a smile,
To have squeezed the universe into a ball[5]
To roll it toward some overwhelming question,
To say: "I am Lazarus,[6] come from the dead,
Come back to tell you all, I shall tell you all"—   95
If one, settling a pillow by her head,
  Should say: "That is not what I meant at all.
  That is not it, at all."

And would it have been worth it, after all,
Would it have been worth while,   100
After the sunsets and the dooryards and the sprinkled streets.

---

[4]**But . . . platter** These lines allude to John the Baptist (see Matthew 14.1–11).
[5]**To have . . . ball** This line echoes lines 41–42 of Marvell's "To His Coy Mistress."
[6]**Lazarus** See Luke 16 and John 11.

After the novels, after the teacups, after the skirts that trail
   along the floor—
And this, and so much more?—
It is impossible to say just what I mean!
But as if a magic lantern threw the nerves in patterns on a screen: 105
Would it have been worth while
If one, settling a pillow or throwing off a shawl,
And turning toward the window, should say:
    "That is not it at all,
    That is not what I meant at all."   110

No! I am not Prince Hamlet, nor was meant to be;
Am an attendant lord, one that will do
To swell a progress, start a scene or two,
Advise the prince; no doubt, an easy tool,
Deferential, glad to be of use,   115
Politic, cautious, and meticulous;
Full of high sentence,[7] but a bit obtuse,[8]
At times, indeed, almost ridiculous—
Almost, at times, the Fool.
I grow old . . . I grow old . . .   120
I shall wear the bottoms of my trousers rolled.

Shall I part my hair behind? Do I dare to eat a peach?
I shall wear white flannel trousers, and walk upon the beach.
I have heard the mermaids singing, each to each.
I do not think that they will sing to me.   125

I have seen them riding seaward on the waves
Combing the white hair of the waves blown back
When the wind blows the water white and black

We have lingered in the chambers of the sea
By sea-girls wreathed with seaweed red and brown   130
Till human voices wake us, and we drown.

⬥ Joining the Conversation: Critical Thinking and Writing

1. What is your response to Eliot's choice of title? Do you think it is effective, or not? Why?

---

[7]**full of high sentence** Borrowed from Chaucer's description of the Clerk of Oxford in the *Canterbury Tales*.
[8]**Am . . . obtuse** These lines allude to Polonius and perhaps to other figures in Shakespeare's *Hamlet*.

2. What is your response to Eliot's epigraph? If he had asked your opinion, would you have advised him to retain it or to cut it? Do you think he should have presented the epigraph not in Italian, but in an English translation?

3. One critic has said, "perhaps the best thing in Eliot's poem is its comedy." Do you agree? Make sure to point to evidence in the text that supports your view.

4. What is your favorite line in the poem? Your favorite image or metaphor? Your favorite passage?

5. How does Eliot's poem end? Do you think it ends effectively, or would you propose a different kind of ending for it?

6. What is the speaker's biggest problem? Is this a problem that you in any way share, or does it seem far removed from anything that has ever troubled you?

7. In poetry or prose, compose a parody of "The Love Song of J. Alfred Prufrock."

8. Prufrock has gone to a therapist, a psychiatrist, or a member of the clergy for help. Write a 500-word transcript of their session.

A Writer's Glossary

analogy. An analogy (from the Greek *analogos*, proportionate, resembling) is a kind of comparison. Normally an analogy compares substantially different kinds of things and reports several points of resemblance. A comparison of one city with another ("New York is like Chicago in several ways") does not involve an analogy because the two things are not substantially different. And a comparison giving only one resemblance is usually not considered an analogy ("Some people, like olives, are an acquired taste"). But if we claim that a state is like a human body, and we find in the state equivalents for the brain, heart, and limbs, we are offering an analogy. Similarly, one might construct an analogy between feeding the body with food and supplying the mind with ideas: the diet must be balanced, taken at approximately regular intervals, in proper amounts, and digested. An analogy may be useful in explaining the unfamiliar by comparing it to the familiar ("The heart is like a pump . . . "), but of course the things compared are different, and the points of resemblance can go only so far. For this reason, analogies cannot prove anything, though they are sometimes offered as proof.

analysis. Examination of the parts and their relation to the whole.

argument. Discourse in which some statements are offered as reasons for other statements. Argument, then, like emotional appeal and wit, is a form of persuasion, but argument seeks to persuade by appealing to reason. (See Chapter 4.)

audience. The writer's imagined readers. An essay on inflation written for the general public—say, for readers of *Newsweek*—will assume less specialized knowledge than will an essay written for professional economists—say, the readers of *Journal of Economic History*. In general, the imagined audience in a composition course is *not* the instructor (though in fact the instructor may be the only reader of the essay); the imagined audience usually is the class, or, to put it a little differently, someone rather like the writer but without the writer's specialized knowledge of the topic.

cliché. Literally, a *cliché* was originally (in French) a stereotype or an electrotype plate for printing; in English the word has come to mean an oft-repeated expression, such as "a sight for sore eyes," "a heartwarming experience," "the acid test," "a meaningful relationship," "last but not least." Because these expressions implicitly claim to be impressive or forceful, they can be distinguished from such unpretentious common expressions as "good morning," "thank you," and "see you tomorrow." Clichés in fact are not impressive or forceful; they strike the hearer as tired, vague, and unimaginative.

compare/contrast. Strictly speaking, to compare is to examine in order to show similarities. (It comes from the Latin *comparare*, "to pair," "to match.") To contrast is to set into opposition in order to show differences. (It comes from the Latin *contra*, "against," and *stare*, "to stand.") But in ordinary usage a comparison may include not only similarities but also differences. (For a particular kind of comparison, emphasizing similarities, see *analogy*.) In comparing and contrasting, a writer usually means not simply to list similarities or differences but to reveal something clearly, by calling attention either to its resemblances to something we might not think it resembles, or to its differences from something we might think it does resemble.

connotation. The associations that cluster around a word. *Mother* has connotations that *female parent* does not have, yet both words have the same denotation, or explicit meaning.

convention. An agreed-on usage. Beginning each sentence with a capital letter is a convention.

denotation. The explicit meaning of a word, as given in a dictionary, without its associations. *Daytime serial* and *soap opera* have the same denotation, though *daytime serial* probably has a more favorable connotation (see *connotation*).

description. Discourse that aims chiefly at producing a sensory response (usually a mental image) to, for example, a person, object, scene, taste, smell, and so on. A descriptive essay, or passage in an essay, uses concrete words (words that denote observable qualities such as *hair* and *stickiness*), and it uses specific language (words such as *basketball* rather than *game*, and *steak, potatoes, and salad* rather than *hearty meal*).

diction. Choice of words. Examples: between *car, auto,* and *automobile,* between *lie* and *falsehood,* between *can't* and *cannot.*

euphemism. An expression, such as *passed away* for *died,* used to avoid realities that the writer finds unpleasant. Thus, oppressive governments "relocate people" (instead of putting them in concentration camps).

evaluation. Whereas an interpretation seeks to explain the meaning, an evaluation judges worth. After we interpret a difficult piece of writing we may evaluate it as not worth the effort.

explication. An attempt to reveal the meaning by calling attention to implications, such as the connotations of words and the tone conveyed by the brevity or length of a sentence. Unlike a paraphrase, which is a rewording or rephrasing in order to set forth the gist of the meaning, an explication is a commentary that makes explicit what is implicit. If we paraphrased the beginning of the Gettysburg Address (page 432), we might turn "Four score and seven years ago our fathers brought forth" into "Eighty-seven years ago our ancestors established," or some such statement. In an explication, however, we would mention that *four score* evokes the language of the Bible, and that the biblical echo helps to establish the solemnity and holiness of the occasion. In an explication we would also mention that *fathers* initiates a chain of images of birth, continued in *conceived in liberty, any nation so conceived,* and *a new birth.* (See Highet's explication of the Gettysburg Address, page 433.)

exposition. An expository essay is chiefly concerned with giving information—how to register for classes, the causes of the French Revolution, or the tenets of Zen Buddhism. The writer of exposition must, of course, have a point of view (an attitude or a thesis), but because exposition—unlike persuasion—does not assume that the reader's opinion differs from the writer's, the point of view in exposition often is implicit rather than explicit.

general and **specific** (or **particular**). A general word refers to a class or group; a specific (particular) word refers to a member of the class or group. Example: *vehicle* is general compared with *automobile* or with *motorcycle.* But *general* and *specific* are relative. *Vehicle* is general when compared to *automobile*, but *vehicle* is specific when compared to *machine*, for *machine* refers to a class or group that includes not only vehicles but clocks, typewriters, and dynamos. Similarly, although *automobile* is specific in comparison with *vehicle, automobile* is general in comparison with *Volkswagen* or *sportscar*.

generalization. A statement relating to every member of a class or category, or, more loosely, to most members of a class or category. Example: "Students from Medford High are well prepared." Compare: (1) "Janet Kuo is well prepared" (a report of a specific condition); (2) "Students from Medford High are well prepared" (a low-level generalization, because it is limited to one school); (3) "Students today are well prepared" (a high-level generalization, covering many people in many places).

imagery and **symbolism.** When we read *rose*, we may more or less call to mind a picture of a rose, or perhaps we are reminded of the odor or texture of a rose. Whatever in a piece of writing appeals to any of our senses (including sensations of heat and pressure as well as of sight, smell, taste, touch, sound) is an image. In short, images are the sensory content of a work, whether literal (the roses discussed in an essay on rose-growing) or figurative (a comparison, in a poem, of a girl to a rose). It is usually easy to notice images in literature, particularly in poems, which often include comparisons such as "I wandered lonely as a cloud," "a fiery eye," and "seems he a dove? His feathers are but borrowed." In literature, imagery (again, literal as well as figurative) plays a large part in communicating the meaning of the work. For instance, in *Romeo and Juliet* abundant imagery of light and dark reenforces the conflict between life and death. Juliet especially is associated with light (Romeo says, "What light through yonder window breaks? It is the east and Juliet is the sun"), and at the end of the play, when the lovers have died, we are told that the morning is dark: "The sun for sorrow will not show his head."

If we turn from imaginative literature to the essay, we find, of course, that descriptive essays are rich in images. But other kinds of essays, too, may make use of imagery—and not only by literal references to real people or things. Such essays may use figures of speech, as Thoreau does when he says that the imagination as well as the body should "both sit down at the same table." The imagination, after all, does not literally sit down at a table—but Thoreau personifies the imagination, seeing it as no less concrete than the body.

The distinction between an image and a symbol is partly a matter of emphasis and partly a matter of a view of reality. If an image is so insisted on that we feel that the writer sees it as highly significant in itself and also as a way of representing something else, we can call it a symbol. A symbol is what it is, and yet it is also much more. We may feel that a passage about the railroad, emphasizing its steel tracks and its steel cars, its speed and its noise, may be not only about the railroad but also about industrialism and, even further, about an entire way of life—a way of thinking and feeling—that came into being in the nineteenth century.

A symbol, then, is an image so loaded with significance that it is not simply literal, and it does not simply stand as a figure for something else; it is both itself *and* something else that it richly suggests, a kind of manifestation of something too complex or too elusive to be otherwise revealed. Still, having said all of this, one must add that the distinction between *image* and *symbol* is not sharp, and usage allows us even to say such things as, "The imagery of light symbolizes love," meaning that the imagery stands for or represents or is in part about love.

interpretation. An explanation of the meaning. If we see someone clench his fist and tighten his mouth, we may interpret these signs as revealing anger. When we say that in the New Testament the passage alluding to the separation of sheep from goats is to be understood as referring to the saved and the damned, we are offering an interpretation.

irony. In *verbal irony*, the meaning of the words intentionally contradicts the literal meaning, as in "that's not a very good idea," where the intended meaning is "that's a terrible idea."

Irony, in distinction from sarcasm, employs at least some degree of wit or wryness. Sarcasm reveals contempt obviously and heavily, usually by asserting the opposite of what is meant: "You're a great guy" (if said sarcastically) means "It's awful of you to do this to me." Notice that the example of irony we began with was at least a trifle more ingenious than this sarcastic remark, for the sarcasm here simply is the opposite of what is meant, whereas our example of verbal irony is not quite the opposite. The opposite of "that's not a very good idea" is "that is a very good idea," but clearly (in our example) the speaker's meaning is something else. Put it this way: Sarcasm is irony at its crudest, and finer irony commonly uses overstatement or especially understatement, rather than a simple opposite. (For a brief discussion of the use of irony in satire, see *satire*, page 656.)

If the speaker's words have an unintentional double meaning, the irony may be called *dramatic irony*: a character, about to go to bed, says, "I think I'll have a sound sleep," and dies in her sleep. Similarly, an action can turn dramatically ironic: a character seeks to help a friend and unintentionally harms her. Finally, a situation can be ironic: thirsty sailors are surrounded by water that cannot be drunk.

All these meanings of irony are held together, then, by the sense of a somewhat bitter contrast.

jargon. Technical language used inappropriately or inexactly. *Viable* means *able to survive*. To speak of a *viable building* is to use jargon. "A primary factor in my participation in the dance" is jargon if what is meant is "I dance because. . . ."

metaphor. Words have literal meanings: A lemon is a yellow, egg-shaped citrus fruit; to drown is to suffocate in water or other fluid. But words can also have metaphoric meanings: We can call an unsatisfactory automobile a *lemon*, and we can say that we are *drowning* in paperwork. Metaphoric language is literally absurd; if we heed only the denotation it is clearly untrue, for an automobile cannot be a kind of citrus fruit, and we cannot drown in paperwork. (Even if the paper literally suffocated someone, the death could not be called a drowning.) Metaphor, then, uses not the denotation of the word but the associations, the connotations. Because we know that the speaker is not crazy, we turn from the literal meaning (which is clearly untrue) to the association.

myth. (1) A traditional story dealing with supernatural beings or with heroes, often accounting for why things are as they are. Myths tell of the creation of the world, the creation of man, the changes of the season, the achievements of heroes. A Zulu myth, for example, explains that rain is the tears of a god weeping for a beloved slain bird. *Mythology* is a system or group of such stories, and so we speak of Zulu mythology, Greek mythology, or Norse mythology. (2) Mark Schorer, in *William Blake*, defines myth as "a large controlling image that gives philosophic meaning to the facts of ordinary life. . . . All real convictions involve a mythology. . . . Wars may be described as the clash of mythologies." In this sense, then, a myth is not a traditional story we do not believe, but any idea, true or false, to which people subscribe. Thus, one can speak of the "myth" of democracy or of communism.

narration. Discourse that recounts a real or a fictional happening. An anecdote is a narrative, and so is a history of the decline and fall of the Roman Empire. Narration may, of course, include substantial exposition ("four possible motives must be considered") and description ("the horse was an old gray mare"), but the emphasis is on a sequence of happenings ("and then she says to me, . . . ").

parable. A short narrative from which a moral or a lesson can be drawn. A parable may, but need not, be an allegory wherein, say, each character stands for an abstraction that otherwise would be hard to grasp. Usually the parable lacks the *detailed* correspondence of an allegory.

paradox. An apparent self-contradiction, such as "He was happiest when miserable."

paraphrase. A rewording of a passage, usually in order to clarify the meaning. A paraphrase is a sort of translating within the same language; it can help to make clear the gist of the passage. But one must recognize the truth of Robert Frost's charge that when one paraphrases a line of good writing one puts it "in other and worse English." Paraphrase should not be confused with *explication*, page 652.

parody. A parody (from the Greek *counter song*) seeks to amuse by imitating the style—the diction, the sentence structure—of another work, but normally the parody substitutes a very different subject. Thus, it might use tough-guy Hemingway talk to describe not a bullfighter but a butterfly catcher. Often a parody of a writer's style is a good-natured criticism of it.

persona. The writer or speaker in a role adopted for a specific audience. When Abraham Lincoln wrote or spoke, he sometimes did so in the persona of commander in chief of the Union army, but at other times he did so in the persona of the simple man from Springfield, Illinois. The persona is a mask put on for a performance (*persona* is the Latin word for *mask*). If *mask* suggests insincerity, we should remember that whenever we speak or write we do so in a specific role—as friend, or parent, or teacher, or applicant for a job, or whatever. Although Lincoln was a husband, a father, a politician, a president, and many other things, when he wrote a letter or speech he might write solely as one of these; in a letter to his son, the persona (or, we might say, personality) is that of father, not that of commander in chief. The distinction between the writer (who necessarily fills many roles) and the persona who writes or speaks a work is especially useful in talking about satire, because the satirist often invents a mouthpiece very different from himself. The satirist—say, Jonathan Swift—may be strongly opposed to a view, but his persona (his invented essayist) may favor the view; the reader must perceive that the real writer is ridiculing the invented essayist.

persuasion. Discourse that seeks to change a reader's mind. Persuasion usually assumes that the writer and the reader do not agree, or do not fully agree, at the outset. Persuasion may use logical argument (appeal to reason), but it may also try to win the reader over by other means—by appeal to the emotions, by wit, by geniality.

rhetoric. Although in much contemporary usage the word's meaning has sadly decayed to "inflated talk or writing," it can still mean "the study of elements such as content, structure, and cadence in writing or in speech." In short, in the best sense rhetoric is the study of the art of communicating with words.

satire. A work ridiculing identifiable objects in real life, meant to arouse in the reader contempt for its object. Satire is sometimes distinguished from comedy in that comedy aims simply to evoke amusement, whereas satire aims to bring about moral reform by ridicule. According to Alexander Pope, satire "heals with morals what it hurts with wit." Satire sometimes uses invective (direct abuse), but if the invective is to entertain the reader it must be witty, as in a piling up of ingenious accusations. Invective, however, is probably less common in satire than is irony, a device in which the tone somehow contradicts the words. For instance, a speaker may seem to praise ("well, that's certainly an original idea that you have"), but we perceive that she is ridiculing a crackpot idea. Or the satirist may invent a naive speaker (a persona) who praises, but the praise is really dispraise because a simpleton offers it; the persona is sincere, but the writer is ironic and satiric. Or, adopting another strategy, the writer may use an apparently naïve persona to represent the voice of reason; the persona dispassionately describes actions that we take for granted (a political campaign), and through this simple, accurate, rational description we see the irrationality of our behavior. (For further comments on *irony*, see page 654.)

style. A distinctive way of expression. If we see a picture of a man sitting on a chair, we may say that it looks like a drawing for a comic book, or we may say that it looks like a drawing by Rembrandt, Van Gogh, or Andrew Wyeth. We have come to recognize certain manners of expression—independent of the content—as characteristic of certain minds. The content, it can be said, is the same—a man sitting in a chair—but the creator's way of expressing the content is individual.

Similarly, "Four score and seven years ago" and "Eighty-seven years ago" are the same in content; but the styles differ, because "Four score and seven years ago" distinctively reflects a mind familiar with the Bible and an orator speaking solemnly. In fact, many people (we include ourselves) believe that the content is not the same if the expression is not the same. The "content" of "Four score and seven years ago" includes suggestions of the Bible and of God-fearing people not present in "eighty-seven years ago." In this view, a difference in style is a difference in content and therefore a difference in meaning. Surely it is true that in the work of the most competent writers, those who make every word count, one cannot separate style and content.

Let C. S. Lewis have the next-to-last word: "The way for a person to develop a style is (a) to know exactly what he wants to say, and (b) to be sure he is saying exactly that. The reader, we must remember, does not start by knowing what we mean. If our words are ambiguous, our meaning will escape him. I sometimes think that writing is like driving sheep down a road. If there is any gate open to the left or the right the readers will most certainly go into it." And let the Austrian writer Karl Kraus have the last word: "There are two kinds of writers, those who are and those who aren't. With the first, content and form belong together like soul and body; with the second, they match each other like body and clothes."

thesis. The writer's position; the proposition advanced.

thesis statement. A sentence or two summarizing the writer's position or attitude. An essay may or may not have an explicit thesis statement.

tone. The prevailing spirit of an utterance. The tone may be angry, bitter, joyful, solemn, or expressive of any similar mood or emotion. Tone usually reflects the writer's attitude toward the subject, the audience, and the self. (For further comments on *tone*, see pages 16–17.)

PHOTO ACKNOWLEDGMENTS

Page 48: Buffalo Bill Historical Center, Cody, Wyoming.

Page 70: Dorothea Lange/FSA Photo/Library of Congress.

Page 71 (top): Dorothea Lange. Copyright © The Dorothea Lange Collection, The Oakland Museum of California, City of Oakland. Gift of Paul S. Taylor.

Page 71 (bottom): Dorothea Lange/FSA Photo/Library of Congress.

Page 73: Dorothea Lange. Copyright © The Dorothea Lange Collection, The Oakland Museum of California, City of Oakland. Gift of Paul S. Taylor.

Page 74 (top/bottom): Dorothea Lange/FSA Photo/Library of Congress.

Page 129: Ansel Adams Publishing Rights Trust/Corbis.

Page 133: George Hight. Courtesy, Natural Museum of the American Indian, Smithsonian N33190.

Page 138: Grant Wood. *American Gothic*, 1930. Oil on beaverboard, 74.3 × 62.4 cm. Friends of American Art Collection. All rights reserved by The Art Institute of Chicago and VAGA, New York, NY (1930.934). Copyright © The Art Institute of Chicago.

Page 144: Pablo Picasso. *Acrobat's Family with a Monkey*, 1905. Goteborgs Kunstmuseum. Copyright © 2003

Estate of Pablo Picasso/Artists Rights Society (ARS), New York.

Page 145: Joanne Leonard/Woodfin Camp Associates.

Page 196: Dorothea Lange/War Relocation Authority/The National Archives.

Page 197: Marion Post Wolcott/FSA Photo/Library of Congress.

Page 233: Courtesy, Amy Tan.

Page 258: Christopher J. Morris/Redux Pictures.

Page 259: PhotoLibrary/GettyImages.

Page 284: Winslow Homer. *Blackboard*, 1877. Gift (Partial and Promised) of Jo Ann and Julian Ganz, Jr., in Honor of the 50th Anniversary of the National Gallery of Art, Photograph copyright © 2002 Board of Trustees, National Gallery of Art, Washington, 1877.

Page 285: Copyright © Ron James.

Page 378: Dorothea Lange/FSA Photo/Library of Congress.

Page 379: Helen Levitt, New York, c. 1940. Copyright © Helen Levitt. Courtesy Laurence Miller Gallery, New York.

Page 420: GettyImages.

Page 428: Jill Posener. *Born Kicking, Graffiti on Billboard, London*, 1983. Copyright © Jill Posener.

Page 429: Fair Street Pictures.

659